Life Histories of
North American Wagtails,
Shrikes, Vireos,
and Their Allies

Life Histories of North American Wagtails, Shrikes, Vireos, and Their Allies

by Arthur Cleveland Bent

Dover Publications, Inc., New York

Published in the United Kingdom by Constable
and Company Limited, 10 Orange Street, London
W. C. 2.

This Dover edition, first published in 1965, is an
unabridged and unaltered republication of the work
first published in 1950 by the United States Government Printing Office, as Smithsonian Institution
United States National Museum *Bulletin 197.*

Library of Congress Catalog Card Number: 65-12257
International Standard Book Number: 0-486-21085-5

Manufactured in the United States of America

Dover Publications, Inc.
180 Varick Street
New York, N. Y. 10014

ADVERTISEMENT

The scientific publications of the National Museum include two series known, respectively, as *Proceedings* and *Bulletin*.

The *Proceedings* series, begun in 1878, is intended primarily as a medium for the publication of original papers, based on the collections of the National Museum, that set forth newly acquired facts in biology, anthropology, and geology, with descriptions of new forms and revisions of limited groups. Copies of each paper, in pamphlet form, are distributed as published to libraries and scientific organizations and to specialists and others interested in the different subjects. The dates at which these separate papers are published are recorded in the table of contents of each of the volumes.

The series of *Bulletins*, the first of which was issued in 1875, contains separate publications comprising monographs of large zoological groups and other general systematic treatises (occasionally in several volumes), faunal works, reports of expeditions, catalogs of type specimens, special collections, and other material of similar nature. The majority of the volumes are octavo in size, but a quarto size has been adopted in a few instances in which large plates were regarded as indispensable. In the *Bulletin* series appear volumes under the heading *Contributions from the United States National Herbarium*, in octavo form, published by the National Museum since 1902, which contain papers relating to the botanical collections of the Museum.

The present work forms No. 197 of the *Bulletin* series.

ALEXANDER WETMORE,
Secretary, Smithsonian Institution.

CONTENTS

INTRODUCTION

This is the eighteenth in a series of bulletins of the United States National Museum on the life histories of North American birds. Previous numbers have been issued as follows:

The same general plan has been followed and the same sources of information have been utilized as in previous bulletins, to which the reader is referred. As this and the previous bulletin were prepared simultaneously and were originally intended to be published as one bulletin, the list of contributors is the same for both volumes and need not be repeated here.

Eighteen complete life histories were contributed especially for this volume; eight were written by Bernard W. Tucker and five by Dr. Winsor M. Tyler; Dr. Alden H. Miller, Wendell Taber, Alexander F. Skutch, Alexander Sprunt, Jr., and Robert S. Woods contributed one each. The same valued assistance was rendered by Dr. Winsor M. Tyler, in indexing, and by Wm. George F. Harris in preparing the egg data and measurements.

The manuscript for this volume was completed in 1943. Contributions received since then will be acknowledged later. Only information of great importance could be added. The reader is reminded again that this is a cooperative work; if he fails to find in these volumes anything that he knows about the birds, he can blame himself for not having sent the information to—

THE AUTHOR.

*Life Histories of
North American Wagtails,
Shrikes, Vireos,
and Their Allies*

LIFE HISTORIES OF NORTH AMERICAN WAGTAILS, SHRIKES, VIREOS, AND THEIR ALLIES

ORDER PASSERIFORMES (FAMILIES PRUNELLIDAE, MOTACILLIDAE, BOMBYCILLIDAE, PTILOGONATIDAE, LANIIDAE, STURNIDAE, AND VIREONIDAE)

By Arthur Cleveland Bent

Taunton, Mass.

Order PASSERIFORMES

Family PRUNELLIDAE: Accentors

PRUNELLA MONTANELLA (Pallas)

MOUNTAIN ACCENTOR

Contributed by Bernard William Tucker

HABITS

There are two records of this Siberian bird in Alaska, the first referring to a specimen taken by C. G. Harrold on Nunivak Island on October 3, 1927, and recorded by Swarth (1928). The second is of a male taken at Camp Collier, St. Lawrence Island, on October 13, 1936, and is recorded by Olaus J. Murie (1938). It was obtained by Mrs. Murie in 1937 from an Eskimo, Jimmie Otiyohok, whose wife had learned to prepare bird skins and who had recognized this as an unusual visitor.

It is only in the more southern parts of its range that this species, like a number of other Arctic forms, is confined to mountains. Farther north, as Seebohm (1901) has pointed out, it is essentially a bird of the Arctic willow swamps. Dybowski (in Taczanowski, 1872) states that in southeast Siberia, though it is tolerably common in spring, only a few remain to breed in the more elevated portions of the mountains. He met with old birds in company with fledged young in the forests of cedar mingled with firs at the foot of the Chamardaban Mountains at the south end of Lake Baikal. More recently Stegmann

1

(1936), writing of the Baikal Mountains, has described the species as mainly characteristic of the subalpine scrub zone and mentions meeting with it in two places in scrub of *Pinus pumila*. He states that the birds were shy and secretive.

Nesting.—Popham (1897), who found six nests in the forests of the Yenisei Valley at Yeniseisk, states that these were "sometimes placed as high as eight feet from the ground in the fork of a willow, and at others quite low down in the stump of a dead tree, and composed of small twigs and dry grass lined with moss and a few hairs." Farther north on the Yenisei, Seebohm (1879) found the species mainly frequenting the willow scrub near the banks of the river and took a nest in latitude 70½°, which was built within a foot of the ground.

Eggs.—The eggs are a uniform, rather deep blue and are doubtfully distinguishable from those of the European hedge-sparrow (*Prunella modularis*), though they are said to tend to be rather paler and smaller. The clutch is 4–6. Jourdain (in Hartert, 1910) gives the measurements of 31 eggs as: average, 18.55 by 13.75; maximum, 20.6 by 14.2 and 19.1 by 14.4; minimum, 17 by 13.2 and 17.2 by 12.6 millimeters.

Young.—No details are recorded.

Plumages.—The plumages are described in Hartert's great work, "Die Vögel der paläarktischen Fauna" (1910). The juvenal plumage is like the adult's, but with colors paler and with flecks of brown on the throat and breast.

Food.—The food consists of insects and other small invertebrates, together with small seeds in summer and almost exclusively in winter. Exact data seem to be almost entirely lacking, but seeds of *Amaranthus* are recorded.

Behavior.—A quiet unobtrusive bird described as very much like its better-known relative the European hedge-sparrow in habits. Like that species it is inclined to skulk in low cover, though, at any rate in the breeding season, it will also perch in and sing from tall trees, when these are present. Seebohm seldom saw it on the wing, but in autumn Miss Haviland (1915) found that birds which were met with flitting about the bushes of the Yenisei Delta frequently took wing and flew a short distance with a jerky, pipitlike flight.

Voice.—The note is a shrill triple call rendered by Seebohm (1901) as *til-il-il* and described by him as titlike. It has a short unpretentious but not unpleasing song, which both Seebohm and Popham (1897) describe as resembling that of the European hedge-sparrow, which is a short, high-pitched warbling strain. It may be delivered either from low cover or, within the limits of forest growth, from well up in a tree, and is at any rate of sufficient merit for the species to be kept as a cage bird by the Chinese.

Field marks.—No field characters have been recorded as such, but it is a small bird of somewhat warblerlike, though fairly robust, build and proportions, with black-streaked brown back, conspicuous black crown and sides of head, separated by a broad pale yellow superciliary stripe, and pale yellow underparts. The striking head pattern and yellow underparts should make it easy to be recognized. Length about 6 inches.

Fall and winter.—David and Oustalet (1877) state that in China at the beginning of the winter cold it settles in gardens and brushwood-covered places, and La Touche (1925), quoting the experience of the Bailey Willis Expedition in 1903–4, states that in the Chili-Shansi Mountains in winter "singly or in pairs they are met in almost every gulch, flitting in and out among the boulders and rugged ledges along the brooks."

DISTRIBUTION

Summer range.—Siberia from the Urals to Bering Sea, north to about 70° in the Yenisei Valley, south to the Altai, Sayansk, Baikal, and Stanovoi Mountains.

Winter range.—North China and Korea. Occasional in the Ural Mountains and stated to occur on passage in the Crimea.

Casual records.—Italy, Austria.

Family MOTACILLIDAE: Wagtails and Pipits

MOTACILLA ALBA ALBA Linnaeus

WHITE WAGTAIL

CONTRIBUTED BY BERNARD WILLIAM TUCKER

HABITS

The white wagtail is an irregular, but apparently not really very rare, visitor to east Greenland, where it has even bred occasionally, and it has been recorded once on the west coast. Winge in his "Grøn-lands Fugle" (1898) was able to quote three records, which include the still unique one for the west coast just mentioned. This refers to a female from Godthaab sent by Holbøll to the Copenhagen Museum in 1849. The other two refer to Angmagsalik, and it is from this locality, the site of the only considerable settlement on the east coast, that information as to the status of the white wagtail in Greenland is chiefly derived. This is due in the main to the careful records of Johan Petersen, the colony superintendent from 1894 to 1915, which are dealt with by Helms in his account of "The Birds of Angmagsalik" (1926). Petersen first observed a white wagtail at Angmagsalik in the spring of 1895, and this constitutes one of the records quoted by Winge. "In 1899 it was seen every day during nesting time in July–August, and on August 21st Petersen saw a young bird. It appeared for the last time on August 31st." He observed another on June 12, 1900, and one was shot on June 10, 1915. On May 15, 1900, he was also informed by a Greenlander from Sermilik, in the same district, that three had been seen there about two days previously. It may be added that Alvin Pedersen (1930) was informed by Greenlanders that the white wagtail was often met with at Angmagsalik. F. S. Chapman (1932), ornithologist on the British Arctic Air Route Expedition, records a nest with six eggs at Angmagsalik on June 16, 1931. He also records one identified near the expedition's base, west of Sermilik Fjord in the Angmagsalik district, on May 10 of the same year and two on May 16, but none were seen there after May 17. Chapman remarks that the white wagtail and several other species which breed in Iceland, only a few hundred miles distant, "all appeared for a few days and then vanished, as if they had overshot their destination."

Alvin Pedersen (1926 and 1930) records white wagtails from the Scoresby Sound district, considerably farther north. One was shot at Cape Stewart on August 24, 1924, and on June 3, 1925, he saw one at Cape Hope and a little later three at a puddle of thaw water. Men working at Cape Hope knew the birds well; they had been seen daily for some days and there were thought to be two pairs. They were not seen, however, after June 9. Another was believed to have been seen and heard at Elvdal on August 15. In his 1930 paper Pedersen records that in 1923 in the second half of March young wagtails were seen in two places. "One can therefore conclude with certainty that the species has bred at Scoresby Sound." Unfortunately, Pedersen's statement is rather ambiguous. It seems obvious that young birds could not have been hatched in Arctic Greenland in March, which seems extraordinarily early for any small birds except snow buntings to be present at all. If birds young in the sense of being in their first spring are meant, then it may be observed in the first place that it seems unlikely that they could have been recognized as such without shooting and secondly that they would only afford evidence of breeding if they were known to have wintered in the country. Of this there is, of course, no evidence whatever and in such a latitude it appears almost, if not quite, impossible. The import of Pedersen's statement is thus obscure, and it is a pity he was not more explicit. It seems logical to suppose that his birds were early migrants.

The above is, to the best of the writer's knowledge, the sum total of published information with regard to the white wagtail in Greenland, and it has seemed desirable to deal with it fairly fully, as the status of this bird in Greenland seems never to have been adequately dealt with in American literature. The A. O. U. Check-list quotes only Godhavn (on the west coast) on the authority of a second-hand statement by Prof. Alfred Newton in the "Arctic Manual" (1875) and ignores the much more numerous records for the east coast, except for the rather vague statement in a footnote "said to breed on east coast (Schiøler)." The Godhavn record is based on the inclusion of *Motacilla alba* in a list of birds obtained at that place in August 1857 by Dr. David Walker in the Ibis, 1860, p. 166, but this was an error, as Professor Newton himself subsequently showed (Yarrell's "British Birds," ed. 4, vol. 1, 1874, p. 549), so that the record should be deleted.

Apart from its visits to Greenland the white wagtail is entitled to a place on the American list on the ground of an occurrence near Fort Chimo, northern Ungava, in August 1883. With regard to this Lucien M. Turner (1885) wrote that four individuals were seen by Alex. Brown and James Lyall, of the Hudson's Bay Co., on August 29, 1883, at Hunting Bay, 4 miles south of Fort Chimo. He added that they described the birds accurately, stating that they were the two parents and two young of the year and that he placed the fullest reliance on their assertion.

The white wagtail, or its British representative, the pied wagtail (*M. alba yarrellii*), is one of the birds which an American ornithologist visiting Europe is almost sure to see, even if he has little leisure for bird observation, for it is much associated with buildings and inhabited places, though in no way confined to such. About farms and villages its liking for nesting in sheds and outbuildings or in crannies in walls attracts it into association with man, and it may be met with even in towns, in the more residential districts where some gardens and open ground are available. Among European small birds it is one of the species for which it is most difficult to define any clear-cut habitat or "biotope," and so far as one can be defined at all it must be partly in negative terms. It is found in a variety of more or less open country, especially, as already noted, about farms, buildings, and cultivation, and preferably, though by no means necessarily, near ponds, streams, or other water. Large closely built-up areas, large uninhabited tracts of moor or marshland and the like, and high elevations in mountains are generally avoided. The same is true of closely wooded country, but here comparatively limited clearings or open ground along the banks of rivers and streams will suffice to attract it. In the high north of Europe it is found mainly near the coast, while in Iceland, according to Hantzsch (1905), it prefers the lower-lying regions especially near standing or running waters and the vicinity of the sea, and displays the same attachment to farmsteads, villages, and inhabited places that it does on the mainland of Europe. It is probable that the relatively frequent records of its occurrence at Angmagsalik are not solely due to the much more regular observation there as compared with other parts of the east coast of Greenland, but again to this liking for the haunts of man— a liking, it should be added, which, at any rate in the breeding season, is sufficiently accounted for by the variety of suitable breeding sites they afford.

The name white wagtail is too firmly established to be altered, but it is a rather absurd misnomer, for the bird has a pied pattern of gray, white, and black. The name is presumably a translation of Linnaeus's "Alba" and has probably been the more readily accepted by English ornithologists because it does serve to express, though in an exaggerated form, the main difference between the black-backed British race or pied wagtail and the paler, gray-backed continental bird. In fact, in this case, as in that of the white rhinoceros, it seems that it must be understood as meaning "not so black"!

Courtship.—The courtship display of *Motacilla alba* seems more elaborate than in most small European passerines. It has been more fully described in the British form or pied wagtail than in the white wagtail proper, but there is no reason to suppose that the races differ in their behavior. The most complete account of the pied wagtail's display is that of Boase (1926).

In the early stages the female is often pursued hither and thither in a graceful, erratic, dancing flight by one, two, or more males which endeavor to induce her to pause long enough for them to posture before her with the head held high and the bill pointing upward at a sharp angle so as to display the glossy black gorget. It is somewhat curious that according to Boase's observations this display of the throat patch appears not to occur in the display of paired birds, but only in the early stages, of courtship in the narrower sense, when males are endeavoring to attract a mate. Further observation on this point is perhaps desirable. In later stages the male frequently approaches the female in a zigzag course, posturing at the same time. Boase describes two variations of this performance. In one the head was moved with a jerky bowing action, a quick flutter of the wings accompanying each return to the normal position. In the other the bird had the head depressed and carried the wing nearest the female expanded, at the same time expanding and depressing the tail and twisting it over to the same side so as to display as much as possible of its upper surface. Displays of this general type, with variations, are not uncommon.

Again, as described by Boase, the male may approach the female with wings drooping and tail spread and depressed, head held low, and the feathers of the rump raised, in a manner recalling a display posture of the European blackbird. Boase does not mention coition as following such displays, but the one just described, at any rate, is a typical preliminary to the sexual act. He does, however, describe in this connection another more striking form of posturing in which the male spreads and erects the tail vertically, with bill inclined upward and wings drooping or slightly spread or sometimes fluttered. The female may or may not respond but, according to Boase, is "generally inattentive, finding interest in a passing fly or in preening, and the whole business may end in a wild pursuit." He records one case, however, where a female joined in a display. He states that he "gives the particulars as they were noted at the time, in spite of the appearance of an error in judging the sexes." "The bird taken to be the male was facing the other when first seen and was bowing rapidly. In the raised position the neck was extended to its limit and the bill was held normally; in the lower position, the neck was retracted, the head being level with the back and the bill slightly uptilted. The other bird, judged to be the female, so far as the plumage gave indication, crept or shuffled with wings and tail moderately expanded and head depressed around the male, which turned so as to face her."

In connection with coition the female is usually passive, merely quivering the wings and raising the tail if responsive or, if not, sometimes actually dashing at and pecking the male.

The above are some of the main types of behavior, but there is a good deal of variation, the displays of wagtails, like those of a good many other small passerines, being by no means stereotyped. The Rev. E. Peake (1926) describes a case, observed on April 29, thus: "The cock approached from ten feet or so away, bobbing his head straight up and down with body flattened out. Then, when he got near, he danced round with wings curved and expanded, and his tail also expanded and drooping, and singing all the time. The hen with tail raised and head lowered stood snapping her bill."

Other minor variations could be added, but the foregoing will suffice. The reader may perhaps be reminded that these observations refer entirely to the British race, since detailed observations on the white wagtail proper of continental Europe are almost entirely lacking. It so happens that the only two brief observations available differ slightly from any recorded for the pied wagtail, but the not inconsiderable variation in the latter race has already been mentioned, and it is most unlikely that there is any real or constant difference in the display behavior of the two forms. One of the two observations referred to was, it must be noted, made on captive birds. W. E. Teschemaker (1913) in an account of white wagtails which nested in an aviary writes:

"The display is very characteristic and interesting. The female crouches on the ground with quivering wings and tail, and beak raised. The male standing sideways to her grovels on the ground, trailing his drooping wings; he then throws himself on that side which is farthest from the hen, the wing on this (the farthest) side drooped and quivering, the other wing raised perpendicularly and also quivering."

In the "Handbook of British Birds" the Rev. F. C. R. Jourdain

(1938, vol. 1) has a note on a pair of white wagtails he saw in Rumania facing one another with the tails of *both* birds almost perpendicularly erected and appearing quite rigid, but unfortunately this somewhat fragmentary observation was all that he could make, as he was passing by in a boat.

Nesting.—Where the white wagtail is a summer migrant the males usually arrive in advance of the females. In Helgoland males have been passing for about three weeks before females begin to appear. The nest is generally built in a recess or cavity of some sort or at least in a more or less concealed position. It may be found in holes in walls and other masonry or in rocks or cliffs, in steep banks, inside sheds or outbuildings, under bridges, in hollow trees or among the roots of trees, in wood stacks, among ivy, and so forth. Commonly it is well above ground level, from a couple of feet or so to perhaps 9 or 10 feet, but it may be merely under a clod in a plowed field or among marram grass on sand dunes. Occasionally it is built in the nest of some other bird, such as a song thrush, blackbird, or fieldfare. The bulk varies a good deal according to the situation. It is made of dry grass, straws, roots, fine twigs, dead leaves, and moss with cup lined with hair, feathers, or bits of wool. It is built by the female only, with the cock accompanying her. It is evident that the female is also mainly concerned in the actual selection of the site, but C. and D. Nethersole-Thompson (1943) state that the male of the pied wagtail also examines possible sites and may "suggest" sites to the female, which she thoroughly tests.

Eggs.—The ground color of the eggs is a slightly grayish or bluish white, closely freckled with gray or brownish, with underlying pale-gray markings often more or less distinct and sometimes with a few hairlike dark-brown streaks. White eggs occur and an erythristic variety has been recorded once. Jourdain (1938, vol. 1) gives the number as four or five to seven as a rule, rarely eight, and he gives the following measurement of 100 eggs: Average, 20.4 by 15.1; maximum, 21.5 by 15 and 20 by 16.2; minimum 18 by 15 millimeters. The breeding season is given by the same authority as from the end of April to early in July, exceptionally later in central Europe, but in Iceland and north Europe often not before June. Eggs may sometimes be found in Iceland by the end of May. It may be recalled that the nest in Greenland recorded by Chapman and already mentioned contained eggs on June 16, but is not known when they were laid.

Young.—Incubation is performed chiefly by the female, though according to Jourdain the male may take some share. The incubation period is 12–14 days. Teschemaker (1913) observed that eggshells were carried away from the nest by birds in captivity.

Both parents feed the young. In the case of the pied wagtail the feces of the nestlings are carried away by the parents, at least in the later stages (Blair and Tucker, 1941), and it is safe to assume that this is true also of the present race. The fledging period is 14–15 days.

Plumages.—The plumages are fully described by H. F. Witherby in the "Handbook of British Birds" (1938, vol. 1). The nestling (described under the pied wagtail, *M. a. yarrellii,* and doubtless not differing in the present race) has smoke-gray down distributed on the inner and outer supraorbital, occipital, humeral, ulnar, spinal, femoral, crural, and ventral tracts, but very scanty on the last two. The mouth is orange-yellow inside, with no spots, and externally the flanges are very pale yellow.

In the juvenal plumage the upperparts are brownish gray, lores and ear coverts dingy, buffish white, breast band dark, smoky brown, rest of breast and flanks buffish gray, throat and belly dull white with a yellowish tinge, wings and tail much as in adult. In the first winter the male is like the adult female, except for having usually rather more black on crown, and the female is also like the adult of that sex but does not show any white on forehead or black on crown as the adult may do. The gray crown has also usually an olivaceous tinge.

Food.—The food consists mainly of insects, principally Diptera, but Jourdain (1938, vol. 1) mentions also Neuroptera, Trichoptera, Ephemeroptera, etc., as well as small snails.

Behavior.—Several of the chief features of behavior are mentioned later under "Field marks." The incessant up-and-down tail motion is one of the bird's most noticeable characteristics. Though largely terrestrial, wagtails perch readily on buildings, fences, and so forth, and somewhat less freely on trees. The mainly insect food is secured chiefly on the ground or in shallow water or in little aerial excursions after flies or gnats. The birds are much attached to the neighborhood of water and may often be seen wading in the shallows of pond, lake, or stream. This association is, however, by no means obligatory, and they may be regularly met with far from water. Farmyards are a popular resort, and the birds will follow the plow in the fields, searching for small worms and burrowing larvae. In the high north they have naturally less opportunity of benefiting by agriculture and cultivation as an extra source of food supply. In Arctic Norway they are mainly coastal birds and may often be seen, as indeed they may be in the other parts of their range, foraging for flies and other arthropods among the debris about high-water mark on the seashore.

Voice.—The principal note, used both in flight and when settled, but especially in flight, is a rather shrill *tschizzik.* There is also a rather more musical *tzi-wirrp* (the *irr* to be pronounced as in *chirrup*) with variants, and the alarm note of breeding birds is an incisive *chick.* The song is a simple, but lively, warbling twitter, consisting largely of slurred repetitions of call notes with variants and modulations. It is delivered on the wing or from a perch or while the bird is running about on the ground and is quite often heard from birds on passage. Indeed, it has very little if any sexual or territorial significance, and one of the major functions served by the song of most birds, that of advertisement to possible mates in spring, seems here to be discharged by the *tschizzik* note, which is uttered persistently from such points of vantage as roofs, walls, or rocks.

Field marks.—The white wagtail and the other races of *Motacilla alba* are very easily recognized, though the separation of the races may be difficult or in some plumages impossible in the field. They are small, slim, long-tailed birds (total length about 7 inches), with a pied pattern of gray, white, and black, spending much of their time on the ground, where they walk and run actively, constantly moving the tail up and down in a very characteristic manner, and the head backward and forward. The flight is equally characteristic, strongly undulating, in a succession of long curves with the wings closed at brief intervals for perceptibly longer than in the case of most small passerines of similar size. The note *tschizzik*, which is freely used in flight, is also distinctive.

In the white wagtail the mantle and rump are clear pale gray, nape and hind part of crown black, forehead, front of crown, sides of face, and belly white. In summer the whole throat and breast are black, but in winter plumage the throat is white bounded by a horseshoe-shaped black bib. The wings and tail are blackish, with double white wing bar and white outer tail feathers. In the female the gray is rather duller than in the male, and young birds in the juvenal plumage are altogether duller and more uniformly grayish without the strong blacks and whites, as described under "Plumages." Differences from *M. a. ocularis* and *M. a. lugens*, the other two races on the American list, are mentioned in the accounts of those forms.

Enemies.—The white wagtail falls a victim at times to various hawks, and in the northern regions the merlin (pigeon hawk) is evidently its chief avian enemy. Greaves (1941) mentions (European) sparrow hawks and peregrine falcons attacking birds at roosts in Egypt. Four-footed marauders, such as rats and weasels, sometimes take toll of the nestlings, and owing to the association with human habitations which has already been stressed the domestic cat must be accounted an important enemy. Hantzsch (1905) particularly mentions prowling cats as special enemies about the farms and settlements of Iceland. In continental Europe the cuckoo frequently lays its eggs in nests of the white wagtail, and as this means that the wagtails can rear no brood of their own, since the rightful young ones are ejected from the nest by the young cuckoo, the cuckoo must be included in the list of enemies.

A list of invertebrate parasites is given by Niethammer (1937), and the same author states that not a few nestlings appear to succumb to the attacks of the larvae of the fly *Protocalliphora caerulea*.

Fall and winter.—The white wagtail is a migrant in the northern parts of its range, and in fall there is a southward movement to the Mediterranean region and Africa. In the British Isles there is a regular passage down the west coast of Great Britain and both east and west coasts of Ireland, consisting, no doubt, mainly of birds from Iceland. It has been shown in Germany (e. g., in Helgoland) that the first arrivals are young birds. Later old and young pass together (Weigold, 1926). In winter quarters, according to most observers, it seems generally to frequent the vicinity of water and may be found either singly or in small parties or in flocks, which may reach very large dimensions. It may, however, also be found well away from water. It is at roosting time that gregarious tendencies are most pronounced, for in regions where many winter, as in Egypt, hundreds and sometimes even thousands will assemble to roost together, and similar gregarious roosting takes place during migration. Reed beds and areas of tangled swamp vegetation are the sites most favored, but buildings and trees (sometimes even in towns), bushes, ivy on walls, and other sites are also made use of. Greaves (1941) has given an interesting account of roosting habits in Egypt, where enormous numbers roost in sugarcane by the Nile. He says: "The birds circle round and up and down, constantly changing directions and calling. It was not clear whether those already down called, but it seemed obvious that the leaders of the flocks were trying to find out the places where others were already roosting, and when the leaders went down the majority followed at once or after making another short flight. Generally, they dropped like stones, with closed wings, until just above the cane, sometimes from a height of forty feet or more. It was exceedingly difficult to assess numbers, but there was no doubt that on favourable occasions a single observer might see as many as 2000. Once down they rarely took to wing again unless disturbed." This was in January. The same kind of thing can be observed on a much smaller scale in Europe. Greaves further states that white wagtails wintering in Egypt "exercised a territorial habit in feeding, and regularly frequented the same garden. A male would dispute his right with another male but generally tolerate a female on his territory, sometimes two, but as observations continued it seemed clear that the association was a loose one. The female for most of the season was in close attendance on the male, and often followed him, but at other times fed alone."

DISTRIBUTION

Breeding range.—Iceland, Faeroes, and practically all Europe from the Arctic Ocean to the Mediterranean and from Portugal to the Urals, but excluding the British Isles, where the form is replaced by the pied wagtail (*M. a. yarrellii*). Also Kolguev, Corsica, Asia Minor, and Syria.

Winter range.—Southern Europe and Africa south to Kenya and Uganda, Belgian Congo (Uele River), Ubangi Shari, Sierra Leone, and Liberia; also Madeira, Palestine, southern Arabia, and Iraq.

Spring migration.—Leaves Equatorial Africa in March. Present in Egypt until early April (late date, May 2). Passage through British Isles mid-March to early in June. Passage of males begins March in Helgoland, that of females from April 9. Reaches breeding grounds in Germany and Holland in March–April, southern Finland beginning of April, and far north of Europe early in May (first arrivals recorded at Vadsö, northern Norway, May 4, and at Ust Zylma, northern Russia, May 12). Arrives southern coastal districts of Iceland at the end of April and beginning of May (early date, April 15).

Fall migration.—Leaves Iceland in August and September (recorded Westmann Islands until October 10). Passage in British Isles mid-August to early in October, in north and central Europe August to October. Even as far north as south Finland some are still passing even in November. Arrives Egypt early October (earliest date, October 7). Reaches Equatorial Africa October.

Casual records.—Jan Mayen, Azores.

MOTACILLA ALBA OCULARIS Swinhoe

SWINHOE'S WAGTAIL

HABITS

This is a northern Siberian race of the common white wagtail of Europe, from which it differs in having a black or dusty streak through the eye and having much more white on the wing coverts.

Its known breeding range in northern Siberia seems to extend from the Yenisei and Lena Rivers eastward to Plover Bay on the Chukotski Peninsula, the nearest point to Alaska, and southward in the interior to Lake Baikal. It is an extremely rare bird in Alaska, and some of the published sight records are open to doubt. Dr. E. W. Nelson (1887) writes: "Although this bird has been taken repeatedly at Plover Bay, Siberia, and thence throughout a large portion of Northeastern Asia, including China and Formosa, to the Lake Baikal region, it appears to be almost unknown in Alaska. In fact its claim as a bird of the Territory rests upon the capture of a single specimen, a young bird in summer plumage, by Captain Kellett and Lieutenant Wood in 'Northwest America', as recorded in the Brit. Mus. Cat. Birds, X, 473." The 1931 Check-list gives two Alaska records, Attu Island and mouth of the Yukon, both sight records. The former is based on the following statement by Lucien M. Turner (1886):

I was looking out of my window on the morning of May 14, 1881, watching the vessel, which was to take me to Unalashka Island, enter the harbor. I saw a bird just beneath the window and on the ground, not more than seven feet from my eyes. At the first glance I supposed the bird to be *Plectrophanax nivalis*. A moment sufficed to convince me that it was not. I ran to get my gun; and, as I opened the door, of the entry-way, to get out, the door opened directly on the bird, which, with a chirp precisely like that of *Budytes flavus leucostriatus*, flew off to a distance of 75 yards and alighted. I approached as nearly as I dared and fired at it, but failed to obtain it, as the gun was loaded with No. 3 shot. It flew off beyond the hills and was not seen again.

This may, of course, have been *ocularis*, but it seems much more likely that it was *lugens*, which is common on the nearby Commander Islands. The record for the mouth of the Yukon is based on the following statement by Dr. Louis B. Bishop (1900) : "On the morning of August 28 the *Robert Kerr*, on which I was a passenger, was hindered from proceeding by a gale and low water on the bar, and was made fast to the bank at the Aphoon mouth of the Yukon. As I came on deck I saw half a dozen white wagtails fly about the vessel and settle in the grass close by. While I returned for my gun they left, but a thorough acquaintance with *Motacilla alba* in Egypt, where it is abundant during the winter, leaves me no doubt that these birds were wagtails." These *probably* were Swinhoe's wagtails, but no specimens were taken.

The most remarkable American record, which is supported by a specimen and so not open to question, is Lyman Belding's (1883) Lower California record; he reports "a single specimen shot January 9, 1882, during a cold gale from the north. It was found on a drift of sea-weed on the beach." His specimen was an adult in winter plumage and was taken at La Paz, near the southern extremity of the peninsula. It seems hardly likely that this wandering waif could have crossed the broad expanse of the Pacific Ocean, unless it had been transported on some ship from southern Asia. It may, of course, have wandered across Bering Strait and then followed the Pacific coastline southward, but it is strange that no other specimen has ever been taken or seen anywhere along this coast south of Alaska.

F. Seymour Hersey (1916), who made two trips to northern Alaska to gather material for this work, published the following report on his experience with Swinhoe's wagtail: "Although this bird has been considered merely a straggler to Alaska, there are reasons for believing that the species is slowly extending its range and becoming established on our coast. During the northern cruise a number of individuals were seen between Kotzebue Sound and Cape Lisburne.

"At Chamisso Island, on August 1, a pair of birds were carrying food into a crevice in the rocks at an inaccessible point on the cliff. One or two were also seen at other points, and at Cape Lisburne I succeeded in shooting a bird which, unfortunately, fell on the farther side of a creek where it could not be found."

Alfred M. Bailey (1926), who spent parts of two seasons in northern

Alaska, says of this wagtail: "Only one specimen was seen on the Alaska side and that at Wales on June 23. While travelling down the coast by dog sled I found a mud nest in an abandoned igloo. The native with me told me it was the nest of a little bird 'all same snowbird, little longer'. It was similar to the nest which I found in the cliff along Providence Bay, but I was unable to carry it with me for possible identification."

N. G. Buxton (J. A. Allen, 1905) found Swinhoe's wagtail abundant around Gichiga and Marcova, in northeastern Siberia, where 17 specimens were collected; he says in his notes: "The first birds arrive the middle of May, but they do not become common before June 1. Before and after the nesting time they are seen in twos and threes about the houses and along the river banks and seacoast, but they never collect in flocks like the Yellow Wagtails, and are seldom seen far back on the tundra. They nest in the crevices in the banks of the streams and along the seacoast and on the ground in the grassy places along the streams. They are good songsters, singing especially while on the wing. They begin to depart the latter part of August and are seldom seen after the middle of September."

Migration.—Swinhoe's wagtail is evidently a common migrant through China. Tsen-Hwang Shaw (1936) records it as passing through Hopei Province in April and again in September and the first part of October. "A few of these birds winter in some warm places within the territory of Hopei province." Vaughan and Jones (1913) write:

> The Streak-eyed Wagtail is an exceedingly common bird of passage at Hong Kong, Macao, and on the Kwang Tung coast generally. Although appearing as early as August 9 on migration, the latter part of September or early October is the more usual time for their advent, when immense numbers may be seen on the cricket-ground and in the Naval dockyard and elsewhere on the island of Hong Kong. The birds on their passage usually roost in the trees, and as many as fifty were observed to crowd themselves, with much bickering, into a small tree in the Naval dockyard. They leave again on the spring migration in April, and probably only breed in the far north of Asia; they do not occur inland, so that their migration is along the coast-line.

Johan Koren, collecting for Thayer and Bangs (1914), reported that "Swinhoe's wagtail arrived at Nijni Kolymsk, on May 15, 1912, and in the autumn of 1911 was observed as late as Sept. 21."

Nesting.—Aside from the probable nests mentioned by Messrs. Hersey and Bailey, no nest seems to have been found in Alaska, but several have been found in Siberia. Thayer and Bangs (1914) say that "a nest with a set of six eggs was taken at Nijni Kolymsk, June 11, 1912. It was built under the roof of a log cabin in the village."

Mr. Bailey (1926) writes: "A nest was found July 5 with five badly incubated eggs, in a little crevice in a crumbling rock cliff facing Providence Bay, about twenty feet from the ground. The nest was of grasses, plastered together with mud and lined with a few feathers, as in a robin's nest. It was fastened rather firmly into the nesting cranny. Unfortunately, I fell with the nest, breaking the eggs. The parent birds hovered overhead all the time I was attempting to climb the rotten walls, one of them having flushed from the nest when I first discovered it."

Theodore Pleske (1928) mentions a nest and six eggs of Swinhoe's wagtail, taken on June 19, 1902, at the mouth of the Elijdep River, of which he says: "The nest is large, solidly built and thick-walled; it is made of dry grass blades of the preceding year interwoven with twigs, sometimes fairly thick, of a small shrub, probably *Betula nana*, and tufts of moss or lichen. The inner layer of the nest is formed of finer grass so arranged that the material becomes finer and finer toward the lining. The cavity itself is abundantly furnished with hair of the wild reindeer very skilfully selected from the finest tufts and in addition a feather of the Snowy Owl (*Nyctea nyctea*)."

A set of five eggs in the Wilson C. Hanna collection was taken near Lake Baikal on May 30, 1898, from a nest situated on the ground, composed of roots and moss and lined with fur.

Eggs.—Five or six eggs generally constitute the full set for the Swinhoe's wagtail. Mr. Pleske (1928) describes the eggs referred to above as follows: "The eggs have a white ground color covered with small spots of a drab brown (Ridgway, Pl. 46, drab) uniformly disposed over the surface and forming a wreath at the large end and a small number of black lines on the large ends of some of the eggs."

Mr. Hanna describes his eggs as ovate in shape, slightly glossy white, and thickly marked, more heavily on the large ends, with fine markings of "buffy brown," "buffy olive," and "light brownish olive."

The measurements of 26 eggs average 20.1 by 15.0 millimeters; the eggs showing the 4 extremes measure 22.0 by 15.8, 17.3 by 14.5, and 19.9 by 14.1 millimeters.

Plumages.—As Swinhoe's wagtail is considered to be only a subspecies of the common white wagtail, its molts and plumages probably follow the same sequence, as fully described in Witherby's Handbook (1919).

In Nelson's "The Birds of Bering Sea and the Arctic Ocean" (1883), facing page 63, there is a fine colored plate of an adult male in full spring plumage, which shows the characters of the subspecies very clearly. And in Turner's "Contributions to the Natural History of Alaska" (1886), facing page 178, there is a good colored plate of the adult and young in winter.

La Touche (1930) says of the immature plumages: "Young birds are entirely dull grey on the upper parts, the forehead grey of a lighter tint, a white eyebrow and a blackish trans-ocular stripe; the sides of the head are mottled with grey, the throat feathers are edged with black and the breast has a blackish crescent-shaped patch. The face and throat are generally suffused with yellow. After the autumn moult the young bird has the forehead and the forecrown white, but the hind crown is grey like the rest of the upper parts. The black begins to appear on the head during the first winter."

Food.—Mr. Shaw (1936) says: "This bird, like several other wagtails, is insectivorous. Its food consists of spiders, beetles, and some other insects and their larvae."

Behavior.—Mr. Hersey writes (1916) : "My failure to secure specimens was due to the excessively restless habits of the birds. When on the ground they were largely concealed by intervening clumps of moss and the general character of the tundra, while they were liable to take wing at a moment's notice and usually flew long distances. Their flight was so erratic that it was exceedingly difficult to shoot them on the wing."

DISTRIBUTION

CONTRIBUTED BY BERNARD WILLIAM TUCKER

Data on winter and summer ranges and migrations are summarized by Paludan (1932), whose paper should be consulted for fuller particulars.

Breeding range.—Northeast Siberia from the Tchuktchi Peninsula west to the Yenisei (Turukhansk) and south to the Stanovoi Mountains.

Winter range.—South China, Formosa, Hainan, Indochina, Tenasserim, Burma, Assam, West Bengal, Philippines.

Spring migration.—Leaves winter quarters in April; last recorded north Kansu May 8, North Chihli May 10, Amurland May 10; arrival at Nijni Kolymsk, northeast Siberia, May 15. Recorded Bering Island from May 9.

Fall migration.—Recorded Nijni Kolymsk as late at September 21; Chihli, September 15 to October 10; Szechwan, September–November; Kwangtung, September.

MOTACILLA ALBA LUGENS Kittlitz

BLACK-BACKED WAGTAIL

CONTRIBUTED BY WINSOR MARRETT TYLER

HABITS

A black-backed wagtail was taken on Attic, now called Attu, Island on May 4, 1913, apparently the first and so far the only record of the occurrence of the species in North America. John E. Thayer and Outram Bangs (1921) published the record of its capture:

During the course of the expedition to the Arctic coasts of East Siberia and Northern Alaska in 1913 and 1914, upon which Messrs. Joseph Dixon and W. Sprague Brooks went as zoological collectors, their power schooner, the "Polar Bear," put into the harbor at Attic Island, the outermost of the Aleutian chain, in early May, 1913. From the deck of the vessel here several black and white Wagtails, recognized as *Motacilla lugens* Kittlitz, were seen flitting about the beaches, and on May 4, one adult male was secured.

This specimen, now No. 21590 collection of John E. Thayer, is the first, we believe to be recorded from North America.

J. D. D. La Touche (1930) in his handbook of the birds of eastern China gives the range of the black-backed wagtail thus:

This fine Wagtail summers in "Kamtschatka, Commander Is., Kurile Is., Askold Is., Hokkaido and N. Hondo (Awomori), and on the Aleutian Is. [?], and its extra-Chinese winter range includes South Japan, the Riu Kiu Is., and Formosa." * * * The Kamtschatkan Wagtail is quite common at Swatow during the winter, but it does not appear to have been noticed by Mell in the interior of Kwangtung or by Vaughan and Jones on the West River. At Foochow it is common enough on passage and a fair number may be seen there in winter as well. * * * At Chinkiang I saw a good many, but chiefly in spring. At Shaweishan it was observed from the 8th March to the 8th May, and in October. This Wagtail is found on wet fields, marshy ground, and mud-flats. I never saw it in the valley of the Min above Foochow, nor in the mountains.

Sten Bergman (1935) gives the following account (freely translated from the German) of the black-backed wagtail in Kamchatka and the Kurile Islands:

The form of white wagtail that breeds in Kamchatka is *Motacilla alba lugens*. It is very common inland as well as on the seacoast, but commoner on the latter. I met it in all parts of the peninsula that I visited during the summer. The first acquaintance that I made with it was on Cape Lopatka, where our ship had a mishap. Here it was everywhere on the seashore, especially on the eastern side, on the rocky shores, where the white wings of the birds contrasted with the dark stones. On the coast of the Pacific Ocean I found it breeding in all the creeks near my camp between Cape Lopatka and Petropawlowsk. Farther north on the same coast Malaise found the black-backed wagtail breeding at Cape Olga, and I found it myself at Ust Kamchatsk. On the Okhotsk Sea I found it in family parties from Cape Lopatka to Bolsheretsk between August 20 and September 2. Malaise found it in the fall of 1921 on Kronoki Lake. In the dry woods the black-backed wagtail is naturally absent. It needs water in order to prosper, and I have never seen one on Kamchatka far from a stream or lake. Its call seems to me identical to that of the white wagtail. Next to the lark, it is the earliest of the small migrants to arrive in Kamchatka. In 1921 I saw the first example in Petropawlowsk on April 22, but sometimes they come even earlier. They generally leave the country at the end of September, but some remain even longer, and I saw a wagtail in Petropawlowsk on October 22.

Motacilla alba lugens builds its nest in many different kinds of places. The normal one is on the shore of the sea or a river, on the ground, not far from water. but the wagtail is also fond of human society and sometimes builds its nest about houses. Building begins in the first half of May. I found a pair on May 14th that were already busy with their nest under the projection of the roof of a house in Petropawlowsk. In Klutschi I found a nest on the roof of a native hut, another on a balagan (a drying rack for salmon), and a third on a boat drawn up on the shore of a river. The nests are large and firm, and are similar to those of the white wagtail. I collected three nests which are now in the Swedish National Museum. The three are almost entirely lined with animal hair, generally from reindeer. Scarcely a feather occurs in any of the nests.

The eggs are laid at the end of May. I found two nests with freshly laid eggs on the 30th and 31st of May near Klutschi. The first pair, whose nest was collected on the 30th of May, immediately began to build a new one about 20 meters from the site of the earlier one in a drawn-up skiff, and had on June 12th a complete nest with five eggs. The building consumed 9 days. The eggs agree in color and size with those of the white wagtail.

The wagtail, except *Hirundo rustica tytleri*, is the only small bird in Kamchatka that seeks human companionship, and nests in houses.

This form breeds commonly on all the Kurile Islands, according to Yamashina. The wagtail is the first of all the birds to arrive in the Kuriles in the spring. After the young have flown, the wagtails are found in family groups along the seashore.

Field marks.—According to Bernard W. Tucker the male in breeding plumage differs from *M. a. alba* and *ocularis* in having a black back. He says that it is much like the pied wagtail (*M. a. yarrellii*) of the British Isles but differs in having the secondaries wholly or largely white and a black streak through the eye as in *ocularis* and that the female and the male in winter have gray backs, or largely gray, and could not be distinguished from *ocularis* in the field; indeed many specimens in the hand appear to him to be separable only with difficulty.

Winter.—The habits are similar to those of other races of *M. alba*. La Touche (1930) states that in China it is found on wet fields, marshy ground, and mud flats.

DISTRIBUTION

Breeding range.—Kamchatka, Kurile Islands, Sakhalin, Yezzo, and north Hondo. Westerly limits somewhat uncertain; recorded from Askold Island and the Amur; but "apparently not on the Amur," according to Hartert and Steinbacher (1938).

Winter range.—Southeast China (Lower Yangtse, Fokhien, and Kwangtung), south Japan, Riu-Kiu Islands, and Formosa.

Spring migration.—Data on migration are summarized by Paludan (1932). Noted passing at Shaweishan, off the mouth of the Yangtse, from March 8 to May 8; arrives Kuriles from early March, but said not to do so in Kamchatka until April–May.

Fall migration.—Gone from Kuriles by end October; recorded at Ussuria and Shaweishan in October and Lower Yangtse in November.

MOTACILLA FLAVA ALASCENSIS (Ridgway)

ALASKA YELLOW WAGTAIL

HABITS

This pretty little bird is our American representative of a wide-ranging species of northern Europe and Asia, from Norway and Sweden to northeastern Siberia. It is one of the few Asiatic species that have wandered across Bering Strait and become more or less firmly established in Alaska, but the yellow wagtail has become more firmly established than the others and is now really abundant in its limited range on this continent, from Point Barrow and Kotzebue Sound to the mouth of the Nushagak River, on the Bering Sea coast of Alaska. It probably breeds also on St. Matthew Island and perhaps on other islands in Bering Sea. On the tundra back of Nome, in July 1911, we were surprised to find the yellow wagtail to be one of the most characteristic and most conspicuous of the small land birds of the region. The young were on the wing then and were much in evidence everywhere, especially in the willow patches and around the small ponds on the tundra, but also on the outskirts of the town. Except near the town they were quite shy, especially when on the ground, but they were constantly flitting about over us, with their peculiar, buoyant, billowy flight and continuous twittering notes.

Dr. Nelson (1887) says that "in the vicinity of Saint Michaels it is one of the most familiar and common land birds, and as one walks over the open tundra its familiar clinking, metallic note strikes pleasantly on the ear. It usually has a preference for the boggy, moss-grown portions of the country." Dr. Grinnell (1900) found it to be "an abundant summer bird of the coast region of Kotzebue Sound." The first specimen he secured "was flushed from the weedy border of a dwarf alder thicket near a pond."

Our Alaska race of this species was once supposed to be identical with the form found in eastern Siberia, *M. f. leucostriatus*, which is decidedly duller in coloration than the brightly colored, olive-and-yellow type form that is found in northern Europe. Our bird is now regarded as distinct from the Siberian race, and is even duller in coloration; Mr. Ridgway (1904) describes *alascensis* as similar to *M. f. leucostriatus*, "but slightly smaller, especially the bill; coloration duller, the yellow of the under parts paler and less pure, the chest more distinctly clouded or blotched with grayish, the olive-green of rump, etc., less pronounced."

Spring.—By just what route the Alaska yellow wagtail reaches its summer home on the Bering Sea coast of Alaska does not seem to be definitely known; and it never will be known until enough specimens have been collected on migration in eastern Asia to separate our bird from the form breeding in northeastern Siberia. It probably follows the same route by which the species originally invaded this continent. Dr. Nelson (1883) says that it "makes its appearance the last of May or the first of June, according to the season." And Lucien M. Turner (1886) says: "This bird arrives about the 12th of June; a few days earlier or later, depending on the opening of the spring." Herbert Brandt (1943) writes: "We did not observe this Palaearctic species as a transient about Hooper Bay during the migration, and it does not seem likely that such a conspicuous bird could escape us had it passed through our region in anything like the numbers that congregated in the mountains a little farther north. It seems probable that this wagtail arrives either from the north or directly across Bering Sea from its Asiatic winter haunts."

Courtship.—Dr. Nelson (1887) writes:

When the male pays his addresses to the female in spring a peculiar performance takes place, somewhat like that of the Yellow Chat. The male starts up from a bank or clump of bushes, and, rising for 20 or 30 yards at a sharp angle, suddenly stiffens and decurves his wings, at the same time slowly spreading and elevating his tail nearly perpendicularly to his body, and in this curious position he floats slowly down until within a foot or two of the ground, uttering a low, clear, and rapid medley of jingling notes which can only be compared to the sound made by lightly rattling together the links of a small steel chain. This performance is very commonly executed over a large snow-bank, as if the bird appreciated the contrast afforded by such a background. As he approaches the ground in his descent he suddenly glides away to a neighboring bush or knoll, whence he repeats the maneuver.

Nesting.—Dr. Nelson (1887) says:

Their nests are usually placed under the edge of a tussock or slightly overhanging bank, bunch of grass, or in fact of any similar shelter, under which they can partially or wholly conceal the nest. Their preference, however, is for grassy borders of a rather steeply sloping bank, along the brow of which they place their nests. As one walks over the grass-covered places frequented by these birds, during the breeding season, he is likely to see a female flutter off her eggs at his feet, and, flying away a few yards, alight and glide away, mouse-like, among the grass with such rapidity that, unless closely watched, she quickly disappears. In some cases she will lie thus concealed for some time, and other times she joins the male at once and circles about overhead.

He says that no two of his seven nests are exactly alike:

The outer portion is usually composed of bits of grass and moss, pretty compactly arranged, with the central cavity well lined with some warm material, such as the hair of dogs and man, or Ptarmigan feathers, or a combination of the three. One nest is built mainly of fine grass lined with a closely felted layer of dogs' hair. The second nest has a thin layer of moss and grass followed by one of feathers, and the six eggs it contains rest upon a layer of silky-brown club-mosses. The third is composed of a felted layer of dogs' hair at the bottom, followed by a thin layer of feathers; this is succeeded by a still thinner layer of club-moss, and the eggs rest upon a felted layer of dogs' hair. The fourth nest is composed of a uniform loosely joined structure of feathers and pieces of grass all mingled into a heterogeneous mass.

Wilson C. Hanna has sent me the data for six sets of eggs of the Alaska yellow wagtail that came to him with the parent birds, five from the Meade River, 100 miles southeast of Barrow, and one from Wales, Alaska. Three nests were in the roots of small willows on the bank of the river, one was in long grass on the river bank, one was on a grassy knoll near some willow roots, and the nest at Wales was "situated at mound at old dwelling place." The nests were made mainly of grasses and fine plant stems, with sometimes a few dead leaves, rootlets, mosses, or feathers. The three nests that he has in his collection are of "rather compact construction"; one has only the finer material for a lining, and another has a good lining of reindeer hair, mouse hair, moss, and a few feathers. The measurements of these nests vary in outside diameter from 4 to 4.5 inches, in inside diameter from 2 to 2.3, in outside depth from 2.5 to 3, and in inside depth from 1.7 to 1.8 inches. Dr. Lawrence H. Walkinshaw (1948) gives a somewhat similar account of the nesting of this species near Bethel, Alaska.

Eggs.—The Alaska yellow wagtail lays four to seven eggs to a set, five and six being the commonest. Mr. Hanna gives me the following description of the 17 eggs in his collection: "The eggs are ovate to short-ovate and are without gloss. At first glance they look like some eggs of the horned lark, but smaller in size. The ground color is 'deep olive-buff' to 'dark olive-buff.' The markings are fine and rather uniform over the entire surface of the eggs, but in at least a few cases heavier on the larger end. The markings are 'light brownish olive' to 'buffy olive'."

Dr. Nelson's description (1887) is somewhat different; of a series of 37 eggs, he says: "The ground color of the eggs varies from a pale-greenish clay to a clayey white, over which extends a profuse confluent mottling, varying from slaty to reddish brown, which, in some cases, almost hides the ground color; in others the spots are large and less numerous, and do not cover the shells so completely. The eggs of the same set usually are of a similar shade and markings, and in but one set can the slightest traces of zigzag markings be found about the larger ends."

The measurements of 50 eggs average 19.1 by 14.4 millimeters; the eggs showing the four extremes measure 20.9 by 15.3, 19.5 by 15.6, 18.0 by 14.4, and 18.5 by 13.2 millimeters.

Young.—Mr. Turner (1886) says that "incubation lasts ten to thirteen days. The young birds are fed exclusively on insect food. They are able to fly in fifteen to eighteen days after hatching. The earliest birds sometimes hatch two broods of young in a season, as young just able to fly have been observed as late as August 18th." When we were at Nome, around the middle of July, the young were fully fledged and on the wing; small parties were often seen about the houses on the outskirts of the town and on the beaches, where they evidently found an abundance of food.

Plumages.—Ridgway (1904) notes no sexual difference in the juvenal plumage, which he describes as "above olive-brown, the wings and tail as in the autumnal plumage; superciliary stripe, malar stripe, and under parts pale yellowish buff, relieved by a conspicuous crescentic patch on chest of sooty black, connected laterally with a submalar stripe of the same color along each side of the throat; bill, legs, and feet brownish."

The postjuvenal molt takes place between July and September. This involves some wing coverts and all the contour plumage, but not the rest of the wings or the tail. It produces a first-winter plumage, which is practically like that of the adult. Ridgway (1904) describes the young male in this plumage as "above plain olive, more grayish on head and rump; wings and tail as in adults; superciliary stripe, chin, and throat pale straw yellow, the first two paler, nearly white; rest of under parts pale buffy yellow or yellowish buff, paler (nearly white) on under tail-coverts; chest tinged with brown, and with a distinct crescentic patch of darker brown; sides and flanks light grayish brown or olive." He describes the young female as similar, but "chest less strongly tinged with brown and with only a few spots of darker brown."

As with some of the Eurasian races, there is probably quite an extensive prenuptial molt in birds of all ages, which involves all the contour plumage, most of the wing coverts and the central tail feathers, though we have not the material to show it in our subspecies. Adults have a complete postnuptial molt, beginning late in July and sometimes lasting through September. There seem to be no winter specimens available that are definitely known to belong to this subspecies, but the winter plumages are probably similar to those of closely allied races, which are fully described in Witherby's Handbook (1919).

Food.—Not much is known about the food of the Alaska yellow wagtail, which probably does not differ materially from that of the species elsewhere. Witherby's Handbook (1919) says that the food of the European race consists "almost entirely of insects (coleoptera and larvae, diptera, orthoptera, larvae of lepidoptera, rhynchota, etc.). Saxby records small worms, larvae, aquatic insects, and small univalves, but these are probably exceptional and diptera constitute bulk of food."

Dr. Grinnell (1900) saw some of these wagtails feeding on salmon-berries, which grew plentifully near the alder thickets. He says also: "Several came around our tents at Mission Inlet daily for crumbs, and if I kept quiet they would come quite close. A wagtail would approach from the nearest grass-patch, sidling along, hopping daintily with ever-changing attitude and canting its head from one side to the other. At every step or two the bird would hesitate a moment before again advancing, its tail nervously twitching up and down. If it spied a crumb, a quick dart and away the bird would fly to a safer rendezvous. The wagtails would also snap up lots of flies."

Behavior.—On July 13, 1911, I was exploring the tundra back of Nome, Alaska. From the top of a low hill I could see a small pond about a mile away and walked over to it, where I found three or four small ponds with wet meadows and marshy ground about them. On the way down over the tundra, as I approached a patch of low willows, I noticed a small bird, which at first I thought was a pipit, flying back and forth in front of me, going over the same space again and again until I became tired watching it and waiting for it to alight. It had a peculiar, billowy, fluttering flight, was twittering constantly, and seemed to be tied to one spot just in front of me, swinging back and forth like a pendulum. I soon saw that it was not a pipit, for I could recognize the bright yellow breast and the conspicuous white tail feathers of the Alaska yellow wagtail. It was my first experience with this lovely little bird, which was really abundant about the willow patches and around edges of the swampy ponds. The peculiar behavior of this individual was probably due to the presence of young in that particular spot. There were plenty of fully fledged young on the wing, but there were probably others in the nests, for we saw adults with food in their bills.

At low tide these birds, especially the young, resorted to the beaches to pick up bits of food left by the receding waves; here they flitted gracefully among the rocks or walked daintily over the wet ground, nodding their heads and flirting their tails after the manner of pipits or the other wagtails. They were always shy on the ground but, if flushed, would come back and circle overhead, where their restless and erratic flight made them difficult to shoot.

Dr. Nelson (1887) writes: "Even during the breeding season they are ever on the alert, and the approach of a stranger to their haunts is sure to bring several of them from bush or flat to protest against the right-of-way. They may be distinguished, while yet far away, by their long, easy, swinging flight, undulating in their course like *Spinus tristis*, or a Woodpecker; drawing near, they circle slowly overhead, constantly uttering the sharp plé-plé-plé, or alighting for a moment upon a small bush or hummock, flirting their tails and moving restlessly about, apparently consumed with nervous impatience, and scarcely have they touched the ground ere they are again on the wing."

Voice.—The courtship flight song is referred to under that heading, and the call note is described above by Dr. Nelson. Dr. Grinnell (1900) referred to the latter note as a faint *pe-weet*, uttered at frequent intervals. These are the notes that I recorded as twittering notes; I never heard any very musical notes, nor anything that could be called a song.

Dr. Lawrence H. Walkinshaw (1948) observed that the "song was usually a high *tzee-zee-zee*, or a *ter-zwee–ter-zwee–zwee–zwee*. The regular rate of singing was about seven times per minute on warmer days during the morning. The birds sang periodically throughout the day, but not continuously."

Field marks.—The yellow wagtails can be recognized by their yellow or yellowish breasts, white throats, and dark cheek patches. Otherwise they closely resemble pipits in appearance and behavior.

Fall.—Dr. Nelson (1887) says that "early in August the old birds commence to disappear, and by the middle of the month are seen only occasionally, although on the 18th of August they have been noted on Saint Lawrence Island. The young remain longer and are found in scattered parties all about the settlements and native houses in the same localities favored by the common Water Wagtail, which occurs sparingly along the coast at this season. The Yellow Wagtail trips daintly along the grassy margins of the muddy spots, its vibrating tail and slender form distinguishing it among the motley crowd of Savanna Sparrows, Lapland Longspurs, and common Wagtails which keep it company."

Mr. Turner (1886), probably referring to the young birds, says:

By the 1st of September the birds of this species collect into small flocks, of eight to twenty in number, and remain as late as September 21st, at which date they have about all disappeared. They generally signalize their readiness to depart by assembling on the low banks, bordering the beach, and dart high into the air to return to the same, or similar, place after a few minutes time. At this particular season of the year they are extremely wary and difficult of approach. * * * I once observed the bird on Attu Island (the westernmost of the Aleutian Chain) on Sunday, October 8, 1880. I chased the bird up and down for two hours, but was not able to get near enough for a shot, as it was very wild. It was evidently on the fall migration, and none were seen after that day. It does not remain on the Aleutian Islands during the breeding season.

Like some other representatives of Asiatic species that breed in Alaska, this wagtail does not migrate down the Pacific coast of North America but prefers to retrace its steps over the ancestral route and migrate down the eastern coast of Asia to its winter haunts in southeastern Asia and the islands beyond, perhaps across Bering Strait or through the western Aleutians.

DISTRIBUTION

Range.—According to the A. O. U. Check-list (1931) the Alaska yellow wagtail: "Breeds in the Arctic Zone in extreme northeastern Siberia and western Alaska from Point Barrow and Kotzebue Sound to Nushagak River; migrates through the western Aleutian Islands to eastern Asia."

ANTHUS SPINOLETTA RUBESCENS (Tunstall)

AMERICAN PIPIT

HABITS

The pipit, apparently a frail but really a hardy bird, seeks its summer home in regions that would seem to us most unattractive and forbidding, among the moss-covered, rocky hills on the bleak coast of Labrador, along the Arctic tundra to northern Alaska, up to 70° on the west coast of Greenland, and then far southward in the Rocky Mountains to Colorado and New Mexico, where it breeds only above tree limits on the wind-swept mountaintops. In the far north and in Labrador it breeds on low hills not far above sea level, but in the mountains its summer haunts become gradually higher as the tree limit rises; on Mount McKinley, Alaska, it breeds from 4,000 to 5,000 feet altitude, in Oregon it is recorded as breeding above 8,500 feet, in Wyoming above 11,000, in Colorado above 12,000, and in New Mexico, at the southern limit of its breeding range, we may find it above 13,000 feet.

On the Labrador coast we found pipits very common all along the coastal strip from Battle Harbor to Cape Mugford, on most of the rocky islands and on the inland hilltops above tree growth. In that region the only tree growth is found in the sheltered hollows back from the coast and in the inland valleys. Elsewhere the coastal strip is mostly bare rock, with a luxuriant growth of reindeer moss, other mosses and lichens clothing the hollows; in the more sheltered places a few small shrubs and dwarfed deciduous trees struggle for existence. Insect life is abundant here during the long days of the short summer, so that the pipits have an ample food supply; they seem to thrive in even the most exposed places.

Spring.—The pipit, although abundant in fall, seems to avoid New England to a large extent on the spring migration, for it is comparatively rare and quite irregular here at that season. Its northward migration seems to be mainly west of the Alleghenies. This point is well illustrated in Milton B. Trautman's (1940) account of the migration at Buckeye Lake, Ohio. "The first migrating American Pipits," he says, "arrived between March 1 and 25. Flocks of moderate or large size, 15 to 500 birds, appeared to be dominant in spring, and only during the very last part of migration were groups of less than 10 birds often observed. The peak of migration occurred from the last of March until mid-April. Then it was possible to record as many as 800 individuals in a day. * * * Throughout spring the species was found principally in recently plowed fields, in wheat fields where the plants averaged less than 5 inches in height, in short-grass pastures, and on the larger mud flats about 'sky ponds', or overflow puddles."

Courtship.—The song flight of the pipit is the most conspicuous part of the courtship performance. This is very well described by Joseph Dixon (1938), who observed it on Mount McKinley, as follows: "On May 20, 1926, high up among the vanishing snowfields on a rocky barren ridge at 4,000 feet, we watched a male pipit in full nuptial flight. It perched on a rock, then flew almost vertically into the sky for a distance of from 50 to 150 feet, singing a single note which was repeated constantly. Then with legs extended, feet spread out, and tail sticking upwards at a sharp angle, this male bird sang steadily as he fluttered his wings and floated down like a falling leaf, usually landing near the place from whence he began his flight."

Dr. Charles W. Townsend (Townsend and Allen, 1907) observed a similar flight-song in Labrador and gives the following information about it:

As he went up he sang repeatedly a simple refrain, *che-whée, che-whée* with a vibratory resonance on the *whée*. Attaining an eminence of * * * perhaps 200 feet from the ground, he checked himself and at once began the descent. He went down faster and faster, repeating his song at the same time faster and faster. Long before he reached the ground he set his wings and tipped from side to side to break his descent. After remaining quiet on the ground for a few moments he repeated the performance and we watched him go up four or five times. On one occasion he was twenty seconds going up, emitting his refrain forty-eight times. In the descent he was quicker, accomplishing it in ten seconds and singing thirty-two bars of his song.

Gayle Pickwell (1947) noticed, on Mount Rainier, Wash., that two males in the vicinity of a female "were battling violently. One of the males was on the near-by snow. The other male plunged down from above with a determination rarely to be observed in avian battles. * * * These pipits fought on the ground as well as in the air. One stayed largely on the snow while the other dashed upon him from above and there was no denying the seriousness of their struggles."

Nesting.—The two nests of the American pipit that I saw on the coast of Labrador in 1912 were probably typical of the species, in that locality at least. The first nest was shown to me on July 6, in the bare, rocky hills of Battle Island, by two of Dr. Grenfell's nurses, Miss Coates and Miss Thompkins, whom I had met in Newfoundland. The nest was very prettily located on the side of a little moss-covered ridge or hummock, in a little valley near the top of the moss- and lichen-covered island; it was sunk deeply into the soft mosses that overhung the entrance on the side of the little cavity; the nest seemed to be made entirely of fine, dry grasses. It contained five eggs, which I did not disturb. The incubating bird was quite tame and, if quietly approached, could almost be touched on the nest.

The other nest (pl. 2) was shown me by an Eskimo, on July 21, near Hopedale. It was similarly located, near the top of a bare, rocky hill, under the overhanging edge of a moss-covered hummock; it was a larger nest than the other and was made of fine twigs and coarse grasses and lined with finer grass; the four eggs that it contained were nearly ready to hatch.

There is little to be said about the nests in other localities, except that they are always placed on the ground in decidedly open situations, but they are almost always more or less sheltered under some outcropping rock or projecting stones, or under the overhang of some eminence. Some dried moss may be placed in the hollow to protect the eggs against the moisture from the ground, but the nests seem to be made almost entirely of dried grasses and to have no other warm lining. A nest mentioned in some notes sent to me by O. J. Murie was "placed in the moss at the edge of a rock, back under a willow root."

Of two nests observed by Gayle Pickwell (1947), "one was in a clump of yellow heather and another beneath the leaves of a purple aster."

Eggs.—The American pipit lays four to seven eggs; four and five seem to be the commonest numbers. They are ovate and have very little gloss. The ground color is grayish white or dull white, sometimes buffy white, but it is often so thickly covered with the markings that it is hardly visible and the egg appears to be of a dark chocolate color, indistinctly marked with small black lines. In the less heavily marked eggs the spots are more distinct and are in various shades of bright or dull browns, from chocolate to hair brown, or in some shades of drab or gray. Sometimes these markings are concentrated into solid color at the larger end. The measurements of 50 eggs in the United States National Museum average 19.9 by 14.7 millimeters; the eggs showing the four extremes measure 21.8 by 15.5, 17.8 by 14.2, and 19.8 by 13.7 millimeters.

Young.—The period of incubation does not seem to have been definitely determined, but it probably does not differ materially from that of closely related European species, 13 or 14 days. According to the observations of Hazel S. Johnson (1933), at Wolf Bay, Labrador, the young leave the nest about 13 days after hatching. The brooding is done entirely by the female, but both sexes assist in feeding the young. "While in the nest the young were fed at quite regular intervals throughout the long July days. My notes show that they were fed as early as 4:30 A. M. (I believe that feeding started even earlier) and continued as late as 8:55 P. M. Rain and fog did not seem to retard feeding activities of the parent birds." Her table indicates that the interval between feedings varied from 5 to 19 minutes; the number of feedings for a 2-hour period varied from 5 to 19; both of these periods were late in the day. She continues:

As the female spent the greater part of her time on the nest, the male brought most of the food during the first six days. Flies and small larvae were the main diet. One large larva or from two to four smaller ones were brought at one time so that each trip represented a fairly constant quantity of food. * * * Sometimes one parent did all the feeding but more often the food was divided and both fed, placing all of it in the mouth of one young bird then removing bits which they gave to others. Very rarely did the female eat any of the food brought by her mate.

After feeding both birds would look expectantly at the nest. When a mass of excreta appeared it was promptly seized and consumed or carried away. In most cases the female secured it but evidently there was some competition between the parents for this privilege. During the last few days of the nesting period excreta were carried off and the nature of its disposal is unknown.

The six young hatched on July 2; the growth of the young was uniform; on July 6 pinfeathers were through the skin, and on the 11th the feathers were out of the sheaths.

They were last seen in the nest in the late afternoon of the 15th. That evening they were out of the nest but nearby. Next morning a hawk was shot near the nest site and was reported to have been attacking young birds. This may account for the fact that but three of the brood were seen on the 17th, with the two parent birds.

Between July 16 and August 3 the family of three young with one or both parents was often seen about the woodpile and house of a local family about 300 yards from the nest site. * * * During the first two weeks out of the nest the young birds seemed to make little effort to find food for themselves but waited until the parent birds brought food and placed it in their mouths. Sometimes the old birds would utter a twittering chirp when food was found, whereupon one or more young would go to the parent to receive it.

Plumages.—Dr. Dwight (1900) describes the juvenal plumage mainly as follows: "Above, hair-brown streaked with black, the edgings of the back pale grayish wood-brown. * * * Below, creamy buff, palest anteriorly, streaked on the throat and breast rather broadly and on the sides faintly with clovebrown. Indistinct superciliary line and orbital ring buffy white; auriculars wood-brown."

An incomplete postjuvenal molt, which involves the contour plumage but not the wings or the tail, occurs mainly in August. This produces a first-winter plumage, which is practically indistinguishable from that of the adult. Dr. Dwight describes this as similar to the juvenal plumage, but "darker above with less obvious streaking and deeper pinkish buff below, the streaking heavier, forming a pectoral band and extending to the flanks; an immaculate pale buff chin. The superciliary line extends behind the eye as a whitish band." Ridgway (1904) says that the young in the first autumn and winter are "similar to winter adults, but upper parts decidedly brown and superciliary stripe and under parts rather deeper brownish buff, with streaks on chest, etc., less sharply defined."

Dr. Dwight (1900) says that the first nuptial plumage is "acquired by a partial prenuptial moult, in April, involving most of the body plumage which has suffered much from wear and become darker above with the buff tints nearly lost below. The extent of the fading is surprising. The new plumage is buff tinged, but wear during the breeding season produces a black and white streaked bird, the buffs being wholly lost through fading." Ridgway (1904) says of this first nuptial plumage: "The species breeds in this plumage, which is very different from the fully adult summer dress, * * * upper parts grayish, as in summer adults, but superciliary stripe and under parts paler (dull pale buffy or dull buffy white) than in winter adults, the chest, sides, and flanks conspicuously streaked with dusky."

Adults have a complete postnuptial molt late in summer, mainly in August, and a partial prenuptial molt, mainly in April, involving most of the contour plumage. Fall birds in fresh plumage are browner above and more buffy below, and spring birds are grayer above and paler below, the spring female being less grayish above, more brownish, and more heavily spotted below than the male; but the two sexes are very much alike in all plumages.

Food.—Forbush's (1929) account of the food seems to cover the subject quite satisfactorily, as follows:

The food of the Pipit consists largely of insects, small molluscs and crustaceans, small seeds and wild berries. More than 77 percent of its food has been found to consist of insects, of which over 64 percent are injurious. The seeds are chiefly weed seeds and waste grain. Professor Aughey found an average of 47 locusts and 4 other insects in the stomachs of some Nebraska specimens. The Pipit takes weevils, bugs, grasshoppers, crickets, plant-lice and spiders. It renders valuable service to the cotton growers of the South by destroying boll weevils. Examination of the stomachs of 68 birds taken in cotton fields showed that half of them had eaten 120 boll weevils. Mr. A. H. Howell says that Pipits pick up weevils throughout the winter, and in the spring they follow the plowman and capture both weevils and grubs. During an outbreak of grain aphids, these destructive insects constituted more than 70 per cent of the food of a Pipit. Mr. McAtee estimated that a flock of these birds then present must have destroyed at least a million of these pests daily.

According to Preble and McAtee (1923), "this species is reported by Hanna to feed during its stay on the [Pribilof] islands in fall migration almost exclusively on maggots on the killing fields. However, the contents of two stomachs, collected August 31, 1914, and September 20, 1916, contained no trace of such maggots. The food in these gizzards consisted of 10 per cent vegetable matter (seeds of a violet, *Viola langsdorfii*) and 90 percent animal matter. The components of the animal food were beetles (ground beetles, *Pterostichus* sp.; and weevils, *Lophalophus inquinatus*), 37 per cent; caterpillars, 33.5 per cent; plant bugs (*Irbisia sericans*), 8 per cent; spiders, 7.5 per cent; flies, 2.5 per cent; and Hymenoptera, 1.5 per cent."

Dr. George F. Knowlton writes to me: "On October 5, 1942, W. E. Peay and I encountered a large flock of the American pipit, extending from the Petersboro foothills in Cache Valley to Collinston, Utah.

The birds were very abundant along the road, feeding among Russian thistle. Hundreds also were feeding in alfalfa and in the wheat stubble, many alighting in plowed fields. Eighteen were collected and an examination of their stomachs revealed: 1 thysanuran; 19 collembolans; 102 Homoptera, 76 being aphids (of which 14 were pea aphids) and 13 leafhoppers. Hemiptera constituted the largest group with 1,527 recognizable specimens, of which 986 were adult and 291 nymphal false chinch bugs and 39 mirids. The 133 beetles included 46 weevils of which 8 were alfalfa weevils, 1 a clover leaf weevil and 19 adult clover root curculios. Ten of the 29 Hymenoptera were ants; most of the 14 Diptera were adults. In addition to the insects there were 8 spiders and mites, 92 seeds and a number of stomachs contained varying amounts of plant fragments."

Practically all the pipit's food is obtained on the ground, in short grass or low-growing herbage, on bare ground or open mud flats, on drifted sea wrack along the coast, and on the salt or brackish marshes along tidal streams. On its alpine breeding ground it has been seen picking up insects on the snowbanks, where they had been blown by the wind. In all such places it walks along daintily on its long legs, picking up seeds or insects from the ground or herbage, sometimes running rapidly in pursuit of an escaping insect. Mr. Cogswell writes to me: "On January 11, 1942, at Dominguez Lagoon, south of Los Angeles, I observed pipits varying their usual ground foraging procedure by perching on the branches of tall weeds growing in the shallow water and reaching for insects (?) among heads of the plants."

Mr. Trautman (1940) reports an interesting feeding reaction: "I saw some 20 individuals of this species on a peat island near the east end of Cranberry marsh. They faced a moderate breeze, and individuals from the group were flying into the air 3 or 4 feet, capturing moderate-sized flying beetles, and then dropping upon the island again. Usually 4 or 5 birds were in the air at once. The continual bobbing up and down was a strange sight, and somewhat resembled that of trout in a pool rising after insects."

Lucien M. Turner says in his unpublished notes that about the whaling stations in northern Ungava, where the carcasses of the white whales are left to rot, incredible numbers of flies are attracted and their maggots "fairly make the earth creep." Great numbers of pipits resort to these places to feast on these larvae. He also saw these birds wading in the shallow pools on the tidal flats, searching for aquatic worms and larvae.

Behavior.—Pipits are essentially terrestrial birds and spend most of their time on the ground, in the fields, meadows, marshes, mud flats, beaches, or on the bare rocks of their summer haunts. Some writers have stated that they never alight anywhere else, but such is certainly not so. In Labrador we frequently saw them walking on the roofs of tilts, where codfish was drying, or alighting on the roofs of the fish houses and even on the roofs of the dwelling houses and on the rocks around them.   On migrations, we often see them perched in trees, on wire fences or fence posts, on the ridge poles of houses, and on telephone or telegraph wires.   Dr. Knowlton writes to me that, in the locality where he collected the birds referred to above, "thousands of pipits were present over an area 6 to 15 miles wide.   The birds would fly ahead of the car, alighting on fence posts and fence wires near the approaching vehicle.   However, when disturbed by a man walking along the road, large numbers would sometimes fly away and alight in the field at some distance from the collector.   They seldom were much disturbed by the firing of a .22 rifle or a small 44x1 bird gun."

When on the ground the pipit walks gracefully and prettily, with a nodding motion of the head, like a dove, and with the body swaying slightly from side to side as he moves quietly along; sometimes he runs more rapidly.   His colors, soft grays and browns, match his surroundings so well, and he moves so quietly with an easy gliding motion, that before we realize that he is there he rises with a large flock of his fellows, as if exploding from nowhere, and they go flying off to some safer spot, twittering as they fly.

Francis H. Allen contributes the following note: "At one time I found the grass fairly 'swarming' with them at a fence corner, and one might have gone within two or three rods without seeing them, so closely did they creep along the ground.   Here one of them stood on a large stone, spread his tail prettily, and scratched his right ear deftly with his right foot.   The books seem to say that when on the ground they wag their tails constantly, but this is not literally true, for the tail is sometimes quiet as the bird walks, and extended straight behind, the whole slender bird presenting a peculiarly flat appearance as he steps daintily along.   I thought that the tail was more constantly wagged when the bird was standing than when he walked."

Observers differ as to the amount of tail wagging and when it occurs, but the pipit belongs to the wagtail family and must indulge in a certain amount of it.   Audubon (1841) stated that the pipit wags its tail when it stops walking; Forbush (1929) says "almost constantly moving the tail"; and others have referred to it as a constant habit.   Probably there is some individual variation in the habit between different birds, or at different times in the same individual. Milton P. Skinner (1928) watched particularly for this habit in North Carolina and found that it was not a constant one.   He noted that "their bodies and tails swung from side to side in time with each step," and says:

In every case this sidewise movement of the tail was an accompaniment of the body movement, and I did not see a single Pipit move its tail *sidewise* independently of the body. But I found there was another movement of the tail, *up and down*, that was sometimes made. Of one hundred and forty birds watched on January 28, 1927, some *tipped their tails up and down* rapidly while walking and while resting on the ground but many of them did not. Ten days later, I noted that only a few of these pipits moved their tails up and down, and that even these movements were noticeable only when the birds alighted after flight, and then there were only two to five movements. On March 1, 1927, I observed that when these birds *stopped walking* they moved their tails more or less regularly, but the motion was not noticeable *while* they walked, and disappeared altogether when they ran.

The pipit's flight is buoyant and undulating, powerful and swift, but rather erratic, as if the bird were undecided where to go or to stop. A large flock of pipits in flight is an interesting sight; they rise suddenly and unexpectedly from almost underfoot, those nearest first and then rank after rank progressively, as if bursting out of the earth; all join into one big flock before our astonished eyes and go sweeping off in a loose, undulating bunch, some rising and some falling in a confusing mass, like so many swirling snowflakes. They swing in a wide circle over the field and back again, swoop downward as if about to alight, then off again as if undecided, and finally drop out of sight on the brown earth in the distance, or perhaps return again and settle near the spot from which they started.

Dr. Witmer Stone (1937) thus describes the actions of a large flock of pipits on a burnt-over area:

After circling in a large arc they came drifting back and settled down near where they were before. Several times later they flushed but always returned to the burnt area. By watching exactly where they alighted I was able to detect them scattered all over the ground, about one bird to each square foot, where thickest. Their backs had a distinct olive cast in the strong light but the streaks on the under parts were only seen clearly when the birds were breast on. They all walked deliberately or sometimes took half a dozen steps in rapid succession, almost a run, though less regular. They all moved in the same general direction and as I moved parallel with them I could see them pressing straight ahead through the grassy spots and between the grass tufts and the stems of the bushes that had escaped the fire. They kept their heads pretty well down on the shoulders and leaned forward, dabbing at the ground with the bill, to one side or the other, apparently picking up scattered seeds of grasses and sedges. The tail was carried parallel with the ground or tilted up a trifle while the tips of the wings hung just below its base. The tail moved a little as the bird advanced but there was no distinct tilting as in the Palm Warbler or the Water-Thrush.

Voice.—The American pipit is not a gifted songster, but the full song as heard on the breeding grounds is rather pleasing. It sometimes sings a weaker suggestion of this song during its spring migration in April and May. Dr. Harrison F. Lewis has sent me the following note on this song: "Pipits sing a good deal when passing Quebec, P. Q., in the spring migration. Here the song is commonly uttered while the birds are on the ground, but I have heard them sing from a tree, in which they perched freely. I do not appear to have any record of this species singing while in flight. The song is simple, but pleasant and attractive. It sounds like *ke-tsée, ke-tsée, ke-tsée, ke-tsée, ke-tsée, tr-r-r-r-r-r-r, ke-tsée, ke-tsée, ke-tsée, tr-r-r-r-r-r-r, ke-tsée*, etc., and is apparently of indefinite duration. Sometimes the little trills are introduced into it frequently, at other times sparingly. The song is not thin, like that of the black and white warbler, but pretty and tinkling, though rather weak."

The song-*flight* has been described under courtship, and the flight-*song*, as heard on the breeding grounds, is described in the following notes from O. J. Murie: "The pipits were generally shy. When I approached one he would fly off with a sharp *tsee-seep, tsee-seep, tsee-see-seep*, then the impulse to sing would come over him and he would flutter his wings and go through his performance. The song was usually a repetition of syllables, *see-see-see-see-see* — —, a peculiar resonant *kr* accompanying and barely preceding each *see*, a quality impossible to describe adequately. This appeared to be the commonest form of the song. Sometimes it was varied, the notes being almost 2-syllabled, as *tsr-ee, tsr-ee, tsr-ee, tsr-ee* — —, and again sounding like *ter-ee-a, ter-ee-a, ter-ee-a* — —. Often it was a quite different form, a clear gliding *swit-swit-swit-swit* — —, or a little more prolonged *swee-swee-swee-swee* — — — —. Frequently a bird would break off on one form of the song and finish on another. The song was usually given on the wing, soaring upward to a height of about a hundred feet, then fluttering downward, finally sailing down to a rock with wings set and raised, and tail elevated. All this time the bird would sing his repetition of the same note, sometimes keeping it up after alighting."

The note that we hear on the fall migration, or in winter, is very short and simple, suggesting the name pipit. F. H. Allen (MS.) says of the flock he was watching: "The birds got up a few at a time generally, uttering as they arose a musical *wit-wit*, or *wit-wit-wit-wit*, with the accent, I should say, on the last syllable. When they were well a-wing, their note was a single, short *proŏt*, very pleasing to the ear."

Mr. Cogswell contributes the following comparison of the notes of two species that are found along our shores and are likely to be confused: "The usual flight call note of the pipit is distinctive of this species, and helpful in separating a distant flying flock from horned larks inhabiting similar areas and with somewhat similar calls. The pipit's note is a sharp *tsip——tsip, tspi-it*, or just *tsip—tsip-it;* the lark's is lower in pitch and much more rolling, not given so sharply—thus, *sleek, slik-seeezik*, or *slik-sleesik*, or just a *sleek, sslik, slik*."

Field marks.—The American pipit is a plainly colored, gray and brownish bird with no conspicuous markings, except the white outer tail feathers; and even these are not distinctive, for several other birds have them, notably the juncos, the vesper sparrow, and, to a less extent, the longspurs. The juncos are not often seen in the haunts of the pipit, and if they were, the color patterns of the different juncos are quite distinctive. The sparrow and longspurs are not so slender as the pipit; they have short, conical bills, and they hop rather than run. The white tail feathers of the pipit show only in flight, but its slender form and sharp bill, together with its habit of walking or running, the nodding of its head, and the frequent up-and-down motion of its comparatively long tail should distinguish it from the others.

Fall.—As soon as the young are able to care for themselves the pipits gather into flocks and begin to drift away from their breeding grounds before the end of August. We begin to see them in New England in September, in flocks of varying sizes from a dozen to a hundred or more, mainly coastwise on the salt marshes, on the mud flats, or along the beaches, but often farther inland along tidal streams, in open fields, and on wind-swept hills. They are commoner here in fall than in spring and usually remain to enliven the brown and dreary landscape until the frosts of late November drive them farther south. By this time the eastern birds have entirely deserted their northern breeding grounds. In the meantime the western birds have drifted down from their alpine heights, above timberline, and are spread out over the plains and lowlands. Migrating birds are often seen in enormous flocks, as some continue their migration beyond our borders into Mexico and beyond.

Winter.—Although the American pipit extends its winter range as far south as Guatemala, most of them spend the winter within the limits of the United States, fairly commonly as far north as California and Ohio; farther north it is rarely seen in winter. Dr. Stone (1937) draws the following pen picture of winter pipits in New Jersey:

On some day of midwinter when there has been no blanket of snow such as sometimes covers the landscape, even at such a supposed 'semi-tropic' region as Cape May, we gaze over the broad monotonous expanses of plowed fields and conclude that here at least bird life is absent. We contrast these silent brown stretches with the swamp edges and their bursts of sparrow conversation or with the old pasture fields where Meadowlarks are sputtering. But let us start to cross these apparently deserted fields and immediately with a weak *dee-dee, dee-dee,* a small brown bird flushes from almost beneath our feet, then another and another, displaying a flash of white feathers in the tail as they rise. In a moment they have settled again farther on and are lost to sight against the brown background as suddenly as they appeared. We advance again and now the ground before us seems fairly to belch forth birds, as with one accord, the whole flock takes wing, and with light, airy, undulating and irregular flight, courses away over the fields, now clearly defined against the sky, now swallowed up in the all pervading brown of the landscape.

In the sand hills of North Carolina Mr. Skinner (1928) saw pipits "only in the largest hay fields, winter-wheat fields, old cornfields where the stalks are all down, and in old cowpea fields." He did not find them in plowed fields. In Florida it is a common winter resident, abundant in the more northern parts; we found it on the Kissimmee Prairie and on old fields and marshes elsewhere; A. H. Howell (1932) says that it is occasionally seen on sand dunes and sea beaches. M. G. Vaiden tells me that it occurs in Mississippi as a migrant in both spring and fall, and "occasionally in winter in great numbers. They are usually found on the slopes of the levee; I have noted flocks of at least 200 feeding on the levee."

Mr. Cogswell (MS.) says of the winter status of the pipit in southern California: "This species is a common winter visitant in all suitable localities below snow level; I have found it most abundantly on wet pasturelands and in the fields bordering coastal marshes, but they are also present in any fields with short or no vegetation. On February 10, 1940, they were particularly abundant in the Chino Creek Valley and all over the nearby rolling hills, where flocks of hundreds foraged on the ground between the rows of growing grain, which completely hid them from view until they flew."

DISTRIBUTION

Range.—The species is circumpolar, breeding in Europe, Asia, and northern North America and wintering south to northern Africa, southern Asia, and Central America.

Breeding range.—The breeding range of the American races of the pipit is in the Arctic-Alpine regions **north** to northern Alaska (Meade River, about 100 miles south of Point Barrow, and Collison Point); northern Yukon (Herschel Island); northern Mackenzie (Kittigazuit, Franklin Bay, and Coronation Gulf); southern Somerset Island (Fort Ross); northern Baffin Island (Arctic Bay and Ponds Inlet); and about 75° north latitude on the west coast of Greenland (Devils Thumb Island). **East** to west coast of Greenland (Devils Thumb Island and Upernivik); eastern Baffin Island (Eglinton Fjord, Cumberland Sound, and Frobisher Bay); Labrador (Port Burwell, Hebron, Okkak, and Battle Harbor); Newfoundland (Cape Norman, Twillingate, and Cape Bonavista). **South** to Newfoundland (Cape Bonavista and the Lewis Hills), southeastern Quebec (Grosse Isle, Magdalen Islands rarely; Mount Albert and Tabletop, Gaspé Peninsula); northern Maine (summit of Mount Katahdin); northern Ontario (Moose Factory); northern Manitoba (Churchill); central Mackenzie (Artillery Lake and Fort Providence); southwestern Alberta (Banff National Park); western Montana (Glacier National Park, Big Snowy Mountains, and Bear Tooth Mountains) ; Wyoming (Big Horn Mountains, Wind River Mountains, and the Medicine Bow Mountains); Colorado (Longs Peak, Mount Audubon, Seven Lakes, Pikes Peak, and Medano Creek) ; central northern New Mexico (Taos Mountains and Pecos Baldy) ; northeastern Utah (Uintah Mountains) ; central Idaho (Salmon River Mountains) ; and northern Oregon (Wallowa Mountains and, possibly, Mount Hood) ; has also been found in summer near the summit of Mount Shasta and Mount Lassen, Calif., but not surely breeding. **West** to Oregon (Mount Hood) ; the Cascades of Washington (Mount St. Helens, Mount Adams, and Mount Rainier) ; British Columbia (mountains near Princeton, near Doch-da-on Creek, Summit, and Atlin; southwestern Yukon (Burwash Landing and Tecpee Lake) ; and the Aleutian Islands and western Alaska (Frosty Peak, Unalaska, the Near Islands, Nunivak Island, Wales, Kobuk River, and Meade River) ; has been found also on St. Lawrence Island.

Winter range.—The pipit occurs in winter **north** to southwestern British Columbia (southern Vancouver Island, occasionally) ; western Washington (Tacoma, Nisqually Flats, and Vancouver); Oregon (Portland, Corvallis, and along the Malheur River) ; Utah (Ogden Valley, Utah Lake, and St. George) ; central to southern Arizona (Fort Whipple, Fort Verde, and Tucson) ; southern New Mexico (San Antonio and Carlsbad) ; southern and eastern Texas (Fort Clark, Kerrville, Austin, Waco, and Commerce) ; occasionally central Arkansas (Van Buren) ; northern Louisiana (Shreveport and Monroe) ; Tennessee, uncommon (Memphis, Nashville, Knoxville, and Johnson City) ; and southern Virginia (Blacksburg, Naruna, and Virginia Beach) ; occasionally north to northern Ohio (Huron and Painesville) ; New Jersey (Seaside Park) ; Long Island (Long Beach and Orient) ; Connecticut (Saybrook) ; and Massachusetts (Newburyport). **East** to the Atlantic Coast States from southern Virginia (Virginia Beach) to southern Florida (Fernandina, St. Augustine, and Daytona Beach, Kissimmee, and Key West rarely). **South** to Florida (Key West, Fort Myers, and St. Marks) ; the Gulf coast to southern Texas (Rockport and Brownsville) ; eastern Mexico (Rodríguez, Nuevo León; Puebla; and Huajuapam, Oaxaca) ; Guatemala; and northern El Salvador (Volcán de Santa Ana), the southernmost place that it has been recorded. **West** to Guatemala (Dueñas) ; Oaxaca (Tehuantepec) ; Sinaloa (Mazatlán) ; Lower California (La Paz and San Quintín) ; the valleys and coast of California (La Jolla, Santa Barbara, San Francisco, Napa, and Eureka) ; western Oregon (Coos Bay and Netarts) ; western Washington (Nisqually Flats) ; and southern Vancouver Island, British Columbia.

The range as outlined applies to all the North American races, of which three are now recognized. The western pipit (*A. s. pacificus*) breeds from southeastern Alaska through the Rocky Mountains of British Columbia and in the Cascades to Oregon; the Rocky Mountain pipit (*A. s. alticola*) breeds in the Rocky Mountain region from Montana to New Mexico; the eastern pipit (*A. s. rubescens*) breeds from Alaska to Greenland south to southern Yukon and Mackenzie to Quebec, Newfoundland, and Mount Katahdin, Maine. In winter the races are mingled.

Migration.—Late dates of spring departure are: El Salvador—Volcán de Santa Ana, April 16. Lower California—San José del Cabo, May 3. Sonora—Granados, May 6. Florida—Pensacola, April 27. Georgia—Athens, May 9. South Carolina—Charleston, April 22. North Carolina—Pea Island, May 16. District of Columbia—Washington, May 14. Pennsylvania—Erie, May 12. New York—Potter, May 16. Mississippi—Biloxi, April 29. Louisiana—Lobdell, May 2. Arkansas—Lake City, April 29. Kentucky—Bowling Green, May 8. Oberlin, May 24. Michigan—McMillan, May 28. Ontario—Rossport, May 29. Missouri—St. Louis, May 2. Minnesota—Lake Vermillion, May 27. Texas—Somerset, May 1. Kansas—Onaga, May 23. Alberta—Genevis, May 26. British Columbia—Okanagan Landing, May 17.

Early dates of spring arrival are: District of Columbia—Washington, February 16. Pennsylvania—State College, February 28. New York—Ithaca, March 15. Massachusetts—Amherst, March 27. Maine—Auburn, May 2. New Brunswick—Chatham, May 6. Quebec—Kamouraska, May 6. Ohio—Oberlin, March 4. Ontario—London, May 1. Michigan—Detroit, March 31. Wisconsin—Milwaukee, April 20. Kansas—Lawrence, March 12. Nebraska—Hastings, March 10. South Dakota—Sioux Falls, March 27. North Dakota—Charlson, April 23. Manitoba—Aweme, April 15; Churchill, May 25. Saskatchewan—Eastend, April 21. Wyoming—Laramie, April 9. Utah—Brigham, April 4. Montana—Helena, April 9. Alberta—Stony Plain, April 8. Mackenzie—Simpson, May 2. British Columbia—Chilliwack, April 6. Alaska—Ketchikan, April 26; Fort Kenai, May 6.

Late dates of fall departure are: Alaska—Wainwright, September 28. British Columbia—Comox, November 9. Mackenzie—Simpson, October 16. Alberta—Glenevis, October 4. Saskatchewan—Eastend, October 16. Montana—Fortine, October 27. Wyoming—Laramie, November 6. Manitoba—Aweme, October 28. North Dakota—Argusville, October 28. South Dakota—Lake Poinsett, November 2. Nebraska—Gresham, November 1. Kansas—Onaga, November 25. Minnesota—Minneapolis, October 31. Wisconsin—North Freedom, November 1. Illinois—Chicago, November 3. Michigan—Sault Ste. Marie, November 8. Ontario—Toronto, November 13. Ohio—Youngstown, November 22. Quebec—Montreal, November 4.

Maine—Machias, November 2.   Massachusetts—Harvard, November
9.   New York—New York, November 27.   District of Columbia—
Washington, December 23.

Early dates of fall arrival are: Alberta—Glenevis, August 19.   Montana—Missoula, September 4.   Minnesota—Hallock, September 4.
Wisconsin—Madison, September 19.   Ontario—Ottawa, September
9.   Michigan—Blaney, September 19.   Illinois—Hinsdale, Septem-
ber 14.   Kentucky—Lexington, October 10.   Tennessee—Memphis,
October 10.   Mississippi—Ellisville, October 19.   Louisiana—New
Orleans, October 10.   Massachusetts—Danvers, September 14.   New
York—Orient, September 2.   Pennsylvania—Doylestown, September
9.   District of Columbia—Washington, September 23.   Virginia—
Wytheville, October 24.   North Carolina—Greensboro, October 17.
South Carolina—Sullivans Island, September 10.   Georgia—Round
Oak, October 16.   Florida—Fort Myers, September 26.   Texas—
Somerset, October 7.   Chihuahua—Chihuahua, October 9; Lower Cal-
ifornia, San Andrés, September 21.

Very few pipits have been banded, and the 10 recovery records are
all of birds retrapped at the place of banding one or two years later.

Casual records.—In November 1848 a flock visited Bermuda, from
which two birds were shot, the date of one specimen being given as
November 26.   The American pipit has been twice collected on the
island of Helgoland, an immature on November 11, 1851, and an
adult on May 17, 1870.   An immature bird was collected on September 30, 1910, on the island of St. Kilda, Outer Hebrides, Scotland.

Egg dates.—Labrador: 21 records, June 10 to July 23; 12 records,
June 18 to 30, indicating the height of the season.

Alaska: 10 records, June 8 to 28.

Colorado: 12 records, June 22 to July 26; 9 records, June 25 to 30.

ANTHUS SPINOLETTA JAPONICUS Temminck and Schlegel

JAPANESE PIPIT

CONTRIBUTED BY WINSOR MARRETT TYLER

HABITS

A single specimen of the Japanese pipit, the only individual known
to have occurred in the Western Hemisphere, was taken on Nunivak
Island, Alaska, on September 10, 1947.   Harry S. Swarth (1934) describes the event of its capture thus:

Harrold's [the collector's] note-book contains the following entry: "September
10, 1927, Cape Etolin, Nunivak Island.   A pipit with bold spotting on a cream
(rather than buff) breast and belly taken on the rocky shore of the Cape.   It
struck me that its flight and actions were not quite typical of the American
Pipit, but its note was not heard.   It is nearly one-half inch shorter by measurement than the average American Pipit."   The capture of this bird (C. A. S. No.

30778, an immature female), the first in North America, has already been recorded (Swarth, 1928, p. 250). Upper mandible brown; lower mandible brown, basal half brownish yellow; iris brown; tarsus and toes yellowish brown.

Swarth (1928), in an earlier paper, reports the taking of this specimen and points out that a previous published record of the Japanese pipit in the Western Hemisphere is erroneous. He says: "There is a prior record for this bird in North America, based upon the capture of one on St. Paul Island, in the Pribilof group, on August 29, 1916. That specimen is in the United States National Museum, and being examined by Dr. Wetmore and Mr. Riley during their scrutiny of the bird here recorded, it proved to be not *japonicus* but a somewhat unusually colored example of *Anthus spinoletta rubescens*. The present is therefore the first recorded occurrence of the Japanese Pipit within the confines of the *A. O. U.* Check-List." Swarth refers to the record of the St. Paul Island bird (G. Dallas Hanna, 1920) and to its refutation (Riley and Wetmore, 1928).

The Japanese pipit breeds far to the north in the Eastern Hemisphere—eastern Siberia, Kamchatka, and the Kurile Islands. It is closely related in appearance and habits to the American pipit. Its breeding grounds lie farther westward than our bird's, extending in Siberia as far west as the Lena River, while the western limit of the breeding range of the American pipit reaches only the northeast corner of Siberia.

Little has been published concerning the Japanese pipit. J. D. D. La Touche (1930), writing of the bird in eastern China, says:

This is a much smaller and darker bird than Blakiston's Pipit. It has a loud double note of alarm, different from the single 'pee' of the Red-throated Pipit. It occurs in flocks in winter on the marshes and wet fields of South-East China of the Lower Yangtse, and in spring is found in green corn at Chinkiang. It moults in April in the latter locality, and may be seen there until about the middle of May and until the end of that month at Chinwangtao. It is purely a marsh and wet-field or meadow bird. * * * This Pipit appears to only straggle down to India in winter, but it is common in the Shan States and other parts of Burma and has also, according to Baker, been taken in other Indo-Burmese countries. * * * The bird was originally described from Japan, and Dr. Hartert gives Kamtschatka, East Siberia, and the Kirile Is. as breeding-range, Japan being only part of the winter-quarters. The nidification is apparently unknown.

La Touche (1920) remarks further: "It migrates in autumn in company with the Wagtails and Swallows, many flocks of which fly by in late August and September. I have seen it in the marshes in October until the 25th of that month. The first arrivals in spring are still in winter dress but soon assume the summer plumage, dark ashygrey, upper parts obscurely spotted, and buffish vinous under parts with a few drop-like spots on the breast and flanks."

A handlist of Japanese birds (Ornithological Society of Japan, 1932) gives the island of Sakhalin as a breeding ground of the Japanese pipit.

Riley and Wetmore (1928) point out the distinguishing characters in the plumage of the Japanese pipit as compared to the American pipit. They say: "It is paler below, with heavier markings, duller, less buffy above, has the wing bars more prominently white, and differs in the coloration of the sides of the head."

Austin Hobart Clark (1910), in his report of the cruise of the steamer *Albatross* in the North Pacific Ocean, says: "I found this bird common in the grassy lowlands near Milne Bay, Simushir, but very shy and hard to get. The males were in full song at the time of our visit, June 23."

Nesting.—Bernard W. Tucker contributes the following note: "The nesting of this race, which was originally described from winter birds in Japan, was long unknown, but in recent years many eggs have been obtained by the Japanese in the Kurile Islands, as noted by Yamashina (1931). In this connection Yamashina gives a reference to a paper by him, 'On a Collection of Birds from Paramushiru Island, North Kuriles', in the Japanese journal Tori, but as this is entirely in Japanese I am unable to state what particulars about nest or eggs are there given. Again, Hartert and Steinbacher (1938) state that in recent years it has also been studied on its breeding grounds by Russian ornithologists, but I have not had access to any Russian data, and the authors quoted give no references."

DISTRIBUTION

CONTRIBUTED BY BERNARD WILLIAM TUCKER

Breeding range.—East Siberia westward at least to the Lena, Kamchatka, and the Kurile Islands. The Sakhalin bird has been distinguished as *A. s. borealis* Hesse, but Hartert and Steinbacher (1938) do not consider this separable.

Winter range.—Japan, Yangtse Valley, Fohkien and Kwantung, Formosa; occasionally in Turkestan.

ANTHUS PRATENSIS (Linnaeus)

MEADOW PIPIT

CONTRIBUTED BY BERNARD WILLIAM TUCKER

HABITS

The meadow pipit is a common European species breeding regularly in Iceland and occurring casually, but evidently not very rarely, on the east coast of Greenland, where it seems certain that it breeds occasionally, though the actual finding of a nest with eggs or young has not been recorded. The earliest record from Greenland is of one received by J. H. Paulsen (1846) taken in 1844 and recorded by him in a footnote to his German translation of Holbøll's "Ornithologiske Bidrag til den grønlandske Fauna." This was the record referred to by Prof. Alfred Newton in the Arctic Manual (1875), which the A. O. U. Check-list quotes. Johan Petersen, who was superintendent of the east-coast colony of Angmagsalik from 1894 to 1915 and whose careful bird observations are quoted by Helms (1926), met with the species repeatedly in that district, though by no means every year. He first observed it in 1903, when four or five were seen by houses in the colony on May 21 and one was shot and sent home to Denmark for identification. The birds remained about in May and June and were seen with young in July. Birds were also seen on a trip to Sermilik Fjord, west of Angmagsalik, at the beginning of June. Petersen records that they were in pairs "and to all appearances they had nests in the vicinity." After this his notes do not mention the species until 1908, when one was seen on May 9 and 12 and was heard singing. In 1912 one was seen on May 5 and one was singing on the mountains on June 11. The latter bird was seen again on July 13, carrying food and behaving in such a way that it obviously had young. On August 10 old and young birds were seen near the colony. In 1913 one was seen on May 12, and finally, on a return visit to Angmagsalik in later years, Petersen again met with the species in August and again on October 10, 1923.

F. S. Chapman (1932), the ornithologist of the British Arctic Air Route Expedition of 1930–31, also met with meadow pipits in the Angmagsalik district. The species was first recorded on May 24, 1931. After this none reappeared till May 28, when, in the observer's words, "a pair started nesting." It is a pity that Chapman was not more explicit on this point and does not state his evidence, since although Petersen's observations leave no reasonable doubt that the species does sometimes breed, it appears, as has already been noticed, that no actual nest has yet been recorded. Considerably farther north, at Cape Dalton, Bertram, Lack, and Roberts (1934) on August 20, 1933, saw a meadow pipit that was probably breeding on rocky ground well covered with vegetation. Just previous to flushing the bird a nest was found composed of grass on the ground in a site typical for this species. Hørning (1939) has recently added two more autumn records, a male shot at Kûngmiut, north of Angmagsalik, on September 6, 1933, and a juvenile female at sea off Cape I. A. D. Jensen on Blosseville coast on August 28 of the same year.

The meadow pipit, a somewhat smaller and more boldly marked species than the American pipit, is a bird of rough grasslands, moors, heaths, sand dunes, and other open country in the breeding season. Though it may be found frequently enough breeding on suitable rough ground in the lowlands, it is more especially a bird of hill country and upland moors. In many parts of the British Isles and Continental Europe there are large tracts of country where the meadow pipit is not only the dominant small bird but almost the only one to be met with at all commonly. As one walks over the moors one may often traverse large areas that are saved from almost complete birdlessness only by the meadow pipits, which from time to time rise ahead of one with their shrill alarm notes, fly a little way with a flitting, jerky action, and drop to the ground again. From about April to June these same moors are enlivened by the dancing forms of the male birds in the air, as each flutters up with his tinkling, feeble, yet cheery little song, which is completed as he glides to the ground again with wings somewhat raised and tail spread.

On the heathy barrens of the high north of Europe beyond the tree limit, the meadow pipit is just as prominent a member of the bird population as on the moors of Great Britain, and it is common, too, in Iceland, whence came, no doubt, the birds that have reached the American Continent. In Iceland, writes Hantzsch (1905), it is characteristic of the hilly grasslands, upland moors, and heathy tracts, and in the mountains ascends as high as it can find a continuous ground vegetation. The bleak lands of the far north are deserted in winter, and even from temperate regions like the British Isles many emigrate, though many remain. The high ground is, however, mostly deserted, and the species becomes common in the lowlands in places where it does not breed. In the more southern parts of its breeding range it is met with chiefly on grasslands in the mountains.

Courtship.—The meadow pipit is one of those small passerines that seem to have no very well defined or regular pattern of display. Miss S. M. Butlin (1940) has recorded the behavior of a male which ran four or possibly five times in front of the female "with stiff, very upright gait, wings slightly away from body and head held rigid and rather bowed while he sang quietly." The female was crouching in the solicitation posture, but the male finished the performance by flying off to a heather clump a few yards away, and coition did not take place although the birds were not disturbed. Miss A. Morley (1940) has witnessed a type of display which has not been recorded by any other observer. She describes how a male which had been moving round the female with slightly drooped wings and cocked-up tail "picked up a large piece of flowering grass and flew with it in his bill for a short way low over the grasses, with a rather slow flight and rapid quivering wings," and this behavior was twice repeated. Drooping of the wings by the male, a common action in sexually excited birds, has also been noted by Caroline and Desmond Nethersole-Thompson (1940), who add that by a dipping action he displays the white beneath the tail. These observers also find that "courtship feeding" of the female by the male is regularly practiced during incubation either on or just off the nest. Whether this behavior also occurs, as in some birds, before incubation begins, when it can be regarded as solely and unequivocally a courtship action, since the utilitarian element entailed in the feeding of the female while she is sitting is lacking, does not appear to have been established. The same observers note that during the pairing period sex chases, although less sustained than those of many passerines, are frequently seen.

Nesting.—The nest of the meadow pipit is built in the open in a depression in the ground—which appears to be often a scrape made by the birds themselves—among grass or in a tuft of rushes or heather, and may be very well concealed or fairly open. It is a cup built of dry grasses and bents lined with finer material and some horsehair. The nest is built chiefly by the female, though the male assists her; she has been seen examining possible nest places some days before beginning to build, but site selection and building may occur on the same day (C. and D. Nethersole-Thompson, 1943).

Eggs.—The eggs are thus described by Jourdain in the Handbook of British Birds (1938, vol. 1): "Ordinary types brown or grey in general appearance, finely mottled or more boldly marbled with varying shades of brown and ashy grey; others are almost uniform ochreous or pale leaden-grey, with dark hair-streaks, and some sparsely or unmarked on pale blue ground. An erythristic type recorded. Average of 100 British eggs: 19.77 x 14.63. Max.: 21.4 x 15.7. Min.: 18.7 x 14.5 and 19.1 x 14 mm." The usual number of eggs in Britain is four or five, sometimes only three and seldom six. But in more northern regions clutches average larger; Blair (1936) found six the usual number in the far north of Norway, and clutches of seven were found on several occasions. In Iceland Hantzsch (1905) found no complete clutch of less than five, a number of six, and one of seven. The experience of other observers in northern regions is similar. In England the season for eggs is from the latter part of April on, though clutches may rarely be found earlier in the month. In Germany it averages rather later; according to Niethammer (1937) it extends from the beginning, or often only from the middle, of May, or not infrequently even from the end of April, to the end of June or occasionally even July. In northern Norway Blair found that the first eggs in a large series of nests examined were laid between June 2 and 19. In Iceland also the first eggs are usually laid at the end of June, though rarely they may be laid at the end of May (Hantzsch). These data are selected as representative from a large amount available with regard to this common European bird. In temperate regions the species is double-brooded, and this appears to be at least sometimes the case even in Iceland, as Congreve and Freme (1930) found fresh eggs on May 28 and also on July 5.

Young.—Only the female incubates. She is regularly fed on or near the nest by the male, though she may occasionally get some food for herself. Incubation begins, according to the Nethersole-Thompsons (1943), with the penultimate or antepenultimate egg, and the period is 13–14 days. When the young hatch the shells are removed, and large fragments have been found away from the nest from which they are presumed to have come (C. and D. Nethersole-Thompson, 1942). Both parents feed the young ones, and the feces are carried away by the parents and dropped in flight or after the bird settles. The latter observation we owe to Lt. Col. B. M. Ryves, an indefatigable observer of the details of the breeding economy of British birds, and Dr. H. J. Moon, whose notes are quoted in a paper on nest sanitation by R. H. Blair and the present writer (1941). Jourdain gives the fledgling period as 13–14 days, but the young are often not fully capable of flight when they leave the nest.

Plumages.—The plumages are fully described by H. F. Witherby in the Handbook of British Birds (1938, vol. 1). The brownish-gray down of the nestling is fairly long and plentiful, distributed on the inner and outer supraorbital, occipital, humeral, ulnar, spinal, femoral, and ventral tracts, but is very scanty on the last two. The mouth inside is carmine, and the flanges of the bill are pale yellow externally. There are no tongue spots, but the tongue spurs are whitish.

The juvenal plumage is much like that of the adult, but the dark central streaks of the feathers of the upperparts are more distinct and the brown edgings smaller. The first-winter plumage is like the adult's.

Food.—The food consists almost exclusively of insects and other small invertebrates obtained on the ground. Jourdain (1938, vol. 1) mentions: "Coleoptera (*Byrrhus, Athous, Cercyon, Longitarsus, Oxytelus, Tachyporus, Limnobius*, etc., and larvae), small Orthoptera, Diptera (*Tipula, Eristalis, Calliphora*, and larvae), Hemiptera, Hymenoptera, and larvae of Lepidoptera. Also earthworms (Saxby), spiders, and occasionally seeds."

Behavior.—Something has been said about general behavior on the breeding ground in the introductory remarks. This is a terrestrial species, the ordinary gait, as in other pipits, being a fairly deliberate walk, though it can also run on occasions. The tail tends to be moved slightly up and down as it walks. It has often been alleged that it seldom or only exceptionally perches in trees, but this is altogether too sweeping a statement. Though admittedly it perches in trees much less regularly than its European relative, the tree pipit, it is not particularly unusual for it to do so in places where trees are present, and this is especially true on migration. It would, however, be fair to say that when the meadow pipit settles in trees it is more often than not only a passing expedient adopted because something has disturbed it on the ground. And, true to its characteristic love of the open, it rarely if ever perches in the cover of foliage. The flight as a rule is rather flitting and jerky, rising and falling in a somewhat erratic fashion rather than regularly undulating as with a good many small birds. Outside the breeding season the species is inclined to be gregarious, though the members of a party or flock generally maintain only a somewhat loose contact.

Voice.—The note when the bird is flushed is a feeble, thin, squeaky *tseep* or *tsiip*, or in point of fact more usually an unbroken string of these shrill notes uttered in quick succession. The call note, heard chiefly on the breeding ground, is a more sibilant and slightly fuller, but still shrill *tissip* or *tisp*, the disyllabic form being typical though not invariable. The opening notes of the song have much the same quality. The tinkling sequence of simple notes gathers speed as the bird flutters up from the ground to, at most, a hundred feet or so and as it planes down again passes into a succession of slightly more musical notes finally becoming a trill, which continues till the singer reaches the ground. On the descent the bird glides down with wings partly spread and inclined somewhat upward and the tail fanned, but there are minor variations in this song flight. At the top of the ascent it may fly a little way more or less level before beginning to drop, or it may even sink a little and rise again, prolonging the song accordingly. The length of the song and the relative duration of the two parts, the rise and fall, vary a good deal. Timings of the total length quoted by E. M. Nicholson (1936) range from 12 to 25 seconds. Shorter, more imperfect versions may be given from bushes, fences, or other low perches or even from the ground. In the south and midland parts of England the period of regular song is from about mid-March to early in July. Occasional song may be heard from mid-February and after the regular song period is over until the beginning of August. As an exceptional occurrence it has been noted as late as mid-September and even October.

Field marks.—An obvious pipit, but rather smaller than the American species, and much more strongly marked, both back and breast being boldly streaked with black. The exact coloring of the upperparts varies from olive or greenish gray to browner shades and the white outer tail feathers are conspicuous when the bird is flushed. It is a bird of open country, little given to perching on trees, though it will do so at times. In Europe it requires to be distinguished from the very similar tree pipit (*Anthus trivialis*), which, as the common name suggests, perches in trees habitually and has a different song. However, as this species has not occurred in America and does not appear likely to do so, it need not detain us further. In the nonbreeding plumage the red-throated pipit also much resembles the present species. The distinctions are given under the field marks of the former bird.

Enemies.—As a bird of open country and a common one at that the meadow pipit is largely preyed upon by hawks. Reference to Jourdain's account of British birds in the Handbook of British Birds (1939, vol. 3) shows that it has been definitely recorded in the dietary of every British-breeding bird of prey that takes birds at all, with the exception of the marsh harrier and the kite. Even the bold peregrine (duck hawk) and the stately golden eagle will condescend to take a meadow pipit on occasions, while it may be said to constitute the main food in the breeding season of the merlin (pigeon hawk), which frequents similar country. It is also largely taken by the hen and Montagu's harriers, near relatives of the marsh hawk of America, also birds of open country, and it quite frequently falls a victim to the European sparrow hawk, which though primarily a woodland bird regularly hunts over open ground.

The meadow pipit is one of the species most commonly parasitized by the European cuckoo.

A list of invertebrate parasites of the species is given by Niethammer (1937).

Fall and winter.—Fall is a time of active movement among meadow pipits, and the movements in the British Islands illustrate on a smaller scale those that take place over the general range of the species. Birds from the northern and more elevated regions abandon these for the winter, and, though many emigrate, some are contented to spread over the lower ground at no very great distance from their breeding haunts, so that the species becomes common in many places where it does not nest or does so only sparingly. It is evident, however, that many of these wintering birds are migrants that have come in from abroad. They are now to be found in flocks and parties on open fields and rough grasslands of all sorts and on waste or cultivated land, with a noticeable liking for wet or partially flooded ground, which also attracts them to the borders of lakes and inland waters and to coastal salt or other marshes. They are also often found feeding on arable land among root crops such as rutabagas or turnips and may be observed picking over debris along tide marks on the seashore. The flocks are largest at the migration period in fall. Later, partly no doubt because many of those in the fall flocks were birds of passage that have passed on, but also as the result of a general tendency to dispersal, the parties are generally smaller. They do not maintain any close coherence; the birds scatter rather widely over their feeding grounds and when approached rise in ones and twos or little groups rather than as a body. At night they roost on the ground, making use of such shelter as offers. It may be provided by the overhanging leaves in a turnip field or by other broad-leaved plants in a marsh or piece of waste ground, by tussocky grass or rushes in the open, or by a young plantation of conifers. Again, birds may sometimes be found roosting off the ground in hedges, but this appears generally to happen in severe or snowy weather.

In the Mediterranean countries, where the species breeds only sparingly on high ground or not at all, meadow pipits are common in winter on essentially the same types of ground described above, and I recall particularly watching many of them, with a sprinkling of water pipits—the European racial form of the pipit of America from the neighboring mountains—feeding on partially flooded land in the precise area north of Naples where at the moment of penning these words the Anglo-American armies are fighting. In North Africa it occurs also in the hills in winter.

DISTRIBUTION

Breeding range.—Iceland, Faeroes, British Isles, and Continental Europe south to the Pyrenees, central France, northern Italy, Yugoslavia, Rumania, and south Russia, east through northern Siberia to the Yenisei.

Winter range.—Far north deserted and range extends to all European Mediterranean countries and North Africa and to southwest and west-central Asia.

Spring migration.—The return passage of birds that have wintered farther south is recorded from mid-March to mid-April on the south coast of England and from as early as mid-February on that of Ireland (Ticehurst, 1938, vol. 1). In Germany passage is described as taking place from March to May, but on Helgoland Gätke (1895) records it as beginning as early as February 24. On the Arctic coast of Norway the first arrivals were not noted by Blair (1936) until May 15, but the first birds reach the south coastal districts of Iceland by the end of April, though the inland regions are not occupied until well into May (Hantzsch). Meinertzhagen's (1930) latest record for Egypt is March 20, but on the north side of the Mediterranean birds are present in some numbers until much later. Alexander's (1927) last date for the Rome district of central Italy is April 13, and this agrees closely with the present writer's for the Naples district, April 12.

Fall migration.—Southward movement of northern birds in Britain from about mid-August to late in October. Emigratory movements from late in September to late in November. From early in September to late in October or November large numbers of immigrants arrive from abroad, some to winter, others to pass on (Ticehurst). In Germany the passage is described as lasting from September to November (Niethammer). Most leave Iceland by the middle or end of September (Hantzsch). Earliest dates in Rome district of Italy, October 4 (Alexander), Naples district, October 5 (B. W. T.), Egypt, end of October, but once September 29 (Meinertzhagen).

Casual records.—Madeira, Canaries.

ANTHUS CERVINUS (Pallas)

RED-THROATED PIPIT

CONTRIBUTED BY BERNARD WILLIAM TUCKER

HABITS

The red-throated pipit is a mainly Siberian species that has occurred accidentally on the west side of the American Continent. The earliest authority for its occurrence quoted by the authors of the A. O. U. Check-list, namely Zander (1854) in the Journal für Ornithologie for 1853, says no more than that its range extends through Asia as far as the islands near America ("bis zu den Inseln bei Amerika"), and although it may be assumed that such a statement was based on actual specimens no other particulars are given, nor has the present writer been able to trace any. Turner (1886), however, records a specimen taken at St. Michael, Western Alaska, in 1867, and Ridgway (1883) another taken at San José del Cabo, Lower California, on January 26, 1883, a rather surprising time of year. Recently Friedmann (1937) has added a third record, of a bird taken on St. Lawrence Island, Alaska, in July 1936, by an Eskimo collector.

The range of the species extends west from Siberia into northern Russia and northern Scandinavia, where it overlaps with that of the meadow pipit, previously described. But whereas the meadow pipit is a widely distributed species in Europe, extending northward to the coasts of the Arctic Ocean, the red-throated pipit is exclusively an Arctic species whose range barely overlaps the northern limits of the forest belt, but on the other hand extends north of Continental Europe to embrace the Arctic islands of Kolguev, Novaya Zemlya, and Waigatz, which the meadow pipit does not reach.

In Arctic Norway, though the habitats of the two species are not rigidly separated, the red-throated pipit appears on the whole to like somewhat bushier and damper ground than does the meadow pipit. In the south of its range it is found on high fells above the tree limit, but in the north it is confined to lower levels, especially near the sea. As described by Blair (1936), "swamps overgrown with dwarf birch and willow and damp grassy flats are the favourite haunts of this pipit," but it also, as he mentions, has a marked predeliction for cultivation and the neighborhood of farmsteads and habitations, where such are available. Thus at Vadsö in Arctic Norway it is common about the little cultivated meadows and damp patches with scrubby growth of *Salix* and birch close to the little towns. I have, however, found it plentiful in a quite different type of habitat from those above mentioned, on the island of Vardö, off the same coast. Here its chosen terrain consisted of a certain amount of grass pasture, a certain amount of heathy ground with the usual Arctic heath association dominated by crowberry *(Empetrum nigrum)*, and considerable outcrops of rock with no scrub at all.

Nesting.—The nest is built on the ground in a recess in the side of a hummock in marshy localities, often sheltered by scrub growth of dwarf birch, willow, or other plants or sometimes, as I have seen it, on the grassy verge of a roadside or near the borders of a meadow near small farmsteads or villages. It is built of dry grass and bents lined with similar but finer material, with occasionally some hair, but without feathers. The owners tend to show up more than in the case of the meadow pipit and, Maj. W. M. Congreve (1936) describes the male as noisy and conspicuous, always giving away the fact that he has a nest in the vicinity.

Eggs.—The eggs are described by Jourdain in the Handbook of British Birds (1938) as variable, ranging from types with evenly freckled markings on a blue-gray ground to an almost uniform ochreous with a dark hair line, or with rich mahogany-red cloudings or bold sepia markings on an olive-gray ground. He gives the following measurements of 100 eggs: average, 19.2 by 14.2; maximum, 21 by 14.3 and 18.1 by 15.1; minimum, 17.1 by 13.9 and 18 by 13.4 minimum. Congreve (1936) considers them less variable than those of the meadow pipit and states that they commonly have blackish spots sometimes with a "penumbra" and to a limited extent bunting-like streaks. According to Jourdain the clutch is usually six, sometimes five, rarely four or seven, and the season is from about mid-June to early in July. Congreve in Arctic Norway found the earliest nest in 1935 (c/7, fresh) on June 20, and fresh or slightly incubated eggs until the end of the month, and Blair (1936) in the same region records full clutches from June 16 to 24, while Williams (1941) in a late season found no full sets until early in July. The experiences of other observers, to much the same effect, are summarized by Pleske (1928).

Young.—Only the hen has been found incubating, and Congreve states that she is fed by the male both on and off the nest. Both parents feed the young, of which, in the short Arctic summer, only one brood is reared. "Injury-feigning" by a bird off a nest is recorded by Williams (1941). An exact fledging period is not recorded.

Plumages.—The plumages are fully described by H. F. Witherby (1938, vol. 1) in the Handbook of British Birds. The nestling has

fairly long and plentiful down of a dark gray-brown color distributed
on the inner and outer supraorbital, occipital, humeral, ulnar, spinal,
femoral, and crural tracts.   The inside of its mouth, as I have myself
noted in northern Norway, is colored a raw-flesh red without spots
and the flanges externally are very pale yellow.   The juvenal plumage much resembles that of the adult female in winter, but the pale
edgings of the feathers of the upperparts are rather smaller and more
buffish and the buff of the underparts more yellowish.   The chin is
buffish white.   In the first winter the male is much like the adult female in winter but may have the chin and throat tinged with buffish
pink.

Food.—Like other pipits the species is mainly insectivorous.   Exact
data are not extensive, but Jourdain (1938, vol. 1) mentions Diptera,
Coleoptera, etc., small worms, and in winter also fresh-water mollusks
and grass seeds.   Haviland (1915) mentions especially mosquitoes,
and indeed it is difficult to see how these pests could fail to figure
largely in the diet of any insectivorous bird on the tundra in summer.

Behavior.—The carriage, gait, and general behavior are those of a
typical pipit.   It perches freely on bushes and fences or, where they
exist on telegraph wires and buildings and on trees.   Miss Maud
Haviland (1915) in Siberia found it a quarrelsome bird.   In winter
it is found in large parties and flocks, which scatter rather widely
over the feeding grounds.

Voice.—The distinctive character of the call note has already been
mentioned.   It is a comparatively full, quite musical, and rather
abrupt *chüp* (the "ü" sound to be pronounced like the French "u"),
quite different from the thin, shrill notes of the other pipits.   It is used
both in flight or when flushed and while perched, and habitually by
migrants as well as on the breeding ground.   A note used by breeding
birds which seems to be more definitely an alarm is a rather hoarse,
shrill *tsweerp*, and from birds chasing one another I have heard a
more rippling *tsrrrrrup*.

The species has a pleasing song superior to that of most pipits.   In
Lapland I found it to be built up of three main types of component,
which, so far as such sounds can be represented crudely by words, might
be rendered as *twee* (repeated about four times, shrill and prolonged),
trrrrrrrr (a little bubbling trill), and *twizz-wizz-wizz-wizz* (more sibilant and usually repeated several times, thus: *twee-twee-twee-twee*,
trrrrrrrr, *twizz-wizz-wizz-wizz*, *twizz-wizz-wizz-wizz*, *twizz-wizz-
wizz-wizz*.   When the song is given from a post or bush it may consist
of a single such sequence, but the fullest and best song is given in the air,
as the bird rises and then parachutes down again with wings half spread
and tail fanned.   It is then more prolonged, consisting of much the
same sequence of three main phrases or types of note repeated two or

more times, with variations, and sometimes linked up with minor warblings or twittering passages. While it is useful to attempt such a necessarily rather prosaic analysis for descriptive and comparative purposes, it conveys little of the general quality of the song. Miss Haviland's description of the bird's "glorious parachute from the upper air to the accompaniment of a rain of melody" seems to the writer rather highly colored, but the song of a good performer is musical, lively, and pleasing, with some rich and rather canarylike notes, and these qualities tend to be enhanced for the hearer in the solitudes where the song is often heard.

Field marks.—The red-throated pipit resembles the meadow pipit, previously described, much more than it does the American pipit; that is to say, it is a distinctly smaller and much more boldly marked bird, with broad black centers to the feathers of the upperparts and prominent black streaks on the breast and flanks. To an experienced European observer it is perhaps even more like the tree pipit (*Anthus trivialis*), but as that species and the meadow pipit are themselves very much alike this refinement need not concern us here. The red-throated pipit, then, is a rather small pipit with the characteristics just mentioned and in spring and summer is easily distinguished from any other by the feature that gives it its name. It must be stressed, however, that this is neither a sharply defined bib nor of a strong red. It is a pale rusty red or rufous tint over the throat and face, generally distinctive enough at fairly close range but varying in its intensity and least developed in some females. In autumn and winter this coloring is lost or much reduced, and there is then little to differentiate it from the meadow pipit except that it is rather more boldly marked above and that the ground color of the upperparts is a warmer brown without the tendency to grayish or greenish shades that so many, but not all, meadow pipits show. About the only really clear-cut difference is that the broad black streaking of the back extends over the rump and upper tail coverts, whereas these parts are practically uniform and unstreaked in the meadow pipit. Obviously this is a difficult character to be sure of in the field, though not impossible if a really good and close view can be obtained. Fortunately, however, a far better field character is provided by the note, which is quite different from that of any of the other pipits, *Anthus spinoletta* included, and should at once attract the attention of anyone with a fair ear for bird calls. It is described under "Voice."

Fall and winter.—In winter quarters the species shows a marked attachment to wet localities, such as damp or partially flooded grasslands, borders of rivers and lakes, marshes, and wet cultivation, though it may be observed more rarely on dry and even arid ground, including coastal sand dunes and the borders of deserts. As a migrant it is generally gregarious in habits.

DISTRIBUTION

Breeding range.—North Scandinavia, north Finland, north Russia (Archangel government), Kolguev, Waigatz and Novaya Zemlya, and across Siberia to Kamchatka, but not the Tchuktche Peninsula.

Winter range.—Africa south to Lake Chad and Lagos in the west, but principally east Africa, south to Kenya and northern Tanganyika; southern Asia, including northwest India, Assam, Burma, the Indo-Chinese countries, South China, and a few even to the Malay islands.

Spring migration.—Leaves Kenya and Uganda from end of March to third week April (latest date April 19). Passage in Egypt from late March till at least April 18 and a few till late in the month (exceptionally late date May 6), and at the mouth of the Yangtse, China, from beginning of April to mid-May. Arrival recorded: Vadsö, northern Norway, June 2; Murman coast, May 20–27; Arctic Circle in Yenisei Valley, June 6. Arrival on western shore of Taimyr Strait on April 18 (Pleske, 1928) presumably abnormal.

Fall migration.—Departure recorded from Golchika at the mouth of the Yenisei, August 15. Passage at mouth of the Yangtse in October. First arrivals noted: Egypt, October 23; Sudan (Darfur) October 25. Early date: Nairobi, Kenya, August 28.

ANTHUS SPRAGUEI (Audubon)

SPRAGUE'S PIPIT

HABITS

Sprague's pipit, or the Missouri skylark, was discovered by Audubon on the Upper Missouri and named for one of his companions, Isaac Sprague, who shot the first specimen near Fort Union on June 19, 1843. Audubon (1844) described and figured it near the end of his great work, and remarks: "On several occasions my friend Edward Harris sought for these birds on the ground, deceived by the sound of their music, appearing as if issuing from the prairies which they constantly inhabit; and after having travelled to many distant places on the prairie, we at last looked upwards, and there saw several of these beautiful creatures singing in a continuous manner, and soaring at such an elevation, as to render them more or less difficult to discover with the eye, and at times some of them actually disappearing from our sight, in the clear thin air of that country."

Audubon's type specimen remained unique until Captain Blakiston, 16 years later, found this species to be quite common on the plains of Saskatchewan and published an account of it in The Ibis for 1863. One of his specimens and Audubon's type were deposited in the Smithsonian Institution. These two specimens were the only ones known to Dr. Coues (1874) until he discovered it while on the survey of the international boundary in 1873, of which he wrote at that time: "It is one of the most abundant birds of all the region along the forty-ninth parallel of latitude, from just west of the Pembina Mountains to as far as the survey progressed this year—about four hundred miles; I had no difficulty in taking as many specimens as I desired. They were particularly numerous at various points along the Souris or Mouse River, where, during our marches or while we were encamped, they were almost continually hovering about us."

The 1931 Check-list gives its breeding range as "from west-central Saskatchewan and southern Manitoba south to western Montana and North Dakota," but it has been reported in recent years as breeding in some localities outside of this range. In 1942, A. D. Henderson told me that Sprague's pipit was then "a rather scarce breeder at Belvedere," Alberta. About the same time, Frank L. Farley, of Camrose, wrote to me: "This splendid aerial songster is a regular summer resident of the open prairies of central Alberta, and in recent years it has appeared in fair numbers in scattered parkland areas that have been cleared and brought under cultivation. It also delights in the open, short-grass plains that surround many of our alkaline lakes and sloughs. The most northerly point at which I have found this pipit was on the south side of Lesser Slave Lake, approximately in latitude 55° N., where a pair was undoubtedly nesting."

Dr. Thomas S. Roberts (1932) states that Sprague's pipit "was once a nesting bird in the southwestern and westcentral parts of Minnesota, but the breaking up of the prairies probably caused it to leave that region many years ago." It is now probably restricted in that State to the Red River Valley, in the northern half of the western border. Dr. Roberts visited that valley in 1928 and says that "it was something of a surprise to find that Sprague's Pipit was one of the common birds of the Valley, its tinkling song being heard high overhead everywhere."

An interesting Michigan record is published by Trautman and Van Tyne (1935), who collected a singing male in Crawford County on June 26, 1935: "On the three days it was observed the bird occupied a territory about a quarter of a mile square of barren 'jack pine plain,' sparsely covered with coarse grasses, sweet fern, and a few small pine and oak saplings."

This habitat, if I understand it correctly, seems to be quite different from the normal haunts of the species, such as the open prairies and the short-grass, rolling plains of Saskatchewan where we found it. Perhaps, with the gradual breaking up and cultivation, as well as the extensive burning, of the virgin prairies, which is rapidly reducing the ranges of all the prairie birds, Sprague's pipit, like the upland plover, is learning to adapt itself to the next-best type of country, such as the above and the parkland areas mentioned by Mr. Farley. When I visited the prairies around Quill Lake, Saskatchewan, in 1915,

I found that the grassy plains had been thoroughly burned over to improve them for grazing purposes; the long-billed curlew, formerly abundant there, had entirely disappeared, and the beautiful little chestnut-collared longspurs were nearly gone. The prairies and their fascinating bird life will soon be merely a delightful memory!

Sprague's pipit, therefore, is probably disappearing from most of its former habitat. William Youngworth, of Sioux City, Iowa, tells me that he spent a few days during the summer of 1939 near Cando, N. Dak., to learn something about this pipit. He says that, although Dr. Roberts (1932) found it so common in the Red River Valley a few years ago, it is not common any more. "One can drive now for hundreds of miles in North and South Dakota and never hear or see a pipit."

Nesting.—Frank L. Farley says in his notes: "For years I tried to find the nest of this bird by careful searching but was never successful. Later, however, I stumbled onto several nests by accident. A few years ago, when sitting in my car on the large open flat on my farm on Dried Meat Lake, my attention was directed to the songs of several of the pipits that were soaring and singing some hundreds of feet above me. It looked up and, just as my eye met one of them, the bird instantly started its downward plunge to earth. On reaching a point about 20 feet from the ground, its mate flew out to meet it. My suspicion that the female had just left its nest was correct as, on going over to where I had first seen it, I had no trouble in locating the nest with five eggs. It is quite probable that further investigation might prove that this meeting of the birds in the air just above their nest is a regular habit."

Audubon (1844) was the first to discover the nest of Sprague's Missouri lark, as he called it; the nest, he says, "is placed on the ground and somewhat sunk in it. It is made entirely of fine grasses, circularly arranged, without any lining whatever."

Dr. J. A. Allen (1874) seems to have been the next to find the nest, of which he says: "The only one found by me was arched over, and being placed in a tuft of rank grass was most thoroughly concealed. The bird would seem to be a close sitter, as in this case the female remained on the nest till I actually stepped over it, she brushing against my feet as she flew off."

Several others have described the simple nests of Sprague's pipit, but the nests are not essentially different from those described above. The most elaborate account of the nesting life of this pipit is furnished by R. D. Harris (1933), who found a nest near Winnipeg, Manitoba, on August 24, 1931, after the young had hatched. The nest was placed on the shoulder of a grass-grown roadway across a pasture field, in a hollow made in muddy weather by passing cattle. Mr. Harris writes:

In a cavity thus formed the nest was placed. Being six inches deep and six inches in diameter, the cavity was much too large for the purpose. The birds had met the situation, however, by filling in the unwanted space to a depth of three inches with dead grass, thus forming a kind of platform beside the nest which undoubtedly was found useful during nesting operations. The nest proper was composed of dried grasses two to six inches long. Unlike the filling, it was packed and woven into a firm structure. The rim was placed level with the filling three inches from the bottom, and the interior measured (after the young had left) three inches in diameter and about one and one half inches deep. It occupied the position farthest from the entrance, with one side resting against the earth wall of the cavity. Overhead, the nest was shielded by a frail roof of dead grass anchored in the plants that stood at the edge of the depression. The entrance hole was barely more than two inches in diameter, and as the grass filling was interposed between it and the nest, the latter could be seen only from a very low angle. This arrangement thus aided concealment.

Eggs.—The set of eggs seems to consist generally of either four or five; rarely a set of six is laid; reported sets of three are probably incomplete. The five eggs found by Dr. Allen (1874) "were rather long and pointed, being 0.90 of an inch in length by 0.60 in diameter. The ground color is dull grayish white, thickly and quite uniformly covered with shall blotches of purplish brown, giving to the eggs a decidedly dark purplish tint. In color the eggs thus somewhat resemble those of *Anthus ludovicianus.*"

The Macouns (1909) quote Walter Raine as saying that "they are something like eggs of the prairie horned lark but are smaller. Some have a pale buff ground, others greyish-white ground, minutely speckled with buff and purplish grey. The eggs can be easily told from small prairie horned lark's eggs by the fine dark brown lines at the largest end of the eggs."

There is a set of four eggs in the Thayer collection in Cambridge. These are ovate and only slightly glossy; the ground color is grayish white; and they are evenly sprinkled over the entire surface with small spots and fine dots of pale olive-brown.

The measurements of 44 eggs average 20.9 by 15.3 millimeters; the eggs showing the four extremes measure 22.6 by 15.7, 21.0 by 16.7, 19.2 by 14.0, and 20.5 by 13.5 millimeters.

Young.—The incubation period for Sprague's pipit does not seem to have been learned. Mr. Harris (1933) found that the female did all the brooding over the young; probably she assumed all the duties of incubation also. The young that he watched remained in the nest for at least 10 or 11 days:

The work of caring for the young in the nest appeared to be assumed entirely by the female. The male was never observed to take part in it. Indeed, the male was detected near the nest only twice, and on both these occasions the female drove it away. The male had ceased its singing rather abruptly about the beginning of August, and was not heard during the course of this nesting. On August 24, the day the nest was found, it was seen with one well-grown young bird, which was presumed to be of the first brood. From this it was concluded that, as in many other species, the male takes charge of the young after they leave the nest while the female proceeds to build another nest and lay the next set of eggs. The young birds of the first nest were noted with the male as late as August 28, but they were doubtless independent of their parents by that time.

The day after the nest was found, Mr. Harris set up his blind 2½ feet from the nest, and the next day he entered it for observation. The bird was shy at first but soon became accustomed to the blind and even the man in it. The birds were supposed to have hatched on or about August 20 or 21 and were watched off and on up to the time that they left the nest on the 31st. The results of his observations on the development of the young are given in too much detail to be included here; only a few points can be mentioned. When the nest was found, on the 24th, he estimated that the young were 3 or 4 days old; their eyelids were separated but incapable of movement; they kept huddled together in the nest and the sense of fear had not developed; a small wingless grasshopper was fed to one of them.

On the 26th, when the blind was occupied for the first time, one of the parents "kept arriving at the nest with food at an average rate of once every four and a half minutes throughout the three hours that I remained in the blind. This bird was presumed to be the female. The other one could be heard circling overhead, uttering the typical pipit '*squi-qui-quick*', for fifteen minutes after I had entered the blind, thereafter it was silent."

On the 26th, when the young had been hatched 5 or 6 days, "down was becoming scanty, and the juvenal plumage was quickly supplanting it. * * * The parent did not brood either on this occasion or at later times. * * * The parent maintained sanitation in the nest by carrying away the faeces in its bill and probably dropping them while in flight. If, however, there were two sacs in the nest at once, one was eaten and the other was carried away. Small sacs were usually eaten." On August 27 and 28, "heavy rains fell, accompanied by strong wind and low temperatures. When examined on the latter day, the birds appeared unharmed by the severe drenching they had received. Their eyes at this date were fully open." During the next two days, the young became increasingly more active and restless; and on the 31st the young left the nest. Three had already left when Mr. Harris entered the blind at 10 A. M.; during the next two hours, the parent came without food several times, as if trying to entice the remaining two young to leave.

Finally, at 12.13, one of the two suddenly scrambled out of the nest and crawled away into the grass, boring forward with its bill and picking its way round the thick clumps. After progressing for about three feet, it squatted down to rest. Here the adult, with a grasshopper in its bill, came upon it and fed it. The young one then moved on for another two feet before resting again. At this point the remaining bird left the nest, and the two were now caught and examined for the last time. * * * The young birds were now very active, and they seized in a flash any opportunity to escape. Although they exerted a remarkable strength at times, they soon became exhausted and were forced to rest frequently. They had as yet found no use for their wings, save as additional limbs with which to balance themselves. Even when the birds escaped from my hand and dropped to the ground, their wings hung limp at their sides. Legs and feet were strong, but the birds could not yet stand upright. * * *

Once the young were out of the nest, the adults changed their attitude completely, reverting to their former secretive habits. They were now almost wholly silent. All flying necessary in the care of the young was done unobtrusively low over the grass. * * * Although the area round the nest was searched diligently, it was not until September 10 that the young birds were again seen. On that date, two of them were flushed from the grass about 100 feet from the nest. One flew for some 200 feet, and the other for 100 feet, before they returned to the ground. A faint 'squick' was uttered by one of them. They had grown amazingly, and were comparable in size and actions to their parents.

Plumages.—Mr. Harris (1933) describes the natal down as "light grey in colour, long and dense; on head, 3 to 10 mm. long, beginning in two rows close together on forehead but diverging gradually to pass over tops of eyeballs; on occiput, in two small clumps 10 mm. long, one on each side; about 10 mm. on scapular region, between elbow and wrist, and on spinal tract—two short clumps on crural tract; one tuft on each side of caudal tract." At the time of nest-leaving, down was still "remaining only on sides of crown, on back and on secondary coverts." He gives a detailed account of the juvenal plumage at this age, to which the reader is referred. The following briefer description by Ridgway (1904) seems more suitable for this work: "Pileum broadly streaked with black and pale buff, the former predominating; scapulars and interscapulars black edged with buff and conspicuously margined terminally with white; rump similarly marked, but terminal margins to feathers buff instead of white; wings and tail as in adults, but whitish or pale buffy terminal margins to middle and greater wing-coverts broader and more sharply defined; under parts as in adults, but white of chin and throat more strongly contrasted with the pale buff or chest, etc."

A postjuvenal molt, involving the contour plumage but not the wings or the tail, occurs in August and September. This produces a first-winter plumage practically indistinguishable from the winter plumage of the adult. The winter plumage of both young and old birds is more strongly tinged with buff everywhere than is the spring plumage; the breast, sides, and flanks, especially, are strongly suffused with deep, rich buff in fall. March specimens are generally in badly worn plumage, and April birds show much fresh plumage about the head and breast, indicating a partial prenuptial molt. The complete postnuptial molt occurs in August and September. The sexes are alike in all plumages.

Food.—Very little seems to have been published on the food of
Sprague's pipit. Dr. Gabrielson (1924) examined 11 stomachs and
found that 2 were filled with seeds of spurge and goatweed; 6 contained grasshoppers and crickets, 75 percent; and the remainder of
the food consisted of Hymenoptera, mostly ants, Coleoptera, Hemiptera, and caterpillars.   Mrs. Nice (1931) mentions weevils, stink bugs,
and false chinch bugs.

During a period of 8 hours Mr. Harris (1933) saw the parent bird
make 91 trips to the nest with food for the young.   In 21 cases the
food was not identified; of the remaining 70 trips, 7 were made with
crickets, 4 with moths, and 59 with grasshoppers.   "Crickets and
moths were brought one at a time, while grasshoppers were brought
at an average rate of 1.58 per trip."

Behavior.—Sprague's pipit is a fascinating but very elusive bird.
We overlooked it in North Dakota and during our first season in
Saskatchewan, probably because we did not know where and how
to look for it or realize the difficulty of seeing or even hearing it.
But, on the plains of southwestern Saskatchewan, thanks to Dr.
Bishop's keen ears, we found it really quite common in 1906, though
more frequently heard than seen.   The males spend much of their
time way up in the sky, almost out of sight; it is only occasionally
that one can be seen, as a mere speck against some white cloud; against
the blue sky it is almost invisible.   When it comes down to the ground,
as it does at long intervals, it is very shy and difficult to approach,
flying off to a great distance in long, bounding, erratic flights.   We
succeeded in collecting very few birds, although we spent considerable
time in fruitless chasing.   I secured only one, shot on the wing at
long range.

Dr. Roberts (1932) says of its behavior:

Sprague's Pipit is a bird that may easily be overlooked.   It should be looked
for high overhead rather than on the ground.   In the nesting-season the characteristic song of the male, floating down from far up in the sky, is the surest
indication of its presence.   The performer may not be easy to locate, but the
song can belong to no other bird.   On the ground it disappears completely in
the prairie grass, walks or runs nimbly away without showing itself and, if
flushed, flies quickly off, appearing much like a Vesper Sparrow.   When it
springs into the air and mounts higher and higher in ascending circles to deliver
its nuptial song and then plunges directly to earth again, it may be mistaken
for a Horned Lark by the casual observer.   The performance is just the same,
but the bird usually goes higher, stays up much longer, and the song is different.
A good glass may show the large amount of white in the tail and the absence
of black markings on the head and breast.   If a glimpse be had of the bird
after it alights on the ground, it will be seen to walk in the manner of the
Horned Lark but with a more dainty, lighter step.   The ordinary flight of the
Pipit is sharply undulatory and erratic, a series of dips and upward
springs, now this way and now that.   When startled from the grass it goes
off in this manner and at the end of the flight turns suddenly backward in its

course and drops abruptly to concealment again. It rarely, if ever, alights except on the ground. Its behavior in these respects is characteristic enough to distinguish it among the other prairie birds with which it is associated.

As to its behavior about the nest, Mr. Harris (1933) discovered that—

the female used a definite route in entering and in departing from the nest. After securing food from an adjoining patch of open grass, it would fly low over the ground directly to about six feet north-west of the nest. Here it would alight and walk along a curving path to enter the nest finally from the south. On leaving, the bird would stand for a few moments on the edge of the depression to watch and listen. Then it would move directly west for about two feet—crossing its path of approach—and again pause at another "listening post." From here it would mount into the air and fly off in search of more food. The path used was always the same, and once known, it could just be discerned because of its slightly trodden appearance. Rarely did the bird depart from the nest without first standing for several minutes at both "listening posts." At these times, the bird's ear coverts were frequently seen to be raised slightly, showing how keenly alert it was. Preening occasionally took place at these intervals also.

Dr. Coues (1874) writes:

In August, after all the broods are on the wing, and through September, I have seen it in considerable flocks; and often, when riding along the prairie road, numbers would fly up at my approach, from the ruts ahead, where they were feeding, to settle again at a little distance further on. These wheel tracks, where the grass was worn away, seemed to be their favorite resorts, where they could run with the greatest ease, and perhaps gather food less easily discovered in the thick grass. They tripped along the tracks with swift and dainty steps, never hopping, and continually vibrating the tail, just like our common Titlark. They were usually associated at such times with numbers of Chestnut-colored Lark-buntings, which seemed to fancy the same places, and with a few Baird's Buntings. These were the only circumstances under which the Larks could be procured without the great quickness and dexterity required to take them on the wing; for the moment they alight in the grass of the prairie, be it scanty or only a few inches high, they are lost to view, their speckled-gray colors blending completely with the herbage.

Voice.—The marvelous flight song of Sprague's pipit has been referred to above. It is one of its most striking characteristics and quite different from the flight songs of other birds. Aretas A. Saunders says, in part, in his notes: "As it flies around, its flight rises and falls. Each time it rises the bird sings; when it falls, he is silent. So the song is heard at intervals as the bird flies about its circle. The song consists of a series of 2-note phrases, each phrase with the first note of the two higher in pitch and each phrase beginning on a little lower pitch than the previous one. I once measured the drop in pitch of a particular singer and found that it was half a tone less than an octave and that the bird sang seven 2-note phrases. But, knowing the amount of variation that exists in the songs of most species, I would not be sure that this song was typical. The song is clear, sweet, and musical but, perhaps because of the distance, sounds rather weak. In some localities choruses of these birds may be heard and, to the lover of bird music, the effect is exceedingly pleasing."

Dr. Roberts (1932) gives a very good description of the song, quoted from some notes of H. W. Gleason, as follows:

At first could be heard three or four sharp "chips" with very decided intervals, followed by a musical repetition of blended, very high-pitched notes sounding like the jingling of a set of tiny sleigh-bells. The accented notes came in regular beats or throbs and gradually diminished in volume until lost to the ear, resembling a very high, fine Veery song but lacking the inflection and given a little slower. The birds being at such a great elevation while singing made it difficult to determine the coordination of the song and flight. It seemed, however, to begin during a short sail on set wings, followed by an ascent in short flights like the Horned Lark, during which came the throbbing part of the song. During the sail the tail was spread and the wings upcurved like those of a singing Bobolink. The song was repeated at short intervals for a period of 15 to 25 minutes as the bird drifted around in wide circles. At the end it descended like a plummet, spreading its wings when almost to the ground and alighting like a Horned Lark. With the aid of a crude triangle and an assistant several rough estimates were made of the height at which the bird sang, which varied from 210 to 325 feet, with a minimum record of 110 feet during a misty rain. It would appear that the average singing height is about 300 feet.

Dr. Allen (1874) says: "Their notes resemble the syllables *jingle*, *jingle*, *jingle*, *jingle*, rapidly repeated, beginning loud and high, and decreasing rapidly in strength and loudness, and are remarkable for their clear metallic ring, their song reminding one of the jingling sound of a light chain when slowly let fall into a coil."

Dr. Coues (1874) gives the following appreciation of the song: "No other bird music heard in our land compares with the wonderful strains of this songster; there is something not of earth in the melody, coming from above, yet from no visible source. The notes are simply indescribable; but once heard they can never be forgotten. Their volume and penetration are truly wonderful; they are neither loud nor strong, yet the whole air seems filled with the tender strains, and delightful melody continues long unbroken. The song is only heard for a brief period in the summer, ceasing when the inspiration of the love season is over, and it is only uttered when the birds are soaring."

Ernest Thompson Seton (1891) writes:

On May 14, I watched a skylark that was singing on high with great devotion; he had trilled his refrain from beginning to end at least twenty times when it occurred to me to time and count his songs. The whole of each trilling occupied 15 seconds, and after I began to count he repeated it from beginning to end 82 times; just as he should have entered on the eighty-third, his wings closed, his tail went up, and down he fell headlong. * * * This singer had serenaded me for about an hour, and I do not think he ranked above his fellows in staying power. * * * When the skylark feels the impulse to sing, he rises from the bare prairie ridge with a peculiar bounding flight, like that of the pipit; up, in silence, higher and higher he goes, up, up, 100, 200, 300, 500 feet; then, feeling his spirits correspondingly elevated, he spreads his wings and tail and pours forth the strains that are making him famous. * * * Once only have I observed this species singing his full song on the ground.

Singing on the ground is evidently seldom indulged in by Sprague's pipit; most observers have never heard it do so; but Trautman and Van Tyne (1935) "on several occasions" in Michigan heard this pipit "sing from the ground and once" they "watched it sing from the top of a small telephone pole. These songs, while identical in pattern with the flight songs, were much less loud and clear."

Field marks.—Sprague's pipit is not easily recognized. Its shyness and its secretive habits when on the ground make it difficult to approach. It has no distinctive and conspicuous field marks except its two pairs of white outer tail feathers, which show only in flight and are shared by some other birds with which it is likely to be associated. It is often associated with vesper sparrows, which have about the same amount of white in the tail; the pipit is a slender bird with a sharp-pointed bill, and it walks or runs; whereas the sparrow is a stockier bird, has a short, conical bill, and it hops instead of walking. The horned lark, one of its frequent companions, also walks, but it has less white in the tail, is not so slender, and has conspicuous black markings on head and breast. The horned lark has a somewhat similar flight song, but, with a good glass, its head and breast markings can be seen. Sprague's pipit closely resembles the American pipit in form and behavior, but it is lighter in coloration and more buffy, less grayish.

Fall.—After the breeding season is over and the young are strong on the wing, these pipits gather into flocks, sometimes of immense size, mingled with horned larks and longspurs, and drift slowly southward to spend the winter close to our southern border, or farther south in Mexico.

DISTRIBUTION

Range.—Interior of North America from southern Canada to southern Mexico.

Breeding range.—Sprague's pipit breeds **north** to central Alberta (Edmonton and Athabaska); central Saskatchewan (Prince Albert and Quill Lake); and southern Manitoba (Aweme, Shoal Lake, and Hillside Beach on southern Lake Winnipeg). **East** to southeastern Manitoba (Hillside Beach and Winnipeg); and western Minnesota (Muskoda and northern Wilkin County). **South** to central western Minnesota (northern Wilkin County); northern South Dakota (Grand River Agency, northern Stanley County, and Harding County); and central Montana (Lewistown and the Belt Mountains). **West** to western Montana east of the Rocky Mountains (Belt Mountains, Great Falls, Teton County, and Browning); and west-central Al-

berta (Red Deer River east of Banff National Park and Edmonton).
Winter range.—Sprague's pipit winters **north** to central Texas (San Angelo, Dallas, and Corsicana); southern Louisiana (Lobdell and Mandeville); and southern Mississippi (Biloxi). **South** to southern Mississippi (Biloxi); southern Louisiana (New Orleans, Avery Island, and Jennings); southern Texas (Galveston, Port O'Connor, Corpus Christi, and Brownsville); through eastern Mexico to Veracruz (Veracruz), Puebla (Puebla), and Guerrero (Iguala). **West** to Guerrero (Iguala); Michoacán (La Salada); and central Texas (Laredo and San Angelo). In fall and winter it has also occurred near Charleston, S. C.; Cumberland Island, Ga.; and Lake Miccosukee, Lukens, Lake Tohopekaliga, and Charlotte Harbor, Fla.

Migration.—Late dates of spring departure are: Louisiana—New Orleans, April 19. Texas—Gainesville, April 14. Kansas—Stockton, April 26. Nebraska—Lincoln, April 26.

Early dates of spring arrival are: Oklahoma—Caddo, February 18. Missouri—Kansas City, March 20. South Dakota—Vermillion, April 14. North Dakota—Jamestown, April 29. Minnesota—Muskoda, April 27. Manitoba—Aweme, April 8. Wyoming—Laramie, April 17. Montana—Great Falls, April 23. Saskatchewan—Eastend, April 7. Alberta—Alliance, May 2.

Late dates of fall departure are: Alberta—Edmonton, September 30. Saskatchewan—Eastend, October 10. Montana—Fallon, September 19. Wyoming—Laramie, September 20. Manitoba—Margaret, October 20. South Dakota—Forestburg, October 30.

Early dates of fall arrival are: Nebraska—Monroe Canyon, Sioux County, October 1. Oklahoma—Kenton, October 2. Texas—High Island, October 31. Louisiana—Lobdell, November 5.

Casual records.—On April 4, 1905, a specimen was collected at Fort Lowell, Ariz.; it was recorded in Yellowstone Park, Wyo., on July 10, 1929. One was present June 21 to 26, 1935, near Lovells, Crawford County, Mich., and was collected on the latter date.

Egg dates.—North Dakota: 3 records, June 7 to 30. Saskatchewan: 5 records, May 19 to June 28.

Family BOMBYCILLIDAE: Waxwings

BOMBYCILLA GARRULUS PALLIDICEPS Reichenow

BOHEMIAN WAXWING

HABITS

The Bohemian waxwing is an elegant bird, a well-dressed gentleman in feathers, a Beau Brummel among birds. He is not so gaudily dressed in gay colors as many other birds are, but his sleek and silky plumage, in softly blended, harmonious shades of modest grays and browns, clothes his shapely form in a most pleasing combination of colors; and the band of white across the wings, the yellow-tipped tail, the chestnut under tail coverts, the black chin, and the red wax tips rather accent than spoil the harmony of the whole; and, above all, the jaunty crest gives the final touch of aristocracy. He is a gentleman in appearance and a courteous gentleman in behavior, as all who have seen him in association with his fellows, or with other species, will attest.

To most of us, these Bohemians are birds of mystery; we never know when or where we may see these roving bands of gypsies. They come and they go, we know not whence or whither, in the never-ending search for a bounteous food supply on which to gorge themselves. On infrequent occasions, far too infrequent in New England, from the vast timbered wilderness of northern Canada small groups, or immense flocks, of these fascinating and erratic wanderers swoop down upon us in winter in the Northern States, and more regularly in the Rocky Mountain regions. According to Dr. Coues (1874), "Prof. Baird mentions that Mr. Drexler saw 'millions' on Powder River, in flocks 'rivalling in extent those of the Wild Pigeon.' " Whence come these vast hordes? It is only within comparatively recent years that a few small breeding colonies have been discovered in different parts of northern Canada. But the total of all these colonies will not begin to account for the enormous numbers of these waxwings that sometimes flock into the States in winter. There must be many more of these, or larger, colonies scattered through the broad expanse of coniferous forests, dotted with muskegs, that extend from Hudson Bay almost to the Pacific slope, most of which region still remains unexplored. A 30-mile trip that I made into the wilderness north of Prince Albert gave me a glimpse of what this country must be like. Perhaps the opening of the Alcan Highway may throw some light on the subject.

Sir John Richardson (Swainson and Richardson, 1831) writes:

This elegant bird has only lately been detected in America, having been discovered, in the spring of 1826, near the sources of the Athabasca, or Elk river, by Mr. Drummond, and by myself the same season at Great Bear Lake, in latitude 65°. * * * It appears in flocks at Great Bear Lake about the 24th of May, when the spring thaw has exposed the berries of the alpine arbutus, marsh vaccinium, &c., that have been frozen and covered during the winter. It stays only for a few days, and none of the Indians of that quarter with whom I conversed had seen its nests. * * * I observed a large flock, consisting of at least three or four hundred individuals, on the banks of the Saskatchewan, at Carlton House, early in May, 1827. They alighted in a grove of poplars, settling all in one or two trees, and making a loud twittering noise. They stayed only about an hour in the morning, and were too shy to allow me to approach within gunshot.

This species is circumpolar in its distribution, and our bird was, for a long time, supposed to be identical with the European bird, but it has since been shown to be subspecifically distinct from the latter, *B. g. garrulus*, as well as from a closely related Asiatic race, *B. g. central-asiae*. Dr. Harry C. Oberholser (1917) has pointed out the differences between the forms. He says that our bird is similar to the Asiatic bird, "but decidely more grayish (less cinnamomeous) both above and below". And he adds: "The North American representatives of this species constitute a well-marked and readily recognizable subspecies which differs from *Bombycilla garrula garrula* in its paler, very much more grayish (less vinaceous or cinnamomeous), coloration both above and below."

The type race has occurred as a straggler in Greenland.

The 1931 Check-list implies that the Bohemian waxwing nests wholly north of the United States, but Dr. Walter P. Taylor (1918) has published several records that indicate that it "occurs, probably rarely, as a breeding bird within our borders in the coniferous forests of the northern Rocky Mountain region, in a district embracing north-western Montana, northern Idaho, and northern Washington."

Harry S. Swarth (1922) found a colony of these waxwings breeding in the lowlands near the upper part of the Stikine River, in northern British Columbia. Just why they were restricted to this limited area, when conditions were apparently equally favorable farther down the river, was not apparent. The terrace or plateau where he found them "extends westward a mile or more, is quite level, and but sparsely covered with forest growth. A year or more before our visit it had been swept by fire and a large part of the timber destroyed. As we saw the place there was very little underbrush of any sort, a great many dead trees, mostly pines with some poplars, and a scattering growth of live trees that had escaped destruction. The conifers were the lodgepole pine (*Pinus contorta*), and were all small trees."

Fifty miles or so down the river, at Doch-da-on Creek, he found the waxwings breeding under slightly different conditions. "This tract was composed mainly of balsam firs of rather large size, with an admixture of cottonwoods and poplars, and with but little underbrush." These woods, though fairly open, were much denser than those mentioned above.

Courtship.—The following short statement by Mr. Swarth (1922) is all that I can find on this subject: "On one occasion one of a pair of waxwings, presumably the male, was seen strutting about and exhibiting his beauties to his mate. Considering that the two sexes are alike in every respect, it seemed rather a superfluous performance, but at any rate the one bird was hopping excitedly about from branch to branch, while the other sat still and looked on. The active performer kept the tail partly spread, wings drooping, and crest raised, and the whole body was held stiffly upright. After several minutes the other seemed to tire of the performance and flew away, followed at once by its mate."

Nesting.—Many years ago, Professor Baird (1865) made the following announcement as to our first knowledge of the nesting habits of this species:

For many years authentic eggs of the Bohemian Chatterer were greatly sought after, but it was not until 1856 that they were brought to the notice of the scientific world, when the late Mr. H. Wolley discovered them in Lapland. Early duplicates from his collection were sold at five guineas each, and although a good many have since been obtained, they are yet considered as great prizes. A nest, with its eggs, of those collected by Mr. Wolley, has been presented to the [Smithsonian] Institution by Mr. Alfred Newton. The only instances on record of their discovery in America are of a nest and one egg by Mr. Kennicott, on the Yukon, in 1861, and a nest and single egg on the Anderson River, by Mr. MacFarlane, both of which, with the female parents, are in the possession of the Institution.

Mr. Swarth (1922), in his excellent account of the breeding colony on the upper Stikine, mentions several other breeding stations that have been discovered since the above-mentioned early records and prior to his own discovery, and gives much interesting information about other phases of the life history of these little-known birds, which will be taken up later. But first I want to include some contributed notes on more recent nestings in some other localities.

Frank L. Farley writes to me: "Bohemian waxwings are apparently as erratic in their selection of nesting territory as they are in their annual wanderings to and from their summer homes. During my early visits to the muskeg country, lying between the Athabaska and the Pembina Rivers, about 100 miles northwest of Edmonton, Alberta, I was not successful in locating nesting pairs, although occasional birds were seen, and the country seemed suitable for such purposes. On such occasions the birds all disappeared before our departure for home. When I visited the region in May 1938, waxwings appeared daily in fair numbers, and several pairs were found nesting toward the end of the month about our camp. On May 28 two nests were located in tall jack pines. One of these contained four and the other six eggs. The nesting trees were about 100 feet apart and were close to an old logging trail that traverses the country between the two rivers. The nests were built on horizontal branches close to the main trunk and about 35 feet from the ground. The nests were made of dry pine and tamarack twigs, intermixed with coarse grasses and tree mosses. The lining is of finer grass, bits of soft black moss, and a fluffy white down, the product of some native plant. The exterior is more or less covered with moss and lichens. The diameter outside is 6 inches and the depth 4 inches. The cup is nearly 3 inches deep and the same in width."

A. D. Henderson contributes the following account: "This beautiful bird is a rather common breeder in the muskeg and sand-hill country north of Fort Assiniboine, with its growth of spruce, tamarack, and pines, and its abundant crop of blueberries, cranberries, and kinnikinnick berries. It nests in spruce and tamarack trees in the muskegs, usually at low elevations. It also nests in pines growing on the high ground. The nests are placed near the top of the tall, slim pines and are so difficult to secure that it is necessary quite often to lash two or more pines together, or pull the tree with the nest into a larger pine nearby. Three nests taken in pines were at heights of 40, 50, and 50 feet. The highest nest of 11 taken in muskegs was 18 feet up and the lowest 4 feet; the rest ranged from 8 to 16 feet up. The birds also nest in the wide-branching pines growing in open situations, and in this case the nests are saddled on the horizontal limbs well out from the trunk.

"The nests are rather flat, and made on the outside of tamarack or spruce twigs, grass, usnea moss, and cocoons; they are lined with a little fine grass, usnea moss, cocoons, and plant cotton, or with tamarack leaves, feathers, or pine needles; some of this lining is, of course, not present in every nest.

"Some pairs breed by themselves, but quite often two or more nests are in the same muskeg at no great distance from each other. On one trip to the muskegs, the birds were entirely absent from their usual haunts. I attribute this to lack of the usual crop of berries, the blossoms evidently being caught in a hard frost the previous season. These birds are also great flycatchers, and, in another season which was very cold and windy and little insect life available, they were not breeding at the usual time and only one nest was found. Few nests are found as compared with the numbers of birds present. They do not breed in the poplar woods around Belvedere."

Wilson C. Hanna has sent me the data for two sets of eggs of the Bohemian waxwing, taken by him at Atlin Lake, British Columbia, on July 14, 1931. Both nests were in balsam firs, 14 feet above the ground; one was at a fork in the main trunk of a small fir, and the other was on a downward-sloping limb against the trunk. The materials used in the construction of the nests were not different from those mentioned above. The larger nest measured 6 by 7 inches in outside diameter by 2.7 inches in depth; the inner cavity was 3.25 inches in diameter and 1.5 inches deep. (Pl. 7.)

Mr. Swarth's (1922) eight Telegraph Creek nests were all in lodgepole pines; one nest was 25 feet, one 10, and one 15 feet from the ground; the others were only 6 or 7 feet up. All the nests but one were on small limbs against the trunk; this nest, found June 24, "was in a lodgepole pine of larger size than most in this locality, in the fork of one of the larger branches, about three feet from the trunk. Both birds were building here at 1 p. m. At 4 p. m. both birds were seen hard at work carrying the nest material elsewhere. When we ceased watching there was very little of the nest left. On July 5 we happened to pass this place and were surprised to see the nest intact and a bird upon it. It yielded a set of five eggs." Of the first nest he says: "Found June 19, nest just begun; June 21, nest completed; June 22, contained one egg; June 24, 3 eggs; June 25, 4 eggs; June 26, five eggs, set taken." Of the nests in general, he says;

The building material was always the same, an outer structure of dead twigs, lending support to a mass of black moss and white plant fiber. Dry grass was used as a lining sometimes but not always. The black moss was the one material that was used in the greatest amount, and it appears in all but one of the nests. This moss grows abundantly on the conifers of the region, depending from the branches in great masses, like coarse hair. The white plant fiber that is also so conspicuous in the nests is from the seed pod of the previous year's dead "fireweed" (*Epilobium angustifolium*).

There was one additional feature in which the nests were all alike, something that could not be preserved. Invariably there was a mass of stuff depending six or eight inches below the nest proper, so loosely attached as to seem on the verge of dropping away. This stuff was mostly the moss and the white plant fiber; usually additional tufts of these materials were adhering to nearby branches.

Of the two nests found at Doch-da-on Creek, 50 miles down the river, he says: "Each was near the top of a fir, about twenty-five feet from the ground, supported upon a branch and by surrounding twigs, and close to the trunk. On July 15 one of these nests was taken, together with a set of three eggs. The other contained two eggs, and was left undisturbed. No more eggs were laid in this nest, the female being still incubating the two eggs some days later."

Several other accounts of the nesting of the Bohemian waxwing have been published, but they are not sufficiently different from some of those mentioned above to warrant quoting them here. Some of them are quoted in Mr. Swarth's (1922) paper, to which the reader is referred.

Eggs.—Mr. Swarth (1922) found one of these waxwings incubating on two eggs for "some days," but usually the set consists of four to six. The eggs are almost exactly like those of the cedar waxwing but decidedly larger. Mr. Swarth describes his eggs as follows: "In color, three of the sets are much alike, a pale glaucous blue, close to Ridgway's 'pale dull glaucous-blue,' but more washed out. This ground color is marked rather profusely with blackish dots and with a few fine, irregular lines, the dots mostly quite small and occurring over nearly the entire egg, though less numerously at the smaller end than elsewhere. There are also obscure underlying spots of bluish, but faintly seen. The fourth set (No. 1821) is more olivaceous, the ground color close to Ridgway's 'mineral gray.' The spots are fewer in number than in the other sets, larger, and more sharply defined."

The measurements of 50 eggs average 24.6 by 17.4 millimeters; the eggs showing the four extremes measure 27.5 by 19.2, 27.3 by 19.4, 21.5 by 17.7, and 22.9 by 15.2 millimeters.

Young.—Apparently no one who has found a nest of the Bohemian waxwing has been willing to allow the eggs to hatch; hence we know nothing about the period of incubation or about the development and care of the young. The eggs were considered worth more than the information. The only hint we have as to the altricial period is that Mr. Swarth found five young in a nest on June 24, which he thought were not more than two or three days old; on July 5, 11 days later, these young birds fluttered from the nest when disturbed; they might not have left the nest voluntarily for two or three days.

Plumages.—Mr. Swarth (1922) shows a colored plate of the young birds, drawn by Maj. Allan Brooks, which gives a better idea of them than any description; the brood consisted of four males and one female. He gives the following interesting description of them:

These young waxwings presented a most striking appearance in life, for to my surprise they exhibited all the characteristic markings of the adult. Not only that, but the yellow tip to the tail was much brighter, more of an orange yellow, than it is in any of the old birds. The wax tips to the secondaries were present in each of the four males but not in the female. Two of the birds had four such tips, one had five, and one had seven, as many as are seen in any of the adults. These wax tips are as large as in many old birds. * * *

The four young males are very much alike in color and markings, the only differences in appearance being those arising from the slight difference in stage of development. The marginal primary markings are present, sharply defined, and in each case bright yellow. In many adults these markings are white. In the young males the terminal tail band is orange-buff, the primary tips, light orange-yellow. In the brightest adult at hand the tail band is light cadmium, the primary tips, lemon chrome. In the young female the tail band is somewhat paler than in the males, though still more orange than in any adult. The primary tips are but slightly tinged with yellow.

A still more remarkable feature in the young males is the fact that in each one the rectrices are distinctly tipped with red. These red tips are not fully developed sealing-waxlike scales such as are on the secondaries, but are produced by red coloration of the terminal portion (4 or 5 mm. in length) of the feather shaft of the rectrix. * * *

While the young birds possess all the markings of the adults, they are appreciably different in general body color. They have a somewhat streaked appearance, though not as much so as in the young cedar waxwing; the whole body is of a duller, darker gray than in the adult, and the young bird has none of the vinous coloring about the head that is seen in the adult. The crest is present but only slightly developed. The young has a dull black line from the nostril to the eye and posteriorly on the head, in resemblance to that on the adult, but in our specimens of young there is just an indication of the black throat. This may be due to the fact that in these birds the feathers of the chin and upper throat are but partly developed.

In full juvenal plumage, according to Ridgway (1904), the malar region, chin, and throat are dull white, the chin is margined on each side by a dusky streak, and the under tail coverts are vinaceous-cinnamon; and Dwight's (1900) description is substantially the same. The latter says that the first winter plumage is acquired by a partial postjuvenal molt, "which involves the body plumage and wing coverts, but not the remiges nor rectrices." He describes it as "everywhere rich drab, grayer below and on rump, fawn-color about the head. A large black chin patch, the black extending to lores and forehead and bordered everywhere by rich walnut-brown."

There seems to be no prenuptial molt in the Bohemian waxwing. One-year-old birds and adults have a complete postnuptial molt, either very late in summer (last of August) or in fall; E. S. Cameron (1908) says this occurs in October; and Witherby's Handbook (1919) says October to November. Dwight (1900) says that young birds become indistinguishable from adults after their first postnuptial molt, adults being somewhat grayer than first-winter birds, with more extensive white markings in the wings and brighter yellow tail band and primary tips.

Except for the smaller and duller black throat, there seem to be no constant sexual differences in plumage, but there is much individual variation in both sexes. The coloration of the female is said to be duller than that of the male, but the most brightly colored bird in the series examined by Mr. Swarth (1922) is a female. "In size (but not in number) of wax wing tips, in 'return margins' of primaries, in yellow on primaries, and in size of white spots on secondaries, it is superior to any of the males. In this bird the wax secondary tips are 7 mm. in length, a size attained by only one or two males." The female parent of the brood of young is a highly plumaged bird. "It has six secondaries of one wing, five of the other, with wax tips, the primary margins are bright yellow, the tail is broadly tipped with yellow, and there is a faint suggestion of red in one or two of the tail feathers."

The presence of wax tips, or their number, did not seem to be dependent on age, sex, or season; they were almost evenly divided between the sexes; out of 45 specimens examined, just 1 (a female) had no trace of a wax tip; in a series of 22 males, 2 had 3 tips, 8 had 6, and 1 had 7 tips, the others being intermediate in this respect; in a series of 16 females, 1 had no tips, 1 had traces of 2, 2 had 3 tips, 7 had 6, and 1 had 7 tips, the others being intermediate.

Food.—On its northern breeding grounds, in summer, the Bohemian waxwing is largely insectivorous, though even there its presence seems to be governed to some extent by the available supply of berries. It has sometimes been referred to as an expert flycatcher; it must be very smart at this, for it has been known to capture such swift and strong fliers as dragonflies. Mr. Swarth (1922) writes:

Waxwings were seen feeding on insects and also on berries and other vege-table matter. About Telegraph Creek, the first week in June, they were usually seen perched on bare branches and making short sallies after flying insects in true flycatcher style. Early in July a berry-bearing shrub (*Shepherdia canadensis*) of general distribution in the region came into bearing, and the waxwings, as well as other species of birds, fed upon the berries of this plant to a great extent. The young waxwings we took from the nest had also been fed upon these same berries.

Dr. Thomas S. Roberts (1932) says: "The Bohemian Waxwing is fond of tree sap, especially that of the sugar maple, and when the sap begins to run in early spring, a leaking tree-trunk will attract a whole flock. * * * With the warm days of early spring, it becomes a 'flycatcher' and may be seen sallying out from the tree-tops in pursuit of the tiny flies and beetles that fill the upper air even before the snow and ice have disappeared. The stomach at such times will be found packed with many hundreds of these minute insects." He gives a long list of berries and fruits eaten, and adds that, in times of stress, it will feed on "rotten apples and cranberries gleaned from garbage cans and dumping places in the rear of residences and stores."

Mr. Farley sends me the following note: "I am told by trappers in the mountains that, in summer, these birds begin to eat the wild raspberries just as soon as they show any signs of ripening, and from that time on, until the berries fall off, the bills and the faces of the birds are smeared with the red juices. During their stay in central Alberta, beginning late in October, their chief food in the country consists of chokecherries, hawthorn, and rose hips, all of which remain on the trees late. As long as these fruits can be had the birds will remain. In the towns and cities, where the shrub *Cotoneaster* is now grown commonly, the Bohemians feed on the blue berries produced on this bush and prefer them to any other food. When feeding on these, their faces and bills are always colored by the blue juices."

Although there is a long list of berries and fruits on which these waxwings feed, the most important two are the berries of the mountain-ash and those of the cedars or junipers; at least these are the foods most often mentioned, and they are probably decided favorites. The mountain-ash berries are so popular with these birds that they will flock to a tree in fruit day after day until it is entirely stripped of its berries and until all those that have fallen to the ground have been picked up. A mountain-ash tree in fruit is sure to attract all the waxwings in the vicinity, provided it has not been stripped of its fruit by starlings, robins, or other birds before the waxwings arrive, for it is one of the most popular of berry-bearing trees or shrubs.

The cedars are more widely distributed and there are many more of them; they provide an abundant food supply for the waxwings. Mr. Cameron (1908) says that, in Montana in winter, these waxwings subsist "entirely on cedar berries, which have a sweet taste and tinge the excrement of the birds red, so that familiar roosting places in the high pines are infallibly marked by the red-stained snow beneath."

Other vegetable foods of the Bohemian waxwing include highbush cranberries, buffaloberries, bearberries, blueberries, wolfberries, snowberries, hackberries, barberries, and the berries of the black alder, American holly, madrona, buckthorn, ivy, asparagus, smilax, kinnikinnick, bittersweet vine, mistletoe, peppertree, dogwood, sumac, laurel, woodbine and the matrimony vine, and doubtless other berries. They also eat frozen apples that hang on the trees or fall to the ground, Russian olives and wild olives, rose hips, wild grapes, persimmons, and figs. They will come to the feeding stations for raisins, dried currants, or minced prunes, and probably for other kinds of dried fruits or berries. They are said to eat the buds of poplars and the seeds of boxelder, black birch, locust, and hollyhock.

Bohemian waxwings are voracious, almost gluttonous feeders; they gorge themselves with all the food their crops will hold, then fly down and take a drink of water or snow and return to the feast; when filled to capacity they fly up into a tree and sit quietly to digest their food, so as to be ready to fly down and eat more. They swoop down in flocks onto the berry-bearing trees or shrubs and keep almost constantly at it until the supply is exhausted.

Dr. Harrison F. Lewis has sent me the following note on a flock that he watched near Quebec City, on February 22, 1920: "At this point two fields were partly separated by a rugged row of thorn bushes (*Crataegus*) of considerable size, on which hung much frozen fruit. Among these bushes and rising high above them stood three or four tall spruce trees. Some of the waxwings were in the spruces, some were in the bushes, and some were on the wind-packed snow beneath. There was much activity, and birds were continually flying back and forth between trees, bushes, and snow. I was able to reach a position among the bushes, at the foot of one of the spruce trees, without disturbing the flock much. I could then see plainly that the waxwings were feeding on the frozen fruit of the thorn bushes, for they would come unconcernedly to within about two rods of me while they were feeding. They swallowed the fruits whole but did so with great difficulty. It seemed as if a bird made five or six unsuccessful attempts to swallow a fruit for every one successful attempt. After failing in one or two attempts to swallow a particular fruit, a bird would drop it and try another, then perhaps drop that and try a third one, and so on. The birds working in the bushes apparently dropped most of the fruit which they pulled from the twigs, but these fallen fruits were immediately mouthed over and some of them finally swallowed by the birds on the surface of the snow. Sometimes the birds, with fruit in their mouths, flew up into the spruces to swallow what they had secured."

Behavior.—The Bohemian waxwing is a well-behaved bird with a gentle and inoffensive disposition, sociable and friendly among its fellows and not hostile toward other species, even in competition for food. Waxwings are often vigorously attacked by robins that try to drive them from the berry-bearing bushes, where they are peacefully feeding, but the waxwings do not retaliate; the angry attacks by the hostile robins only cause them to step quietly aside and await their turn. Audubon (1842) published an interesting account, given to him by Thomas McCulloch, which illustrates the devotion of one of these birds to its wounded companion; it returned again and again to its fallen friend, uttering notes of alarm and warning, and flying against it in its efforts to urge it to escape from danger, until it paid with its life for its friendly solicitude.

It is very tame and confiding in the presence of human beings, being quite unsuspicious and easily approached, as illustrated by the following observation by Thomas D. Burleigh (1930) :

The birds on the University campus have gradually increased until now there are fully eight hundred of them there; they feed on the ground or in the thickets where the bushes are full of berries, and are remarkably tame, allowing anyone to walk up within a foot of them; two lit on me as I stood watching them, one on my shoulder and one on the top of my head, the latter bird remaining there for several minutes; a few minutes later, I held out my hand full of berries and one bird actually lit on my arm and standing on the sleeve of my mackinaw ate the berries without paying the slightest attention to me.

The Bohemian waxwing shows its sociability by its pronounced flocking habits; even on its breeding grounds it is often seen moving about in flocks, and it seems to prefer to nest in communities. S. F. Rathbun has contributed the following notes on flock behavior :

"December 22, 1919. This morning we again heard these waxwings and found them in the same locality where we had seen flocks on two other occasions. The flock was a large one, a majority of the birds being perched in or near the top of a large maple tree; all were headed directly into the wind, which seems to be customary when any appreciable wind is blowing; individuals were constantly dropping down to feed on the berries in some adjacent mountain-ash trees. As usual, there was a constant movement in the flock, birds continually leaving and returning to it; and, to judge from the sound, the greater number were uttering their soft, rolling notes that are so pleasing to hear.

"A striking and very noticeable feature of a flock is that, when disturbed, nearly all the birds will take wing and circle around a number of times until they come together in a close and compact body; then it appears as if at the same instant all were impelled by the same impulse to alight, and the flock will sail up to the chosen spot on stiffly extended wings, this action being uniform on the part of each individual; and during these various evolutions the soft, lisping notes of the birds are always much in evidence.

"In these flocks of waxwings other species will sometimes be found in limited numbers, robins and cedar waxwings most commonly. It is amusing to see the robins resent the presence of the Bohemians feeding upon the berries; the former would frequently make a dash at them and try to drive them away, but this was futile, as the latter simply shifted their positions and resumed feeding.

"On another occasion we saw a large flock that numbered nearly 2,000 birds, the majority occupying the tops of several small trees. Near the base of one of the trees, grew a tall, decorative rosebush, and as the bush had many hips, numbers of the birds attempted to alight therein to feed, but its branches, being too weak to sustain them, would continually give way, causing a constant commotion; the birds kept fluttering and interfering with one another and dislodging many hips, which fell to the walk beneath, to be eaten by the birds alighting there. The sight of these many birds in active motion reminded one of bees swarming about a hive."

Bohemian waxwings are seldom seen singly, though one or two may be seen occasionally in a flock of cedar waxwings, with which they seem to be on friendly terms and to have similar habits. Mr. Rathbun mentions in his notes one that he saw entirely alone and a long way from home; while he was crossing the Gulf of Alaska, and was some 20 miles offshore, one solitary individual came aboard the ship and perched on one of the stays of the stack for nearly half an hour and then flew off low over the water toward land.

P. M. Silloway (1903) says of their flight behavior:

They were continually fluttering upward or outward from the tree-tops, hovering in air like kingbirds capturing insects a-wing. Their aerial movements were much like those of swallows over water, as they sailed, fluttered, or hovered with expanded tail, or mounted obliquely upward with rapidly beating wings. Frequently a crowded company of them would fly outward from some tree in which they had been sitting, keeping together in undulating flight, veering abruptly upward or downward or sidewise in capricious evolution.

Voice.—As a vocalist the Bohemian waxwing is no star performer. Mr. Swarth (1922) says of it:

Under ordinary circumstances the only sound uttered by the waxwing is a sibilant call note much like that of the more familiar cedar bird. While notes of the two species are of the same character, still they are distinguishably different. This difference may, perhaps, be indicated by describing the cedar bird's call as a hiss, the Bohemian waxwing's call as a buzz. The note of the latter is somewhat coarser; the listener has an impression of hearing a series of very slightly separated notes, rather than of a continuous sound such as the cedar bird utters.

Mr. Cameron (1908) says that "when flying the birds keep up an incessant twittering, so that high passing flocks are immediately recognized by their call of *zir-r-r-r*—a sort of trill. * * * The weak voice of a single waxwing is inaudible except at very close quarters, but hundreds together produce quite a volume of sound." Ralph Hoffmann (1927) remarks that the note, 'given when the birds wheel off in flight is a low rough *scree*, with more body than the sibilant call of the Cedar Waxwing."

Dr. Harrison F. Lewis (MS.) watched a flock, near Quebec, that "seemed to be 'all talking at once', and the result was a continuous and fairly loud noise. The ordinary note seemed to resemble that of the cedar waxwing but was shriller and lighter in tone, resembling also the loud sibilant note often uttered by the robin. Besides a continual shower of these notes, there seemed to come from the flock an unceasing, jumbled twitter, much like the twitter of a large flock of slate-colored juncos, contentedly feeding."

Field marks.—A Bohemian might easily be mistaken for a cedar waxwing. It is a larger bird, but size is sometimes deceptive where there is no direct comparison. The underparts of the cedar waxwing are largely yellowish, but decidedly grayish in the Bohemian, and the latter has a black chin and a conspicuous white bar across the wing, and the under tail coverts are a rich brown.

Enemies.—Frank L. Farley writes to me: "Pigeon hawks must take a heavy toll of the Bohemian waxwings while they are gathering in the Rockies and foothills to commence their wanderings to the south. On several trips after big game into these regions, I have seen large flocks of a hundred or more birds, sitting motionless and apparently fearful, on the top branches of a solitary leafless tree, out in an opening. If one looks about, he is almost certain to see a pigeon hawk perched in a nearby tree top, patiently watching the waxwings. The birds seem to know that they are safe, if they remain in the tree, but, if one puts them to flight, the hawk is off in a flash and easily takes one before the flock gets a hundred yards from the tree."

Mr. Cameron (1908) says that, in very severe weather, when the waxwings were somewhat stupified by the cold—

they became the prey of ranch cats. A very fine male which our cat brought to me on Feb. 13, 1899, was quite fat after eighteen days of a cold wave during which 45° below zero was registered. I do not think that many Waxwings fall victims to Prairie Falcons, as they betake themselves to thick cover when the latter are about. On March 6, 1904, my wife and I approached within two yards of a flock of Waxwings, which refused to leave a low cedar when a Rough-legged Hawk was sailing above.

Winter.—It is probably failure of the food supply, rather than cold weather, that sends the Bohemians southward in winter. Mr. Cameron (1908) reports them as abundant winter residents even during the most severe winters, when the temperature goes down to 31° or 45° below zero. Given food enough, they seem to be able to stand the most intense cold.

This species seems to be present regularly, in varying numbers, but apparently every winter, in Montana and in the Rocky Mountain region as far south as Colorado. It appears less regularly, and usually in smaller numbers, in Missouri, Illinois, Ohio, Pennsylvania, New York, and New England, these localities being far removed from its breeding grounds. Where food conditions are favorable, its winter sojourn may begin early in October and continue beyond the middle of April; the exact dates for different localities will be given under "Distribution."

There have been several well-marked invasions recorded, in which these waxwings appeared in unusual localities and in enormous numbers. The most conspicuous flights occurred in the winters of 1908–09, 1916–17, 1919–20, and 1930–31. The first of these reported invasions covered such widely separated localities as New England, Iowa, and Colorado. The New England records are given in detail by Horace W. Wright (1921), to which the reader is referred. For Iowa, Miss Althea R. Sherman (1921) reported that—

on December 29, 1908, the day the Bohemian Waxwings arrived, a vast flock of birds was seen by two observers at points a half mile apart. * * * The first observer was Mr. Jerome Jones, who stated that soon after daylight a vast flock of birds flew over his head, "millions of them" he estimated; that they covered the sky and were several minutes in passing. * * * The other observer was Mrs. D. A. Wright, whose description of the flock was written down soon after it passed and was substantially as follows: About eight o'clock in the morning she saw a flock, containing thousands of birds, fly northeast. They flew as closely together as birds ever do and covered a space from two hundred to three hundred feet in width and were two or three minutes in passing. She believed they were Bohemian Waxwings, nine of which for the following eighteen days frequented her mountain ash tree. There seems to be no other species to which to assign the birds of this great flock.

During the winter of 1916–17 there was a great invasion of these waxwings throughout the western part of the country, at least from Washington to Colorado. Mr. Rathbun has sent me the following account of the birds that visited Seattle:

"The great incursion of the winter of 1916–17 will long be remembered, for many, many thousands of individuals of the species were in the region at that time. As nearly as can be ascertained, this species made its first appearance about December 10, in flocks of considerable size; but, on the 26th or 27th, the great body of the birds arrived numbering thousands of individuals, which thereafter for some considerable period could be observed almost every day within a comparatively restricted area some six miles in length along the eastern border of the city, adjacent to Lake Washington. This was accounted for by the fact that within this particular section there was an abundant food supply in the form of the berries of the madrona tree (*Arbutus menziesii*), which had fruited with unusual abundance the past season, and of which the waxwings appeared very fond; it was not uncommon at times to count in one of the larger trees upward of five hundred of the birds.

"Always associated with the waxwings were flocks of the western robin (*Turdus migratorius propinquus*); of this species the individuals numbered several thousands; and at times when suddenly startled, this immense body of birds would arise, scattering in every direction, and then begin to congregate in flocks. On some occasions, they would all amalgamate into one vast flock and, after flying about, would again break up into small flocks; these would alight in the berry-laden trees and immediately resume feeding, until again disturbed, when these evolutions would be repeated. At all times the soft, rolling chatter of the many waxwings could be heard, which added to the interesting spectacle. On one particular occasion apparently all the individuals in a large portion of the section became associated, forming a flock that by careful estimate was an eighth of a mile in length and of considerable width.

"Many times, in these flocks of Bohemian waxwings, we observed a few cedar waxwings and, in the same locality, small flocks of pine siskins and willow goldfinches, which would sometimes mingle with the former in flight, but disassociate when the waxwings alighted.

"About January 25, the supply of madrona berries in this section became practically exhausted, and thereafter the waxwings were seen in smaller flocks and became scattered throughout the city in quest of suitable food. On many occasions the birds were seen in the parks of the city and about the residences where there was shrubbery that might bear berries; this continued until about February 15, after which date we have failed to note them."

Several observers have commented on the abundance of Bohemian waxwings in Colorado during that winter, where the species may be a fairly regular winter visitor in the mountains, but is rarely seen in large numbers in the foothills, towns, and cities. Frederick C. Lincoln (1939) writes:

The most impressive invasion of this bird to be recorded in the history of Colorado ornithology occurred in February 1917, at which time I estimated that at least 10,000 were present within the corporate limits of the city of Denver. Large flocks were to be found in all of the city's parks, where they frequented fruit-bearing shrubbery particularly the Russian olive. Many citizens tried to feed the visitors and after vainly offering bread crumbs and seeds of various kinds, finally discovered that canned peas were very acceptable. The last previous occurrence of the species in large numbers in that section was in 1908.

The most widespread and perhaps the greatest invasion of all came in the winter of 1919–20. Mr. Rathbun refers to this in his notes from Seattle; the first waxwings were seen there on November 25, and they increased in numbers from then on, reaching their maximum in December and January and decreasing in February; the last one was noted on March 1.

Gabrielson and Jewett (1940) write: "The Bohemian waxwing is an irregular winter visitor over most of the State but appears most regularly in the mountain valleys about the base of the Blue Mountains. * * * In the winter of 1919–20 there occurred a big invasion of these birds, and they were present in numbers in Portland, Corvallis, and other points in western Oregon as well as over most of eastern Oregon, reaching at least as far south as Adel, Lake County, where Gabrielson collected a bird out of a flock of approximately three hundred on April 3, 1920."

This invasion extended to Nebraska, where large flocks were seen all over the State. Many hundreds were seen also in northern Illinois. This flight also reached New England, as far south as Massachusetts, but in comparatively small numbers. According to Horace W. Wright (1921), there had been a somewhat heavier invasion of New England during the latter part of the winter of 1918–19. There was a marked spread of Bohemian waxwings in Colorado in the winter of 1930–31, but it was not nearly of the magnitude of that which occurred in 1916–17. Gabrielson and Jewett (1940) report that the birds appeared again in numbers during the winter of 1931–32, "going far south into California, according to published reports."

DISTRIBUTION

Range.—The Bohemian waxwing breeds in wooded sections of the northern part of the Northern Hemisphere, wandering irregularly southward in winter, sometimes in immense flocks.

Breeding range.—The Bohemian waxwing is a vagrant and is irregular in its occurrences. Comparatively few nests of young have been found, and the outlining of the range where they may be found breeding in North America depends to a large extent on records of birds seen in the breeding season. This area extends **north** to northern Alaska (Kobuk River, Fort Yukon, and the Porcupine River above Coleen), northern Mackenzie (Aklavik, Fort Anderson, Leith Point on Great Bear Lake, and Fort Reliance); northeastern Saskatchewan (Theitaga Lake); and northern Manitoba (Churchill), the easternmost point. **South** to northern Manitoba (Churchill and Cochrane River); southern Alberta (Flagstaff, Buffalo Lake near Alix, Red Deer, and Banff); northwestern Montana (Glacier Park and Granite Park); northern Idaho (Sandpoint); and central Washington (Lake Cle Elum). It has also been found in summer near the east base of Mount Evans, Colo., at about 12,000 feet altitude. **West** to central Washington (Lake Cle Elum); central British Columbia (mountains near Alta Lake, Quesnel, Hazelton, Telegraph Creek, and Atlin); southwestern Yukon (Burwash Landing); and to central and western Alaska (Chitina Moraine, Mount McKinley National Park, Nulato, and Kobuk River).

Winter range.—The winter wanderings of the Bohemian waxwing are very irregular, probably influenced to a large degree by food supply. They may be present by the thousands in one year and then not be seen again for a long time. These "winter" occurrences frequently are not until late in winter or even spring. The area over which the species has occurred in winter or spring extends **north** to southeastern Alaska (Juneau); southwestern Mackenzie (Fort Liard); central British Columbia (Francois Lake and Puntchesakut Lake); southern Alberta (Buffalo Lake and Sullivan Lake); southern Saskatchewan (Eastend, Regina, and Yorkton); southern Manitoba (Brandon, Portage la Prairie, and Selkirk); southern Ontario (Lake Nipissing, Algonquin Park, and Ottawa); southern Quebec (Montreal and Quebec); Prince Edward Island (Tignish); and Nova Scotia (Pictou). **East** to Nova Scotia (Pictou and Halifax); southern Maine (Bangor and Auburn); and eastern Massachusetts (Bolton and Taunton). South to eastern Massachusetts (Taunton); Connecticut (Torrington); Pennsylvania (Atglen); central Ohio (Delaware and Quincy); central Indiana (Richmond and Indianapolis); southern Illinois (Villa Ridge); northwestern Arkansas (Fayetteville and Winslow); Kansas (Topeka, Wichita, and Hays); a single record in northwestern Texas (Palo Duro Creek, Randall County); Colorado (Colorado Springs, Salida, and Grand Junction); one record in central northern New Mexico (Gold Hill); northern Arizona (Grand Canyon and Mojave; and a single occurrence in the Baboquivari Mountains in southern Arizona); and southern California (Danby, Daggett, Victorville, and Claremont). **West** to western California (Claremont, Berkeley, and Eureka); western Oregon (Carlton and Portland); Washington (Olympia, Seattle, and Bellingham); British Columbia (Esquimalt, southern Vancouver Island; and Vancouver); and southeastern Alaska (Ketchikan, Wrangell, and Juneau).

Migration.—The Bohemian waxwing is not migratory in the ordinary sense of the term, but a few dates of fall arrival and spring departure may be useful to show the erratic nature of its movements. Dates of fall arrival are: Quebec—Montreal, November 23. New York—Ithaca, November 28. Michigan—Sault Ste. Marie, October 26. Illinois—Waukegan, November 26. Minnesota—St. Paul, October 24. South Dakota—Yankton, November 29. Colorado—Fort Morgan, October 13. Wyoming—Yellowstone Park, October 27. Montana—Fortine, September 11.

Dates of last seen in spring are: Montana—Great Falls, May 14. Wyoming—Laramie, April 5. Colorado—Denver, May 20. North Dakota—Fargo, April 18. Minnesota—Duluth, April 25. Wisconsin—Madison, March 23. Illinois—Chicago, April 18. Ohio—

Youngstown, May 14. New York—Rochester, March 26. Massachusetts—Boston, April 27. New Brunswick—Scotch Lake, April 28. Quebec—Quebec, April 12.

Banding records.—During an invasion in March 1932, several Bohemian waxwings were banded at Waukegan, Ill. One banded on March 23 was found dying on April 11 at Milwaukee, Wis., and one banded on March 25 was caught alive on April 15 at Craik, Saskatchewan, where it was kept until it died on May 1.

A bird banded at Summerland, British Columbia, on February 15, 1933, was killed on March 20, 1934, at Silver City, S. Dak.

During an invasion of Bohemian waxwings in Denmark in 1944, a bird was captured that had been banded on Helgoland in December 1941, during the previous invasion.

Casual record.—A specimen of the Old World race (*B. g. garrulus*) was collected June 14, 1931, from a flock of four at Cape Tobin, Liverpool Land, near the outlet of Scoresby Sound, East Greenland.

Egg dates.—Alberta: 24 records, May 24 to June 13; 17 records, May 29 to June 6, indicating the height of the season.

British Columbia: 39 records, June 11 to July 24; 20 records, July 8 to 16.

BOMBYCILLA CEDRORUM Vieillot

CEDAR WAXWING

CONTRIBUTED BY WINSOR MARRETT TYLER

HABITS

Cedar waxwings impress us as being unlike most of the birds we know. We see them commonly in flocks or small companies through the greater part of the year, but we never know just when they will appear, or how numerously, for the movements of these flocks do not conform to the regular northern and southern swings of migration that the majority of North American birds make to and from their breeding grounds. Moreover, unlike most birds, there is no close relationship between the time of their arrival on their nesting grounds and the commencement of breeding.

When we become well acquainted with the waxwing we look upon him as the perfect gentleman of the bird world. There is in him a refinement of deportment and dress; his voice is gentle and subdued; he is quiet and dignified in manner, sociable, never quarrelsome, and into one of his habits, that of sharing food with his companions, we may read, without too much stress of imagination, the quality of politeness, almost unselfishness, very rare, almost unheard of, in the animal kingdom. His plumage is delicate in coloring—soft, quiet browns, grays, and pale yellow—set off, like a carnation in our buttonhole, by a touch of red on the wing.

Alexander Wilson (Wilson and Bonaparte, 1832), writing of this attractive decoration, says: "Six or seven, and sometimes the whole nine, secondary feathers of the wings are ornamented at the tips with small red oblong appendages, resembling red sealing-wax; these appear to be a prolongation of the shafts, and to be intended for preserving the ends, and consequently the vanes, of the quills, from being broken and worn away by the almost continual fluttering of the bird among thick branches of the cedar. The feathers of those birds which are without these appendages are uniformly found ragged on the edges, but smooth and perfect in those on whom the marks are full and numerous."

Spring.—Spring begins late with the cedar waxwings, for although many move northward into New England in January and February and often linger for weeks, sometimes in great numbers, attracted by a plentiful supply of food, these apparently are merely wandering flocks (noted under "Winter"). The breeding birds of the Transition Zone, the real spring birds, do not arrive, it is thought, until well into May, and even then they do not start nesting until long afterward.

William Brewster (1906) ably summarizes their movements in the region about Boston, Mass., during the first part of the year. He says:

The seasonal movements of the Cedarbird are somewhat erratic and not as yet fully understood. There is apparently a double migration northward, the first flight—which is much the heavier of the two—reaching eastern Massachusetts anywhere between the last of January and the first of March. The birds which compose it appear suddenly, often in very large flocks, and make themselves peculiarly conspicuous by roaming restlessly over the country, frequently visiting densely populated localities to feast on the berries of the mountain ash, the English hawthorn, Parkman's apple and other cultivated trees. They also eat asparagus berries, and they are especially fond of the berries of the red cedar or Virginia juniper. They disappear almost completely before the end of April, presumably going further north to breed, although this has never been definitely established.

The second flight, which arrives in May, is believed to be made up chiefly, if not wholly, of the birds which pass the summer with us. They appear in pairs or in small, scattered flocks which are seen almost everywhere but most frequently in apple orchards.

Courtship.—Cedarbirds spend so great a portion of the year gathered together in flocks, and when thus assembled, contrary to the custom of most birds, pay so much attention to one another, that it is often difficult to decide whether to regard some of their actions as indicating courtship or to consider them an expression of the comradeship or courtesy that seems to pervade their behavior. The passing of a berry back and forth between two birds, or along a line of birds, a procedure we may watch sometimes even in winter, may have developed from courtship feeding, and the delicate little dance, in which one of two birds hops close to the side of the other, then takes one short hop away, and back again, over and over, may have its origin in courting behavior developed in an unusually social species, although the dance may take place long before the breeding season.

Aretas A. Saunders (1938) says: "In early July one sometimes sees what appears to be courtship in these birds. At such a time, the action of the one I suppose to be the male suggests a young bird wishing to be fed. His wings tremble and whirl about, suggesting the wing motions with which a starling often accompanies its songs. The notes at such times are the beady, somewhat rattlelike ones, rather than the clear whine that this species uses most commonly."

P. M. Silloway (1904) reports: "Two waxwings were sitting near each other on a lower branch of a fir, about twenty feet from the ground. They were evidently courting. He would sidle over to her, rub his breast against hers, rub his bill caressingly upon hers, and then sidle back to his former place. Then the other bird would go through a similar performance."

Margaret Morse Nice (1941) describes the behavior of a pair of waxwings while they were building their nest: "I first became aware of the parents of my birds on June 19," she says, "when I heard what I took to be incessant begging from a baby bird; it proved to be the female waxwing begging from her mate with voice and violent wing movement. He fed her four times, but she continued to beg, crowding against him. Later I saw a waxwing take a piece of nesting material to a near-by cedar. On the 20th she was again begging for ten to fifteen minutes at a time."

The two following quotations are charming, clear descriptions of the courtshiplike play, one between a pair of birds, the other between members of a large flock. Speaking of a day early in summer, Harriet McCoy (1927) says:

As we came up to some sumac and other shrubs, we saw a slight movement, as of birds, near the ground. Looking closer, we were delighted to see two Cedar Waxwings perched together on a branch in a little space clear of foliage. We saw after a moment, that they seemed to be engaged in a dance or game, and we watched, half doubting our eyes. One bird had a tiny flower or very new leaf in its bill. The other, standing perhaps 6 inches away, all at once hopped close, took the leaf, and with one hop came back to its position. There it stood, straight, its posture being perhaps a cue to the other bird, who now approached and, to our wonder, received the leaf, gave one hop back and stood erect. There was rhythm and precision about the little exercise which made it appear a conscious performance on the part of the birds and one which they seemed to enjoy greatly. We thought we had never seen anything with such a pretty grace and delicacy of movement and color. They repeated it several times and when they flew off at last, we were left with a feeling of having been audience to a scene in a fairy play.

Caroline M. Stevens (1911) writes:

Coming through an apple orchard one noontime in May, 1909, I stopped to watch a large flock of Cedar Waxwings feeding on the apple blossom petals, and then it was my good fortune to see as pretty a sight as could be imagined among birds. The attention of the birds seemed about evenly divided between eating petals and playing a sort of game. Looking from tree to tree I saw it going on all around me.

It was a game for two. One bird, taking the initiative, with a petal in his mouth, suddenly flew to his chosen playmate, alighting close beside him on the twig, at the same instant offering the petal (once it was a bit of green leaf). The other bird, though apparently taken unawares, was quick enough to catch it on the instant it was offered. Immediately, with the petal, he hopped side-wise just one small hop away from the first bird. After a pause of perhaps a second, back he came close to the bird and offering the petal, which the first bird on the instant caught from his bill, hopped away with it just one hop, paused a second, then very suddenly hopped back, offering the petal, all just as the other bird had done. And so they passed the petal back and forth, not three or four times, but twelve and fifteen times, until, tiring of the play, they flew apart, or the petal, with much hasty snatching from bill to bill becoming tattered and too small for use, was indifferently eaten by one of the birds.

In the moments of pause before the always sudden re-offering of the petal, each bird looked straight ahead; the one with the petal as if trying to conceal from the other the instant he meant to come back with it, and the one awaiting the petal as if the rules of the game forbade his watching to see when it was coming. Yet he was plainly tense and watchful, and only once did I see a bird fail to get the petal. In that instance the other bird gave him another chance at it, when he got it all right, and the game continued. But for this element of competition, this apparent keenness to take the other bird unawares, which gave the spirit of a sport to the performance, it would have more the aspect of a "dance," for it was measured, dignified, and dainty, with the quality of an old-time minuet.

Certainly throughout the time I watched, it had no observable connection with courtship, however indirectly the mating season may be responsible for it. The choosing of a partner seemed wholly casual and disinterested, and when the game palled, the birds separated as casually.

Nesting.—We in New England think of the cedar waxwing's nest as rather large, made of twigs, dry grass, and stalks of weeds, with perhaps a few feathers and bits of twine put together loosely and clumsily, but Forbush (1911) states that "in the South it is comparatively small and compact," a structure more in accord with its dainty owner.

Thomas D. Burleigh (1923) describes two nests found in Idaho: "The first * * * was fifteen feet from the ground in the top of a small slender larch at the edge of some underbrush at the side of a road. It was compactly built of larch twigs, grasses and moss, lined with the dry needles of the western white pine. The second * * * was six feet from the ground in a small Douglas fir at the edge of a field, and was built of weed stems and wool, lined with wool and dry pine needles."

Albert W. Honywill (1911), speaking of nests in Minnesota, says: "Nests were sometimes located in the Norway pines, from the noise made by the young in calling for food. Usually these nests were placed upon the extreme ends of the branches and were inaccessible. They were generally composed almost entirely of usnea moss."

O. M. Bryens (1925) points out the cedar waxwing's preference for wool as nesting material:

The material composing the nests of the Cedar Waxwing (*Bombycilla cedrorum*) in this locality [Michigan] consists chiefly of wool and moss. Their nests also contain a considerable amount of small twigs, and if they are near hemlocks, they are largely of the twigs of that tree. One hemlock tree in particular that I saw Cedar Waxwings getting twigs from one summer, stands nearly on top of a hill, and was nearly killed by fire. Many of the lower branches had died, and thus there was a large amount of twigs. Cedar Waxwings were observed coming to this tree for twigs and returning to the nests, just as birds come and go from a drinking fountain.

Before there were sheep on the grounds where these observations were made, the Cedar Waxwings used the moss that hangs in rather long strings, and is found especially on tamarack, balsam, fir, and other conifers, but also on maple and birch. After sheep were present the moss was found to be used very little in the construction of the nests. Much wool was available from the barbed wire fences and some from low bushes. On the lane fences the three lower wires held wool that sheep had lost when reaching through the fences, and it was no uncommon sight to see Cedar Waxwings along the fences gathering this material during the nesting season. The past two years the grounds have not been pastured to sheep, and thus there has been no wool, and I find that the waxwings are again using the moss in their nests. Thus it appears that wool is the substance that will be used if the birds can secure it. The nests are at times lined with short stems, such as those that bear the seeds of the maple.

Mary B. Benson (1920) relates her experience in supplying twine and strips of cloth for the cedarbirds' use.

[I] began putting out string, as usual hanging it upon a clothes line on the back porch. Within half an hour the Waxwings spied it and began carrying it to the apple tree. They made no efforts to collect twigs or any other nesting material. * * *

My supply of twine threatening to become exhausted, I began tearing old cloth into strips about one-half an inch wide and from five to twelve inches in length. This, the birds liked even better; and they at once redoubled their efforts. How fast they worked, and what yards of cloth they used. * * *

I experimented with colors, and although they apparently preferred white, they did use several strips of bright pink outing flannel when the supply of white cloth was low. * * *

We called it [the nest] "The Waxwing's Rag Bag".

Edward R. Ford writes to Mr. Bent of the "habit of the cedar waxwing of taking material from active nests of other species of birds for use in its own nest." "On three occasions," he says, "I have seen it take bits from kingbirds' nests; in two instances the nests were abandoned by the owners (in one case the structure was rendered so flimsy as to allow the eggs to fall to the ground); the third nest, however, did not suffer so much, and the kingbirds did not desert it. I have also observed cedarbirds taking material from the nest of a yellow-throated vireo."

The height of the nest above ground varies considerably. Thomas D. Burleigh (1925) describes one in Georgia "forty-five feet from the ground at the outer end of a limb of a large white oak," and another "fifty feet from the ground in the top of one of the larger trees."

A. Dawes Du Bois records in his notes four nests, found in Minnesota, New York, and Wisconsin; the Price County, Wis., nest was 8 feet from the ground in a fork and between upright branches of a small plum tree in a garden; the other three were in apple trees, at heights ranging from 6 to 20 feet above ground; the highest nest was near the end of a branch of a large, old apple tree on a constantly traveled, dusty, public road. A nest in an orchard was built chiefly of grass blades and stems, with a few slender, woody twigs, the longest 6½ inches; a coarse, stiff straw of grass measured 7¼ inches, but most of the material was comparatively soft; one very slender grass stem, folded twice, was 15 inches long; there were numerous long shreds of grass and a few weed stems were intermingled. Outwardly this nest had a slovenly, rather formless appearance, but the inner portion was a well-formed and compactly-woven cup, lined with long, fine rootlets, together with grasses and a very few small bits of plant down. It measured externally 5 to 6 inches in diameter by 3.5 in height; the internal diameter was 2.5 and the depth 1.95 inches.

He says of another nest: "On the 7th of September I lifted this nest from the branch with the intention of dissecting it. Feeling something squirming within, I placed it on the ground and a white-footed mouse came out through a hole in the side, with a family of very young, blind sucklings clinging to her teats."

Dr. Paul Harrington mentions in his notes a nesting colony of cedar waxwings in a clump of white pines near Toronto, Ontario. "There were 11 nests in all within a radius of 25 feet, on horizontal pine limbs, all within 20 feet from the ground. One nest had four fresh eggs, one held two, and two others had one egg each; five other nests were more or less complete, and two were half finished. I returned to examine these nests a week later and all were deserted." On another occasion he found a nest containing five fresh eggs, on which both parent birds were incubating; "they were sitting in the same direction, and this apparently had been a common practice, as the nest was quite markedly shaped, so as to allow both birds to sit comfortably in the nest."

Charles W. Richmond (1888) says: "The Cedarbird does not nest till late in the season, and is sometimes eccentric about choosing a nesting place. A nest found within the city limits [Washington, D. C.] was situated in a lamp post. * * * It will forsake its nest on the slightest provocation, even after laying one or more eggs."

Aretas A. Saunders (1938), writing of Allegany State Park, New York, says: "Nests of the cedar waxwing are found in various trees or shrubs in and about the school grounds, chiefly in the Aspen-Cherry and camping grounds areas, but sometimes in Maple-Beech-

Hemlock. The nests are mostly rather high up. * * * Occasional nests are lower down. One in 1927 was only six feet from the ground in a staghorn sumach (*Rhus typhina*). One in 1935 was in a willow and about four feet from the ground."

James E. Crouch (1936) states: "The measurements of a typical Cedar Waxwing's nest are as follows: Outside depth, 4–4½"; inside depth 3–3¾"; outside diameter, 4½–5"; inside diameter 3–3¼"; and thickness of walls 3/4–1 3/4". The nest is completed in five to seven days and egg laying starts immediately. * * * One egg is laid each day until the complement is completed, and incubation starts at the laying of the first egg. Regardless of this fact they all hatch at the same time." Mr. Crouch's observations were made in the vicinity of Ithaca, N. Y.

Aretas A. Saunders (1911) reports on an interesting study of an unusual nesting, "ten nests of the Cedar Waxwing [at West Haven, Conn.] in a small tract of about five acres," an instance of the close association characteristic of the bird being carried into the nesting season. Even when flying off to procure food, the birds traveled in small companies. Mr. Saunders says: "The parent birds from the different nests made trips for food in small flocks, usually of four or five. The cherry trees where most of the food was obtained grew along the shore about a quarter of a mile from the nests. The small flocks usually gathered in the tops of a few dead stubs that stood above the thicket, and left these in a body for the cherry trees, returned in the same manner when the food was obtained and then scattered slowly to their respective nests."

Mr. Saunders (1911) adds: "Late in November, after the leaves had fallen, I visited the thicket again to see how many Waxwing nests in all were there. I found seven more nests evidently of this species, making a total of seventeen. These other nests were some distance from the ones I studied and much more scattered. All of the seventeen, however, could be included within a radius of 150 yards."

Mr. Saunders (1911) says: "I watched incubating birds for some time and so far as I could tell, only the female performs this duty." James E. Crouch (1936) concurs with this statement, saying, "Incubation was performed entirely by the female," but Dr. Arthur A. Allen (1930) states that both birds "take turns sitting on the eggs."

Crouch (1936) describes thus the building of the nest:

Nest building is an interesting process. I watched the construction of one nest placed in the forking branch of a willow tree. The birds worked very vigorously both in bringing material and in shaping the nest into form. Although they both carried materials, one bird seemed to do most of the shaping and weaving together of the nest. As nearly as I could tell, it was the female which did this shaping. However, because of the similarity of plumage, it may be that I was mistaken in this observation. Inasmuch as there is contradiction in the literature on this point, it must be studied further. The birds work very close together. They both come to the nest with their bills full of cattail down or small twigs. The male deposits his on the nest and the female then follows with hers. She stays and by much twisting and turning of the entire body and use of the bill, the material is woven into the nest. When this is finished, she calls and is joined by the male, who usually waits nearby, and they then fly off together for more materials.

Speaking of the return of waxwings to a former nesting locality, Saunders (1911) says:

Evidently Waxwings do not necessarily return to the same locality in which they have nested before.

It is evident that the presence or absence of Waxwings in a given locality is due to the abundance or lack of a supply of the berry or fruit that forms the major part of their food. A later experience in the vicinity of Bozeman, Montana, confirms this. During the summer of 1908 there were no Waxwings that I observed in the vicinity of Bozeman. The next year, however, they appeared in June and were abundant throughout the summer. During this time I found two Waxwing nests in shade trees along the streets of Bozeman and could doubtless have found many if I had had time for search. In this region the service berry (*Amelanchier alnifolia*) forms the principal article of food. This berry was very abundant about Bozeman in 1909 and correspondingly scarce in 1908. During the summer of 1910, in a few short visits to Bozeman, I again found Waxwins quite common and service berries fairly abundant.

The waxwing breeds later in the season than most birds do, at a time when many of the berries and fruits, which the bird uses as food for its young, are ripe. Normally it breeds in July or early August, but sometimes much later. W. J. Hamilton, Jr. (1933) reports a bird incubating four eggs on September 27 near Ithaca, N. Y.

Eggs.—[AUTHOR'S NOTE: The cedar waxwing lays three to five eggs, rarely six. These are usually ovate and have little or no gloss. They closely resemble the eggs of the Bohemian waxwing, having the same peculiar coloration, but they are, of course, smaller. The ground color is pale bluish gray, pale "mineral gray," or "glaucous-gray." They are sparingly marked with dots or small spots of black, or blackish brown, scattered more or less irregularly over the surface. Some eggs show underlying spots or blotches of pale shades of drab.

The measurements of 50 eggs in the United States National Museum average 21.8 by 15.6 millimeters; the eggs showing the four extremes measure 24.4 by 15.8, 22.4 by 16.3, 18.8 by 15.2, and 20.3 by 14.7 millimeters.]

Young.—The length of the cedar waxwing's incubation period is given by various writers as follows: Saunders (1911), 12 days; Burns (1915), 10 to 12 days; Knight (1908), about 14 days; Forbush (1911), about 14 days; Crouch (1936), 12 to 16 days.

Aretas A. Saunders (1911) gives a careful description of the development of young waxwings. He says:

The young when born are perfectly naked, without the natal down found in most young birds. The first few days they grow in size only. By the fourth day a row of small black pimples shows along the middle of the back where the first feathers are starting through. In six days the feathers of the back and the wing quills come through and pimples begin to show on the breast. By seven or eight days the eyes begin to open and more pimples appear on top of the head. In eight or nine days the head and breast feathers appear, the feathers and the wing quills come through and pimples begin to show on the breast. By ten to twelve days the throat and tail feathers appear, the wing quills and head feathers break their sheaths, and the creamy white streak above the eye, a mark of the young birds only, begins to show plainly. By twelve to fourteen days the eyes are wide open and all the feathers are unsheathed or unsheathing except those forming the black patch on the forehead and about the eyes. These feathers are last of all to appear and do not break the sheaths till about the fifteenth day or later, sometimes after the young have left the nest. This fact appears to have led some writers to state that young Waxwings do not have this black mark. By fourteen to eighteen days the young are fully fledged and leave the nest shortly, being able to fly a little as soon as they leave. For a few days after leaving they may usually be found in the vicinity of the nest, the whole brood perched together in a row, with necks stretched and bills pointing up in the air in the same manner as the adults.

Of brooding he says: "After the young hatch the female broods closely for several days until they become partially feathered and the eyes begin to open. During this time she seldom leaves the nest and never for more than an hour at a time. After this she broods but little in the daytime but continues to brood at night until the young are about twelve days old. I believe the male does not brood at all." Mr. Saunders states that the young birds left the nest when approximately 16 days old, and that the parents "feed the young only at long intervals, rarely as short as fifteen minutes and usually of from three quarters of an hour to an hour or more."

George G. Phillips (1913) illustrates the tameness of young cedar waxwings by a personal experience he had with a brood whose parents had disappeared. He raised them by hand, feeding them with berries and later on bread and milk. They became very tame, and even after he liberated them they came to him like pets. "Wherever I was about the place," he says, "they were liable to appear. Each morning as I stepped on the porch their cry greeted me, and instantly four little monoplanes would be coming full speed toward me. I always threw up my arm for a perch, and they would suffer me to carry them thus about the grounds and to the house."

Two other writers, Mrs. Whittle (1928) and Mrs. Nice (1941), report in detail studies of captive young cedar waxwings to which readers are referred.

The juvenal cedar waxwing seems rather disheveled in comparison with its spruce parent: the streaks on the breast and the restriction of the black about the eye detract from the trim stylishness of the adult.

Plumages.—[AUTHOR'S NOTE: Dr. Dwight (1900) describes the juvenal plumage of the young cedar waxwing as follows:

Above, including sides of head and wing coverts, olive-brown. Below, paler with darker broad fused stripes on the throat, breast, sides and flanks, the chin paler, the abdomen and crissum dull white often yellow or buff tinged. A crest not well marked is found on the crown. Anterior frontal feathers, lores and partial orbital ring dull black; posterior quadrant of orbital ring, submalar streak and narrow superciliary line white or pale buff. Chin bordered laterally by dull black. Wings and tail slate-black, the primaries ashy edged, occasionally some of the secondaries tipped with bright vermillion wax-like appendages, the tail terminated with a lemon-yellow band, the rectrices also occasionally but infrequently tipped with similar red appendages.

A partial postjuvenal molt, involving the contour plumage and the wing coverts, but not the rest of the wings or the tail, begins in September. This produces a first-winter plumage, which is practically indistinguishable from that of the adult, the brown being much lighter, the crest well marked, and the breast not streaked. The red appendages on the wings and tail are usually more frequent in adult than in young birds.

The nuptial plumage is acquired by wear, which is not very obvious, and a complete postnuptial molt occurs in both one year old birds and adults, usually beginning in September. The sexes are practically alike in all plumages, though the female usually has less black on the chin, and perhaps fewer red appendages.]

Food.—Waldo L. McAtee (1926) gives the following comprehensive summary of the cedar waxwing's food:

The Cedar-bird gets five-sixths of its food from the vegetable kingdom and at times is destructive to flowers of fruit trees, and later to the ripening fruit especially of cherries. Sometimes local control measures are necessary to preserve the crop.

Destruction of cultivated fruit is an index to the natural feeding habits of the bird, wild fruits being decidedly favored. Those most frequently taken are juneberries, strawberries, cedar berries, and the various wild cherries. The only other vegetable food of importance in the diet of the Cedar-bird is flowers.

The animal food (one-sixth of the whole) comprises quite a variety of items, of which beetles probably are most important. Leaf beetles, including the locust leaf beetle (*Odontota dorsalis*), and weevils are forms detrimental to the forest. Carpenter ants, sawfly larvae, caterpillars, cicadas, and scale insects are other tree pests eaten. The other noteworthy items of animal food are crane-flies, spiders, mayflies, dragon flies, and stone flies.

The Cedar-bird in some places is called Cankerbird, on account of a marked fondness for cankerworms, and it has a great reputation also as a foe of the elm leaf beetle. In New England it has several times been observed to clean up local infestations of this pest. The species has been observed to clear orchards of the tent caterpillars and to feed also on larvae of the forest tent caterpillar, the willow sawfly, the basket-worm of cedar, and the spotted willow leaf beetle.

Except in the orchard of ripening cherries, the Cedarbird is a desirable visitor. Although ordinarily it may not be highly useful, at times evidently it attacks some pests in a wholesale way. Then, just as it is able to do much harm by feeding in flocks on buds or fruit, it is able to do much by massed attack on some destructive insect. Its record in this respect is excellent.

H. H. Kopman (1915) speaks of the cedar waxwing's feeding in Louisiana: "At New Orleans, little is seen of it until about Feb. 1, when it arrives to feed on the fruit of hackberry and Japan privet, and the flowers of the elm. It later feeds on the blossoms of the pecan, and finally on the fruit of the mulberry."

The voracious appetite of the cedarbirds has attracted many comments. Forbush (1911) exclaims: "Such gourmandizers as they were! They ate until they could eat no more, only to sit about on the branches or play with one another awhile, and then eat again." And Audubon (1842) remarks:

The appetite of the Cedar-bird is of so extraordinary a nature as to prompt it to devour every fruit or berry that comes in its way. In this manner they gorge themselves to such excess as sometimes to be unable to fly, and suffer themselves to be taken by the hand. Indeed I have seen some which, although wounded and confined in a cage, have eaten of apples until suffocation deprived them of life in the course of a few days. When opened afterwards, they were found to be gorged to the mouth.

Charles H. Rogers (1907) mentions cedarbirds drinking the sap flowing from broken maple trees, and Prof. Maurice Brooks, writing to Mr. Bent, says: "We were in the spruce belt on Gaudineer Knob, Randolph County, W. Va., searching for red crossbills. The spruces were in bloom, the carpels hanging with tiny drops of a sweetish gum. This is a favorite food of the crossbills, and we saw, on one occasion, a large flock of cedar waxwings feeding steadily on these flower carpels. It was not a case of eating insects in the flowers; with glasses we watched the birds strip off and swallow the flower parts themselves."

There are several records of cedarbirds eating the petals of apple blossoms. William Brewster (1937) speaks of the birds thus, as he watched them on May 14, 1905:

The apple trees at the Farm were in full bloom to-day. On one of them we found a party of 5 Cedar Birds * * * all of which were busily engaged in picking off and devouring the *petals* of the blossoms. I watched them at close range (about 20 feet) for fully 15 minutes. During this time each bird must have eaten a dozen or more petals. These were sometimes swallowed whole (not without some difficulty), sometimes torn into halves before being swallowed. As the birds remained nearly motionless the whole time, simply bending down and taking the petals within easy reach without exercising any apparent choice, I was convinced that they were eating only the petals and not selecting those that may have had insects on them. This habit of the Cedar Bird (if it be really a habit) is quite new to me.

Among others, Ben. J. Blincoe (1923) has also observed this habit repeatedly, and Ralph Hoffmann speaks of it in his manuscript notes.

Cedar waxwings are adroit flycatchers. We frequently see them, generally in small companies, flying out from a high perch, oftenest, perhaps, over a river or pond, to snatch up insects gathered in large assemblies. The birds appear as adept as the true flycatchers and, like them, return as a rule to a perch after each capture. William Brewster (1906) speaks of their turning their flycatching skill to the snapping up of tiny snowflakes floating in the air. He says: "When no insects are on wing Cedarbirds sometimes practise the art of fly-catching on inanimate but rapidly moving objects. Thus on March 1, 1866, I saw the members of a large flock engaged in chasing and cap-turing whirling *snowflakes*, at which they launched out in quick suc-cession from the upper branches of a tall elm. * * * Probably the birds were only amusing themselves, although they may also have en-joyed slaking their thirst with snow fresh from the clouds."

At first the young are fed on insects, presumably by regurgitation, but early in their lives, within a few days after hatching, berries are added to their diet. The adults bring the berries to the nest several at a time, stored temporarily in the gullet. W. E. Shore, of Toronto, Ontario, writes to Mr. Bent an amusing account of their delivery: "Having set up the camera at a nest in an apple tree, I retired to the blind to wait and was surprised to find that within 15 minutes both parents were back in the tree, but apparently empty-mouthed. How-ever, one bird hopped to the side of the nest, and the two well-feathered young shot their heads up and opened their bills, action which I con-sidered overly optimistic. But they apparently knew their business, for, as I watched through the binoculars, the adult gave a slight jerk of his head, and to my surprise a ripe, unbroken cherry appeared in his bill. This was promptly dropped into the bill of a young one, and again the head jerked, and another cherry appeared. This happened seven times; then the bird flew off, and the mate came to the nest and went through the same performance. The whole thing so resembled a magician producing cards out of thin air with the time-honored twist of the wrist and jerk of the hand that I could almost hear the word 'Presto' emanating from the solemn-faced birds as they continued to produce cherry after cherry."

Howard L. Cogswell says in his notes from Pasadena, Calif.: "This species is often very abundant throughout the cities in winter, especially in sections where camphortrees and peppertrees are planted. Of late years the peppertrees, long a recognized favorite for berry-eat-ing birds, have been yielding poorer and poorer crops in the Los An-geles area. As a consequence, in the Pasadena area at least, the wax-wings and their often-present associate, the robin, are now to be seen chiefly in the camphortrees used extensively to line the streets of resi-dential districts. From their arrival in numbers in November until about February 1, the small cherrylike drupe of this tree seems to be the chief food of the waxwings. Then, when these are gone, they turn to the various berries on ornamental bushes in gardens, such as *Pyracantha, Cotoneaster*, and *Eugenia*. Many times I have also seen waxwings eating from persimmons and apples allowed to remain on the trees until overripe. Outside the city, they feed on toyon, mistletoe, coffeeberries, the fruits of the sycamore tree, and wild grapes in the lowland willow regions."

Mr. Du Bois (MS.) watched some cedar waxwings that "were feeding on geometrid caterpillars, which were defoliating the trees. They picked the caterpillars from the leaves, and sometimes they struck them against a twig or branch before eating them. They were particular to wipe their bills on the branch after eating. Sometimes a bird would make a little fluttering jump to get the caterpillar, or occasionally would taken one in midair. One bird flew out from a branch and seized a caterpillar that was hanging by a gossamer thread several feet away. He lighted on a branch, with the caterpillar in his bill, before eating it."

Behavior.—One of the most conspicuous features in the behavior of the cedarbird is its tameness. Albert W. Honywill, Jr. (1911), gives a striking instance of this trait in a wild bird he met in Minnesota: "On Aug. 4, 1908, four young birds were found that were not quite able to fly. While arranging them to be photographed one of the old birds came and fed them. The old birds appeared to be fearless, and fed the young ones blueberries and wild cherries while I held them enclosed in my hands, and even tried to get to their young when I pushed them gently aside."

There are several records showing how readily the young birds adapt themselves to confinement. As an example, Mrs. E. A. Matteson (1924) says of a fledgling waxwing, injured soon after leaving the nest:

He became the joy of the household. He was given a large, roomy cage, with the door left open by day. * * * Very soon he began to sit on a paper in my friend's lap, unthread the machine when she sewed, peep into the work-basket to pull bits of threads, snap his bill quite sharply and pick at one to assert his rights, and, in his playful mood, when one tells him to dance he prances all along the perch with wings drooped, with a very graceful movement of the head and his crest erect. * * * He will hop upon the shoulder of the master of the house and drink milk from a spoon. He is perfectly happy, will pass an open window never thinking of going out—in fact, is afraid of the outside world. * * * Dandy is a little over eight years of age, and still active and bright.

Alexander Wilson (Wilson and Bonaparte, 1832), in his inimitable manner, points out the indifference with which the cedarbird regards a scarecrow: "Nor are they easily intimidated by the presence of Mr. Scarecrow; for I have seen a flock deliberately feasting on the fruit of a loaded cherry tree, while on the same tree one of these *guardian angels*, and a very formidable one too, stretched his stiffened arms, and displayed his dangling legs, with all the pomposity of authority."

The berry-passing habit is mentioned under "Courtship." Between two birds, back and forth, it is common enough, but the passing of a berry along a row of birds is much more rarely seen. We may watch a flock of cedarbirds for days and see no trace of it; in fact many authors, Wilson and Audubon, for example, do not mention the habit at all. Nuttall (1832), however, on the authority of "my friend S. Green, Esq., of Boston," says: "This friendly trait is carried so far, that an eye-witness assures me he has seen one among a row of these birds seated upon a branch dart after an insect, and offer it to his associate when caught, who very disinterestedly passed it to the next, and each delicately declining the offer, the morsel has proceeded backwards and forwards before it was appropriated."

One hundred years later Dr. Thomas S. Roberts (1932), an unquestioned authority, describes the habit thus: "Even more surprising, they may be seen to pass some titbit, a ripe cherry most likely, from one to the other all along the line and then back again, several times in succession without any bird being impolite enough to eat it!"

Of the birds in the air Dr. Dayton Stoner (1932) says: "In their flights a close order is maintained and sometimes a large flock will suddenly wheel, the members behaving as a unit and, darting downward, alight as a group in the top of a tree, whence thereupon a chorus of low, tremulous whistles soon proceeds."

Crouch (1936), writing of the relations of cedar waxwings toward other birds, says:

They always seem to be friendly. While I was watching the birds on July 15, another Waxwing made its appearance. It happened that the female was off the nest at that time, and instead of there being a fight, as one might expect, there was nothing of the kind. The female merely flew quickly to the nest and covered the eggs, while the other two birds sat on a branch about eight feet away. This same procedure is followed when other species come close to the nest. A Catbird approached to within two feet of the nest one day. There was no fight. They merely flew at him, and one bird went on the nest. The other sat close by for a few minutes and then flew off. Similarly, a Chickadee visited the nest and hopped right into it and picked around. The owner came onto the nest directly, but did not chase the Chickadee away. He stayed within a few inches of the nest, peering about with curiosity.

Dr. Arthur A. Allen (1930) makes the point that cedarbirds have nothing to gain by fighting, for their food is of such a nature that there is either more of it than they could consume before it spoils or else there is none at all. Since they can fly long distances to feeding places, they do not need to defend a feeding territory about their nests.

Charles H. Feltes (1936) gives an interesting account (summarized also in Bird-Banding, vol. 6, p. 104, 1935) of trapping and banding 4,010 cedar waxwings in California. He attracted the birds with a bait of dried raisins and was especially successful when he left live birds in the traps as decoys.

Arthur E. Staebler and Leslie D. Case (1940) note an instance of "community bathing of the Cedar Waxwing," another example of their social behavior. They say: "Between 55 and 60 Waxwings were in a small aspen tree next to a pool of stagnant water in a depression on the beach of Lake Michigan. Some of the birds were bathing in the water while others were sitting quietly or preening themselves in the tree. Periodically one or several of the bathing birds would fly up into the tree and almost immediately they would be replaced at the pool by others from the tree. Thus there were always about 15 or 20 birds from the flock bathing at any one time."

Bradford Torrey (1885) gives us this delightfully dainty snap-shot of the cedarbird: "Taking an evening walk, I was stopped by the sight of a pair of cedar-birds on a stone wall. They had chosen a convenient flat stone, and were hopping about upon it, pausing every moment or two to put their little bills together. What a loving ecstasy possessed them! Sometimes one, sometimes the other, sounded a faint lisping note, and motioned for another kiss. But there is no setting forth the ineffable grace and sweetness of their chaste behavior."

Voice.—The cedar waxwing's voice is very high in pitch, something like a hiss with very little tone quality, except when the note is uttered at its highest pitch and given with increased intensity, when it becomes almost a long, clear whistle. Even then the voice is not loud and does not carry far, but when heard from near at hand it is sharply piercing. Generally we detect an effect of vibration in a prolonged hiss, owing doubtless to the breaking up of the note into many minute parts. The division is so coarse, sometimes, as to give the note a rattling effect, sometimes so fine as to be nearly imperceptible. The variability of this simple sound enables the bird, in our imagination at least, to express different degrees of emotion—content, excitement, or alarm. Thus Helen Granger Whittle (1928), who for 18 months cared for a young cedarbird, whose flight feathers never developed, found that it had a wealth of notes. "Only one was loud," she says, "a piercing danger note, and even that was sibilant in quality. A modification of this note, softer and reiterated, was a complaining note, his only tiresome vocalization. His 'dinner' note called for food; he had a bedtime note, and what I called a 'nesting' note." Mrs. Whittle also reports that her bird, which on post-mortem examination proved to be a female, used to sing. "On November 6th," she says, "as his cage stood in a sunny window and I was busy at a little distance, I was delighted and amazed to hear from him a little song. * * * This first song was not long, and not at all loud, but it was distinctly musical and pleasing. It was made up of little trills, interspersed with his usual soft single notes. * * * It was a nearly continuous warbling, a varied arrangement of short trills, some higher, some lower, with a few connecting or finishing single notes, and occasionally a glide. One needed to be rather near to get all the modulations, as the voice was soft."

N. S. Goss (1891) mentions thus a similar song: "They are generally spoken of as birds without a song, and their feeble attempt is hardly worthy to be called one; they do, however, at times, utter low, warbling notes, with tremulous wings, in a manner expressive of love and joy; in sound very similar to their lisping call notes, but much softer. It is evidently not intended for outsiders, for its voice is scarcely audible twenty paces away."

William Brewster (1906) calls attention to a note, evidently of rare occurrence. He says:

Various writers have asserted that the Cedar Waxwing has no vocal utterances other than the thin, hissing calls which are familiar to everyone. I have heard it give a succession of loud, full notes, rather mellow in quality and not unlike some of those which Tree Swallows use in spring. On several occasions I have known them to be uttered by a single Waxwing that had just left a feeding flock and was circling rather high in air, over a field, performing what looked like a song flight. I suspect, however, that these swallow-like calls represent cries of alarm or of apprehension, rather than song notes, for sounds very like them are often made by wounded Waxwings.

Aretas A. Saunders (1935) records a striking note, saying: "Only once have I heard any other sound [beside the common note] from this species. Then, when I found and caught a bird that had broken its wing against a wire, it literally shrieked with fright. The sound was high-pitched, loud, and strident, strongly suggesting the voice of the Kingbird."

In his studies of "Vibration Frequencies of Passerine Bird Song," Albert R. Brand (1938) says: "The difference in frequency between the first three [birds showing highest frequency], Blackpoll, Grasshopper Sparrow and Cedar Waxwing, is only about a half a note, and is so small and the pitch so high, that an ear would have to be remarkably accurate to recognize the pitch difference."

Margaret Morse Nice (1941) points out the usefulness of the cedar waxwing's voice. She says: "A peculiarity of the Cedar Waxwing was its habitual use of the characteristic note whenever it took flight. This species has nothing in its plumage resembling 'banner markings'; its 'flight note' is evidently an important device for keeping the flock together, and it must be particularly valuable with this bird that is apt suddenly to take off on long flights."

Field marks.—There is no mistaking the cedarbird—a little, pale-brown bird with a conspicuous crest—for any other species except the Bohemian waxwing. This larger bird has a white patch in the wing and is chestnut under the tail, whereas the cedarbird has no white in the wing and has a white crissum.

Enemies.—The cedar waxwing has no special enemies, only those that prey commonly on most small birds. In the time of the older ornithologists, however, the bird was shot for food, and the slaughter of great numbers was made easy by their habit of flying in close flocks.

Audubon's (1842) remarks on the subject are interesting in these days of wildlife conservation. He says: "They fatten, and become so tender and juicy as to be sought by every epicure for the table. I have known an instance of a basketful of these little birds having been forwarded to New Orleans as a Christmas present. The donor, however, was disappointed in his desire to please his friend in that city, for it was afterwards discovered that the steward of the steamer, in which they were shipped, made pies of them for the benefit of the passengers."

Herbert Friedmann (1929) speaks of the cedarbird as "an uncommon victim" of the cowbird. He says: "This is to be expected when we consider that this bird starts nesting after the laying season of the Cowbird is well past its height. There are cases on record from various places—New York, Connecticut, and Montana. Aside from these few records there are no data available."

In a later paper on this subject, he (1934) adds two records, both in western Canada.

Fall.—If we look for the waxwings in New England in the fall, after their late breeding season is over and the young are fully grown, say in mid-September, we often find them collected in a small flock of a dozen or so, perched high in a dead tree or in the top of a leafless bush. For a time they sit erect, silent, and motionless; then, in a body—a half dozen or more perhaps—they start out into the air on a steady flight, flying with a few rapid flips of the wings, then a short pause, a flight slightly undulating like that of English sparrows. At first we may surmise that they are flycatching, pursuing the insects that are abundant in the air at this season of the year, but as we keep the birds in our eye we see that they neither turn nor pause, but hold straight onward in a protracted, uninterrupted flight. They may even pass out of sight, 200 or 300 yards away, flying all together, but in a loose flock, and if we wait, watching for their possible return, we see that they do return, back to the same tree, even to the same branches they left not 5 minutes before. Here they rest for a while, standing straight up on their perches, like little falcons, silent as before.

Some few, however, may not have flown with the others but stay behind at their temporary headquarters; on the next flight, however, every one may fly away, leaving the tree empty while they make a circuit far out and back. In these long flights the birds are nearly silent—we hear from them only an occasional faint, hissing whisper.

The flights are perhaps taken for exercise in which the young birds join, and they may serve as a preparation for a long migration later in the season.

Winter.—Cedarbirds appear to us at their best advantage when they arrive in New England in the late winter months or early in spring and gather in large flocks in the trees where there is a bountiful food supply. The "cedar pastures," to use an old New England term, furnish one of their favorite foods, and the cultivated rowan trees, the European mountain-ash, laden with red berries, supply another. One of these trees, which stood for years in my front yard in Lexington, Mass., was a rendezvous of the cedarbirds almost every winter and spring. Long before my time the tree had been famous for its cedarbirds, which by their numbers and tameness often attracted the attention of merely casual passersby. From my windows I could study the birds at short range for hours at a time, and the following glimpses of them, adapted and condensed from the records in my journal written with the birds only a few yards away, show their behavior at this season of the year.

A company of the birds often drops into the tree from high in the air, way above the surrounding elms, coming down almost perpendicularly with wings closed until just before they come to rest in the ash tree. They begin at once to pick off the berries. They seem in a hurry, as if ravenously hungry, and eager to get at the food. They lean downward to reach the berries hanging in a cluster below them, snatch one, and, pulling it free, straighten up, and, with the bill almost vertical, manipulate the berry until they get a good hold on it. Sometimes in throwing the head back, they give the berry a little toss and catch it again; sometimes, but very rarely, they drop a berry in this way. When feeding they almost always remain near together, often side by side, not scattered widely in the tree, but they are restless and move constantly from one branch to another.

They eat their fill, then fly up to the branches of an overhanging elm where they remain quiet for many minutes. In spite of the strong wind they appear not to seek shelter from it but between their visits to the ash tree sit in little groups, often in rows, high on the exposed elm branches, facing the blustering, biting wind, riding the swaying branches. When perched thus they squat down close to their perch and lean forward so that their backs are almost parallel to the ground, their heads drawn backward and downward close to the body between the shoulders. Sometimes they drop to the ground and drink from a puddle of melted snow, then fly back to the ash tree, pulling off the fruit again and tossing the berries about before swallowing them. There is a constant restlessness in the flock. There may be 75 or more birds in the tree, all busily feeding, and five minutes later not a bird is in sight. Sometimes as many as half the flock, 30 or more, will leave the tree suddenly, twist rapidly around the tops of the elm trees, then, rising clear of the branches, steer straight northward and disappear in the distance.

The restlessness so characteristic of these winter flocks sometimes mounts to seeming panic. Yet this feeling, apparently, seldom spreads to all the members of the gathering. Even when a large proportion sweeps away into the air, the remainder may continue to feed on, uninfluenced by the exodus of the others. Also, those that leave the tree in these precipitous flights do not start necessarily from adjacent branches, but quite the reverse: one flies from here, near us, another from the opposite side of the tree. Indeed, one of two birds sitting side by side may fly, leaving the other undisturbed. Very different from the behavior of a flock of sparrows in this regard! And all the time, whether they are feeding or resting between meals, the birds keep up their gentle, hissing whisper.

Nathan Clifford Brown (1906) describes an impressive migration of cedarbirds and robins that he saw at Camden, S. C., on February 4, 1905. He says:

When I first looked out of doors, Robins and Cedar-birds were flying over in large numbers, going about west-northwest. It soon became evident that the flight was unusual, and at twenty minutes to nine o'clock I took up a position at a window from which I had an unobstructed view for long distances towards the east, north and west. Here for an hour and a half, pencil and paper in hand, I endeavored to count the passing birds.

The Robins flew in open order and were little more numerous at one time than another. The Cedar-birds, however, though many of them also went by in open order, were mostly gathered in masses containing from twenty to four hundred birds or more each. They swept along very rapidly. Their largest masses suggested scudding clouds and were decidedly impressive. The Robins moved a good deal more slowly. Both species flew at altitudes varying from twenty to one hundred yards from the ground, and most of the birds passed within a distance of one hundred and fifty yards from my window,—none, I think, farther away than about an eighth of a mile.

At ten minutes past ten o'clock I was obliged to take up some work which was awaiting me. But I frequently looked out of the window after that hour, and could detect no diminution in the number of passing birds until after one o'clock P. M. All the afternoon they flew by in gradually diminishing numbers, a good many Robins tarrying for brief periods in the fields before my window. Throughout the day the direction of the flight was the same, and there was practically no retrograding: altogether I saw less than a hundred birds coming back, all Robins.

I found that I had counted a total of twenty thousand four hundred birds in the hour and a half, at least fourteen thousand of which were Cedar-birds. These figures are much inside the mark. Between ten minutes past ten A. M. and one o'clock P. M. twice the number of birds that I had previously counted must have gone by. A multitude had passed before I began counting. Ten thousand, at the lowest estimate possible, must have followed during the remainder of the afternoon. In the course of the day, therefore, many more than sixty thousand birds passed over that part of Camden which I overlooked. I believe that seventy-five thousand—fifty thousand Cedar-birds—would be too low an estimate. The path of the flight also extended south of my position at the window. I cannot say how far it extended, and I can offer no estimate of the number of birds which passed on that side.

R. H. Palmer (1922) speaks of meeting the cedarbird in winter in various parts of Mexico: at Tehuantepec, which is "but a hundred feet or so above sea-level, is very hot, and has an abundance of irrigated tropical vegetation"; at Mexico City, which "is at 7,600 feet elevation, and has a cool climate; its vegetation is of the Oregon or northern California type"; at Monterrey, which "but a few hundred feet above the sea, is very hot, and has the floral and faunal aspect, as well as the climate, of southwest Texas. All of which goes to show that the Cedar Waxwing in winter shows little choice among different climates and surroundings."

Wilbur F. Smith (MS.) reports waxwings lingering in large numbers, estimated at 5,000 birds, on St. Armands Key, Fla. Under date of March 26, 1943, he writes to Mr. Bent: "The flocks of waxwings are still about Sarasota. They completely cleaned up the fruit of the cabbage palms on the key and then moved to the mainland and fed on the palm berries there. The mulberries are ripening, and the birds eat these also. Today I watched a flock of several hundreds gathering the fruit from one of these trees."

A. F. Skutch (MS.) sends to Mr. Bent the following account of the waxwings in their winter quarters in Central America:

"The cedar waxwing is a regular winter visitant to Central America, fairly abundant in the Guatemalan highlands, increasingly rare farther southward and at lower elevations. It reaches its southernmost known limit in Costa Rica, where it is not often seen. One of the latest of the immigrants to arrive, it rarely appears before January. In my two years in the Guatemalan highlands, I failed to see a single bird during the closing months of the year, although during these months I was constantly afield, in 1933 on the Sierra de Tecpán (7,000–10,000 feet), in the Department of Chimaltenango; while during the following year I traveled widely, largely by horseback, over the western mountains. Yet in February 1933 the birds suddenly appeared in large flocks on the Sierra de Tecpán and were repeatedly seen until the following May 12. They frequently linger well into May and even in Costa Rica have been recorded as late as May 7.

"The sociable nature of the cedar waxwing is not altered by its sojourn between the Tropics. The birds are almost always found in flocks, containing from a dozen to perhaps 100 individuals, although groups of more than 50 are in my experience rare. Occasionally a lone bird is seen, or two or three together. As in the more northerly parts of their range, they perch close together in exposed positions well up in the trees, delivering their low, far-away, lisping notes, each so slight an utterance, yet so stirring in its multiplication by scores of voices.

If the flock be divided between neighboring trees, some of the birds will constantly be passing back and forth between them; and of a sudden, with a whir of wings, the entire company take the air, wheels about, and comes to rest again in some more distant tree. At higher elevations in Guatemala, the resting flocks of waxwings are often joined by a group of silky flycatchers (*Ptilogonys cinereus*), which usually choose the topmost twigs as their perches. Of all the resident birds of the country, these gray, slender, restless creatures are the waxwings' nearest—although still distant—relations; and the birds themselves seem to recognize the fact!

"While many migrants, once they have reached their winter range, appear to become as sedentary as the local birds, the cedar waxwing is inveterately a wanderer, rarely remaining long in one locality, but suddenly appearing, lingering a few days or a week or two, then roaming away again. These movements bring them into the most varied sorts of country: heavy forests of the upper levels of the Tropical Zone as well as the pine and oak woods of the highlands, arid as well as humid districts. They are as fond of berries in their winter as in their summer home.

"Central American dates are: Guatemala—Sierra de Tecpán, 7,000–10,000 feet, February 5 to May 12, 1933; Finca Mocá, 3,000–4,000 feet, January 5, 1935; Antigua (Griscom), May 15. Costa Rica—Basin of El General, 3,000–4,000 feet, March 1 to May 7, 1936; Vara Blanca, 5,500 feet, April 16–24, 1938."

DISTRIBUTION

Range.—From central Canada south to western Panama.

Breeding range.—The cedar waxwing breeds **north** to southeastern Alaska (Ketchikan; has occurred north to Juneau); north-central British Columbia (Kispiox Valley, mouth of the Ingenika River, and McLeod Lake); northern Alberta (Peace River, Lesser Slave Lake, and McMurray); northern to central eastern Saskatchewan (Methye Portage, Island Lake, and Cumberland House); central Manitoba (Chemawawin, Grand Rapids, and Berens Island); central Ontario (Kenora, Lac Seul, Kapuskasing, and Moose Factory); southern Quebec (Lake Mistassini, Godbout, Seven Islands, and Natashquan); and central eastern Newfoundland (Glenwood). **East** to Newfoundland (Glenwood and Searton); Nova Scotia (Cape Breton Island, Halifax, and Yarmouth); the Atlantic Coast States south to Maryland (Easton); Virginia (Lynchburg and Roanoke) and in the mountains to extreme northern Georgia (Cornelia). **South** to northern Georgia (Cornelia and Tate); western Tennessee (Athens); central Kentucky (Eubank and Bardstown); southern Indiana (Wheatland and New Harmony); southern Illinois (Mount Carmel, Olney, and Odin); central Missouri (St. Louis, St. Charles, and Warrensburg); eastern

Nebraska (Falls City, London, and Fort Calhoun) ; eastern and northern South Dakota (Yankton, Sioux Falls, Aberdeen, and Harding County) ; Montana (Terry and Billings) ; northern Utah (Ogden and Lehi) ; and northern California (Eureka). It has bred occasionally in Colorado (nest found near Fairplay and spotted young found in the Denver region). **West** to northwestern California (Eureka) ; western Oregon (Fort Klamath, Corvallis, and Portland) ; western Washington (Cape Disappointment, Shelton, Seattle, and Bellingham) ; western British Columbia (Vancouver Island, Francois Lake, and Hazelton) ; and southeastern Alaska (Ketchikan). Within this area the cedar waxwing is irregular in occurrence, sometimes present one year and absent in other years. Because of its late time of breeding, the species sometimes migrates so late that it is reported to breed farther south than it does.

Winter range.—Roving flocks of cedar waxwings have been found in winter to southern Canada (Toronto and Ottawa) and well toward the northern boundary of the United States. The area in which they are found in winter with some regularity is **north** to northwestern Washington (Lake Ozette and Seattle) ; northeastern Oregon (Weston) ; central California (Grass Valley, Fresno, and Death Valley) ; southern Arizona casually (Phoenix and Tucson) ; central northern New Mexico (Arroyo Seco) ; northeastern Colorado (Denver and Fort Morgan) ; southern Nebraska (Red Cloud) ; central Missouri (Warrensburg) ; southern Illinois (Odin and Mount Carmel) ; southern Michigan (Grand Rapids, casually, and Ann Arbor) ; northern Ohio (Toledo, Cleveland, and Youngstown) ; and through central Maryland to Delaware (Smyrna). **East** to Delaware (Smyrna) ; Maryland (Cambridge and Crisfield) ; and the Atlantic coast south to central Florida (Titusville) ; rarely southern Florida (Royal Palm Hammock and Upper Matecumbe Key) ; western Cuba, occasional in winter or migration (Matanzas and Habana) ; Quintana Roo (Cozumel Island) ; central Honduras (La Ceiba and Siquatepeque) ; Costa Rica (Volcán de Irazu and Guayabo) ; and western Panama ("Chiriquí"), the southernmost record. **West** to Costa Rica (valley of the Río General) ; western Nicaragua (San Rafael del Norte) ; El Salvador (Volcán de Conchaqua) ; western Guatemala (Duenas, Tecpam, and Finca Mocá on the Pacific slope) ; Oaxaca (Puerto Ángel) ; Guerrero (Acapulco) ; Jalisco (Ameca) ; Nayarit (Tepic) ; Lower California (Cape San Lucas, Comondu, and La Grulla) ; western California (San Diego, Buena Park, Catalina Island, San Francisco, and Eureka) ; western Oregon (Medford and Portland) ; and northwestern Washington (Lake Ozette).

The cedar waxwing occasionally visits the West Indies, where it has been reported from Jamaica, the Cayman Islands, and the Dominican Republic ; also in the Bahamas and Bermuda.

Spring migration.—Late dates of spring departure area: Costa Rica—basin of Río General, May 7. Guatemala—Antigua, May 15. Puebla—Tehuacán, May 7. Lower California—San Telmo, June 4. Florida—Pensacola, May 30. Alabama—Autaugaville, May 25. Georgia—Athens, May 27. South Carolina—Charleston, June 3. Mississippi—Pass Christian, June 2. Louisiana—Shreveport, May 26. Arkansas—Rogers, May 31. Texas—Kerrville, May 23. Oklahoma—Tulsa, May 24. Kansas—Harper, May 21. Arizona—Phoenix, May 25.

Early dates of spring arrival are: Massachusetts—Essex, March 8. Vermont—Wells River, March 25. Maine—Presque Isle, April 20. New Brunswick—Fredericton, April 13. Quebec—Quebec, March 29. Ontario—Ottawa, February 22. Indiana—La Fayette, March 11. Michigan—Houghton, March 13. Iowa—Iowa City, February 21. Wisconsin—Milwaukee, February 17. Minnesota—Red Wing, February 28. Manitoba—Brandon, April 3. Saskatchewan—Eastend, May 9. Wyoming—Guernsey, May 6. Montana—Billings, May 17. Alberta—Carvel, May 17. British Columbia—Courtney, May 15.

Fall migration.—Late dates of fall departure are: British Columbia—Chilliwack, October 20. Alberta—Camrose, October 3. Montana—Fortine, October 22. Wyoming—Laramie, November 22. Saskatchewan—Yorkton, October 27. Manitoba—Aweme, October 8. North Dakota—Fargo, October 20. South Dakota—Faulkton, November 15. Minnesota—Minneapolis, November 6. Wisconsin—Superior, November 5. Michigan—Jackson, November 19. Illinois—Rantoul, November 9. Ontario—Toronto, October 11. Quebec—Quebec, October 31. Prince Edward Island—Charlottetown, October 21. New Brunswick—Scotch Lake, October 10. Maine—Portland, October 21. Massachusetts—Boston, November 15.

Early dates of fall arrival are: Texas—Corpus Christi, October 20. Louisiana—New Orleans, October 10. Mississippi—Edwards, October 20. Georgia—Round Oak, September 25. Alabama—Montgomery, October 20. Florida—Daytona Beach, October 22. Guatemala—San Lucas, October 26.

Banding records.—Since 1934 several thousand cedar waxwings have been banded at Modesto, Stanislaus County, Calif. Recoveries of these birds have shown migration northward through California to Idaho, Oregon, and Washington, and also some very erratic movements. One bird banded in February was captured the following winter near Redlands, Calif. Many birds banded in the Prairie Provinces of Canada and the Upper Mississippi Valley have been found the following winter in the Gulf States from Texas to Alabama. The recoveries of seven birds banded in eastern Massachusetts show a wide winter distribution: one was found in Texas; three in Louisiana; and one each in North Carolina, Georgia, and Alabama.

A bird banded at Modesto, Calif., on February 17, 1935, was killed on January 8, 1938, at Phoenix City, Ala., and another banded at the same place on April 14, 1935, was killed at Meridianville, Ala., on March 29, 1937. Both of these records were carefully verified. Another Modesto bird banded on April 23, 1939, was killed the following fall at Holden, Utah. One banded at McMillan, Mich., on the Upper Peninsula, on July 2, 1936, was found dead on March 19, 1937, at Muscogee, Fla.

Casual records.—Early in 1850 two specimens were collected at Stockton-on-Ties, England.

On September 19, 1925, a young cedar waxwing came on board a ship at latitude 41°58′ N., longitude 59°34′ W.; this was more than 300 miles from the nearest land.

Egg dates.—New York: 65 records, June 2 to September 27; 36 records, June 15 to 24, indicating the height of the season; 14 records, July 2 to 30.

Illinois: 11 records, June 7 to August 19.

Maine: 14 records, June 11 to August 7; 9 records June 19 to 28.

Oregon: 12 records, June 6 to July 28; 7 records, June 20 to 28.

Family PTILOGONATIDAE: Silky Flycatchers

PHAINOPEPLA NITENS LEPIDA Van Tyne

PHAINOPEPLA

HABITS

CONTRIBUTED BY ROBERT S. WOODS

On the deserts of the Southwestern United States, the glossy black phainopepla, with its arboreal and aerial habits, contrasts strikingly with its prevailingly tawny or grayish neighbors, which scurry over the sun-baked soil or seek the shelter of the sparse shrubbery. The phainopepla, however, also finds congenial surroundings in parks and estates whose semitropic verdure somehow seems a more appropriate setting for the bird's graceful, refined beauty and gentle manner.

The range of this subspecies extends from central California, southern Utah, and central western Texas southward through Lower California and northwestern Mexico, the typical form occurring farther south in Mexico. Some of the birds winter locally within the United States, principally in the southern deserts of California and Arizona. On the coastal slope of southern California the phainopepla is ordinarily found neither in the mountains nor in the lower valleys, but rather on the oak-covered mesas near the foothills and long watercourses where arborescent shrubs are common. It has, however, been reported by James Stevenson (1933) from an altitude of 6,200 feet near Mount Pinos, on June 12, 1932, and, more surprisingly, a female was seen by L. E. Hoffman (1933) at an altitude of 5,500 feet in the San Gabriel Mountains on December 30, 1932, with a foot of snow on the ground. East of the principal mountain ranges of southern California the phainopepla occurs mainly in the mesquite association, though W. E. D. Scott (1888) reported meeting with it at every point in south-central Arizona visited by him up to an altitude of about 5,000 feet. In connection with his studies of the Lower Colorado Valley, Dr. Joseph Grinnell (1914) wrote: "Everything indicated that this bird was common as a permanent resident of the region. It was, however, closely restricted to two narrow belts paralleling the river, one on each side; namely, as constituting the mesquite association. The close coincidence of the range of the bird with the plant association in question was here clearly due solely to the preferred food afforded in constant and abundant quantity by the berries of the mistletoe parasitic upon the mesquite. * * * In certain places, as on the Arizona side above Mellen, and on the California side opposite Cibola, this bird was, within the riparian strip, the most abundant single species."

The outstanding attributes of this bird, in the eyes of those who named it, are revealed by a translation of its scientific name: *Phainopepla* (fā-ī′ nō-pĕp′là), from two Greek words meaning "shining robe"; *nitens*, a Latin word also meaning "shining"; *lepida*, from the Latin and meaning "charming." Probably no one has more vividly expressed the general impression produced by the phainopepla than did Bradford Torrey (1904), after making its acquaintance in southern Arizona:

What I call the Phainopepla's elegance comes partly from its form, which is the very perfection of shapeliness, having in the highest degree that elusive quality which in semi-slang phrase is designated as "style;" partly from its motions, all prettily conscious and in a pleasing sense affected, like the movements of a dancing-master; and partly from its color, which is black with the most exquisite bluish sheen, set off in the finest manner by broad wing-patches of white. These wing-patches are noticeable, furthermore, for being divided into a kind of network by black lines. It is for this reason, I suppose, that they have a peculiar gauzy look (I speak of their appearance while in action) such as I have never seen in the case of any other bird, and which often made me think of the ribbed, translucent wings of certain dragon flies.

Doubtless this peculiar appearance was heightened to my eyes, because of the mincing, wavering, over-buoyant method of flight (the wings being carried unusually high) to which I have alluded, and which always suggested to me the studied movements of the dance. I think I never saw one of the birds so far forget itself as to take a direct, straightforward course from one point to another. No matter where they might be going, though the flight were only a matter of a hundred yards, they progressed always in pretty zigzags, making so many little, unexpected, indecisive tacks and turns by the way, butterfly fashion, that you began to wonder where they would finally come to rest.

Spring.—On the Pacific slope of California, where few of the phainopeplas winter, they make their appearance in numbers during the latter half of April, as a rule. They are usually first noticed as small companies of males, which perch on the tops of trees and make frequent, seemingly aimless flights. This would suggest some type of courtship activity, except that few females are seen at that time. At no time during the season, in fact, are the females nearly as much in evidence as the males; unless the former are actually much fewer in numbers, they are comparatively quiet and inconspicuous in their habits.

Nesting.—On the deserts nesting begins 2 to 3 months earlier than on the coastal slope. At Palm Springs, according to M. French Gilman (1903), "it would seem that most of the young are hatched in March and April and that in some instances nest building must begin in the latter part of February." Dr. Grinnell (1914) found both eggs and young in April in the Lower Colorado Valley. West of the mountains, on the other hand, nesting begins during the latter part of May, while June witnesses by far the greatest portion of this activity, which seems to end in July, with but one brood raised. It has been surmised that a first nesting might take place on the desert and a second in the coastal region, but Mr. Gilman continues: "Possibly some of the birds rear two broods a year, but from the fact that some adult birds fail to pair and nest in this vicinity [Banning], I am inclined to think that but one brood is raised. Probably those hatched in March on the desert return there to nest the following March; while those hatched in the San Gorgonio pass, in June and July, nest there the following summer." Dr. Alden H. Miller (1933) doubts that any coastward migration occurs after the early desert nesting period, remarking: "In my experience I have been unable to detect any general exodus of breeding Phainopeplas from the deserts even in May when adults and young are common in these regions."

In the desert portion of the phainopepla's breeding range, nests have been reported in mesquites, cottonwoods, hackberries, and willows, for the most part. In coastal California, sycamores, oaks, and orange trees are frequently used, together with many other trees and tall shrubs. Near the Papago Indian Reservation in southern Arizona, Herbert W. Brandt (MS.) says "it preferred for its nesting tree the densely foliaged hackberry, where an abundance of concealment is offered for its comparatively small, well camouflaged nest. The latter is saddled on a small fork near the outer margin of the foliage, usually in the middle third of the tree. In the drier areas small mesquites may be occupied, especially if the tree contains a dense clump of mistletoe. Then the bird builds down in the center of this common parasite, mounting its home astraddle of the supporting limb." In orange trees about 10 to 15 feet high the nests are placed in the upper third of the tree, in the outer foliage but usually well concealed from an observer on the ground. Twenty-one nests at

Azusa, Calif., most of them in orange trees, were situated at heights of 6 to 11 feet, averaging 8½ feet.

Mrs. Harriet Williams Myers (1908), who watched the building of many nests in sycamore trees, observed that nearly all of them were in upright crotches. A large proportion of the nests mentioned by others are described as placed in forks, either vertical or horizontal. Reporting on San Diego County observations, F. E. Blaisdell (1893) says: "The nests are placed at varying distances from the ground, from four to even fifty feet. The materials used are prickly or viscid. The fruit and leaves of some of the members of the Borage family have the preference, together with the leaves and down of species of *Gnaphalium*, all being bound together by spiders' web; the interior of the nest is thinly lined with bits of wool, hair and down." Also in San Diego County were the nests described by Florence Merriam Bailey (1896):

By following the birds as they flew from the pepper trees, I found four nests. They were all on the border or in the midst of dense chaparral. * * * all were built in low oaks, two not eight feet above the ground, and two under five. One was in a narrow socket between two small branches, and another was placed on a horizontal limb. All the nests were broken up, and the three that I took after they were deserted were made of about the same materials: small bits of plant stems, oak blossoms and other small flowers. The materials were so fine that, although I sat within a few yards of the nests when the birds were at work, I rarely saw them bring anything, except in the few instances when they came with grass dangling from their bills.

As soon as I began to watch the Phainopepla's nests, I discovered that the males did almost all the building. This was especially surprising because in direct opposition to the laws of protective coloration, for their black plumage and white wing markings made them striking figures as they went about their work.

As Mrs. Bailey states, nest-building seems to be almost exclusively the duty of the male. The female may occasionally visit and carefully inspect the unfinished nest, but according to most observers she seldom offers any active assistance, and may actually be driven away by her mate. That there are individual variations in this regard, however, is indicated by observations of Dr. Barton W. Evermann (1882) in Ventura County, Calif. He says: "Two or three pairs of these Flycatchers were soon detected in their nest-building, and I watched them for several evenings with much interest. Both male and female worked at the nest, each bringing and placing its own material." In the light of present knowledge, it seems likely that he may have concentrated his attention on one pair and assumed their cooperation to be typical of all.

The nest is notably shallow and appears small for the size of the bird, though neat and compactly constructed. Mr. Brandt (MS.) writes: "The five nests measured by us varied but little in size and measured about 2½ inches in total height, 4½ inches in outside diameter, and 2¼ inches in inside diameter, while the U-shaped bowl was 1½ inches deep." Measurements of a nest at Tombstone, Ariz., as given in F. C. Willard's notes, are somewhat smaller: Diameter outside 3¾ inches, inside 2½ inches; depth outside 1½ inches, inside 1 inch. Dr. Evermann (1882) remarked that "the cavity in most of them is more nearly the form of an ellipse than a circle. The wall of the nest is generally thicker at one end of the ellipse than elsewhere."

In parts of central Lower California the breeding season seems to be intermediate between those of the two distinct regions in the United States, as indicated in a report by Griffing Bancroft (1930):

These birds are plentiful in José María Cañon, but they become progressively less so as one travels eastward. They are gregarious to the extent of perhaps a dozen pairs in especially favored spots where the mesquite is at its best and food supply is exceptional. They are absent, locally, from altitudes of over a thousand feet.

The breeding season opens the middle of April but does not reach its height for another month. The season is 6 weeks later than is that of the phainopepla of the Colorado Desert, but it is slightly in advance of that of the birds of the San Diegan District. In California we expect to find the nests resting against the larger limbs of trees. In the San Ignacio region nearly all were placed in mistletoe or suspended beneath it. That condition, however, is not peculiar to this region, for I have observed the same thing near Ensenada.

The nests were typical, small and built of fine gray plant down reinforced with tiny twigs and leaves. They were ordinarily placed 8 to 12 feet above the ground, though some were much higher.

The number of eggs in a set is either two or three, the latter being more common and an exception to the very general rule that the San Ignacio birds lay more sparingly than do their northern counterparts. The variations in the individual eggs, in shape, size, and markings, were pronounced. Some were practically spherical and others extremes of elongation.

With the laying of the eggs the female begins to assume a more direct responsibility in the nesting operations, though the duty of incubation seems to fall principally to the male, at least during the daylight hours. The birds are rather easily disturbed while on the nest, and they fly about with anxious cries as long as the intruder remains near.

Eggs.—Mr. Blaisdell (1893) says: "The eggs are two (frequently), three (usually), or four (rarely), in number." While sets of four seem to be exceedingly unusual, the relative frequency of two and three egg sets may be in part a matter of locality. In relating his early experiences in Ventura County, Calif., Dr. Evermann (1822) wrote:

Six of the seven nests contained three eggs each, the other but two. Dr. Cooper and Capt. Bendire, the only naturalists who appear to have found the nest of this species before me, never found more than two eggs in a set. Dr. Cooper found a single nest near Fort Mojave, on April 27. Capt. Bendire, in the season of 1872, found fourteen nests in the vicinity of Tucson, Arizona, and not one contained more than two eggs, "and in three instances the nest contained but a single egg and the bird hard setting upon that." * * * He says: "The small number found by me is unquestionably due to the fact that in southern Arizona they raise two and perhaps three broods, while in California, where we found them, they raise but one."

With respect to the last statement, the evidence as to the number of broods raised in southern Arizona is not entirely clear. Referring to the foothills of the Santa Catalina Mountains, Mr. Scott (1885) says: "That there is a wide difference in the time of the breeding of different pairs in the same locality cannot be doubted, but my experience leads me to believe that here, at least, only one brood is raised during the season." Later, however, he writes (1888): "It apparently breeds throughout its range, raising at least two broods and probably three." In the earlier paper, Mr. Scott also states that "the number of eggs would seem to be quite as frequently three as two." More recent writings on the habits of the species in Arizona cast no further light on the subject.

The measurements of 50 eggs average 22.1 by 16.0 millimeters; the eggs showing the four extremes measure 25.7 by 16.7, 24.1 by 18.0, 19.3 by 15.2, and 20.4 by 14.7 millimeters.

Young.—The incubation period is given by Frank L. Burns (1915) as 16 days and by Frank F. Gander (1927) as 15 days; but two sets timed by the writer hatched in 14 days. W. L. Dawson (1923) says: "The young are hatched upon the fourteenth day after the deposition of the last egg; and they would look much like blackberries a little under-ripe, if their appearance were not relieved by generous tufts of long white down. The edges of the mouth are bright yellow, but the lining proper is flesh-colored. The parents do not feed by regurgitation; but berries are carefully crushed and perhaps invested with parental mucus before being fed." Mrs. Myers (1908) describes the feeding of the young as follows: "As near as I could tell, berries and tiny insects formed the chief part of the diet. When the birds fed pepper berries, or nightshade, the berries were taken from the mouth down into the neck, and back several times before feeding. In the case of the insects they seemed to be carried in the throat, extending down into the neck, from which they were brought up by a sort of pumping motion, not violent, however, like the finches."

In the care of the young the female does at least her full share of the work. In one nest so situated that it could be conveniently watched without alarming the birds, the young were fed by the female only, at intervals of 3 to 6 minutes except during the middle of the day, when longer rest periods were taken.

The aspect of the nestlings is made distinctive by the erect, pointed crest, which begins to develop on the crown with the appearance of the first pinfeathers. They differ from the young of most birds in their willingness to leave the nest and return voluntarily before they are ready to abandon it permanently. Two nestlings frightened from the nest about two days prematurely, returned as soon as they had recovered from their alarm; and Mrs. Myers (1909) tells of one young bird flying and hopping about in the tree for 12 minutes, then flying back to the nest.

The young remain in the nest for about 19 days, a period not only longer than that of the majority of the smaller passerine birds, but apparently much more constant, the shortest time reported being 18 days.

Plumages.—On the bodies of the newly hatched young, long white down covers the lower back, fringes, and wings and forms a circlet or halo around the bare crown of the head. Some of the filaments on the wings approximate 1 centimeter in length. The exposed upper surfaces of the body are slaty black, the skin gradually becoming more transparent toward the median lower parts. Pinfeathers begin to appear about one week after hatching, and by the tenth or eleventh day the beginnings of the crest are quite apparent on the forehead. Vestiges of down still cling to the feathers of the head when the young are nearly ready to leave the nest.

The following data have been abstracted from a treatise on the postjuvenal molt, by Dr. Alden H. Miller (1933):

The sexes are identical in the juvenal plumage and are extremely similar to the adult female. The body plumage is slightly browner throughout than is that of the adult female, but this appears to be due in part to the looser structure of the vanes of the feathers of the juvenile, which permits exposure of some of the basal parts of the feathers * * *.

Contrasted with the adult female, the light-colored edgings on rectrices, on middle, greater, and marginal coverts of the forearm, and on the inner secondaries of juveniles are less definitely set off from the gray parts of these same feathers and are duskier or buffier. The major feathers of the wing and tail are often a lighter shade of dark brown than in adult females.

Dr. Miller shows that there are pronounced individual and geographic variations in the completeness of the postjuvenal or first fall molt. "The admixture of plumage can be adequately studied only in the male Phainopepla. In this sex brown juvenal rectrices, remiges, and coverts stand in sharp contrast with corresponding glossy black feathers gained in the postjuvenal molt. * * * Not infrequently the mixture of plumages and feather types produce grotesquely pied male individuals. * * * It would appear that the immature male Phainopepla has differentiated sexually at the time of the first fall molt sufficiently to stimulate deposition of black pigment in rectrices, remiges, and coverts. If any of these are not molted, there is, of course, no chance for this differentiation to find expression." The group from coastal and central California averages higher in juvenal feathers than the birds from the desert regions, perhaps because of the earlier breeding of the latter. Of the postjuvenal body plumage he says: "The body plumage of females is a nearly uniform olivaceous mouse gray and is not distinguishable from that of adult females. In the first-year male the body plumage is highly variable. * * * The replacement of body feathers proper, in the postjuvenal molt, is as far as known always complete, and the apparent admixture of body plumage is the result entirely of the variety of feather types that may be produced during the course of this molt, not a mixture of feathers of various ages as in the wing and tail."

Food.—The food of the phainopepla consists mainly of various kinds of berries and winged insects, the former undoubtedly predominating. On the deserts the principal portion of its diet, according to many observers, is made up of the berries of mistletoe parasitic upon the mesquite. In the desertlike washes along some of the watercourses of southwestern California is found a buckthorn, *Rhamnus crocea*, whose small scarlet berries are a favorite food; berries of juniper, elder, and various species of *Rhus* are also said to be eaten. In settled districts the birds are often seen eating the red berries of the peppertree, *Schinus molle*, which is abundantly planted as an ornamental. Another exotic item of diet highly appreciated by the phainopepla is the rather succulent, sweetish petals of the Paraguay guava, *Feijoa sellowiana*. When one of these large shrubs is in bloom late in spring, several of the birds will often congregate in it, busily picking off the petals. I have never seen them show interest in any fruit larger than a small variety of mulberry.

Of its food habits in the foothills of the Santa Catalina Mountains north of Tucson, Ariz., Mr. Scott (1885) says: "All through July and August, and for the greater part of September, the birds remained abundant, feeding on the various berries and small fruits which became ripe as the season progressed, and wherever such fruit as they liked was at all abundant they paid little attention to any other kind of food, though insect life fairly teemed in and about the berries that attracted the birds. They showed a particular fondness for a kind of wild grape, and hunted the country through for such fruit, in parties of from ten to forty."

Behavior.—One may well doubt whether most phainopeplas ever have any contact with the ground during their lives, except perhaps for the purpose of drinking. All their actions plainly express their preference for the air rather than the earth: they perch on the topmost twigs of trees and shrubs, and when going from place to place, their flight is likely to follow a course far above the straight line that is the shortest distance between the two points. The flight, though not rapid, appears leisurely rather than labored, and, as pointed out by Bradford Torrey, previously quoted, it has a peculiarly buoyant

quality.   When a company of the birds is seen flitting idly about, they
strongly suggest a flock of giant butterflies.

The males, particularly, often carry on flycatching activities from
elevated perches, sometimes by sallies in regular flycatcher fashion,
but frequently by hovering and fluttering about in the air in a seemingly aimless and befuddled manner.   It is often difficult to determine
whether these peculiar maneuvers represent the prosaic pursuit of
food or some odd form of play.   It is noticeable that the hunting of
winged insects always is conducted at a considerable height and never
by low swoops over the ground as is often the case with flycatchers.
Mrs. Bailey (1896) further describes some of the habits and manner-
isms of the phainopepla:

In feeding, the birds occasionally flew against a bunch of berries, as Chickadees
do, clinging while they ate; and I once saw one hover before a bunch while
eating, as a Hummingbird whirrs under a flower.   More frequently they lit
on a branch from which they could lean over and pick off the fruit at leisure.
I never actually saw them eat anything but peppers, but at one time when the
brush was full of millers, the birds seemed to be catching them; and they sometimes made short sallies into the air as if for insects.   They did this much as a
Kingbird does, flying up obliquely and going down the opposite side of the angle.

Their flight was interesting.   In leaving the pepper trees to go back to
their nesting ground, they uniformly rose obliquely high into the air—sometimes,
I should judge, as high as one hundred feet—and then flew on evenly, straight
to their destination, several pairs going so far that they would disappear up a
side cañon, or, as black specks, would be lost in the fog down the valley.   When
watching the flight of Phainopeplas, Mourning Doves often passed close beside
me, and I was struck by the contrast in motion.   The Dove cut the air, swerving
to one side as it flashed by, and its free whirling flight served to emphasize the
calm, even rowing of the Phainopepla.   Occasionally the birds flew in an undecided way, still high and even, but changing their direction by sudden jerks.
Frequently, when nearing the nest tree, a male would close his wings and shoot
obliquely down, tilting his tail for a brake.   One of them used to fly in at a
height of about ten feet, waver as he came near, as if slowing up, and then
after turning his head to look down and place the nest, tilt down in the usual
labored way, his tail pressing the air.   Not until he was nearly through building did he discover that it was easier to slow up in time to fly down to the nest.

According to John Cassin (1854), this species, described from
Mexico by Swainson in 1838, was first added to the known fauna of the
United States by Col. George A. McCall, inspector general in the
United States Army, while on a tour of duty in California in 1852.
It is, therefore, interesting to read Colonel McCall's own impressions
of the "black flycatcher," as given by Cassin:

The first opportunity that I had for observing the manners of this bird, was
afforded me in 1852, while travelling from *Valle-cita* to *El Chino*, in California.
On that occasion, as I left the country bordering the desert, and began to ascend
the hills, my route followed the course of a mountain brook, whose clear waters
were at intervals shaded with gnarled and scrubby oaks.   In approaching one
of these clumps of trees, I remarked a number of dark-colored birds, which

afterwards were found to belong to this species, darting upwards from the topmost branches, and after diving and pitching about in the air for a moment, returning again to the dead branches with the lively port that proved them to be engaged in the agreeable pastime of taking their insect prey. A nearer approach showed them to be light and graceful on the wing; but less swift and decided in their motions than most of the true Fly-catchers. There were about a dozen in company, and they presented a pleasing sight, as three or four together were constantly either pitching upwards to a considerable height in the air, or gliding silently back to their perches. In these aerial evolutions, the bright spot on the wing which is formed by broad patches of white on the inner webs of six or seven of the quill feathers, and is visible only when the wing is spread, gleamed conspicuously in the sunshine, and formed a fine contrast with the glossy black of the general plumage. I sat upon my horse, watching their movements for some time, and I now perceived that two of their numbers were of a dusky hue, and without the wing spot to which I have referred; but I could discover no difference in their manners or their style of flight. I, therefore, had little doubt of their being adult females; for although at that period of the year (June 20) the young birds might have been well grown, yet there is generally a want of decided character in the unpractised flight of young birds, which betrays them to the sportsman's eye. * * *

However, on my attempting to approach still nearer, these birds became alarmed, and winging their way to the hill-side, alighted on the scraggy bushes scattered among large projecting rocks, where they resumed their sport, rising lightly into the air and darting about after insects, which seemed to be abundant. I followed—but they were now on the *qui vive*, and, without permitting me to get within gun-shot, flew from bush to bush, as I advanced, keeping all the while in a loose irregular flock, and still pursuing their sport of fly-catching. In this way they continued to ascend the hills, until the broken character of the ground abruptly stopped my horse. Having, however, dismounted, I clambered over the rocks, and at last succeeded in killing two of them. These were alike in plumage—black, with the wing spot; and one of them, which I dissected, proved to be a male.

As I journeyed on towards the Sierra Nevada, I met, during several days succeeding, these birds, either in small companies, or singly; and subsequently I found a few individuals between *El Chino* and *Los Angeles;* but they were invariably black, with the white wing spot. And I never on any occasion, except the one I have referred to, saw one of those clad in dusky garments, which I had supposed were females.

The accuracy of this account of approximately a century ago is attested by its close agreement in practically every particular with the writings of more modern ornithologists, including the comments on the apparent scarcity of females. Incidentally, there seems to be no reason to suppose that the phainopepla's living conditions have changed greatly since that date, except on the sites of cities and towns; food supplies may even have been increased in some places.

Voice.—The most frequent utterance is a liquid *quirt* or *perp*, repeated at intervals of one or two seconds. This call has rather a worried sound and does, in fact, often indicate anxiety; at times, however, it is kept up almost interminably without ascertainable reason. Other notes of the phainopepla have been well described by Mrs. Bailey (1896):

In watching the birds at their nests, I found that they had a number of calls. The commonest was uttered in the same tone by both male and female, and was like the call of a young Robin. In giving it, they flashed their tails, showing the square corners conspicuously. The male also had a harsh cry of warning, drawn out like *ca-rack* or *ca-ra-ack*. In addition, he had a scold and a note suggesting the Meadowlark. The Phainopepla's ordinary song had some weak squeaking notes, but it also had phrases of rich blackbird quality, recalling the *o-ka-lee* of the marshes. One of these was a high keyed *whee'-dle-ah*. Other parts could be roughly syllabified as *kit-er-ah-at* and *cher-nack'-ec*. The song in flight was bright and animated. I once heard a bird break out as he came down from a sally into the air, and he often flew away from the nest singing. Sometimes I thought he even sang in the nest. * * * Indeed, to me the Phainopepla's song was pleasing in spite of its jumbled notes, not merely because of the flute-like quality of some of its tones, but pre-eminently because of the bright, vivacious way in which it was uttered.

Field marks.—Both sexes may be recognized by the high crest, slender form, the flaring end of the tail, and by their characterisuic manner of flight. When the male is in flight, the disklike white wing patches contrasting with the otherwise black plumage are unmistakable. Even the nestlings may be rather easily identified by their erect crests. The adults seldom lower their crests—perhaps only when angry or when facing a stiff wind.

Enemies.—Obviously, few if any of the phainopepla's enemies are terrestrial. Although the birds express marked disapproval of cats, it is hard to see how the latter would be able to harm them, except in cases of disabled adults or young birds fallen from the nest. While no reports are at hand, their nests undoubtedly suffer to some extent from the smaller climbing and flying predators. Dr. Herbert Friedmann (1929) lists this species as "apparently a rare victim of the * * * Cowbirds," with but one record known. Concerning any possible enemies which might attack the adults, there is little information.

To be classed as a persecutor rather than a dangerous enemy, the mockingbird displays an unreasonable spite against the phainopepla, pursuing this inoffensive bird upon every opportunity. Mrs. Myers (1909), telling of the successive nesting failures of a pair of phainopeplas, surmised that abandonment of their nesting sites might well have been the result of persistent persecution by mockingbirds.

With only two or three eggs to the set, and with but one rather slow-growing brood yearly in some localities, at least, the phainopepla's mortality rate must be unusually low as compared with that of other passerine birds. The impression received in field observation of the species is definitely that of a shy, timid bird, perhaps even more by reason of its manner than its actions. Possibly this constant attitude of wariness and suspicion is of substantial benefit in prolonging its life span and making unnecessary a high rate of increase.

Fall.—Regarding the postbreeding dispersal, Harry S. Swarth (1904), in writing of the Huachuca Mountains in Arizona, says: "About the end of July, 1902, a movement began from the lower valleys up into the mountains, and during August the Phainopeplas were most numerous throughout the oak region, up to about 5000 feet. At this time they were in loose straggling flocks of from six to a dozen birds, young and old together, and were generally seen sitting in the tree tops and feeding for the most part, as flycatchers."

Most of the phainopeplas leave the Pacific slope of California during the month of August, though stragglers are often seen in September or October, or occasionally in midwinter. Whether some of these individuals winter in the deserts of southeastern California and southern Arizona, or whether they all pass over the desert regions to winter farther south, seems not yet to have been determined.

DISTRIBUTION

Range.—Southwestern United States and Mexico.

Breeding range.—The phainopepla breeds **north** to central California (Marysville, perhaps the Lassen Peak region, and Murphys); probably southern Nevada (Tempahute Range); southwestern Utah (St. George and Zion National Park); central Arizona (Campe Verde and the Salt River Wildlife Refuge; wandering north to Keams Canyon); southwestern New Mexico (Silver City, Fort Webster, and Elephant Butte); and southwestern Texas (Pine Springs, probably). **East** to southwestern Texas (Pine Springs, Cathedral Mountain, and Boquillas; and has occurred, apparently as a wanderer, as far east as San Antonio); Nuevo León (Galeana); Hidalgo (Cuesta Tesqueda); Puebla (Tehuacán); and **south** to Oaxaca (Tehuantepec). **West** to Oaxaca (Tehuantepec); Puebla (Huehuetlán); northwestern Durango (Rosario); Lower California (Cape San Lucas, La Paz, San Fernando, and Ensenada); and western California (San Diego, Santa Catalina Island, Santa Barbara, San Antonio Valley, Stockton, and Marysville).

Winter range.—While the phainopepla is migratory to some extent, it has been found almost as far north in winter as in summer, and it does not seem possible from present information to outline a definite winter range as distinct from the breeding range.

The range as outlined for the entire species includes two subspecies. The eastern phainopepla (*P. n. nitens*) occurs from southwestern Texas through eastern Mexico to Oaxaca; the western phainopepla (*P. n. lepida*) occurs from central California and southwestern New Mexico, south through western Mexico to Durango and southern Lower California.

Eggs dates.—Arizona: 34 records, April 4 to June 19; 18 records, May 13 to 30, indicating the height of the season.

California: 150 records, February 23 to July 15; 20 records, March 8 to 29; 84 records, June 1 to 30.

Mexico: 24 records, April 10 to June 3; 15 records, May 11 to 28.

Family LANIIDAE: Shrikes

LANIUS BOREALIS BOREALIS Vieillot

NORTHERN SHRIKE

HABITS

The great northern shrike, or butcherbird, is known to most of us only as a rather uncommon winter visitor throughout the northern half of the United States, where we see it as a solitary sentinel perched on the top of a tree, looking for some luckless small bird, or hovering over an open field, ready to pounce on the timid little mouse as it threads his winter runway. Either bird or mouse is to be added to his larder, impaled on a nearby thorn or crotch, as the butcher hangs his meat; hence the appropriate name of butcherbird (pl. 15).

Few of us have been favored to see it in its summer home, for it breeds as far north as the spruce forests extend and comes south only when scarcity of food compels it to do so. We found it fairly common all along the coast of Labrador, from Hopedale to Nain and Okkak, wherever there was any considerable growth of fair-sized spruces. According to Lucien M. Turner (MS.), it was not very common at Fort Chimo, Ungava. Westward from Hudson Bay it begins to intergrade with the northwestern subspecies (*invictus*).

Nesting.—There are three sets of eggs of the northern shrike in my collection, all taken by the Rev. W. W. Perrett at Hopedale, Labrador. They were all placed in spruce trees, about 12 feet from the ground, nicely hidden by the branches, and all were very bulky affairs. The first nest was discovered by seeing the male bird carrying food to the female while she was sitting on the nest; the nest contained only two eggs, on June 7, 1915, but the data slip says "incubation just begun"; the nest was made mainly of twigs, grass, feathers, rags, and deer hair.

This same pair of birds built another nest in the same patch of woods, about 150 yards from the first nest, from which he took a set of four fresh eggs on June 17, 1915; these birds had built their new nest in seven days; as there were no eggs in it on the 13th, the bird must have laid an egg each day. The third set of six fresh eggs was taken on June 3, 1918. The three nests were all made of similar materials.

There is another set of six eggs of this shrike in the Carnegie Museum, taken by Mr. Perrett in the same locality on June 17, 1918, for which W. E. Clyde Todd has sent me the data. The nest was constructed of similar materials and was located 8 feet from the ground in a spruce tree. This was evidently the second set from the same pair of birds from which my set of six eggs was taken on June 3. This second nest was located about 400 yards from the first; it had been built and the six eggs laid in the short time that intervened.

Eggs.—The usual set for the northern shrike may consist of two to nine eggs, though I believe that any sets of less than four are incomplete and that the large number of nine is unusual; probably four to six are the usual numbers. What few eggs of this species I have seen are ovate or rounded-ovate and nearly lusterless. The ground color is grayish white or greenish white, and they are usually heavily spotted or blotched over the entire surface, seldom having the spots concentrated at one end, with olive-brown, dull olive, or pale dull brown, and with underlying spots and blotches of different pale shades of Quaker drab or lavender. The measurements of 31 eggs average 26.7 by 19.5 millimeters; the eggs showing the four extremes measure 28.0 by 20.0, 27.0 by 20.5, and 25.9 by 18.5 millimeters.

Plumages.—A very full account of all the plumages of all the North American shrikes has been published by Dr. Alden H. Miller (1931), to which the reader is referred; his descriptions are given in too much detail to be quoted here. Dr. Dwight (1900) describes the juvenal plumage of a specimen taken in Labrador, as follows: "Above, brownish mouse-gray with indistinct vermiculations, especially on the rump. Wings black, a white area at bases of primaries; the coverts, tertiaries and secondaries edged with wood-brown, or pale cinnamon mottled from irregular extension of the color, and similar tipping on the rectrices which are black, the lateral ones largely white. Below mouse-gray, nearly white on mid-abdomen, indistinctly vermiculated, more marked on sides and crissum. Bar through eye dull clove-brown; lores grayish."

A partial postjuvenal molt occurs, mainly in July and August, which involves the contour plumage and the wing coverts, but not the rest of the wings or the tail, producing a first winter plumage, which Dr. Dwight (1900) describes as follows: "Above, French gray washed with brownish gray, the rump grayish white. Lesser coverts cinereous gray, the median black, the retained greater coverts dull black buff tipped. Below grayish white with indistinct dusky vermiculations except on the chin, abdomen and crissum. Tail black, the three outer rectrices with much white. Lores grayish. Bar through eye dusky."

He says that the first nuptial plumage is "acquired by a partial prenuptial moult in March which involves the anterior part of the head, chin and throat. A whiter chin and black lores are acquired, young and old becoming practically indistinguishable. A good deal of the vermiculation is lost by wear of the feather edges." Dr. Miller (1931) says that this molt, "as far as known, occurs in March and April and is associated with the change of the bill from brown to black." And he adds that the young bird frequently loses, at this molt, "large, but often irregular, areas of the brown first fall plumage from the back, head, and shoulders."

Dr. Dwight (1900) says that the adult winter plumage is acquired by a complete postnuptial molt, which Dr. Miller (1931) says occurs in July and August, "perhaps also early September." According to Dr. Dwight, this adult winter plumage differs from the first winter plumage "in having a white wing band on the greater coverts, the tertiaries and secondaries with white edgings, the wings and tail jet-black, including all the coverts. The back is grayer without the brownish tint of the young bird."

The above remarks apply to the male; in the female the sequence of molts and plumages is the same. Ridgway (1904) says that the young female, in first winter plumage, is "similar to the young male of corresponding season but browner, the color of upper parts approaching isabella color, the scapulars, lower rump, and upper tail-coverts washed with cinnamon-buff, under parts more or less washed with the same, especially on sides and flanks, greater wing-coverts edged with the same, and white at tips of secondaries and rectrices more or less buffy." In the adult female, the gray of the upper parts is less pure than in the male, darker and more or less tinged with olive, the black of the wings and tail is duller, and the white markings are more restricted.

Food.—Dr. Sylvester D. Judd (1898) writes of the food of the northern shrike: "During its winter sojourn it renders a threefold service by killing grasshoppers, English sparrows, and mice. The birds and mice together amount to 60 percent, and insects to 40 percent, of the food from October to April. Grasshoppers constitute one-fourth of the food, and are equal to twice the combined amounts of beetles and caterpillars. * * * In the stomachs of the 67 butcherbirds examined 28 species of seed-eating birds were found. Of these 3 were tree sparrows, 5 juncos, and 7 English sparrows; the others could not be determined with certainty."

In the early days of the English sparrow in this country, while they were being protected, northern shrikes became so abundant on Boston Common that men were employed to shoot them, lest they destroy the sparrows. In this connection, Dr. Judd remarks: "It is to be hoped that in other cities this enemy of the sparrow will be protected instead of persecuted. If there were 6 butcherbirds in each of 20 New England cities, and each butcherbird killed 1 sparrow a day for the three winter months, the result would be a removal of 10,800 sparrows. Since two sparrows could raise under favorable conditions four broods of 5 each, the increase would be tenfold, so that those destroyed by the butcherbirds, if allowed to live, would

have amounted at the end of the first year to 118,800, and at the end
of the second year to 1,306,800 individuals."

In addition to the three named above, he lists the following birds
that this shrike has been known to kill: Chickadee, snow bunting,
downy woodpecker, vireo, kinglet, field sparrow, goldfinch, siskin,
myrtle warbler, mourning dove, cardinal, longspur, and horned lark.

Among mammals, meadow mice (*Microtus*) seem to be the most
frequent victims, but Judd also lists the white-footed mouse (*Peromys-
cus*) and the harvest mouse (*Reithrodontomys*). He continues:

Carrion is sometimes eaten. Prof. F. E. L. Beal, while at Ames, Iowa, in
January, 1880, saw a butcherbird fly over the brown frozen prairie to a carcass
of a cow, where it lit on one of the ribs and greedily tore off shreds of the flesh.

Active insects are much more liable than sluggish ones to fall victims to the
butcherbird, because objects which at rest can not be discriminated are instantly
seen when moving. Thus it happens that flying grasshoppers and running beetles
form a large proportion of the food of this bird. Grasshoppers and crickets
(*Orthoptera*), which are eaten during every month from October to April, form
24 percent of the total volume of food, and for October and November together
these insect pests form more than half of the food. Compared with *Orthoptera*,
the beetles (*Coleoptera*) eaten are of minor importance, amounting to only 6
percent of the food. More than half of these beetles belong to the family
Carabidae, the members of which prey upon insect pests. Caterpillars were
contained in one fifth of the stomachs examined, and during the months of
January and February amount to 8 percent of the volume of the stomach contents. Dr. A. K. Fisher collected in March two stomachs that were full of
caterpillars. Even the bristly Isabella caterpillar is eaten, an object apparently
as edible as a chestnut bur. Cutworms were found in several instances, but
moths were seldom met with. Ants, wasps, flies, and thousand legs are sometimes eaten, and spiders constitute 3 percent of the food; but bugs (*Hemiptera*)
were not detected during our laboratory investigations, though a cicada supposed to have been impaled by a shrike was found by Mrs. Musick, at Mount
Carmel, Mo. * * *

The present investigation shows that beneficial birds form less than one-
fourth of the food of the butcherbird. It also shows that the butcherbird, in
addition to being an enemy of mice, is a potent check on the English sparrow, and
on several insect pests. One-fourth of its food is mice; another fourth grasshoppers; a third fourth consists of native sparrows and predaceous beetles and
spiders, while the remainder is made up of English sparrows and species of
insects, most of which are noxious.

The amount of insect food taken by the northern shrike, as stated
above, seems surprising. The stomachs examined must have been
taken largely in the southern extremes of its winter range, or in fall
or spring, for the shrike would not be likely to find flying or crawling insects in New England or in the Northern States in the dead of
winter; but grasshoppers are often available in New England in
October, and even in some Novembers, and other insects in March.

Dr. Miller (1931) adds the following birds to the list mentioned
above, as taken by the species, including both subspecies: Hairy
woodpecker, phoebe, white-winged crossbill, redpoll, titmouse, bush-

tit, and robin.   Charles B. Floyd (1928) adds song, white-throated, and fox sparrows and the starling to the list of victims and says:

Several reports are at hand of unsuccessful attempts to capture White-breasted Nuthatches, English Sparrows, Downy Woodpeckers, etc.   In several cases where a Shrike pursued Nuthatches, the latter escaped capture by entering a hole in a tree or a nesting-box.   The Downy Woodpecker often out-manoeuvred its pursuer by constantly turning and dodging in the air rather than by flying away in an attempt to escape by speed, as do almost all the other small birds. Twice this winter I have personally watched a Shrike attempt to capture a Downy Woodpecker from above.   Each time that the Shrike swooped to strike the bird, the Downy turned quickly in the air at a sharp angle, the Shrike overshooting its mark.   It then turned with much more effort than the woodpecker, and again took up the pursuit.   So long as they were in sight—and I saw the Shrike swoop a number of times—the Woodpecker continued on its way apparently unafraid, and dodged each attack with ease.

Several observers have seen shrikes chasing blue jays or found one of the jays impaled in the usual shrike fashion.   Ora W. Knight (1908) adds the pine grosbeak to the list of the shrike's victims.   William Brewster (1936) gives the following account of a shrike in pursuit of a brown creeper:

When I first saw him, he was in hot pursuit of one of the Brown Creepers and both birds were about over the middle of the river and scarce a yard apart.   The Creeper made straight for the big elm which stands at the eastern end of the bridge.   When he reached it, the Shrike's bill was within six inches of his tail, but he nevertheless escaped; for an instant after the two birds doubled around behind the trunk the Shrike rose to the topmost spray of the elm, where he sat for a minute or more, gazing intently downward, evidently watching for the Creeper.   The latter, no doubt, had flattened himself against the bark after the usual practice of his kind when badly frightened and he had the nerve and good sense to remain perfectly still for at least *ten minutes*.   My eyes were no better than the Shrike's, for it was in vain that I scanned the trunk over and over with the greatest care.   Feeling sure, however, that the Creeper was really there, I waited patiently until at the end of the period just named he began running up the trunk, starting at the very point where I had seen him disappear.   It was one of the prettiest demonstrations of the effectiveness of protective coloration that I have ever witnessed.

In the same publication, he vividly describes the capture and killing of a field mouse:

As I watched a Shrike it flew from the topmost spray of a small maple into some alders and alighted on a horizontal stem about a foot above the level of surrounding snow but directly beneath; as I afterwards found, the snow had thawed quite down to the ground, leaving a trench about two feet deep by three or four inches wide, into which the Shrike, after peering intently for a moment, suddenly dropped with fluttering wings and wide opened tail.

Within a second or less it reappeared, dragging out a Field Mouse of the largest size.   The moment it got the Mouse fairly out on the level surface of the snow it dropped it apparently to get a fresh hold (as nearly as I could make out it had held it up to this time by about the middle of the back).   The Mouse, instead of attempting to regain its run way, as I expected it would do, instantly turned on its assailant and with surprising fierceness and agility sprang directly at its head many times in succession, actually driving it backward several feet although the Shrike faced its attacks with admirable steadiness and coolness and by a succession of vigorous and well aimed blows prevented the Mouse from closing in.

At length the Mouse seemed to lose heart and, turning, tried to escape. This sealed its fate for at the end of the second leap it was overtaken by the Shrike, who caught it by the back of the neck and began to worry it precisely as a Terrier worries a Rat, shaking it viciously from side to side, at the same time dragging it about over the snow which, as I could plainly see through my glass (I was standing within ten yards of the spot) was now freely stained with blood. I could also see the Shrike's mandible work with a vigorous, biting motion, especially when it stopped the shaking to rest for a moment. When it finally let go its hold, the Mouse was evidently dead.

After the shrike had carried off the mouse in its claws, partly eaten it and hung it in a fork, Mr. Brewster examined the mouse.

The Shrike had not touched any part of the body but the skin had been torn away from the entire neck and the muscles and other soft tissues were almost entirely gone from the shoulders and sternum to the base of the skull. The body was untouched and the skull showed no signs of injury, but the cheek muscles had been eaten pretty cleanly away as had also the entire throat with the tongue. Both eyes were whole and in their sockets. This examination confirmed the conviction which I formed while watching the Shrike and Mouse struggling together, viz. that the bird killed the Mouse partly by *throttling*—that is by choking and shaking it and partly (perhaps chiefly) by cutting open its neck on one side. No attempt was made to stun the Mouse by striking at its skull, such blows as I saw delivered being evidently intended merely to keep the Mouse at bay until the Shrike could close with it and get it by the neck as it finally did.

Mr. Brewster's close observation and careful description shows what is perhaps the shrike's usual method of killing rodents, and I can find very little evidence to the contrary, but Mr. Forbush (1929) says that John Muir "saw a shrike go down into a gopher hole and drive out half a dozen young gophers, and hovering over one after another as they ran, it killed them all by blows delivered from its powerful bill on the back of each one's head."

Dr. W. S. Strode (1889) tells the following story of a mouse-hunting shrike:

Not long since a young farmer invited me out to his field near town where he was husking shock corn, to see a "Mouse Hawk," as he called it, catch mice. On coming to where he was at work I looked about for the Shrike but did not see it until he pointed to a tree two hundred yards away where it sat on the topmost twig. Pretty soon a mouse ran from the shock, when it came almost with the rapidity of an arrow, and seizing the mouse in its bill flew away with it to the woods across the river, but in a short time it was back again at its perch on the tree where it did not remain long until another mouse ran out from the shock. In order to test the bird's boldness I pursued this mouse, but undaunted it flew almost between my feet and secured it, and apparently not liking its hold it alighted a few rods away and hammered the mouse on the frozen ground, and then tossing it in the air caught it by the throat as it came down. He then again flew off to the woods. This proceeding the farmer assured me would be repeated many times in the course of the day, and that every mouse would be carried to the strip of woods just over the river. Subsequently a chopper told me that he had found a honey locust tree in this woods that had mice stuck all over it on the thorns.

The northern shrike has two principal methods of hunting, watchful waiting and active pursuit.   The former method is the one usually employed, as in the above accounts, in securing mice; the bird perches patiently and motionless on some commanding tree, post, or wire, ready to pounce suddenly on its unsuspecting quarry; mice may be secured also by hovering over their runways in the fields and meadows. Grasshoppers, crickets, and other moving insects may be taken by watching for them, hovering over the fields, or by active pursuit on the ground, though I have not seen the latter method mentioned. But birds must be caught by active pursuit in the air or by chasing them through the trees and bushes; in the latter case the birds escape more often than they are caught by seeking the shelter of dense growth where the shrike is less adept in penetrating the thickets and dodging through the tangles of branches and twigs; cedars and other dense evergreens offer excellent havens of refuge for small birds.   Small birds easily recognize the difference between a shrike and some other harmless bird, and immediately "freeze" in their tracks, or seek shelter in the nearest dense cover.

The shrike is a fairly swift flier, but is often not able to catch a smaller bird in a straightaway flight, especially if it resorts to dodging, at which the heavier bird is less adept.   The shrike's usual method is to rise above its victim and dive down upon it, felling it to the ground with a stunning blow from its powerful beak, which often proves fatal by breaking the little bird's neck or its back.   The shrike follows it to the ground immediately and, if necessary, kills the bird with a blow at the base of the skull or by biting through the vertebrae of the neck. Small birds often escape from such attacks by mounting higher and higher in the air, so that the shrike cannot get above them, and then suddenly darting downward into thick cover.

Having killed its bird, the shrike seizes it by the neck or shoulders in either its bill or its claws, or both, and flies away with it.   Mr. Floyd (1928) made a number of inquiries on this point and received replies from 23 observers, 13 of whom reported that the prey is carried in the bill, 7 said in the claws, and 3 had seen both bill and claws used.   By some one of these methods the bird is carried to the shrike's larder and impaled on a thorn or a sharp stub on some tree or bush, on the barb of a barbed-wire fence, or some other similar point; often the bird is hung by its neck in the acute angle of a fork in a branch or twig. Mice are hung up in the same way, to be immediately devoured or saved for future reference.   The feet and claws of the shrike are evidently not strong enough to hold the quarry firmly while it is being torn apart, and some additional support is desirable; hence this characteristic habit. If the shrike is really hungry, its prey is gulped down almost entirely, flesh, feathers, fur, and most of the bones, only a few of the larger feathers and bones being discarded. These indigestible portions of the food are disgorged later in the form of pellets, which are often found where shrikes have been feeding. Edwin A. Mason sends me the following description of a pellet that he took from a bird-banding trap where a shrike had been feeding on a junco: "Including a 10-mm. tip, or tail, the pellet was 40 mm. long and 10 mm. thick, consisting largely of matted feathers; scattered through the mass could be seen small pieces of bone, some identifiable as from the skull, one tarsus with foot attached, and one fragment of bone obviously from the main body skeletal structure." A very brief period of time had elapsed between the ingestion and the regurgitation of the indigestible material.

Mr. Floyd (1928) mentions "several pellets which measured from half an inch long to one and one-eighth inches. They averaged three-eighths of an inch in diameter."

The northern shrike often kills more mice or birds than it can use at once, to many of which it never returns, and these are left to dry or rot. It has been known repeatedly to enter a bird-banding trap, kill all the birds in it, and not eat any of them. It sometimes dashes into a flock of redpolls or goldfinches, knocking out several of them, perhaps for the mere sport of killing them. Mr. Floyd (1928) writes: "A shrike that was seen to enter an electric-car barn in pursuit of an English Sparrow killed all the Sparrows in the barn, without thought of itself or pausing to eat any of its victims."

In captivity it will eat almost any kind of raw meat, will kill living birds and eat them, or eat dead birds or mice, though it seems to prefer mice to any other food. It will come to a feeding station to eat suet or hamburg steak, even when live birds are in the vicinity. Dr. Charles W. Townsend (1933) says: "On a warm March day I watched a Shrike fly-catching from the top of a tree. He pursued a large bee and missed it, but by a quick turn he caught it. * * * Once I saw two on March 9 hovering about the dry thatch-grass cast up on the beach, apparently picking up flies and spiders."

Behavior.—Much of the behavior of the northern shrike has been referred to above. The outstanding traits of this bloodthirsty rascal are boldness, fierceness, and savagery in its fearless and relentless pursuit of its prey, utterly regardless of obstacles or the presence of man. Nuttall's (1832) historic account illustrates its audacity:

Mr. J. Brown, of Cambridge, informs me that one of these birds had the boldness to attack two Canaries in a cage, suspended one fine winter's day at the window. The poor songsters in their fears fluttered to the side of the cage, and one of them thrust his head through the bars of his prison; at this instant the wily Butcher tore off its head, and left the body dead in the cage. * * * On another occasion, while a Mr. Lock in this vicinity was engaged in fowling, he wounded a Robin, who flew a little distance and descended to the ground; he soon heard the disabled bird uttering unusual cries, and on approaching found him in the grasp of the Shrike.

He snatched up the bird from its devourer; but having tasted blood, it still followed, as if determined not to relinquish its proposed prey, and only desisted from the quest on receiving a mortal wound.

Dr. Brewer (Baird, Brewer, and Ridgway, 1874) writes:

Its bold audacity and perseverance are quite remarkable, and are often displayed, in the fall, in the manner in which it will enter an apartment through an open window and attack a Canary, even in the presence of members of the family. * * * In one instance the writer was sitting at a closed window reading, with a Canary hanging above him. Suddenly there was a severe blow struck at the pane of glass near the cage, and the frightened Canary uttered cries of alarm and fell to the bottom of its cage. The cause was soon explained. A Shrike had dashed upon the bird, unconscious of the intervening glass, and was stretched upon the snow under the window, stunned by the blow. He revived when taken up, and lived several days, was sullen, but tame, and utterly devoid of fear.

Mr. Floyd (1928) writes: "Northern Shrikes are particularly destructive and annoying about a feeding or banding station. Their audacity is well known. They do not hesitate to seize a bird newly banded when it flies from the bander's hand, and they enter a trap, barn, room, or hen-house with absolute unconcern when birds or mice are seen there. In the trap they kill all the birds there before considering how they may escape or pausing to eat." He says that, "when intent upon the capture of its next meal, the Shrike loses all sense of fear of man," and tells how Mrs. Richard B. Harding was unable to drive one away from the vicinity of her trap, in which there were some birds, "and only after she secured a broom and actually struck at the intruder several times, did it give up and abandon the premises."

In its summer home in Labrador, the northern shrike seemed to be very tame, and we saw no signs of aggressiveness toward the few small birds that live there; probably it was living largely on insects. On August 18, 1912, I watched one for some time in Dr. Hettasch's small garden and in the woods around it. It was flying in its direct slow flight from one tree to another, or perching on a topmost twig, its body held erect, and flirting its tail up and down, or holding it straight out behind horizontally. Occasionally it darted out from its perch to chase some flying insect, or dropped down to the lower branches of a larch, where it seemed to be feeding on the buds and tender shoots, though probably it was finding insects there. When making a longer flight to a more distant tree, it flew more swiftly in a slightly undulating course, alternating a few rapid wing strokes with downward glides in woodpeckerlike curves. If flying low, as it often did, as if to keep behind cover, it would suddenly swoop upward in an abrupt curve to reach its perch on a treetop. Occasionally, it would hover like a sparrow hawk over an open space, as if looking for mice or insects.

Francis H. Allen says in his notes: "A shrike I watched mousing over river meadows in Millis, Mass., January 25, 1931, hunted mainly by hovering. It would start off with two or three bounds in the air and then rise almost vertically for perhaps six to ten feet—that is practically vertically at the top of the rise—and then hover for some time, turning its head from left to right to scan the grassy marsh. It was a very pretty performance."

Wendell Taber tells me of a rather unusual action that he saw: "As it sat on a twig the bird suddenly *jumped* to another twig slightly to one side and somewhat lower. I estimated the horizontal distance at about eight inches and the vertical descent at about six inches. The jump was accomplished entirely by leg and body motion, with the wings remaining folded throughout. The branch on which the bird landed was strong enough, so that no visible motion took place under the impact of the bird's landing."

I have never seen a northern shrike on the ground, nor can I find anything in the literature as to its method of progression there. It must jump or hop vigorously in pursuit of grasshoppers or crickets. Dr. Miller (1931) says that "loggerhead shrikes hop but do not walk. In moving sideways or backward one foot is moved independently of the other. While hopping, the body is held erect and the head held high unless the bird is engaged in investigating objects close to the ground." Probably the northern shrike progresses in a similar manner.

Voice.—I did not hear the northern shrike sing in Labrador. The singing season had evidently passed, as the young birds were fully grown and the molting season was at hand. The only notes I heard were a variety of twittering, chattering, squealing, or whistling notes, with occasional gurgling warbles in soft tones. Other observers of Labrador birds do not mention its song.

The males, and sometimes the females, have often been heard singing at various times during their sojourn in the United States and much has been written about it. Aretas A. Saunders writes to me: "I first heard it many years ago in March, before I kept definite notes of singing. The only records I find of hearing the song in late years are November 8, 1921, March 25, and April 8, 1922. It is a long-continued song, suggesting that of the mockingbird, but containing more harsh notes."

Francis H. Allen describes it in his notes as a "song of indeterminate length, composed of caws and scraping notes and short, very pleasing liquid trills, with occasional whistling notes. The notes may be single and staccato, or given in series of three or four in the manner of a mockingbird. The whole is a formless, disjointed performance. When fleeing from an attacking crow, a shrike sounded a prolonged rattle of high-pitched 'beady' notes—like *pip-pip-pip-pip*, etc., uttered very rapidly."

Eugene P. Bicknell (1884) writes:

I have heard a variety of notes from it in October, on its first arrival, and in November; but its highest vocal achievement is in late winter and early spring. * * * An unusually vocal bird was observed on February 10, 1877—a morning when winter seemed quietly relaxing from long-continued severity. Perched in the sunlight, on the topmost spray of a tall oak, on an eminence commanding an expanse of changing landscape, it was alternately singing and preening its beautiful plumage. The song was a medley of varied and rather disconnected articulations, an occasional low warble always being quickly extinguished by harsh notes, even as the bird's gentle demeanor would soon be interrupted by some deed of cruelty.

Frederic H. Kennard records in his notes the capture of a singing shrike on his grounds, and says: "I heard its warble, but having seen a robin before I saw the shrike, I thought it must be a young robin practicing, so like were the notes. I thought, however, that the young robin was mighty hoarse, so went to investigate. On dissection, this singing shrike proved to be a female." A similar experience is thus recorded by Dr. Arthur Chadbourne (1890): "On the morning of April 8, 1890, when walking through the Fresh Pond Swamps at Cambridge, I heard a Butcher Bird (*Lanius borealis*) in full song. The bird was an usually fine singer, and quite a mimic, its medley of notes suggesting a combination of the Brown Thrasher and the Blue Jay, with an occasional 'mewing' sound much like the common Catbird. It was shot, and on sexing proved a female, the ovary being considerably enlarged."

Several other observers have referred to the shrike's power of mimicry. Mr. Forbush (1929) adds the song sparrow to those named above, and says: "One day Mr. Wm. C. Wheeler, who can imitate many bird songs, whistled the song of a Robin as he approached a Northern Shrike. The bird immediately mocked his rendition of the song, and repeated it after him thrice."

Field marks.—Shrikes look superficially somewhat like chunky mockingbirds with thick heavy heads and bills, but there is a black band on the head, through and behind the eye; in the adult shrike the back is clearer, gull gray, browner in the young, and the breast is vermiculated with dusky; there is also much less white in the wings and tail; the latter is proportionately shorter than in the mockingbird. Its posture and behavior are quite different. The loggerhead shrike is slightly smaller and is purer gray above and whiter below than the northern shrike.

Enemies.—The worst enemy that the northern shrike ever encountered was the man with the gun on Boston Common, who killed over 50 of the birds in a single winter, many years ago, to protect the English sparrows soon after their importation. The tables are turned now, for one of the best things the shrike does is to help reduce the numbers of this ubiquitous foreigner, so the shrikes are now welcomed in the cities.

Harold S. Peters (1936) lists only one louse, *Philopterus subflavescens*, as an external parasite on the northern shrike.

Winter.—The northern shrike comes southward to spend the winter in varying numbers at more or less regular intervals, depending probably on the variations in its food supply in its summer home. Sometimes it is abundant in New England in winter, sometimes rare, and sometimes entirely absent or very local. They were reported as very abundant in the winter of 1878–79. Mr. Floyd (1928) called attention to a decided invasion in the winter of 1926–27, in Maine, New Hampshire, Vermont, Massachusetts, Rhode Island, Connecticut, New York, and New Jersey, and they were unusually plentiful in Nova Scotia. He corresponded with bird-banders from New England to Virginia and learned that "during the six months from October to April, sixty-two Shrikes were reported destroyed by banders, while eight were banded and released." He attempted to learn whether the abundance of shrikes coincided with the heavy invasions of redpolls, siskins, and other small northern birds, on which the shrike might prey, but the data accumulated did not confirm this theory; in fact, there was only one year out of eight in which the small birds and shrikes were both abundant.

David E. Davis (1937) has made a study of this subject and says in his interesting paper on it:

The Northern Shrike (*Lanius borealis borealis*) has attracted attention by its occurrence in New England and adjoining States in large numbers in certain years. Since the species is predatory, a correlation with the well-known cycle of mice (*Microtus* spp., *Dicrostonyx* spp.) was suspected. * * * A thorough examination of the available literature was made for records concerning shrike invasions. It was soon apparent that the Christmas Bird Census in "Bird-Lore" supplied the only data which could be used to compare one year with another. These records are here presented in a graph showing the number of birds observed per census for each Christmas period. * * * That there is a definite cycle is at once apparent from the graph. The average is 4.2 years. It should be noted that there are two five-year periods and no three-year periods. The winters of maximum abundance are 1900–01; 1905–06; 1909–10; 1913–14; 1917–18; 1921–22; 1926–27; 1930–31; 1934–35. That there was a maximum in the winter of 1900–01 is supported by Brewster (1906) who states that shrikes were not seen in 1902, 1903, or 1904, but were rather common in 1901. * * * It is quite obvious that the mice increase and periodically die out. During the increase of mice, the predators likewise increase. * * * When the mice disappear the predators first exhaust other prey and then either migrate or die.

Range.—In the Eastern Hemisphere: to the limit of trees from Norway to western Siberia; in winter south to central France, northern Italy, western Rumania, and central Russia. In America, from Alaska and northern Canada to the central part of the United States.

Breeding range.—The American races of the northern shrike breed **north** to the limit of trees in northern Alaska (Lower Noatak River, Kobuk Valley, and Seward Creek near Circle); central Yukon (Ogilvie Range); northern Mackenzie (Fort McPherson, Fort Anderson, McVicar Bay on Great Bear Lake, and Fort Reliance); northern Manitoba (Lac du Brochet and Churchill); and northern Quebec (Chimo). **East** to northern Quebec (Chimo and Indian House Lake); and Labrador (Lake Melville and the east coast). **South** to Labrador (Lake Melville); central Quebec (possibly Anticosti Island, Lake Abitibi); northern Ontario (Moose Factory and Fort Severn, probably; casually to Ottawa and Toronto); central Saskatchewan (Prince Albert and Carlton House; casually to Qu'Appelle); northern Alberta (Athabaska Delta); northern British Columbia (Thudade Lake and Atlin); southwestern Yukon (near Burwash Landing); and southern Alaska (Homer, mouth of the Chulitna River, and Nushagak). **West** to western Alaska (Nushagak, Kigluaik, and the Noatak River).

Winter range.—The northern shrike probably winters occasionally nearly as far north as it breeds but winter records from much of that region are scarce. In the southern part of its winter range it is quite irregular, and it is likely that its southward wanderings are in search of food. Insofar as actual records go, this shrike winters **north** to central Alaska (Flat, Toklat River, and Chilkat); central British Columbia (Francois Lake and probably Thudade Lake); central Alberta (Belvedere, Edmonton, and Camrose); central and southern Saskatchewan (Cochin and Lake Johnstone); southern Manitoba (Aweme, Lake St. Martin, and Hillside Beach, Lake Winnipeg); central Quebec (Great Whale River, Quebec, and Bonaventure Island); and northern Newfoundland (Hare Bay). **East** to Newfoundland (Hare Bay, Salmonier, and Tompkins); Nova Scotia (Antigonish and Bridgetown); New Brunswick (Grand Manan); the New England States and Long Island (Orient); and occasionally central New Jersey (Morristown and Barnegat Bay). **South** to central New Jersey (Barnegat); southeastern Pennsylvania (Philadelphia, occasionally); Maryland (Baltimore); District of Columbia, rarely: North Carolina, rare or accidental (Pea Island); West Virginia (White Sulphur Springs, rarely; northern Ohio (Salem, Oberlin, and Toledo); occasionally southern Indiana (Bloomington and Vincennes); rarely southern Illinois (Mount Carmel); central Missouri

(St. Louis, St. Charles, and Columbia); southern Kansas (Wichita and Coolidge); accidental at Fayetteville and Van Buren, Ark., and at Decatur, Tex.; south-central Colorado (Pueblo, Colorado Springs, and Salida); northern Utah (Ogden); central western Nevada (Reese River, Lahontan Valley, and Carson); and northern California (Rolands Marsh and Marysville); also occurs rarely or accidentally south to north central New Mexico (Las Vegas and Santa Fe); central Arizona (Flagstaff and Prescott), southwestern Utah (St. George), and central California (Sacramento). West to central California (Marysville); western Oregon (Grants Pass, Corvallis, and Blaine); western Washington (Seattle, Sequin, and Bellingham); western British Columbia (Crescent, Courtney, and Francois Lake); and Alaska (Chilkat, Bethel, Akiak, and Flat).

The above ranges for the species in North America are divided into two geographic races. The northern shrike (*L. b. borealis*) breeds east of Hudson Bay; the northwestern shrike (*L. b. invictus*) breeds from Alaska to Manitoba.

Migration.—From the available records the northern shrike appears to be quite irregular in its migratory movements. Dates of spring departure are: Pennsylvania—Harrisburg, March 10. New York—New York, April 17. Massachusetts—Harvard, April 4. Maine—Wells, April 26. Ontario—Ottawa, April 18. Ohio—Oberlin, April 3. Michigan—Grand Rapids, March 29. Iowa—Grinnell, March 31. Wisconsin—New London, March 23. Kansas—Manhattan, March 29. Nebraska—Neligh, March 31. South Dakota—Vermillion, March 28. North Dakota—Charlson, March 12. Manitoba—Margaret, April 6. Saskatchewan—Indian Head, April 21. Colorado—Yuma, April 4. Wyoming—Laramie, April 15. Montana—Bozeman, April 3. Washington—Pullman, April 8. British Columbia—Okanagan Landing, April 20.

Early dates of spring arrival are: Mackenzie—Fort Liard, April 2. British Columbia—Atlin, April 18. Alaska—Fairbanks, March 31.

Late dates of fall departure are: Alaska—Bethel, November 7. Yukon—Forty Mile, October 12. Mackenzie—Simpson, October 12. British Columbia—Atlin, October 12.

Early dates of fall arrival are: British Columbia—Chilliwack, September 27. Washington—Tacoma, October 11. Montana—Fortine, September 27. Wyoming—Yellowstone National Park, October 15. Colorado—Colorado Springs, October 2. Saskatchewan—Eastend, October 2. Manitoba—Aweme, October 3. North Dakota—Argusville, October 16. South Dakota—Pierre, October 21. Nebraska—Lincoln, October 27. Kansas—Onaga, October 19. Minnesota—Lanesboro, October 18. Wisconsin—La Crosse, October 18. Iowa—Keokuk, October 19. Michigan—Sault Ste. Marie, October 9. Illinois—Glen Ellyn, October 24. Ontario—Toronto, October 15.

Ohio—Youngstown, October 16.   Pennsylvania—Erie, September 21.
Maine—Phillips, October 19.   New Brunswick—Scotch Lake, October 17.   Massachusetts—Danvers, October 31.   New York—Orient, October 22.   District of Columbia—Washington, November 7.

From the few banded northern shrikes the two recoveries available are of some interest.   One banded at Hepburn, Saskatchewan, on July 4, 1931, was found dead on September 23, 1931, at Cross Timbers, Mo.; and another banded at Harwich, Mass., on November 8, 1934, was found dead about April 1, 1936, at Clarenceville, Quebec.

Casual records.—Eight specimens have been collected in Bermuda: October 31, 1846; January 23, 1847; March 12, 1850; January 1872; January 1, 1876; and three without dates.

Egg dates.—Alaska: 2 records, May 21 and June 27.

Labrador: 3 records, June 3 to 17.

Mackenzie: 3 records, May 20 to June 11.

LANIUS BOREALIS INVICTUS Grinnell

NORTHWESTERN SHRIKE

HABITS

This western race of the northern shrike was described by Dr. Joseph Grinnell (1900), who says of it:

L. borealis invictus differs from *L. borealis borealis* in larger size, paler coloration dorsally and greater extent of white markings.   These differences are fairly comparable to those between the southwestern *L. ludovicianus excubitorides* and *L. ludovicianus* proper. * * *

During the fall the Northwestern Shrike was met with in the Kowak Valley rather sparingly.   Single individuals would be seen, one or two in a day's tramp, in the willow bottoms where they were the terror of the redpolls.   On only one occasion did I see more than one in a place. * * * None were seen after October 26th, until March 22nd, when one was secured.   During April and May they became fairly common, that is, for shrikes.

Harry S. Swarth (1926) was evidently not greatly impressed with the wisdom of recognizing this race.   He found that there are Alaskan birds "that lie well within the range of variation of eastern birds, and there are one or two eastern birds with white markings on the tail feathers nearly as extensive as in any western ones."   After examining a series of over 80 specimens, about equally divided between eastern and western birds, he writes: "There are a number of winter birds in this series from points lying between the Great Lakes and the Rocky Mountains, and nearly all of these I am unable to allocate to an eastern or a western race with any degree of assurance.   Thus, while recognizing in the northern shrike a tendency toward development of the characters ascribed to *invictus* in the western part of its habitat, it seems to me so impossible to define the boundary between an eastern and a western race, or to identify most winter birds taken south of the breeding range, that I am disinclined to use different names for the variations exhibited."

Dr. Alden H. Miller (1931) does not agree with the above, saying: "I cannot agree with Swarth (1926, pp. 135, 136) that it is impossible to define the boundary between the eastern and western races of this species, difficult as it is to identify some winter specimens. The boundary line between the breeding ranges is poorly known, I believe, only as a result of the extremely meagre collections of breeding birds from critical localities."

His distributional map shows an area of intergradation from the west coast of Hudson Bay westward for breeding birds, and directly southward from that area into the United States for wintering birds. It is interesting to note that this is just where one would expect to find the intergrades that Mr. Swarth had difficulty in identifying! He says that "an immature specimen from Fort Churchill, Manitoba, taken in July may be considered intermediate between the two races although its dimensions are those of *invictus*." This seems to demonstrate, as satisfactorily as our present knowledge will allow, that *invictus* is the breeding form from this point westward.

Nesting.—Neither Dr. Grinnell nor Mr. Swarth found a nest of this shrike, but Roderick MacFarlane (1908) took a fine nest of the northwestern shrike at Fort Anderson, northern Mackenzie, on June 11, 1863; it was in a spruce tree, 7 feet from the ground; he describes it quite fully, as follows:

It is in many respects in striking contrast with the nests of its kindred species of the Southern States of the Union, far exceeding them in its relative size, in elaborate finish, and warmth. It is altogether a remarkable example of what is known as felted nests, whose various materials are most elaborately matted together into a homogeneous and symmetrical whole. It is seven inches in diameter and three and one half in height. The cavity is proportionately large and deep, having a diameter of four and one-half inches and a depth of two. Except the base, which is composed of a few twigs and stalks of coarse plants, the nest is made entirely of soft and warm materials most elaborately interworked together. These materials are feathers from various birds, fine down of the eider and other ducks, fine mosses and lichens, slender stems, grasses, etc., and are skilfully and artistically wrought into a beautiful and symmetrical nest, strengthened by the interposition of a few slender twigs and stems without affecting the general felt-like character of the whole.

Several nests have been reported, from the more southern portions of Canada, as placed in deciduous trees, but these were probably extra large nests of white-rumped or migrant shrikes.

There is a beautiful nest of this shrike, taken by Johan Koren in Alaska on May 21, 1913, in the Thayer collection in Cambridge. It is a bulky nest, nearly 9 inches in external diameter and about 4 inches in height; the inner cup is over 4 inches in diameter and 2½ inches deep. It is made of coarse grasses and weed stalks, inner bark, and plant down, reinforced with fine and coarse twigs, and thoroughly mixed throughout with white ptarmigan feathers, with which it is also profusely lined, forming a soft, warm bed. It was placed 12 feet from the ground in a cottonwood tree and contained the unusual number of nine handsome eggs.

W. E. Clyde Todd has sent me the following note from Arthur C. Twomey: "A nest of this shrike was found on June 20, 1942, on the outer fringe of the transitional willow community that divides the coniferous forest from the true tundra. It was located six miles west of the southwest tip of Richards Island, Mackenzie River Delta, N. W. T., Canada. The nest was in a dense growth of willows about twelve feet from the ground. It was a large, bulky structure made up of dead willow twigs, dry sedges, grasses, and strips of willow bark. It had a deep inner cavity that was completely lined with a half inch layer of winter ptarmigan feathers. The five half-incubated eggs were well insulated against the rapidly changing temperatures."

Eggs.—The nest described above by MacFarlane (1908) contained six eggs, and he reports another nest that contained eight. The eggs are evidently indistinguishable from those of the northern shrike. He describes them as "of a light greenish ground, marbled and streaked with blotches of obscure purple, clay colour and rufous brown." The measurements of 14 eggs average 27.3 by 20.4 millimeters; the eggs showing the four extremes measure 28.1 by 20.0, 27.3 by 21.0, 26.3 by 20.7, and 26.5 by 20.0 millimeters.

Young.—In the Atlin region of northern British Columbia, Mr. Swarth (1926) collected a brood of six young, "just able to fly," on June 30. "The young birds, huddled together in a spruce thicket, were being fed by one parent, which escaped. * * * The young birds were extremely noisy; it was the incessant squalling for food that drew our attention, from a distance. Their stomachs were well filled, mostly with insect remains, including some small *Coleoptera;* in one stomach there were parts of a very young ptarmigan chick, including the bill."

Plumages.—Mr. Swarth (1926) writes: "A notable feature of the shrikes in juvenal plumage is their gray coloration. In the freshly acquired first winter plumage there is a decidedly brown tone both above and below, but, save for the wing markings, none of this appears in the juvenal stage. This plumage is mostly clear gray, slightly darker on the dorsum, and finely vermiculated below."

An adult male, collected on July 28, "is in the midst of the annual molt. Above and below the old feathers are extremely pale colored. The underparts are almost pure white, the old feathers having lost every vestige of the dusky vermiculations. Such markings show plainly enough on the new breast feathers, just coming in."

Food.—Dr. Grinnell (1900) saw a northwestern shrike "carrying prey to a clump of spruces further up the channel where there must have been a brood of young. On one occasion the bird was carrying a redpoll, but usually it was a lemming or meadow mouse. Once he had grasped in his claws a lemming so heavy that it dragged in the water as the bird flew laboriously across the river." The stomach of an adult collected by Mr. Swarth (1926) held insect remains.

Behavior.—Ernest T. Seton (1911) writes:

One afternoon I heard a peculiar note, at first like the *"cheepy-teet-teet"* of the Pine Grosbeak, only louder and more broken, changing to the jingling of Blackbirds in spring, mixed with some Bluejay "jay-jays," and a Robin-like whistle; then I saw that it came from a Northern Shrike on the bushes just ahead of us. It flew off much after the manner of the Summer Shrike, with flight not truly undulatory nor yet straight, but flapping half a dozen times—then a pause and repeat. He would dive down near the ground, then up with a fine display of wings and tail to the next perch selected, there to repeat with fresh variations and shrieks, the same strange song, and often indeed sang it on the wing, until at last he crossed the river.

S. F. Rathbun (1934) says: "On one occasion we paced this shrike in flight. For more than a mile the bird flew alongside the road or over it and in front of us as we drove, at no time distant more than one hundred feet. The shrike was flying at the rate of thirty-two miles when we first contacted it, but as we kept up with it the bird imperceptibly increased its speed to forty-two miles, and once for an instant reached forty-five miles.

"This test was very fair. There was no wind blowing, and the shrike maintained an almost direct flight either in front of, or nearly at the side of the automobile."

LANIUS LUDOVICIANUS LUDOVICIANUS Linnaeus

LOGGERHEAD SHRIKE

HABITS

CONTRIBUTED BY ALEXANDER SPRUNT, JR.

Among the earliest ornithological memories of the writer is the search for nests of the "French mockingbird" amid the myrtle bushes of the back beach of Sullivans Island, near Charleston, S. C. On this narrow barrier of sea sand, which has figured so largely in history since the days when Sir Peter Parker's fleet was turned away by the batteries of palmetto-logged Fort Moultrie, many Low Country bird records have helped make ornithological fame locally. It was a happy hunting ground for several kindred spirits of schoolboy days, and birds' eggs were mediums of exchange for various and sundry other specimens of beach and marsh. In few other areas since has the writer ever found the loggerhead shrike such a characteristic bird and will always associate it with this spot for it was among the first half dozen species of his "life list."   Though having shown it to many others for their "first" since, long acquaintance with it has not dimmed interest in its attractive way of life.

Misunderstood and rather frowned upon by the uninformed, the loggerhead is one of the decidedly beneficial and valuable birds of its range and its activities are a natural asset of no mean proportions. As its name implies, it was described from Louisiana, by Linnaeus, but the bird is no more typical of that State than many other parts of its habitat.

Spring.—There is little change in the seasonal numbers of the loggerhead in most of its range except in the northern limits.   Elsewhere the population remains largely static as the species is resident throughout most of the country it frequents.   Certainly, numbers in coastal South Carolina, Georgia, most of Florida, and the Gulf coast do not vary appreciably.   In North Carolina (eastern) there is a slight southward movement in fall and a return in spring but it is not pronounced.   Some confusion may exist in that State by the overlapping occurrence of *L. l. migrans* and the difficulty of differentiating between the two in the field.   That both *ludovicianus* and *migrans* occur together there has been demonstrated by T. D. Burleigh, who secured specimens of each at Tarboro, Edgecombe County, N. C., in January 1931 (Pearson and Brimley, 1942).

Courtship.—The courtship performance is not particularly elaborate or widely commented upon.   It is undertaken with much fluttering of the wings and some spreading of the tail in display on the part of the male.   Considerable erratic chases of the female occur at times, the birds twisting and turning almost like sandpipers over the surf, for apparently the female does not take very kindly to watching the male display at length.

Audubon (1842) was somewhat cavalier in his opinion of this phase of the loggerhead's way of life.   He says flatly that "the male courts the female without much regard, and she, in return, appears to receive his haughty attentions with merely just as much condescension as enables her to become the mother of a family, whose feelings are destined to be of the same cold nature."   He follows this later in his account with a quotation from the Rev. John Bachman as follows: "You speak of the male showing but little attachment to the female. I have thought differently, and so would you were you to watch him carrying * * * a grasshopper or cricket to her, pouncing upon the Crow and even the Buzzard, that approach the nest, and invariably driving these intruders away.   Indeed I consider these birds as evidencing great attachment toward each other."

Living in the same area from which Dr. Bachman wrote these words, and where he saw so much of the loggerhead, the writer agrees with him completely. He has never noted any trait that would tend to prove that the loggerhead was lacking in domestic responsibility.

Nesting.—This species is an early nester, even in regions where early nesting is indulged by other avian forms. It is another point of similarity to the birds of prey, for the loggerhead is decidedly reminiscent of that order in many ways. Though Florida shows the earliest dates for nesting (which is to be expected) there is not a great deal of difference between it and coastal South Carolina or Georgia. In all of these the loggerhead sometimes begins nest-building in February, but March is more nearly normal.

Arthur H. Howell (1932) lists February 9 as an early Florida record, this nesting being near Gainesville. The birds usually begin to build in the Lake Okeechobee region late in February, and are incubating during the first week of March. In the Pensacola area (much to the north and west) the latter part of March is more typical, and F. M. Weston (MS.) states that the first brood is raised by "early April." Nests with eggs found by him in mid-May he says are "almost certainly a second brood." Similar dates are typical of southern Georgia. Fresh eggs on or after the middle of May in either region are doubtless a second laying.

C. H. Pangburn (1919) believes that the loggerhead is the third commonest nesting bird in Pinellas County, Fla., and that the young are flying the last week in March. S. A. Grimes (1928) puts it second in the Jacksonville area, outnumbered only by the mockingbird.

Dr. E. E. Murphey, of Augusta, Ga., has a nesting date of March at that locality. Arthur T. Wayne (1919) states that he was informed by G. R. Rossignol that the latter found a nest and five eggs at Savannah on February 15, 1919. Nest-building by this pair began on January 16. This is a very early date and may be considered the earliest Georgia record.

Nesting in South Carolina in some years varies little from that in Florida. Wayne (1910) has noted birds mated by mid-February and says that nests are often built late that month. Bad weather in March frequently delays nest construction, however, and not infrequently the birds abandon original efforts and start new nests. Average time for the Charleston region is late in March. Files of the Charleston Museum show that incubating birds were found by F. M. Weston on March 18, 1913, and March 19, 1911. Wayne's earliest breeding record was March 13, 1917. The writer found a nest with five fresh eggs on March 28, 1914. While living in the city of Charleston he was accustomed to find nests of this species every year on the street in front of his home. There was a line of small live-oak trees planted there (the area was all "made" land, having been reclaimed from the Ashley River), and their thick, tough twigs were ideal nesting sites.

One tree, about 12 or 15 feet high, across the street from his house, always had a nest in it every season, and in 1924 one was built and the young raised by mid-April. On June 22 another nest was built in the same tree about 5 feet from the first one (same pair of birds doubtless), which was still in excellent condition. H. K. Job visited the writer while the first nest was in use and photographed it.

In the northern rim of its range (eastern North Carolina) the loggerhead nests noticeably later than elsewhere. T. Gilbert Pearson and the Brimleys (1942) list fresh eggs as having been found in Columbus County on May 6, in Bladen County, May 7, completed nests but no eggs. At the same date, however, young just out of the nest were seen! Probably late April would be normal for many breeding pairs, just about one month later than South Carolina birds. Again, at the western terminus of its range the loggerhead is late. Dr. H. C. Oberholser (1938) states that "it breeds in Louisiana from April to June, and there is record of eggs as early as April 16." If the latter is an early date for Louisiana it is obvious that the loggerhead is far behind its eastern dates in its western home.

The nest itself is built at medium elevations, never very high and seldom close to the ground; 8 to 15 feet is normal. It picks out heavily twigged growth, though its early habits often reveal the nest to any observer as it is completed before the leaves come out. Young oaks are favorites, and these, of course, retain their leaves. Such trees are widely used in coastal South Carolina, and the species often nests in towns and cities, even on streets carrying considerable traffic.

The loggerhead is a good architect and builder. Though somewhat bulky, the nest is well made and lasts long after its usefulness is over. The materials are usually thick twigs, firmly woven and lined with rootlets or fibers and, in the rural sections, often padded with cotton. The latter is a characteristic item among a varied range of material. Others are string (often used), feathers of various kinds, hair, palmetto fiber, weeds, small sticks, grass, "rabbit-tobacco" (everlasting), rags, and occasionally paper. M. G. Vaiden, of Rosedale, Miss. (MS.), once found a piece of blue bottle glass in a nest!

Both sexes work on the nest and very assiduously. Incubation consumes 10 to 12 days, and both male and female engage in the duty. S. A. Grimes (1928) gives 14 days for incubation.

E. R. Ford (1936) gives an account of an unusual nesting site with regard to elevation, which he found at Fort Lauderdale, Fla., on March 5. The birds began building that day "on one of the lower branches of a long-leafed yellow pine. The site was a little more than fifty feet from the ground. * * * Except on one occasion, I had never seen the nest of any Shrike more than eight or ten feet up, [and] I made it a point to observe this one particularly." This height is very abnormal and can be considered the extreme.

Two broods are usually raised, though in coastal South Carolina there are often three in a season. It is interesting to note that Audubon's (1842) account is contradictory in that he says in the early part of his biography of the species that "loggerheads rear only one brood in the season" and later, quoting Rev. John Bachman, that "this species breeds twice in a season." The latter is the correct statement, applying to the greater part of the range.

An example of what amounts to practically colony nesting of the loggerhead is furnished by M. G. Vaiden, of Rosedale, Miss. He says (MS.) that on April 9, 1937, he was driving near the site of the old town of Concordia (Miss.) now inundated by the river. Along the levee was a hedgerow of dwarf thorn bushes or small trees (*Crataegus uniflora*), and shrikes were noted flying in and out of them. Careful investigation revealed that nearly every tree held occupied nests, and 14 were found in 13 trees! Eight nests contained eggs; the others were either just completed or still building. Eggs were found in them a few days later. This is a remarkable observation, and the writer has never heard it approached, but Mr. Vaiden says that he once saw another similar instance. This was the finding of seven nests in thorn trees along an unused road also in Mississippi. No two nests were more than 60 feet apart, and it was not over 200 feet from the first to the last nest in a straight line down the road. The writer has often found two or three loggerhead nests in trees fairly close together, the distance of a city block for instance, but never anything that would justify an illustration of colony nesting.

S. A. Grimes (1928) gives an interesting observation of communal use of the same nest by loggerheads as follows:

A nest about eight feet up in an oak, found March 15th, 1925, was built on a thrasher nest of the preceding year. Revisiting this nest a week later, I was much astonished to find seven eggs in it, and two broken eggs on the ground below. The eggs were obviously not all laid by the same bird, for five were of a dark ground color and minutely speckled with dark brown, whereas the set of four, two of which were on the ground, were of a much lighter ground color * * * and there were three solicitous Loggerheads berating me on all sides. This was a plain case of avian bigamy. The nest was destroyed a night or two later, apparently by someone's treacherous house cat. Within a day or two, the "pair" began making a new nest fifteen feet up in a pine sapling * * *. On April 5th, this nest held five dark eggs and one light egg. Nine days later it contained three light-colored eggs and only four of the dark variety, and in the grass beneath were two of the less densely speckled eggs. This nest subsequently met the fate of the first. At least nineteen eggs, but from them not one Loggerhead to enhance, with futile loquacity and sprightliness, the attractiveness of a bit of shaded street or tree-lined field.

Eggs.—[AUTHOR'S NOTE: The sets of eggs laid by the loggerhead shrike may consist of four to six eggs, though four and five are probably commoner numbers than six. These are practically indistinguishable from those of other races of the species, which are well described under the California shrike. The measurements of 50 eggs of this southeastern race, in the United States National Museum, average 24.2 by 18.7 millimeters; the eggs showing the four extremes measure 25.9 by 18.3, 23.6 by 19.9, 22.3 by 18.7, and 23.4 by 17.8 millimeters.]

Plumages.—[AUTHOR'S NOTE: The sequence of molts and plumages is the same as for the migrant shrike, to which the reader is referred.]

Food.—The local name of the loggerhead in many localities, i. e., butcherbird, is indicative of the popular opinion of its food habits. However, popular opinion in this case, as in so many others, is often erroneous in its conclusions. The basis for the rather generally held belief that the species is injurious lies in the undoubted fact that it sometimes does take small birds. This habit, however, is not widely or even generally indulged and is much more the exception than the rule. The condemnation of the bird for it, therefore, is again reminiscent of the treatment meted out to the birds of prey, so widespread and detrimental to that group.

In certain respects the loggerhead exhibits predatory habits, and if such a combination can be visualized it might be said to be a passerine raptor! Not possessing talons with which to grip prey while feeding, it resorts to the well-known and thoroughly characteristic trait of impaling its victims upon thorns, barbed wire, or other sharp projections; hence the local name butcherbird.

Naturally, what birds are taken are small ones. Little of definite information appears in the literature regarding specific varieties, but there is much generalization. Sparrows and warblers appear to make up the bulk of small-bird prey. The writer has seen myrtle warblers (*Dendroica coronata*) victimized on at least two occasions, and English sparrows (*Passer domesticus*) are fairly often taken in cities and towns, probably because of the ease with which they are secured.

Wright and Harper (1913) relate that they saw a loggerhead chasing a red-cockaded woodpecker (*Dryobates borealis*) in the Okefenokee Swamp in southeastern Georgia and found the remains of one young and one adult bluebird (*Sialia sialis*) on a stump, also the work of the shrike. Pearson and the Brimleys (1942) record the finding of the dried body of a myrtle warbler on a thorn by C. S. Brimley and a similarly treated chipping sparrow (*Spizella passerina*) by Pearson. The brains of the sparrow had been eaten from a cavity in the back of the skull. Observations by F. H. Craighill are quoted by these authors to the effect that he has seen "young birds" hanging in small plum trees but apparently no identification was made of the young. Craighill is further quoted as saying: "Last week I saw a shrike pursuing a small bird with evident felonious intent. I had never before seen that here [Rocky Mount, N. C.] except when there was snow on the ground and shrike food was scarce." Again, there is no identification of the "small bird."

H. L. Stoddard writes me that a shrike got into a banding trap of one of his neighbors near Beachton, Ga., and killed a chipping sparrow. "The queer part of the thing was that there was a stiff straw through the sparrow's neck," he says. "I went down and got the bird and found that the shrike had pinched at the neck and broken it in several places. The only explanation of the presence of the straw that occurs to me is that the instinct to hang prey on a twig or thorn is a very strong one. The shrike would have been unable to eat the sparrow in the usual way as there was no place in the trap to hang it (and shrikes are probably unable to hold prey in the feet as do birds of prey). Hence it had worked the stiff straw through the neck in an attempt to anchor the bird for eating. At first glance this would seem impossible, but when we remember the skill in nest-building it does not seem so remarkable. The straw was stuck through between the gullet and windpipe just above the breast in the exact spot where shrikes usually hang the small birds they kill."

E. G. Holt (1913) watched a loggerhead near Barachias, Ala., kill a mockingbird (*Mimus polyglottos*). It was during a severe freeze, and the shrike attacked and pinned down the mocker, striking it repeatedly with its beak and soon killing it. Holt then interrupted proceedings by picking up the dead bird and examining it; then, as he held it in his outstretched hand, the shrike returned and attempted to take it. Subsequent observation revealed that it removed the mockingbird's entrails through a small hole above the kidneys.

Loggerheads rather frequently incur the wrath of owners of canaries in attacks on these cage birds. When a cage is placed on a porch or anywhere outside, it seems to be an irresistible attraction to shrikes in the vicinity. When one alights on the cage it produces panic in the canary, which, instead of remaining in the middle of the perch where it would be perfectly safe, often sticks its head out between the bars. Thereupon it is clipped neatly off by the shrike, or so pierced by its beak that death is the result. The writer's mother lost three canaries in this way while summering on a beach resort near Charleston, S. C., a place where loggerheads were abundant.

The food of the loggerhead is nearly entirely animal in character. Food of eastern shrikes is wholly of this category, though examination of some of the western subspecies showed that vegetable matter amounted to 2.5 percent (F. E. L. Beal, 1912). Professor Beal's researches further revealed that the eastern bird shows a breakdown of 68 percent insects, 4 percent spiders, and 28 percent vertebrates. These studies were based on the contents of 88 stomachs. Distinct seasonal variation appears in the food take, for it has been established that the warm seasons show a preponderance of insect prey secured, while in winter the greater part consists of mice and small birds.

Among the insects the Orthoptera compose the largest item. Grasshoppers and crickets make up 39 percent. In August and September these constitute 70 percent of the total food, though they are taken in every month of the year. Among the crickets, which are not so acceptable as grasshoppers, the so-called wood cricket is often taken, numbers of the genus *Stenopelmatus* being particularly noticeable. These insects usually live under leaves and stones and avoid light but not to the extent of remaining undetected by the remarkable vision of the loggerhead.

Beetles are eaten to the amount of somewhat in excess of 16 percent. Ground beetles (Carabidae) and carrion beetles (Silphidae) compose 7 percent of this total; the rest are harmful varieties. Ants and wasps are represented by only 3 percent, the latter outnumbering the former. Moths and caterpillars form 4 percent. Bugs, flies, and a few other odd insects total 5 percent.

Spiders make up 4 percent of the loggerhead's diet, while the vertebrates (28 percent) include mammals, birds, and reptiles. Of these, mice compose by far the bulk. A. H. Howell (1932) quotes Judd (1898) as saying that mice are taken "at all seasons and in winter comprise half the food." He adds that "birds make up only 8 percent of the food for the year." Certainly, this predilection of the loggerhead for mice, and the fact that half the winter food is made up of these animals, should go far to prove the great value of the shrike to agricultural interests. Audubon went the length of saying that mice "form the principal food of the grown birds at all seasons."

Alexander Wilson (Wilson and Bonaparte, 1832) wrote that on the rice plantations of Carolina and Georgia "it [the loggerhead] is protected for its usefulness in destroying mice." He describes it as sitting near stacks of rice and "watching like a cat; and as soon as it perceives a mouse, darts on it like a Hawk." Evidently the loggerhead was more appreciated in Carolina then than it is now.

Occasionally, extraneous items appear in the shrike's food, or attacks are made on forms not usually associated with its diet. N. C. Longee, of Gainesville, Fla. (Howell, 1932), saw a shrike bring a number of large, live cattle ticks to a barbed-wire fence and impale them thereon. Howell once saw a lizard being eaten. F. M. Weston (MS.) states that he witnessed near Pensacola, Fla., the chase of a bat by a shrike on "a bright summer day," but the animal eluded two attacks and escaped. The writer has seen a loggerhead chase a bat once and failed to secure it. Weston adds that he once found a small terrapin of "quarter-dollar size" that had been taken and impaled by a loggerhead. E. S. Dingle, of Huger, S. C., writes (MS.) that he saw a loggerhead kill a frog, fly away with it in the beak for a short distance, and then transfer it to the feet in flight. The frog was carried about 200 feet in this manner to a live-oak tree.

Audubon (1842) quotes the Rev. John Bachman as saying: "I have seen one [shrike] occupy himself for hours in sticking up [on thorns] * * * a number of small fishes that the fishermen had thrown on the shore * * *. The fishes dried up and decayed."

Pearson and the Brimleys (1942) give an interesting observation on a shrike "larder" in a residential section of High Point, Guilford County, N. C. It was composed of "no less than fifteen small snakes" impaled on the thorns of a bush. They also state that F. H. Craig-hill, of Rocky Mount, N. C., found a loggerhead's cache of a snake, a crayfish, and a grasshopper.

Alluding once more to its bird-killing propensities, observations by S. A. Grimes, of Jacksonville, Fla. (1928), reveal that the loggerheads "take fledgling English Sparrows from their nests in holes made by woodpeckers. Perched in the entrance, heedless of the frantic chatter-ing of the sparrows without, the Shrike, in each instance, appeared to be having no little difficulty in seizing one of the young sparrows. The squealing victim was invariably held by the head. On one occasion the struggling sparrow succeeded in freeing itself, but was recap-tured and promptly thrust on a barb of a nearby fence."

Behavior.—The loggerhead presents a striking combination of absolute immobility and intense activity. To see one sitting on a telephone wire awaiting prey is to see a bird as motionless as if it were cast in bronze. The next moment it may be dashing through the air like a winged meteor to pounce accurately upon a spot many yards away. These alternating periods of activity and inactivity are very characteristic.

Essentially a bird of open country, it is a still hunter in the main and always chooses an elevated and conspicuous perch. This may be the topmost twig of a tree or bush, roadside wires or fences, or any such advantage giving a wide and uninterrupted view. Charlotte H. Green, however (1933), states that the bird has "another method of hunting. Like the crows, he sometimes sneaks upon his victim from the ground." She gives no specific observation relating to such procedure, and it must be a rather uncommon occurrence. The writer has never happened to witness it in his long experience with the species, and certainly it is not freely indulged.

The vision of the loggerhead is phenomenal, even for a bird. That it can and does see insects at remarkable distances is unquestioned. When living in the Battery Section of Charleston in an area then being developed residentially, the writer has often sat on the porch and watched loggerheads hunting in adjacent vacant lots. Frequently a bird would pitch off the wires and glide, or fly, 50 to 70 yards in a direct line to a spot in the grasses and seize a grasshopper. No hov-ering or hesitancy is shown in these sudden dashes. The bird goes directly to a specific spot, and there is no doubt whatever that the intended prey was seen before the bird left the perch.

Weather affects the activity of the loggerhead because it reacts on the food supply. S. A. Grimes (1928) says: "Two of the elements greatly facilitate the capturing of food for the Shrike. Heavy rains drive the subterranean inhabitants to the surface, where they are exposed to the bird's keen sight; and the grass fire, routing number-less insects, form a veritable cornucopia for this and other species." Weather has adverse effects also as witnessed by F. M. Weston, of Pensacola, Fla., who says (MS.): "After the prolonged freeze of January 1940, both shrikes and sparrow hawks (*Falco sparverius*) disappeared from this region for the rest of the winter." The ab-sence of two species sharing the same sort of food leads him to believe that intense and *prolonged* cold "did away with the winter insect life right down to the grass roots" a most reasonable and logical conclu-sion.

The flight of the loggerhead is accomplished by very rapid vibra-tions of the wings, an almost labored fluttering, it seems. It does not, however, give the impression of wasted energy. Periods of sail-ing intervene, and the course is usually at low elevations. When se-lecting a perch it sweeps upward to it in a steep glide. When leav-ing, it drops a few feet, then catches the air with the wings, and pro-ceeds with the characteristic rapid beats. The speed attained in flight has been given by Gordon Aymar (1935) at 22 to 28 m. p. h. based on "specific records."

A sidelight on the flight is indicated by A. L. Pickens, of Paducah, Ky., who writes (MS): "Another name for the loggerhead shrike in the South is cotton-picker, probably from its bobbing waves of flight above the cotton rows, as if darting down here and there to pluck off a fleece." The writer has never heard this name applied to the bird anywhere in its range but would think that its derivation would be much more apt to apply to the frequent use of cotton in nest-building than the "probable" reason given above.

The outstanding trait of the loggerhead is its habit of impaling victims on thorns, barbed-wire fences, and similar sharp projections. This accounts for the local name so universally in vogue—butcher-bird. Supposedly, it is done for the reason of storing a food supply, but probably also to assist in tearing the prey apart in many cases, as the loggerhead does not have very strong claws. The future food supply idea is, no doubt, much more applicable to the northern shrike (*Lanius borealis*), for the food in the loggerhead's range is so abun-dant and constantly available that there is rarely an occasion when the bird has to resort to already secured prey. Conversely, there are doubtless times when the northern bird is hard put to it in winter and uses a larder far more frequently. Regarding the loggerhead, indeed, many have questioned whether it ever does return to impaled prey. The frequent finding of dried bodies of birds, snakes, and insects by many observers, ignored completely by the bird, leads to such an impression.

Pearson and the Brimleys (1942) states: "Whether this bird hangs up food for future use has not been definitely established. The authors of this book have not known shrikes to return to the grasshoppers, beetles * * * that they had impaled." However, it is certainly the case that this *is* sometimes done. H. L. Stoddard (MS.) writes me: "There used to be a question in my mind as to whether shrikes ever returned to their food caches, after such prey had dried out through hanging on a twig or wire. I settled this question to my satisfaction one day in the yard here at home [Sherwood Plantation, Grady County, Ga.]. Noticing a shrike flying through the yard with a sizable object, I grabbed up a clod and threw it at the shrike, which dropped the object. This proved to be a brittle dead twig about 2 inches long, to which firmly adhered the dried remains of a myrtle warbler. Evidently the shrike had returned to prey hung many days before and in trying to remove the warbler had broken off the twig that anchored it."

So, then, it is safe to conclude that the loggerhead does not ordinarily return to impaled prey but occasionally does so.

Curiously enough, Audubon (1842) makes this remarkable statement: "I have never seen it attack birds, nor stick its prey on thorns in the manner of the Great American Shrike." Whether he means that he did not actually see this accomplished, or whether he never found any evidence of it, is not clear, but it seems that the latter was meant. If so, it is almost beyond belief, since he spent much time in the loggerhead's range, and it would be most natural to conclude that he would have found something of the sort during his expeditions. He does, however, quote the Rev. John Bachman, who wrote him that he had "never found either this or the Northern Shrike return to such prey for food. * * * I have seen them alight on the same thorn bush afterwards, but never made any use of this kind of food."

Some evidence that the loggerhead occasionally indulges in a kind of play, reminiscent of certain hawks, is contained in an observation related to me by Herbert R. Sass, of Charleston, S. C. He happened to be watching a pigeon sitting on the roof of his house one day, when a loggerhead suddenly appeared in the air behind and above the pigeon and, diving straight at it, struck it a resounding blow in the back! The startled pigeon was knocked completely off the roof and fell several feet before recovering its balance and spreading its wings. No effort was made by the shrike as a follow-up; apparently it simply indulged a sudden impulse, as it cannot be supposed that it meant to seek the pigeon as prey.

An observation by E. J. Reimann (1938) reveals a rather unusual encounter between a loggerhead and a yellow chicken snake (*Elaphe q. quadrivittata*) at Marco Island, Fla. While perhaps an indication of an attempt to secure food, it may have been an instance of the tendency to play, similar to that above, for the size of the snake would rather preclude the idea of the bird being able to despatch it. At any rate, Reimann says that noting a group of men watching something on the ground, he found the shrike attacking the snake. He says:

> The snake would crawl forward over the ground, and the shrike would fly down from a telegraph wire and, hovering over the snake, would pounce down, grasp the snake by the tail, rise in the air about six inches, and let the tail drop. The snake would immediately fall into a defensive coil and the shrike would alight on the ground about two feet away. It remained there until the snake again wandered off; then it would hover, pounce, and grasp the tail as before. Sitting along a telegraph wire close by, were four newly fledged young shrikes * * * a Mockingbird was also perched on the wire, but the young shrikes took no part in the combat. Due to coming dusk, the shrikes finally moved off and I threw the snake under an old building, to save it from the crowd that had gathered there.

Another instance of a shrike-snake encounter is submitted by M. G. Vaiden (MS.), but it appears to be directly an attempt at securing food. Driving along a country road on July 4, 1926, he saw a shrike flying across ahead of him carrying, with great difficulty, a snake in its beak. At last it reached the top of a telephone pole, and there a real battle took place. The snake was very much alive and twisted, beat, and turned energetically while the shrike kept striking at it with its beak. After several minutes of watching, he states, "I broke up this feeding, as I had more feeling for the snake than for the shrike." Throwing a clod or two at the pair was enough to drive the bird off, and the snake dropped to the ground, still alive but somewhat "bunged up." It proved to be a rough-scaled green snake (*Opheodrys aestivus*) and measured 16½ inches long. He concludes by adding: "Unfortunately I did not weigh this reptile, but I know that the shrike was handling much more than its own weight. The lifting power of the shrike must be more than the average expected of small birds." This is a very interesting observation as it reveals the loggerhead as proportionately more powerful than the bald eagle (*Haliaeetus leucocephalus*). The latter is said by most authorities to be unable to lift more than its own weight, or at the maximum, very little more. The shrike in the foregoing account was handling "much more" than its own weight, though Mr. Vaiden does admit that the snake was not actually weighed. None the less, it is a striking illustration of the virility and determination embodied in this passerine species.

The loggerhead maintains definite territorial limits and protects them assiduously. S. A. Grimes states that he has often noticed that "each pair of shrikes has an apparently well-defined domain of its own, which it holds defiantly to the exclusion of others of its kind." Other species often nest in fairly close proximity, however, without molestation.

Some observers have considered the loggerhead as a quarrelsome species, but, though instances of it no doubt take place, the writer has never been impressed with this as a characteristic. On the whole, the bird gets along very well with its avian neighbors, some of which are very close neighbors at times. Audubon (1842) had a rather poor opinion of the loggerhead's disposition, for he says, in explanation of his drawing, that "I have given you, kind reader, the representative of a pair of these Shrikes, contending for a mouse. The difference of plumage in the sexes is scarcely perceptible; but I have thought it necessary to figure both, in order to shew the quarrelsome disposition of these birds even when united by the hymeneal band."

Voice.—Though the loggerhead has little reputation in vocal performance, it has always seemed to the writer that what attainment is reached has been rather cavalierly treated in the literature. Few descriptions of its notes are complimentary! While it can hardly be said to be a singer, its efforts in spring are worthy of some notice and, in certain individuals at any rate, possess a surprisingly melodious quality. It is true that such notes are interspersed with others anything but musical, but the general effect is a liquid tone that is definitely pleasing.

Howell (1932) says: "The birds are not noisy but most of their notes are harsh and unmusical; occasionally one makes an attempt at singing, which Chapman describes as 'a series of guttural gurgles, squeaky whistles and shrill pipes.'" It is the impression of the writer that *all* male shrikes "make an attempt at singing" during the nesting season. In coastal South Carolina and the Okeechobee region of Florida he feels certain that the song is indulged by all mated birds. Shrikes are abundant in both areas, and the writer is intimately acquainted with them. While "guttural" is apt enough to describe many of the notes, and it is the case that "most of the calls are harsh and unmusical," this applies more to the alarm and call notes than the song, if this term can be employed. Some of the latter are very liquid, flutelike, and appealing, so much so that many observers are surprised to find them issuing from a loggerhead.

Peterson (1939) is rather more generous in his comments, saying that the song of the loggerhead is "similar to that of the Northern Shrike," which he describes as "a long-continued thrasher-like succession of phrases, harsher on the whole than the Thrasher's song." It is this writer's experience that the loggerhead's efforts are seldom "long-continued," but it is refreshing to hear the bird compared to the thrasher! One could ask little better.

Peterson has an able foundation in his comparison in a statement made long ago by one who knew the loggerhead well—the Rev. John Bachman, of Charleston, S. C.   It was this genial gentleman's observations that considerably augmented Audubon's account of the loggerhead in the Birds of America, the latter saying without reservation that "my friend the Rev. John Bachman has had much better opportunities of studying them."   In regard to the vocal efforts he (Bachman) wrote Audubon (1842) : "You say it has no song.   This is true in part, but it has other notes than the grating sounds you attribute to it.   During the breeding season, and indeed nearly all summer, the male * * * makes an effort at a song, which I cannot compare to anything nearer than the first attempts of a young Brown Thrush * * *.   At times the notes are not unpleasing, but very irregular."

Yet another allusion to similarity with the thrasher's song comes from A. L. Pickens, of Paducah, Ky., who writes (MS.) : "At times I have had to pause and take note to determine whether the birds' notes, softened in spring by the mating urge, and in fall and winter by distance, might not be thrasher, sparrow, or bluebird.

A. T. Wayne (1910) states: "Although the song of this species is considered by most ornithologists to be hard and unmusical, I have heard a few individuals which sang very sweetly."

Economic status.—Aside from its undoubted value to agriculture in its considerable destruction of injurious small mammals and insects, a fact well recognized by informed people, the loggerhead assumes added importance to stockmen by reason of a comparatively recent discovery.   At the 1929 meeting of the American Ornithologists' Union in Philadelphia, a paper was read by Dr. Eloise B. Cram (1930) dealing with birds as factors in the control of a stomach worm in swine. While the details of it cannot be quoted here it is of great interest to note the conclusions reached.   The investigation resulted "from the discovery made by H. L. Stoddard several years ago that the Loggerhead Shrike (*Lanius l. ludovicianus*) in northern Florida, chiefly in Leon County, and in southern Georgia, chiefly in Grady County, were infested with large numbers of roundworms encysted in the wall of the digestive tract.   These parasites were identified by the writer as spirurid larvae and the infestation as a case of aberrant parasitism * * * the larvae being in a host other than the correct final host and therefore incapable of further development."   Careful study was undertaken of birds so infested, and it was found that the dung-beetle (*Phanaeus carnifex*) remains in shrikes' stomachs were "practically one hundred percent heavily parasitized with the same larval roundworm as was found in the shrikes."   Extensive feeding experiments were carried out in order to find the final host of the parasite, larvae taken from shrikes being fed to a series of experimental animals. Coming to the summary of the entire undertaking the writer quotes Miss Cram again:

Larval roundworms found * * * encysted in the walls of the digestive tract of Loggerhead Shrikes * * * were identified * * * as *Physocephalus sexalatus,* the adult form of which occurs in the stomach of swine. The dung beetles * * * were found to serve as the first and normal intermediate hosts of the parasite in this locality [northern Fla. and southern Ga., in counties above named]. Reencystment of the larvae was found to occur in a wide variety of animals * * *. It is pointed out that beetle-consuming animals, of which birds are the most important, are therefore a significant factor in limiting the degree of infestation of swine with *Physocephalus sexalatus* in such an area.

This is a most interesting account and revelation and should be of value to those engaged in hog-raising probably in other parts of the Southeast. The loggerhead is an abundant bird in the cattle-ranch areas of Florida, notably the Lake Okeechobee and Kissimmee Prairie regions, and it may be that its value in that area is equal to good done in the more northern parts of the State. At any rate it is commended to all who are interested in the welfare of the loggerhead and its economic importance to humanity, directly and indirectly.

Field marks.—The loggerhead is hardly to be confused with any other species except the mockingbird. To the latter, however, it bears such a resemblance that many inexperienced observers confuse the two birds, though the similarity is largely superficial. Casual acquaintance on the part of the general public has resulted in the often heard local name of "French mockingbird," but even this term infers that there is a variation between the two for, as some put it, the prefix "French" implies a more striking appearance and the result is a fancy mockingbird!

A. L. Pickens states (MS.) : "The Cherokee Indians appear to have confused the mockingbird with the loggerhead under a common name meaning "heads-it-eats" or "head-eaters," which has given rise to the legend among them that the mockingbird attains its wonderful powers of mimicry by eating the heads (singing parts) of other birds."

The shrike, however, is a much chunkier bird than the mocker, and the gray is markedly lighter in shade, much resembling that of the gray kingbird (*Tyrannus dominicensis*). The large head, which is the reason for the name loggerhead, is always very noticeable even in silhouette; while the black line through the eye, amounting almost to a mask, is easy to see and contrasts sharply with this lack in the mockingbird.

The entire plumage pattern is very contrasting, the blacks, grays, and whites being distinctly defined and not blending. The tail while at rest appears very slim, and the heavy forepart of the bird suggests a somewhat top-heavy appearance. Unlike the larger northern shrike there is no barring on the breast.

These characters, together with the habit of the bird in selecting such conspicuous perches and its rapid vibratory flight, combine to render it plainly distinctive after a little experience in the field.

DISTRIBUTION

Range.—Southern Canada to southern Mexico.

Breeding range.—Shrikes of the loggerhead group breed **north** to central northern Washington (Twisp and Riverdale); recorded in extreme southern British Columbia (Chilliwack, Osoyoos, Midway, and Edgewood) but no positive evidence of breeding; south-central Alberta (Edmonton and Camrose); southern Saskatchewan (Carlton, Quill Lake, and Yorkton); southern Manitoba (Lake St. Martin and Winnipeg); southern Ontario (Emo, Midland, Rutherglen, and Ottawa); southern Quebec (Montreal and Kamouraska); and southern New Brunswick (Scotch Lake and St. John). **East** to New Brunswick (St. John); southern Maine (Bangor, Waterville, and Saco); northwestern Massachusetts (Williamstown); western Connecticut (Winchester); New Jersey (Elizabeth and Cape May), and the other Atlantic Coast States to southern Florida (Homestead). **South** to southern Florida (Homestead and Fort Myers) the Gulf coast to southern Texas (Galveston, Victoria, San Antonio, and Marathon); southern Coahuila (Diamante Pass); southwestern Tamaulipas (Gómez Farías); western Veracruz (Las Vigas); to Oaxaca (Tehuantepec). **West** to Oaxaca (Tehuantepec); Guerrero (Chilpancingo); Lower California (Cape San Lucas, San Ignacio Lagoon, and San Quintín); California (San Diego, the Santa Barbara Islands, Fresno, San Francisco, and Oroville); Oregon, east of the Cascades (Tule Lake and Ashland); central Washington (Yakima and Chelan); and southwestern British Columbia, possibly (Chilliwack).

Winter range.—In winter the races of the loggerhead shrike withdraw somewhat from the northern part of their breeding range. At that season they are found **north** to northwestern Washington (Blaine and Dungeness); southern Oregon (Klamath and Tule Lakes); western and southern Nevada (Carson and the Charleston Mountains); southwestern Utah (St. George); central Arizona (Flagstaff, Fort Verde, and the Salt River Wildlife Refuge); southern to central New Mexico (Silver City, Elephant Butte, and Albuquerque); northwestern Texas (Palo Duro Canyon); northern Kansas (Stockton, Manhattan, and Lawrence); occasionally to Nebraska (Scotts Bluff and Stapleton); central Missouri (Concordia, Columbia, and St. Charles); southern Illinois (Mount Carmel); southern Kentucky (Russellville); Tennessee (Nashville and Johnson City); central Virginia (Sweet Briar); District of Columbia (Washington); and central New Jersey (Princeton); rare or accidental north to Wauwatosa, Wis.; Toledo, Ohio; Toronto, Ontario; Rochester, N. Y.; and Concord, N. H.

The range as outlined is divided into several subspecies or geographic races. The typical race, the loggerhead shrike (*L. l. ludovi-*

cianus), breeds in the Southeastern States from central Louisiana through southern Alabama and Georgia to southern North Carolina and southward; the migrant shrike (*L. l. migrans*) breeds from southeastern Manitoba to northeastern Texas and eastward north of the range of the typical race; the white rumped shrike (*L. l. excubitorides*) breeds from central Alberta and southwestern Manitoba south to eastern California, northern Arizona, and central Texas; the Sonora shrike (*L. l. sonoriensis*) breeds from the Colorado Desert of California and northwestern Lower California east through southern Arizona and New Mexico, south to northern Sinaloa, Durango, and Chihuahua; the California shrike (*L. l. gambeli*) breeds from southern British Columbia (probably), southwestern Montana, and western Wyoming to the Cascades in Washington and Oregon and south to central California, west of the Sierras, and thence along the Pacific coast to about San Diego; the island shrike (*L. l. anthonyi*) is resident on the islands of Santa Cruz, Anacapa, Santa Rosa, and Santa Catalina, Calif.; Mearns's shrike (*L. l. mearnsi*) is resident on the island of San Clemente Island, Calif.; Grinnell's shrike (*L. l. grinnelli*) is resident in northern Lower California south to about latitude 29°; Nelson's shrike (*L. l. nelsoni*) is resident in southern Lower California.

Migration.—Only the migrant and white-rumped shrikes are truly migratory, but in the following dates no attempt has been made to divide the races.

Early dates of spring arrival are: Pennsylvania—McKeesport, March 24. New York—Rochester, March 15. Maine—Phillips, March 22. New Brunswick—Chatham, April 6. Quebec—Montreal, March 27. Ohio—Oberlin, March 2. Ontario—London, March 22. Indiana—Notre Dame, March 4. Michigan—Ann Arbor, March 23. Illinois—Rantoul, February 28. Wisconsin—Milwaukee, March 10. Missouri—Columbia, March 11. Iowa—Keokuk, March 2. Minnesota—Stillwater, March 18. Kansas—Topeka, March 6. Nebraska—Chadron, February 15. South Dakota—Yankton, March 24. North Dakota—Charlson, March 25. Manitoba—Aweme, March 28. Saskatchewan—Eastend, March 28. Colorado—Colorado Springs, March 2. Wyoming—Douglas, March 5.

Late dates of fall departure are: Wyoming—Laramie, October 15. Colorado—Denver, November 2. Saskatchewan, Indian Head, November 2. Manitoba—Aweme, October 28. North Dakota—Jamestown, December 18. South Dakota—Sioux Falls, November 14. Nebraska—Lincoln, November 19. Kansas—Wichita, November 27. Minnesota—St. Paul, October 26. Iowa—Marshalltown, November 14. Missouri—Concordia, November 15. Wisconsin—Unity, November 4. Illinois—Chicago, November 13. Michigan—McMillan, October 26. Indiana—Bloomington, November 30. Ontario—Ottawa, October 18. Ohio—Salem, November 20. New York—Orient, December 9. Pennsylvania—State College, November 17. New Brunswick—Scotch Lake, October 14. Maine—Lewiston, November 24.

The majority of the returns of banded shrikes have been at or near the place of banding. A few recovered at distant points may be quoted. One banded at Carmangay, Alberta, on June 25, 1933, was killed December 22, 1933, at The Grove, Tex., and another banded at the same place on July 16, 1933, was killed on October 6, 1934, at Granger, Tex. One banded at Amenia, N. Dak., on April 7, 1932, was killed on September 8, 1932, at Chriesman, Tex. A bird banded on June 9, 1929, at Whittemore, Mich., was found on September 5, 1929, at Ramer, Ala. A bird banded as an adult was killed at the same station five years later, being then at least six years old.

Casual records.—The loggerhead shrike is reported as of accidental occurrence on Andros Island, Bahamas. A specimen collected at Churchill, Manitoba, on July 1, 1938, has been determined to be a white-rumped shrike; a pair of undetermined race bred near Churchill in 1940.

Egg dates.—Arizona: 53 records, March 10 to June 17; 28 records, April 1 to 26, indicating the height of this season.

California: 126 records, February 24 to July 1; 70 records, March 15 to April 15.

Florida: 44 records, February 19 to July 6; 22 records, March 20 to April 11.

Illinois: 90 records, April 4 to July 5; 57 records, April 15 to 30.

New York: 29 records, April 25 to June 28; 18 records, April 25 to 29.

Ontario: 17 records, April 5 to June 2; 9 records, May 6 to 9.

Texas: 11 records, March 23 to June 4; 5 records, May 4 to 26.

LANIUS LUDOVICIANUS MIGRANS Palmer

MIGRANT SHRIKE

HABITS

Considerable confusion existed in the minds of the earlier writers on American ornithology as to the subspecific status of the small shrikes of the loggerhead group that breed east of the Mississippi Valley and north of the Gulf States and the Carolinas. The breeding birds of this northeastern section have been referred by various authors, from the time of Audubon on, to either the southern loggerhead, the western white-rumped, or even rarely to the large northern shrike, *L. borealis.* I remember very distinctly submitting a shrike that I shot near Cape Vincent in northern New York, during my youth, to that careful and eminent ornithologist William Brewster; I was in doubt about it and asked him to identify it; he called it, with some hesitation, a white-rumped shrike, *L. l. excubitorides*, but admitted that it was not quite typical. This was, of course, some time before *migrans* was recognized.

Even as late as 1895 the second edition of the A. O. U. Check-list gave the breeding range of the loggerhead shrike, *L. l. ludovicianus*, as extending northeastward to New England, but restricted *excubitorides* to breeding west of the eastern border of the Great Plains. The confusion and misunderstandings were finally cleared up by William Palmer (1898), who described and named the migrant shrike, *L. l. migrans*, as a distinct subspecies. His historical synopsis gives an interesting account of all the misunderstandings that had prevailed since the days of Wilson and Audubon, to which the reader is referred, as it is too long to be included here. He gives the distinguishing characters of the adult males of the two eastern races as follows: Loggerhead shrike: "Above dark slaty; beneath almost immaculate white; bill large and stout, swollen toward tip; hook large and coarse, gently curved downwards; tail longer than wing." Migrant shrike: "Above bluish gray; beneath pale slaty; throat white; bill smaller, regularly tapering; hook delicate and sharply bent downwards; tail shorter than wing." This wing-to-tail ratio follows the usual rule, that birds having long migration routes have relatively longer wings than those that do not migrate.

He gives the range of the loggerhead shrike as "from middle Louisiana eastward along the Gulf Coast and its indentations; throughout Florida, and eastward into North Carolina. Extending from this range to an indeterminate distance up the valleys, though generally confined below the 100-foot contour line. Non-migratory except at its more northern and its higher habitat." And that of the migrant shrike as "from Maine, Vermont, and Canada to Minnesota; southwards into North Carolina and the Ohio Valley to the Plains. Absent in winter from its more northern and higher habitats and migrating in the autumn toward the Atlantic Coast and into the Carolinas, Tennessee, and lower Mississippi valley. Breeding almost entirely above the 500-foot contour in the valleys, casually up to about 2000 feet, and to within about 50 miles of the coast in Maine. From Canada and the edges of the plains intergrading into *excubitorides*."

"From the distribution here given," says Palmer, "it will be noticed that there is a considerable hiatus between the breeding ranges of these two forms. This is evidently caused by the fact that the interval between the 100-foot and the 500-foot contours is a part of the great coastal plain forest region of the south, a region unsuited to shrikes, and in which they do not breed."

All shrikes love open country, thinly wooded regions, scrubby country, clearings, meadows, pastures, and thickets along roads and

hedges, especially osage-orange hedges.   Ora W. Knight (1908) says
that, in Maine, "it is largely a bird of civilization, frequenting the
hedgerows, wayside trees, telegraph wires and peaks of houses, and
I have never seen them at any distance from cultivated lands."   Although the loggerhead shrike is common in the flat pinewoods of
Florida, its northern relatives seems to largely avoid pinewoods and
dense deciduous woods, though it sometimes breeds in the more open
stands of fir trees in the northern part of its range.

Prof. Maurice Brooks sends me the following interesting comment
on the distribution of the migrant shrike in West Virginia: "For some
reason migrant shrikes are rare in West Virginia west of the Allegheny
crests, becoming common or locally abundant in the river valleys of
the eastern portion of the State.   Whether or not there is any correlation, it is interesting to plot the distribution of this bird and the rainfall within the areas of its presumed range.   Common in the Middle
West where rainfall averages around 30 inches or below, it becomes
scarce or absent in the Allegheny foothills of Ohio and western West
Virginia, where the precipitation shows a sharp increase to 35 or 40
inches.   In the West Virginia regions where rainfall is heavier, 50 or
60 inches, it is, so far as we know, completely absent as a breeding
bird; but to the east, where the Allegheny Mountains throw the valleys
into a rain shadow, the bird reappears in good numbers.   This may be
accidental, but the gap in distribution cannot be accounted for by any
known factors of food, temperature, or place to impale victims."

Territory.—Mr. Knight (1908) says: "A pair of birds occupies the
same locality year after year, that is to say I have found nests in the
same trees or group of trees, and many times on the very same limb
from which a nest or nests had been taken in years previously.   The
eggs also were of the same type so that it was evidently the same birds.
*   *   *   In one case the male bird was killed and the survivor soon
found a mate and had another nest in the same locality within a month.
The next season the female was killed, the male shortly found a new
mate in the same way and another nest was built, and the eggs laid
therein were of a different type.   *   *   *   I have knowledge of one
pair being in the same locality for ten years, and of several other pair
for only a year or so less than this."   He does not refer to any attempt
at defense of the territory, as observed by Dr. Miller (1931) in the resident California shrike.

Migration.—The migrant shrike is well named, as it is more migratory than its southern relative, with which it has been compared.   Its
migration range is not extensive, for it has been known to spend the
winter occasionally as far north as southern New England, where,
however, its migrations have been fairly well marked.   Evidence
seems to indicate that this shrike originally entered New England from

the west and that the northward migration in spring is mainly west of the Alleghenies and then eastward into New England. I have never seen it in southeastern Massachusetts in spring and only rarely in fall; but Wendell Taber tells me that he has seen it in eastern Massachusetts on at least four occasions during March, once quite near my home and twice even on Cape Cod. In fall, however, it apparently moves southward, or southeastward, toward the coast and then follows a coastwise route, east of the Alleghenies, to its winter haunts. From the more western portions of its summer range the fall migration seems to move in a more southern, or southwestern, direction to winter haunts as far west as Louisiana and Texas.

Nesting.—The nesting habits of the migrant shrike do not differ materially from those of the species elsewhere, except that in some localities it seems to select more often some isolated tree along a highway and often at a considerable height in an exposed situation. In northern New England and in eastern Canada, nests have been found in conifers, firs, spruces, and pines.

Henry Mousley (1918) mentions a nest found near Hatley, Quebec, in a solitary, tall fir tree by the side of a road and not far from his house. The lower branches of the tree had been cut off, and the nest was placed 34 feet from the ground in a dense portion of the tree, so that it could not be seen from the ground. "The foundation of the nest consisted of fir twigs, rootlets, string and that favorite material of most birds here, the stalks and flower heads of the pearly everlasting. The lining was formed of wool, plant down, and a good supply of feathers, and the dimensions were as follows, viz.: outside diameter 6, inside 2¾ inches; outside depth 4½, inside 2¼ inches." He located the second nest of this pair 8 feet up in an apple tree, only 85 yards distant, and suggests that the shrikes may have selected the fir tree because there was no foliage for concealment on the deciduous trees and thickets when the first nest was built. However that may be, there are a number of other records of nests in conifers, up to 20 feet in spruces and firs and down to as low as 4 or 5 feet in stunted spruces. Owen Durfee mentions in his field notes a nest 13 feet from the ground, in plain sight, in an elm tree and another in a pine, both by a roadside near Lancaster, N. H.; and Frederic H. Kennard records in his notes for the same locality a nest 18 feet up in a spruce tree growing by the road in front of a farmhouse.

It must not be inferred from the above records that the migrant shrike does not nest in other situations in this general region, for it has often been found nesting here in apple trees in orchards, in other low trees, and in such thorny bushes and thickets as it uses elsewhere.

A. Dawes Du Dois has sent me his data for seven nests in Illinois. Four of these were in osage-orange hedges or bushes; one was in an apple tree in an orchard, 15 feet from the ground; one was 12 feet up in a small tree by the side of a little-used lane, with no attempt at concealment; and the lowest nest was only 5 feet from the ground in a wild crab-apple tree in a pasture.

Dr. Miller (1931) lists, in addition to those mentioned above, as among the many types of trees and bushes used as nesting sites by the migrant shrike, oaks, hawthorn bushes, cottonwoods, willows, and wild plum trees, at heights ranging from 4 to 18 feet. Margaret M. Nice (1931) records two nests near Norman, Okla., that were 30 and 40 feet above the ground, respectively; both were in elm trees; the latter seems to be the record height for this subspecies. Dr. Thomas S. Roberts (1932) states that a pair of these shrikes built a nest in an old grackle's nest and that another pair used an old catbird's nest, in Minnesota.

Eggs.—The migrant shrike lays four to six eggs, rarely seven. The eggs are practically indistinguishable from those of the species elsewhere, which have been well described by Dr. Miller under the California shrike. The measurements of 40 eggs average 24.7 by 18.6 millimeters; the eggs showing the four extremes measure **26.4** by 19.5, 26.3 by **19.9, 23.0** by 18.6, and 24.0 by **17.6** millimeters.

Young.—The full account given by Dr. Miller under the California shrike is so satisfactory that it does not seem necessary to say anything here about the incubation of the eggs and the care and development of the young, though some authors have credited the migrant shrike with a shorter period of incubation and a longer altricial period for the young. Probably Dr. Miller's figures are correct, and doubtless the two races do not differ much in these respects. Apparently two broods are often raised in a season in the north, and probably usually in the south. The male has often been seen feeding the young of the first brood while the female is laying eggs for the second brood.

Plumages.—A very full account of all the plumages of all the North American shrikes has been published by Dr. Alden H. Miller (1931), to which the reader is referred, as the descriptions are given in too much detail to be quoted here. Dr. Dwight (1900) describes the juvenal plumage of *migrans* as follows: "Above, drab-gray, faintly vermiculated and with pale buff edgings; rump slightly paler. Wings and tail black, a white area at the bases of the primaries, the coverts and tertiaries buff tipped, palest on the tertiaries; the outer rectrices largely white, the central ones buff, with terminal mottling. Lores, orbital region and auriculars dull black. Below, dull white on chin, abdomen and crissum, washed on breast and sides with very pale buff or drab, vermiculated with dusky subterminal bands on each feather. Bill and feet dusky becoming black."

The first winter plumage is acquired by a partial postjuvenal molt, "in September and October, which involves the body plumage, tertiaries, wing coverts and tail, but not the rest of the wings. Similar to previous plumage but grayer above and the vermiculations absent or very indistinct on the breast. Above, plumbeous gray, paler on rump, the posterior scapulars white.

"Wings and tail black except for the brown juvenal primaries, secondaries and primary coverts, the lesser coverts plumbeous, white tips to the new tertiaries and white terminal spots on the lateral rectrices. Below, dull white with dusky vermiculations sometimes faintly indicated. A broad, black bar through the eye."

He says that in both young and old birds there is a partial prenuptial molt in February and March, "which involves chiefly the chin, throat and head, and a few scattering feathers elsewhere, but neither the wings nor the tail." All individuals have a complete postnuptial molt, mainly in September, but sometimes beginning in July or August, and sometimes prolonged into October or even November.

Food.—The migrant shrike eats fewer mice and birds and more insects than the northern shrike does. The northern bird is with us in the States only in winter, when insects are scarce; but the migrant finds insects abundant in its summer home and fairly common in the south in winter. Shrikes are almost omnivorous and will take what animal food is most readily available. The following report by F. H. King (1883) on the contents of stomachs collected in Wisconsin is interesting as showing the variety of food eaten and the proportions of each: "Of fifteen specimens examined or observed, one had eaten seven moths; three, five caterpillars; two, eleven diptera, among them five crane-flies; nine, eighteen beetles, among them three ground-beetles, three carrion-beetles and two leaf-chafers; five, twenty-two grasshoppers; two, two crickets; three, six May-flies; two, four snails. Two had killed three birds—one, a Canarybird, and one, two Warblers; two, two mice. One of the birds was shot while in the act of killing a meadow mouse (*Arvicola riparia*)."

William Brewster (1938) saw a migrant shrike impale a bank swallow, a bluebird, and a pickerel frog. Others have reported small sparrows as killed by this shrike, as well as shrews, snakes, lizards, and tree frogs. But all the vetebrates eaten form but a small proportion of the food. Invertebrates, mainly insects, form the bulk of the food, of which Orthoptera make up the largest item; but beetles, both beneficial and harmful, cutworms, butterflies, cicadas, wasps, and spiders are also included in the food.

Frank T. Noble (1902) published an interesting account of a migrant shrike that met its match in an attempt to capture a small gartersnake, about 18 inches long. The snake had wound itself around the bird's neck and had nearly strangled it. Mr. Noble was unable to uncoil the snake until he severed it with a pair of scissors and released the badly frightened bird.

Behavior.—The behavior of this species in foraging and impaling its prey has been so fully described by Dr. Miller under the California shrike, that it need not be repeated here. Mr. Brewster (1938) watched some of these shrikes in their normal behavior and says of their flight: "On leaving their perches, whether the latter were fence posts or telegraph poles, they invariably shot down at a steep angle, as if aiming at some object on the ground and then skimmed off swiftly across the field only a foot or two above the turf, rising and falling in long, graceful but gentle (or shallow) undulations, moving their wings very rapidly at the beginning of each upward curve and then closing them for an instant just as a Woodpecker or Goldfinch does when pursuing its similar 'galloping' flight. During the exceedingly rapid beat of the wings their light markings were alternately displayed and concealed, giving a flickering effect as of a small bit of looking-glass flashed in the sunlight."

This shrike also has a conspicuous hovering flight, hanging suspended in the air on rapidly vibrating wings, like the hovering flight of the sparrow hawk while scanning the ground below in search of prey, its wings serving only to hold it stationary in one spot. While perched, it frequently raises and drops its tail, spreading it during the motion and then closing it and letting it hang.

Voice.—So much has been written about the song and other notes of this species under the other subspecies that there are only two items worth mentioning here.

Harold M. Holland writes to me from Galesburg, Ill.: "On a bright, early May morning several years ago, having stopped my car opposite a migrant shrike's nest in a hedgerow bordering a country road, I became aware of an unfamiliar bird song close by and was surprised to find that this emanated from the shrike occupying the nest. With head slightly raised, it sang for two or three minutes, a low-pitched, pleasing little jumble of notes that lacked the least trace of harshness, as if singing softly to itself, in perfect contentment. Both the unusual 'song' and singing from the nest remain lone occurrences in a long acquaintance with this species."

Saunders and Dale (1933) heard a migrant shrike singing on the wing in Middlesex County, Ontario, on May 24, 1928: "On entering the field we heard a clear whistle that reminded us of a Sandpiper's note. On tracing this to its source we found the Shrike sitting on a fallen dead apple tree. It flew as we approached and alighted on a thorn bush. The next note resembled that of a Nighthawk. It flew again and as it was on the wing it uttered a rolling call similar to that given by the Bartramian Sandpiper, a bird which, by the way, lives in the same field as the Shrike."

LANIUS LUDOVICIANUS EXCUBITORIDES Swainson

WHITE-RUMPED SHRIKE

HABITS

This is the paler race of the species that is found in the western plains of Canada and the United States, from the eastern border of the Great Plains to the western edge of the Great Basin, and from the plains of the Saskatchewan in Canada to the southwestern desert regions and northern Mexico.

Ridgway (1904) describes it as "similar to *L. l. migrans*, but gray of upper parts decidedly paler (between slate-gray and no. 6 gray), changing abruptly to white on upper tail-coverts; white of scapulars more extended (occupying practically the whole of scapular region) and more abruptly contrasted with gray of back; forehead and supraloral region paler gray than crown, sometimes whitish; under parts purer white; size averaging slightly larger."

Dr. Miller (1931) says of its haunts in general:

This race is found chiefly in arid, short grass or desert savanna, plains areas. In these regions the original terrane is rarely modified by small farms. In the north the range of this race includes some areas of more luxuriant grassland. The birds forage out over the plains but usually they are to be found near the timber, principally cottonwoods, along water courses. * * * In Texas the race is found irregularly in regions where scattered oaks and mesquites occur. Throughout its summer habitat *excubitorides* encounters comparatively arid conditions with the exception of some northern parts of its range in Canada. Life-zones occupied are Upper and Lower Sonoran, locally Transition in the north.

Between Quill Lake and Prince Albert, in northern Saskatchewan, I saw a few white-rumped shrikes near the northern limit of their summer range; the country here was rolling, largely open grassland, but with scattered ponds, bogs, and muskegs in the hollows, and with many groves of poplars or aspens on the highlands; it was only thinly settled with villages and small farms.

I have no record of having seen it in southwestern Saskatchewan, though it doubtless occurs there.

Nesting.—In southern Arizona we found the white-rumped shrike to be a very common bird and saw a number of their nests, as we drove along the roads; most of the nests were easily seen in the thorny bushes by the roadside, usually not much more than 4 or 5 feet from the ground. Along the road leading to the Chiricahua Mountains we saw several nests in the soapweed yuccas; one of these was a very pretty nest, made of whitish weed stems with white cottony blossoms, giving the nest a soft fluffy appearance; the six eggs in it were so heavily incubated on April 26, 1922, that we did not collect it. But the next day, near the Dragoon Mountains, we took a set of six perfectly fresh eggs; the nest was 8 feet from the ground in a small blackjack oak in open country; it was built on top of an old mockingbird's nest and was made mainly of weed stalks with the leaf and blossom buds on them, mixed with grasses, straws, and fine twigs; it was lined with finer material of the same kind and with a few feathers. Another set was taken on May 1 from a nest near Hereford that was 4 feet from the ground in a small hackberry by the roadside. An exceptionally high nest was found on May 27 near Fairbank, in the San Pedro Valley; this was 15 feet above the ground, near the end of a branch of a large willow.

A set of seven eggs in my collection, taken by Fred M. Dille, in Weed County, Colo., came from a nest "in the lower, tangled branches of a scrub willow, 7 feet from the ground."

Dr. Miller's (1930) two proposed races, *sonoriensis* and *nevadensis*, both of which we have always included within the range of *excubitorides*, seem to have somewhat different preferences as to nesting sites, owing, of course, to the difference in environment. Of the former, the southwestern desert race, he (1931) says: "Mesquite, screw bean, palo verde, smoke-bush, and other desert trees and bushes of similar size afford nesting sites for this race. At Palm Springs, California, I have found several nests fairly well concealed in clumps of mistletoe in mesquite trees ranging in height from seven to fifteen feet above ground. Where broadleaf trees occur these shrikes may make use of such shelter for nesting." Of the more northern race, he says: "Nesting sites of *nevadensis* include willows, cottonwoods, atriplex, Joshua trees, mesquites, *Purshia*, *Lepargyrea argentea*, and *Artemisia tridentata*. Nests may be placed as low as two feet in sagebushes. A nest taken at Lancaster, Los Angeles County, California, was located about five feet from the ground on a hanging limb of a Joshua tree." For the more northern and eastern race, to which he restricts the name *excubitorides*, he says that "principal among the nest sites of this form are the cottonwood and willow trees along the water courses in the Great Plains region." E. S. Cameron (1908) mentions a Montana nest "in the fork of a box elder" and another "in a cedar."

Dawson and Bowles (1909) say of the nesting of this shrike in eastern Washington: "The nest is a bulky but usually well-built affair, placed habitually in a sagebush, or a greasewood clump, with wild clematis for third choice. The structure is designed for warmth and comfort, so that, whenever possible, to the thickened walls of plant fibers, cowhair, or sheep's wool, is added an inner lining of feathers, and these not infrequently curl over the edge so as completely to conceal the nest contents."

Dr. Jean M. Linsdale (1938) records four Nevada nests in buffalo-berry bushes, 2½ to 4 feet above ground, one 3 feet up in a sagebush and one in a wormwood only 18 inches from the ground, the lowest I have seen recorded.

Eggs.—The white-rumped shrike lays four to seven eggs; six seems to be the commonest number, four uncommon and seven rare. They are practically indistinguishable from the eggs of the species elsewhere, which are so well described under the California shrike. The measurements of 40 eggs average 24.8 by 18.4 millimeters; the eggs showing the four extremes measure 27.4 by 18.3, 26.2 by 19.6, 21.8 by 18.3, and 24.9 by 17.3 millimeters.

Food.—In a general way the food of the white-rumped shrike is similar to that of the other races of the species, due allowance being made for what its environment provides. In the southwestern deserts, where reptiles are plentiful, it seems to eat many kinds of lizards and small snakes.

William Lloyd (1887) gives a good idea of its food in western Texas: "It lives on grasshoppers when it can procure them, and in winter, when the weather is severe, takes to carrion. I found one in January, 1884, so gorged from feeding on a dead sheep that it could not fly. In the Davis Mountains it lives in winter on large coleoptera. In spring it occasionally kills birds. I have seen *Spizella socialis arizonæ*, *Vireo belli*, *Polioptila cærulea*, and others, amongst its victims, and in summer it has a fancy for nestlings."

G. F. Knowlton and F. C. Harmston (1944) give a detailed list of the stomach contents of 65 white-rumped shrikes collected in Utah, to which the reader is referred.

Other habits are similar to those of the species elsewhere. It is a migratory subspecies, withdrawing from the more northern portions of its range in the fall and spending the winter in the Southwestern United States and Mexico.

LANIUS LUDOVICIANUS GAMBELI Ridgway

CALIFORNIA SHRIKE

HABITS [1]

CONTRIBUTED BY ALDEN HOLMES MILLER

Over a large part of North America south of the great transcontinental forests, loggerhead shrikes may be found in open country and broken woodland. But it is chiefly well to the southward, as in California and in Florida, that the species is numerous enough to become a conspicuous element in the bird life. The California loggerhead shrike, *Lanius ludovicianus gambeli*, westernmost race of the species,

---

[1] Derived largely from Miller, "Systematic Revision and Natural History of the American Shrikes (*Lanius*)," 1931.

is especially common in the Great Valley of California and in coastal southern California. To the northward in eastern Oregon and Washington and the northern part of the Great Basin it occurs rather sparsely in juniper and sagebrush land. Aggressive, vigorous, and decisive in its actions, and contributing strident bursts of sound and also varied melodic trills to the auditory ensemble, it is likely to be one of a person's first bird acquaintances in those regions where it flourishes. Shrikes are drawn to roadsides by desirable perches on fences and power lines, and in such places their conspicuous foraging actions and their interesting butchering habits are easily watched, as is also their nesting activity, which centers in isolated clumps of trees or tall bushes. Through the spring and early summer the wheedling cries of large families of hungry young shrikes are an ever-present sound, typical of the parched plains and gently sloping hills of a lowland California countryside.

Loggerhead shrikes hunt by watching from fixed positions, and long unobstructed views are required. Food typically is taken on the ground and is seen from above. These instinctive methods demand that the bird live in the open but where there are good lookout posts. Dense brush and continuous woodland or forest would not permit normal operations. Further than this, these shrikes seem to do best where there is little or but moderate rain and fog, especially in the summer season. Agricultural developments within the range of the California shrike have probably favored this bird by providing trees in open plains areas without diminishing significantly the exposed ground surface where they hunt.

North of California, shrikes are largely migratory, but south of latitude 40° their populations are resident. Migration is never a conspicuous affair in this bird, although on the Colorado Desert California shrikes winter regularly with Sonora loggerhead shrikes, *Lanius ludovicianus sonoriensis*, which are permanently resident there. Where I have most closely watched California shrikes in Contra Costa County, Calif., and in the Lower San Joaquin Valley, no movements of more than local type have been detected.

Territory.—Unlike many passerine birds, shrikes display territorial behavior throughout the year. Late in summer and in fall, resident California shrikes are completely solitary, and males and females defend feeding territories. The annual territorial cycle then may be said to begin at the close of the breeding season early in July when family groups are disintegrating. Typical was the action of an adult male observed on July 3, 1929, at Firebaugh, Fresno County. Two young were pursued seemingly in an endeavor to chase them from the vicinity. The adult sang at frequent intervals and attempted to attack three young captive shrikes that I had in camp. No other adult shrike was permitted to come about the singing posts of this male.

Several other adult shrikes were stationed in adjacent territories at distances of 200 to 400 yards. That one of these birds was the female parent of the young is highly probable. Elsewhere solitary females were collected which were acting in the same manner as this male.

Early in August apparently the same male shrike was observed at Firebaugh. No young were in evidence, and other shrikes repeatedly were chased from the territory with much vigor. The bird was singing as frequently as in July but was in the height of the annual molt. When shot, it proved to have gonads decidedly smaller than is normal for the breeding season. At this same time several hundred solitary shrikes were noted in the San Joaquin Valley; not one pair was seen.

By November some few California shrikes have become paired. Members of a pair were seen 30 yards from one another near Firebaugh, and members of another were watched as they amicably occupied perches on fence rails on either side of a small country road. A census on three days late in November revealed only three and a doubtful fourth pair out of 93 individuals watched long enough to determine their status.

Pair formation seems to involve trial chases and begging notes, which doubtless aid in revealing the sex of a bird, or better, in inducing appropriate differentiated response in birds of opposite sex. An apparent example of incipient sexual interest was noted on November 30. A shrike that had been watched for a short time was soon chased violently high into the air by the owner of the area. The chase was accompanied by the sharp note, *bzeek*, several times repeated, indicative of excitement and usually associated with combat. The intruder was followed to the edge of the territory, whereupon the defender stopped and engaged in a sexual display commonly seen in the breeding season. This consisted of fluttering the wings and of begging notes similar to the actions of females during the laying and incubating periods. The bird that had been chased from the territory showed no response, and the bird giving the display ceased and returned to one of its lookout posts. Unfortunately, both individuals were not obtained; the bird that had been driven away proved to be an adult male.

The two birds obviously were not paired at the time. There was some form of sexual excitement in one of them, presumably a female. The chasing perhaps was a sexual flight but, judged from nuptial activities observed in the spring season, the flight represented a defense of territory. It appears to me that sexual excitation was awakening in the defending bird but was not yet sufficient to overcome the impulse to remain in solitary possession of the feeding territory. At this season a few individuals had yielded to sexual impulses so far as to tolerate association in a territory with a member of the opposite sex. Most of the birds, however, either were in the undecided condition of these two birds or were inactive sexually. It is significant that some pairing activity occurs previous to any perceptible increase in the gonads.

In the vicinity of the Pinole, Contra Costa County, Calif., early in January 1930, I located several single shrikes and studied and mapped their territories. Later, at the time when these shrikes paired and nested, there was no change in the size or limits of the territories, two birds and finally the entire family remaining within the confines of the area once occupied by but one of the parents. In most cases the sex of the original owner of the territory used for nesting was not known with certainty. In one instance a territory was first located when seemingly but one bird was present. This bird later proved to be a female, fortunately, in this case, mating with a bird sufficiently different in coloration as to be individually distinguishable in the field. The female, when discovered on February 7, I followed about over her territory for some time, and so I was able to outline the area occupied. Had the bird been paired at this time, I am confident from other experiences that the mate would have been seen. By February 10 a male had joined this female and they were constantly close together.

Other solitary birds were found to be joined by mates late in January and still others not until March. Occasionally some minor shifts in the territorial limits may be made when the winter territories are converted into breeding territories, in one observed instance with the seeming purpose of including a desirable nest tree. The complete abandonment of some winter territories is inevitable if pairs are to be formed; disappearances of this kind were noted in a few instances in January.

The size and shape of the territory, whether breeding or feeding, are dependent upon several factors, namely: the floral habitat occupied, whether an open prairie or a moderately wooded area; the concentration of the food supply and the provision of nest sites; the local abundance of the species; and the local associational or physical barriers.

There is a marked difference in sizes of territories in California, and this apparently is correlated with habitat and concomitant variations in food supply. Territories in grassy hills and meadows with scattered oaks, eucalyptus, and lines of willows ranged from 11 to 14 acres in size in Contra Costa County, but in semidesert terrain consisting of much bare ground, widely spaced bushes, and few trees; in Kern County (race *Lanius ludovicianus nevadensis*) territories consisted of 25 to 40 acres.

In parts of the northern San Joaquin Valley, where the shrike population is large, nearly every individual's territory is bounded on all sides by other shrikes. But in the neighborhood of Pinole shrikes hold territories limited by physical and associational barriers. Thus, one pair was bounded to the south and northeast by steep hills, not prohibitive to shrikes, but not so desirable as the flat meadow which they occupied. To the east this pair was limited by the holdings of another pair of shrikes; I witnessed several encounters between them. To the west there was no change in association, no physical barrier, and no other shrikes, yet this pair moved only a limited distance in a westerly direction. Habit and lack of need for further foraging ground apparently had fixed the western boundary.

The defense of a territory is coincident partly with the foraging habits of the bird, which keep it in more or less conspicuous, open places. While a strike is hunting for food it can at the same time see large parts of its territory. Detection of invaders is by sight, less commonly by sound. When not engaged in active feeding, which often is conducted from low perches, the shrike always tends to mount to some high exposed position of observation. Here its ready visibility aided by characteristic form and contrasting markings serves to advertise at considerable distances its possession of the area. This advertisement is aided by song and by the familiar series of 4 to 10 or 12 screeches of progressively diminishing intensity. Loggerhead shrikes are in the greatest degree silent during the nesting season, at which time adult birds have reached the annual minimum in numbers and territorial boundaries are well established. More constant, though less ecstatic, songs and screeches are given late in summer and in autumn when competition in the possession of territories is more severe. The rhythmic summer song then seems certainly to be given for the purpose of warning invaders. A bird in summer or fall perched quietly on a wire or tree top suddenly, and without apparent reason, will break out with its series of violent screeches. No other shrike appears, the bird is not watching any particular prey, and it settles back again into quiet waiting. The screech seems merely an expression of the bird's presence, an indication of a potential aggressiveness to defend its position.

At Pinole I once witnessed a vigorous attack by the defender. Members of the resident pair were sitting on fence posts about 10 yards apart, one bird, probably the male, singing occasionally. A succession of sharp notes (*bzeek*) was heard from a third shrike, which had appeared at the edge of the territory about 60 yards distant. This was immediately answered by similar notes from the defending "male." The invader sang a few trills, then came closer, approaching the "male" of the resident pair and sat on the adjacent fence post. The "female" of the pair was on the opposite side of the defending "male," which sat facing the invader. The two "males" remained rigidly on guard, neither moving in the slightest. One of them, I could not be sure which, gave a few song trills. After about five minutes both birds suddenly jumped into the air, the defending "male" came within striking range, and a series of sharp clicks of the bill and a few screeches, low buzzing notes, and staccato vocal notes were heard. The flight of the two continued for a few yards, when the defender returned to the "female," which had remained quiet and seemingly undisturbed throughout the performance. The repulsed invader towered in a most erratic manner and flew high over the hills at the edge of the valley half a mile away, apparently most intent on departing with rapidity.

In each territory there is usually what may be termed a headquarters. The roosting place, so far as known, is situated here and usually also the nest, if the territory is used for breeding purposes. The headquarters provides good lookout perches, feeding facilities, and some sort of bush or tree for shelter at night. It is occupied during a large part of the day. In many territories, nevertheless, subsidiary headquarters exist. If one wishes to locate a shrike in a known territory, a search in two or three favorable localities usually reveals the bird's presence. Evidently, therefore, all parts of the territory are not used equally, yet territories are defended in their entirety.

The requisite for roosting places seems to be some support above the ground within a screen of overhanging limbs. Roosts are marked by conspicuous fecal deposits. In one instance the nest was built within 6 feet of a roost that had been used for a considerable period previously by the female. The male roosted about 15 feet away in a similar location among dense limbs, the site not being well marked probably owing to his recent arrival on the territory. Arrival at the roost is commonly 35 to 40 minutes after sundown and departure in the morning about half an hour before sunrise.

Courtship.—Two aspects of courtship should be recognized. The first type of activity apparently serves to reinforce the pair's bond. It does not immediately lead to copulation and it normally occurs early in the season. Typical is the following: On January 24, members of a recently mated pair were seen sitting one foot apart on a telephone wire. The birds flew from the wire, one closely following the other. Upon alighting on a fence one of them gave a series of screeches of the usual rhythm but of a peculiar metallic quality, a note found to be associated always with nuptial activities. The two birds then hopped and flitted back and forth from fence wires to fence post in what might be called a mock pursuit. After perching quietly for several minutes on the fence, one bird attempted to alight on the post occupied by the other shrike, whereupon the two again engaged in mock pursuit. Still later one of the birds crouched near the other, fanned its tail, and at the same time tipped its tail upward. This action was followed by more of the metallic screeching, the performer twice flying back and forth 20 feet above the mate, which remained perched on the fence. The flight was erratic and zigzagging with vertical undulations and changes in pace. It is believed that the bird performing this nuptial flight was the male.

This behavior has also been seen in the period following the destruction of a set of eggs. In some instances hovering is interpolated in the nuptial flight. Such hovering is performed at greater height from the ground than that which commonly is seen when shrikes are in pursuit of prey. It is similar to the hovering of excited parents while in defense of small young.

The second type of courtship consists of the feeding of the female by the male. The female postures, flutters the wings, and calls much in the manner of a juvenal shrike. This begins in the final stages of nest-building and continues through the laying and incubating periods. However, the feeding is much more of a routine affair after the set is laid, and one does not then note the extreme posturing and excitement of the laying period. Begging by the female often follows upon her noticing the male in the act of capturing food, whereas at other times her actions seem to arise purely from some internal sexual urge. The female in this type of courtship is the aggressor. The male usually is quiet and nonresponsive to the female and may consistently move away from her advances. If he does respond to her entreaties, it is by rapidly and quietly approaching with food in the bill, which food is snatched from him by the female. If he responds in a more purely sexual manner, it is by a few quickly repeated ecstatic song trills. I have never seen any strutting or display of plumage by the male at this time. Often there is a noticeable increase in the amount of song delivered by him, although this is not given while in close company of the female but from one of the higher perches in the territory.

Between these two phases of courtship there is a period of variable length, when the members of a pair hunt during most of the day, remaining within 50 yards or less of one another but rarely showing any other signs of attachment or of sexual interest. The male usually takes the initiative in moving about from post to post within the territory. At this time neither bird sings to any great degree. Such singing as does occur is performed normally by the male. But the female may sing, although only briefly.

Nesting.—The pair, when searching for nest sites, makes an inspection of various densely branched trees and bushes near the headquarters of the territory. Both birds may spend 15 minutes at a time hopping about through thickets of a sort not commonly frequented while feeding.

The nest sites have certain general characteristics. Preference is shown for locations in dense bushes or small thickly grown trees at medium heights, rarely less than 3 feet or more than 25 feet from the ground. Where possible the nests are hidden below the crown of the bush or tree and are placed on limbs that afford ample support for the comparatively heavy structure. The use of old nests as foundations for building new structures frequently is recorded. I have observed this in at least five nests of *gambeli*.

Nests have been found by me in live oaks, willows, various orchard trees, cypress, sumac, saltbush, blackberry vines, acacias, peppertrees, and eucalyptus trees. The greatest height at which a nest has been noted is 30 feet from the ground in the top of an acacia. Bancroft informs me of the nesting of this race in loose tangles of baling wire about 4 feet high and 6 feet long. Grinnell (1911) records an instance in comparatively barren terrain of nesting between two upright boards of a support for telephone wires.

The materials used in building the nests are extremely varied and dependent on local supply. Shrike nests commonly have an ample substructure of twigs, usually not more than one-quarter of an inch in diameter. Occasionally the nest is a more or less homogeneous cup lacking a base of sticks. Grass is seldom used extensively, but stalks of various annuals are employed, often taking the place of sticks or twigs. The lining ordinarily is heavy, forming a thick felted cup with a wide margin, which frequently projects outward a distance of an inch over the stick framework. The lining includes cottonlike substances principally, with smaller amounts of hair, feathers, rootlets, and bark. The lining is especially variable according to the local supply of materials. In sheep country much use is made of wool.

Wide variation occurs even in nests from the same vicinity. A female of a pair at Pinole built an extremely inferior type of nest early in the spring of 1930. The framework was of small twigs and rootlets, rarely over 2 millimeters in diameter, which basal structure extended not more than 1 inch beyond the narrow rim of the nest cup. The lining was not over one-quarter of an inch in thickness and was composed of willow catkins, hair, and a few strips of bark. Likewise, the nest cup was unusually small, barely 3 inches in diameter and 2 inches deep. A second nest of the same sort was built by this pair, which was only slightly more substantial than the first. The first nest had become dislodged from its precarious position among the small twigs of a willow and had allowed the small young to fall to the ground. In contrast to the efforts of this pair was the series of three nests built by another female, each of which was lined to the extent of nearly an inch in thickness. The cups of these nests were 4 inches across, and the maximum diameter of the entire substructure of one of the nests was 12 inches.

Nests may be situated well braced in crotches of large limbs, against boards or other artificial supports, or among the fine dense twigs of bushes, trees, and vines. The desirability of large limbs as supports seems to be indicated by the fate of three nests I have observed near Pinole. The young in these nests were allowed to fall to the ground or the nests became dangerously tilted as a result of placement among small branches a centimeter or less in diameter.

The female builds the nest with little or no active aid of the male. The difficulty of distinguishing male and female in the field makes it hard to be sure that this is always true. To judge from the actions of pairs in which the sexes of the birds were known, the male usually follows the female while she is gathering material, and he may go with her to the nest but, in my experience, has not been seen to touch the nest or to bring material to the female (see however, Johnson, 1938, with respect to *Lanius ludovicianus migrans*). He may sit within a foot of the female while she is building. California shrikes are extremely shy while engaged in nest construction and will cease activity when the nest is approached within 60 yards. It is difficult, therefore, to observe the manipulation of material at the site, which is usually well hidden from view. Foraging for material is conducted, for the most part, within a radius of 50 yards of the nest. The greatest distance that I have observed a bird transport substances designed for the nest is 100 yards. Nevertheless, on occasion it is fairly certain that materials are obtained at even greater distances from the nest. One female was seen to go to an old Bullock's oriole's nest constructed of hair and tug vigorously at the edge, finally securing small pieces of the rim which it carried directly to its own nest.

Eggs.—With *gambeli*, in the vicinity of San Francisco Bay, sets of seven eggs are as common as those of five, six being the usual number. In San Diego County, Calif., on the other hand, Bancroft states that *gambeli* lays five or six eggs, usually five. Likewise, I have taken numerous complete sets of five eggs in western Los Angeles County.

The time of laying of first sets ranges from April and early in May in the north to late in March and early in April in the San Diegan district of California. Occasionally sets of eggs are found in February in southern California. Second broods and replacement of destroyed nests may prolong the laying period into the early part of July.

Eggs of the loggerhead shrike vary from dull white to either light neutral gray or buff in ground color. The spots are usually small, the maximum diameter in most eggs being about $2\frac{1}{2}$ millimeters, but occasionally spots and splotches as large as $6\frac{1}{2}$ millimeters occur. The sharply defined surface markings vary from neutral gray to various tones of yellowish brown and umber. There also are indistinct light gray spots deposited in layers beneath the surface of the eggshell. Occasionally, fine black scrawlings appear near the large end of the eggs. Spots are more concentrated at the large end but rarely are grouped into pronounced blotches with intervening unpigmented areas. A wreath of spots about the large end rarely is present. Out of 150 eggs of *Lanius ludovicianus* examined by me, 6 instances of reversal of the color pattern, that is, heavy pigmentation on the small end of the egg, have been noted. Four of these examples were in the same set of eggs.

The measurements of 97 eggs average 24.1 by 18.5 millimeters; extreme measurements are 26.9 and 22.0 for length and 19.4 and 17.3 for width. The average and extreme weights of 100 eggs weighed by Hanna (1924) and myself are: 4.64 gm. (5.7–3.6).

Incubation.—The female alone incubates and begins to cover the eggs usually with the laying of the next to last egg of the set. The incubation period is 16 days.

The female leaves the nest only for short intervals and depends largely upon the male for her supply of food. Usually the female attempts to return and cover the eggs within five minutes after having been flushed from the nest, unless she is an especially wary individual. When settling upon the eggs the shrike usually spends several seconds in moving about rather vigorously, adjusting the clutch so that it will be well covered and included between the two ventral feather tracts on the breast and belly. The incubating bird faces in various directions while on the nest, often turning toward an observer as if better to watch for danger. It has been repeatedly recorded in my notes that eggs in sets are arranged in a definite order in the nest according to the direction in which the bird previously had been facing during incubation. Sets of six eggs usually are arranged in a double row of three, the row paralleling the long axis of the bird's body. The aligning of the eggs in a double row appears best suited to the brooding of a large sized set by a bird of the narrow proportions of a shrike.

The male feeds the female while she is either on the nest or in the near vicinity of it when she has left incubation to meet the male. The food is not placed in the mouth but, as during the period before incubation, is snatched from the male's bill and is swallowed at once or, if necessary, first is broken into pieces or impaled. When fed while incubating, the female either stands up in the bottom of the nest or else remains settled on the eggs and allows the male to approach close enough to enable her to reach the food in his bill. When the pair is not at the nest, the male usually does not approach the female but waits for her to come and take the food from him.

At a nest at Pinole, between 6 and 6:30 A. M., the female was fed five times. On this date, March 31, 1930, sunrise was at 6:16 A. M. Later in the morning the male did not appear at the nest more frequently than every half hour, and on a later date in the afternoon, 45 minutes elapsed without feeding. Occasionally the female may forage for herself within 50 yards of the nest tree; especially is this done if the male is absent. An estimate of the source of the food supply of the incubating female would place responsibility for the provision of at least 80 percent upon the male.

The boldness displayed by the birds when the nest is approached by an observer is highly variable. They are less audacious than when there are young present. Some individuals approach within 2 feet, whereas others do not approach within 100 feet or more. Similarly, some females tolerate an approach while incubating of 1 or 2 feet, others leaving the nest at distances of 50 to 100 feet. Any one bird will vary in its boldness to remain on the nest, depending on the weather conditions, not on the advance of incubation.

Demonstrations at the nest in an endeavor to repulse an intruder include clicking notes, prolonged jaylike notes, *schgra-a-a*, and to a lesser degree the customary series of intense screeches of progressively diminishing intensity. Snapping of the bill has been observed during a rush toward the observer. In their excitement the tail frequently is fanned, and also flicked sideways or up and down, the feathers of the back and head are elevated, the body is depressed with the head lowered, and the beak often is held open. Such attitudes are alternated with periods of fear when the feathers are adpressed to the body and the head raised accompanying a retreat, or anticipated retreat, to safer distances. The female has been seen suddenly to start begging during the height of her excitement. On other occasions shrikes have been seen hovering in the air over the nest tree or about the head of the observer. In some pairs the male is the more active defender, while in others the female is the more aggressive of the two. Nevertheless, when there is no major disturbance in progress, the male is usually the one to chase other species of birds from the vicinity of the nest site.

Young.—As the young crack open the shells, the greatly dried allantois may stick to the abdomen and cause the lower half of the shell to remain in contact with the bird. Once a female was watched while she sat quietly on the nest on the morning of the day when five of the young hatched. She was seen to stand up suddenly, move to the edge of the nest, and then tug and pull at an empty eggshell, which after three or four efforts was freed from the nest, carried to a distance of about 20 yards, and there dropped.

Young just hatched are bright orange with apricot-yellow bill and feet; the skin is smooth with few wrinkles and down is nearly lacking, being limited to two single rows of short white neossoptiles on each of the posterior abdominal regions of the ventral tract and a few similar neossoptiles on the elbows.

For at least an hour after hatching the young bird does not beg for food, but soon after commences to raise the head when it is touched or when the nest is jarred. The margin of the open mouth is conspicuously outlined with yellow, but the inside of the mouth is a deep pink with no special markings.   Faint thin notes, *tsp*, *tsp*, are given by the young as the head is held unsteadily upward.

The actions of the adults during the first day are not especially different from their actions during the incubation period, and there is no increase in their efforts to defend the nest. The female broods nearly as constantly as during incubation. The male procures almost all the food for the family and delivers it to the female, which either passes it on to the young or eats it herself. On several occasions a male was seen to approach the nest and sit beside it while the female was absent. He refrained from sitting on the nest and did not feed the young. The food that is brought to the nest is of such small size as to be, to the observer, invisible within the bill of the adult. Dark-colored parts of insects may be discerned through the skin of the under surfaces of the young. What appeared to be the elytra of small beetles, one-half centimeter in length, were visible in one instance.

On the third day a captive nestling disgorged a pellet 11 millimeters in length containing parts of dermestids and the hard muscular portions of the digestive tracts of snails I had fed to it during the morning of the same day. Also included in the pellet was a nearly complete femur, 9 millimeters long, of a small grasshopper that had been fed by the parents at least 24 hours previously. When passing fecal masses the hind quarters are elevated and the head thrust down. The fecal mass is inclosed in a firm mucous envelope, in a position from which it readily may be removed by a parent.

In the wild the parents had difficulty in inducing young to raise their heads, for, several times, the female upon approaching with food waited on the nest edge and, failing in her attempt to feed the young, swallowed the food herself. On another occasion, when the young failed to respond, she gave a faint, low-pitched, burred note, which resulted in an immediate begging for food. Seemingly an auditory stimulus had been necessary to arouse the brood. I then approached the nest, found the birds nonresponsive to touch or to jarring of the nest, and attempted a rough imitation of the nest call that the female had just given. The response was immediate, several heads being raised. Apparently at this age the young are able to receive sufficient food early in the morning to satisfy their hunger for a period of several hours lasting through the middle of the day.

On the fourth day the male was observed to feed the young for the first time and at the same time was heard to give the nest call similar to that given by the female. The male fed only when the female was absent from the nest. If she was present, food was delivered to her. A large part of the food brought by the parents is now visible in the bill. It was estimated that the female by this time is responsible for the capture of about 40 percent of the food of the family. She still spends much time brooding and occasionally eats food brought by the male, but rarely begging for it. The young may be left unbrooded for periods of 20 minutes, whereas earlier they were left for but intervals of about 5 minutes even at midday. The anxiety of the female to cover the young is regulated by the temperature. Late in the evening attempts to return to the nest while I was weighing the young were more frequent and bold than at midday when temperatures were as high as 75° F.

Brooding still occupies 50 percent of the time of the female on the sixth day. The male and to some extent the female are much more demonstrative against intruders than previously, coming closer and making more elaborate attacks upon them. Frequently adults have flown at my head, coming within a foot. It has been reported by several competent observers that at times the parent will even strike the intruder during these attacks. Late in the afternoon at one nest the young were hungry continuously, opening their mouths in response to all manner of stimuli and attempting to swallow fingers or even the wings of other nestlings that, through jostling, happened to be placed inside their open mouths. Nevertheless, the parent fed but three times in 45 minutes.

On the seventh day the brood in one nest was banded. The female, when allowed to return, eyed the nest and picked at the bands, soon lifting one of them up as though extracting a fecal sac. Finding the band attached to the young, she made a more vigorous effort and finally pulled the band and the leg up above the rim of the nest. The next effort dislodged the juvenile, and the female started to leave the nest with the band in her bill and the young dangling beneath. She flew only 6 feet in the direction of the customary depository for fecal masses and then fluttered to the ground. Considerable consternation was registered by both parents; they inspected the juvenile as it lay on the bare ground and screeched and hovered over it. After 10 minutes the female returned to the nest to brood. Fearing that the bird on the ground had been deserted completely, I replaced it in the nest. Subsequently, at each visit to the nest, the female made an effort to remove the bands but never again proceeded so far as to extract a young bird. Finally, after about 10 such efforts at intervals of 5 or 10 minutes, each effort decreasing in intensity, the bird ceased to pick at the bands. Through repeated trial and error she had come to recognize that this type of foreign material could not be removed successfully from the nest. After the juvenile that had been dropped to the ground was returned to the nest, the female several times left the nest and hovered and hopped about the spot where it had been. The inference would be that the shrike does not sense the number of young in its brood; furthermore, it returns to its young by reason of a memory for location, not necessarily because the young are sighted or heard.

By the twelfth day the young cannot yet stand upright on the metatarsus and hold their heads erect, yet they keep the eyes open and watch objects that move about near them. When the parents are screeching, the young refuse to open their mouths and they lie quiet and low in the nest. After the parents have been absent for several minutes, they respond to touch with the hunger reaction and seem to lose their fear. The fear attitude is reestablished with the recurrence of screeching and fluttering by the adults. The food call changes from *tsp* to a husky *tcheek*. The adults now become much warier, and brooding practically ceases. When away from the nest, the female often sits near the male while he forages, as during the period previous to nest-building. She procures at least half of the food of the young. Occasionally she begs feebly from the male and may receive food, which she eats herself. The male seldom brings food to be delivered to the young by the female, but instead he feeds it directly to them.

By the fifteenth day the young are well feathered, the tips of the remiges forming a continuous flight surface. The weight of juveniles on the sixteenth day nearly reaches that of adults, there being no decline in weight previous to this time although the rate of increase is relatively more gradual during the two or three days preceding. It is likely that in the wild a marked drop in weight follows departure from the nest. In the brood raised in captivity a decline of about 4 or 5 grams accompanied the first efforts of the young to hop about outside of the nest box. At this age the young in the wild squat low in the nest when approached by the observer and, when pulled from the nest, jump and flutter in their efforts to escape. They are belligerent and peck at the hand when captured. Handling of the young, and their screeches, make the adults frantic, and at such times both parents, in their excitement, have been heard giving the begging notes. When the juveniles are left on the ground they hop about giving a note indicated as *screig*, which is uttered at intervals of 10 to 20 seconds. The sound appears to be a "location note," that is, it serves to indicate to the parents the changing locations of the young. The young progress on the ground by hopping, the entire length of the metatarsus touching the ground. In trees and bushes they perch and jump distances of 3 to 6 inches, often falling and fluttering frantically as they cling to twigs and regain their balance. Progression on the ground or in trees is always upward. Young once removed from the nest when replaced usually will not remain but move off through the surrounding brush and, reaching a distance of several feet, sit motionless. In one instance, however, three young returned to a nest from the surrounding tree, a distance of at least 10 feet.

On the twentieth day four of the young at a nest near Pinole still were perched on the much flattened and excrement-stained nest, which for only the preceding four days the parents had failed to keep clean. The young hopped off through the trees while I was yet 6 feet from the nest. This day may be considered as the normal time of final departure from the nest when broods are unmolested.

Feeding still occurs at short intervals. It was estimated that the solitary female parent of one brood brought food 24 times between 9 and 10 A. M. on the twentieth day. Most of the foraging was done within 70 yards of the nest. The six young of this brood all were in the nest tree or in the willow adjacent; they occasionally gave the "location note." When the female appeared in flight moving toward the nest tree, the typical rhythmic wheedling or begging notes were given simultaneously by many, if not all, of the juveniles. This note had not been heard previous to the twentieth day. This latest and final type of food call of the young is accompanied by a flutter of the wings. Parent birds during this period are shy and usually do not attack intruders unless the young are captured or caused to move from their hiding places in the foliage of trees and bushes.

Between the twenty-sixth and thirty-fifth days the parents continue to feed the young, but at the same time the young are learning to forage for themselves. By the end of the period the juveniles frequently drop to the ground and feed, although they beg and follow their parents when the adults are in sight. The young still tend to stay grouped together but now perch in conspicuous places much of the time. As early as the thirtieth day the young range over the entire territory but make their headquarters near the nest.

Captive birds began drinking water and attempting to bathe on the thirtieth day. When 39 days old a bird sang the usual juvenal, mockingbirdlike song for the first time, the first efforts being, to the human ear, rather grotesque. The clicking vocal notes develop on the twenty-fifth day in a feeble, but recognizable, form; impaling of food items begins about the fortieth day.

Second nestings are begun while the adults are still feeding young of the first brood, but not all pairs undertake a second brood. One pair had a new nest with fresh eggs when the young of the first brood were 46 days old.

Plumages.—The natal down is scanty and is white (see p. 167). The juvenal plumage, which is acquired almost entirely before the young leave the nest, is lighter colored and less compact than that of the adult.

Juvenal coloration is as follows: UPPERPARTS: pileum and hind neck smoke gray, each feather with two dusky bars; back olive-gray, each feather usually with narrow smoke-gray tip and a dusky bar; lateral scapulars dull white distally, each with a distinct bar near tip followed by a less distinct bar proximally; the more median scapulars (not the interscapulars) and bases of lateral scapulars light olive-gray; rump and upper tail coverts light drab or clay color, each feather with two dusky bands; frontal tufts gray; bristles black; lores gray; antorbital, suborbital, and auricular regions varying from dull black to hair brown. UNDERPARTS: chin and throat white; malar region vermiculated with dusky and frequently sparingly tipped with black; breast, sides, and flanks light smoke gray, each feather with two dusky bars; belly and under tail coverts white with dusky spots and bars occasionally occurring on tips. WINGS: primaries dull black, both webs white basally (except outer web of No. 10) but with white more abruptly defined on outer web; primary 5 slightly tipped with light buff, primaries 4, 3, 2, and 1 with progressively broader dull white tips; secondaries dull black fading basally to gray on margin of inner webs; tips of distal secondaries dull white changing to vinaceous-buff or cinnamon-buff on inner secondaries; greater secondary coverts with clay color tips and median subterminal dots or bars; all middle and upper marginal coverts of forearm similarly tipped and barred with cinnamon-buff. TAIL: four middle rectrices black, with 2.0 millimeter tips of clay color or cinnamon-buff, frequently with a subterminal buff not separate from tip; other rectrices black, extensively but unequally tipped with light buff or white; outer webb of outermost rectrices entirely buff or white.

The first annual plumage is acquired by a partial postjuvenal molt in which the body, plumage, and a variable number, but not all, of the primaries and secondaries are replaced. The white-tipped juvenal primary coverts are retained throughout the first year, these together with the browner juvenal flight feathers serving to distinguish the first-year birds from adults. There is a prenuptial molt of limited extent, involving a few body feathers only. (For detailed description of postjuvenal plumages and the variations in completeness of the postjuvenal molt, see Miller, 1928 and 1931.)

Food.—The food of the American shrikes has received special treatment by Judd (1898) and by Beal and McAtee (1912). From an inspection of the reports of stomach contents of birds collected by me and from my own field observations, I am inclined to think that shrikes possess an almost indiscriminate taste for all sorts of animal matter. That is to say, if food properly attracts the attention of a shrike and if it is within its power to obtain it, there are few kinds of animals that are rejected because of unsuitable flavor or consistency. For example, millipeds and beetles that possess odors obnoxious to human beings are eaten by shrikes, although perhaps without relish.

Judd shows that vertebrate food of loggerhead shrikes may amount to as much as 76 percent of the diet during the winter months, but during the remainder of the year it is only 28 percent of the total food taken. However, samples of the stomach contents of *gambeli* in winter show it never takes as much as 70 percent of vertebrate food. Both Judd and Beal and McAtee have mentioned the fact that *gambeli* seems to take fewer birds and mammals than do the eastern races of the species. This is believed to be due to a more constant supply of insects throughout the year in the range of *gambeli* in California. Beal and McAtee estimate that vertebrate food during the entire year amounts to only 12 percent in the western races, principally *gambeli*.

In the San Joaquin Valley of California small rodents occur in the stomachs of shrikes more commonly late in summer than in winter. At this season there is a flux in the populations of *Reithrodontomys* and *Perognathus* in California. Specimens of *gambeli* taken about alfalfa fields, grainfields, and orchards usually have captured no mice. Contrasted with these conditions are those found in areas in the San Joaquin Valley where the sparse native brush is undisturbed, more small rodents having been taken by the shrikes in these localities.

Birds, chiefly small passerines, at no time comprise more than 15 percent of the food.

In regions where reptiles are common, these animals may amount to 7 or 8 percent of the diet. Some of the forms recorded as eaten or impaled are: *Uta* sp., *Sceloporus* sp., *Cnemidophorus tessellatus*, *Phrynosoma*, *Gerrhonotus*, *Diadophis*, and *Thamnophis*. Snakes as long as 18 inches may be successfully attacked.

Among the insects, the Orthoptera are variously estimated as constituting 30 percent to 75 percent of the total food. The higher percentages recorded for insects of this order occur at the times of year when grasshoppers increase to plague proportions. Bryant (1912) concluded that grasshoppers at Los Banos, Calif., reached an abundance of 20 to 30 per square yard during a plague in July 1912. At such times California shrikes were found to eat 47 percent of grasshoppers alone. Aside from the many species of grasshoppers and locusts preyed upon by *Lanius ludovicianus* should be mentioned the Gryllidae and *Stenopelmatus*. In California, *Stenopelmatus* is eaten particularly during the rainy season when it may be encountered frequently in fields or pasturelands.

Members of the Coleoptera comprise only 20 percent of the bulk of the food but are represented by a large number of individual animals. Of the 20 percent, the Carabidae contribute 7 percent.

In summarizing the factors that govern the kinds of food eaten by shrikes, I should mention first the factor of the size of prey. Animals too small to compensate for the energy expended by a shrike in procuring them mark the lower limit of size. The maximum size of prey is determined by the limits of the powers of the shrike to overtake and kill large-sized animals. When large animals are available, these perhaps are preferred to smaller animals, since one or two captures with the aid of the impaling reactions may provide food for an entire day. Secondly, in any habitat at any particular season there exists one or more optimum types of prey, that is to say, animals that by reason of their abundance in the habitat and the efficiency with which they may be captured are most commonly used as food. Obviously, the efficiency with which food is captured in turn depends on a delicately adjusted equilibrium between the many protecting devices on the part of the prey and the detecting powers of the shrikes.

Behavior.—The most profitable method of foraging, although not the one commonly observed, is what I have termed active hunting. This activity occurs usually early in the morning and at dusk in the evening. The actions as seen in *gambeli* consist principally of perching on objects 6 inches to 6 feet above ground where prey clearly may be seen moving within a radius of a few yards. At times the ground or low bushes are resorted to, and the bird hops about in these places in search of animals. The shrikes in moving rapidly from perch to perch fly close to the ground. Instead of waiting indefinitely on a perch until prey is sighted, if food is not secured from a certain post within a minute or two, the bird moves on to another part of its territory. Much or all of the territory may be covered in a short time as a result of these tactics.

Contrasted with active hunting is passive hunting, which is noted commonly during a large part of the day at times other than when adults are engaged in feeding young. It is conducted from relatively high perches that at the same time may serve as territorial lookout posts. Food is captured at distances from the perches of 10 to 150 feet, and there are extended intervals, often 10 to 30 minutes in duration, when no food is taken. The passive form of hunting occurs when digestion and pellet formation are in progress, the results of the early morning active hunting.

A less common method of foraging is the capturing of insects in the air, the birds maneuvering as do kingbirds, although in an awkward fashion. Dragonflies are caught in this manner. The actions consist of darting out into the air at insects as they fly past, the shrike often towering many feet above its perch.

The flight toward prey on or near the ground commonly is a nearly vertical or diagonal plunge either with set wings or, if necessary, accompanied by rapid wing motion. Hovering frequently is observed at the end of the approach flight and is either a searching device or serves to allow the bird better to judge the succeeding stages in the attack. Shrikes are adept at following prey that may fly or run from them. They are aided in this by the short, rapidly moving wings and long tail, which enable them to change rapidly the direction of their flight.

The worrying of prey that is difficult to kill is most persistent. Captive shrikes often spend half an hour at a time in attempting to kill large-sized mice and, failing in their efforts, will worry the mice at intervals during the greater part of a day.

The initial thrust at prey is with the bill. The effective motion is not a pounding or driving action with the end of the beak but a rapid biting motion of the tip of the lower mandible against the tomial tooth of the upper mandible. The killing mechanism, then, is a quick cut or snip of the bill.

After the initial successful thrust with the bill, a series of rapid biting motions follows and sometimes also shaking or pounding of the prey against the ground or perch. In the case of large animals a shrike commonly stands motionless for several seconds, and often minutes, after the animal is dead before further disposing of its catch.

The impaling habit of shrikes is the result of a lack of sufficiently powerful feet to hold the prey while it is being torn to pieces, thorns or crotches being used in order to hold the food while it is being eaten. Once a shrike has killed or injured its prey to the extent that it is incapable of escape, the food is further disposed of in one of two different ways: it is either impaled or else almost immediately eaten. If the food is smaller than about a centimeter in its greatest dimensions, it is swallowed at once or is taken to an elevated feeding or lookout post and there eaten.

Occasionally the feet are used to grasp small prey so as to obtain a fresh hold with the bill. The degree to which the foot is used in this way varies with individual shrikes. When food is held in one foot, the bird does not use that foot to support its weight. I have failed to note any instances of shrikes holding their prey against a perch or against the ground by standing on it, as do jays and hawks. To peck at or tear at food in the foot, as occasionally is done, the shrike seems required by its structure to hold the foot forward of the position normally taken in perching.

I have seen caged birds repeatedly attempt to ingest food that they either had failed to break up by impaling or feared would be taken from them, with the result that they were forced to disgorge. Several times I have seen the foot used to extract objects which were stuck in the mouth. In these instances the foot was not thrust into the mouth but passed along the side of the head, the claws catching hold of projecting parts of the food at the angle of the mouth.

As a rule large objects that must be impaled before being eaten are carried during flight, in the bill, but occasionally in the feet. Esterly (1917) reports the actions of a California shrike as follows:

The shrike flew against a window pane near where I was, and dropped a dead "White-crown." When the sparrow was picked up again it was seized by the neck, and the shrike flew off with it. But before it had gone more than a yard, and while about a foot in the air, the shrike released its hold on the neck of the prey, and, without hesitating or altering its course, caught the sparrow in its feet. The flight was continued for about fifteen yards, and then the shrike dropped to the ground. It started off at once and the same behavior was repeated; the prey was picked up by the neck with the beak and this hold was given up, while flying, for the hawk hold. The substitution is almost instantaneous; the burden does not drop perceptibly and the flight is continuous and steady.

This observation on behavior, although entirely reliable, must be considered as abnormal, for most shrikes certainly do not handle their prey in this fashion.

With large-sized prey, shrikes resort to special impaling stations within the territory. The variety of impaling devices is great and indicates a generalization of the inherited reaction, permitting individual adaptability in the matter of finding and experimenting with the most effective means for the fixation of food. The first attempts of juveniles at impaling have been noted in cage birds. These consist of dragging the food along the perches with a jerking motion, the head held low and the long axis of the bill paralleling the perch. If nails are provided in the perches, the food on encountering these obstacles offers resistance to the bird, which continues to tug and may on occasion thus firmly lodge the food on the nails. Subsequently, small bits are picked from the impaled mass, first gently, but later they are torn loose with great vigor.

Well-known examples of trees and plants used for impaling are orange, yucca, saltbush, and some cactuses. The use of barbed wire is widespread wherever this is available. Ends of broken branches also are used extensively. I have observed a California shrike slip the abdomen of a *Stenopelmatus* over a broken willow twig one-fourth of an inch in diameter, fitting it on tightly, and then proceed to tear off bits from the open anterior end of the abdomen. My cage birds became accustomed to impaling upon the split end of a small broken branch as well as upon nails driven through their perches.

If shrikes are hungry when large prey is impaled, they eat enough to gorge themselves thoroughly. As much a 7 grams of food may be eaten at a single feeding. If the impaled food amounts to more than this in bulk, the remainder may be left hanging. The shrike returns to the food during succeeding hours and usually eats it to the last morsel. As a storing device, impaling is useful for periods of a day or two only, unless climatic conditions favor the preservation of the animal food for longer intervals of time. Impaled objects are comparable to the kills of large predatory mammals, and, so long as they are still edible, the shrike returns to them unless more recent kills occupy its attention. Storage in its true form involves gathering together a considerable quantity of food for future use without at the time partaking of it extensively. The object of the American shrikes' habit of impaling, then, is not truly storage. When concentration of impaled objects does occur it is due to the habitual return of the shrike to a successful impaling station because of the facilities available there for the ready handling of the prey, not because of a desire to store or concentrate food.   In inspecting numerous shrike impalings I find that where abundant impaling situations, such as barbed-wire fences, are at hand, the unfinished meals of shrikes are distributed along such fences at considerable intervals.   Concentrations of impalings such as often do occur probably result from a scarcity of impaling facilities in a territory.

A considerable portion of the deserted impalings consists of parts of animals that would seem to be less desirable as food.   Jaws of lizards, the hard heads of *Stenopelmatus*, partly picked bones of mice, and the wings and tails of birds are samples of deserted parts that appear on the average more abundantly than do soft-bodied insects and the flesh of vertebrates.   Recent, although deserted, impalings do not appear in the same abundance at all times of year in California. During the middle of winter they are rare, and I have never found them where young or brooding females were being fed.   The season of their greatest abundance is late in summer and in fall.

Voice.—Most of the utterances of California shrikes have been mentioned in earlier sections, but they may here be reviewed.   The spring song of the male consists of short trills or combinations of clear notes repeated a number of times, yet varied in rhythm, pitch, and quality.   For example, each of the separate parts or units of the song may be primarily a trill with three or four distinguishable throbs in it.   The quality of the trill often is described as liquid, but the trill also contains harsher, burred qualities.   Added to this trill are clear, usually sharp, descending or ascending terminal notes. Other songs lack a trill, two or three clear or burred notes, variously accented and pitched, constituting the unit of song.   Still other individuals precede a trill by clear notes.   The most characteristic features of the California shrike's song are not pitch or the structure of the unit song of a series but rather the rhythmic repetition of song units and certain general tonal qualities impossible of description or even exact imitation.   The units of song are repeated at an average of one every two seconds, but the rhythm may be more rapid if the song unit is especially short.

The feeding territory song of *gambeli* given late in summer by males and females alike is of the same general construction as the spring song but appears to contain fewer high clear notes and more notes rough in quality and resembling the quality of the harsh screeches or begging notes.

Immature birds give a decidedly different song of a continuous sort, consisting of short screeches, gurgles, trills, and clear notes in a succession quite pleasing to the human ear.   It is the continuous type of song that has led observers to claim that shrikes imitate other birds. However, I have consistently failed to detect anything in these songs that could definitely be called imitation.   Captive juveniles that never had heard songs of other birds or of shrikes uttered primitive songs identical with those given by wild shrikes.   Such songs of cage birds are purely instinctive and unlearned.

The screech or call note consists of 4 to 10 or more harsh forceful utterances of diminishing intensity, the first notes slightly higher pitched and shorter than the terminal notes, although pitch is difficult to detect in a sound so thoroughly discordant.   A metallic variation of this call note occurs during nuptial displays.

Single notes, *schgra-a-a*, of a quality less sharp than that of the screeches, variously repeated and resembling the huskier notes of *Cyanocitta stelleri*, are given by birds while defending their nests. These notes are each longer in duration than a single screech of the call-note series.   This type of note also may be given while a logger-head shrike is worrying prey it cannot readily kill.

Staccato clucking notes are heard during attacks upon invaders or when birds are in a defensive attitude.

The pulsating or begging notes of young and the begging notes of adults are extremely similar, although slight differences in quality may be detected.   The *tsp* and *tcheep* of young in the nest, fear notes of juveniles, the juvenile's "location note," *screig*, and the nest call of the parents have earlier been described.

There is but one note given by cage birds that I have failed to hear in the wild and have not seen mentioned in the literature.   This is a low-pitched chuckle of weak intensity, which cage birds give when approached and when completely at ease, that is to say, when they are not frightened or in any way excited.

Captive nestlings develop perfectly all the notes of wild shrikes with the exception of the rhythmic types of song.

Enemies.—Unfortunately little is known concerning causes of death in California shrikes.   These birds are moderately large, aggressive, and well equipped to fight, and it is difficult to understand what happens to the relatively large number of young hatched annually.

Instances of death other than by shooting I have noted have occurred as a result of accident caused by automobiles on roadways.   Robertson (1930) includes in his discussion of death of birds on roadways records of ten California shrikes found dead during one year on the roads bounding a region roughly 10 square miles in an area in southern California under his daily observation.   He concludes that the most likely cause of death is collision with automobiles and that death is not caused to any extent by collision with overhead wires or by shooting. Birds probably are struck down by automobiles most commonly early in the morning, for the road surfaces at that time are well baited with insects injured during the night. A shrike while killing prey is likely to be practically oblivious to surrounding dangers, and its powers to spring rapidly into the air are relatively poor.

A shrike at Firebaugh, Calif., after retiring to its roost was heard to give repeated frantic screeches when a horned owl perched on a pole nearby. A barn owl, which approached and perched near the roost shortly after the horned owl had left, provoked no such outburst from the shrike. E. L. Sumner, Jr., has found the remains of shrikes in horned-owl nests. Captive birds are greatly disturbed on being confronted with dead hawks or owls. Similar fear is displayed when hawks, cats, or dogs come near them. Therefore, there is some evidence to indicate that shrike populations experience losses through the feeding activities of large predatory birds and mammals.

The known parasites of shrikes rarely produce death and cannot be considered as contributing importantly to the death rate.

Despite our ignorance concerning the causes of death in shrikes, the life expectation of individuals can be estimated by indirect means. Usually in *Lanius ludovicianus* first-year birds make up about 50 per cent of winter populations. This means that annually half of the breeding population of the preceding season die and are replaced by first-year birds. If we assume that a family group in the spring consists of two adults and six juveniles, the succeeding year would, on the average, result in the death of one of these adults and five of the juveniles. Most of the juveniles would be lost before leaving their parents or during the first summer and autumn. Therefore, the juvenal and immature death rates are high, and the average life expectation of young upon leaving the nest is only about four months. The group of immatures that successfully passes the first winter, later, as breeding birds, constitutes 50 percent of the total breeding population. Theoretically, during each succeeding year this same group must undergo a 50 percent annual reduction by death.

LANIUS LUDOVICIANUS NELSONI Oberholser

NELSON'S SHRIKE

HABITS

The shrikes of this species living in the southern two-thirds of the peninsula of Lower California have been separated by Dr. Oberholser (1918) under the above name. He describes the form as "similar to *Lanius ludovicianus gambeli*, but bill larger; white terminal areas on outer rectrices much smaller; upper parts averaging darker, though with the upper tail-coverts more conspicuously whitish; lower surface more tinged with grayish, particularly on the posterior portion." He gives as its distribution: "The southern two-thirds of Lower California, including the adjacent islands, north to 29°30″ north latitude."

Griffing Bancroft (1930) says of the haunts of Nelson's shrike: "There are shrikes near Santa Rosalia. In any small cañon which runs back from the Gulf and which also contains a few trees, three or four, perhaps a breeding pair, of these birds are apt to be found. They nest near San Ignacio Lagoon and among the sand dunes along with the Desert Thrasher. They occupy, intermittently, the terrain between these extremes, but only in associations either of low brush or of isolated trees. On the whole they are to be listed as rare birds."

Nesting.—Bancroft says on this subject: "The breeding season is well under way in March and does not extend beyond April. Either three or four eggs are laid, in bulky nests of tree moss. There is no lining in the cup. The building material, which is the same throughout, is itself soft enough for the eggs." Dr. Miller (1931) says that, of the three nests found by Mr. Bancroft, "one was in a Joshua tree, one against a bank and covered with a creeping vine, and one in the heart of a growth of tumble weed." There is a set of four eggs of this shrike in the Charles E. Doe collection, at Gainesville, Fla., that was taken by Mr. Bancroft at a later date, March 30, 1932, at Playa María, Lower California. The nest was said to have been of "fine end tops and moss," and located 3 feet from the ground in a frutilla bush.

J. Stuart Rowley writes to me: "In the Cape region of Lower California, I found this shrike not very abundant and exceedingly wary to approach within gun range. One nest was located near Todos Santos on May 22, 1933, containing four fresh eggs, which are smaller than the average size of the northern races. The nest was very well concealed in overhanging vine tangles, but was typically of shrike construction."

Eggs.—The eggs of Nelson's shrike are apparently like those of other races of this species. The measurements of 18 eggs average 24.9 by 18.3 millimeters; the eggs showing the four extremes measure 26.5 by 18.5, 26.0 by 19.5, and 22.8 by 17.1 millimeters.

LANIUS LUDOVICIANUS ANTHONYI Mearns

ISLAND SHRIKE

HABITS

Two races of this species have been described from the Santa Barbara Islands, off the coast of southern California, but only the above-named form is recognized in the 1931 Check-list. Dr. Mearns (1898), in naming this subspecies, remarks: "This Shrike is naturally to be compared with *Lanius ludovicianus gambeli* Ridgway, the form common on the adjacent coast of California, but differs in being very much darker as well as smaller. It is, in fact, darker than the darkest eastern specimens of *L. ludovicianus.*"

Mr. Ridgway (1904), in comparing it with the eastern bird, calls it the "darkest of all the forms of this species. Similar in coloration to *L. l. ludovicianus*, but gray of upper parts still darker (nearly slate color), especially on pileum, and more uniform, the scapulars almost wholly deep gray; white spot at base of primaries much smaller; under parts of body much more strongly tinged with gray, becoming distinctly gray (about No. 6) on sides and flanks; lateral rectrices with much less of white, this extending only about 22 mm. from the tip on inner web of exterior rectrix."

He restricts this form to Santa Cruz Island, and names a new subspecies from San Clemente Island *L. l. mearnsi*, which he characterizes as "similar to *L. l. anthonyi*, but upper tail-coverts abruptly white, more white on scapulars, white spot at base of primaries larger, and under parts of body much less strongly tinged with gray. In white upper tail-coverts, greater extent of white on posterior scapulars and at base of primaries, similar to *L. l. gambeli*, but gray of upper parts very much darker (quite as dark as in *L. l. anthonyi*), and with much less of white at base of primaries and on lateral rectrices."

Ridgway's new form, *mearnsi*, was at one time accepted by the A. O. U. Committee on Nomenclature, but after its validity had been questioned by a number of writers the name was discarded, and it never appeared in the Check-list. The latest authority on this group, Dr. Alden H. Miller (1931), however, recognizes *mearnsi* as the bird of San Clemente Island, remarking: "Of all the subspecies of *L. ludovicianus*, *mearnsi* is the most isolated race and is among the most sharply characterized subspecies of the species. Although not to be considered as a distinct species, it is surprising to note the doubts that ornithologists have entertained concerning the valdity of this race."

He says of the range of *anthonyi*:

The islands of Santa Catalina and Santa Cruz off the coast of southern California comprise most of the range of this subspecies. Santa Rosa Island may possess a considerable population but thus far few records for this island have appeared. Parts of Santa Cruz Island are forested with live oaks and the Monterey pine. In August 1922 I found shrikes in the pines and acacias at Prisoner's Harbor and also in the scattered live oaks in the cañon leading from this point toward the interior of the island. Much of the habitat, however, consists of grasslands with small bushes in the cañons. The hills and cañons which the shrikes frequent are often exceedingly precipitous. Likewise, on Santa Catalina Island much of the habitat consists of steep hillsides covered with scrub oak, toyon, ironwood, and, in places, dense stands of opuntia cactus. * * * San Clemente Island is more arid than those islands of the Santa Barbara group on which *anthonyi* occurs."

Nesting.—Dr. Joseph Grinnell (1897) found a shrike's nest on April 2, 1897, on San Clemente Island: "The nest was in a small bush growing out from the side of a cañon, and was composed mostly of sheep wool, with an admixture of weed stems and grasses. Five slightly incubated eggs constituted the set. They are not different from eggs of true *L. l. gambeli* of the mainland."

Dawson (1923) records two nests found on Santa Cruz Island, near Prisoners Harbor, one 6 feet up in an acacia tree and the other in a pollard willow. The first nest contained six eggs and the second held five; in both cases there were two distinct types of eggs in the nest, with three shrikes in attendance. Dr. Miller (1931) says that "Mailliard (1899, p. 42) found two nests on the same island, one placed in a brush pile, the other in a gum (eucalyptus) tree."

Eggs.—The four, five, or six eggs laid by the island shrike are apparently indistinguishable from those of the bird of the mainland. The measurements of 30 eggs average 25.0 by 17.5 millimeters; the eggs showing the four extremes measure **26.1** by 18.3, 24.9 by **19.7**, and **24.4** by **13.2** millimeters.

Behavior.—One of the most prominent characteristics of the island shrike seems to be its shyness or its wildness. Dr. Mearns (1898) writes:

All who have seen it regard it as one of the wildest of birds. On his visits to San Clemente, in 1888 and 1889, Mr. Townsend was unable to obtain a specimen. In 1894, Mr. Anthony and myself procured a single one—with difficulty, although Shrikes were seen daily. At night, when we went out to shoot bats, Shrikes would dash about us, uttering loud, harsh screams, differing from the voices of any Shrikes I have heard elsewhere. In the daytime they never permitted us to come within range of them.

Dr. Grinnell (1897) found the birds on San Clemente equally shy: "This bird was without question the shyest and hardest to be secured of any on the island. Indeed it was as shy as any hawk I ever saw. It was tolerably common; that is, two or three could be generally seen during an hour's walk. There was a pair in the neighborhood of the windmill where we were camping, and nearly every morning a little after daybreak the male would perch either on the windmill or on the topmost twig of a brush pile on the opposite side of the ravine, and utter its defiant shrike notes. The rustle of the tent door or the click of a gun lock, however, was sufficient to send him up over the ridge, not to appear again for hours."

Family STURNIDAE: Starlings

STURNUS VULGARIS VULGARIS Linnaeus

STARLING

HABITS

There are some 60 species of starlings widely scattered over the Eastern Hemisphere, though none indigenous in Australia or in New Guinea. We have only two resident species in North America, both introduced and long suspected to be of doubtful value. The subject of this sketch is supposed to be of the same subspecies as that found in western Europe, of which there are many allied races in Europe and Asia.

The starling is a dominant species, well fitted to survive in the struggle for existence, as shown by its successful competition with other species, by its steady increase in a strange land, and by its remarkable spread over new territory, of which we have not yet seen the end. The literature of American ornithology is flooded with references to its spectacular progress. This whole story might well be filled with this interesting phase of its life history, but space will permit only a brief outline of its spread and the tremendous increase in its numbers; only the highlights among the hundreds of references can be shown.

We probably shall never know how many unsuccessful attempts have been made to introduce the starling into North America; Edward H. Forbush (1927) mentions the following introductions: "Cincinnati, Ohio (1872–73); Quebec, Canada (1875); Worcester, Massachusetts (1884); Tenafly, New Jersey (1884); New York City (1877, 1887, 1890, 1891); Portland, Oregon (1889, 1892); Allegheny, Pennsylvania, and Springfield, Massachusetts (1897); and Bay Ridge, New York, about 1900." Apparently all these attempts were failures except those made in New York City in 1890 and 1891. May Thacher Cooke (1928) mentions an unsuccessful attempt made at West Chester, Pa., before 1850.

Authorities differ somewhat as to the numbers of starling liberated by Eugene Scheifflin in Central Park, New York, and as to the exact dates. Mr. Forbush (1927) says that 80 were liberated on March 16, 1890, and 40 more on April 25, 1891. Miss Cooke (1928) says that 80 birds were released in April 1890 and 80 more the next year. It is generally accepted, however, that 60 birds were introduced in 1890 and 40 more in 1891; Dr. Chapman (1925) states that there were only 100 birds liberated in all, and he ought to have known. From this small nucleus have descended all the vast hordes that now overrun the country.

For the first six years, while the birds were becoming established, they were confined to greater New York City, including Brooklyn and Staten Island, though stragglers were reported in Princeton, N. J., in 1894. Then, as the population built up, the fall and winter wanderings began in search of new territory in which to establish a breeding range later. By 1900 they had appeared at New Haven, Conn., Ossining, N. Y., and Bayonne, N. J. Dr. Stone (1937) reported them at Tuckerton, N. J., in 1907, and Dr. Townsend (1920) saw the first one in 1908 in eastern Massachusetts. During that and the next two years, the starlings wandered over most of Massachusetts, up to the New Hampshire border, and over eastern Pennsylvania. Robie W. Tufts tells me that the first one was seen near Halifax, Nova Scotia, on December 1, 1915. By 1916, according to Kalmbach and Gabrielson (1921), its postbreeding wanderings extended from "southern Maine to Norfolk, Va. On November 10, 1917, one specimen was collected as far south as Savannah, Ga. Inland it has been seen at Rochester, N. Y., Wheeling, W. Va., and in east central Ohio." During the next 10 years starlings were variously recorded as far north as southern Ontario, as far west as Wisconsin, Iowa, and Illinois, and as far south as Louisiana, Mississippi, Alabama, and Florida. E. C. Hoffman's (1930) map shows the range for the winter of 1929–30 as extending west to southeastern Wisconsin, eastern Iowa, including most of Missouri, southeastern Kansas, much of Oklahoma and Texas, and extending practically to the coasts of the Gulf States. It is interesting to note that the western limit of this range roughly parallels the 1,000-foot contour line.

Some interesting extreme wanderings were recorded in 1931 and 1932 at Churchill, Manitoba, Moose Factory, James Bay, and the Gaspé Peninsula, Quebec. Frank L. Farley tells me that one appeared at Camrose, Alberta, in May 1934 but none have been seen since. L. M. Dickerson (1938) has published a map showing the western migration frontier of the starling in the United States up to February 1937; this touches South Dakota and eastern Nebraska and includes a large part of Kansas and most of Oklahoma and Texas. In 1939 the starling crossed the Mexican boundary, had reached Colorado and New Mexico, and appeared at Norway House in northern Manitoba. A. D. Henderson writes to me that, on September 21, 1940, he observed the first starling he had seen in Belvedere, Alberta; it was perched on a poplar tree with several blackbirds. Russell K. Grater tells me that he saw a large flock at Mount Carmel, Kane County, Utah, on January 2, 1941; "this flock was apparently drifting and was seen only the one day." Last, but most interesting of all, comes the westernmost record from Stanley G. Jewett (1942), who reports a flock of about 40 starlings seen in Siskiyou County, Calif., in January and a specimen collected there on February 4, 1942. Gabrielson and Jewett (1940) state that "in 1889 and 1892, the Portland Song Bird Club released 35 pairs of Starlings in Portland. These birds established themselves and remained for a number of years, but some time about 1901 or 1902 disappeared." So, unless these California birds were survivors from that Oregon importation, which seems unlikely, the starling had at last reached the Pacific slope.

The extension of the breeding range of the starling lags about 5 years behind its spread as a fall and winter wanderer. According to Dr. Chapman (1925), the starling began to breed soon after its release in Central Park in 1890, for a nest was found under the eaves of the northeast wing of the American Museum of Natural History that year, for which the museum "may claim the doubtful honor of being the birthplace of the first European starlings to be born in this country."

The following outline of the extension of its breeding range is taken mainly from the published maps of Dr. Chapman (1925), Kalmbach and Gabrielson (1921), and Miss Cooke (1928), together with a large number of published records that are deemed to be reliable. Up to 1896 it was not known to breed outside of greater New York, including Brooklyn and Staten Island. In 1900 and 1902 it was found breeding near Norwalk, Conn., and Elizabeth, N. J. By 1906 its breeding range had covered about one-half of Connecticut and about one-half of New Jersey; and by 1910 it had covered practically all these two States and extended its range into southern Massachusetts, and into Rhode Island. During the next four years it occupied practically all Massachusetts, about one-quarter of New York, the eastern quarter of Pennsylvania, and practically all Maryland. Between 1916 and 1920, it extended its breeding range farther inland into Maine, New Hampshire, and Vermont, covering most of New York, three-quarters of Pennsylvania, and a large part of Virginia. During the next six years, up to 1926, its range expanded northward to cover all New England, except northern Maine, some of southern Ontario, southeastern Michigan, most of Indiana, eastern Kentucky and Tennessee, northeastern Georgia, and the uplands of South Carolina.

Mr. Tufts tells me that the first Nova Scotia nest was found on June 26, 1928, on a golf course in Halifax, and says: "Since then, they have become exceedingly abundant in our Province." During that and the next 10 years, the starling was reported as breeding on Cape Breton Island, southern Quebec, the Chicago area and other parts of Illinois, Nebraska, Arkansas, Mississippi, and northern Florida. How much farther it has progressed since these data were accumulated (1942) remains to be seen.

Miss May Thacher Cooke has contributed an interesting history of the spread of the starling, based on the records of the Fish and Wildlife Service, which appears at the end of the distribution for this species.

As the starling became established in a given area, it began to increase rapidly until its numbers approached the saturation point, when it was forced to expand its range. Thus, there was a continuous increase going on behind the advancing pioneers, and this is still continuing. Two interesting studies of this advance and the following increase have recently been made, based on the figures given in the Bird-Lore Christmas censuses. W. J. Cartwright (1924) has compiled these census figures in two very significant tables; the first table shows that there was only one census report from one State, New York, in

1900, but there were 79 reports from 10 states in 1923; the second table shows that the number of birds reported increased from 4 in New York in 1900 to 15,388 reported in the same 10 States in 1923. These tables do not claim to be absolutely accurate, as many rough estimates have been made by the census-takers, nor do they come anywhere near representing the total population at any one point, but they show interesting trends.

Another interesting study has since been made by Dr. Leonard Wing (1943) on data collected from the same and other sources. His maps and figures show the spread and increase of the starling, as compared with the more rapid spread and greater increase in numbers of the English sparrow, and are well worth careful study, for only a few points can be mentioned here. One table shows the steady increase in airline spread of the starling in different directions during the different periods from 1901 to 1940. Based on the census reports, the spread increased from the 1901 to 1905 period to the 1936 to 1940 period as follows: For birds traveling westward, from 15 to 1,917 miles; for birds spreading west-southwest, from 21 to 1,898 miles; and for birds spreading north-northwest, from 78 to 727 miles. It appears that the spread was more rapid through the Southern and Southwestern States than through the Northern States; it also shows that more rapid progress was made in recent than in earlier years. The figures from published sources are somewhat higher, but the trend is similar, and the rate of increase is remarkably steady, in both cases. He says in his summary: "The rate of spread, as measured by percentage of area covered, was fastest in the 26–30 years (1916–1920) after its introduction.

"The area covered by 1940 is calculated as 2,717,161 square miles for the Starling which is still spreading. For the English Sparrow, the area is calculated as 3,676,427 square miles.

"The Starling is not limited by low altitudes but has reached areas more than 6,000 feet above sea level."

The following pertinent note was sent to me by Prof. Maurice Brooks in 1942: "The most notable thing which can be said of the starling in West Virginia is that it has not been able to establish itself in our mountain forests, so far at least. Harvey Cromer, who has spent 60 years at Cheat Bridge, Randolph County, and has kept his eyes open, showed me two starlings he shot there about 15 years ago. He regarded them as a great curiosity, since he has never seen others there before or since. I do not know of any other records for the birds in the spruce belt."

The above observation is not to be wondered at, for it is a well-known fact that starlings in their wanderings prefer to frequent rural and farming districts, or even towns and cities, rather than forests and mountain regions. Consequently, as such settlements are found mainly in the valleys, the birds have followed these routes in crossing what mountain ranges they have encountered in their travels.

Milton B. Trautman (1940) says of the increase at Buckeye Lake, Ohio: "In 1922 no Starlings were recorded in the area. In 1929, 8,000 were noted in a day."

Now that the starling has spread so rapidly southward and westward and has increased so enormously in its northeastern range, it has probably reached the limits of its abundance in some eastern sections of the country, and we may expect to find its numbers falling off in some places. Dr. Clarence Cottam (1943) has published some evidence of this decline in the agricultural districts of western New York, based on studies made there in 1932 and again in 1942. He writes: "For about 15 years the Starling has been the most abundant bird in northeastern United States. Accurate counts of such an abundant, gregarious, and active species are almost impossible. * * * Although no exact figures can be given, it seems evident that peak numbers were reached six or eight years ago, a small but noticeable decline taking place each succeeding year."

Referring to the western New York area, he concluded, after the second study, that "it was doubtful whether, in the summer of 1942, the area contained 25 per cent of the concentration found there in 1932.

"A similar but less noticeable reduction of the enormous wintering flocks is believed to have occurred in the District of Columbia region, although the birds are still overabundant and constitute an annoyance of major proportions in the Capital City. No careful study of populations has been made, but a number of competent ornithologists who have been connected with the Starling problem for many years have repeatedly expressed their belief that there has been an encouraging reduction in the size and number of these flocks. The writer is of the opinion that there has been a reduction of 15 to 25 per cent in the population wintering in this section during the past eight years."

Migration.—The European starling is largely sedentary in Great Britain, though some emigrate in the fall and return in February and March. But from late in September until early in November, "vast numbers arrive from central and north Europe; * * * some winter and some pass south," according to Witherby's Handbook (1919). There seems to be a decided migratory movement, northeasterly in the spring and southwesterly, on the European Continent, the birds which breed in the Scandinavian countries and other parts of northern Europe spending the winter in Spain, the other Mediterranean countries, and northern Africa. It is fair to assume that our birds inherited from their European ancestors an instinct for this northeast-southwest trend in migration. This tendency is shown in the way the species has spread in this country, mainly in these two directions. The southwestern spread has been more pronounced than any others;

this may be because the natural flocking instinct of starlings has led
to their association with grackles and blackbirds, which were drifting
southward in large flocks in the fall.   Our starlings have probably
not yet fully developed the migratory habit in its strictest sense, that
is, regular north and south migrations at definite times, such as those
made by our native birds, but they are learning fast from their blackbird associates in both spring and fall.

Many starlings remain in the more northern portions of their range
all winter, many others make only short flights or wander about in a
haphazard way, but there is a general fall movement toward the south
and great winter concentrations at points far south of the breeding
range.   In their southern roosts and concentration areas, the starlings
are intimately associated with the great flocks of grackles, red-winged
and rusty blackbirds, and cowbirds; and when these birds start northward early in spring, the starlings flock along with them.

There are apparently two quite distinct migration routes in the
eastern United States, both northeastward in the spring and southwestward in the fall.   One of these follows the Atlantic Coast States
from New England to the Southern States, east of the Alleghenies.
The other is an inland route, entirely west of the Alleghenies, from
eastern Quebec to the Gulf States.   This latter route is well illustrated
in the maps shown in an excellent paper by Edward S. Thomas (1934),
based on the results obtained by the banding of 7,062 starlings at
Columbus, Ohio, in 1927, 1928, and 1929, and the recoveries from them
up to April 4, 1932.   The maps show that, with very few exceptions,
the spring and summer recoveries were from points northeast of
Columbus and the fall recoveries were mainly from points southwest
of that locality.   He makes the following pertinent conclusions in
his summary:

1. The European Starlings banded at Columbus, Ohio, are highly migratory.
2. A large proportion, if not the great majority of the birds banded at roosts at
Columbus nest in northeastern Ohio, Pennsylvania, New York, eastern Ontario,
and Quebec.   3. Many of them winter to the southwest of Columbus, one of them
at least, as far as Merigold, Mississippi.   4. The evidence indicates that a very
small percentage of the birds banded at the large roosts at Columbus are permanent residents.   5. The individuals passing through Columbus migrate in a
northeast-southwest direction, closely parelleling the direction of flight of the
species in continental Europe.

Nesting.—Starlings are not very particular as to where they place
their nests, nor are they at all particular about the care of them.
Their nests are slovenly and often filthy with the large amount of
excrement voided by the young during their rather long stay in the nest
and by the parents while attending them.The nests are sometimes occupied for several years in succession, and the accumulated mass of half-
rotted material becomes quite foul.   Such slovenly habits have caused

many complaints, where nests have been built over doors or windows, or behind blinds.

Almost any old hole or cavity will serve for a nesting site, but a preference seems to be shown for natural cavities in trees, or in old or new holes made by the larger woodpeckers, such as the flicker or red-headed woodpecker. I have seen a starling watch a flicker excavating its nest hole until it reached the proper depth to suit the former, when the flicker would be driven out and a starling's nest be built in the hole. The flicker excavates a new hole but is again driven out; and this procedure may be repeated until all the starlings in the neighborhood have been supplied with homes, or until the flicker becomes discouraged and moves off to the nearest woods, where it can nest in peace.

Nests in trees may be anywhere from 2 feet to 60 feet above ground, but they are usually between 10 and 25 feet up. Woodpecker holes in telephone poles, fence posts, or dead snags are often occupied. Holes made by hairy woodpeckers may be used occasionally, but these are usually in the woods where the starlings do not like to go; the holes made by the downy woodpecker are too small.

Starlings are serious competitors of the bluebird, tree swallow, English sparrow, and other birds of that size that nest in bird boxes, and to a less extent of the purple martin, but often these birds are able to defend their homes. They cannot enter boxes having entrance holes less than 1½ inches in diameter. Crested flycatchers nest in natural cavities in old apple orchards, must meet some competition from starlings. On June 8, 1941, W. George F. Harris and I hunted through an old orchard in Raynham, Mass., where crested flycatchers and wood ducks had nested for a number of years. The orchard was infested with starlings, large numbers of the young, fully grown in their juvenal plumage, were flying about, evidently the products of first broods, and their parents were laying their second sets of eggs, one of which we found. We flushed the flycatcher from her nest and were surprised to find that it contained six eggs of the flycatcher and one of the starling. Incubation had started in three of the flycatcher's eggs, the other three and the starling's egg being perfectly fresh, indicating that the starling had probably laid its egg in the flycatcher's nest before the latter's set was complete, perhaps while she was off the nest.

While tree cavities, woodpecker holes, and bird boxes are favorite nesting sites, the starling loves to nest in any convenient cavity it can find in or on barns, outbuildings, deserted houses or schools, under eaves of houses or those of dormer windows, about the cornices or in the towers of buildings in cities, and in church steeples or belfries. Mr. Forbush (1927) writes: "By prying off a plank of the floor above a chime of bells in a Long Island church-tower I was enabled to enter the chamber above, where about thirty nests of Starlings were occupied by young birds. Concealed in this dark chamber and watching the feeding of the young I noted that every 15 minutes when the chimes were rung some of the machinery struck the planks beneath my feet with a sound like that of a sledge-hammer."

Witherby's Handbook (1919) says that, in England, they sometimes nest in the ivy growing on the walls of buildings. W. A. Smith, of Lyndonville, N. Y., tells me that he has heard of starlings nesting in the branches of a tree, and he sent me a nest which he thought was a starling's that was built on the ground in a "grassy meadow." He tells me the following story: "We have a motor on an upstairs floor of our factory; it is enclosed with a partition which rises from floor to ceiling and is about 3 by 3 feet square; there is a small hole through the concrete-block siding right near the motor, made for the purpose of admitting fresh air to the motor. The starlings found this and decided on it as a nesting place. The motor being somewhat in their way, they proceeded to cover it up with nesting material. I noticed them carrying nesting material to the hole, as it was visible from my office window. They continued to carry material for several days. After I thought it was time for eggs, I went up to see what was in the nest. I found the largest starling's nest I have ever seen or heard about; a bushel basket would not begin to hold it. They were successful in raising their brood, as the motor was not being used at the time."

Starlings' nests have also been found in holes in haystacks, holes in cliffs and banks, such as the old burrows of kingfishers and bank swallows, and in cavities among rocks or heaps of stones. Kalmbach and Gabrielson (1921) state that "nests have been found on fire escapes, hay tracks, and barn doors, behind window shutters, and even in open boxes erected for pigeons. * * * The clogging of hay tracks or tracks of barn doors with their nests is occasionally a source of trouble, and the infesting of the immediate vicinity of their homes with bird lice is complained of when they build about water tanks, poultry houses, etc."

Starlings sometimes build their nests near those of other starlings, or even near the nests of other species, with no appearance of antagonism nor fear of molestation. Dr. Chapman (1925) "heard of five pairs of starlings nesting simultaneously in the hollow limbs of a single willow tree." Mr. Forbush's experience with the colony in the church steeple, referred to above, is a more striking example of colonizing. Mr. Trautman (1940) writes: "In 1928, 2 pairs nested in the attic of a deserted schoolhouse, and at the same time and within 10 feet of a pair of Barn Owls, and in the same year 2 occupied Starling nests were found on the same side of a tree and about 3 feet apart, while between them was the occupied nest of a Red-headed Woodpecker." I have often seen starlings fly from their nests in the bases or sides of the huge stick nests of ospreys, where they find convenient crannies. In 1942 I saw a starling drive away a flicker from its new nest in a large sycamore stub and appropriate it for its own use; on the other side of the stub, about 3 feet away, was a saw-whet owl's nest with a brood of young. One of F. W. Braund's (MS.) nests was 10 feet below an occupied sparrow hawk's nest.

As the nests are built in cavities, there is no necessity for building a well-made and compact nest. The cavity is loosely filled with a mass of material in sufficient quantity to fill the space up to within a few inches of the entrance. This material consists mainly of coarse and fine grasses and straws, with sometimes rootlets, small twigs, corn husks, a few green leaves mixed in, and occasionally bits of cloth, paper, string or other trash; the lining may consist of finer pieces of grass, or small or large amounts of poultry feathers; the latter are often mixed into the body of the nest. The size of the nest depends on the size of the cavity, but the inner cup is usually about 3 inches in diameter.

Eggs.—The starling usually lays four or five eggs, often six, rarely seven, and as many as eight have been recorded. These are mainly ovate to elliptical-ovate and have a slight gloss. The color is very pale bluish or greenish white, often nearly white. W. A. Smith tells me that he has a set in his collection in which the eggs "are a pure, pearly white, without a trace of blue color; they were collected from the nest of a partially albino starling." I have no record of any spotted eggs. Bernard W. Tucker sends me the measurements of 100 British eggs; they average 30.2 by 21.2 millimeters; the eggs showing the four extremes measure **34.9** by 21.0, 34.1 by **22.4,** and **27.2** by **19.8** millimeters.

The measurements of 50 American eggs are somewhat different; they average 29.2 by 21.1 millimeters; the eggs showing the four extremes measure **31.4** by 21.4, 30.5 by **22.5, 26.9** by 20.0, and 27.9 by **19.8** millimeters.

Young.—The period of incubation is variously reported as 11 to 14 days, but most authorities agree on the latter figure. The duties of incubation are shared by both sexes. The young are said to remain in the nest until they are fully fledged, or for a period of 2 to 3 weeks; they can then fly well; this protracted nest life in a closed nest tends to reduce the mortality in the young. The total nesting cycle, nest-building, incubation, and nest life of the young is therefore about 40 days.

Kalmbach and Gabrielson (1921) write:

Nestling starlings are fed by the parents largely on insects. For the first week both parents take part in the feeding operations, but in several nests that were under observation the female was left to do all the work during the latter part of the nestling period. When 3 or 4 days old the young are very noisy and give the feeding call in lusty chorus in response to almost any sound.

Later, they learn to distinguish the approach of the parents and respond only to their notes or appearance. Other noises or vibrations cause them to crouch silently in the bottom of the nest, and no amount of coaxing will persuade one of them to stir or make a sound.

Two broods are usually raised each year and sometimes there are three. The first of these leaves the nest about June 1 and the second late in July. Fledglings which may have been from either a belated second or third brood just from the nest were collected as late as September 12, at Bay Shore, N. Y.

As soon as the first brood leaves the nest small flocks of young starlings can be found feeding on grasslands or roosting at night in trees or buildings. These flocks grow rapidly in size and by mid-July often number into the thousands. During the day no adult birds are found in these early flocks and very few appear until after the completion of the molt in September; both old and young, however, occupy the same nightly roost.

Lony B. Strabala (1926), of Leetonia, Ohio, spent a long day watching a pair of starlings feeding their young, on which he reports: "During the whole day that I watched, * * * I saw them feed the young 121 times." During the day he was away from the nest at meal times for 2 hours and 50 minutes, but he saw them make their first feeding at 4:32 A. M., and their last trip at 7:21 P. M. "They were feeding their young fifteen hours and twenty-three minutes, they made an average while I watched them of around 10 trips an hour so in the whole fifteen hours and twenty-three minutes they would make no less than about 155 trips in one day of which the male made 74 and the female 47 of the 121 trips I saw them make. The male carried out excrement 20 times while I was watching and the female 23 times. The shortest interval between feeding was one minute and the longest was 45 minutes. During the whole day they were not seen to feed the young anything but insects and worms as far as I could tell."

Dr. Witmer Stone (1937), writing of conditions at Cape May, N. J., says: "When the young first leave the nest they follow a parent, presumably the female, on the lawns of the town, running rapidly after her and jostling one another in their greed to get the food she is finding for them. This often continues until the birds are full-grown and seem perfectly able to shift for themselves. By July 1 we may see flocks of young numbering one hundred or more, all in their plain gray dress, arising from the fields of cut hay where they find an abundance of insect food; other flocks all composed of young were seen on July 2 and 7 in different years about the hogpens which are to be found on the edges of marsh and woodland, where the garbage from the town is hauled."

William Lott (1939), of London, Ontario, found a flicker feeding a brood of three feathered young starlings; the nest was a typical starling's nest; he saw the flicker make several trips with food before he caught her on the nest; he raised the question whether the starling may have built its nest in the flicker's nesting hole and the latter hatched the eggs.

R. A. Johnson (1935) conducted a study on a lot of starling nests in an old barn at Oneonta, N. Y., for the purpose of determining the success of the birds in raising their broods. He says:

Notes were recorded on the success of seventeen nests. Six of these were early or May nests of 1933 and 1934. Eleven were second or June nests of 1933. All of these second nests came at the time of the beginning of the drought of 1933.

The seventeen nests produced seventy-nine eggs, hatched fifty young, forty of which were reared. It is very interesting however to compare the success of the early or May nests with the late or June nests. The six early nests produced twenty-nine eggs, hatched twenty-six young and fledged twenty-six young. The eleven late or June nests produced fifty eggs, hatched twenty-four young, of which only fourteen were fledged. During the incubation period for the June nests the severe drought of that summer set in, which was, in my opinion, the main factor in causing the low percentage of success for the second nests.

Plumages.—The small nestling starling is fairly well covered with long, drab-gray, or grayish-white natal down, longest and darkest on the head, but present on practically all the principal feather tracts. The juvenal plumage is fully acquired before the young leave the nest, including considerable development of the flight feathers. In this plumage, the young bird is very plainly colored and entirely unlike the adult. The upperparts, including the wings and tail, are brownish "mouse gray"; the underparts are only a slightly paler shade of the same color, fading out to whitish on the throat and chin; the abdomen is streaked with grayish white; and the wings and tail have narrow buffy edgings.

The starling is one of the few American birds that have a complete postjuvenal molt, which takes place between July and September, depending upon the date of hatching; for birds of the first brood in New England, this occurs mainly in August. James Lee Peters (1928) has published a detailed account of this molt, to which the reader is referred. He says that molt of the body plumage occurs simultaneously with that of the primaries and tail, beginning with the inner, or first, primary and ending with the outer, or tenth. He has seen this molt practically completed by August 19, and in another case, perhaps a bird from a second brood, not until the end of September. The molt begins soon after the wings and tail are fully grown, the first of the glossy green, white-tipped feathers appearing on the flanks, and the last of the juvenal plumage disappearing on the head.

Dr. Dwight (1900) describes the first winter plumage very well, as follows: "Everywhere bottle or purplish green with metallic reflections, the feathers above with cinnamon terminal spots, smallest on the head, the feathers below with white spots. Wings and tail greenish black edged with cinnamon, the wing quills having a pale terminal spot bordered with black."

Young and old birds are now much alike, but the cinnamon spots and edgings are more deeply colored in young birds, the chin is whitish, the forehead buffy, the spots are larger and rounder, especially below, and the body feathers are more rounded, less pointed.

There is no spring molt, but wear and fading have practically eliminated most of the spotting, especially on the underparts and head. The bill, which was mostly dusky in the fall, becomes lemon-yellow before spring. Adults and year-old birds have a complete postnuptial molt, beginning sometimes in June but usually from July through September. This produces the heavily spotted fall plumage, which is changed by wear, as in the young bird. Females are like the males, but the colors are usually duller, the body feathers are shorter, less pointed, and the spotting is heavier. Females usually have less yellow, or less brilliant yellow, in the bill at any season than the males. Dr. Lawrence E. Hicks (1934) says that, "as the breeding season approaches," the basal half of the lower mandible "becomes conspicuously bluish white to bluish gray in the males and pinkish white to pinkish gray in the females."

Food.—The most comprehensive report on the food of the starling is contained in Kalmbach and Gabrielson's (1921) excellent paper on the economic value of this bird, from which most of what follows is taken. The examination of 2,301 stomachs showed that 57 percent of the food for the year was animal matter and 43 percent vegetable. The highest percentage of animal food was taken in April, 91.22 percent, and in May, 94.95 percent; it dropped to the lowest point in February, 28.17 percent; but the average for the four months, December to March, was 31.5 percent, a remarkable showing. Vegetable food reached its maximum in July, 52.67 percent, nearly all mulberries and cherries.

Insects formed 41.55 percent of the total food, "a greater proportion than is shown in the food of most of our native birds of similar habits." It reached its maximum in October, 57.8 percent. About half of the insect food, 19.59 percent, consisted of various beetles, largely weevils.

Most prominent among these was the clover leaf weevil (*Hypera punctata*), which does considerable damage to the clover crop; 1,125 starlings had fed on this pest, both winter and summer. A number of other species of weevils were found, including the strawberry crown girdler and the bluegrass billbug. "It is evident that the starling is a very effective enemy of such weevils as feed on grass or forage crops. This is particularly noticeable in regard to the clover pests, and it is safe to assert that *the starling is the most effective bird enemy of the clover weevil in America.*"

The Carabidae, or ground beetles, amounted to 5.71 percent for the year but rose to 13.02 percent in August, only a small part of which were of the beneficial, predatory species. A long list of other beetles follow in the report, among which are May beetles, the adults of the notorious white grubs, dung beetles, the injurious Japanese beetle, rove beetles, leaf beetles, click beetles, darkling beetles, and the famous potato beetle.

Orthoptera, among which the shorthorned grasshoppers (Acrididae) and crickets (Gryllidae) predominated, constituted 12.41 per cent of the annual food of the adult starlings examined. * * * A conservative estimate of the annual loss in this country due to the grasshoppers is $50,000,000. This would be much greater were it not for the controlling influence of insectivorous birds. Some of these, among which may be placed the starling, secure practically all of their insect food during September and October from this source, stopping thereby the depredations of millions of these insects and preventing the future development of countless millions more. * * * When hay fields are being cut and raked in the latter part of August and early September, flocks of juvenile starlings secure practically all their sustenance from these insects, supplemented with wild black cherries (*Prunus serotina*) and elderberries (*Sambucus canadensis*). * * * Of the 2,301 stomachs of adult starlings examined, 538 contained the remains of caterpillars; 20 contained pupae; and 30, adult Lepidoptera.

In one bird's stomach "were the remains of no less than 40 caterpillars, which formed 98 percent of the food." The starling has distinguished itself as a most effective enemy of that notorious pest, the cutworm; it has been observed doing exceptionally good work on the army worm; and has been seen feeding on the larvae of the cabbage butterfly. Only a few tent caterpillars and other hairy species have been found in its food. "One reason for not finding more spiny or hairy caterpillars may be explained by an incident observed at Norwalk, Conn., where a starling was seen to eat a tent caterpillar much after the fashion of the Baltimore oriole, by forcing out the soft parts and leaving the hairy skin hanging on the limb."

Among other insects eaten they mention Hymenoptera, mostly ants and a few ichneumons and bees, Hemiptera, and Diptera in small quantities. And the remainder of the animal food consists of millipeds, spiders, land snails, earthworms, sowbugs, and remains of animal garbage; fragments of a crab, a few beach fleas, and the bones of a salamander were also found.

The vegetable food consists of cultivated and wild fruits and berries, grain, and seeds. The most serious complaint against the starling is its fondness for cherries. "In 1915, on a farm near Closter, N. J., trees that should have produced $50 to $60 worth of cherries yielded only $10 worth, a loss due largely to starlings. At Bristol, Conn., a flock of about 300 starlings entirely stripped a single tree of its 1916 crop in less than 15 minutes. At Rowayton, Conn., six cherry trees were entirely stripped of their fruit by robins and starlings in 1916." But in the 2,301 stomachs examined, only 169 contained cultivated cherries, forming 2.66 percent of the annual food, or a maximum of 17.01 percent in June. "During the months of June and July, the robins obtained 24.58 per cent and 22.71 percent, respectively, of their food from cultivated cherries, quantities half again as great as those consumed by starlings in the same months." Probably very little damage is done to strawberries, in spite of some complaints, or to other small fruits. Some apples, pears, and peaches have been pecked into and ruined on the trees, but the extent of the injury seems to be over-rated. Only 45 of the 2,301 stomachs examined contained pulp or skin of apples, and in 23 of these cases the birds were taken in winter and spring. No grapes were found in the stomachs examined, though the starling is said to eat grapes, especially in the vineyards of France.

Together with large flocks of grackles, red-winged blackbirds, and cowbirds, starlings visit the fields of sweet corn, when it is ready for the market, and do considerable damage by tearing open the ears and eating enough of the juicy kernels to render the ears unsalable; but most of this damage is evidently done by the other black birds, for only 52 out of the 2,301 starlings had eaten any corn; moreover, most farmers do not distinguish starlings from immature redwings, so that the starlings have often been unjustly blamed. The starling has also been accused of pulling up sprouting corn and other grains, pecking at tomatoes, and pulling up and injuring various other truck garden plants, but the aggregate damage is apparently not great, except in a few small city gardens.

Wild fruits constitute 23.86 percent of the starling's yearly food, reaching a maximum of 40.88 percent in August. Early in the summer they eat mulberries and Juneberries (*Amelanchier*), then blackberries and wild cherries; later on they take the berries of the sour gum and Virginia-creeper, and elderberries, and in fall and winter they eat bayberries and the seeds of the sumacs and other species of *Rhus*. "Wild fruit enters into the winter food in the following percentages: November, 41.80; December, 36.44; January, 19.98; February, 32.90." Other vegetable food consists of poison-ivy seeds, garbage refuse, seeds of ragweed, foxtail grass, etc.

The stomachs of 309 nestlings of all ages were examined, from which it appeared that the food items were mainly the same as for the adults, though there was a larger proportion of soft-bodied insects, 95.06 percent against 82.36 percent for the adults at the same season. "To very young birds caterpillars are especially attractive. Only 3 of the 79 nestlings estimated to be less than 6 days old had failed to eat these larvae." Cutworms and the white grubs of the May beetle were prominent and spiders were most conspicuous, being present in 182 of the 325 nestling stomachs examined. Cherries were eaten by 30 of the nestlings, mostly during the last few days of their nest life.

That young starlings are heavily fed is shown by the following observation:

In nine days a total of 390 feedings were recorded, in 14 periods varying in length from 30 minutes to 4 hours and 41 minutes. One hundred and four of the feedings were by the male and 286 by the female. An average of one feeding every 6.1 minutes was maintained for the whole period of observation, 31 hours and 10 minutes. The highest rate was recorded on the morning of May 18, which was probably the seventh day of the nestlings' life. A feeding every 3.2 minutes was maintained for 4 hours and 41 minutes. The lowest rate, once every 11.7 minutes, occurred on May 25, the day before the young left the nest. * * * When it is borne in mind that the parent birds would often bring in three or four cutworms, earthworms, or grasshoppers, or an equal bulk of miscellaneous insect food, at a single trip, one may gain an idea of the quantity of food required to develop a brood of young starlings.

In conclusion, they say as to the economic value of the starling: "Most of the starling's food habits have been demonstrated to be either beneficial to man or of a neutral character. Furthermore, it has been found that the time the bird spends in destroying crops or in molesting other birds is extremely short compared with the endless hours it spends searching for insects or feeding on wild fruits. * * * The individual farmer will be well rewarded by allowing a reasonable number of starlings to conduct their nesting operations on the farm. Later in the season a little vigilance will prevent these easily frightened birds from exacting an unfair toll for services rendered."

It is interesting that their investigation of the economic value of the starling abroad was favorable. After presenting some of the evidence, they say: "Summing up, it may be said that in Europe the verdict on the starling is distinctly favorable; of 35 works dealing in a general way with the economic status of the bird, only 7 report adversely. It is noteworthy, moreover, that the findings of all the thorough and more scientific investigators have been in favor of the species, although some authors admit that at present starlings are too numerous in some localities."

Starlings are generally seen feeding on the ground, where most of their insect food is undoubtedly obtained, or resorting to trees and bushes for their fruit and berries, but Kalmbach and Gabrielson (1921) mention two other rather unusual methods of feeding, as follows:

Connected with the capture of Hymenoptera is one of the oddest activities of the starling. While primarily terrestrial feeders, soon after the first of August young starlings were seen catching insects on the wing, much after the fashion of true flycatchers. From a perch on a dead upper limb the birds would spy insects several yards away, fly out, and dexterously capture them. Later, after the first of October, starlings changed their tactics, adopting methods similar to those of swallows or martins in securing flying insects. The best illustration of those activities was furnished in northern New Jersey on a calm day above a warm, sunlit meadow. Here a dozen or more starlings were sailing about and capturing insects at a height of about a hundred feet from the ground. Under such conditions one not acquainted with the starling would certainly have mistaken the birds for martins, for, combined with a form which is quite similar, was the flight evolution, which imitated the martins perfectly.

Many ants in the winged stage are captured by starlings in their aerial evolutions, some are picked up on the ground, and others are secured from the branches of trees. On September 5 a number of juvenile starlings were noted diligently searching for and picking up food from the upper branches of a spruce. To some extent their actions imitated those of chickadees or warblers, though they were not so sprightly. One of these birds was collected and its stomach found to be filled with ants.

All the above account of the food and feeding habits of the starling has been condensed from the extensive report by Kalmbach and Gabrielson (1921), which leaves little more to be said. Doubtless many other kinds of insects, small animals, fruits, and berries are eaten that are not mentioned above, and the list will be added to as the bird extends its range into other types of country, and as more observers are watching them. For instance, E. A. McIlhenny (1936) saw them feeding, on Avery Island, La., upon the berries of the cassena, hackberry, camphor, and chinaberry trees and upon other berry-bearing trees, shrubs, and vines, flocking in countless numbers with robins and cedar waxwings.

Mr. Forbush (1927) says: "It takes practically all grains, including corn, and digs up the seed in planted or sowed fields. It takes the young sprouts of such garden vegetables as beans, peas, lettuce, onions, radishes, beets, carrots, muskmelons, squashes and tomatoes and young flowering plants as well. * * * In pastures it follows the cattle or sheep, catching the insects that the animals stir up, or actually alighting on their backs in search of ticks or other insects." See, also, a paper by Clarence Cottam (1944).

Short-grass fields, pastures, or lawns are favorite feeding places, where the ground is easily reached; they do not like to feed in long grass. On my lawn in the center of the city, I can see from a few to many starlings almost any day when the ground is bare, winter or summer, zigzagging over the lawn and probing into the ground. I do not want to shoot them to learn what they are eating, for I know that they are feeding on enemies of the grass, perhaps the larvae or pupae of the Japanese beetle. My flowering crabapple trees fruit profusely nearly every year; and before the tiny apples are ripe the starlings and some robins flock to them day after day, until the trees are entirely stripped of their fruit; and for a long time after that, they may be seen on the ground under them, picking up the fallen apples.

For a further study of the economic status of the starling, the reader is referred to Mr. Forbush's (1927) extensive remarks on the subject and to E. R. Kalmbach's (1922) discussion of the food habits of the species in England as compared with those of this bird in America, which illustrates what can happen to change its status when it becomes too numerous. Whereas in moderate numbers it may be a very useful bird, it may increase to such an extent as to become very detrimental.

Behavior.—Starlings are shy, timid, nervous birds. It is almost impossible to approach them within gunshot range in open country. If, when they are feeding in a cherry tree, a gun is fired at them, the survivors will fly away and not soon return, more scared than hurt as a rule. It is impossible to exterminate them, or even materially reduce their numbers. Their caution is their salvation. I often watch them feeding on my front lawn, which extends unprotected to the sidewalk; usually a person walking by, or certainly one stopping to look at them, will send them flying up into the trees; even a passing vehicle may produce the same effect.

On the ground they walk with short, mincing steps and a waddling gait on their rather short legs, running or hopping occasionally if in a hurry; they do not seem to forage systematically but wander over the lawn in a haphazard manner. Milton P. Skinner (1928) says that when a flock is moving forward, "Starlings have the peculiar habit of hopping up in the air from eight to twelve inches and forward at the same time a foot or more. These hops are rather frequent, four per cent or more of the flock being in the air at the same time." It is interesting to watch a large flock feeding on some wide expanse of grassland; the whole flock seems to progress by "rolling" over the ground, all moving in the same direction, those in the rear ranks rising, flying over the crowd and settling in front of the slowly moving ranks, thus securing the first chance to feed on fresh ground.

Starlings show to best advantage in flight; their ordinary short flights sometimes seem slow and feeble, but, when well under way and going somewhere, the flight is strong, swift and direct, with rapid strokes of the short, pointed wings, interspersed with periods of sailing on stiff pinions. Miss Cooke (1928) says that "they are swift flyers, at times traveling as fast as 49 miles an hour." Everett W. Jameson (1942) timed the speed of a starling that flew parallel to his automobile for over half a mile in still air at 55 miles an hour.

The spectacular flight maneuvers of a large flock of starlings are most remarkable, and they always attract the enthusiastic admiration of the beholder, as they wheel, turn, and swing into fantastic formations with marvelous precision, with no apparent leader but all responding as if one individual, rivaling in their coordinated movements the flocking instincts of some of the smaller shorebirds that we like to watch whirling in clouds over the marshes. Many writers have referred to this interesting flight, but the following words of Dr. Chapman (1925) are fully as good as any:

A thousand, five thousand, ten thousand birds mount to the sky, animated by one impulse—the flock becomes a ball symmetrical as a globe in outline; suddenly, with no suggestion of disorder, it lengthens to an ellipse which a moment later, narrowing in the middle and concentrating at the ends, simulates a dumbbell in form. Again a change, and a dusky snake undulates across the heavens only to telescope on itself and become a ball again.

But little less spectacular are the great roosts resorted to by the young after the breeding season and by young and old starlings in fall and winter, often with hordes of grackles, red-winged blackbirds, cowbirds, and robins. Early in the season, late in summer and early in fall, enormous numbers roost in trees, and in cattail swamps or other marshes. But, when winter comes, the flocks of starlings seek better protection in or on various buildings in the towns and cities, though many continue to roost in shade trees along the streets as long as the leaves remain on the trees. Many congregate in barns or in church towers in the villages, while others resort to public buildings in the large cities, roosting in the ventilators on the roofs, on ledges under the eaves, on cornices, on the tops of windows or on the capitals of pillars, wherever they can crowd into some sheltered spot. Many starling roosts have been described in print, but only a few can be mentioned here.

Hicks and Dambach (1935) made some observations on a large roost in an oak thicket on the southward-facing slope of a ravine near Zanesville, Ohio, through the fall and until cold weather drove them out in January:

The aerial manœuvres performed before the final roost movements were little short of miraculous. To see more than 30,000 birds flying in unison and in close formation is a truly worth-while sight. The black, moving cloud of starlings took on fantastic shapes as the birds swerved to one side, swooped down, or performed other movements, each bird following the path taken by its predecessor. The manœuvres were performed so regularly that we gave them names and recognized the same movements repeatedly night after night. At times the moving mass of birds resembled a huge bullet hurtling through space; at other times it consisted of a continuous revolving circle, or resembled a waving flag, a darting fish, a conventional comet, a most spectacular dark sinister-looking waterspout. These manœuvres took from 45 to 60 minutes each night. During this time the starlings actually were on the wing for about 30 minutes, and maintained an average speed of a little more than 30 miles an hour. * * *

And this exercise was in addition to perhaps 20 to 90 miles of flying by each bird during the day. * * *

Activity in this roost was apparent at the first sign of daybreak. The birds, in a vociferous garrulous mass, swarmed like an excited cluster of honey-bees through the dense tangle of the thicket until twelve minutes before sunrise. Then, within eight minutes, the whole group took wing, rising in several well-defined waves. Next a few aerial manœuvres were performed over the roost in mass formation, the groups gradually breaking into a number of small units, each unit taking a definite route, which was found to be the same each day.

Loefer and Patten (1941) describe an interesting roost in a rocky gorge near Lexington, Ky., as follows:

At this scenic spot between Fayette and Madison Counties the river has cut through solid rock marking a very narrow valley hedged in by rocky walls and slopes which mark the channel of long ago. * * * Fairly large and closely planted deciduous trees line the bank, and smaller trees, including some cedars, cover the more gentle slope which extends for about a hundred and twenty-five yards from the river bank to the highway. * * *

Intensive observations were made at the roost this year (1941) during the month of March. On fair evenings the birds began to appear in the trees along the top of the gorge at about six o'clock. They seemed to converge in small flocks from all directions during the next half-hour. The smaller flocks aggregated into larger ones, but did not descend to the roost until about dusk, probably because the inhabitants of the valley in attempting to break up the roost, shot into the flocks frequently. The skillful maneuvering by the close formations of these large flocks as they veered sharply first in one direction and then in another while flying around before settling was an impressive sight not easily forgotten by any observer. When the birds settled, the trees appeared, from a few hundred yards distant, as though in full leaf. The small grove in which the birds settled did not exceed four acres, but the birds were so numerous that many limbs of the trees were broken and dung in places was four inches deep. It was impossible to estimate accurately the total number of blackbirds. Local ornithologists set the figure at anywhere from a half to around several million. * * * Of the three species seen at the roost, Starlings (*Sturnus vulgaris vulgaris*) were by far preponderant, outnumbering Bronzed Grackles (*Quiscalus quiscula aeneus*) at least twenty-five to one. A number of Cowbirds (*Molothrus ater ater*) were there during early March, but few were seen late in the month.

Kalmbach and Gabrielson (1921) say of a New Jersey roost:

At a roost in a marsh along the Hackensack River an opportunity was afforded to watch the starlings congregating. As early as 3 o'clock in the afternoon flocks of a dozen or two could be found gathering in the hayfields in the vicinity, or perching on dead chestnuts, singing and preening their feathers. Most of these were juveniles with the molt extending up as far as the neck. They would fly alternately to the hay stubble, which was heavily infested with grasshoppers, and then to the tree tops when flushed. By 4 o'clock a flock of a hundred or more had gathered. * * * With the approach of evening the birds would rise and perform numerous flight evolutions, in which they displayed wonderful coordination of action. This was best observed when they would fly in the direction of the sun, and the flashes of light coming from their glossy backs appeared as coming from a single mirror instead of from several hundred bodies acting independently but in perfect unison. * * * As dusk approached, the birds had worked their way toward the Hackensack River, where they gathered in compact flocks, singing in the tree tops along the bank. A few were seen feeding with a large number of red-wings on the tidal flats along the edge of the marsh. When darkness finally came the starlings in the tree tops sailed out over the marsh and joined their relatives, perching on the cat-tail flags for the night.

Mr. Kalmbach (1932) tells us something about the city roostings of starlings in Washington, D. C., where he and others did some extensive banding in winter roosts. Fully a thousand starlings roosted in ventilators on top of the Post Office Department Building on Pennsylvania Avenue, in December 1927, but they were not easily caught there; they abandoned the roost and promptly changed to the tower of the First Presbyterian Church, where as many as 2,000 repaired nightly; 1,241 starlings were banded there on March 2, 1928. In the winter of 1928–29, starlings were banded in the tower of the Metropolitan Memorial M. E. Church.

The Starlings in the first of the towers visited, which is an old one, occupied various ledges and nooks in the wall as the cross braces. At a certain level there was a series of box-like cavities in the wall construction, each about two feet wide, three feet deep, and six inches high. These were filled with Starlings for their entire depth with scarcely room for another, and, despite an outdoor temperature of well below freezing, I am confident a thermometer placed among the birds would have registered close to that of their own bodies. We ourselves were able to keep perfectly comfortable, even though working bare-handed on cold nights, by frequently delving arms' length into one of these cavities to drag forth a double handful of Starlings. This habit of dense crowding is quite different from that displayed by Starlings when roosting in trees or on the exterior of some buildings where there is ample room. In such locations the birds appear to resent close association and aim to keep between each other a space equal to the width of a bird.

The starlings also roosted in such numbers on the outside of the old Land Office Building and the Patent Office that men had to be hired to drive them away. "On the 9th of February 1931, a crew of eight men, four to each building, started a crusade against the roosting birds. Cat-o-nine tail whips of short poles with several strands of flexible wire attached were used to lash the ledges beneath the eaves. The men operated from the roof of the building."

This was carried on for four nights in succession, and "since then, these two buildings, which together harbored probably in excess of 6,000 birds, have been free of Starlings."

In a nearby community in Virginia, "a mixed flock of English Sparrows and Starlings roosted, to the great distress of the owner of the property, in ivy covering the brick walls of a large and stately dwelling. A plea for some relief led to an experiment in the use of calcium cyanide dust as a fumigant."

After several repetitions of this treatment the birds left and never returned. Various other methods have been employed, more or less successfully, to prevent or break up starling roosts; where the birds roost on outside ledges of buildings, these could be screened or slanting boards be placed on them, or the birds could be driven away by shooting at them with slingshots or air rifles; shooting with shotguns is most effective, but in many places it is objectionable or illegal; shooting Roman candles into roosting trees is sometimes effective and not objectionable; the use of the city fire hose will drive them out; but all these devices must be followed up persistently to be successful. Where starlings roost inside buildings, they can be killed with poisonous gases, but these are dangerous and should be used only by an expert; and they can be eradicated by frequently disturbing their slumbers. For a full discussion of this subject, the reader is referred to a mimeographed circular by Mr. Kalmbach (1937).

In its relation to other species the starling is not above criticism. It has been severely condemned on two counts, competition with various native species for nesting sites and consumption of too much of the available food supply on which our birds largely depend in fall and winter. Whether the harm done on either of these counts has been overestimated is an open question, when we consider the economic value of the starling as one of the greatest destroyers of noxious insects, as shown above. The study of its food habits indicate that the starling is of more economic value than the robin, English sparrow, or flicker, with which it competes for food or nesting sites, and it has a better food record than such beneficial birds as the catbird, red-winged blackbird, or grackle; but the economic value of the bluebird and the purple martin might be considered greater than that of the starling.

In its search for nesting sites, the starling comes into competition with domestic pigeons, screech owls, sparrow hawks, flickers and other large woodpeckers, crested flycatchers, purple martins, bluebirds, tree swallows and house wrens, or other hole-nesting birds that build their nests in open cavities in trees, or in bird boxes that have entrance holes large enough for them to enter. But the starlings cannot occupy a box, if the entrance hole is an inch and a half in diameter or less, where the smaller birds would be safe.

Starlings either preempt the nesting site before the others have had a chance to occupy it, in which case their ownership is seldom disputed, or they actually evict the rightful owners after their nest is built, or even contains eggs or young. Probably the flicker is the most frequent victim of these aggressive tactics, about which much has been published. The following case, reported by Kalmbach and Gabrielson (1921) is typical:

In contests with the flicker the starling frequently makes up in numbers what disadvantage it may have in size. Typical of such combats was one observed on May 9, at Hartford, Conn., where a group of starlings and a flicker were in controversy over a newly excavated nest. The number of starlings varied, but as many as 6 were noted at one time. Attention was first attracted to the dispute by a number of starlings in close proximity to the hole and by the sounds of a tussle within. Presently a flicker came out dragging a starling after him. The starling continued the battle outside long enough to allow one of its comrades to slip into the nest. Of course the flicker had to repeat the entire performance. He did this for about half an hour, when he gave up, leaving the starlings in possession of the nest.

They tell of another case in which the flickers were finally successful in raising a brood which was nearly ready to leave the nest. "Whenever this flicker relaxed its vigilance for a moment one of the starlings would immediately make a dart for the nest opening. A scuffle would ensue in which both flicker and starling would come tumbling to the ground and a few feathers would fly." This conflict continued for several days, until the young flickers left the nest unharmed. Even then the starlings did not use the nest.

On several occasions starlings have been known to remove the flicker's eggs, or pull out the young birds and throw them to the ground, in order to occupy the nest hole. That they sometimes kill the adult flicker in shown by the following observation by Lewis O. Shelley (1935) :

The first year the Flickers were driven away before the eggs were laid. The next spring, a pair of Starlings desirous of the new nest-hole for their second brood, killed the young Flickers and they, or another pair, threw out the dead birds, and nested. The third year, hearing a great to-do of Starling squawks and whistles, I was in time to see a Starling pursue the female Flicker and strike her at the base of the skull when she alighted at the nest-hole. Examination proved that the victim was killed instantly, the Starling's bill having pierced the skull and brain. Since then several nesting Flickers, presumably killed in this same manner, have been brought to me. In 1933 I saw a female that was paralyzed from an attack ; she tried several times to climb up the tree and finally fell back and died.

Kalmbach and Gabrielson (1921) mention a number of occasions on which starlings have attacked other birds, and some on which they seemed to get along amicably with their neighbors. "One martin house at Norwalk, Conn., was occupied by a pair of sparrow hawks on one side and three pairs of starlings on the other. At Hadlyme, Conn., a colony of fully 50 pairs of martins conducted unmolested their nesting operations under the close scrutiny of starlings that nested nearby." One of two martin houses at Adelphia, N. J.—

was occupied by starlings, and when a pair of martins appeared and attempted to take up the other abode a fight occurred. A starling was observed going into the martin house, and after pulling out one of the inmates dragged out the nest material.

The martin was subsequently attacked whenever it approached and it finally left the premises. * * * The single record of starlings attacking a red-headed woodpecker comes from Baltimore, Md., where a combat was observed over a nest cavity in a telephone pole. * * * At Ambler, Pa., two nestling robins were killed by starlings, the victims being dispatched by powerful pecks on the head.

At East Norwalk, Conn., a starling was seen to peck and break all the eggs in a robin's nest. * * * Single attacks on a Baltimore oriole's nest and the young of a chipping sparrow were reported. * * * At Middletown, R. I., it was found necessary to wage constant warfare on the starlings to keep them from nesting in one pigeon loft, where they appropriated for their own domestic affairs the boxes put up for the pigeons. They carried in so much material that they filled the boxes and on one or two occasions dragged it in so rapidly as actually to barricade the setting pigeons, which were entirely unresisting.

At Norwalk, Conn., a pair of bluebirds started to build nests in three different boxes, one after another, but the starlings removed all the nesting material, and it was not until the bluebirds found a box provided with a 1⅝-inch opening that they were able to lay a set of eggs. But, in some cases, bluebirds and starlings were noted nesting peaceably in close proximity.

In summing up the evidence on this phase of behavior, they say:

While instances such as those cited are numerous and often have resulted fatally to the birds attacked it must be borne in mind that this information is the compilation of more than six months' constant investigation, during which time no opportunity to secure data on this point was overlooked. Bluebirds are common and generally distributed in the sections thickly settled with starlings, and although observers have noted their disappearance in small areas confined to a dooryard or two, it is the opinion of those who are qualified to judge the general abundance of these birds that in Connecticut and northeastern New Jersey, bluebirds have either held their own or increased in numbers in the last few years. * * * The flicker also will be driven from the vicinity of houses, but it, too, will always find a refuge in wilder situations to which the starling seldom goes. In those parts of Connecticut, New York, and New Jersey where the starling has been a common bird and in competition with the flicker for at least 15 years the latter still maintains as conspicuous a place in the bird world as it does in other parts of these States where the starling is not yet common.

Mr. Forbush (1927) says that starlings have "been known to kill young game birds. Mr. Perry S. Knowlton, of Essex, Massachusetts, says that he saw a small flock of Starlings attack five young pheasants 'about as large as robins' and kill two of them. The Starlings struck the young birds with their bills, piercing the skull about at the ear where the blood oozed out."

Dr. Dayton Stoner (1932) writes: "Mr. William Parker, who lives about one and one-half miles southwest of Lakeport [N. Y.], says that in many places the starling has driven away the English sparrows from the vicinity of barns and other buildings. With the dispersal of the sparrows the barn and cliff swallows, more desirable birds than either the sparrows or the starlings, have come in. Swallows will not build where sparrows congregate in any numbers, but starlings and swallows seem to get on without much conflict. * * * The starling and the purple martin will sometimes nest side by side without hostilities."

Leo A. Luttringer, Jr. (1927), relates the following tragedy which he saw near Harrisburg, Pa.; "Several Starlings besieged a mother Robin on the nest and one ran its bill through the eye, killing the bird almost instantly. In pulling the bill from the eye of the Robin, the entire eye was torn from the socket."

Whatever the verdict against the starling may be on the score of competing with our native birds for nesting sites, or for attacking them aggressively, there is no doubt that where starlings are abundant there is a just complaint against them for serious competition with such birds as robins, catbirds, cedar waxwings, and other berry-eating birds for their late summer, fall, and winter supply of wild fruits and berries. There is little evidence to prove that they regularly drive away other birds from such food supplies; large numbers of starlings and robins feed together on the fruiting trees and shrubs in my yard in apparent harmony; except for occasional slight squabbles between the starlings themselves when feeding on the ground, I have never seen any signs of conflict between them, though I frequently stop to watch them as I sit at my desk. But, when they swoop down on the berry-bearing trees and shrubs in big flocks, they soon strip them of all fruit, including what falls to the ground, and when these are gone, the other birds must look elsewhere for their food and are thus effectively driven away. Starlings often drive away small birds from feeding stations, sometimes even the aggressive blue jay.

Charles A. Urner (1936) made an interesting observation on a starling that was robbing a robin of its hard-earned grubs: "Each time a Robin would stop, look or listen and start to dig for a grub the Starling was at its side, would drive it away and procure the located food for its own young. When more than one Robin stopped and started to dig at the same moment the Starling was greatly agitated. It would run from one to another and occasionally it did little but cause confusion, and nobody ate."

I have seen very little evidence of hostility or signs of quarreling among the starlings on my lawn, but Francis H. Allen has sent me the following note: "Starlings are active birds and apparently enjoy excitement. A group of eight or ten one October afternoon walked, ran, and hopped and flitted about on my lawn, feeding on insects and fallen pears. There were many hostile tilts between different couples. Sometimes an apparently determined advance of one individual upon another would end in an aerial tilt, sometimes in nothing at all. The running appeared to be actual running, not the rapid walk characteristic of the species. Probably one or two combative individuals started this little Donnybrook Fair, and the imitative instinct brought the others in. It broke off suddenly but while it lasted it was a lively and noisy affair."

J. C. Tracy writes to me: "Starlings were observed upon several occasions to be acting in a most peculiar manner with English walnuts (*Juglans regia*) which had fallen to the ground from a large walnut tree. The birds were apparently using the oil from the outside part of the nuts to preen their feathers, although the reason for the action may, of course, simply have been coincidental. The starlings would insert their beaks in the soft outer shells of the nuts, and then in the next move quickly turn their heads and apparently preen their necks and wings. At any rate, it was obvious that the birds were not eating the nuts; to all intents and purposes there was something about the green outer shells that they liked. Whenever an intruder starling would approach one already at work, he would be greeted by a good stiff fight; there were not a great many nuts on the ground and competition for the bill-sticking ritual was extremely keen. It is quite possible that some oily substance found in the nutshells was appealing to the birds, and they were using it for some purpose in connection with their plumage."

Clarence F. Smith has sent me the following note on undesirable behavior of starlings: "Foresters have made the statement that starlings in increasing numbers are taking the seeds of longleaf pine, thus raising a potential problem in reforestation of this important tree. Another particularly important action of the starling relates to injury of livestock, particularly cattle. The starlings seem to attack the cattle to obtain ox warbles, but they also feed on the flesh and blood of the animal attacked."

Voice.—A group of starlings sitting in a tree top and tuning up for the spring chorus is rather painful to watch in their attempts at song; and the series of squeaks, chatters, creaking rattles, chirps, and wheezy notes is far from pleasing to the ear; but these are often interspersed with long-drawn, cheerful whistles, which are almost humanlike and easily imitated. And Dr. Chapman (1925) says: "Less often heard is the starling's musical soliloquy which, with fluttering wings, he delivers, from a more or less exposed position. * * * But if the notes of adult starlings have merit, the voice of young starlings uttering their food call is exceedingly disagreeable, harsh, rasping, and insistent; inspired by no higher emotion than that which arises from an apparently unfillable stomach, it rends the air with discord."

The starling has acquired considerable fame as a mimic, and much has been written about it. Francis H. Allen has sent me the following notes on this subject: "An incomplete list of imitations I have heard from starlings—always given when the bird is singing, as is the case, I think, with other birds that mimic—includes the *bob-white, bob-bob-white,* and the scatter call of the bobwhite, the strident single note of the killdeer, the *kee-up* of the flicker, song-notes of phoebe and wood pewee, the distant cawing of a crow, and notes of black-capped chickadee, bluebird, ruby-crowned kinglet, northern yellow-throat, English sparrow, meadowlark (song), oriole, grackle, cowbird, and golfinch.

"The *pewee* note of the wood pewee used to be so frequent an imitation that some New England ornithologists were led to believe it a native note of the starling, but it was learned that that note was not used by the starling in England. Later, in my neighborhood at least, the starlings used the *pewee* note less frequently, but specialized on the flight notes of the cowbird.

"Gradually these notes—the long ascending note followed by two short ones—were altered by hurrying the last two notes, and standardized in that form, so that it was always easy to distinguish the imitation from the original genuine cowbird notes. Recently, however, our starlings have practically discontinued use of the cowbird's notes and have taken up the wood pewee's again, though using them less frequently than formerly. It seems clear that individual starlings learn their imitations quite as much from one another as from the original authors of the notes and that fashion plays a large part in the choice. * * *

"In feeding young in a hole in an apple tree, in the absence of myself and two lurking cats, a pair of starlings used a long-drawn, low-pitched, grating note and a rapidly repeated note resembling the call note of the downy woodpecker. Both notes were once given by a bird with insects in its bill."

Mr. Forbush (1927) "adds to its repertory, notes, songs or calls of the Wood Thrush, Robin, Bluebird, Chickadee, Tufted Titmouse, White-breasted Nuthatch, Red-breasted Nuthatch, Catbird, House Wren, Carolina Wren, Chestnut-sided Warbler, Barn Swallow, Purple Martin, Scarlet Tanager, Field Sparrow, English Sparrow, Crossbill, Goldfinch, Slate-Colored Junco, Meadowlark, Bronzed Grackle, Baltimore Oriole, Red-winged Blackbird, Cowbird, Crow, Blue Jay, Redheaded Woodpecker, Kingfisher, Wood Pewee, Phoebe, Red-eyed Towhee, Red-shouldered Hawk, Bob-white, Guinea Fowl and Killdeer, and rather imperfect imitations of the calls of both species of Cuckoo. The imitations of some performers are excellent, some of those of others are less so, but all are recognizable, even to the barking of a dog or the mewing of a cat."

Various other observers have listed the following additional birds as imitated by the starling: Herring gull, sora rail, whippoorwill, nighthawk, chimney swift, solitary sandpiper, greater yellowlegs, hairy and downy woodpeckers, yellow-bellied sapsucker, sparrow hawk, mockingbird, brown thrasher, horned lark, myrtle warbler, summer tanager, purple finch, white-throated sparrow, and cardinal.

The above are impressive lists and, if accurate and reliable, would seem to place the starling in the front rank of mocking birds, rivaling our famous mockingbird, which it is said to mock. Many of these notes are quite easily recognized, but some others not so, and it would seem to one whose ears are not sharply attuned to the niceties of bird music that some observers have stretched their imaginations. However, the starling in England is said to be able to imitate almost anything and in captivity can be taught to whistle tunes and even articulate words.

The power of mimicry is not shared equally by all individual starlings; many of them never indulge in the habit; some do much more than others. My collaborator, Dr. Winsor M. Tyler (1933), a man with the keenest and most discriminating ears, listened for nine years for evidence of mimicry and heard only the notes of the cowbird imitated, perhaps half a dozen times in all. He was skeptical about the bird's ability as a mimic, until one day he heard "in ten minutes, thirteen notes of ten different birds, given by a flock of Starlings—perhaps by one Starling; an accumulation of audible evidence to convince the stubbornest juror."

Starlings sing in fall as well as in spring, and sometimes sing in their winter roosts at night. According to Albert R. Brand (1938), the pitch of the starlings voice is somewhat below the average of passerine bird song; the highest note has about 8,225, the lowest about 1,100, and the approximate mean about 3,475 vibrations per second; the average for passerine birds is above 4,000 vibrations per second, or around the highest note of the piano keyboard.

Field marks.—Among a crowd of other black birds the starling can be distinguished by its trim, compact figure, its short tail, and its long bill. In breeding plumage its glossy, sleek breast and head show greenish and purplish reflections, and its bill is bright yellow. In fall its body plumage is covered with conspicuous whitish and buffy dots. The young bird, during its first summer, is colored much like a young cowbird, but its long bill will distinguish it. It can be recognized in flight by its sharply pointed wings, its widely spread and short tail, and by its manner of flight, as described above. After one has learned to know it, he should be able to recognize it almost as far as it can be seen.

Enemies.—Cats sometimes catch young starlings and perhaps an adult occasionally. Almost all the swift-flying hawks have been recorded as preying upon them at times, particularly the duck hawk, Cooper's hawk, and the sharp-shinned. Hicks and Dambach (1935) write:

During the flight manoeuvres several Cooper's hawks and one sharp-shinned hawk were observed repeatedly preying upon the starlings. On one occasion a Cooper's hawk flew swiftly to the centre of a giant oak tree, making a kill and scattering, as if by explosion, the 2,000 starlings perched on the branches. Two screech owls and a barn owl were known to visit the roost, as were also a fox, several opossums, and many weasels. The gregariousness of the starlings made them easy prey; but, because of the small numbers of predators, such losses were negligible.

That starlings recognize hawks as enemies is shown by their peculiar method of mass attack. When a hawk appears near a large flock of starlings, these birds gather into a dense formation and pursue the hawk, sometimes enveloping the confused predator in a great rolling cloud of black birds. This generally results in the ignominious retreat of the bewildered hawk before the overwhelming numbers of its pursuers. A somewhat similar performance is described in the following note from Francis H. Allen: "One October day I saw a red-shouldered hawk sitting in the dead top of a tree when some starlings flew into the tree. The hawk flew off and a flock of perhaps 25 or 50 soon gathered and followed him about in the air, occasionally one or two swooping at him, but most of the time the flock simply keeping above him wherever he went. The flock became augmented for a time, but before long all but what might have been the original nucleus left him. I watched the performance for a quarter of an hour or so, and the hawk soared high and covered a considerable distance in his circling flight, but the starlings, in close formation, as is their custom in flocks, stuck to him. Sometimes he would rise above them, but only for a moment, for they would speedily regain and keep the ascendant, though the pursuit carried them much higher than starlings ordinarily fly. Again once in September I saw a large band of starlings pursuing an osprey. In the short time before they abandoned the chase I could not see that the large bird paid any attention to them, but shortly after that the same band was seen sporting with a sparrow hawk, and in this case the hawk flew about among them as if in play."

In their competition for nesting sites, starlings have sometimes found that flickers, bluebirds, and even English sparrows were more than a match for them and have had to retreat, though the reverse is usually the case.

Joseph B. Sommer (1937) found that a large number of starlings examined in Illinois were infested with internal parasites; 132 birds were examined, among which 51 "were hosts to one or more parasites, all of which were found in the intestinal tract." External parasites identified by Harold S. Peters (1936) included three species of lice, one mite, and one tick.

We probably have not been bandings birds long enough to learn the maximum age to which starlings live. Mr. Thomas's (1934) banding records in Ohio "indicate that a very small proportion of Starlings attain an age of five years, although a fair number reach an age of four and many attain the age of three years." But since then, birds have been reported that were six years old and even eight years old.

Dr. Friedmann (1934) published the only record I have seen of a cowbird laying an egg in a starling's nest; I doubt if it ever hatched.

Fall.—After the young starlings have completed their postjuvenal molt, the flocks of young birds that have been wandering about by themselves join with the flocks of adults in preparation for migration. They inherited the migratory instinct from their European ancestors, but in this country they had no established route of migration. This had to be learned from other birds. Being naturally gregarious and apparently fond of association with other species of similar habits, they naturally joined with the grackles, red-winged-blackbirds, and cowbirds in their autumnal wanderings and in their great roosts, eventually following them southward. But, as Dr. Alexander Wetmore (1926) says, "the blackbirds in question habitually fly from 22 to 28 miles per hour, while the starling as regularly travels at a rate of 38 to 49 miles per hour. The two speeds are so incompatible that it might be difficult for the species to keep together in prolonged flight." Therefore, it appears as if the grackles and others led the way and the starlings followed. The grackles seem to be the first to appear at the more southern roosts, to be joined later by increasing numbers of starlings, until the latter far outnumber the other black birds. This indicates that the greater part of the starlings start on their migration later in the season than the others but eventually catch up with them on account of their increased speed.

Winter.—Although enormous numbers of starlings follow the black-birds southward, large numbers spend the winter as far north as southern Canada and New England. For example, P. A. Taverner (1934) reports Jack Miner's experience with it at Kingsville, Ontario: "There the Starlings found winter roost in his planted pine grove, resorting to it in such numbers as, by their dropping, to smother the foliage, over-fertilize the ground, and finally to kill all the trees in the plantation. This in spite of an active campaign against them in which truck loads of the birds were trapped and shipped to the cities to assist in feeding the needy."

Severe winter storms and extremely low temperatures often result in great mortality in the more northern roosts. Odum and Pitelka (1939) report such a disaster at Urbana, Ill., in February 1939. The roost was estimated to contain 25,000 birds, starlings, cowbirds, grackles, and redwings, over 95 percent of which were starlings. A heavy rainstorm, accompanied by a wind velocity of 48 miles an hour, which blew down a number of trees, was followed by a sudden drop in temperature to below freezing. This resulted in the death of about 4 percent of the birds in the roost, among which 570 starlings were actually counted, and perhaps as many as 1,000 may have perished.

Forbush (1927) mentions a report from Carl E. Grant that "after the severe weather of January, 1925, he found in an area of less than an acre in a pine grove near Wenham Lake about 500 dead Starlings and innumerable parts of others, which had been partly eaten. He counted 22 dead Starlings in a space less than two feet square where, apparently, they had crowded together for warmth."

Records from various sources indicate that approximately 70 percent of these birds that winter in the north are males. The others go south and so overcrowd the southern resorts that the robins, cedar waxwings, and other berry-eating birds are hard pressed to find sufficient food.

DISTRIBUTION

Range.—The starling is a native of Europe, where it breeds from the British Isles, northern Norway, and Russia south to southern Russia, northern Italy, and southern France; during the winter it is found somewhat farther south in the Mediterranean region. Since its introduction in North America in 1890 it has spread throughout the United States, southern Canada, and to northern Tamaulipas, Mexico.

Breeding range (1949).—In North America the starling breeds **north** to southern Alberta (Brooks) ; southern Manitoba (Norway House and Steeprock) ; central Ontario (Port Arthur, Kapuskasing, Lake Nipissing, and Ottawa) ; southern Quebec (Blue Sea Lake, Quebec, Riviere-du-Loup, and Natashquan). **East** to eastern Quebec (Natashquan) ; Newfoundland (Tompkins and St. John's) ; the Atlantic coast south to northern Florida (Jacksonville). **South** to northern Florida (Jacksonville and Pensacola) ; central Mississippi (State College) ; northwestern Arkansas (Rogers) ; southeastern Kansas (Clearwater) ; and central Mississippi (State College) ; southern Louisiana (New Orleans, 1949) ; etc. **West** to eastern Kansas (Clearwater and Newton); eastern Colorado (Denver) ; eastern and northern North Dakota (Fairmont, Lower Souris Wildlife Refuge, and Des Lacs Wildlife Refuge) ; and southern Alberta (Brooks).

The northernmost records of occurrence are: Alberta (Belvedere, 1940) ; Manitoba (Churchill, 1940, and York Factory, 1934) ; Ontario (Fort Albany, 1940, and Moose Factory, 1931).

Winter range.—During the winter the starling is found over much of its breeding range, though in somewhat less numbers in the north, and south to the Gulf coast, west at least to central Texas. Many of the occurrences farther west have also been in winter.

Egg dates.—Massachusetts: Early April to July. New Jersey: 12 records, April 10 to May 16. Utah: 7 records, April 9 to May 7.

History of its spread.—After many attempts to introduce the starling into North America it was "successfully" introduced in Central Park, New York, in 1890 and 1891, and for six years was confined to the limits of greater New York. After that the increasingly rapid spread began which in little over a half century took it to the Pacific coast. A study of the chronology of this spread shows that it was not a steady progression but somewhat spasmodic; a big expansion in one year followed by several years while the territory gained was filled in and little new occupied. How much transportation has helped in this spread is problematical, but some long jumps have suggested that birds may have been "stowaways."

By 1912 starlings were breeding from eastern Massachusetts to eastern Pennsylvania and winter flocks had reached Washington, D. C. They continued to move southward in winter until northern Florida (Amelia Island) was reached by individuals in 1918, by which time breeding birds had reached southern Maine. The first specimen from west of the Allegheny Mountains was collected in 1916 at West Lafayette, Ohio; Canada was reached in 1919 at Brockville, Ontario; by 1925 they were breeding at Ottawa, and individuals had arrived in Nova Scotia. The mountains having been crossed there was a noticeable southwestward drift in winter. A flock reached southern Louisiana (near Baton Rouge) in December 1921, and by 1926 many small flocks were present in winter. By this time the breeding range had been extended to western Ohio and northern Georgia. Many of the first winter records were of starlings found in blackbird roosts. By 1928 the breeding range was approximately to the Mississippi River from southern Wisconsin to Tennessee. The extension of the breeding range into the Southeastern States has been slow. Many birds are present in winter. No evidence of nesting in Florida was reported until 1932 (Pensacola) and 1937 (Jacksonville).

The next 10 years saw marked progress westward in the Northern States. In 1938 starlings bred in northwestern North Dakota (Des Lacs Wildlife Refuge), western Minnesota (Madison), eastern Nebraska (Uehling), and northwestern Arkansas (Rogers). Young birds banded that summer at Des Lacs Refuge furnished in the following winter the first records for Montana (Lindsay) and Saskatchewan (Tyvan).

Meantime the advance to the southwestward also had been rapid. The first record for Texas was a bird found dead at Cove in 1925, but by 1932 others had reached the eastern edge of the plains in this State and in Oklahoma. In November 1939 it reached the Rio Grande at El Paso and Albuquerque, N. Mex.; and crossed the river into Mexico where a flock of 25 was seen 9 kilometers south of Nuevo Laredo, Tamaulipas. An individual spent the winter of 1938–39 in Colorado, 10 miles south of Monte Vista. In 1937 starlings followed the Platte River into Wyoming as far west as Parco, and the following year were found near Denver, Colo. They may have bred in Colorado in 1942, but the first positive record was made at Lowry Field, near Denver, in May 1943.

To date (May 1949) no breeding has been recorded from west of the Rocky Mountains although there are records of occurrence from every State. The Alleghenies were crossed in 1916, and 25 years later the Rockies were crossed, starlings have been observed in 1941 at Jackson, Wyo., and Corvallis, Mont. From there (apparently) they reached Moscow, Idaho, and Lake Malheur, Oreg., in 1943 and Pullman, Wash., in 1945. Portland, Oreg., was reached from the east in 1947. In 1889, 20 pairs had been released there and the species persisted until about 1901.

California was entered from both north and south. In January 1942 a specimen was collected from a flock of about 40 near Tulelake, Siskiyou County; and in December 1946 one was taken at Chino, San Bernardino County, the species having crossed Arizona that year. In January 1947 a flock of eight wandered up to the Okanagan Valley to Oliver, British Columbia, thus completing the roll call of the United States and Provinces of Canada.

Some idea of the extensiveness of starling migrations may be gained from a few banding records. Several thousand starlings have been banded, the majority in winter roosts. The recoveries of banded birds indicates that the population of these roosts are drawn from a wide area. Much banding has been done in winter roosts in central Ohio and recoveries have been received from Quebec, Ontario, Michigan, Indiana, Missouri, Tennessee, Mississippi, New York, Pennsylvania, and Maryland. The most distant was from Ste. Marie Beauce, Quebec, 14 months after banding.

A bird banded at Columbus, Ohio, March 11, 1927, was taken at Charleston, Mo., on January 28, 1928, and was the second specimen from west of the Mississippi River.

A bird banded as a nestling on June 8, 1936, at Ottawa, Ontario, was found dead on February 25, 1937, at Thurmont, Md. Another banded at the same place on June 22, 1936, was captured on December 26, 1936, at Ozark, Ark.

In August 1938 several young were banded at Des Lacs Wildlife Refuge near Kenmore, N. Dak. One of these was shot at Lindsay, Mont., on February 19, 1939; another was found dead at Billings, Mont., on February 14, 1939, and third at Tyvan, Saskatchewan, in May 1939.

A few records of longevity obtained through banding are of interest. A bird banded at Washington, D. C., on March 23, 1928, was caught in a pigeon loft at Mount Vernon, N. Y., July 8, 1936. One banded at Columbus, Ohio, February 16, 1929, was recaptured at the same place on March 23, 1939. One banded at Overbrook, Pa., on November 24, 1931, was found on March 4, 1939, at Narbeth, Pa. Another banded at Ardmore, Pa., on May 14, 1938, was retrapped at the same station on May 15, 1942.

Casual records.—A specimen was sent from Greenland in 1851 to the Royal Museum at Copenhagen. In a collection at Godthaab, Greenland, there are four specimens taken as follows: Julianehaab, September 10, 1925; Fiskenaessit, November 7, 1925; Angmagassalik, early summer 1926; and Godthaab, May 13, 1927. In the Berlin Museum was a specimen taken in Labrador about 1878. A specimen was taken in spring about 1917, near Betchewun, Quebec. All these records suggest the possibility that they may have come from Europe rather than from the introduced birds.

On March 3, 1929, a dying bird was picked up at St. George, Bermuda.

On October 5, 1936, at Myggbukta, on the east coast of Greenland, two specimens were taken from a flock of five, which were identified as *S. v. zetlandicus*. This was following an exceptionally hard gale at sea.

AETHIOPSAR CRISTATELLUS CRISTATELLUS (Linnaeus)

CRESTED MYNAH

HABITS

Another foreign bird of questionable value has established a foothold in North America, much to the regret of the bird lovers of this country and causing much apprehension as to its spread and as to its effect on our native avifauna. If it proves to be as aggressive and as dominant as that other member of the starling family that has overrun our country, its coming will indeed be a calamity. But perhaps we are too apprehensive. Perhaps our climate may not suit it or some of our natural barriers may hinder its spread. And perhaps it may not prove to be so undesirable as we fear. In its native home in China it does not seem to be too unpopular. J. D. D. La Touche (1926) writes: "The Chinese Crested Mynah is *the* characteristic bird of the plains and lowlands of cultivated South China, ascending in Yunnan to the plateaux of that province. It is the faithful companion of the husbandman, following the plough in winter to gather the insects and worms brought to the surface, often in the fields using the back of the cattle as a perch, and doubless ridding them of many an unpleasant parasite. * * * On the whole it is a useful bird, being in great part insectivorous and granivorous, but not a devourer of field crops. In gardens, however, it probably levies toll on the vegetables and fruit."

Most of what follows is taken from a comprehensive paper on the species by Scheffer and Cottam (1935), to which the reader is referred for many interesting details and references and which can only be partially condensed in this account. They summarize its present status and prospects in North America as follows:

The crested myna, or Chinese starling, was introduced into British Columbia about 1897 by persons unknown, possibly by an oriental resident of the Vancouver district. The first specimens taken by a naturalist were collected in 1904. The increase of the bird in its new home was slow, peak numbers having been reached about 1925 to 1927, and there appears to have been no increase during the next few years. Apparently only one brood a year is raised in the Vancouver district.

Climatic conditions do not appear to favor the crested myna in British Columbia, as regards either increase in abundance or extension of range. Its further dispersal to the north seems barred by high mountains and forested interior; to the west and south are ocean straits; hence any further spread would apparently have to be to the east or southeast.

J. A. Munro (1922) writes:

Nothing definite is known regarding the introduction of this species to Vancouver. One story has it that a large wicker cage containing a number of these birds, consigned to a Japanese resident, was broken open in transit from one of the Oriental liners and the birds escaped. Other stories are to the effect that its introduction was deliberate. * * * The increase of this species has not been as spectacular as that of the House Swallow [sparrow], but within the last few years it has been steady and they are gradually spreading from Vancouver into the rural districts. In common with the House Sparrow, they frequent the city streets in order to feed on the undigested grain in horse-droppings. The curtailment of this food supply that followed the change from horse-traffic to motor-traffic no doubt served to check their increase as it has also reduced the Sparrow population.

Referring to the increase in the numbers of the crested mynah in Vancouver, William N. Kelly (1927) says that he "first observed them early in 1909 at their roosting place on the building at the southwest corner of Cordover and Carrall Streets. There were not many in the colony at that time, possibly a few hundreds. Now their main roosting territory takes in about four city blocks adjacent to the original rookery, and they have also been observed congregating in smaller bands to roost in the East End of the city, the West End, and extending to New Westminster. It is estimated by some that the colony now exceeds 20,000 birds. They have also been reported from Bellingham, Washington."

The above estimate seems high, but it evidently refers to the concentration in winter roosts; probably less than half of that number remain to nest within the city. In considering the chances of a widespread invasion of the crested mynah into the United States, it must be remembered that its natural habitat is in the comparatively warm climate of central and southern China, and that the countries into which it has been introduced and has succeeded in raising more than one brood a year, such as the Philippines, are tropical or semi-tropical. Should it become established in California, it might spread over the warmer portions of this country. But it probably would not thrive in the colder climate of our Northern States, as has the European starling which came from colder climate.

F. W. Cook reported to Scheffer and Cottam (1935) that on August 13, 1929, he observed a party of 12 mynahs about a mile from the head of Lake Washington on Sammamish River, Wash., though they were not seen again. And in February 1924 one was seen in Portland, Oreg., as recorded by Wood (1924) and others.

Nesting.—La Touche (1926) says of the nesting habits of the crested mynah in China: "The breeding-season is from April onwards, and I have taken hard-set eggs on the 29th of May. There are probably two broods, as in Kwangtung the latest date given by Vaughan and Jones for fresh eggs is the 4th of July. These authors give the bird as double-brooded for the majority. All kinds of situations are taken for the nest: holes in buildings, hollow trees, Magpies' nests, and often, according to the same authors, Kingfishers' nests are favourite sites. The materials consist of all kinds of rubbish, and every nest invariably contains a snake slough."

Scheffer and Cottam (1935) write:

The nesting time of the crested myna in the Vancouver district covers about 10 to 12 weeks in May, June, and July. * * * The crested myna is not so confiding and persistent as the English sparrow (*Passer domesticus*), but where persecuted or unduly disturbed, it will usually abandon its homemaking to try elsewhere. * * *

For nesting sites, the crested myna apparently requires a nearly enclosed space. It does not incline to build, like the robin or the English sparrow, on supports partly in the open or with semishelter. In fields and woods, the nests are usually made in the tree holes that sometimes result from decay in the dead stubs, but more frequently from excavations made by flickers (*Colaptes cafer*) or other woodpeckers. As many as half a dozen or more such holes occupied by mynas may sometimes be seen in a single tree trunk on logged-off and burned-over land that has a covering of low, second-growth trees and shrubs. About the city the nests are commonly made in enclosed shelters formed by the cornices, eaves, chimneys, and drain spouts of buildings. Sometimes they are in the boxing of guy wires on line poles. Mynas will also occupy tree boxes placed for them or for other birds.

The nests themselves are mere collections of trashy materials assembled from any available source not too remote for economy in flight, such as bits of grass and weeds, foil, cellophane, and other candy and gum wrappings, feathers, snake skins, rubber bands, and fine rootlets. * * *

The following summary was made of notes kept by Scheffer and Cumming on the nesting of a pair of crested mynas in a tree box placed in a garden at Vancouver: The pair first appeared at the nesting site on April 14 and spent 14 days in building the nest, the first egg being laid April 28. Five days were required to complete the clutch, one egg each day. * * *

It is difficult to learn by direct observation just when the season of brood rearing naturally closes; for, because of the bird's association with human habitations, many nests are inadvertently broken up from time to time, and the nesting pairs are forced to seek new sites and try again. Sometimes, too, the birds or their nests are disturbed with hostile intent by city dwellers who do not care to have the foreign intruders about the premises. The crested myna is not so confiding and persistent as the English sparrow (*Passer domesticus*), but where persecuted or unduly disturbed, it will usually abandon its home-making and try elsewhere.

Vaughan and Jones (1913), writing of southeastern China, say: "The Mynah breeds plentifully at Hong Kong and elsewhere on the Kwang Tung coast, where, as a rule, some hole in a building, the top of a waste-water pipe, or still more frequently the deserted hole of one of the Kingfishers, is made use of. In the latter, a sort of step is always scratched at the lower portion of the orifice, which is also consider-ably enlarged. Up the West River and inland the favourite site is an old Magpie's nest, though ruinous old pagodas and holes in trees are also made use of, and the deserted nest of *Graculipica nigricollis* is sometimes resorted to. In suitable situations breeding-colonies are often found."

Eggs.—The usual set for the crested mynah consists of four or five eggs, sometimes six and rarely seven. La Touche (1926) says the eggs are "greenish blue, the surface smooth and glossy." Wilson C. Hanna tells me that a set of five eggs in his collection are elliptical-oval and very slightly glossy; they were collected by R. A. Cumming in South Vancouver, British Columbia. Their color is uniform "light Niagara green." Vaughan and Jones (1913) state that eggs pure white in color have been taken, and that "eggs with a few spots have occurred later on in the season."

The measurements of 19 American eggs average 30.6 by 21.7 millimeters; the eggs showing the four extremes measure 33.2 by 21.4, 31.5 by 23.0, and 28.5 by 19.0 millimeters.

Young.—Referring to the nest observed by Scheffer and Cumming, Scheffer and Cottam (1935) say:

On the evening of May 15, the first egg was found to be hatched, and all the eggs were pipped, an incubation period of 14 days. The young birds left the nest and perched on a branch 27 days after hatching. After that they were fed or were aided in feeding by the parent birds for about 7 days, when, on June 19, they were able to shift for themselves. The actual lapsed time, therefore, from the first appearance of the mynas at their nesting site until the fledglings were able to care for themselves was 66 days, a surprisingly long period and one that would seem to preclude the habitual rearing of a second brood in this locality and latitude. Accurate observations by Cumming through several years of intimate field acquaintance with the species seem to strengthen conclusions reached by Scheffer. * * * A nesting pair has been observed to feed its young as late as the first week in August, but most of the broods are out much earlier. Whether the species is commonly two-brooded is a matter difficult to determine without banding studies.

Plumages.—Young birds in juvenal plumage in June are dull, sooty, dark brown above and below, without any gloss; the crest is only rudimentary, barely discernible; the wings and tail are like those of the adult, nearly black, but the white tips on the lateral rectrices are lacking; the under tail lacks the white tips. I have seen young birds in full juvenal plumage up to August 25, indicating that the post-juvenal molt comes later. Adults have a complete postnuptial molt from August to October; some birds complete this molt before the end of August, others not until late in October.

Food.—Scheffer and Cottam (1935) give the following summary of the food of this species:

In the laboratory study of the food habits of the crested myna, which was undertaken after the field studies of 1931–32, 117 adult and 20 juvenile stomachs were examined. These were collected over the 8-month period from May to December. Stomach analyses and field observations show that the bird is decidedly omnivorous, with a partiality for fruits and for foods from such unsavory sources as garbage dumps and manure piles. Availability seems to be the chief factor in its choice of food. The average monthly diet of adults was 38.89 percent animal and 61.11 percent vegetable matter, with fruits of various species aggregating 32.49 percent, insects 22.44 percent, garbage 14.6 percent, and leafy vegetable material 8.57 percent. The nestlings are predominantly insectivorous. During the latter part of summer self-feeding juveniles and adults are highly frugivorous.

Favorite feeding grounds are in the Chinese gardens, where manure and garbage piles have been allowed to accumulate. Here "they may flock together in small groups or in numbers up to a hundred or more. It is not uncommon for the birds to feed about an abattoir, pigpen, corral, or pasture, and while foraging frequently to associate with crows (*Corvus brachyrhynchos*), English sparrows, and gulls (*Larus* spp.)."

Their table showing the percentages by month of the various food items breaks down into the following monthly averages for the following items: Flies, 11.04 percent; moths and caterpillars, 4.99 percent; wasps, bees, and ants, 1.85 percent; bugs, 1.72 percent; beetles, 1.24 percent; grasshoppers, etc., 0.45 percent; miscellaneous insects, 1.15 percent; spiders, 2.82 percent; earthworms, 4.08 percent; wild fruits, 27.80 percent; cultivated fruits, 4.70 percent; and grain, 2.54 percent. Although most of the insects eaten are injurious or neutral, a few useful forms are taken, such as predacious ichneumonoid wasps, of which 16 were found in one stomach, and useful ground beetles.

The mynah does good work in the destruction of house flies, which it finds in the garbage and manure piles in larval and adult stages. "No fewer than 225 pupae, 20 larvae, and 1 adult of the housefly were found in one stomach and more than 200 larvae and pupae were found in two others. Three additional July stomachs each contained more than 100 of these flies." Tent caterpillars, cutworms, and measuring worms, all very destructive, made up the larger part of the lepidopterous food.

The mynah's record on its vegetable food is not so good. About one-third of its food consists of fruits and berries; most of these are wild varieties, such as elderberries, wild cherries, blueberries, crowberries, snowberries, salmonberries, loganberries, and serviceberries, as well as the fruits of cascara, dogwood, mountain-ash, sumac, and nightshade; but a substantial amount of the food consists of cultivated cherries, strawberries, raspberries, and blackberries, and some damage is done to apples and pears, cabbages, and lettuce; the amount of grain eaten is small and is mainly waste grain picked up in the fields after harvesting or taken from garbage or manure piles.

Mr. Kelly (1927) says that the eggs of smaller birds "form a large part" of the diet.

It can be seen from the above account that there is a great potentiality for harm in the feeding habits of the crested mynah; if it should become very abundant in the fruit-raising districts of the Pacific States, it could do an immense amount of damage. It might prove even worse than the European starling, which has a far better record as a destroyer of harmful insects. For this reason, its spread should be carefully watched and controlled before it is too late.

Behavior.—La Touche (1926) says of the habits of the crested mynah in China:

At night it roosts in company with other Starlings and with Jackdaws and other *Corvidae* on tall bamboos and trees to the accompaniment of * * * the usual shrieks and cries peculiar to the Starlings. Companionable as it is with the ploughman and workers in the fields, it is wary and shy with the suspected stranger. But, taken at the nest and brought up by hand, the Crested Mynah makes a most delightful pet, distinguishing its owner and becoming exceedingly tame and familiar. I have had many of these birds, and, but for their accipitrine failing which they share with the Crow family, they make quite the most enjoyable bird-companion one can have. They are good talkers, equal to most Parrots, and are docile and easily taught. With the Chinese this Mynah is a valued cage-bird, and great numbers are reared by hand every spring in South China.

One of the worst things that can be said against the mynah is that it competes with some of our most useful species in its nesting habits and in its feeding habits; berry-bearing trees and shrubs are soon stripped of their fruit, so that our native birds have to look elsewhere for their food supply; it not only drives away our hole-nesting birds from their accustomed hollows in the trees or from bird boxes, but it destroys their eggs or young in order to preempt the site. As a result, many of native woodpeckers, bluebirds, and wrens have disappeared from sections where they were once common. The mynahs have also been reported as destroying the eggs and young in open nests, such as those of robins; these were probably taken for food.

Scheffer and Cottam (1935) write:

In conflict with the flicker, the myna shows tact and persistence. If a new home of the former is under construction in a tree stub, the mynas will wait patiently for its completion, coming around occasionally to note progress. When it is ready for use, several pairs of the intruders may contest for its possession, giving the impression that they are "ganging up" on the unfortunate home builder. The result is always the same—eviction of the woodpecker tenants. When the myna wishes to build its home where a native bird has already made progress in rearing a family, it tosses out both eggs and young with little ceremony. * * *

For a time after dispersal from the nests, late in summer and early in fall, crested mynas are associated in small groups, probably family parties remaining about the old nesting sites or in flight to and from feeding grounds. This habit was particularly noticeable at the time of the first visit of Scheffer to the Vancouver district, in August. It is in considerable contrast to the flocking habits of Brewer's blackbirds, which assemble in great numbers at this season. * * *

Though sometimes observed feeding with other birds, particularly Brewer's blackbirds, in the gardens and grainfields of the Fraser River delta, the myna has shown no disposition to drift with them in migration, and at roosting time, it clannishly associates with its kind. When rougher weather comes on, these birds resort more and more to close-foliaged trees for shelter or roosting at night, and for accommodations for larger groups than family parties.

The large myna roost in the heart of Vancouver city, near the waterfront, in the glare of street lights and the confused noise of traffic, has been the subject of much comment and many reports for several years. This section is but little occupied by the birds each year until early winter, when they begin to assemble at evening in large numbers. Almost from the earliest recalled time of the arrival of the mynas, their noisy roosts have been associated with the Christmas season, and the birds have been known locally as "Christmas birds." * * *

First arrivals at the roost were noted between 3 and 4:30 p. m., and from that time until nearly dark the mynas drifted in by twos, threes, half dozens, or as many as 15 to 20 in a flock. Apparently the larger groups had assembled en route. Most of the birds came down one street, from the east, flying remarkably low, scarcely over the tops of the cars, and swung up steeply to perch about the eaves and cornices of the buildings, where new arrivals joined in the noisy chatter of greeting from those earlier on the roost. After a time some would fly to the ground or pavement in search of bits of food. * * * In the morning the mynas left the roost as soon as it was fully light and scattered to feed. In a walk of 3 miles eastward into the suburbs, Scheffer and Cumming observed the birds singly or by twos and threes on small trees or on house roofs in the residential district.

Voice.—The same authors say: "Scheffer finds the whistling notes always cheerful, in the nesting period even quite musical. Several calls may be recognized, the longer ones including a rolling trill, and all are distinguishable from the songs of our native birds by their peculiar 'foreign accent.' At roosting time in the winter season there is more or less chatter from flocking numbers. In his acquaintance with these introduced birds, Scheffer has noted no calls in imitation of native species. In its own habitat the myna is sometimes credited with being a mocker."

La Touche (1926) says that the Chinese bird is a good talker: "Its voice is loud, but often musical and always cheery, and it has a pleasant song mixed with a variety of hard, throaty, Starling notes."

Field marks.—The crested mynah is a well-marked bird, a short, chunky, glossy black bird, about the size of a robin; it has a prominent crest hanging forward over its yellow bill, a short tail with narrow white tips, and a large white patch in the wing, most conspicuous in flight. It has a somewhat labored, straightaway flight, by which it can be distinguished at a distance from a robin or a Brewer's blackbird. On the ground it usually walks instead of hopping.

DISTRIBUTION

CONTRIBUTED BY BERNARD WILLIAM TUCKER

Range.—South China from south Yunnan to the Yangtse Valley inclusive. Reaching in Shensi to the Hanchong-fu Valley. Introduced in the Philippines. As an introduced bird in North America, established in the district of Vancouver, British Columbia; described in 1921 as extending perhaps 20 miles east and west and about the same distance north and south, comprising North Vancouver, Sea

Island, Lulu Island, and other parts of the Fraser River Delta, east
to New Westminster and Coquitlam and south to Ladner. Single
individuals or small parties recorded as far afield as Portland, Oreg.
(1924), Bellingham, Wash. (1927 or earlier), Chilliwack, British
Columbia (1930 or earlier), near the head of Lake Washington
(1929), and Vancouver Island (1937).

Egg dates.—British Columbia: 6 records, April 28 to June 2.
China: 2 records, May 29 and July 4.

Family VIREONIDAE: Vireos

VIREO ATRICAPILLUS Woodhouse

BLACK-CAPPED VIREO

HABITS

This well-marked and handsome vireo was discovered by Dr. S. W.
Woodhouse while attached to Capt. L. Sitgreaves's expedition down
the Zuni and Colorado Rivers. He took two specimens, both males,
near the source of the Rio San Pedro in western Texas on May 26,
1851. About three years later a third specimen was taken by J. H.
Clark, one of the naturalists of the Mexican Boundary Commission,
not far from the same locality. Not much more was learned about it
until William Brewster (1879) got in touch with Edmund Ricksecker and W. H. Werner, who had acquired three sets of eggs, taken
in Comal County, Tex., in 1878. Mr. Werner gave Mr. Brewster
considerable information about this, then very rare, vireo. He found
them in the northwestern part of Comal County, along the Guadaloupe
River. "They were not very plenty; I noticed during my rambles
ten to twelve specimens in a radius of about ten miles, in the course
of six weeks. The peculiar song of the male first attracted my attention, and as soon as I saw the bird I was sure that it belonged to
the Vireo genus. They seemed to prefer mountainous districts; at
least I always found them in such localities. They frequented low
brushwood, and built their nests from three to four feet above the
ground."

Since then, much has been learned about the distribution and habits
of the black-capped vireo. It is now known to breed from southwestern Kansas, southward through Oklahoma and southwestern
Texas, and to winter in Mexico at least as far south as Sinaloa.

In Kansas, Col. N. S. Goss (1891) found them quite common in
summer in the deep ravines in the gypsum hills. "These birds are
very local in their distribution, and, until of late, very little has been
known in regard to their habits. They inhabit the oak woods upon
the uplands, and the bushes and trees in the ravines on bluffy prairie
lands."

C. D. Bunker (1910) describes somewhat similar nesting haunts in Blaine County, Okla.: "In the locality of which I speak, the canyons were about three hundred and twenty feet deep, with outcroppings of gypsum rock from bottom to top, with a strong salt stream running at the bottom. The only fresh water for miles was a spring on the ridge, a quarter of a mile above the head of the canyon. The canyon walls, and gulches leading to the canyons, were studded with clumps of bushes, mostly dog-wood, scrub-oak and similar shrubs forming ideal cover for vireos, of which *Vireo belli* was not uncommon. On one occasion a nest of a Bell Vireo was found in the same bush with that of a Black-cap."

George F. Simmons (1925) says that its haunts in central Texas are "typically, scrub-oak ridges, ravines, and canyons. Hottest imaginable places on sterile ridges or backbones among peaks of the small mountains or limestone hills of central Texas, among clumps of scrub oak, cedar, broad-leaved deciduous bushes, and chaparral brush, scantily scattered among small mountain live oaks and shaded mountain Spanish oak thickets on steep, sterile, rocky slopes of peaks which break in endless strata down to the valleys below; scrub oak thickets; oak thickets along bottoms of dry ravines; vine-grown thickets on canyon walls."

Nesting.—We are indebted to Mr. Brewster (1879) for the first published account of the nesting habits of this vireo, in which he says that "to Mr. Werner is due all credit for discovering the first authentic nest of the Black-capped Vireo known to science. Those received by Mr. Ricksecker were collected May 26 and June 13 respectively." That was in 1878, in Comal County, Tex. The former came to Mr. Brewster and was said to have been built in a "red-oak tree." Mr. Brewster describes it as follows: "It is suspended in the fork of two very slender twigs, and is in every way after the usual type of Vireonine architecture. In a few points of detail, however, it differs slightly from any Vireo's nest that I have seen. Although, generally speaking, of the ordinary cup-shaped form, the walls are unusually thick and firmly felted, and the entrance being very much contracted, the bulging sides arch over the mouth of the nest, giving to the whole a nearly spherical shape."

After confessing his lack of knowledge of Texas botany, he writes:

The great bulk of the structure, however, is made up of fine strips of reddish bark, probably from some species of cedar, layers of small, delicate, bleached leaves of a former year's growth, a few coarse grasses, one or two catkins, and several spiders' cocoons. These are firmly bound together, and the whole attached to the forked twigs above by fine shreds of vegetable fibre, caterpillars' or spiders' silk, and sheep's wool. The lining is of fine grasses and what appear to be the slender needles of some coniferous tree, the whole being arranged with that wonderful smoothness and care which belong to the highest order of nestbuilders alone. * * * Greatest external diameter, 2.90; external depth, 2.25; internal diameter at mouth, 1.30 x 1.68; internal depth, 1.40; greatest thickness of walls, .63.

Of the measurements of the other nest, he says: "The greatest diameter is 3 inches; inside diameter, 1.75 inch; depth, 1.80 inch; thickness of walls, from .45 to .60 of an inch."

Mr. Simmons (1925) says of the nest location in central Texas: "2 to 6, rarely 15, usually 4, feet from the ground, suspended from horizontal forked twig of small scrub oak, live oak, Spanish oak, or elm bush or stunted tree, usually among low shin oaks and elms and dwarf plum thickets on dry hillsides near a stream, a habitat never frequented by the White-eyed Vireo; in tangled thickets of dewberry; in low trees on edge of thick mountain shrubbery; less commonly, in deep shady ravines where the White-eyed Vireo places its nests."

Mr. Bunker (1910) says of the nests found in Blaine County, Okla.:

The nesting habits of the Black-cap are unlike Bell's, in that it always builds in the center of a bush or rather in a clump of bushes instead of on the outer edge, slips away upon the approach of an intruder, and if singing or scolding in a bush, you may depend upon it, that the nest is nowhere near. * * *

Nests were found at the bottom of canyons, and steep canyon walls, uplands, and little draws leading to the canyons. They nested in jack-oak, dogwood, wild plum, China berry and like shrubs. No matter where the nest was built, on bottom lands, or ravines, the bush in which it was placed was always above high water mark. * * *

I was fortunate enough to watch the construction of one nest from start to finish. The weaving was accomplisht after the fibers had all been attacht to the forked twig, and hung down like a fringe. The female would dart down from a nearby twig, catch the end of a fiber in her bill, fly up to the opposite side of the fork, draw up the fiber a little at a time, turning her head from side to side, as if studying her work, and then secure it.

Eggs of the eastern, and more often those of the dwarf, cowbird are sometimes found in the nests of this vireo.

Eggs.—Three to five eggs may make up the full set for the black-capped vireo, but four seems to be the commonest number. These are ordinarily ovate in shape, but some are slightly pointed and others are somewhat elongated. The shell is smooth, without gloss, pure white in color and always (?) entirely spotless. The measurements of 50 eggs averaged 17.6 by 13.1 millimeters; the eggs showing the four extremes measure **19.3** by 12.7, 18.8 by **14.7, 16.0** by 12.7, and 16.7 by **12.2** millimeters.

Incubation.—The period of incubation does not seem to have been determined. Both sexes assist in the duties of incubation and usually stick so closely to the nest that they can almost be touched. Nothing seems to have been published on the development and care of the young, but probably both parents do their shares of this work. Mr. Simmons (1925) says that "usually one, rarely two, broods" are raised in a season.

Plumages.—Mr. Ridgway (1904) says that the juvenal plumage is similar to that of the adult, "but without black or clear gray on head, which is replaced by grayish brown or brownish gray; olive-green of back, etc., browner; white of under parts and head markings much less pure, strongly washed with pale buff or brownish buff, the sides and flanks more brownish olive-green."

The sexes are alike in the juvenal plumage, but quite different after the postjuvenal molt. For many years it was thought that the sexes were alike in all plumages, as they are in most of the vireos, but now it seems to be well-established that the black head markings of the male are replaced by slate-gray in the female; the wing bars and light edgings of the tertials are yellow in the male and whitish in the female; the olive-green of the back is duller in the female and the white of the underparts and head is less pure than in the male. The iris in both sexes is said to be light brick red: Van Tyne and Sutton (1937) call it "a striking shade of light, clear, reddish brown—this shade in sharp contrast to the whiteness of the eye ring and blackness of the cap."

I have seen no molting birds.

Food.—There seems to have been no comprehensive study made of the food of the black-capped vireo. Mr. Simmons (1925) makes the brief statement that it "feeds low among the dwarf shin oak and scrub oak or dwarf plum thickets on ridges and dry hillsides, searching for caterpillars, other insects, and their eggs."

Behavior.—Mr. Simmons (1925) says that it is "observed singly or in pairs. Very shy and quick, dodging in and out among thick foliage of bushes, and from one dense clump to another; alert, active, and energetic, hopping and flying briskly about, generally keeping close to cover of bushes."

Evidently the quiet demeanor and deliberate, leisurely movement, so characteristic of most vireos, are quite lacking in the blackcap, for all observers seem to agree on its restless activity. Some say that it can be easily approached to within a reasonable distance and is really not very shy, but that its constant hopping and flitting about in the thick foliage make it a difficult bird to collect. Several have mentioned being able to almost touch it on the nest when incubating. Van Tyne and Sutton (1937) observed that "the birds were given to dropping from one perch to a lower perch, letting their bodies swing downward while still holding tightly with their feet, then suddenly letting go."

Voice.—The black-capped vireo must be a very striking and quite versatile singer, but one easily recognized when the form of its song is once learned. Mrs. Nice (1931) listened to one singing in Oklahoma, of which she writes:

He sang continuously, giving an extraordinary variety of phrases, all of them harsh, vehement and unmusical. One phrase (*tee war twit*) reminded me of a

Chewink in its timing and pitch, others of a Chat. The number of phrases given per minute was 31, 31, 29, 28, 32. A different bird gave 29 in one minute. Intervals between beginnings of phrases varied from 1.8 to 3 seconds. No phrase was given more than once at one time. I was not able to record all of his expressions, but the following are samples: *hee-hee chúr, hee prér, chee-chee-chee-chee, hee-hee-hee, whit whit whit, sissiwit heé, hay party, ter para chée, wheep, hur wee chée.*

The phrases of another bird across the creek were all somewhat different from those of the first bird. Some that I recorded are: *which er chée* (a Chewink-like note), *dee dee dee, what kée, whip chúr whip kée.*

Mr. Simmons (1925) calls the song, "varied, reminiscent of that of the White-eyed Vireo, but less emphatic and more of a gentle warble; somewhat like the song of the Bell Vireo, but much slower and more distinct, less of a helter-skelter roundelay; a subdued, low, sweet, persistent musical warble, neither hurried nor slow, as though the bird were making insistent efforts to pronounce its name; * * * also interpreted as a loud, emphatic, liquid *there now, wait-a-bit* or *come here, right-now-quick*. First and second usually alternate at regular intervals; first and sixth end with a peculiar, fine, tinkling, bell-like quality which is very attractive. * * * Sings from arrival in March until mid-August, frequently from the nest after the manner of the Bell Vireo. A hoarse alarm note."

William Lloyd (1887) says that "the song is loud, clear, and very musical, and the singer generally selects some blasted pecan stump for the site of his vocal efforts. The female has also a song, sweet, but not particularly noticeable."

Field marks.—The conspicuous black and white head pattern of the male is diagnostic and that of the female is only duller in color. No other vireo even approaches this, and there is no other bird within its habitat for which the black-capped vireo might be mistaken.

DISTRIBUTION

Range.—Southern Kansas to central Mexico.

Breeding range.—The breeding range of the black-capped vireo seems to be very restricted. Nests have been found **north** to central southern Kansas (Comanche County, one record); north-central Oklahoma (Stillwater and Tulsa). **East** to east-central Oklahoma (Tulsa and Spencer); and central Texas (Dallas, Waco, Austin, New Braunfels, and Castroville). **South** to south-central and southwestern Texas (Castroville, Medina, High Bridge, Langley, and the Chisos Mountains). It seems probable that it breeds also in northern Coahuila, but at present no data are available. **West** to southwestern Texas (Chisos Mountains, Glass Mountains, and San Angelo); southwestern Oklahoma (Wichita Mountains Wildlife Refuge); and central southern Kansas (Comanche County).

Winter range.—So far as is known the black-headed vireo in winter is confined to the southern half of Sinaloa. Specimens from Volcán Toluca, Mexico, on September 11, and Santa Leonor, Tamaulipas, on April 12, were probably migrant individuals.

Migration.—Few records are available. The dates of occurrence in Sinaloa are from September 22 to March 20. In Texas they have arrived at Kerrville by March 19 and have been seen at San Angelo to September 25.

Casual records.—The black-capped vireo has been taken in eastern Nebraska twice; near Bellevue, on June 19, 1894, and at Meadow, on May 19, 1921. Both localities are just south of Omaha.

Egg dates.—Oklahoma: 7 records, May 20 to July 20.

Texas: 26 records, April 17 to June 23; 13 records, May 15 to June 3, indicating the height of the season.

VIREO GRISEUS GRISEUS (Boddaert)

WHITE-EYED VIREO

HABITS

The typical white-eyed vireo is widely distributed and well known throughout the eastern half of the United States. Its range extends northeastward into eastern Massachusetts, where it is only locally distributed. I know of only a few places in my section of the State where it can be found, mainly in low, swampy, briery thickets along the banks of some tiny stream. We always look for it in these places and seldom fail to find it, though it is more often heard than seen. This vireo was formerly quite common in the vicinity of Cambridge, Mass., but has since become scarce; William Brewster (1906) says of its haunts there: "During the years of their comparative abundance their favorite summer haunts were briery thickets covering swampy or very moist ground, but scattered pairs were occasionally found nesting in upland pastures among barberry bushes or other low growing shrubs."

Referring to its haunts in Greene County, Pa., Dr. Samuel S. Dickey (1938) writes: "In habitat the White-eyed Vireo shows partiality to swamps, swales, and glades; yet, in districts from which such features are lacking, it is found inhabiting old fields grown up in a variety of native vegetation. Favorites among areas so chosen seem to be those where the cover consists of saplings of maple and elm associations; or of small trees and shrubs such as wild plum, witch hazel, burning bush, and the dogwoods and willows, and even an alder stand. The ground cover may be of such growth as cat-briers (*Smilax* sp.), wild oats grass (*Danthonia spicata*), ground pine (*Lycopodium complanatum* var. *flabelliforme*), or other associated plants."

Prof. Maurice Brooks writes to me: "This is a bird that has been steadily enlarging its breeding range within the central Appalachian region during the past 20 years. In the early days of this century, these vireos were found only in the less elevated river valleys of the State [West Virginia]. About 1920 they appeared in fair numbers in Upshur County, at elevations up to 1,800 feet. Within comparatively recent years, they have become common at Morgantown, only a few miles from the Pennsylvania border, and they are to be found in a few of the southwestern Pennsylvania counties.

"The white-eye is partial to brushy country, rather than to the larger forests, conditions which have followed the death of the American chestnuts from bark disease have favored the spread of the birds. A typical region in which the birds are abundant will have a fringe of standing dead chestnut trees, surrounded by numerous chestnut sprouts, and covered with grape vines, Virginia creeper, and other climbers. Here the birds seem completely at home. Farther to the south they reach elevations well above 2,000 feet, and nest in rhododendron and American holly thickets."

Farther south and west its haunts seem to be of the same general character, where it may sometimes be found in such places as one would look for the other low-nesting vireos, the black-capped or Bell's, or with such birds as catbirds, brown thrashers, chats, and certain wrens.

Courtship.—The only note I can find on this subject is the following by Bradford Torrey (1885): "Pretty soon a pair of the birds appeared near me, the male protesting his affection at a frantic rate, and the female repelling his advances with a snappish determination which might have driven a timid suitor desperate. He posed before her, puffing out his feathers, spreading his tail, and crying hysterically, *yip, yip, yaah,*—the last note a downright whine or snarl, worthy of the catbird. Poor soul! he was well-nigh beside himself, and could not take no for an answer, even when the word was emphasized with an ugly dab of the beloved's beak. The pair shortly disappeared in the swamp."

Nesting.—The only nest of the white-eyed vireo that I ever succeeded in finding in my home territory was unexpectedly discovered in Rehoboth, Mass., on June 6, 1908, in what was, to me, an unlikely locality for this vireo, which we had always found singing in low, damp thickets. The locality was an old abandoned cemetery on high, dry land near a village; arborvitae trees had been planted in regular rows and had grown up to considerable size, 20 to 25 feet in height; after many years of neglect the spaces between the trees had been largely overgrown with small wild cherry trees, other saplings, and thickets of blackberries and other underbrush. While hunting through this area, where brown thrashers, catbirds, and purple finches were nesting, we were surprised to hear the unmistakable song of a white-eyed vireo. A thorough search resulted in finding the nest, suspended from a forked twig of a small wild cherry sapling, 20 inches from the ground, in a little thicket of underbrush and briers between two of the arborvitae. The nest was a beautiful structure, woven mainly of strips of inner bark and grasses, mixed with soft plant fibers and plant down, bound together with spider's silk, and lined with fine grasses; it was prettily decorated externally with green mosses, lichens, bits of paper, and pieces of wasps' nests, a large piece of the latter forming a tip at the bottom of the long nest (pl. 25). While I was photographing the nest, both birds appeared; they seemed much concerned and were quite fearless, one of them alighting on the nest in front of the camera. The nest contained four fresh eggs.

Another eastern Massachusetts nest is recorded in Frederic H. Kennard's notes for May 26, 1912. It was placed in the middle of a tangle of *Viburnum dentatum* bushes, about 3 feet from the ground; it was attached to a twig so slender that when the bird sat on the nest, the twig hung down at a sharp angle; fortunately, the nest was too deep for the single egg to fall out. The bird sat fearlessly while four people walked to within six feet of the nest, and he almost crawled under her before she left.

While collecting with W. George F. Harris, near Old Lyme, Conn., on June 2, 1934, he found a white-eyed vireo's nest, about 3 feet above the ground, suspended from a fork of a horizontal branch of a small yellow birch, in a briery thicket. It was beautifully made and very deep; the exterior was composed of small pieces of rotted wood and shreds of bark held together with cobwebs; it was lined with fine plant stems and a few pieces of fine dry grass.

Frank W. Braund has sent me the data for two of the nests in his collection; one nest, taken in Adams County, Ohio, on June 6, 1939, was in a small crotch at the end of a limb in a dense wild plumb tree, 4 feet up, in a honey locust grove; the other was taken at St. Petersburg, Florida, on April 22, 1942, in an extensive field of gardenias; it was 2 feet above the ground, attached to a small crotch at the end of a branch of a large gardenia.

M. G. Vaiden, of Rosedale, Miss., writes to me of his experience with the white-eyed vireo in his State: "I have record of 11 nests. Generally this bird nests in or near openings in heavy woodland among the broken and fallen limbs, where vines, blackberry bushes, etc., have grown up forming a tangle. The nests are placed 3 to 6 feet above ground. The nests here are generally very poorly made affairs when looked on from the outside. A nest I have in my collection, along with four eggs, would have been overlooked completely, had we not seen the bird carrying leaves to the nest. The nest is composed of, we might say, a cluster of old leaves of oak, pecan, and maple, lined with fine rootlets and grass; yet the construction of the actual nest is composed of larger sticks, grasses, and rootlets, forming a very pretty nest, should one remove the outer layer of leaves. The nest was in a bramble thicket where an old limb had fallen.

"I have found this bird nesting along a drainage ditch in Allen Gray wood, which is composed of some 10,000 acres of virgin timber. I have found them nesting deep into these woods, but always selecting a site where the growth was greatest, yet near a partial opening in the woods."

There are nine nests of the white-eyed vireo in the Thayer collection in Cambridge that vary considerably in location, size, and composition. They were placed in various small trees and bushes at heights varying from 26 inches to 5 feet. The largest nest was taken by Arthur T. Wayne at Mount Pleasant, S. C.; it measures 3 inches in outside diameter and 3½ in height; the inside diameter is 2 inches and the depth of the cup 2 inches; it is prettily made of various plant fibers and is profusely decorated externally with small dry leaves (apparently green when added), delicate strips of thin, buffy inner bark, soft woody fibers, spider cocoons, cotton, wool, etc.; it is lined with very fine grasses and hairlike fibers. There are six nests from Georgia that have the sides and bottoms completely covered with large flakes of soft, thin, buff-colored inner bark, held in place by spider silk and fine fibers. Another nest, from Bristol, R. I., is similarly decorated with thin strips of light-colored inner bark and the rim is tightly bound with wool and cotton.

Nests mentioned in the literature do not differ materially from those mentioned above. They have been found placed in a great variety of trees and shrubs, at heights varying from 1 to 8 feet above the ground, probably occasionally higher. The nests are quite different in shape from the nests of the red-eyed vireo, which are cup-shaped; the nests of the white-eyed vireo are shaped like an inverted cone, more or less long and narrow and quite pointed at the bottom; the nest that I collected in Rehoboth was not measured, but, judging from my photograph, I should think that it was over 4 inches long.

Eggs of the different races of the cowbird are often found in the nests of this and the other subspecies; in fact, this species is a common victim of the parasite.

Eggs.—The white-eyed vireo lays three to five eggs to a set, usually four. The eggs are generally ovate, rarely more elliptical or slightly pointed. They are pure, lusterless white and are marked with a few widely scattered small spots or fine dots of dark brown or blackish; sometimes these dots are so minute and so few as to make the egg appear immaculate; very rarely there are a few small blotches around the larger end. The measurements of 50 eggs in the United States National Museum average 18.7 by 14.0 millimeters; the eggs showing the four extremes measure **21.8** by 14.5, 18.8 by **15.2, 17.1** by 13.5, and 17.3 by **12.7** millimeters.

Incubation.—The duties of incubation are shared by both sexes, and the period has been set at 12 days and at 16 days; probably the average period is somewhere between these limits, as it is with other vireos. Aretas A. Saunders (1915), who watched a nest from the time the first egg was laid until the eggs hatched, determined that the period was 15 days. He learned to recognize the sexes by their different behavior and by the song of the male. He says:

The two birds showed marked individuality in the matter of fearlessness, the male being much more so than his mate. * * * Frequent visits to the nest found sometimes one bird and sometimes the other incubating. The female always left the nest when I was several feet away and scolded me from a distant point in the thicket. The scolding usually brought her mate to the vicinity, and he never failed to take up his position on the eggs immediately unless my hand was actually on the nest. As time went on his courage increased until he would actually peck at my fingers before leaving. * * * [On one] occasion the bird pecked vigorously at our fingers, and absolutely refused to oblige us by getting off. We finally had to remove him forcibly. He showed such resistance to this that we could do it in no way except to grasp him by the bill and thus lift him off.

We seem to have no data on the development of the young, nor any information as to their care and feeding, but it seems fair to assume that the male does his share of this work, as he does in nest-building and incubation. Apparently only one brood is raised in a season in the North, but probably at least two in the South.

Plumages.—The young white-eyed vireo in juvenal plumage is much like the adult, but the upperparts are duller and browner, dull brownish olive-green; the line over the eye and the orbital ring are grayish white or brownish white, instead of yellow; the underparts are dull grayish white, buffy on the throat, and strongly washed on the sides, flanks, and crissum with yellowish or buffy; the iris is grayish or brownish, and does not become white until the next spring.

Dr. Dwight (1900) says that the first winter plumage is acquired "by a complete postjuvenal moult beginning about the middle of August. The juvenal dress is worn much longer than that of the other Vireos, becoming rapidly ragged from the thicket-loving habits of the species and thus probably its complete renewal is a necessity." But he says that he is not sure that the complete postjuvenal molt occurs in all specimens. Mr. Forbush (1929) says that the postjuvenal molt is incomplete, as with other vireos, involving the body plumage and the wing coverts, but not the rest of the wings or the tail. I am inclined to think that Forbush is probably right, for I can find no birds renewing wing or tail feathers at the postjuvenal molt in a considerable series that I have examined.

The first winter plumage is practically the same as the winter plumage of the adult, but young birds can be recognized by the gray iris. The spring plumage is produced by wear, without molt, the colors becoming brighter. Adults have a complete postnuptial molt from late July to September. The sexes are alike in all plumages.

Food.—The food habits of the white-eyed vireo are wholly beneficial, with the exception of the negligible number, 1.36 percent, of the useful ladybird beetles (Coccinellidae) taken, and a few useful Hymenoptera. And it eats no valuable fruits or berries. Dr. Edward A. Chapin (1925) says in his report on the contents of 221 stomachs of this species: "Nearly nine-tenths of all the food eaten by the white-eyed vireos is composed of insects, spiders, and other animal matter; of this all but 3.96 percent is of insects. * * * Moths and butterflies and their larvae (caterpillars) make up slightly less than one-third of the food of this species and form the most important item of the diet. Of this portion, 20.66 percent is represented by caterpillars. * * * The yearly average for the adult forms is 9.83 percent, which with the caterpillars makes a total percentage of 30.49."

Hemiptera (bugs), including stink bugs and scale insects, are preyed upon regularly at all seasons. Beetles of all kinds make up 12.78 percent of the total food; these include the leaf-eating forms, weevils, ladybirds, scarabs, and the wood-boring beetles, all but the ladybirds being injurious. Hymenoptera and Diptera together amount to 11.64 percent, including wasps, bees, ichneumons, and flies. Grasshoppers make up 13.25 percent of the annual food, other insects 3.74 percent, spiders 3.59 percent, and other animal food, including snails and the bones of a small chameleon, 0.37 percent.

"In the spring and fall months foraging for suitable food compels the birds to turn to the berries and small fruits, which are usually to be had in almost any locality. In January 22.93 percent of the entire food is vegetable, in February only 5.62, still less from March to July, in August 16.2, and in the next two months the percentage rises to 32.37. The vegetable food is composed of such berries as those of sumac, dogwood, wild grape, and wax myrtle, and has no economic importance."

Behavior.—Mr. Saunders (1915) expresses it very well when he says that the white-eyed vireo, when its nest is approached, "is one of the most fearless birds that we have. Perhaps I might have written one of the tamest birds, for that is the way many people would express it. But the bird does not show the confiding familiarity with man that such birds as the Chickadee and Chipping Sparrow show and thus could not properly be called tame. It keeps away from man, seeking out the wildest tangle of green-brier thickets for its habitat and nest. It is only when man seeks it out, and finds the secret of its nest that it becomes at all 'tame,' and such tameness is better called fearlessness."

In spite of its bravery on its nest, it is at other times most restless, shy, and retiring; we often hear it singing in the depths of its shady retreats, but it seldom shows itself or mounts to some open perch to sing; and, if we try to enter its haunts to catch a glimpse of it, it promptly fades away and we hear its voice from some more distant point.

Dr. Chapman (1912) remarks: "If birds are ever impertinent, I believe this term might with truth be applied to that most original, independent dweller in thickety undergrowths, the White-eyed Vireo. Both his voice and manner say that he doesn't in the least care what you think of him; and, if attracted by his peculiar notes or actions, you pause near his haunts, he jerks out an abrupt 'Who are you, eh?' in a way that plainly indicates that your presence can be dispensed with. If this is insufficient, he follows it by a harsh scolding, and one can fancy that in his singular white eye there is an unmistakable gleam of disapproval."

This display of an irritable temperament is most pronounced when its nesting haunts are invaded; then it is that it shows its petulance and irascibility by skipping about and scolding in a state of great excitement. But at other times it may behave quite differently, showing decided traits of curiosity and inquisitiveness, a desire shown by some other birds to investigate more closely any stranger within its haunts. At such times if we sit, quietly, and partially concealed in its home thicket, it will approach stealthily, hopping from one low twig to another and looking us over, coming silently to within a few feet of us. It is an interesting bird of strongly marked characteristics.

Voice.—Aretas A. Saunders contributes the following full account of the striking song of this species: "The song of the white-eyed vireo differs markedly, not only from other vireos, but from all other birds. It consists of three to nine (commonly five to seven) distinct notes, some short but emphatic, others longer and strongly accented, some slurred or otherwise connected, and others separated from all other notes by short pauses. Phonetic sounds are common in the song and stand out distinctly. Songs are likely to begin and end with a short emphatic note like *chick* or *tick*, but not all do this. Most songs contain a loud, accented *whee*, or a slurred *wheeyo* or *wayo*. Examples would be: *Chick! ticha whéeyo chick!; chick tick wheée chickero chick!; chick wháy! chick wayo! tick to! tickata yăă tick!;* and there are many others.

"Each individual has several songs and commonly sings one over and over a dozen times or so and then changes to another. The greatest number of different songs I have recorded as definitely from one individual is four, but I believe they have more variations than this. The difficulty lies in positively identifying the same individual from day to day. They wander about and are not always singing

in the same locality from day to day, and in spite of the great variation in the song, two different individuals often sing the same song.

"I have 105 records of the song, but two are duplicates of others,
so that the collection contains 103 different songs. It seems quite
probable that many more than this could be recorded. In a number
of my records I have recorded the fact that two different birds sang
the particular song.

"The pitch of the song varies from D'''' to F♯'', two tones less than
two octaves, but the greatest range of one individual is 5½ tones, half
a tone less than one octave. The greatest range in any single song is
four and a half tones, from A''' to C'''.

"The song period begins with the arrival of the bird in the spring
and continues to early August, my average last date being August 8.
But I have but four years of records, having been out of the breeding
range of the species many summers. The song is revived after the
molt, in late August or September, my dates varying from August
30, 1917, to September 20, 1907, and the last song averaging September 9. I have records at this season for ten years, but in a good many
years have heard no singing at this season."

Francis H. Allen gives me a record of what he considered "to be
a somewhat unusual song, heard in Dover, Mass., in 1903—*chip-ăă-
chip-a-wheéoo-chip*, the second syllable nasal and 'catty'. I used to be
in the habit of rendering the song as *pip-i-tweeo, who-are-you*. Besides the regular and distinctive song, the white-eyed vireo sometimes gives various catbirdlike or chatlike chips, chucks, and mews
that seem to form a part of the song performance."

An almost countless number of various renderings of the songs of
this versatile performer, mostly more or less similar to those mentioned above, have been written by other observers. Some have put
them into words, such as the following from Robert Ridgway (1889):
"In Bermuda they are interpreted as '*gingerbeer, —quick*,' while in
Illinois the writer has heard them translated by boys into '*chick' ty-
beaver, —lim'ber, stick*, with special emphasis on the first syllable of
each word." Both of these seem to be very expressive.

The white-eyed vireo has quite a reputation as a mimic, but whether
the fancied imitations are really copied from other birds, or whether
they are only demonstrations of the bird's own talents as an accomplished vocalist, is open to question. We may hear such a volume
of varied songs coming from the hidden depths of some dense thicket,
that it would seem as if many kinds of birds were competing in chorus.
Ralph Hoffmann (1904) has "heard it give the *chip-churr* of the Tanager and the *dick-you* of the Chewink." Mr. Forbush (1929) gives it
credit for "fairly good fragmentary imitations of songs or notes of
the Song Sparrow, Robin, Flicker, Catbird, House Wren, Goldfinch,
Whip-poor-will, Yellow-breasted Chat, House Sparrow, Towhee,

Carolina Wren, Warbling Vireo, Summer Tanager, Wood Thrush and others, and although its imitations are not as accurate as those of the Mockingbird, or even as those of the Starling, they are easily recognizable." The notes of the catbird and the chat are so well imitated that, as all these birds live in similar thickets, it is easy for the listener to be deceived. Bradford Torrey (1904) recognized the notes of the crested flycatcher mingled with its song.

Field marks.—The white-eyed vireo is a small, very active vireo, bright olive-green above and tinged with yellow on the sides of its white underparts; the space in front of and around the eye is yellow, these being white in the larger blue-headed vireo; but the best field mark is the very conspicuous white iris; and its song is unmistakable.

DISTRIBUTION

Range.—Eastern United States and southeastern Canada to Guatemala and Honduras.

Breeding range—The North American races of the white-eyed vireo breed **north** to southeastern Nebraska (Vesta and Falls City; possibly Homer) ; southern Iowa (Council Bluffs, Grinnell, and Coralville) ; southern Wisconsin, rarely (Lake Koshkonong; occurrences have been reported from Madison, New London, and Milwaukee) ; southern Michigan, probably (Kalamazoo, Ann Arbor, and Detroit) ; southwestern Ontario (London, Woodstock, and Toronto) ; central New York (Rockport, Ballston Spa, and Troy) ; southern Vermont (Bennington, possibly farther north) ; southern New Hampshire (Jaffrey, Manchester, and Boscawen) ; southeastern Maine, probably (recorded from South Harpswell) ; and Gaspé County, Quebec (one record; L'Anse Pleureuse). **East** to Gaspé County, Quebec (L'Anse Pleureuse) ; New Brunswick (Fredericton and St. John, probably) ; southeastern Maine (South Harpswell) ; Massachusetts (Boston and Woods Hole) ; and the Atlantic Coast States, south to southern Florida (Miami, Key Largo, and Key West). **South** to southern Florida (Key West) ; the Gulf coast to southern Texas(Brownsville) ; and northeastern Mexico (Matamoros and Gómez Farias, Tamaulipas; and Matlapa, San Luis Potosí). **West** to San Luis Potosí (Matlapa) ; southeastern Coahuila (Saltillo) ; western Nuevo León (Monterrey) ; central Texas (Rio Grande City, Kerrville, Mason, and Henrietta) ; central to northeastern Oklahoma (Fort Reno and Copan) ; eastern Kansas (Neosho Falls, Lawrence, and Manhattan; a casual record in Ellis County) ; and eastern Nebraska (Vesta and Homer, and has occurred west to Kearney).

Winter range.—The white-eyed vireo is found in winter **north** to southern Texas (San Antonio and Cove) ; southern Louisiana (Avery Island, Thibadeau, and Baton Rouge) ; southern Mississippi (Edwards and Biloxi); southern Georgia (Thomasville, Tifton, and Savannah); and southeastern South Carolina (Charleston). **East** to southeastern South Carolina (Charleston); Florida (Daytona Beach, St. Lucie, Miami, and Key Largo); western Cuba, rarely (Habana and Isle of Pines); and the Swan Islands (Caribbean Sea). **South** to the Swan Islands; northern Honduras (Tela); and central Guatemala (Bananera and Cobán). **West** to Guatemala (Cobán); Oaxaca (Chivela); western Veracruz (Orizaba); Puebla (Metlaltoyuca); Hidalgo (Jacala); eastern San Luis Potosí (Angostura); western Nuevo León (Monterrey); and southern Texas (Mission and San Antonio). Resident in Bermuda.

The ranges as outlined include all the North American races of the white-eyed vireo of which there are five. The typical race, the southern white-eyed vireo (*V. g. griseus*), breeds on the Coastal Plain from eastern Texas to northern Florida and along the Atlantic coast northward to northeastern North Carolina; the northern white-eyed vireo (*V. g. noveboracensis*) breeds from east-central Texas to western North Carolina and Virginia, northward. The Key West vireo (*V. g. maynardi*) breeds in southern Florida from the Florida Keys northward to Tarpon Springs and Anastasia Island; the Rio Grande vireo (*V. g. micrus*) breeds from the Rio Grande Valley of Texas southward to Nuevo León and San Luis Potosí, Mexico; and the Bermuda vireo (*V. g. bermudianus*) is resident in Bermuda. Other races occur in Mexico, Central America, and the West Indies.

Migration.—The latest date of spring departure from Habana, Cuba, is April 10.

Early dates of spring arrival are: South Carolina—Columbia, March 1. North Carolina—Charlotte, March 13. Virginia—Lawrenceville, April 4. District of Columbia, Washington, April 10. Pennsylvania—State College, April 29. New York—Collins, April 27. Arkansas—Helena, March 18. Tennessee—Nashville, March 31. Kentucky—Eubank, April 7. Ohio—Columbus, April 17. Indiana—Terre Haute, April 18. Texas—Somerset, March 7. Oklahoma—Caddo, March 25. Kansas—Wichita, April 20. Nebraska—Omaha, May 9.

Late dates of fall departure are: Nebraska—Kearney, October 20. Kansas—Onaga, September 15. Oklahoma—Copan, September 18. Texas—Victoria, November 6. Missouri—Columbia, October 6. Arkansas—Delight, October 10. Louisiana—Monroe, October 15. Illinois—De Kalb, October 3. Indiana—Indianapolis, October 5. Ohio—Austinburg, October 3. Kentucky—Versailles, October 12. Tennessee—Athens, October 10. Alabama—Wheeler Dam, October 22. New York—Rhinebeck, September 30. Pennsylvania—Jeffersonville, October 12. District of Columbia—Washington, October 28. Virginia—Sweet Briar, October 31. North Carolina—Hendersonville, October 18. South Carolina—Clemson College, October 29. Georgia—Macon, November 12.

Dates of fall arrival are: Cuba—Habana, October 2. Guatemala—La Libertad, November 10.

Casual records.—Coues (1874, p. 100) records a specimen, without date, taken "on the upper Missouri" by F. V. Hayden. From the account of the exploring expeditions it seems probable that this specimen was collected in 1874 in South Dakota. Several individuals are reported to have landed on a steamer in Lake Huron, October 9, 1939, about 50 miles south of Detour, Mich. A specimen was collected on August 24, 1933, at Cyanthanis, Cochise County, Ariz., about 15 miles east of Pearce. A specimen was collected on April 14, 1909, at Staniard Creek, Andros Island, Bahamas.

Egg dates.—Connecticut: 22 records, May 17 to June 13; 16 records, May 30 to June 10.

Florida: 16 records, April 18 to July 9; 8 records, May 4 to 31, indicating the height of the season.

Georgia: 28 records, March 22 to June 13; 14 records, May 7 to 30.

Texas: 29 records, April 1 to June 14; 15 records, May 14 to 29.

VIREO GRISEUS MAYNARDI Brewster

KEY WEST VIREO

HABITS

The 1931 Check-list and Howell's "Florida Bird Life" (1932) both imply that this subspecies is confined to the Florida keys, where it seems to be a resident, but Holt and Sutton (1926) record it as breeding in extreme southern Florida. And Mr. Ridgway (1904) extends its range northward on the coast of Florida as far as Tarpon Springs and Anastasia Island; he says, in a footnote, that these specimens from the more northern points are not typical of *maynardi*, but nearer to that than to the more northern form.

Mr. Brewster (1887) in naming this race, describes it as "in size and proportions similar to *V. crassirostris*, the bill equally large and stout. Coloring more like that of *V. noveboracensis* but grayer above, the yellow beneath paler (but of the same greenish or lemon tinge) and equally, if not more, restricted." In other words, the Key West vireo differs from our common white-eyed vireo of the north in having a longer and stouter bill, grayer upper parts, and more restricted, paler yellow sides. The most typical birds are found in the Florida keys and birds in progressive stages of intergradation occur northward.

Alexander Sprunt, Jr., who has spent much time on the keys and elsewhere in southern Florida, has sent me the following notes on it:

"Found to be common on most of the keys from Key Largo to Key West. On some of them it is about the only land bird in evidence, except doves and mockingbirds, for hours on end. Its note is almost constant, and the song is heard in any of the winter months. Heard one on Lower Matecumbe, March 3, 1932, which was singing as enthusiastically as though nesting. Frequents the red mangrove (*Rhiziphora mangle*) and occurs on the smaller keys of Florida Bay, notably Bottlepoint, Low, Manatee, and the Tern Keys. Found rather sparingly about Cape Sable, in my experience, though at East Cape Canal at times they are to be noted by reason of the call notes and song. Here, as in the keys, it is partial to the red mangrove. Of course, on some keys there is no other growth. Have not observed it north of Little Shark River above Whitewater Bay, though it may stray up the west coast for some distance. Very tame as a rule, not noticing an observer only a few feet away. I could notice no marked variation from habits of *V. griseus*, indeed it seemed almost identical in every way, except at times the larger bill was apparent. Heard and seen casually, it was a white-eyed vireo and no more."

Nesting.—While walking through a hammock, 3 miles west of Flamingo, near the southern tip of Florida, with Guy Bradley, the warden who later gave his life in the cause of bird protection, I unexpectedly came upon a nest of this vireo on April 28, 1903. It hung directly in our path, suspended 3 feet above the ground from the slanting twigs of a "salt bush" that overhung the narrow path; this is a peculiar, slender, thorny shrub, which Guy said has red berries on it in the fall. The nest was beautifully made of strips of inner bark, soft vegetable fibers, skeletons of leaves, plant down, mosses, lichens, spiders' nests, etc., and was lined with fine grasses and *Usnea* lichen. It held three eggs well advanced in incubation. I shot the parent bird and later identified it as this subspecies.

Holt and Sutton (1926) say: "Mr. Semple has sent the Carnegie Museum a beautiful nest with two eggs which he found, April 23, twenty-five miles south of Coconut Grove. He closely observed the parents many times, and waited several days to make sure that two eggs constituted the complete set. The nest is two inches deep and about three inches in diameter outside, and one and one-half by two and one-half inches inside. It is thinly but securely bound by spider-webs and lined entirely with fine shreds of palm-fiber, and was placed at the tip of a branch of a large bayberry bush."

There is a nest and four eggs of the Key West vireo in the Thayer collection in Cambridge, taken at Key West on May 29, 1890. It was suspended from the fork of a small twig on a "low, bushy tree"; it is a bulky nest and deeply hollowed, measuring three inches in diameter by three inches in depth outside; the inner diameter at the top is only one and one-half inches, but the top is much overhung, so that it is wider below; the inner cup is nearly two inches deep. It is thick-walled and made of various plant fibers, palmetto shreds, coarse mosses and lichens, strips of inner bark, many dead and bleached leaves, and some wool and spider nests, all bound with very fine fibers and spider silk; it is lined with very fine grasses.

There are three nests of this vireo, containing three or four eggs each, in the Doe collection in the University of Florida, all of which came from Key West. One was collected by J. W. Atkins on May 4, 1885, in a pendent fork of a bush, 5 feet up. The other two were taken by Mr. Doe on June 26, 1939, and on June 18, 1940; both of these were in myrtle bushes, 3 feet and 5 feet above the ground, respectively, one on the edge of a golf course and the other on the edge of a roadway. The latter he describes as "a beautiful pure white nest plastered with fine bark." He says in his notes that the nests of the Key West vireo "are the most beautiful of the species, but hard to locate in the thick foliage. Key West was a paradise for birds, but now gone, as all this country has been taken over for war purposes."

Eggs.—The Key West vireo incubates two to four eggs, probably most often three. These are similar to those of the common white-eyed vireo. What few I have seen are ovate and lusterless white, with a very few small spots and fine dots of very dark brown near the larger end. The measurements of 26 eggs average 18.5 by 13.9 millimeters; the eggs showing the four extremes measure 19.9 by 14.0, 18.17 by 14.9, and 17.5 by 13.2 millimeters.

The molts, plumages, food, behavior, voice, etc., are apparently very similar to those of the species elsewhere.

VIREO GRISEUS BERMUDIANUS Bangs and Bradlee

BERMUDA VIREO

HABITS

Bangs and Bradlee (1901) named and described this race of the white-eyed vireos as follows:

In general similar to *V. noveboracensis* (Gmel.). Wing much shorter (the wing of *V. noveboracensis* often reaching 65 mm. in length) [in *bermudianus* it is less than 60 mm.]; tarsus longer; general coloration much grayer, less yellow and olivaceous. The color varies much individually; in extreme examples the whole upper parts are olive gray, only slightly shaded with olive green on rump and sides of interscapulum; the supra-loral region pale grayish yellow; wings and tail edged with olive gray; lower surface dull grayish white, sides and flanks olive gray faintly tinged with dull olive green; wing-bands pure white. The other extreme approaches more nearly to *V. noveboracensis* except that the back and head are always much more suffused with olive gray, and the sides and flanks always dull olive green, not sulphur-yellow. The usual style of coloration is about halfway between these extreme examples. * * *

The notes and song of *V. bermudianus* are not at all the same as those of *V. noveboracensis*. The usual note is a harsh scolding or querulous mew, often varied to a clear warble—*chic-hà-chic-a-choo-choo-weecoo; chic-choo-choo-weeeoo-*

weet, its song being surprisingly varied. It is one of the familiar birds of the islands, very tame and found everywhere, and very different in all its ways from its shy, retiring continental relative.

It is apparently resident in Berumda throughout the year, as their specimens were collected in winter.

A single egg in the United States National Museum measures 18.3 by 12.7 millimeters.

Capt. Savile G. Reid (1884) has considerable to say about the white-eyed vireo of the Bermudas, from which I quote:

The smallest and one of the commonest resident Bermuda birds, familiar to all through its sprightly ways, loud song, and astounding impudence. It is termed locally, "chick-of-the-village," or "chick-choo-willie," from its note. This is, however, very variable, and hardly any two birds give it the same rendering. One has a prefatory "chick," in addition; another tacks the extra "chick" on at the end of his version; while others cut it short, or jumble it all up together at random. One particular variety is "ginger-beer-quick," a call very much adapted to the climate of Bermuda. In short, there is no end to the variations; and a stranger might well imagine, as I did myself at first, that there was more than one species present. * * *

It would be a waste of time and valuable space to describe the pretty pensile nest of this species, so familiar to all ornithologists. I have found it usually from 3 to 12 feet above the ground, in cedars, mangroves, Bermuda "holly," pomegranate, and lemon trees, but most commonly in cedars. I never met with more than *three* eggs or young in one nest in the islands; authors assign four or five to the genus. The eggs average .71 inch by .52 inch, white, with a few dark-brown or black dots; some are entirely white. * * * This is a sad little torment to the collector. It comes hissing and scolding within a foot of one's head, puffing itself out with malignant fury. I have touched one with my gun in the thick bushes before it would budge an inch. And when one is on the *qui vive* for rarities among the big cedars, the little wretches will come from all parts to irritate and deceive one, playing all sorts of antics on the topmost branches, apparently imitating the movements of a *Dendroëca* or other *Sylvicolidae*, in order to induce one to waste a charge on them. Several times they succeeded with me; and on one occasion, the bird having lodged at the top of a very ugly-looking tree, I tore my hands and clothes to pieces in my anxiety to secure the supposed prize. But in spite of this I have a great regard for the cheerful, restless little fellows, whose presence does so much to relieve the monotony of the everlasting cedars. They are very dexterous in catching insects among the foliage, their manner of feeding seeming to be intermediate between that of a Flycatcher and a Warbler. You can hear the "snip" of their mandibles as they secure their prey for a considerable distance. I have seen one catching flies off the back of a cow, jumping vigorously at them from the ground, and "snipping" them off neatly as they buzzed round the recumbent animal.

VIREO GRISEUS MICRUS Nelson

RIO GRANDE VIREO

HABITS

The small white-eyed vireo, as we used to call it, is found in north-eastern Mexico, Tamaulipas, Nuevo León, and San Luis Potosí. Its range extends into the United States only in the Rio Grande Valley of Texas, mainly in Cameron and Hidalgo Counties. It is the smallest of the races of the white-eyed vireos, similar to our northern bird, but duller colored and with a paler wash of yellow on the flanks.

We found the Rio Grande vireo common around Brownsville, Tex., and discovered two nests, one on May 24 and one on May 25, 1923. The first was 5 feet from the ground, suspended from a lower branch of an ebony tree near the town; it was a pretty nest, new but deserted; so I took it, but it blew out of the car and was lost. On the following day, while hunting through the dense thickets along a resaca, we found the second nest, 3 feet up in a small bush, containing four heavily incubated eggs; the eggs could not be saved, but the nest is now before me. Externally it measures 2½ inches in diameter by about the same in height; the internal diameter at the top is about 1½ by 1¾ inches, and the depth of the cup is about 2 inches; the rim is somewhat incurved and is very firmly attached to the supporting twigs, being securely bound with spider webs and woolly substances; the walls of the nest are not thick, but they are very firmly woven, with dead leaves, a few green leaves, many pieces of paper from wasp or hornet nests, strips of thin inner bark, lichens and spider nests, all reinforced with fine grass fibers and securely bound together with spider silk; the lining is of very fine grasses and white hairs; a few rootlets and bits of wool have been worked into the body of the nest.

Dr. Herbert Friedmann (1925) also found the Rio Grande vireo common around Brownsville, of which he says: "This Vireo sings and acts just like the typical form in the northern states. Its nest is harder to find than most Vireos' because of the density of the foliage of the places in which it nests and also because the nests are placed towards the inside of the mesquite clumps instead of on out-hanging branches as are the nests of the Red-eyed Vireo. According to Camp this bird is very commonly parasitized by the Dwarf Cowbird. Only four nests were found, of which two were empty and the other two had three eggs each."

There are four nests of the Rio Grande vireo, containing from three to five eggs each, in the Thayer collection in Cambridge, all collected by, or for, F. B. Armstrong in Tamaulipas, Mexico, between April 2 and 11. They are mostly like my nest, as described above, but one very pretty nest is made largely of lichens and mosses held in place by some very fine twigs and bound with the usual amount of spiders' silk. The nests were placed 3 to 6 feet above the ground. The largest nest measures about 3 inches in diameter and about the same in height externally.

The eggs are characteristic of the species. The measurements of 30 eggs average 18.0 by 13.6 millimeters; the eggs showing the four extremes measure 19.1 by 13.7, 18.3 by 14.2, and 16.6 by 13.2 millimeters.

HUTTON'S VIREO

HABITS

The typical form of Hutton's vireo inhabits the Pacific slope, from Vancouver Island southward through Washington, Oregon, and California, west of the high Sierras, to about latitude 30° in northwestern Lower California. Two other races have been described from Vancouver Island and from Washington, but they are not now recognized on the A. O. U. Check-list.

Throughout most of its range, it seems to be partial to the growths of the evergreen oaks, where it lives at all seasons. As Clark C. Van Fleet (1919) says: "One always associates the Hutton Vireo in his mind with the live oaks. I always think of this little fellow as the spirit of the live oak tree. The tree stationary, unconscious until livened by its spirit, in whose unfolding bosom the spirit lives and dies."

Howard L. Cogswell writes to me: "This vireo is much less common in the Los Angeles area than farther north around Santa Barbara, where it is found at all times in every small canyon or oak region. In the Pasadena area there are five or six oak areas on the outskirts of the city in each of which one or two are found regularly. I have also seen Hutton's in the broader mountain canyons in sycamore, maple, and oak associations, in the tall chaparral of Griffith Park, Los Angeles, and in the willow regions along the lowland streams."

Grinnell and Storer (1924) write: "Four species of vireos or 'greenlets' are found in different portions of the Yosemite section during the summer months but only one, the Hutton Vireo, remains in the region through the winter as well. This vireo is almost exclusively an inhabitant of the live oaks and golden oaks and this choice of habitat is doubtless the basis for the continuance of the bird here during the winter months. These 'evergeen' oaks furnish forage in the form of insects throughout the year, as is shown by the number of warblers and kinglets which resort to these trees during the colder months. The Hutton Vireo, by being restricted to this type of tree, is assured of food in all seasons, and does not need to migrate."

Ralph Hoffmann (1927) designates its habitat as "in the live oaks west of the Sierras and in young firs west of the Cascades." Samuel F. Rathbun tells me that it is a resident throughout the year in western Washington, and "is most often to be found in or about the dense second growth of conifers that are of considerable size."

Nesting.—Mr. Van Fleet (1919) gives the following good account of the nesting habits of Hutton's vireo in Sonoma County, Calif.:

About the first and second weeks in March home-building is begun. The site being properly chosen, both birds begin the task. The round, deep-cupped structure is built entirely of Spanish moss, the first strands being woven on both sides of the chosen crotch, with loose ends hanging down; as the building goes on these hanging ends are woven together at the bottom and the nest begins to take shape. As the structure progresses the moss that goes to build it becomes finer and finer and each strand is woven in with a weaving motion of the bill. When the nest will support the weight, each bird, after it has placed the material it has brought, pops in and works with feet and body to round out and cup the structure.

Most of the material for the nest is collected within a radius of 35 to 50 yards of the nest, but seldom in the immediate vicinity of the site and never from the same tree. * * * Building progresses slowly or rapidly, as the weather permits. I noted one pair commence and complete a nest in about four days; normally a week, two, or even a greater length of time is required on account of the frequent showers we have in March and April. Sometimes a few days elapse between the completion of the nest and the depositing of the first egg, but usually the female commences to lay and does so daily until the setting is complete. Incubation is begun at once. * * *

The nest is usually built back from some open or clear space. It is almost useless to look in the first fringe of trees about the clearing; usually the nest is to be found in the second or third row of trees from the opening. The only exception I have ever noted was a nest in a live oak in the middle of an open pasture. Although the tree was fairly thick, the nest was deserted before an egg was laid. * * * The nest is placed from 7 to 25 feet up, and well out at the end of a branch, usually very well concealed. As a matter of fact unless discovered building, the nest is almost impossible to locate. On one occasion I discovered a nest by the fact that its occupant, presumably the male, was singing while on the nest. I judged this to be a rather uncommon occurrence. The nest blends so well with its surroundings that sometimes, even though I have formerly located the nest, I have had difficulty in locating it again.

All his nests but one were placed in live oaks; one "was located in a small live oak tree about seven feet from the ground. It would have been impossible to have seen it from any angle except directly above, unless led to it by the birds. Fronds of Spanish moss hung all about it, part of one frond being woven into one side of the nest. * * * An unusual nest was one located in a manzanita bush under a live oak."

Though Hutton's vireo may show a preference, in California at least, for the evergreen oaks as nesting sites, it also nests in some other trees, shrubs, or saplings. Mr. Dawson (1923) mentions a nest in a bay tree and two in willows. Grinnell and Linsdale (1936), at the Point Lobos Reserve, found two nests in ceanothus and two in pines, none over 7 feet from the ground.

Mrs. Wheelock (1904) says that "in the valleys and foothills of California the Hutton Vireo builds its nest among the branches of the scrub oaks."

Thomas D. Burleigh (1930) found two nests in western Washington, one near Kirkland and one near Tacoma, both in Douglas firs; one was "35 feet from the ground at the outer end of a limb of a fir, and was built entirely and compactly of light green usnea moss, lined well with fine grasses"; the other was a similar nest and similarly located, 25 feet up. There is a set of eggs in my collection, taken

by Henry W. Carriger near Sonoma, Calif., that came from a nest
about 16 feet from the ground in a laurel; it was apparently of usual
construction, but was said to have been lined with fine grasses, a few
feathers, and a little hair.

Mr. Dawson (1923) gives the following good description of a
Hutton's vireo's nest: "An example before me is a three-quarter
sphere composed of sycamore down, and the familiar gray-green
usnea (a lichen, of course, but we all call it 'moss') lashed together
with cobwebs. The edges are made fast to forking twigs of live oak,
and are exquisitely rounded, while a convenient twig below supports
the bottom of the nest in graceful security. The nesting hollow, almost as deep as it is wide, is daintily lined with the finest of dried
grasses. Its dimensions are three inches in width by two and three-
quarters in depth, outside; and two and three-eighths in width by one
and three-quarters in depth inside."

Mr. Rathbun mentions in his notes a nest found by D. E. Brown,
in Pierce County, Wash., that "was 6 feet above the ground and attached to the end of a somewhat drooping branch of a spirea."

Eggs.—The Hutton's vireo's set usually consists of four eggs, sometimes only three, and very rarely five. The usual shape is ovate, but
some eggs are slightly more pointed and some a little more elongated.
The shell is smooth but without gloss. They are pure white and
rather sparingly marked with a few small spots or fine dots, mostly
near the larger end, of dark or light browns, or reddish brown. Some
eggs appear to be nearly spotless.

The measurements of 40 eggs average 18.0 by 13.2 millimeters; the
eggs showing the four extremes measure 20.0 by 14.2, 17.0 by 12.5,
and 17.5 by 12.0 millimeters.

Young.—Mr. Van Fleet (1919) writes:

Incubation is performed by both parents, and it is during this period that
they are most wary against the detection of their treasures. I have seen
one bird dive into the nesting tree, make the change at the nest and the other
bird leave, so rapidly, that it seemed as though but the one bird had entered
and left the tree. * * * About two weeks after incubation is started the
nestlings are hatched and by the time the month is out they are ready to take
their first trials of flight. The nestlings are fed by both parents during their
stay in the nest. I watched four fledglings being fed for a period of about an
hour; they were visited every five minutes on an average during this period.
The nestlings were partially covered with feathers at the time and were keeping the parents very busy filling their hungry mouths.

Mrs. Wheelock (1904) says that the young "are fed by regurgitation
for five days and, after that, the food is usually reduced to pulp before
being given to them. It consists almost entirely of small tree-worms,
green and white, the latter sometimes seeming, by their whiteness, to
be fruit worms. The intervals between feeding are unusually short,
ranging from three minutes to half an hour."

Plumages.—According to Ridgway (1904) young Hutton's vireos, in juvenal plumage, are "similar to adults, but much grayer olive above, under parts much paler (chin, throat, and chest very pale olive-grayish), and auricular and suborbital regions pale as throat, etc., thus reducing contrast with pale orbital ring and supraloral line."

Young birds apparently have a partial postjuvenal molt, mainly in August, which involves the contour plumage and the wing coverts but not the rest of the wings nor the tail. The first winter plumage is practically indistinguishable from that of the adult. Adults have a complete postnuptial molt that sometimes begins at the end of July and may continue through September.

Food.—Dr. Edward A. Chapin's (1925) report on the food of the Hutton vireos is based on the study of 77 stomachs, only 70 of which contained enough food for use. Furthermore, none of these were collected in March, April, May, or November, and so the results are not as satisfactory as they might be. There was a preponderance of animal food, 98.23 percent, made up of insects and a few spiders, but none of the small mollusks usual with other vireos. Nearly 46 percent of the food consisted of bugs (Hemiptera), nearly half of them stink bugs. Caterpillars, moths, and butterflies made up nearly one-quarter of the total food; beetles 13.25 percent, of which 8.12 percent were the useful ladybird beetles and 2.75 percent weevils. Other insects were eaten in small quantities, but spiders were found in all stomachs, averaging 2.05 percent. These vireos seem to eat too many ladybird beetles and not enough caterpillars, to compare favorably with other vireos.

Professor Beal (1907), in his earlier report, mentions among the Hemiptera: "Assassin-bugs, leaf-bugs, stink-bugs, leaf-hoppers, jumping plant-lice, and bark scales." In the somewhat less than 2 percent of the vegetable food, he adds: "One stomach contained a few seeds of elderberries, two contained those of poison oak, and these with a few galls and some rubbish make up the whole of this part of the food."

Behavior.—Hutton's vireo is a quiet, modest, unobtrusive bird that must be sought for to be seen in its shady retreats, where its olive-green plumage blends so well with the foliage that it is far from conspicuous and it is not sufficiently active to attract attention. Mr. Van Fleet (1919) describes its behavior very well as follows:

The Hutton Vireo is not a bird likely to draw attention to himself. There is no fluttering of wings or hasty glances here and there for food, such as distinguishes the Kinglet; no hammering or pounding and gay chattering or scolding, in the manner of the Plain Titmouse. His sober mantle of olive green is not less subdued than his movement from branch to branch, and tree to tree, his quiet peering under leaves and bark scales, where he takes toll of the teeming insect life. Occasionally a large insect will fall his prey; he will then stop and diligently snip off the wings and legs before attempting to swallow it. Rarely, he will dive forth from the protection of the trees at a passing insect, very much in the manner of a flycatcher; but on his return to the protection of the green foliage his flycatcher propensities desert him and he usually goes full tilt into the cover rather than show himself longer than necessary.

All observers agree that this, like most other vireos, is very tame and confiding, or rather fearless, as shown in its attachment to its nest. It is usually necessary to lift the bird off its nest in order to see the eggs. Mr. Dawson (1923) mentions an extreme case, in which J. H. Bowles, in attempting to collect a set of eggs, "had been obliged to cut away a large willow branch, and the foliage was so heavy and so one-sided that the branch had turned over in his hands, insomuch that the Vireo's nest, which hung near the tip, was nearly upset, lacking nearly an eighth turn, that is, a quarter of a half, of being upside down. But the bird clung to the nest, and it was her presence alone which saved the eggs! Even when the branch was hauled in, she required to be removed by hand. A large experience with this bird, unfolding with the years, shows it to be, without exception, the most confiding species within our borders."

Under the name Anthony's vireo, which is now discarded, Mr. Burleigh (1930) writes of its habits in northwestern Washington:

This little Vireo may be fairly plentiful here but it is so quiet and inconspicuous that it is easily overlooked and may therefore be thought scarcer than it really is. It is certainly unlike any of the other vireos with which I am familiar for I rarely heard it utter a sound, and during the spring it oddly enough became even more retiring and nothing even slightly resembling a song was heard. At intervals throughout the winter single birds were seen feeding in underbrush in the short stretches of woods, frequently with restless flocks of Kinglets, but I soon realized that unless actually looked for they possibly would not have been noticed."

Mr. Rathbun watched a pair of Hutton's vireos during their nest-building activities for over an hour and witnessed a display of hostility by the hard-working female against her less active mate; he writes in his notes: "During the time occupied by this work the male sat near where first seen, and ceaselessly uttered his notes. As soon as the female had completed her work on the nest, she flew directly at her mate, attacking him, and the birds for a moment struggled together, the male seeming to be rather on the defensive; then suddenly the female flew away closely followed by her mate. These actions on the part of both birds were repeated several times subsequently. Invariably, after the female finished her work on the nest, an attack on her mate would follow, the last seen being to all appearances the most vicious, for in this instance the birds fell to the ground in their struggles."

Voice.—If Hutton's vireo is not a brilliant singer, it is certainly a persistent one, as shown by some song records sent to me by Mr. Rathbun, who watched one singing and being answered by another for a long period. He says that, at a distance, the note "sounds somewhat like *tcher-ree*, the first syllable being quickly given but prolonged and somewhat accented, the second with a rising inflection; and the repetition of this note or call was so rapid and so long continued that I timed the bird. I found that it was repeated at the rate per minute of 61—67—62—75—25—20—57—71—a slight intermission and then 40, this representing a succession of minutes." Several other somewhat similar records were made, sometimes in a higher and sometimes in a lower key, for periods of six consecutive minutes, the last of which was the most rapid and protracted of them all. "Following the lapse of seven minutes, the notes again began to be given in a slightly higher key. This record was per minute, 52—78—78—71—74—73—71—63—69—71—66—15, covering a time of eleven minutes and a few seconds. The total time of this was 675 seconds, during which the note was given 781 times, this proving a complete record or performance, as the bird was not again heard for quite a long time. When once more heard it was some distance away. These notes were given with much regularity and rapidly, and at times some were of less strength than at others, though all were clear. When quite close, the note sounds much like *ser-ree*. During my stay both birds were quite often heard and seemed to be calling to each other."

Mr. Cogswell writes to me: "Hutton's 'song' is usually a repetition of two notes, the second either higher or lower than the first, with the accent on the higher note—

> *chée-*   *chée-*   *weén,*   *weén,*
>   *wee,*   *wee,* etc., or *chu–*   *chu–*   etc.

When not singing, these vireos often give a simple, light *kip, kip, kip* call note, and this or their song is sometimes preceded by an odd mewing twittering. In addition, they give a nasal grating (scolding?)_ note. Many times, though, a bird will sing repeatedly for as much as 15 or 20 minutes, and then become completely silent for as long a period or more."

Mr. Van Fleet (1919) writes:

During the fall and winter this Vireo's liquid note is seldom heard and then but a contented bar or two while feeding. But at the first breaking of winter into spring his notes become more frequent. The nuptial song is a constant repetition of a single note, often for a prolonged period. It is like the twanging of a bow string in one key, *quid, quid, quid,* repeated indefinitely. The above is not an attempt to reproduce the note, as it has more liquid quality and there is a slight cadence in it ranging higher towards the end of the note. In some individuals it is given a slight trill like water over stones. The earliest I have heard their song, if song it could be called, is in the first week of February, and it is to be heard from then on until late summer."

Other published accounts of the vocal efforts of Hutton's vireo do not differ greatly from the above descriptions, but Ralph Hoffmann (1927) adds that "it has besides a *tschuk tschuk* uttered in a low inquiring tone, and a low *whit whit*."

Field marks.—Hutton's vireo is a small vireo, but not the smallest; it is smaller than Cassin's or the western warbling vireo, but larger than the least vireo. It is the greenest of all the Pacific coast vireos. It has a prominent eye, with an incomplete white eye ring, set in a rather large round head, and has two faint white wing bars. It might easily be mistaken for a female ruby-crowned kinglet, with which it is often associated in winter, but it is larger, has a stouter bill, its movements are more deliberate, with less flicking of the wings, and its notes are entirely different.

Enemies.—Mr. Van Fleet (1919) says that "as the nest is strongly anchored to green wood and deeply cupped the danger of accident or disease is reduced to a minimum. The nests are invariably so well concealed that a marauding jay or squirrel has little chance of discovering it, unless by accident. In fact I have never found but one raided nest." But the dwarf cowbird succeeds in finding it occasionally.

Winter.—Hutton's vireo is resident all winter throughout practically all of its breeding range, in its usual haunts among the evergreen oaks and some of the conifers, firs in the north and pines and cypresses in the south. At that season, it is often found associated with kinglets, various warblers, bushtits, chickadees, and other small birds that frequent such localities. It is often heard singing during the latter part of February.

DISTRIBUTION

Range.—From southwestern British Columbia to central Mexico; not definitely migratory.

Breeding range.—The Hutton's vireo breeds **north** to southwestern British Columbia (San Josef, Vancouver Island; Kingcome Inlet and Chilliwack, possibly); northwestern Washington (Bellingham and Tacoma); western Oregon (Portland); through the interior of California (Baird, Grass Valley, and Big Creek); southeastern Arizona (Santa Catalina Mountains, Graham Mountains, and Chiricahua Mountains); extreme southwestern New Mexico (Cloverdale and the Animas Mountains); and southwestern Texas (Chisos Mountains). **East** to southwestern Texas (Chisos Mountains); Coahuila (Diamente Pass); and Tamaulipas (Miquihuana). **South** to Tamaulipas (Miquihuana), Durango (El Salto); Sinaloa (mountains south of Babizos); and the Cape region of Lower California (Miraflores). **West** to Lower California (Miraflores, Victoria Mountains, San Ramón, and Ensenada); the coastal region of California (Escondido; Santa Catalina, San Rosa, and Santa Cruz Islands; Santa Barbara, Santa Cruz, Oakland, and Eureka); western Oregon (Grants Pass and Coos Bay);

western Washington (Ozette Lake) ; and Vancouver Island, British Columbia (Victoria and San Josef).

The range as outlined includes all the North American races of the Hutton's vireo, of which four are recognized. The Vancouver vireo (*V. h. insularis*) is found on Vancouver Island and possibly the adjacent mainland; the typical race (*V. h. huttoni*) breeds west of the Cascades in Washington and Oregon and west of the Sierras in California to about latitude 30° in northwestern Baja California; Stephens's vireo (*V. h. stephensi*) breeds from southeastern Arizona to southwestern Texas, south to northern Nayarit and Tamaulipas; Frazar's vireo (*V. h. cognatus*) breeds in the Cape district of Lower California. Other races are resident in Mexico and Central America.

Though there seems to be some seasonal movement of individual Hutton's vireos, no definite migratory movement can be distinguished.

Egg dates.—Arizona: 10 records, May 10 to June 24; 6 records, May 28 to June 9.

California: 57 records, February 22 to June 20; 24 records, April 24 to May 26, indicating the height of the season.

Washington: 12 records, May 2 to June 26; 9 records, June 4 to 23.

Lower California: 1 record, May 10.

VIREO HUTTONI STEPHENSI Brewster

STEPHENS'S VIREO

HABITS

This pale southwestern subspecies is found in southern Arizona, New Mexico, central western Texas, and southward to Tamaulipas and the northern part of the Mexican Plateau during the breeding season at least.

William Brewster (1882) described this race and named it in honor of Frank Stephens, who collected and sent him a series of five specimens including the type. The wing of *stephensi* is decidedly longer than that of typical *huttoni* and its coloration is much lighter and duller. In comparing the two races, he states that whereas *huttoni* is "olive-green above and olivaceous-yellowish beneath," with "no clear white anywhere"; *stephensi* is "grayish-ash above with no decided olive-green excepting on the rump and tail. Beneath brownish-white, untinged with yellowish excepting on the sides and crissum. Wing-bands pure white and nearly confluent."

Mr. Stephens found it "not uncommon in scrub-oaks" (Brewster, 1882) in the Chiricahua and Santa Rita Mountains in Arizona, and near Fort Bayard in New Mexico, where it seemed to be confined to the mountain ranges. Mrs. Bailey (1928) reports it in the Animas Mountains, N. Mex., from 5,800 to 8,100 feet.

Harry S. Swarth (1904) says of its status in another range of Arizona mountains:

Possibly this species remains in the Huachucas [sic] Mountains throughout the winter, but I am inclined to doubt it, and if it does it must be in very limited numbers. I secured a single bird as early as February 20th, but no more were seen until March 2nd, when another was taken; about the middle of March they became more abundant, though not a common bird at any time, and soon after the middle of the month were already in pairs. Upon their first arrival they were found mostly in the live oaks near the base of the mountains, but the breeding range seems to lie between 5000 and 7500 feet. During the breeding season these vireos were very quiet and inconspicuous, and were most easily overlooked; but after the middle of August they began to appear in considerable numbers, and were more abundant at this time than at any other.

In Brewster County, Tex., Van Tyne and Sutton (1937) "found the Stephens' Vireo fairly common in the Chisos Mountains above 6400 feet." In the same mountains, Herbert Brandt (1940) heard this vireo singing "in a canyon-floor oak grove, * * * nearly erect on a dead limb." Based on a small series of specimens in fresh plumage, he gave the birds of this region a new name, *Vireo huttoni carolinae*, in honor of his wife; Dr. Oberholser had told him that they "proved much darker above and rather darker below" than typical *stephensi* from farther west.

Nesting.—Frank C. Willard (1908) saw a pair of Stephens's vireos building a nest in "a scattering growth of oak brush" on a steep hillside in the Huachuca Mountains, Ariz. He says:

The female was evidently using some cobweb. After it was placed to her satisfaction the male took a turn at re-arranging it. During all the time I watched him he did this and several times he brought material which he invariably dropped, none of it ever finding its way into the nest. On June 5 the female was sitting. She did not leave the nest until touched. * * * The nest is a wonderful piece of bird architecture. It is composed of a frame work of fine grass holding together a thick mat of oak down almost as compact as felt. The prongs of the fork are entirely covered with the down held on by cobwebs. There is a scanty lining of fine grass tops. As is the case with the Plumbeous, the seeds are all removed from the grass tops used in the lining. The nest has a yellowish appearance. * * *

On June 10th an intruding Jay helped me locate a nest with three well-feathered young. The nest was in Carr Canyon and was placed at the top of a black oak sapling growing out of the side of the canyon. The nest was fifteen feet from the ground and seventy-five from the bed of the canyon which is very deep with precipitous walls. The male came with a caterpillar but seeing me would not go to the nest. The female, however, fed the young and brooded them without paying much attention to me. * * *

On May 22 another bird was seen building, the nest being almost completed, apparently. June 3rd no bird was around and June 12th, when I again visited it, the nest had entirely disappeared. Not a vestige was left. I climbed up to examine the fork where it had been and it was cleaned off completely.

Mr. Willard and I had a similar experience in 1922. On May 1 we saw a pair of Stephens's vireos building a nest about 6 feet up in a clump of oak saplings in the lower part of Ramsay Canyon in the Huachucas. We did not go near it, for fear of frightening them away and remembering his previous experience with these shy birds. But our caution was of no avail, for, when we visited the spot on May 10, the nest had so completely disappeared that we could not even find a trace of it; evidently the birds had entirely removed it after they learned that we had discovered their secret.

There are three beautiful nests of this vireo in the Thayer collection in Cambridge that were taken in the Chiricahua Mountains, Ariz. The first, taken by Virgil W. Owen on May 28, 1906, was attached to a horizontal crotch in the topmost branches of an ash tree on the bank of a mountain stream, 16 feet above the water and well-concealed in the new foliage. The second was also taken by Mr. Owen, on June 2, 1906; it was "18 feet up and near the top of a slender olive oak tree which was growing near a stream"; it is suspended between small twigs close to a vertical branch and was apparently well shaded by a spray of leaves just above it, which are still attached to the branch; this is the largest of the three nests, measuring externally 3 by 2½ inches in diameter and nearly 3 inches in height; the internal diameter at the top is about 1½ inches, but it is much wider within, as the rim is much incurved; the inner cup is nearly 2 inches deep. The third nest, taken by H. H. Kimball on June 24, 1908, was 15 feet from the ground, attached to some small twigs under a crotch of a sycamore limb. All these nests were more or less well-concealed in the foliage, much of which came with the nests.

The nests are all alike in general appearance, looking like cup-shaped, yellowish-buff sponges, quite different from any vireos' nests that I have ever seen. At first glance they appear to be made entirely of this yellowish-buff down, so completely and profusely are they covered with it, even enclosing the supporting twigs; the down probably was gathered from oaks, but perhaps from sycamores. But, on close inspection, it appears that this material is strongly reinforced with fine grasses, lichens, and a few green leaves, the whole being firmly bound together with spider silk. The lining consists of very fine yellow grass tops. Altogether, they are works of art.

In the Chisos Mountains in Texas, Van Tyne and Sutton (1937) saw a pair of Stephens's vireos building a nest that "was swung from a clump of mistletoe which grew in an oak, and was about twelve feet from the ground."

There is a set of three eggs in my collection, taken by Frank B. Armstrong in Tamaulipas, Mexico, on April 18, 1908, from a "nest of fine hay, hair, bark, cobwebs and lichens, suspended from a limb 4 feet high in a thicket."

Eggs.—The usual set for Stephens's vireo is three or four eggs, perhaps rarely five. They seem to be indistinguishable from those of Hutton's vireo. Those that I have seen are sparingly marked with very dark brown or blackish, but others have mentioned markings in lighter shades of brown. The measurements of 25 eggs average 18.1 by 13.6 millimeters; the eggs showing the four extremes measure 19.5 by 13.6, 17.5 by 14.5, 16.9 by 13.6, and 18.2 by 13.2 millimeters.

Plumages.—The molts and plumages are apparently in the same sequence as those of the species elsewhere. Van Tyne and Sutton (1937) say that a male in juvenal plumage, collected on July 18, "is paler and browner above than the adult, with broad edgings of bright yellowish green on the outer webs of the flight feathers. The throat is much like that of the adult, but the belly is whiter in the center and more buffy on the sides." Mr. Swarth (1904) says:

Specimens taken the middle of August are in the midst of the moult, but some secured the first week in September have nearly completed the change. Birds taken at this time are generally rather darker and more olivaceous than spring specimens, with more greenish-yellow on the edges of the wing and tail feathers. Aside from these seasonal differences the series of specimens I secured here shows very little variation in color, and I took none which approach *huttoni* very closely; but I have a male specimen of *huttoni* taken at Los Angeles on December 6th, 1898, which is almost indistinguishable from autumnal examples of *stephensi;* being quite as pale in coloration, but having rather more greenish-yellow streakings on the sides and flanks than is the case with that race. The bill is also of the larger size which distinguishes the coast race.

VIREO HUTTONI COGNATUS Ridgway

FRAZAR'S VIREO

HABITS

This is another pale race that is resident in the Cape San Lucas district of Lower California. Mr. Ridgway (1904) describes it as "similar to *V. h. stephensi*, but wing averaging decidedly shorter, tarsus longer, and coloration paler. Adults with olive-gray of upper parts slightly paler and greenish olive of rump and upper tail-coverts much less pronounced, under parts whiter, the chest, etc; much less strongly tinged with olive-buff. Young with under tail-coverts, anal region and lower abdomen much less strongly tinged with buff."

William Brewster (1902) remarks that "Lower California specimens of Stephens's Vireo have larger bills than those from Arizona, but I can discover no other differences." His specimens were collected by M. Abbott Frazar, for whom the subspecies was named. He says of its haunts:

Mr. Belding, who was the first to detect Stephens's Vireo in Lower California, gives it in his list of mountain birds as "common above 3,000 feet altitude," but "not observed below this." Mr. Frazar found it numerous among the pines on the Sierra de la Laguna in May and early June, but none of the specimens killed there showed any signs of breeding. He also met with it at San José del Rancho

In July, although not in any numbers. During his second visit to La Laguna, the last week of November, two birds were shot and several others seen on the very summit of this mountain, and a few days later (on December 2) a single specimen was taken at Triunfo, indicating that at least a few individuals winter in the Cape Region, to the northward of which, on the Peninsula, this Vireo has not yet been noted.

Nesting.—Not much is known about the nesting habits of Frazar's vireo. J. Stuart Rowley seems to be the only one that has seen its nest. He says in his notes: "On May 10, 1933, on the sierra above Miraflores, while I was eating lunch in the shade of some trees, a dull green bird flashed before me and without a sound flew directly to a nest not 20 feet from me and started brooding. All that was visible from where I sat was the basket nest with a large black eye peering over the edge at me and watching my every move. Upon approaching, the female silently flushed from the three eggs, which were slightly incubated. This was the only nest of this species I found; in fact, it was the only instance of observing these birds which I had throughout the whole Cape region."

In response to my request for further information, Mr. Rowley writes to me: "Not being a botanist, I am not certain as to the species of trees in the area where this nest was located, but the prevailing cover here was oak, a small, scrubby form, and it was in this type of tree that the vireo nest was located. The surroundings were typical Sierra de la Laguna canyon country, being dry, rather steeply sloping country, full of flora which has thorns and continually raises the very devil with one's clothes. The nest itself was made of small fibres and soft downy material, with a predominant covering of a local lichen, abundant in the oaks, so that the nest was cleverly and well concealed among the leaves."

Charles E. Doe, who now has this set of eggs, probably with the original data, tells me that the nest was pendent in the fork of a low, thorny oak, about 4 feet from the ground; it measured 3 inches across the top and was 2 inches deep. He describes the eggs as "pure, dull white, faintly dotted at the larger end with almost black, brown dots." They measure 0.78 by 0.55, 0.76 by 0.54, and 0.72 by 0.56 inch, or 19.7 by 14.0, 19.3 by 13.7, and 18.3 by 14.3 millimeters.

VIREO BELLI BELLI Audubon

BELL'S VIREO

HABITS

Audubon (1844) discovered this species on his Missouri River expedition and named it in honor of his companion J. G. Bell, who procured the type specimen on the same day that Harris's sparrow was discovered, May 4, 1843. He says of its haunts: "This species, like other Vireos of the smaller class, is usually found in the bottom lands along the shores of the Upper Missouri river, from the neighbourhood of the Black Snake Hills as far as we went up that river; finding it in many instances, whether in the bottom lands, overgrown with low shrubbery, or along the borders of ravines that discharge the water accumulating during the spring meltings of the snows that cover the upper country prairie land."

The species, *Vireo belli*, is widely distributed over the western United States and northern Mexico, but the type race is found only east of the Rocky Mountains, from southern South Dakota, northern Illinois, and northeastern Indiana to eastern Texas and Tamaulipas.

Like the white-eyed vireo, Bell's is a denizen of low dense thickets, preferably along the banks of a river or some small stream. Where the ranges of the two species overlap, they are often found in similar haunts or in the same thickets. Bell's vireo seems to show a preference for thickets of wild plum or small, densely leaved plum trees. But it is also often found in thickets of hazel bushes, alders, haws, willows, or dogwoods, specially those that are overgrown with a tangle of wild grapevines.

In Texas, according to George F. Simmons (1925), its habitats are: "Mesquite flats and mesquite prairie forests; tangled brush and brier patches in open country; mesquite thickets bordering open prairie or cotton fields; lines of bushes and trees along country roads and fence rows between cultivated fields; brush fringing woods or roadsides; osage-orange or bois-d'arc hedges; orchards; plum thickets on prairie or on country hillside."

Spring.—Of the spring migration in Central America, Dickey and van Rossem (1938) write: "From April 5 to 9, 1927 a marked wave of this species was migrating through the beach scrub and more open parts of the woodland at Barra de Santiago. As the males were then in full song, they were naturally more conspicuous than would otherwise have been the case. Even so, it was obvious that large numbers were passing through, and in the low growth along the peninsula as many as a dozen birds were in sight or sound at one time. The evidence of a fall and spring migration in El Salvador, without the detection of a single winter visitant, argues that some individuals, at least, winter considerably to the southward."

Nesting.—Harold M. Holland, of Galesburg, Ill., writes to me: "During the past 40 years or so, upward of a hundred nests of Bell's vireo have been examined by me in this west-central Illinois locality. None of these has contained more than four vireo eggs, which is the normal complement. Fresh eggs have been noted from May 25 to June 15. The characteristic and unmistakable song, when heard in proper season where surroundings offer a favorable site, is indication usually of a nest near at hand.

"Forbush, in the 'Birds of Massachusetts' [vol. 3] states that the nest is 'lined with soft substances, such as down or hair,' and others have mentioned down and hair. Linings of the nests observed by me could not be even remotely regarded as of soft substances. While occasionally a horsehair may have been worked into the lining, neither plant down, poplar, nor willow 'cotton', nor similar materials, though often easily available, have been included.

"Typical nests of this locality may be described as composed exteriorly of soft, grayish plant strips and shreds, fibers, leaf fragments, and small pieces of bark, neatly lined almost invariably with fine, brownish grass stems. The exterior, especially at the rim, as well as the lining, may be supplemented by spider web and cocoons.

"Two nests before me provide fair examples of measurements: (1) exterior diameter, 2⅜ by 3 inches; interior diameter, 1½ by 1¾ inches; exterior depth, 3⅜ inches; interior depth, 1½ inches. (2) exterior diameter, 3 inches; interior diameter, 1¾ by 1⅞ inches; exterior depth, 3 inches; interior depth, 1¼ to 1¾ inches."

Many years ago, A. Dawes Du Bois sent me some notes on Bell's vireo. On June 5, 1913, he watched a pair of these vireos near Lincoln, Ill., "in a raspberry patch adjoining an orchard and thus located their nest, which was fastened to a raspberry stalk about 2 feet from the ground. The little twig, which had formed one prong of the fork in which the nest was originally built, had broken loose so that the nest hung from one side only, and the four eggs were not very secure in a wind. Beneath the nest on the ground was the empty shell of a fresh cowbird's egg, about one third of it, at the large end, broken away as if by the bill of a bird. I suspect that the vireos had thrown it out." He took this nest and the eggs, but the birds built another nest and raised a brood in the same raspberry patch; they had fully grown young on July 21.

Some years later, Mr. Du Bois (1940) published an account of this and two other nests, which he found near Springfield, Ill., in 1922 and 1923. One of these "was two and a half feet from the ground, in a haw bush at the edge of a brier patch." It "was composed of bark shreds, plant fibers, numerous thin, paperlike dried leaves, and some bits of newspaper; lined with fine grass stems and a very few coarse hairs." One of the others "was three feet from the ground, exceedingly well hidden, in a bushy wild crab, in a narrow but dense thicket." It was similar in construction.

Pitelka and Koestner (1942) made a study of five nests of Bell's vireo in central Illinois. "These consisted of three attempts at nesting and a fourth successful nesting of one pair together with one successful nesting of a second pair. Nest building lasted 4 to 5 days. * * * Cowbird interference was probably the cause of desertion of the first two, and possibly three, nests of one pair. At each of these nests, desertion occurred after removal of one host egg.   Nest building was done by the female."

In 1926 Mrs. Nice (1929) followed the fortunes of a pair of Bell's vireos for two months on the campus of the University of Oklahoma; they built three nests, all of which were destroyed by a cat, in one case after the young had hatched and in the other two cases while there were eggs in the nests.   The first nest was in a honeysuckle bush, 15 inches from the ground; it "was largely made of birch bark (from an introduced tree near-by) ; spider webs, cocoons and bark fibres were on the outside, while fine pieces of peppergrass stems and horse hair served as lining."   This nest was destroyed on June 3 or 4, and by the 14th the birds had built a new nest and laid four eggs; this second nest was 75 yards away, three feet from the ground, in a hydrangea bush in a row of bushes.   On June 25, this nest had been torn out. The next day she "discovered that the foolish little birds had returned to their first bush and had started a nest three feet from the ground." On July 2, the first egg had been laid, but a similar disaster befell this third attempt three days later.

In Texas, Mr. Simmons (1925) records nests as placed from "1.12 to 10, once 25, average 3, feet from ground."   He says that the nest is "nearly always in a low mesquite tree; occasionally in cedar elm, winged elm, Texas black-fruited persimmon, Mississippi hackberry; black willow, prickly ash; honey locust, or bois d'arc bush."   He adds the following to the usual materials employed: "Bits of wool; rarely, tiny bits of twigs, rootlets, Indian tobacco weed, feathers, cast-off snake-skin, string, lichens, moss, bits of cotton, rags, and pieces of wasp nest.   * * *   Occasionally nests have false bottoms built over eggs of the Dwarf Cowbird, the birds preferring a second story to building a new home."

In addition to the above-mentioned situations, nests have been recorded in cottonwood, dogwood, and apple trees, in lilac, osage-orange and hazel bushes; and doubtless other kinds of trees and bushes are used as nesting sites; most of the nests have been less than 5 feet above ground, much less on the average.

Two very unusual nests are worth mentioning.   George W. Morse, of Tulsa, Okla. (1927), reports a double nest, the second having been built two-thirds of the way around the first and containing two eggs while the young were still in the first nest and nearly ready to fly; the second nest later contained four eggs, when he collected it.   Baird, Brewer, and Ridgway (1874) report a nest, taken by B. F. Goss, near Neosho Falls, Kans., which, "unlike others of this family, is lined with down, and the fine long hair of some animals, instead of with vegetable stems."   With the exception of a similar statement by Forbush (1929), probably based on the same authority, I can find no mention

of such a lining in all the many references to this species in the
literature.

Eggs.—Bell's vireo lays three to five eggs to a set, but four seems to
be the commonest number. Those that I have seen are ovate, or
somewhat pointed ovate, and lusterless white, with a few fine dots
of dark brown or blackish, scattered mainly about the larger ends.
Others have reported spots of lighter brown or reddish brown. Some
eggs, and apparently some entire sets, are nearly or quite spotless.
Rarely, an egg is more heavily spotted. The measurements of 50
eggs average 17.4 by 12.6 millimeters; the eggs showing the four extremes measure 18.8 by 12.7, 17.0 by 13.2, 16.5 by 11.9, and 16.8 by
11.4 millimeters.

Young.—All observers seem to agree that incubation normally
lasts for about 14 days, and that this duty is shared by both sexes.
Pitelka and Koestner (1942) found that "incubation began after
laying of the first egg and lasted 14 days. Nestling life lasted 11
days. * * * Both sexes participated in incubation and care of
young." Mrs. Nice (1929) states that in one of her nests there were
four eggs on May 15, there having been only one egg on May 12;
"three of these hatched May 28, the last, May 29; hence, incubation
must have started with the third egg and lasted 14 days." Of the
feeding of the young, she says:

> The meals were brought at a rapid rate, once every 4.9 minutes during five
> and a half hours of watching. To be sure, some of these 75 meals, at least five
> and perhaps a dozen, went into the female's crop, so that the young received
> food once every five minutes on an average, or three times an hour for each little
> bird. The male fed 54 times, the female 21. * * *
>
> In this fragmentary study of the home life of a pair of Bell Vireos, the
> enthusiasm of the male throughout the cycle was delightful to witness—his
> intense interest in nest building, his exuberance while incubating, and his
> devotion to the young both in occasionally brooding them and in assuming the
> major part of the task of feeding them. * * * The average duration of
> brooding was 13 minutes on the part of the female and three for the male. Both
> parents ate the feces the third and fourth days and carried them away after
> that, the female disposing of seven in the five hours, the male of eight.

Mr. Du Bois (1940) says that during an "hour and forty-four
minutes of watching, the young were fed seven (or possibly eight)
times, mainly with smooth caterpillars; they were examined on four
occasions without being fed, and were twice brooded. * * * Both
birds stood at the fork side of the nest, on one branchlet or the other
(never on the unsupported edge), to inspect or to feed." He
continues:

> The newly hatched young were of a pinkish or reddish color. When one
> day old they remained entirely naked. Examination through a reading glass
> disclosed no trace of down or filament on any part of the reddish flesh-colored
> skin. The lining of the oral cavity was slightly yellowish, without markings.
> The wings were slender but relatively rather long.

At the age of five and a half days, though the nestlings had grown much larger, their eyes did not appear to have opened, and they continued to be almost naked. A narrow blackish tract had started along the anterior portion of the median line of the back, adjacent to the neck; edge of wing was thickly sprouted; and there was slight indication of sprouting on crown and hind head, and in the caudal tract. Nothing on rump or posterior portion of back. Under parts showed barely an indication of broad, extensive tracts along the sides, these showing whitish rather than blackish. At this age one of the nestlings demonstrated a lusty voice for so small a creature—a squeaking noise.

Plumages.—According to Ridgway (1904), the young Bell's vireo in juvenal plumage is much like the adult, "but pileum and hindneck soft drab, back and scapulars dark drab, under parts nearly pure white, with sides, flanks, and under tail-coverts tinged with sulphur yellow, wing-bands more distinct, and tertials edged with yellowish white or pale sulphur yellow."

Apparently the molts are similar to those of other closely related vireos, a partial postjuvenal molt in July and August, no prenuptial molt, and a complete postnuptial molt late in summer.

Food.—Dr. Edward A. Chapin's (1925) report on the summer food of the Bell vireos, was based on the examination of 52 stomachs, collected from May to August, inclusive. "Nearly all (99.3 per cent) of the food taken is of animal origin, such forms as bugs, beetles, caterpillars, and grasshoppers predominating." Hemiptera (bugs) make up 34.43 percent of the summer food. Of Orthoptera, the average percentage is 18.52. Dr. Chapin continues:

No other species of vireo of which the food habits are known takes so large a quantity of such bulky insects as grasshoppers, locusts, and the like. Though the present species is one of the smallest in size, it includes in its diet for July enough of the orthopteroids to make 34.88 per cent of that month's food. * * * About one-fifth (20.63 per cent) of the subsistence of the Bell vireos during the summer is made up of caterpillars, and of adult moths and butterflies, and their eggs. As the last-named items are rarely found in a stomach, the figures given refer mainly to the first two. * * * Beetles of all kinds make up 15.26 per cent of the summer food of the Bell vireos. Ladybird beetles are taken in moderate numbers and form 2.19 per cent of the total food. Weevils (6.09 per cent) and leafbeetles (3.98 per cent) account for most of the remainder of coleopterous food. * * * Hymenopterans of all sorts (bees, wasps, etc.) amount to 6.44 per cent of the total diet. * * * The rest of the animal food of the Bell vireos is composed of a few miscellaneous insects and spiders and a very few snails, spiders (2.71 per cent) being the most important. * * * It is not until July that the Bell vireos feed on wild fruits. At that time 1.57 per cent of the subsistence is of vegetable matter.

In his summary, he remarks: "Grasshoppers, locusts, caterpillars, and moths are frequently injurious to man's best interests, as also are many of the hemipterans. The percentage of these insects in the food of birds of this species is 73.58, nearly three-fourths of the total. Of the remainder about half the beetles and hymenopterans are injurious. This will add about 11 percent, leaving about 16 percent of the food of debatable import. As the small quantity of vegetable matter eaten is of no economic significance it may be disregarded. Ladybird beetles are about the only beneficial forms that the birds take, and these are not consumed in very great numbers."

Behavior.—Ordinarily Bell's vireo is a timid, shy, retiring little bird, but when incubating, brooding, or feeding its young it shows considerable fearlessness, coming freely to the nest even in the near presence of an intruder; it has somtimes been touched by the human hand while bravely defending its eggs or young. The male is quite as devoted as the female, and generally remains near his incubating mate, singing joyously in the same bush or in one nearby. But, at other times, this vireo is active and restless, disappearing into its leafy retreats on the least alarm; it jumps and flits about in the bushes so rapidly that it is difficult to catch a glimpse of it, though it may be watching the observer from behind some sheltering foliage. Its actions remind us of that other dweller in low shrubbery, the white-eyed vireo. It is often found in similar thickets with the white-eye, or with the black-capped vireo in Oklahoma or Texas, where the ranges of these species overlap. As Pitelka and Koestner (1942) say, "individuals are seldom seen above six or seven feet in shrubby vegetation and their flights are usually made low over openings between thicket patches."

Voice.—Mrs. Nice (1931) writes:

There is no music in the Bell Vireo's refrain, but it possesses a quaint charm in its air of enthusiasm, in the rapid jumble of it all. It may be phrased *whillowhee, whillowhee, wheé;* sometimes there are three *whillowhees.* Either song may end with a rising or falling inflection. When the bird is thoroughly in the mood, his rate is a song every 3 seconds, but this rapid pace is seldom kept up as long as a minute, 15, 16 and 17 songs a minute being the highest numbers I have recorded, while 8 or 12 are more commonly heard. As for hour records, a nesting bird sang the following number of times: 32, 56, 57, 61, 70, 99, 131 and 254. These birds seem to sing all day long and all summer long, although in August their zeal diminishes; the last songs are heard from the 13th to 21st of September.

Unlike most birds the male sings a great deal in the home bush; in the 9 hours of observation 388 songs were given there and 417 elsewhere. He even sings while sitting on the eggs. On June 22 during a 41 minute session of incubation, the absurd little bird gave 30 songs.

Elsewhere (1929) she noted, on September 6, 1925:

The Bell Vireo sings a little each morning. One day we saw him eating berries of black alder, in the meantime singing his regular *jiggledy jiggledy jee;* he also had a scolding kind of song—*zip zip zip zip zip zip zee.* Sometimes this was preliminary to the ordinary song, sometimes not. * * *

The scold, *chee chee chee chee,* is the most expressive utterances, given by both male and female. A sputtering *spee spee,* heard from the male during nest building, appeared to be a courting note. The juvenile call note is a single, nasal *pink*. A cuckoo-like *kuk kuk kuk kuk kuk* was heard August 12, and a loud *unk* on July 10; the significance of these notes is unknown.

Mr. Du Bois (1940) writes: "The principal song of the first male was a rather long continuous sentence, usually declarative, ending quite emphatically, but sometimes ending with a rising inflection as though asking a question. The form was somewhat on the order of a warble, but the effect was never very musical. The same bird had an entirely different song, with loud harsh squeaks as a prominent element—a performance difficult to describe, and certainly unique in bird music."

Mr. Skinner (1925) gives somewhat similar renderings of the song, and mentions a "call, a harsh scolding, though not so harsh as similar calls of the White-eyed Vireo; uttered as bird moves about tree and bush in search of food. In presence of intruder, a short, exceedingly quick, scolding *too-weea-skee* or *ter-weea-wee*."

Pitelka and Koestner (1942) says: "On July 2, Koestner recorded an exchange of place on the nest when, as the male left, the female approached and sang twice. The occurrence of female song in this species was not ascertained further (although suggestive evidence had been recorded on June 22 and 26)."

Field marks.—Bell's vireo has no very conspicuous field marks; it is a plainly colored little bird in merging shades of gray and olive; it has a rather inconspicuous whitish eye ring and one or two whitish wing bars; and its sides and breast are faintly washed with yellowish. It is mostly to be seen in the haunts of the white-eyed vireo, which has a very conspicuous white iris, or in thickets with the black-capped vireo, which shows a decided black cap.

It is smaller than the other vireos, and its song is distinctive.

Enemies.—As it builds its nest so near the ground, its young are easy victims for the cat. Undoubtedly cats and cowbirds are its worst enemies. Mrs. Nice (1931) reports that of 17 nests found in Cleveland County, Okla., 15 were failures, 4 due to cowbirds and at least 3 to cats. Elsewhere (1929) she says that out of nine failures, seven were due to cowbirds; but in no case was a cowbird raised. The first three attempts at nesting studied by Pitelka and Koestner (1942) were failures, probably due to interference by cowbirds. Dr. Friedmann (1929) says that Bell's vireo is a common victim of two races of cowbirds; he has dozens of records in his files. Roy Quillin wrote to him that the vireo "will sometimes build another layer, or, rather, add a layer of lining, and cover up the eggs of the cowbird. They must often push the foreign eggs from the nest, as I have seen many, many eggs of the cowbird on the ground under a nest of this species. Yet the Bell's vireo will hatch the eggs in the majority of cases."

Other observers evidently do not quite agree with Mr. Quillin in his

last statement. The evidence seems to indicate that the vireo will
usually desert the nest, if imposed upon by a cowbird. George A.
Moore (1928) writes from Stillwater, Okla.:

> We found ten nests, all constructed in the same manner and of much the same
> material. All were located within one hundred yards of the first one found.
> One nest had a Cowbird egg only; one had a vireo egg and a Cowbird egg; one
> had a vireo egg; another had two dead vireos (young) and one vireo egg that
> had not hatched; the others were empty. From all appearances the nests were
> all built that season. One nest was so high in a slender bush that we could not
> see into it.
>
> The incident suggests to me the possibility that Bell's Vireo leaves its nest
> when bothered by the Cowbird, moves over to a new site and builds a new nest.
> There were only the two vireos in the ravine.

Harold M. Holland writes to me from Galesburg, Ill.: "Cowbirds
are responsible for the abandoning of many nests, and I rather believe
that the Bell's contribution toward increasing our cowbird population
may be considered relatively small."

Pitelka and Koestner (1942) write: "Both incubating adults and
young apparently suffer infestation by the northern fowl mite, *Lip-
onissus sylviarum* (Can. & Franz.). On July 2, the adult bird on
nest No. 4 pecked and scratched its breast while on the nest. The
mites were numerous on the following day when the young hatched.
A heavier infestation was recorded at the nest of pair B, containing
three young on July 11; on July 14, two young left the nest and a
third was found dead in the nest. On July 15, the rim of this nest
and adjoining twigs were covered with 'thousands' of mites which
dropped to the ground in a continual little shower."

Range.—Western United States south to El Salvador.

DISTRIBUTION

Breeding range.—Bell's Vireo breeds **north** to north central and
southeastern California (Red Bluff and the Mount Lassen region,
Owens Valley, and Death Valley); southern Nevada (Ash Meadows);
central Arizona (Fort Mojave, Fort Verde, Salt River Wildlife Refuge, and the Graham Mountains); specimens have been collected in
April at St. George, southwestern Utah; southern New Mexico (Gila
River and San Antonio); extreme eastern Colorado (Holly, Wray,
and Julesburg); has been reported from Wyoming (Freezeout Mountains); central northern Nebraska (Thedford and Valentine); southeastern South Dakota (Yankton, Sioux Falls, and Dell Rapids);
southern Minnesota, casually (Minneapolis and Winona); southern
Wisconsin (La Crosse and Madison); and northeastern Illinois (Chicago). **East** to eastern Illinois (Chicago, Urbana, and Fox Prairie);
western Tennessee (Memphis, one record); east-central Arkansas
(Stuttgart); eastern Texas (Marshall, Houston, Corpus Christi, and
Point Isabel); and central Mexico (Jacala, Hidalgo). **South** to cen-

tral Mexico (Jacala) ; central Durango (Río Nazas) ; central Sonora (Ures) ; and northern Lower California (San Fernando). **West** to western Lower California (San Fernando and San Telmo) ; and southwestern and central California (San Diego, Santa Barbara, Sargent, Sacramento, Marysville, and Red Bluff).

Winter range.—The winter range of the races of the Bell's vireo is discontinuous, but present information is inadequate to assign the range of each race. The species occurs in winter in the Cape region of Lower California as far north as Santa Margarita Island; in the tropical region of southern Sonora as far north as Ures and probably in northern Sinaloa. It is found from southern Guerrero (Coguca and Chilpancingo) through Oaxaca (Chivela and Tehuantepec) to Guatemala (Ocos, Sacapulas, and Gualam) ; and in El Salvador (Barra de Santiago and Divisadero). The species has been reported to reach northern Nicaragua, but no records of specimens are at present available.

The range as outlined includes the entire species, which has been divided into four subspecies or geographic races. Bell's vireo, the typical race (*V. b. belli*), breeds from Colorado to Illinois south through eastern Texas to Tamaulipas; the Texas vireo (*V. b. medius*) breeds from southwestern Texas to central Mexico; the Arizona vireo (*V. b. arizonae*) breeds from southeastern California to southwestern New Mexico south to Sonora and Chihauhua; the least vireo (*V. b. pusillus*) breeds in central and southwestern California south to about latitude 30° in Lower California.

Migrations.—Early dates of spring arrival are: Texas—Austin, March 26. Oklahoma—Tulsa, April 15. Missouri—Concordia, April 13. Illinois—Quincy, April 18. Iowa—Ames, April 30. Kansas—Manhattan, April 22. Nebraska—Stapleton, April 24. South Dakota—Dell Rapids, April 24. Arizona—Tucson, March 21. California—Santa Barbara, March 7.

Late dates of fall departure are: California—Azusa, October 3. Arizona—Tombstone, October 20. Colorado—Fort Morgan, October 6. New Mexico—Chloride, September 20. South Dakota—September 5. Nebraska—Red Cloud, October 1. Kansas—Onaga, September 27. Iowa—Grinnell, September 12. Missouri—Columbia, October 3. Oklahoma—Oklahoma City, October 18. Texas—Cove, October 15.

Casual records.—A specimen was collected in Durham, N. H., on November 19, 1897; a specimen has been recorded as taken at Detroit, Mich., on May 26, 1885, but the original label has been lost and the correctness of the locality has been questioned; a specimen in fall migration was collected on Deer Island, Miss., September 18, 1939.

Egg dates.—Arizona: 35 records, April 24 to July 1; 18 records, April 29 to May 29, indicating the height of the season.

California: 105 records, April 7 to June 27; 58 records, May 11 to June 10.

Illinois: 18 records, May 25 to July 6; 11 records, May 25 to June 5.

Kansas: 26 records, May 20 to July 1; 15 records, June 7 to 16.

Texas: 47 records, April 25 to July 1; 24 records, May 13 to 29.

VIREO BELLI MEDIUS Oberholser

TEXAS VIREO

HABITS

In southwestern Texas, Presidio, Brewster, and Kinney Counties, and farther south in Mexico, we may find this subspecies.

According to Ridgway (1904) it is "similar to *V. b. bellii*, but coloration paler and tail averaging longer; pileum and hindneck brownish gray instead of grayish brown; olive of back, etc., grayer; under parts whiter, with olive-yellow of sides and flanks much paler; under tail-coverts and axillars white, yellowish white, or very pale sulphur yellow."

Referring to Brewster County, Van Tyne and Sutton (1937) write:

The vociferous Texas Vireos were common in the thick tangles of mesquite and willow along the desert draws and about springs and cattle ponds. Occasionally a few were found at a distance from surface water, but they were always much more numerous where water was available.

Since the male usually sings when an intruder approaches, a fairly accurate estimate of their abundance could be made. The Texas Vireo is unquestionably one of the most common inhabitants of the mesquite thickets of the region.

On May 4, 1935, they located two nests in willow trees along the Rio Grande, "one with two slightly incubated eggs, and one newly made and ready for eggs. On May 11 we found a nest four feet from the ground with four young about five days old in a mesquite bush."

The nesting and other habits seem to be similar to those of the species elsewhere. The measurements of nine eggs average 17.0 by 12.7 millimeters; the eggs showing the four extremes measure 17.5 by 12.2 and 16.5 by 13.2 millimeters.

VIREO BELLI ARIZONAE Ridgway

ARIZONA VIREO

HABITS

This might be called the desert race of the species, found along the Colorado River in southeastern California, in southern Arizona and southwestern New Mexico, and from central western Texas southward into Chihuahua and Sinaloa.

Ridgway (1904) describes it as "similar to *V. b. medius*, but still paler and grayer, the back and scapulars brownish gray, like pileum and hindneck, the sides and flanks faintly washed with more grayish olive-yellow; tail and tarsus decidedly longer. Young with under parts pure white, the sides, flanks and under tail-coverts tinged with pale sulphur or primrose yellow; pileum and hindneck light pinkish gray, approaching écru drab; back and scapulars vinaceous-drab."

Dr. Joseph Grinnell (1914) met with the Arizona vireo at all stations all the way down the Colorado River, it "being one of the most characteristic avifaunal elements in the riparian strip". He says further:

The bird foraged in all of the component associations, but was perhaps best represented in the willow association, especially where there was an undergrowth of guatemote (*Baccharis glutinosa*).

On the Arizona side above Bill Williams River, March 14, I was able to make some observations on local distribution. Here the willow association was narrow but well defined, and the vireos were closely confined to it. A singing male occupied each segment of about 200 yards in this belt, just about the same spacing as the Lucy warbler in the adjacent mesquite belt. Each pair of vireos was closely delimited in the forage beat by that of its neighbor.

Each pair in its own area actively resented encroachment by others of its own species. The vireos worked a rather low zone of foliage, from the ground up to a height of six or eight feet.

In Arizona, in 1922, we found this vireo only at the lower levels, in the valley of the San Pedro River, where it frequented the narrow strips of willows, small cottonwoods, and underbrush along the irrigation ditches, and in the extensive mesquite forest near Tucson. In the former locality the willow association was full of birds, roadrunners, Abert's towhees, Sonora yellow warblers, desert song sparrows, and Sonora redwings.

W. E. D. Scott (1888), however, found them "breeding throughout the region up to an altitude of 4000 feet. In the Catalinas they arrive about the 25th of March and by April are common. They are apparently mated on arrival, and at once proceed to build nests and lay eggs. Two broods are generally raised and three eggs are commonly found to form the brood. They leave the Catalinas early, by September 5, but are to be found on the plains about Tucson much later."

Nesting.—The only nest of the Arizona vireo that I collected was taken on May 27, 1922, near Fairbank, in the San Pedro Valley. It was suspended 8 feet from the ground between two twigs and close to the stem of a slender willow near one of the irrigation ditches. The nest, now before me, is a typical vireo basket, none too firmly attached to the two twigs and made of various vegetable fibers, conspicuous among them being split shreds of sacaton and Johnson grasses, which grew in profusion in the surrounding fields; mixed with these are strips of soft inner bark, finer grasses, bits of willow cotton, plant down, pappus, spider nests, etc., and considerable cattle hair, all firmly bound together; the lining consists of the very finest grass tops with a little cattle hair. It measures about 3 by 2½ inches in outside diameter and at least 2 inches in outside depth; internally it measures about 2¼ by 1¾ in diameter and about 1½ inches in depth. It contained four fresh eggs, two of the vireo and two of the dwarf cowbird.

A nest taken by Frank Stephens and sent to William Brewster (1882) was "pensile between the forks of a small mesquite branch about five feet from the ground, in a thicket of weeds and brush." A nest found by Dr. Grinnell (1914) in the Colorado Valley "was attached to the forking stalk of a guatemote five feet above the ground. It would appear that many nests meet with disaster from their being built, as they so often are, in openings between thickets. These openings serve as passage ways for browsing cattle, which as they crowd through, force the supporting branches aside and demolish the nests. Evidence of a number of instances of this type of catastrophe came to notice. * * * A nest found April 24 on the Arizona side, five miles above Laguna, was located three and one-half feet above the ground on a horizontal willow branch, beneath and darkly shaded by several small willow trees growing close together at the margin of an overflow slough."

Eggs.—The set of eggs for the Arizona vireo seems to consist of either three or four, perhaps most commonly three. These numbers often include one or two eggs of the dwarf cowbird. The eggs of this subspecies are apparently indistinguishable from those of Bell's vireos elsewhere. The four eggs taken by Dr. Grinnell (1914) were "dotted very sparsely about the large ends with bay and hazel." The measurements of 30 eggs average 17.0 by 12.6 millimeters; the eggs showing the four extremes measure 18.5 by 12.9, 17.2 by 13.2, 16.0 by 12.4, and 16.1 by 12.2 millimeters.

Enemies.—This, like other races of Bell's vireo, is a common victim of cowbirds.

VIREO BELLI PUSILLUS Coues

LEAST VIREO

HABITS

The name least vireo was appropriate when applied to all the vireos of this species in the far West and Southwest, as it formerly was; but it seems to be a misnomer for the California race, as its measurements indicate that it is slightly larger than either the Arizona or the Texas race.

Ridgway (1904) describes it as "similar to *V. b. arizonæ*, but still grayer above and whiter beneath; the upper parts between olive-gray and mouse gray without distinct tinge of greenish olive except on rump and uper tail-coverts (and there obviously only in fresh plumage) ; under parts nearly pure white, including under tail-coverts, the sides and flanks washed with pale olive-gray or grayish olive, but with only the merest trace of yellow tinge; wing and tail averaging longer. Young with upper parts decidedly paler and grayer, and under parts of body, with under tail-coverts, pure white throughout."

The haunts of the least vireo in California are similar in a general way to those of Bell's vireo in the Central States, mainly dense thickets of willows and low bushes along streams or damp places, or in alder thickets in wet bottom lands. In the Lassen Peak region, according to Grinnell, Dixon, and Linsdale (1930), "it lived for the most part near the ground in the stream-side willow thickets. Individual birds were seen also to forage into grapevine tangles, valley oaks, and live oaks. * * * The closest avian associate of the least vireo was the yellow warbler. For example, a mid-river island in the Sacramento two miles or so above Red Bluff, and comprising about ten acres, harbored on May 7 three singing male vireos and eight singing male warblers. But in foraging, the vireos kept near the ground, below about the 3-foot level, while the warblers kept mostly above that level."

Nesting.—Grinnell and Storer (1924) record a completed nest that they found in the Yosemite region on May 8, 1919 :

It was in deep shade under a thicket of willows and white alders which grew on the lower slope of a pile of gravel left by a gold dredger. The nest was 19 inches above the gravel, and instead of being placed in one of the stout crotches of the adjacent alder it had been lashed to a slender fork on the brittle stem of a weed of the previous season's growth. This was only 7 feet from the margin of a pool of quiet water. In form the nest was a well rounded, deep and rather thin-walled cup with slightly inrolled rim. It was composed of dry shreds of plants felted compactly with down from cottonwoods and willows. Outside, it measured 2 inches in height and 2½ inches in greatest diameter, while the interior was 1½ inches deep at the center and about 1⅝ inches across the opening.

In what was once called Nigger Slough, near Los Angeles, on May 30, 1914, we found a least vireo's nest containing two eggs; it was hung in a fork of a slender willow sapling in a thicket of these trees, 7 feet above the damp ground; in construction, it was similar to the one mentioned above.

The nests often contain cowbirds' eggs, as do all other races of this common host.

Eggs.—The eggs are like those of the species elsewhere. The measurements of 40 eggs in the United States National Museum average 17.4 by 12.7 millimeters; the eggs showing the four extremes measure **19.1** by 12.2, 18.0 by **13.2**, and **15.8** by **11.2** millimeters.

Behavior.—Grinnell, Dixon, and Linsdale (1930) watched a pair of these vireos on April 23, 1928, in what may or may not have been part of a courtship performance: "The birds were in willows and sparse brush along a small stream in the hills. One, probably the male, was singing and keeping within one meter of the other, both moving through the low branches, feeding. The singing bird kept its tail spread and frequently gave it a twitch, spreading the feathers still more. Also at intervals the tail was pushed downward to a nearly vertical position."

James Murdock, of Glendale, Calif., writes to me: "An experience with a least vireo, concerning the stealth with which it sometimes approaches its nest, may interest you. A friend and I watched a pair of birds moving in and out of the willows in a stream bed near Santa Ana, Calif., and we soon felt that we had located the area in which the nest was placed. Time after time we would search this area and find nothing. Finally, in desperation, we decided to stand on the outskirts of this area, absolutely still (as nearly as we could manage it) and more or less hidden in the thick branches of the willows. My friend did not succeed in standing very still, but regardless of his movements, we soon saw the bird enter the branches at the usual place. What was our surprise to see the bird turn sharply in flight just after it had entered the tree area and fly directly to a branch that was hanging down just over the head of my friend. Then the bird seemed to disappear. The mystery was solved only when we began to search every inch of this branch. Concealed from our view, directly above the spot on which my friend had been standing, was the tiny nest with the bird in it. We were able to touch the bird in the nest and she did not fly. We must have looked at it directly more than 15 times before it could be seen."

Voice.—Grinnell and Storer (1924) give two descriptions of the song of the least vireo, somewhat different from those given for the eastern Bell's vireo: "To one observer the song sounded like this: *we-cher*, *che we, che we-chey? we cher, che we, che we, cheey.* Each set of syllables was uttered rapidly, with a distinct rest between the two." The other song was uttered by the male while he was following the feeding female. "This song was transcribed on the spot as *wretchy*, *wretchy, wretchy, wretchy, wree? wretchy, wretchy wretchy, wretcheur, wreer.* The *r*'s here indicate a burred or rolling quality; and the whole song was, as usual, hurried in its delivery. The question-and-answer inflection was striking."

Field marks.—The least vireo is decidedly smaller than the other California vireos, except Hutton's, and slightly smaller than the latter. Hutton's vireo is more stockily built, its plumage more fluffy, its movements more deliberate, and its white eye ring and *two* white wing bars are more conspicuous. The least vireo is slimmer in outline, it is very active in all its movements and its general coloring is grayish, rather than greenish; it lives in the low thicket, rather than in the trees, and its song is quite distinctive. One of its two whitish wing bars is often inconspicuous or worn away to obsolescence, so that it shows only *one*.

VIREO VICINOR Coues

GRAY VIREO

CONTRIBUTED BY WENDELL TABER

HABITS

Parched and barren foothills of the higher mountains baking in the searing heat of the interior of southern California—such is the favorite haunt of the gray vireo. Camped near the upper edge of the shelf rising sharply in some 3 or 4 miles from the floor of the Mohave Desert to the almost sheer-rising massive wall of the San Gorgonio Mountains, I arose one frigid May 18 when the thermometer was most certainly in the low forties if not in the thirties and started in pursuit of what was obviously a gray vireo singing joyously nearby. Cold or heat, it seemed to matter little. A few minutes of quiet trailing with the inevitable tantalizing fleeting glimpses were finally rewarded: the bird appeared on the outside of a bush and greeted me with the full benefit of his song, which was rendered even more superb by the unusual setting. I have spent far more time chasing down a Canada warbler deeply intrenched in a boggy forest in the East, as well as many others of our eastern forest dwellers, and can but wonder whether the well-known elusiveness of the gray vireo is not merely a matter of comparison with other western species in a country where low, dense foliage is comparatively lacking.

Other gray vireos were singing in the vicinity. The terrain was a dry wash several hundred feet above the Mohave and within perhaps a mile of the mountain bulwark. Juniper and cholla cactus were the most common forms of vegetation. Other birds in the immediate vicinity were western gnatcatchers, Lawrence's goldfinches, and desert and black-chinned sparrows. Unpleasantly, if not significantly, a good-sized rattlesnake turned up altogether too near our sleeping spot.

Grinnell and Swarth (1913) limit the distribution of the gray vireo in the San Jacinto region of southern California to the "*Adenostoma minor* association, of the Chaparral major association, of the San Diegan faunal division, of the Upper Sonoran Zone," chiefly on the Pacific side of the mountain. They found the species between about 3,000 and 6,500 feet altitude. On one occasion the species was among pinyons. Of primary importance, they bring out the fact that being preeminently an inhabitant of dry chaparral the species conflicts with no other member of the genus. On one occasion this species, the western warbling vireo, and the Cassin vireo were all heard simultaneously. "The notes of the latter two, however, re-sounded respectively from the alder-lined ravine bottoms, and from the golden or black oaks of the cool slopes, while the gray vireo sang from the chamissal on the hot, steep slopes." Likewise, they heard both the Hutton's and the gray vireos from the same stand, "the former, however, from the golden oaks, the latter, as usual, from the brush belt adjacent." To make representation in the genus complete as far as normal distribution is concerned, they also found both the gray and the least vireos in one short stretch, "the former in some chamissal straggling down the west wall to the lowest limit of its range, the latter species in some guatemote and chilopsos along the stream bed." They summarize the relationships of the various members of the genus as follows: "The presence of no less than five closely related species of one family in so limited a region is obviously closely depend-ent upon the separate, sharp, associational and zonal preferments of each. The warbling, Cassin and Hutton vireos are arboreal foragers; the least and gray vireos brush foragers; but the least is riparian, while the gray is distinctly a dry-slope forager." They conclude that the gray vireo "has only been able to find its way into the avifauna of southern California from a Sonoran center of dispersal, through the existence of an associational niche not occupied by another vireo."

Grinnell (1922) found an adult pair on the west slope of Walker Pass in northeastern Kern County, Calif., on July 25, 1922. The location was at an altitude close to 4,500 feet on a steep, north-facing hillside, Upper Sonoran Life Zone, but in a semiarid phase of it. "The birds were in sparse brush (*Garrya, Kunzia, Artemisia tridentata,* and *Cercocarpus betulaefolius*); and a digger pine and a pinyon both grew within one hundred feet of where they were discovered."

W. E. D. Scott (1885) took a specimen in Arizona on April 1 "in a pretty rolling grass country, where the trees are rather scattered, and at an altitude of 3500 feet." He says further:

On the San Pedro River foothills of Las Sierras de Santa Catalina, at an altitude ranging from 2800 feet to 4000 feet (which is here the point of meeting of the mesquite timber and the evergreen oaks), [the species] is, excepting the Least Vireo (*Vireo pusillus*), the commonest form of Vireo, being fairly abun-dant. * * * The two altitudes mentioned seem to be about the limits of the species while breeding, and most of the birds secured were obtained between 3000 and 3500 feet altitude. * * * The locality where the species is most abundant is where the mesquites terminate and the oaks begin; there being of course a sort of gradual transition and no well or clearly defined line, the two forms of trees being mingled about equally, I have found that the smooth flat mesas, and the broad open bottoms of the wider cañon are quite as much frequented by them as the rough and broken hillsides, and it is difficult to ride about anywhere between the altitudes above mentioned, without hearing the very characteristic song of the species.

It is interesting to note that on June 26 he did find one bird well up within the oak belt.

Nesting.—Grinnell and Swarth (1913) found a nest in the upper tangle of a greasewood (*Adenostoma fasciculatum*). This nest was 33 inches from the ground, which was sloping, and was discernible for several yards though well surrounded by the sparsely leaved greasewood twigs. Another nest, also found on the same date, May 21, in the same kind of a bush, was 36 inches above the ground. The nests are "similar to other vireo's nests in shape and semi-pensile attachment. The main support is at the rims, but their situation among the close-set, obliquely upright, stiffish stems of the greasewood afforded some support by minor twigs." They give details as follows:

The measurements of the nests are, respectively, of each of the two nests in each respect: outside diameter, about 76, 73 mm.; inside diameter, 48, 47; outside depth, 54, 59; inside depth, 41, 43. The nests are composed largely of silvery gray weathered grass and plant fibers, usually with the vascular bundles unraveled. Some of these elements were evidently grass blades, some stems of plants, and others the shredded bark of weed-stalks. There is an admixture of tenacious spider-web, and portions of spider cocoons; on the very outside, in both cases, are many unbroken, tridentate, gray leaves of the sagebrush. Internally the nests are lined with a distinct layer of slender, disintegrated, hairlike fibers of great length, so that the inner surfaces of the nests are firm and smooth, but porous.

Florence M. Bailey (1928) describes New Mexico nests as being "in thorny bushes or trees, 4 to 6 feet from the ground, occasionally supported underneath or on sides; made sometimes of mesquite bark and loosely woven coarse grass, lined with fine grass, but also made of plant fibers, spider web, and cocoons, lined with long vegetable fibers and decorated with sagebrush leaves." She describes, however (1904), a nest found in junipers at Montoya, northeastern New Mexico, which was composed "principally of shreds of bark, apparently the soft juniper bark, and, unlike ordinary vireo nests, was unadorned."

W. E. D. Scott (1885) found a number of nests in Arizona of which one was "about seven feet from the ground, in smooth, flat country, at an altitude of about 3500 feet." Another nest was built near the center of a mesquite and was about 6 feet from the ground in an upright V formed by two upright limbs. Although admitting that the rim of the nest was attached for almost half an inch of its circumference to a small twig on one side, and for an inch to another twig on the other side, he states: "The bottom of the nest outside does not quite rest in the angle of the V, but the sides rest firmly against the limbs forming it, and the result is a Vireo's nest resting in a crotch, and in no degree pensile."

Yet another nest he describes as—

built in a kind of thorn bush, almost at the extremity of one of the upper and overhanging branches, six feet from the ground. It is composed externally of the dry outside skin or bark of a coarse kind of grass, rather loosely woven. But immediately beneath this loose, external layer is a wall of the same material, very closely and strongly woven. The lining of the nest, which is very distinct from the walls, extends throughout the interior. It is much thicker on the bottom of the structure, but extends up to the rim, where, however, it is thin. It is composed of fine dry grasses, arranged on the sides of the nest in concentric layers, much as the horsehairs are placed in the nest of *Spizella domestica*. On the bottom this arrangement does not obtain, but the grasses cross one another seemingly at random, forming a soft mat. The walls are uniformly about one-fourth of an inch in thickness, and the shape of the entire structure is that of a half sphere. The external diameter at the rim is two and three-fourths inches, and the diameter at the same point inside is two and one-quarter inches. The depth outside is two inches, and inside one inch and three-quarters. The nest is attached at the rim for almost the entire circumference very much like a Red-eyed Vireo's nest, but here the resemblance ceases, for it is not fastened to the many small twigs, on which it rests, that pass diagonally downward, so that it is not even a semi-pensile structure. The thorns of the bush, which are from an inch and a half to two inches long and very sharp, protect the nest in every direction, for the whole is entirely surrounded by twigs and small branches.

He states further: "The structure is, as a whole, very symmetrical, but is widely different from that of other Vireos which breed in the neighborhood."

James Murdock, of Glendale, Calif., in a letter to Mr. Bent, states that the nests he has found have usually been small and without any colors that stand out against the background; the spot is, therefore, quite difficult to see. He says that on one occasion he found the nest "only after watching the bird hop repeatedly from branch to branch in the chaparral, always seemingly following the same routine. This bird usually entered from the left side of the tree and progressed by hopping from branch to branch around the outside of the bush facing me and then by going through the bush back nearly to the spot at which it first perched. I found the nest near this location."

Wilson C. Hanna writes to Mr. Bent: "My notes record 13 nests, and these have been between 2½ feet and 8 feet from the ground, averaging 4 feet. The host shrubs have been about equally divided between big sagebrush (*Artemisia tridentata*), antelope-brush (*Purshia glandulosa*), and greasewood chamise (*Adenostoma fasciculatum*), and a single nest each in mountain-mahogany (*Cercocarpus betulaefolius*) and pinyon (*Pinus monophylla*)."

Eggs.—Scott (1885) discovered a nest in Arizona on May 26 which was apparently finished, with the female sitting very close. He says: "Daily visits to the spot showed the same circumstances obtaining until May 30, when the first egg was laid; and then an egg was laid daily until June 2, when the laying was completed, four eggs being in this case the full set." He says further that the eggs are "rather rounded in general shape, though one end is somewhat sharper than the other. The ground-color is rosy when fresh, becoming a dead white when blown, rather sparsely spotted with irregularly shaped dark umber brown dots, chiefly at the larger end." With one egg broken, he gives the measurements of the others as ".77 x .59, .78 x .58, and .75 x .57 inches." Another nest found on June 6 "contained three slightly incubated eggs, which do not vary in color from those already described, except that the spots are of a slightly redder brown, and they are more concentrated at the larger end. The eggs are rather smaller and even more rounded in general shape than the other set spoken of, being but little more pointed at one end than at the other. They measure .72 x 53, .70 x .55, and .68 x .53 inches, respectively."

Grinnell and Swarth (1913) describe the eggs as "pure white in color, with numerous abruptly-defined minute dots and spots of not more than one-half millimeter diameter, nearly all agglomerated around the large ends. In color these markings are mostly very dark, of clove brown and sepia tones; a few approach drab. The eggs measure: no. 74: 18.3 x 14.5, 18.7 x 14.0, 18.8 x 14.1; no. 75: 17.8 x 14.7, 17.8 x 14.6, 18.2 x 14.7."

Frank Stephens (1890) gives measurements as 0.73 by 0.57, 0.74 by 0.55, 0.74 by 0.55, and 0.77 by 0.53 inch, with color similar to those described by Scott.

The measurements of 31 other eggs average 18.0 by 13.5 millimeters; the eggs showing the four extremes measure 19.7 by 13.9, 18.6 by 14.6, 17.2 by 12.4, and 17.7 by 12.2 millimeters.

Young.—Florence M. Bailey (1904) found a nest with three newly hatched young at Montoya, N. Mex., on June 15. But W. E. D. Scott (1885) in Arizona found fully fledged young shifting for themselves on June 4 and on the same day "found a pair of these birds just starting to build: but this was the second brooding, as the female of the pair, which I took before I discovered the nest, clearly showed." Again, he took on May 26 "two young males that had just left the nest and were under the care of the male parent bird."

Coues (1878) says of the young: "A specimen just from the nest is brownish-gray above, white below, without a trace of olivaceous or yellowish on the body; the quills and tail-feathers have yellowish-olive edgings, rather stronger than in the adult, and there is a slight whitish bar across the ends of the greater coverts. The bird bears a superficial resemblance to a small faded specimen of *V. plumbeus*, but is quite different."

Ridgway (1904) says: "Texture of plumage looser and much softer than in adults; coloration similar, but the gray of upper parts slightly more brownish, white of under parts purer, and pale edgings to remiges and rectrices and tips of greater coverts tinged with pale olive."

Plumages.—W. E. D. Scott (1885) says of his series of 42 males and 12 females, all of which except one were taken between April 1 and June 11, "They present very little variation in size or color, and the young in first plumage do not differ materially from the adult birds."

Frank Stephens (1890) considers the California birds different from those east of the Colorado River in breeding area. He says: "The most prominent difference between the two forms is the darker color above, combined with the greater amount of whitish edging on wing and tail, in the California form."

Grinnell (1922) collected a male out of a pair at Walker Pass, Kern County, Calif., on July 25, 1922. He says that the bird "proved to be in molt, with only two of the old tail-feathers remaining and with new feathers showing where old ones had fallen out, in the wings and in most of the body tracts. The weight of the bird was 12.5 grams."

Grinnell and Swarth (1913) describe an adult male secured on August 27 as being in nearly full fresh fall plumage. "The annual molt is very nearly completed, only the outermost primaries being still partly unsheathed." They say further:

Since there is in all probability no spring molt, even partial, this bird presents the true color characters of the species. As compared with the better known spring plumage, conspicuous among various species of the family for its general plumbeous tone, the freshly acquired plumage is not so distinctly gray save about the head. The whole dorsum, the outer surface of closed wing, and, more appreciably, the rump and upper tail coverts, are pervaded with a tinge of green; the sides and flanks have a conspicuous tinge or mixture of primrose yellow; and there is a faint buffy suffusion across the chest. All these tints are evidently very much reduced, or obliterated altogether, through the intervening months of wear and fading, until spring brings the notable gray cast again.

With more material than had been available to Frank Stephens, they came to the conclusion there was no basis for systematic separation of the California birds from the Arizona ones. They conclude, in this respect, as follows: "From a consideration of its distribution as now known, it appears probable that the gray vireo has invaded California from the south-central plateau region of western North America, within relatively recent times."

Food.—Frank Stephens (1878) comments as follows: "I have never seen them catching insects in the air, as some other Vireos do, but have observed them scratching on the ground like a Pipilo."

From the only two stomachs examined by the Biological Survey, Dr. Edward A. Chapin (1925) could obtain only a hint as to the food of the gray vireo: "Caterpillars and a small moth were found in one stomach, together with a stink-bug (*Prionosoma podopioides*), a tree hopper (*Platycentrus acuticornis*), and a tree cricket (*Oecanthus*). In the other stomach two dobson flies (*Chauliodes*), a small cicada (*Tibicinoides hesperius*), and a long-horned grasshopper made up the greater part of the contents; two beetles (*Acmaeodera neglecta* and *Pachybrachys*) complete the list."

Behavior.—Grinnell and Swarth (1913) found the species a constant accompaniment of the belts of the two species of chaparral bushes, *Adenostoma sparsifolium* and *A. fasciculatum.* They say: "While adhering closely to the cover of these plants, it foraged also through scrub oak, manzanita, and ceanothus, occasionally into four-leafed piñon (*Pinus parryana*) or sagebrush (*Artemisia tridentata*). The forage depth of this vireo is between one and five feet above the ground, rarely any higher. A person may follow a bird around for twenty minutes, keeping track of it by the oft-repeated song, without catching a view of it above the level of the chaparral tops."

Grinnell (1922) witnessed a particularly interesting variation from the foregoing of which he writes as follows: "From the bushes she went into the pinyon tree before mentioned, and thence into the digger pine, reaching the unusual height of some fifteen feet above the slope at the base of the tree. Her head was turned from side to side at frequent intervals, especially when she approached and eyed me curiously at a range of not more than 12 feet." He also brought out the fact that most of the time the tail drooped below the axis line of the body.

H. W. Henshaw (1875), finding adults with fledged young on July 8, says: "The parents manifested the utmost solicitude, and flew to meet me, uttering a variety of notes, now flying to the edge of the thicket, and remonstrating with me with harsh cries of anger and alarm, now returning to their young, and with earnest warning notes endeavoring to lead them away from a spot which to them seemed fraught with danger." The young were still dependent on the old for food.

W. E. D. Scott (1885) on May 26 found a "female sitting on the nest, and the male singing in the bushes close at hand. The female was very tame, and in order to see the interior of the nest I was obliged to touch her with my fingers before she would leave her home. Several times afterwards, in watching the progress of laying, I was obliged to repeat this action, and once had to lift the bird out of the nest."

J. Van Tyne and G. M. Sutton (1937) collected a pair in Brewster County, Tex., and commented on three birds seen about "the habit of flicking their long tail nervously as the gnatcatcher does."

A. J. van Rossem (1932) speaks of the bird as "far from typical of the family in habits for its quick, jerky movements and cocked-up tail led us more than once to mistake it for a wren."

Voice.—H. W. Henshaw (1875) says of the song, "One of the most beautiful I had ever heard from any of the family," an opinion with which the writer, who has heard nearly every species of vireo in the United States, concurs.

Grinnell and Swarth (1913) say: "The presence of the gray vireo is most easily ascertainable through the peculiar and far-reaching song." Describing the song, which they attribute to the male only, they state: "The song of the gray vireo is loud and full-toned, in volume and quality. In these respects it reminds the hearer strongly of the Cassin Vireo, yet with the twang and less deliberate utterance of a western tanager. In measure, and in the suggestion of alternate rising and falling inflection, it recalls the least vireo.

Grinnell (1922) mentions the "broken, post-nuptially rendered song of the male—intermittent and sketchy, yet distinct enough from the songs of other vireos to be recognized at once." Speaking of the female he said: "The only note she gave was a low harsh *churr* or *shray*, given now and then as she hopped slowly through the twiggery."

Frank Stephens (1878) says: "They sing pretty steadily, the song consisting of a couple of syllables repeated with different inflections, something like *chu-wee*, *chu-wée*, *chu-wée*, generally pausing a little after three or four notes. Sometimes the order is reversed. This seems to be the song of the male, as the only female that I am positive of having heard, sung more like *V. pusillus*. Sometimes when alarmed they will scold like a wren, when near to them, as they are singing, a sort of whistling sound can be heard between the notes."

Ralph Hoffmann (1927) in an attempt to reduce the songs to syllables gives them as "*chee wi*, *chee wi*, *choo* or *che weet*, *chee; che churr weet*."

W. E. D. Scott (1885) describes the song as "composed of single whistling notes, generally delivered rather slowly, and seemingly with hesitation, and in an abstracted way, as if the performer were thinking the while of other affairs; and yet frequently this sort of abstraction seems cast aside, and the same series of notes are given with a precision and brilliancy that calls to mind a fine performance of a Scarlet Tanager, or even of a Robin."

Field marks.—Roger T. Peterson (1941) points out that the species "has a *narrow white eye-ring* but differs from other Vireos having similar eye-rings by having *no wingbars* or one faint one." The song and the habit of flicking the long tail nervously as the gnatcatcher does are the most readily noticed characteristics.

Elliott Coues (1866) describes the bird as follows: "Tail very long; as long as the wings; decidedly rounded; * * * The wings are short and remarkably rounded. * * * The colors of the species are almost exactly those of *plumbeus;* * * * in form the two birds are widely diverse. It is a smaller species than *plumbeus*, but its greatly elongated tail make the total lengths of the two nearly the same. * * * It is unnecessary to compare *vicinior* with any other species, it is so very dissimilar from them all."

DISTRIBUTION

Range.—Southwestern United States, Lower California, and the western coast of Mexico.

Breeding range.—The gray vireo breeds **north** to southern California (Saugus and Walker Pass, possibly); southern Nevada (Grapevine Mountains and probably Oak Spring); southwestern Utah (Beaverdam Mountains and has occurred north to Salina); northeastern Arizona (Keams Canyon); is casual or accidental at Lamar, Colorado; and extreme western Oklahoma (Kenton). **East** to western Oklahoma (Kenton); east-central New Mexico (Pajarito Creek near Montoya); and western Texas (Guadalupe Mountains near Frijole). **South** to western Texas (Frijole); southwestern New Mexico (Apache and Silver City); southern Arizona (Tombstone and Santa Catalina Mountains); and northern Lower California (San Rafael Valley). **West** to northern Lower California (San Rafael Valley) and southern California (Campo, San Jacinto Mountains, Riverside, and Saugus).

Winter range.—In winter the gray vireo is as yet known only from the coast of Sonora (San Esteban and Tiburón Islands to Guaymas) and the Cape region of Lower California. There is also a specimen, accidental or in migration, from Irde, Durango, taken on August 13, 1898.

Migration.—In Sonora the extreme dates of occurrence are September 15 to April.

Dates of spring arrival are: Texas—Frijole, April 30. Arizona—Santa Catalina Mountains, April 1. California—Mecca, March 26.

Dates of fall departure are: California—San Jacinto Mountains, August 27. Utah—Salina, August 22. Arizona—Grand Canyon, September 14.

Egg dates.—Arizona: 7 records, May 20 to June 6.

California: 12 records, April 20 to July 4; 6 records, May 21 to 29, indicating the height of the season.

VIREO FLAVIFRONS Vieillot

YELLOW-THROATED VIREO

HABITS

This handsome vireo, the most brilliantly colored of the family, is widely distributed over the eastern half of the United States and southern Canada, but it is not equally common everywhere throughout this wide range, and it is uncommon or rare in many places. When I was a boy it was a common bird in southeastern Massachusetts, and we often saw its beautiful nests in our shade trees and orchards; but now, alas, it is only a happy memory; I have not seen one here for many years. It has probably gone from many another of its former habitats. I have always suspected that its disappearance was largely due to the extensive spraying of our shade and orchard trees. The red-eyed vireo, also, seems to have been driven away from our home grounds and the shade trees along our streets, probably for the same reason, but it is still common enough in our deciduous woodlands. The yellow-throated vireo, in my experience, has never been as much of a woodland bird as the redeye and far less so than the closely related blue-headed vireo. Dr. Brewer (Baird, Brewer, and Ridgway, 1874) expresses it very well as follows: "All the older ornithological writers, in speaking of the Yellow-throated Vireo, repeat each other in describing it as peculiarly attracted to the forest, seeking its solitudes and gleaning its food chiefly among its topmost branches. Such has not been my experience with this interesting and attractive little songster. I have found no one of this genus, not even the gilva, so common in the vicinity of dwellings, or more familiar and fearless in its intercourse with man."

It is only fair to say, however, that Dr. Brewer's observations were evidently made near Boston, Mass., where its haunts were much as they used to be here. In other portions of its range, and to some extent in the east, it may be found on the edges of woodlands, in groves and in open stands of oaks, maples, and other hardwood trees, but seldom in the dense forests. Dr. Dayton Stoner (1932), referring to the Oneida Lake region in New York, writes: "It seems to be more widely dispersed in early spring than later when its local distribution becomes more restricted, being then confined largely to orchards and groves, the vicinity of cottages and summer camps, tall roadside trees and those in the villages about the lake. I have been particularly impressed by the numbers of yellow-throated vireos about the villages of Bridgeport and Cleveland during the summer. Wooded tracts composed largely or solely of tall maples, wild black cherry and other hardwoods * * * also appeal to this vireo."

Probably in such localities the yellow-throated vireo would be likely to survive longer than in the much-sprayed roadside trees and orchards of Massachusetts.

Nesting.—The yellow-throated vireo builds the handsomest nest of any of the vireos, even prettier than the best examples of the nests of the blue-headed vireo, and fully as well decorated as the nests of the hummingbird, wood pewee, and blue-gray gnatcatcher, though differing from all these in shape and suspended from the prongs of a forked twig. The general construction of the nest is similar to that of other vireos, but it is very well made and firmly attached to the supporting twigs. In one before me the supporting twigs are entirely concealed by the masses of cobwebs and other material that have been tightly drawn over them and covered with lichens; the whole body of the nest is almost completely covered with small bits of variously colored tree lichens, all held securely in place by numerous fine strands of spider silk; the deep cup, with its thick walls and incurving rim above it, is neatly lined with fine grass tops. It measures approximately 3 inches in outside diameter and about 2½ inches in outside depth; internally the cup is about 2 inches in diameter at the top and 1½ inches deep; the bulging sides make the inner cavity wider below the rim, thus giving the eggs or young more security as the nest is swayed in the wind.

The nests of the yellow-throated vireo are placed in a variety of deciduous trees, but rarely in conifers. The height from the ground varies from 3 feet to 60 feet; apparently most of them are over 20 feet up. A nest was built in a tuliptree close to my house, about 20 feet above the ground, attached to a forked twig that projected from a horizontal branch in the middle of the large tree, and within a few yards of my dressing-room window. The nest, now in my collection, is beautifully decorated with the egg cases of spiders and green and gray tree lichens, firmly secured with spider silk and lined with fine, dry needles of the white pine. I have found a number of nests in old, neglected apple orchards; these were also fully camouflaged with lichens picked from the branches and trunks of the old lichen-covered trees, so that they blended beautifully with their surroundings and were easily overlooked.

Dr. Brewer (Baird, Brewer, and Ridgway, 1874) writes:

All of its nests that I have ever met with have been built in gardens and orchards, and in close proximity to dwellings, and they have also been exclusively in comparatively low positions. In one of the most recent instances a pair of these birds built one of their beautiful moss-covered nests in a low branch of an apple tree that overhung the croquet ground, within a few rods of my house. It was first noticed in consequence of its bold little builder flying in my face whenever I approached too near, even before its nest contained any eggs. The grounds were in frequent use, and the pair were at first a good deal disturbed by these constant intrusions, but they soon became reconciled to their company, and would not leave their position, even though the game was contested immediately under their nest, which was thus often brought within a foot of the heads of the players. Before this nest was quite finished, the female began her duties of incubation. Her assiduous mate was constantly engaged at first in completing the external ornamentation of the nest with lichens and mosses, and then with a renewal of his interrupted concerts of song. These duties be varied by frequent captures of insects, winged and creeping, most of which he duly carried to his mate.

Edward R. Ford sends me the following notes: "Of 14 nests of the yellow-throated vireo, found in Newaygo County, Mich., my notes lack desirable detail because of the height at which they were placed, 25 to 40 feet from the ground. However, all nests had this in common: They were placed *within* the crown of the tree on small, sturdy branches at right angles to the trunk, or to a large upright fork thereof. At the point of attachment to the supporting branch, the nests were within from 12 to 20 inches of the trunk or fork. Except in two instances of comparatively low nests, they were built in rather large oaks or, once, in a wild cherry. One low nest was in a small oak, the other in an apple tree. Four nests were placed near, or directly above, the roof of some cottage or outbuilding near the shore of Hess Lake. All the nests found were not far from the lake, and some were in the woods, apart from man-made structures.

"An unusual circumstance was the use of a repaired and redecorated nest of the previous year. This brought forth a brood in the first part of June. One pair was observed to carry nesting material to two separate sites, about 20 yards apart. On the second day work ceased at one site, near a building, but was continued at the other until the nest was completed. Like other vireos, this species is strongly attached to the nest. One bird that I attempted to remove by lifting it from the nest was so obdurate that I gave up, fearful of damaging the contents."

A. Dawes Du Bois writes to me: "In 1933, while selecting a spot for planting some wild anemones, I chanced to see a yellow-throated vireo at work on a nest in a basswood tree near the corner of our house. The nest could be seen from the bathroom window, which was about on a level with it and only 25 feet away. The nest seemed about in the midstage of construction. Both birds were working industriously; sometimes one would come before the other left. The procedure was of three kinds: (1) to place material inside of the nest; (2) to work from outside the nest, pulling material upward and outward over the rim and over the supporting twigs; (3) to get inside the nest and work with the feet, shaping and enlarging the nest, and stretching it to greater depth. The last action showed plainly from the outside, as the bird pushed the nest out into humps in various parts of the bottom.

"The vireos worked all the next day (May 20). They chased invading birds away with a vim. On two occasions, when a bird was working inside the nest, I observed that its body was in practically a vertical position, head in bottom of nest, tail approximately straight up. They continued to work at the nest on the 21st. Once I saw her carrying a large patch of white cocoon material.

"I did not see them doing any work on the 22d. On the 23d the wind blew a gale all day, bringing a dust storm in the afternoon. Twice, in the afternoon, I saw one of the birds working at the rim of the nest, where it was attached to the branchlet, probably repairing damage. The next morning the nest was pretty badly wrecked; and the wind continued. When I returned in the afternoon it had been blown out of the tree. I found it on the ground; evidently it had not been completed."

N. S. Goss (1891) found a nest of the yellow-throated vireo, in the timber near Neosho Falls, Kans., "attached to branches of a very small horizontal limb of a large hickory tree, about twenty feet from the ground, and ten feet below the limbs that formed the top of the tree. In the forks of the tree the Cooper's Hawks were nesting, and I discovered the Vireo and its nest in watching the Hawks—or rather the man I had hired to climb the tree to the Hawks' nest." He continues:

I have since noticed these birds in the woodlands on several occasions, and on the 18th of May, 1883, while strolling along the south bank of the Kansas River, near Topeka, in the timber skirting the stream, I had the pleasure to find a pair of them building a nest in a honey locust, about sixteen feet from the ground, and eight feet from the body of the tree. The nest was fastened to the forks of a small horizontal branch. The frame of the nest appeared to be completed. The birds were busy at work, the female lining the nest with small, hair-like stems, the male covering the outside with soft, lint-like fibrous stripplings from plants (these closely resembling the limb and its surroundings), and dotting it over with lichen. * * * As the female stood upon the top of the nest, with head down and inside, I could not see the manner of arranging the lining; but as she kept walking around upon the rim, I could, in imagination, see her plaiting and weaving in and out the hair-like stems. It was very easy and interesting, however, to see and note the actions of the male, as he deftly worked the material into the framework, running the longer, fibrous, thread-like strips through, and then quickly springing upon the top, and fastening them on the inside. Then he would rearrange the outside, stopping a moment to inspect the work, and then off in search of more material, occasionally warbling a few notes on the way; but he was silent at the nest, while I remained so near.

John Hutchins (1902) gives a full account of the building of their nest by a pair of yellow-throated vireos close to his house in Litchfield, Conn.:

The discovery of the nest-building was made, as is so often the case, by seeing the bird gathering material. We were passing near the stable, when underneath its rather deep eaves a small bird was seen to be fluttering, and we thought she was caught in a strong spider's web, as before now I have found our Humming-bird; but instead of this the bird was gathering web for her uses, and soon flew away to the front of the house, where we lost sight of her; but on coming up cautiously we had the great joy of seeing her fastening the first sticky threads of her new home to some outstretched twigs of a small low-growing elm branch close by our window. * * * The birds began their building on Sunday morning, June 2. By the following Saturday, June 8, the nest was completed, so that they took about one round week of not hurried, but of quite incessant work to complete their home-making. * * *

The material for the nest was almost all of spider-web. * * * And there were occasional thread-like shreds of some coarser fiber in the Yellow-throats' building, but by far the larger part was of the twisted films of the spider. * * * The birds built the rim of their nest stout and strong, twisting the web about the twigs and over and over upon itself where it stretched from twig to twig till I wondered at their ingenuity and patience. Their little beaks reminded me of the needle of the sewing machine with its eye at the pointed end. * * * Inside and outside the little heads would reach, with the prettiest turns and curvetings imaginable, till, as the nest grew deeper, the work was done more and more from the inside. Then it was gathered together at the bottom, with side joined to side. When this part of the work first took place the nest seemed to be strangely lacking in depth and had an unshapely look altogether.

But this was the point where the full revelation came to me of how the deepest part is shaped. I saw the bird at this stage inside the nest raise her wings against the upper rim and the twigs which held it and strain with her wings upward and her feet downward till the nest itself grew so thin that I could see through it in places. Then they began again, for the most part from the inside, weaving in more material to thicken and strengthen sides and bottom where these had become thin and weak through the stretching. This was done many times over until the proper depth and thickness were both secured. The nest after being stretched out in this way would be like the coarse warp of a fabric on a loom, and into this the little weavers wove their silken threads.

After this came the embellishing with the bits of lichen. These were brought, and fastened on by means of little filmy threads of the spider drawn from the surface of the nest and fastened down over the moss.

Samuel A. Grimes has sent me two fine photographs of Florida nests (pl. 33), one in a blackjack oak and one in a loblolly pine. Nests have been found in other trees than those mentioned above, mostly in various oaks and maples, but also in beech, chestnut, and elm; probably some other trees could be added to the list. About one week seems to be the average time required to build the nest.

Eggs.—The yellow-throated vireo lays three to five eggs to a set, usually four. The normal shape is ovate, but some are slightly pointed and some are more oval. They are the handsomest and most heavily marked of any of the eggs of the vireos. The ground color varies from pure white to creamy white or pinkish white, these tints often remaining persistent in the collector's cabinet. They are quite strongly spotted, mostly at the larger end, with various shades of brown, reddish brown, chestnut, vinaceous-cinnamon, dark brown, blackish, or different shades of drab or lavender; some of the spots are large enough to be called blotches, even such as occur on kingbirds' eggs, but such extremes are very rare; even more rarely, an egg may be nearly, or quite, immaculate. The larger spots often show a washed-out effect around their edges. The measurements of 50 eggs average 20.8 by 14.9 millimeters; the eggs showing the four extremes measure 22.8 by 16.0, 17.9 by 13.6, and 18.8 by 13.2 millimeters.

Young.—The period of incubation for the yellow-throated vireo seems to be about two weeks, and the young remain in the nest for about the same length of time. Very little study of this subject seems to have been made, but Mr. Hutchins (1902) gives us the following information on it: "After the sitting proper seemed to have begun it was in about two weeks' time that we saw the first signs of life in the nest. The male bird took his part with the female in the incubating. He would bring food to her as she sat upon the nest and, I am

not quite sure, but think that she did the same with him. * * *
My Yellow-throats were very faithful to their young, of which there
were three. The male fed them as attentively as did the mother. On
July 7, nearly a month from the beginning of the brooding, the first
young bird left the nest. It seemed to take good care of itself, keeping to the trees, and the next day the other two followed it."

He discovered great clutching power in the feet of one of the young
that he picked up on the lawn. This was evidently of great service
to the young while tossed about in the nest, for he says: "Through
many thunder storms which came to us in that month of June I have
seen that slight branch from the body of the elm whip in the blast
as if it would be torn from its setting in the great trunk. The nest
would be top-down and driven every way, and yet never a fledgling fell
from its place. No wonder there had come a development of clutching
power !"

Plumages.—Dr. Dwight (1900) says that the natal down of the
yellow-throated vireo is drab, and he describes the juvenal plumage
as "above, smoke-gray. Wings and tail black, edged with olive-gray,
the secondaries and tertiaries with olive-green (the two inner tertiaries white edged), the greater and median coverts with dull white
forming two wing bands. Below, silky white, the chin, throat and
sides of head pale canary-yellow, the orbital ring, ocular region and
superciliary stripe still paler."

A partial postjuvenal molt, involving all the contour plumage and
the wing coverts, but not the rest of the wings or the tail, occurs in
July and August. This produces the first winter plumage, which is
practically indistinguishable from that of the adult. The upperparts are now bright olive-green, the wing bars are pure white, and the
throat and breast are bright canary yellow.

The sexes are much alike in all plumages, but the female is usually
somewhat paler than the male in adult plumage. There is apparently no spring molt, and wear and fading are not pronounced.
There is a complete postnuptial molt late in summer, mainly in
August.

Food.—Reporting on the contents of 160 stomachs of the yellow-
throated vireo, collected during the months of April to September,
inclusive, Dr. Edward A. Chapin (1925) says: "The yellow-throated
vireo eats comparatively little vegetable food, practically none during
April and May, none during June and July, less than 2 percent in
August, and less than 9 percent in September. The average for the
year is only 1.74 percent. Among the items specifically determined
were sassafras berries and seeds of wild grapes. No cultivated fruit
of any kind was found."

The animal food was made up of 95.82 percent insects, 2.38 percent
spiders, and 0.06 percent other animal matter.

Lepidoptera, butterflies and moths in their various stages, constituted the largest item, more than 42 percent of the whole, of which caterpillars amounted to more than half of this, 23.1 percent. Most of the adults were moths, 19.35 percent. Hemiptera, true bugs, occupied second place, stink bugs amounting to 15.5 percent, and the remaining 7.62 percent including such forms as assassin bugs, scale insects, and leafhoppers. "Beetles of all kinds, making up 12.9 percent of the yearly food, stand third in the diet. Ladybird beetles, usually plentifully found in the stomachs of vireos, in this species amount to less than 1 percent of the total." The injurious beetles eaten include weevils, wood-boring forms (Buprestidae and Cerambycidae), the plant-feeding Elateridae, dung beetles and leaf chafers (Scarabaeidae), leaf beetles (Chrysomelidae), and ladybird beetles (Coccinellidae). Diptera make up 7.36 percent, Hymenoptera 5.07 percent, and other insects 4.92 percent. No honey bees were identified, but there were some sawflies and ichneumon-flies. The other insects eaten include grasshoppers, crickets, locusts, dragonflies, cicadas, mosquitoes, midges, and plant lice.

Behavior.—On its nest the yellow-throated vireo, like the blue-headed vireo, is a close and steadfast sitter, allowing close approach and even handling; it cannot easily be driven from its nest and must often be removed forcibly, sometimes with difficulty. It seems quite fearless in the presence of humans; Francis Orcutt (1928) tells of one that came and fed a young bird several times while he held the little one in his hand, perching on his thumb or finger. It is, however, sometimes quite aggressive when its nest is approached, attempting to drive away the intruder by scolding and threatening to attack him. Dr. Brewer (Baird, Brewer, and Ridgway, 1874) writes:

They are somewhat confiding and trustful of man, are readily approached, and soon become so well acquainted with those among whom they have a home as to fearlessly come to the windows of the house in pursuit of spiders or flies, and even to enter them. In the latter case they cannot readily make their exit, and soon lose their self-possession, beating their heads against the walls and ceiling in vain attempts to get out, unless caught and released. In one instance a young bird, that had entered my barn-chamber, became so entangled in cobwebs, around his wings and feet, as to be unable to escape again. When taken in the hand, and his meshes one by one picked out from about his feet and quills, he was very docile, made no resistance or outcry, nor any attempt to escape, until he was entirely freed from his bonds, although it required some time and care to accomplish it. When entirely freed from these clogs, and permitted to go, he flew away very deliberately to a short distance, and occupied himself with dressing his disordered plumage.

Voice.—Aretas A. Saunders has given me the following elaborate account of the song and call notes of this vireo: "The song of the yellow-throated vireo is long continued, consisting of short phrases separated by pauses. In this respect it is like the songs of the blue-headed and red-eyed vireos, but there are a number of differences, some apparent when we listen carefully to the bird, others appearing only when the song is recorded and studied.

"The yellow-throated vireo's song is slower than those of the other vireos, the pauses between phrases being longer. The quality of the sound is rather reedy and less clear than the others. The pitch is lower. The number of different phrases is less, and the bird is inclined to repeat two to four of them in a regular order. The notes of the phrases are usually slurred together, so that they sound like *eeyay*, *ayo*, or *ahweeo*, etc.

"In the records I have of 52 different birds the pitch varies from C ′ ′ ′ ′ to B ′ ′. Only one bird sang to C ′ ′ ′ ′, the majority having A ′ ′ ′ or G ′ ′ ′ for the highest note. The rate of singing varied from one phrase every four-fifths of a second to one every 2 seconds. Individuals possess five to nine different phrases, but frequently sing only two or three of them for so long a time that patient listening is required to get them all. The phrases are commonly of two or three notes. In all my records there are just two phrases of four notes, and none with more than that. Two-note phrases that slur downward are much commoner than those that slur upward; that is, *ayoh* is a commoner phrase than *oway*. In the same manner in 3-note phrases, such a phrase as *oweeah* is commoner than *eeoway*.

"The period of song is from arrival early in spring to early in August. The song is revived again late in August or early in September. It is impossible to give definite dates of cessation, for though each individual stops singing for a time, that time is so short, and the difference in individuals so great, that there is no certain period of complete silence for the species, and one cannot be sure, when birds are heard in mid-August, whether it is the last of the regular period or the beginning of the revival. The song is not heard in September every year, but in 14 years in which I have definite dates, the average is September 8, and the latest September 18, 1939.

"The yellow-throated vireo has a soft musical call note running down in pitch, and with a trilly sound. I have written it in my notes as *whree-whree-orrrr*. An alarm note is a series of notes, also descending in pitch, *chi-chi-cha-cha-chu-chu*. Both of these notes bear a strong resemblance to corresponding calls used by the blue-headed vireo."

Mr. Skutch writes to me from Costa Rica: "Like the blue-headed vireo, the yellow-throat sings much in its winter home. It is in a songful mood upon its arrival late in September or October; and although it may fall silent during the wet closing months of the year, from January until its departure in late March or April, it frequently delivers its queer, halting song. Indeed, in many parts of its winter range, the species is so rare that it would probably be overlooked but for its habit of proclaiming itself at a season when most of the migrants—and a large proportion of the resident birds, too—are songless."

Mr. Ford mentions in his notes "a disturbed trill, which may be likened to the wing sound of a flushed mourning dove, albeit much diminished. This seems to be used only when the bird is in attendance upon the young. Its scolding note is unlike the whining complaint of the warbling vireo and the red-eye. It is a sort of chatter, in tone similar to that of the agitated house wren." These are, apparently, the same notes as those described above by Mr. Saunders.

Francis H. Allen writes to me: "A call note that I have heard in May and which may be connected with courtship is a low *hew*. Another record of a note heard in early May reads something like *sswink* or *sswinkel*." Elsewhere (1922) he describes another song: "The song consisted of several repetitions of a high-pitched note with rising inflection, suggesting the goldfish's call note, but less clear and less prolonged, followed by shorter, indefinite notes and then by the rolling trill, then more of the high-pitched notes, and so on—a sort of continuous performance, perhaps not always in this precise order, but having the trills interspersed with these long and short notes. The characteristic chatter of the yellow-throated vireo was also thrown in occasionally. The bird dropped this song presently and began its ordinary song."

E. P. Bicknell (1884) observed one of these vireos singing on the wing:

On May 21, 1882, I observed a pair flying about among an open group of trees; one was being followed by the other; but their motions betrayed none of the excitement of pursuer and pursued; their flight was so easy and leisurely that it was almost restful to watch them. For more than a minute they continued slowly circling about among the trees, within a space of a few rods, passing in and out among the branches; several times the leading bird appeared about to alight, but feeling its pursuer close at hand continued its course. The rear bird was constantly giving utterance to its full song notes, which fact probably accounts for its uninterested manner as pursuer; for it seemed so engrossed with the feat of singing during flight that it could give little heed to the chase. Both birds finally alighted peaceably among the branches, the follower alighting first.

This may have been part of a courtship display, in which the male was showing off his powers of song.

Albert R. Brand (1938) found that the pitch of the yellow-throated vireo's song was far below the average for passerine birds; the approximate mean was 2,750, the highest note 3,825 and the lowest 2,325 vibrations per second.

The fact that the yellow-throated vireo has been heard to sing the song of the blue-headed vireo, several times by competent observers, and that the bluehead has been observed to sing the yellowthroat's song, suggests that these two closely related species may occasionally hybridize; and there is some evidence to support this theory. William Brewster (1906) reported that, during two seasons, a blue-headed vireo repeatedly sang both songs in his garden; and he suggested the possibility that it *might* have been paired with a yellow-throated vireo, though he had no evidence to prove it. Dr. Charles W. Townsend (1920) says: "On May 8, 1919, a bird that sang the wild clear song of the blue-headed vireo so that there seemed to be no mistake about its identity turned out to be be a yellow-throated vireo." And Bagg and Eliot (1937) have this to say on the subject.

Throughout the fifteen years 1921–35, according to Prof. Eliot, the Smith College Yellow-breast has sung the same song. * * * In 1930 (but not again) another male took up quarters in the same neighborhood who sang two songs—his own species' and the Blue-headed Vireo's. Inspection showed that he looked darker, especially about the head, than normal for his kind; and suspicion was at least aroused that in the scarcity of Yellow-throated females his father (presumably the Smith College male), perhaps widowed, had persuaded a Blue-head to mate with him, the year before. * * * In Agawam on May 26, 1936, the song of a blue-head, seeming very out of place, was looked up and found to issue from a typical-looking Yellow-breast (Eliot). Apparently the *flavifrons* coloration is "dominant" in hybrids. Probably it was that of the two species' common ancestor, and *solitarius* originated as a northern variant or "sport". * * * On June 22, 1936, near Mt. Tekoa (not at all Yellow-breast country), Mr. Dietrich studied a Blue-head with a yellow wash on the throat and "incomplete eye-ring"—possibly the effect of Yellow-breast blood?

This is an interesting theory, but it is strange that no hybrids have found their way into collections!

Field marks.—The yellow-throated vireo should be unmistakable, with its brilliant yellow throat and breast, only slightly less brilliant in the female than in the male, its olive-green back and its double, white wing bars. No other northern vireo is so brightly colored. It is much more deliberate in its movements than any of the warblers, less slender in form, and has a heavier bill. It looks something like a pine warbler, but this warbler frequents the pines, whereas this vireo is almost always seen in deciduous trees. Its color pattern is somewhat like that of the yellow-breasted chat, which is seldom seen away from dense thickets, is larger, and has a much longer tail; the behavior of these two is very different. The contralto voice of the yellowthroat will also distinguish it from other vireos.

Enemies.—Probably the principal reason for the almost complete disappearance of this and other vireos from our New England urban and suburban districts has been the wholesale spraying of our shade trees. Ludlow Griscom (1923) wrote of the New York City region: "Our handsomest Vireo was formerly a common summer resident throughout the area from early May to the middle of September. While many of us had noted a slow but steady decrease in numbers in the last 20 years, no one was prepared for the sudden and rapid disappearance of this species since 1917 over the whole suburban section, where it is now a rare bird." And more recently Bagg and Eliot (1937) write: "In the early years of this century, the shade trees it so loved were persistently sprayed with poison for the elm beetle, gypsy moth, etc. Many Vireo-nests were ruined and many Yellow-breasts died from eating poisoned larvas. The bird became uncommon and has remained local." It is hard to believe, and impossible to prove, that the birds, once so common here, have all perished from eating poisoned larvae; it seems likely that some have been forced to look elsewhere for their accustomed food, which they fail to find in their former foraging grounds; however, there are plenty of unsprayed trees, teeming with caterpillars and beetles, in all of our towns; but the vireos do not seem to have found them. There is some other reason, which we do not understand, that has caused the loss of this beautiful vireo.

Dr. Friedmann (1929) had reports of some 50 cases, from a number of different States, in which the yellow-throated vireo had been imposed upon by cowbirds, and says that the vireo occasionally buries the cowbird's eggs in the lining of the nest, if it has no eggs of its own at the time. Edward R. Ford writes to me from Michigan: "I am reasonably certain that nests started after the first week in June were those of birds whose first attempt was unsuccessful, and that failure in the first instance was due to the cowbird. Of five successful nests, the last feeding of the young in the nest was observed May 31, June 8, July 15, July 23, and August 10, respectively. It will be noted that in three cases success was attained after the end of the cowbird's laying cycle which, here, seems to be about July 1. The two low nests mentioned above were parasitized. One of these was deserted after two cowbird's eggs had been removed; the other after the intrusion of two cowbird's eggs and the ejection of one of the eggs of the vireo."

Harold S. Peters (1936) mentions two external parasites, a louse, *Myrsidea incerta* (Kellogg), and a mite, *Megninia tyrelli* (Haller), that have been found on this vireo.

Fall.—During the fall migration yellow-throated vireos wander about quite extensively and are likely to be seen almost anywhere that there are trees and in many places where they were not to be found during the breeding season. They sing more or less in September and are then more in evidence than the silent migrants. Their migration is evidently leisurely, for though most of them leave New England in September or earlier, Mr. Skutch tells me that he has not seen them in Costa Rica before October 20. Mr. Forbush (1929) says: "When the single brood has been raised the parents take them to the berry pastures and they pass the molting season amid the fruiting thickets and are ready for their long southward journey by September, if not before."

Winter.—Mr. Skutch writes to me: "The yellow-throated vireo winters throughout the length of Central America, from Guatemala to

Panama, on both coasts and in the mountainous interior up to an altitude of (rarely) 5,000 feet. It is at home in a variety of habitats, ranging from the heavy rain-forest to the low, thorny scrub and cacti of such arid regions as the middle Motagua Valley in Guatemala and the coast of El Salvador. In most parts of its wide and varied winter range it is far from abundant; but on February 1, 1935, I found it rather common in the arid scrub and low, open woodland near Cutuco, on the dry coast of El Salvador. Among the shade trees of the great coffee plantations on the Pacific slope of Guatemala, between 2,500 and 3,500 above sea level, I found it present during the winter months in somewhat greater numbers than in most parts of its Central American range—yet still far from common. These vireos do not form flocks; and one almost never sees two together; but individuals may attach themselves loosely to mixed flocks of small birds."

DISTRIBUTION

Range.—Southern Canada to Colombia.

Breeding range.—The yellow-throated vireo breeds **north** to southern Manitoba (Aweme and Hillside Beach, probably, and Winnipeg); southern Ontario (Kenora, possibly, South Magnatawan, Beaumarais, and Ottawa); southern Quebec (Pelissier, Montreal, and Hatley); and central Maine (Ripogenus, Dover-Foxcroft, and Calais). **East** to Maine (Calais and Portland); the Atlantic Coast States to about central Florida (New Smyrna and Glencoe). **South** to Florida (New Smyrna, Oxford, Brooksville, and very rarely to Pensacola); southern Mississippi (Pearlington); southeastern Louisiana (New Orleans and Thibodaux); and central Texas (Houston and Kerrville). **West** to central Texas (Kerrville and Gainesville); eastern Oklahoma (Hartshorne, Tulsa, and Copan); eastern Kansas (Winfield, Topeka, and Manhattan); eastern Nebraska (Red Cloud and Greeley); eastern South Dakota (Yankton and Sioux Falls); eastern North Dakota (Hankinson, Fargo, and the Turtle Mountains); and southern Manitoba (Aweme). From the records it appears that within the last generation the yellow-throated vireo has extended its range southward or at least has increased in members in the southern part of its breeding range.

Winter range.—In winter the yellow-throated vireo is found **north** to southern Veracruz (Tres Zapotes and Santecomapam); Yucatán (Chichen-Itzá); and Quintana Roo (Cozumel Island). **East** to Quintana Roo (Cozumel Island and Chunyache); British Honduras (Toledo district); eastern Guatemala (Gualan); eastern Nicaragua (Bluefields); Costa Rica (Guapiles); Panama (Boquete), and Colombia (Santa Marta district and Perico). **South** to Colombia (Perico and Santa Elena). **West** to Colombia (Santa Elena); Panama (Garachine); Costa Rica (San José and Liberia); western Guatemala (San José and Colombia); Chiapas (Huehuetán); and Veracruz (Tres Zapotes).

Migration.—Late dates of spring departure are: Panama—Barro Colorado, March 12. Costa Rica—Valley of El General, April 16. El Salvador—San Salvador, April 8. Guatemala—Moca, March 6. British Honduras—Mountain Cow, April 14. Mexico—Chiapas; San Benito, March 12. Cuba—Habana, April 11. Florida—Fort Myers, April 3.

Early dates of spring arrival are: Florida—Pensacola, March 11. Georgia—Beachton, March 19. South Carolina—Charleston, March 21. North Carolina—Statesville, March 27. Virginia—Lawrenceville, April 4. District of Columbia, Washington, April 1. Pennsylvania—Beaver, April 26. New York—Watertown, April 29. Massachusetts—Boston, May 4. Vermont—Wells River, May 2. New Hampshire—East Westmoreland, May 2. Louisiana—Rigolets, March 2. Tennessee, Memphis, March 28. Kentucky—Bowling Green, April 15. Illinois—Olney, April 18. Ohio—Columbus, April 18. Michigan—Ann Arbor, April 25. Ontario—London, May 5. Missouri—St. Louis, April 10. Iowa—Keokuk, April 26. Wisconsin—Madison, April 29. Minnesota—Lanesboro, April 27. Texas—Kerrville, March 15. Kansas—Manhattan, April 22. North Dakota—Argusville, May 15.

Late dates of fall departure are: North Dakota—Fargo, September 6. Kansas—Lawrence, September 29. Texas—Fredericksburg, October 15. Minnesota—St. Paul, September 27. Wisconsin—New London, September 20. Iowa—National, October 3. Michigan—Detroit, September 23. Indiana—Notre Dame, October 11. Ontario—Guelph, October 10. Ohio—Youngstown, October 4. Kentucky—Danville, October 6. Tennessee—Nashville, October 7. Arkansas—Jonesboro, October 6. Mississippi—Ariel, October 14. Louisiana—New Orleans, October 11. New Hampshire—Jaffrey, September 5. Massachusetts—Williamstown, September 20. New York—Rhinebeck, October 2. Pennsylvania—Harrisburg, October 4. North Carolina—Arden, October 10. South Carolina—Spartanburg, October 8. Georgia—Athens, October 14. Florida—Gainesville, November 12.

Early dates of fall arrival are: Florida—Pensacola, September 3. Cuba—Habana, August 31. Mexico—Yucatán—Chichen Itzá, October 6; Oaxaca—Tepanatepec, October 27. Guatemala—Colomba, September 30. El Salvador—Divisadero, October 3. Nicaragua—Greytown, October 4. Costa Rica—San José, October 4. Canal Zone—New Culebra, November 3.

Casual records.—A specimen of the yellow-throated vireo was collected at Flatts, Bermuda, on March 24, 1931; another was collected in Nevada at Crystal Spring, Pahranagat Valley, Lincoln County, on May 29, 1932.

Egg dates.—Arkansas: 3 records, April 24 to July 4.

Massachusetts: 19 records, May 16 to June 14; 14 records, May 30 to June 9, indicating the height of the season.

New York: 20 records, May 24 to June 30; 16 records, May 31 to June 14.

VIREO SOLITARIUS SOLITARIUS (Wilson)

BLUE-HEADED VIREO

HABITS

The yellow-throated vireo may be more brilliantly colored, with its bright yellow throat, but, to my mind, the subject of this sketch is the handsomest of the vireos. His gray-blue head is accented by a pair of pure-white spectacles, eye rings, and loral stripes; in marked contrast are his olive-green back, his pure-white throat and breast, and his yellow sides. The soft color tones combine to make a most charming picture of pleasing loveliness. He appears to be a well-groomed aristocrat among birds. In addition, his song is delightfully rich and varied, to which we always stop and listen. And his gentle, trustful manners, as we try to stroke him on the nest, have endeared him to all who know him. He is a lovely and a lovable bird.

I had seen the blue-headed vireo as a migrant in southeastern Massachusetts, but it was some years before I came to know it as a breeding bird; this was mainly because I did not know where to look for it, until one of my rivals in egg collecting reported finding a nest in a grove of white pines (*Pinus strobus*). Since then we have learned to look for it in the white-pine woods, with which this section of the State is well supplied. It is a forest-loving bird, and we practically never find it breeding anywhere but in woods where these pines or hemlocks make solid stands or at least predominate; often, however, such woods contain scattering growths of gray birches, wild apple trees, or sapling hardwoods of various kinds, in which the vireos like to build their nests.

It may be purely accidental, but it is an interesting fact that we have often found the blue-headed vireo nesting in a tract of pines occupied by a pair of breeding Cooper's hawks; I find six such cases recorded in my notes, and once the vireo's nest was within 50 feet of the occupied hawk's nest; but we have never found this vireo nesting in similar woods where sharp-shinned hawks were breeding. We never saw anything to indicate that the Cooper's hawks ever harmed the vireos, or their young, but it might have been different with the sharpshins! Perhaps the vireos have learned to trust the larger

Accipiters. They evidently prefer the same type of woodland as the hawks; hence this apparent community of interest. I once found a pair of blue-headed vireos building a nest in a similar tract of pine woods where a pair of barred owls had a nest.

In the Allegany State Park, New York, Aretas A. Saunders (1938) says that "they inhabit both the Maple-Beech-Hemlock forest and the areas modified for camping, and seem to be rather more common on the campaign areas or about their edges, apparently liking the edge of the open area and having no fear of man's presence. Where much undergrowth is removed, however, they do not occur, as there are then no nesting sites near the ground, and it is my experience that the nest is rarely placed very high."

Leonard Wing (1939) says that, in the Upper Peninsula of Michigan, "the Blue-headed Vireo lives in the heavier growth of Jack Pine."

Spring.—The spring migration of the blue-headed vireo seems to be quite prolonged. Alexander F. Skutch tells me that few are seen in Central America after April 19, only one being seen after that on the 28th. Yet the species arrives in Massachusetts around the middle of that month, Forbush's (1929) earliest date being April 11. We look for them in numbers before the end of April, in the vanguard of the migrating hosts of small birds, along with the black-throated green and yellow warblers, the towhee, catbird, and brown thrasher, but at least a week ahead of the other vireos.

Territory.—Mr. Saunders (1938) writes:

One difference in habit between this bird and the red-eyed vireo is that of wandering about when singing, apparently with no fixed singing tree. This habit makes it difficult to determine territory and to get a definite count of birds. This would be more difficult if it were not for individual differences in songs. This wandering habit keeps singing birds moving about over a considerable area, and I have known them to sing now and then in the same tree in which a red-eyed vireo sings regularly. In such cases there is no jealousy or animosity shown on the part of either species. Such observations leave me holding some doubts about the territory theory, both in vireos and some other birds. It would seem that the two species should be rivals for food, nest sites and nesting materials. Yet their territories, if they have such, frequently overlap with no hostility between them, at least in late summer. If there is some sort of territory in this species, it seems to be larger than that of the red-eyed vireo. Singing males are not very close together, and nests not near each other.

Courtship.—Dr. Charles W. Townsend (1920) says: "Twice I have been favored with a sight of the courtship performance. The male puffs out his yellow flank feathers very conspicuously and bobs and bows to the female, very slim in contrast, and sings repeatedly meanwhile with many variations to his song."

In a patch of swampy woods back of a pine grove, I once watched a pair of blue-headed vireos for a considerable length of time and followed them about, as they seemed to be making love to each other;

the female was in the lead, but the male was not far behind her, displaying his charms. He sang his loud, rich, two-note song, so much like the song of the yellow-throated vireo in tone, at regular intervals. But he varied it occasionally, especially when near his mate, with a series of sweet, warbling notes in a subdued tone, *cher wee, sweech, sweech, sweech*, to which she generally replied in a similar strain, as they came together for an interchange of caresses. Near there I found their new nest.

Nesting.—All the nests of the blue-headed vireo, at least a dozen, that my companions and I have found in eastern Massachusetts have been in, or on the borders of, white-pine woods, seldom in clear, thick stands of *Pinus strobus*, but more often in mixed woods of pines, hemlocks, oaks, and other deciduous trees where the pines or hemlocks predominated. I find only two exceptions to this rule in the literature. C. W. and J. H. Bowles (1892), of Ponkapog, Mass., report a nest that "was about eight feet from the ground on the lowest branch of a thirty-foot live oak. This was in a grove of other oaks of the same size. This, we think, is an exceptional case, as all our other nests were built in coniferous trees." And Dr. T. M. Brewer (Baird, Brewer, and Ridgway, 1874) says: "In the summer of 1870 a pair built their nest in a dwarf pear-tree, within a few rods of my house."

F. H. Kennard reports, in his field notes, a nest 12 feet from the ground in a small pine, and Owen Durfee's notes record a nest that was 26 feet up and 10 feet out from the trunk of a large pine. He and I once found a nest, 5½ feet from the ground, in a white-cedar sapling under a large hemlock in swampy mixed woods. Mr. Kennard's notes mention one that was only 4 feet up in a small hemlock under some large pines. All our other local nests were in saplings of deciduous trees, mostly oaks, but also gray birch, beech, hickory, and walnut. The lowest was 3½ feet up in an oak sapling and the highest 20 feet in a slender oak.

Farther north the nests are generally built in coniferous trees, Mr. Kennard's notes mention a nest at Averill, Vt., that was about 6 feet up in a slim spruce on the bank between a trail and a stream, and one at Duck Lake, Maine, in a spruce. Robie W. Tufts writes to me from Nova Scotia: "With but one exception, all nests of this species have been found in coniferous trees of various kinds. The single exception was a nest found in a wild apple tree. Conifers were close by."

Dr. Wing (1939) writes: "June 26, 1932, I found a nest under construction at the Lake Superior State Forest, twenty-six miles northwest of Newberry, Michigan. The birds had chosen a thirty-five-foot Jack Pine tree for attaching the pensile nest, which was in the fork of a horizontal branch twenty feet from the ground and three feet from the trunk of the tree. Lichens and shreds of birch bark composed the framework of the nest, and thin dry grasses served for lining."

Mr. Saunders (1938) says of the nests of the blue-headed vireo in the Allegany State Park, New York:

They range from four to 30 feet from the ground; in fact, with the exception of one nest in an area of mature timber on Red House creek, all nests I have seen have been ten feet or less from the ground. They are placed in beech, sugar maple, yellow birch and hornbeam trees and probably other species, but these species are most abundant in the forest and therefore most commonly used. I think the bird does not have any special preference for one species over another.

The nests are indistinguishable from those of other vireos. Under natural conditions they are composed of bark, leaves, bits of moss and some grasses, strips of yellow birch bark, in this region, being a conspicuous material. About camps they frequently use paper, and are evidently just as fond of newspaper as is the red-eyed vireo. Tissue paper, cellophane and a piece of chewing gum wrapper have all been found in the nests. One nest was gaudy with strips of colored tissue paper that had been supplied to the birds by a student at the school. One nest back on the mountainside that had no such artificial materials, had three porcupine quills woven into its rim.

C. M. Jones (1887), of Eastford, Conn., found three nests in laurel bushes, between 8 and 7 feet above the ground, and one suspended near the end of a long horizontal branch of a hemlock tree, about 5 feet from the ground. Most of the nests reported by others have been almost, or quite, within reach from the ground.

The hanging, basketlike nests of the blue-headed vireo, like those of other vireos, are suspended by their upper rims, often none too securely, from the supporting twigs. The nest may be at the forked end of a long, slender branch of a tree, between the prongs of a forked twig, or between two twigs projecting side by side from the upright stem of a sapling; and it is almost always close to where the prongs start to fork, or close to the stem of an upright.

The nests that I have seen vary considerably in size, neatness, and kind of materials used in their composition. Most of the materials mentioned in the above descriptions are likely to be found in one or another of the nests. Brief descriptions of three nests before me will illustrate some of the variations. One nest, built early in the season, is not beautiful but is one of warmest and coziest cradles for an early brood of vireos that I have seen; the body of the nest is made mainly of strips of inner bark of grapevine, various soft plant fibers, many fine rootlets, pieces of thread and fine grasses, mixed with lichens, bits of mosses, bunches of rabbit hair, bits of cotton and soft feathers, including a large downy feather of a great horned owl; it is neatly lined with some peculiar hairlike filaments, light yellow and red at the base, which I think are the roots or stems of club mosses; on this lining are a few small downy feathers, a little cow hair, and a little rabbit fur.

The second might be considered an average nest, built in July and very insecurely attached to a forked twig of a swamp white oak; it is prettily made of strips of inner bark of various kinds, bits of lichens, and mosses and decorated externally with many pieces of paper from the nests of wasps or hornets and a few spider nests; it is profusely lined with fine needles of the white pine. It measures about 3½ by 3 inches in external diameter and about 2¼ inches in external depth; the inner cavity is about 1½ inches in depth and about 2 by 2¼ inches across the top, with very little overhang.

The third came to me from Lancaster, N. H., taken by Fred B. Spaulding. It is the largest, most compactly built, and handsomest nest that I have seen of this species, perhaps more typical of northern nests than of those with which I am familiar. It is securely attached to two diverging twigs close to the upright stem of a sapling with a quantity of usnea and fine strips of outer bark of the yellow birch. The bulk of the nest is made up largely of various lichens and mosses, mixed with bits of small dry leaves, bits of fine string, and spider nests, all apparently firmly interwoven with narrow strips of the outer bark of the yellow birch, with which the exterior of the nest is profusely decorated. It is smoothly lined with very fine grass tops and a few hairlike rootlets. Externally it measures about 3 by 3½ inches in diameter and 3½ inches in depth; internally it measures about 2 by 1¾ in diameter and about 1½ inches in depth, the walls being very firm and thick. The above measurements do not include the extent to which some of the loose streamers of the birch bark hang below and around the nest.

I have twice watched blue-headed vireos building their nests. Both of the pair help in this work, though the female seems to do most of it and to be the dominant influence, the male's part consisting mainly of bringing material. At the beginning of the nest a few hanging loops of soft fibers are attached at both ends to the supporting twigs; as these increase and the bag is formed, the ends are securely bound to the twigs by strips of usnea or fine shreds of inner grapevine bark, forming the rim of the nest; some spider web may be used for this purpose, but it does not seem to be much in evidence in the nests that I have seen; apparently the bluehead does not use so much of it as do other vireos. The rest of the material is worked in between the hanging loops, and finally the lining is added and the interior is shaped by the turning of the bird's body in it. The birds are very apt to desert an unfinished nest, if watched, as happened in the two cases that I observed.

Eggs.—The blue-headed vireo lays three to five eggs in a set, usually four. These are usually ovate in shape, but some are quite pointed. The ground color varies from pure white to creamy white. They are rather sparingly spotted or dotted, mostly near the large end, with light brown, dark brown, reddish brown, or blackish. The measurements of 50 eggs average 19.5 by 14.4 millimeters; the eggs showing the four extremes measure 21.8 by 14.7, 19.6 by 15.3, 17.0 by 14.1, and 18.1 by 13.4 millimeters.

Incubation.—F. L. Burns (1915) says that the period of incubation is 10 to 11 days, but this must be based on insufficient information, for the other vireos require a somewhat longer time; no further data on the subject seem available. Mr. Saunders (1938) remarks that his experience "indicates that the period of incubation is at least 11 days long, but, up to date there has been no opportunity to determine its length definitely."

Both parents share the duties of incubation and are devoted to the care of the young. They change places on the nest at regular intervals regardless of the near presence of human observers. Sometimes when we drive the female from the nest the male will take her place within a few feet of us. They are usually very close sitters and often must be lifted off the nest if we want to examine the eggs. Mr. Saunders (1938) says: "Changing places is accompanied by a call by which the incubating bird notifies its mate. The mate answers with the same call, and comes immediately. The call is a soft, rather, low-pitched trill, running downward in pitch at the end, like 'tiprrrrrr.' This call is interpolated in the song by some individuals."

The male sings regularly while incubating, and probably the female does to some extent; Mr. Saunders (1938) remarks: "It is impossible to distinguish sexes by plumage or by habits about the nest, and my observation that the female sings is based on observing two birds, both in song, one singing while incubating and the other answering from near-by trees."

Dr. Cornelius Weygandt (1907) writes:

The comradeship of the two during incubation had been very winning. As one sat upon the eggs the other would come flying swiftly to a dead limb above and then drop to the little branch from which the nest swung, landing not a foot away from it. Here the incoming bird would mew, ever so caressingly, and the bird on the nest would answer in the same low tone. Sometimes the interchange of greetings would be followed by interchange of positions, the sitting bird first unsettling itself gently from the eggs and then flitting off to alight beside its mate. The incomer would lift itself into the nest as deftly and then after a few more mutual mews the relieved bird would be off to the oak-tops. Once the sitting bird, this time I suppose the male, sang while brooding on the nest when the other returned.

Young.—Mr. Saunders (1938) says:

Singing takes place all through the incubation and while the young are still very small, but it gradually ceases as the young grow larger, and is heard not at all after they are five or six days old, and is only resumed after they have been out of the nest nearly a week and are able to shift for themselves. *   *   *

When feeding young, the adults are rather more concerned than they are when incubating, perhaps not for themselves, but they do not entirely trust a man near the young.   An alarm call, used at such a time, is a protesting "shŭ shŭ shŭ shŭ shŭ." Even this note is gentle when compared with the alarm notes of most birds.

Young are fed by both birds, chiefly on insects, of which span-worms are the most conspicuous and easily identified.   One student observed a dragon fly fed to the young, wings and all.   From her description it was apparently *Aeschna umbrosa*, a fairly large species.   It is not probable that a vireo could catch a fully matured adult dragon fly, but in the morning, when the insects have just emerged from the nymph stage, their wings are soft and they are incapable of flight, and easily caught.

When the young are out of the nest, parents are still busy feeding them for a few days.   At such times, if the young are near the ground, the parents still show little fear of man, and come to feed them in front of groups of people and camera lenses.

The very early and very late dates at which eggs have been found suggest that two broods are sometimes raised in a season, as seems to be the case with the mountain vireo.

Plumages.—The juvenal plumage of the blue-headed vireo is much like that of the adult in pattern, but the general coloration is duller. Dr. Dwight (1900) describes it, in part, as "above, drab, tinged with green, pileum and auriculars drab-gray. * * * Below, pure white, tinged on flanks and crissum with primrose-yellow.   Obscure superciliary stripe, loral and orbital regions white; a dusky anteorbital streak."

The first winter plumage is acquired by a partial postjuvenal molt in August and September, which involves the contour plumage and the wing coverts but not the rest of the wings nor the tail.   In this plumage the young bird is practically indistinguishable from the adult, though the head and back are more or less tinged with brownish and the white of the underparts is less pure.   Both old and young birds usually, though perhaps not always, have a partial and irregular prenuptial molt in March and April, at which a few or more feathers are renewed on the head, back, throat, and breast.

The sexes are practically alike in all plumages, though the coloration of the female is usually duller.

Food.—The Biological Survey had 306 well-filled stomachs of the blue-headed vireos and 23 other stomachs only partially filled, on which Dr. Edward A. Chapin (1925) based his report on the food of this species.   The animal matter, 96.32 percent of the entire food, consisted almost entirely of insects, the few spiders included amounting to 2.63 percent and the snails 0.25 percent.   Lepidoptera, in all stages, were the largest items, averaging 38.8 percent for the whole year; caterpillars were eaten in greatest numbers in March (41.56 percent) and in September (40.39 percent) ; the greatest consumption of adult moths came in July (18.38 percent).   Hemiptera, true bugs, formed the second largest item, averaging 20.13 percent for the year, stink bugs (Pentatomidae) predominating.   Dr. Chapin writes:

During the winter months hibernating pentatomids constitute one of the most important sources of food for the blue-headed vireos, as shown by the November and January percentages of 48.7 and 29.02, respectively.   *   *   *

Considering the enormous numbers of beetles available, it is somewhat surprising that not more are eaten. The blue-heads manage to seek out enough, however, to make up 13.51 percent of their entire diet. Of this, the ladybird beetles make up 4.88 percent, or more than a third. It is certain that there are not a third as many ladybird beetles as all other beetles combined; and thus it must be considered that the blue-headed vireos, like the warbling, either find these brilliantly colored forms in abundance in their environment or else make special search for them, a most undesirable habit economically. Roughly, a second third of the total bulk is composed of the metallic wood borers, the longicorns, and the click beetles. The remaining portion includes, among others, the weevils, which comprise 1.8 percent of the food.

The average of Hymenoptera for the year was 6.86 percent, and of flies, Diptera, 4.29 percent. Other insects eaten include stoneflies, dragonflies, grasshoppers, crickets, and locusts (6.56 percent for the year).

The small percentage of vegetable food was mostly "in the form of fleshy fruits, such as wild grape, dogwood, viburnum, and wax myrtle. No cultivated fruit was identified, and it is practically certain that none is eaten." The average for the year was 3.68 percent, but in January it formed nearly a quarter of the total food, 24.37 percent.

Aaron C. Bagg (Bagg and Eliot, 1937) says: "The height of the Blue-head's migration coincides with the emergence of tent-caterpillars. At Holyoke on May 10, 1926, I watched one of these Vireos take most of the young caterpillars in one web, then fly to another and repeat the heavy meal."

Alexander F. Skutch writes to me: "Once in the highlands of Guatemala I saw a blue-headed vireo pick up a very long caterpillar, possibly an inch in length. At first the bird seemed puzzled to know what to do with it, and crossed to the other side of the tree with the larva dangling from its bill. Here he laid it along a twig, held it there with a foot, and took a few nibbles or tugs at it. Then he took it in his bill again, still nearly or quite intact, and swallowed it whole. The habit of using the foot for holding food, while it is torn apart with the bill, appears to be very imperfectly developed among the vireos, but has attained a high degree of efficiency in the related families of shrike-vireos (Vireolaniidae) and pepper-shrikes (Cyclarhidae)."

The blue-headed vireo lives mainly in the trees of the forest and obtains most of its food among the twigs and foliage, where it gleans quietly and thoroughly. But Ora W. Knight (1908) says: "I have also on several occasions seen one of these birds spring into the air after passing insects after the style of a Flycatcher, in fact this manner of feeding would seem to be more characteristic of this species than of any other Vireos with which I am acquainted."

Behavior.—One of the chief characteristics of the blue-headed vireo is its tameness or fearlessness, or perhaps its confidence in man or its indifference to his presence. Its gentle demeanor when its nest is approached is in marked contrast to the aggressive tactics employed by some other vireos and by many other birds. There is seldom any scolding or great excitement and no attempt at attack, but a brave display of parental devotion. Many a bird-lover has enjoyed the thrill of stroking the incubating bird on its nest, or perhaps lifting it off without even being pecked in the attempt, and then seeing it settle down in the nest again with apparent confidence. It is a gentle little parent that soon wins our admiration and our affection. Perhaps it will even sing almost in our faces as it returns. With patience one may be persuaded to take food from our fingers when incubating or brooding. But individuals are not all alike; some will quickly leave the nest, if we come anywhere near it, and will not return to it while we are in the vicinity.

With all its tameness and tolerance of humans, the blue-headed vireo is not a sociable bird; it does not seek the company of man or the security of our home grounds; it is seldom seen in our yards and gardens or in the shade trees of village streets and city parks, except on migrations. It is rather a recluse of the woodlands, the solitudes of the forests, often well hidden in the foliage of the tree tops; we must seek it there in its shady retreats, if we would make its acquaintance. If we follow the lead of its rich song, we may see it sitting quietly on some outstanding branch near an opening or among the lower branches of a forest tree. It may remain in one spot for a long time or move about very deliberately while feeding, for it is far less active in its movements than the smaller vireos. Quiet dignity and an air of calm repose seem to dominate its behavior in the security of its woodland home.

Voice.—Aretas A. Saunders contributes the following account of the music of this vireo: "The song of the blue-headed vireo is long-continued, made up of phrases separated by short pauses. It is the highest in pitch of the common vireos of eastern United States, and of exceedingly sweet, clear quality. The phrases are delivered more rapidly than those of the yellow-throated vireo, but more slowly than those of the redeye. On the whole it is the most pleasing of the vireo songs.

"From a study of the records from 37 individuals, the pitch varies from E♭ ′ ′ ′ ′ to B′ ′, two tones more than an octave. The rate of singing is about one phrase to a second, or a second and a half. The phrases themselves are delivered slowly, the slurred portions being long-drawn-out and strongly accented. Each individual uses 9 to 15 different phrases. These are delivered in a varied order, which avoids the monotonous repetition found in the yellow-throated vireo. Phrases are composed of two to six notes. Two-, three-, and four-note phrases are common, while five- and six-note ones are rather rare. The notes of the phrases are sometimes connected by slurring and sometimes by abrupt changes. In phrases of three or more notes both kinds of changes may occur in the same phrase. Such phrases are character- istic of the song, and a help in distinguishing it from other vireos. Such phrases may be written *aweeto, teeaytoay, taweetayo*, etc.

"On the breeding range in midsummer, this bird sometimes runs all its phrases together, omitting the pauses, producing a warble of 15 or 20 notes, the song then suggesting that of the warbling vireo. This song is heard commonly in the spring migration in April, and occa- sionally in fall in October.

"On the breeding grounds the period of song lasts till about the third week in August. Then individuals cease singing for a time but revive the song in late August. Definite dates are difficult to determine, how- ever, for some individuals revive the song before others have ceased the main period of singing. Where the species is common one or more birds are likely to be heard in song every day in the summer."

Francis H. Allen sends me the following notes: "I have heard from both birds of a pair, in June, a faint trumpetlike note uttered with the bill almost closed. Sometimes the note was sounded more emphati- cally with the bill opened a little more. It then had a more strident character. I have also heard the tin-trumpet note in August, some- times with a variant in two syllables, *tee-weh*. The chatter of the blue- headed vireo resembles that of the yellow-throated but is not so loud.

"August 25, 1911—One feeding in trees in a drizzling rain uttered continually a rather harsh, nasal *see-a*, sometimes more distinctly dis- syllable, like *see-weep*. Once he gave a succession of similar but short notes, like *she-she-she-she-she*. All the notes were more like the char- acteristic harsh note of the red-eye than the other call-notes I have heard from this species. This may have been a young bird (so far as could be seen in the rain and without a glass, it was not in full plu- mage), but it was well enough grown to take care of itself, and it was alone.

"One cold afternoon with spits of snow in early May, one of two blue-headed vireos in a hawthorn tree near my house sang *sotto voce* with snatches of catbirdlike song, a trill, and, later, phrases of the regular song but faint."

The following note from Mr. Skutch is interesting: "Contrary to prevalent impression, the majority of North American birds that win- ter in Central America may be heard singing here. Most of them rarely sing until the time for their northward departure approaches, yet a few are tuneful even in the midst of the northern winter. Con- spicuous among these are the yellow-throated and blue-headed vireos. With the possible exception of the orchard oriole, the blue-headed vireo is more songful while in Central America than any other of the winter visitants. Early in January 1935 they sang much among the shade trees of the Finca Mocá, a great coffee plantation on the Pacific slope at the base of the Volcán Atitlán. Their song resembled that of the red-eyed vireo but was sweeter and more varied and was interspersed with pleasing little warbles uttered in a low, soft voice. On the morning of January 13 all the blue-headed vireos I met, four in number, were singing persistently. Of course, a singing bird is far more likely to attract attention than one which is silent. At noon I came upon two that were singing against each other from neighboring trees. One repeated all the notes of the other, as if in rivalry. They continued this as long as I stopped to listen but did not lose their tempers and clash, as so often happens under these circumstances. It is rare to hear wintering birds sing in January and exceedingly rare to hear them sing so much as these vireos sang.

"In the highlands I often heard the blue-headed vireos sing during April. When two came together they sang against each other like the birds on the coffee plantation. *Viree*, one said; and other repeated *viree*. Then the first called *vireo;* and *vireo* answered the second. They continued this pretty conversation for some minutes."

Many years ago, when my hearing was good, I wrote down my impression of the song as *kwee*^{eee}, with a rising inflection as in the redeye's song, or *kew*$_{ew}$, with a falling inflection; sometimes there was only the *kew*, or a short *keweék;* again there was a rich and full *koy week*, or *per cheet*. The first combination was the commonest, but it was often varied by the second.

The literature contains many references to the beautiful song of the blue-headed vireo, but there is little that need be added to the above accounts. William Brewster (1906) mentions an interesting bird that "had two songs, one perfectly characteristic of his own species, the other indistinguishable from that of the Yellow-throated Vireo. These songs were invariably kept distinct, the notes of one never being interpolated among those of the other; nor was the bird ever known to change from one to the other save after a well-marked interval of total silence." Dr. Thomas S. Roberts (1932) writes:

The song is to be distinguished from the Red-eye's especially by two curious characteristic phrases which are introduced at frequent intervals. These may be recalled by the syllables *wheop-teu*, the first note sharp and quick, the last prolonged; and the other couplet by the words *johnny-cake*, rapidly uttered. Later in the season, mid-July, the song may consist almost entirely of these notes and is then a curious medley of *wheop-teu, wheop-teu, johnny-cake, johnny-cake, wheop-teu*, and so on, with now and then a few sweet, vireonine notes. At the end of the season, early in August, the *wheop-teu* call is all that remains and this rings through the forest, an unmusical reminder of the beautiful song to be heard no more until the coming of another nuptial awakening.

Field marks.—It is only in the brightest light that the head of the blue-headed vireo appears at all blue, and then it is only a bluish gray; in shadow, or at a distance, it appears a dark slate-color. But the pure white eye ring and the white stripe in front of the eye, the "spectacles," are conspicuous at considerable distance. On the nest the gleaming white throat, in sharp contrast with the dark head markings, shows plainly above the rim of the nest. The two white wing bars, which the red-eyed vireo lacks, the pure white breast, and the yellow sides are good field marks.

Enemies.—Undoubtedly some eggs and young are destroyed by predators, such as blue jays, crows, chipmunks, squirrels, and perhaps snakes, as many rifled nests have been found. Based on my experience, mentioned above, Cooper's hawks do not molest them even when nesting nearby; and Mr. Forbush (1929) says that the vireos also nest in the same woods with goshawks and red-tailed and sharp-shinned hawks.

The blue-headed vireo is a common victim of the cowbird; if the cowbird's egg is laid before the vireo has laid any of her own, the vireo may cover it up and lay her eggs in the upper story; Dr. Friedmann (1929) says that the bluehead does this more often than the other vireos; but, after any of her own eggs are laid, she will not cover them. Unless the alien eggs are removed, the poor vireos will probably raise only young cowbirds.

Harold S. Peters (1936), in his list of external parasites, mentions only one tick (*Haemaphysalis leporis-palustris* Packard) found on this vireo.

Winter.—Arthur T. Wayne (1910) says that "this vireo winters abundantly in the great swamps which are in close proximity to our [South Carolina] coast. That it is a common bird in the months of December, January, and February there is no question, for I have often seen and counted as many as ten individuals in the course of a few hours. On mild days in winter the birds sing with some vigor, but it is not until March that the full volume of song is heard."

Arthur H. Howell (1932) says that, in Florida "in winter it is often found in low, swampy thickets." Dickey and van Rossem (1938) say of the blue-headed vireo in El Salvador: "The center of abundance of this very common winter visitant was along the upper edge of the Arid Lower Tropical Zone, in other words in the coffee districts at about 3,500 altitude. In numbers it compared favorably with the warbling and Philadelphia vireos, but of course was much more in evidence. The smaller species are ordinarily silent or at least do not sing, but the familiar song of *solitarious* may be heard throughout the winter. This species, far more than the warbling and Philadelphia vireos, was likely to accompany the composite flocks of visiting warblers."

Mr. Skutch writes to me: "The blue-headed vireo winters in northern Central America but has not been recorded south of Nicaragua. In Guatemala it is abundant through the winter months. Avoiding extremes of altitude, it yet spreads over a wide vertical range, from 2,000 to 9,000 feet above sea level. In December and January I found it rather abundant among the shade trees of the coffee plantations on the Pacific slope, at 3,000 to 4,000 feet above sea level. At higher elevations it frequents the forests of oak, alder, pine, and arbutus. During the year I passed on the Sierra de Tecpán in the Department of Chimaltenango, I found it wintering in small numbers between 8,000 and 9,000 feet. True to its name *solitarius*, it never forms companies of its own kind; yet it is not entirely a hermit, for a single blue-headed vireo is often met in one of the mixed flocks of small birds that are so conspicuous a feature of the highlands during the winter months. The nucleus of each flock is made up of the excessively abundant wintering Townsend warblers, and about this gathers a motley assemblage of warblers of other kinds, vireos, flycatchers, woodhewers, hairy woodpeckers, etc. Only with extreme rarity will the blue-headed vireo which has attached itself to a flock tolerate the presence of a second individual of its kind.

"On the Sierra de Tecpán, the blue-headed vireo arrived on October 10, 1933. My latest spring date for the same year was April 28; but after the 19th I saw only this single individual. Griscom (1932) gives the extreme dates for the presence of this vireo in Guatemala as October 15 and April 27."

DISTRIBUTION

Range.—North-central Canada to Nicaragua.

Breeding range.—The solitary or blue-headed vireo breeds **north** to southern British Columbia (Comox, Puntchesakut Lake, and Sixteen-mile Lake); central western Alberta (Grand Prairie and Peace River Landing); southwestern Mackenzie (Nahanni River, Simpson, Hay River, and Fort Smith); northeastern Alberta (Chippewyan); central Saskatchewan (Lake Ile-a-la-Crosse, Emma Lake, and Hudson Bay Junction); central Manitoba (Grand Rapids and Knee Lake, probably); Ontario (Port Arthur, Moose Factory, Lake Abitibi, Algonquin Park, and Ottawa); southern Quebec (Blue Sea Lake, Quebec, Grand Greve, and probably Seven Islands); and extreme southwestern Newfoundland (Tompkins). **East** to southwestern Newfoundland (Tompkins;); Nova Scotia (Baddeck, Pictou, and Halifax); Maine (Calais, Ellsworth, and Portland); Massachusetts (Boston, Taunton, and New Bedford); Connecticut (New Haven); northern New Jersey (Lake Mashipacong); and south through the Appalachian Mountains to northern Georgia (Brasstown Bald, Oglethorpe Ridge, and Burnt Mountain). In comparatively recent years the mountain vireo of the southern Appalachians has extended its range to lower altitudes, and in North Carolina has been found breeding at Statesville and Charlotte, and a few times at Raleigh, and in Georgia at Athens and Round Oak. **South** to northern Georgia (Burnt Mountain), northeastern Ohio (Ashtabula); extreme southern Ontario (Point Pelee); southeastern Michigan (Rochester); southern Wisconsin (Racine, North Freedom, and Prairie du Sac); central Minnesota (North Pacific Junction, Brainerd, and Itaska State Park); northern North Dakota (Pembina and Turtle Mountains); eastern Wyoming (Sundance and Laramie); central Colorado (Boulder, Denver, Colorado Springs, and Trinidad); central New Mexico (Santa Fe, Las Vegas, and San Antonio); western Texas (Guadelupe Mountains, Davis Mountains, and Brewster County); northern Chihuahua (San Diego and Pachico); central Sonora (Moctezuma), and northern Lower California (Sierra San Pedro Mártir). A resident race is found in the Cape district of Lower California. **West** to northern Lower California (Sierra San Pedro Mártir); western California (Campo, Pasadena, Almaden, Oakland, and Eureka); western Oregon (Coos Bay, Corvallis, the mountains near Tillamook, and Portland); western Washington (Vancouver, Seattle, Lake Crescent, and Bellingham); and western British Columbia (Victoria, Comox, and Puntchesakut Lake).

Winter range.—In winter the solitary vireo is found north to northern Michoacán (Cerro Patamban and Zamora); possibly north to southern Sonora (Tesia); Puebla (Metaltoyuca); Nuevo León (Monterrey); southern Texas (Harlingen, Houston, Cove, and Silsbee); southern Louisiana (Avery Island and New Orleans); southern Mississippi (Biloxi); southern Alabama (Prattville, occasionally); Georgia (Milledgeville and casually to Atlanta and Athens); and southern South Carolina, casually (Aiken, Summerville, and Charleston). **East** to coastal South Carolina (Charleston and Port Royal); Georgia (Savannah and St. Marys); Florida (St. Augustine, New Smyrna, and Royal Palm Park); Quintana Roo (Chunyaxche), and El Salvador (Mount Cacaquatique); and occasionally to northern Nicaragua (San Rafael del Norte). **South** to El Salvador. **West** to El Salvador (Mount Cacaquatique and Barra de Santiago); Guatemala (Duenas and Huehuetenango); Oaxaca (Tehuantepec and Juquila); Guerrero (Tlalixtaquilla and Chilpancingo); Michoacán (Cerro Patamban); the Cape region of Lower California (Cape San Lucas), and possibly southern Sonora (Tesia), and in small numbers in the vicinity of Tucson, Ariz.; a single record of winter occurrence at Pasadena, Calif. It is a rare migrant of winter resident in western Cuba (Habana).

The ranges as outlined apply to the species as a whole, which has been separated into five subspecies or geographic races. The typical race, the blue-headed vireo (*V. s. solitarius*), breeds from southwestern

Mackenzie eastward and south to central Alberta, southern Manitoba, northern Minnesota, southeastern Michigan, northeastern Ohio, Massachusetts, and the mountains of central West Virginia and Pennsylvania; the mountain vireo (*V. s. alticola*) breeds in the Appalachian region from southern West Virginia and Virginia to Georgia; the plumbeous vireo (*V. s. plumbeus*) from northeastern Nevada, Utah, and southern Montana south to Arizona and northern Sonora, western Texas, and the mountains of Chihuahua and Veracruz; Cassin's vireo (*V. s. cassini*) breeds from central British Columbia, southeastern Alberta, and northwestern Montana, through Idaho, western Nevada, and California to northern Lower California; the San Lucas vireo (*V. s. lucasanus*) is resident in the Cape district of Lower California. Other races are resident in Central America.

Migration.—Late dates of spring departure are: Guatemala—Tecpam, April 28.   Mexico—Guerrero—Chilpancingo, April 20.   Tamaulipas—Victoria, May 1.   Florida—College Point, April 23. South Carolina—Aiken, April 22.   Virginia—Naruna, May 4.   District of Columbia—Washington, June 2.   Pennsylvania—Doylestown, May 24.   New York—Orient, May 3.   Louisiana—Grand Isle, April 6.   Mississippi—Biloxi, April 14.   Arkansas—Winslow, May 8.   Missouri—Columbia, May 28.   Indiana—Bloomington, May 17.

Early dates of spring arrival are: Georgia—Dalton, March 8.   South Carolina—Spartanburg, March 26.   North Carolina—Raleigh, March 9.   West Virginia—White Sulphur Springs, April 1.   District of Columbia—Washington, April 6.   Pennsylvania—Berwyn, April 8. New York—New York, April 16.   Massachusetts—Amherst, April 19. Maine—Ellsworth, April 21.   Nova Scotia—Wolfville, April 25.   New Brunswick—Scotch Lake—May 2.   Quebec—Montreal, May 3.   Tennessee—Knoxville, April 4.   Illinois—Chicago, April 27.   Ohio—Sandusky, April 14.   Michigan—Ann Arbor, May 1.   Ontario—Hamilton, April 25.   Missouri—St. Louis, April 20.   Iowa—Marshalltown, April 29.   Wisconsin—Madison, May 2.   Minnesota—Red Wing, May 1.   Kansas—Harper, April 26.   Manitoba—Aweme, May 2.   New Mexico—Chloride, April 26.   Colorado—Boulder, April 18.   Wyoming—Laramie, May 7.   Montana—Columbia Falls, April 26.   Alberta—Glenevis, May 8.   Mackenzie—Simpson, May 22.   Utah—St. George, April 16.   Idaho—Coeur d'Alene, April 19.   California—Twenty-nine Palms, March 24.   Oregon—Pinehurst, April 15.   Washington—Shelton, April 8.   British Columbia—Courtenay, April 3.

Late dates of fall departure are: British Columbia—Okanagan Landing, September 15.   Washington—Seattle, September 10.   Oregon—Eugene, October 13.   California—Santa Barbara, November 7. Alberta—Islay, October 1.   Montana—Fortine, September 18.   Wyoming—Laramie, October 16.   Utah—Ogden, October 6.   Colorado, Beulah, October 17.   Manitoba—Aweme, September 30.   Minnesota—

St. Paul, October 6. Iowa—Iowa City, October 15. Missouri—Columbia, October 20. Arkansas—Hot Springs, November 1. Wisconsin—Beloit, October 19. Michigan—Blaney Park, October 8. Ontario—Toronto, October 20. Ohio—Toledo, October 27. Indiana—Indianapolis, October 2. Kentucky—Bowling Green, November 4. Tennessee—Nashville, November 9. Newfoundland—Tompkins, September 18. New Brunswick—Scotch Lake, October 22. Quebec—Montreal, October 6. Maine—Dover-Foxcroft, October 27. Vermont—Wells River, October 19. Massachusetts—Marthas Vineyard, October 25. New York—Rhinebeck, October 20. Pennsylvania—Philadelphia, November 4. District of Columbia—Washington, November 5. West Virginia—Bluefield, October 27. Virginia—Lawrenceville, November 13. North Carolina—Weaverville, November 24.

Early dates of fall arrival are: Minnesota—Lanesboro, August 24. Iowa—Hillsboro, August 23. Ohio—Oberlin, September 12. Illinois—Glen Ellyn, September 10. Arkansas—Monticello, August 29. Louisiana—Thibodaux, August 21. Mississippi—Oxford, October 2. District of Columbia—Washington, September 6. Virginia—Naruna, August 12. South Carolina—Charleston, October 23. Georgia—Round Oak, October 7. Alabama—Greensboro, October 23. Florida—Pensacola, September 21. Mexico—Guerrero, Taxco, October 10. Guatemala—Tecpan, October 10.

Egg dates.—Arizona: 15 records, May 20 to July 9.

California: 100 records, April 26 to July 9; 52 records, May 20 to June 6, indicating the height of the season.

Massachusetts: 57 records, May 14 to July 29; 32 records, May 30 to June 18.

North Carolina: 16 records, April 12 to June 16; 8 records, April 18 to May 9.

Washington: 37 records, May 1 to July 3; 20 records, June 3 to 16.

VIREO SOLITARIUS ALTICOLA Brewster

MOUNTAIN VIREO

HABITS

The mountain vireo deserves its name as an inhabitant of the mountains and adjacent valleys of the Appalachian Mountain system, the most typical birds being found in western North and South Carolina, eastern Tennessee, and northern Georgia. The 1931 Check-list extends the range northward to Maryland, but probably *alticola* intergrades with typical *solitarius* somewhere in Maryland, the Virginias, and Pennsylvania. Prof. Maurice Brooks, in some notes he has sent me, points out the folly of trying to define too closely the ranges of subspecies by "creating an artificial barrier on the political boundary made famous by Mason and Dixon. * * * The situation as regards these vireos is exactly paralleled by slate-colored and Carolina juncos, and by black-throated blue and Cairns's warblers; in each case the southern birds are supposed to just reach the Pennsylvania border, where they are met by their northern relatives. It happens that all three species are abundant in the mountains on both sides of the line, and it is obvious that no sharp limits between the races can be defined; there is constant meeting and interbreeding."

I have sometimes been criticized because we have not attempted in this series of bulletins to outline accurately the ranges of the subspecies; the above remarks illustrate very clearly the futility of trying to do so in nearly all cases; in only a few isolated instances can this be done satisfactorily.

The summer range of the mountain vireo in the regions roughly outlined above extends from about 1,200 feet above sea level in the valleys to over 6,000 feet on mountain summits. In winter it retires from the mountains and lives in the lowlands of South Carolina, Georgia, and northern and central Florida.

William Brewster (1886) described and named this subspecies from specimens collected in Macon County, N. C. He says:

This new form may be easily distinguished from *solitarius* by its larger size, heavier bill, and different color of the upper parts. In *solitarius* the crown and sides of the head are clear, pure ash, in strong contrast with the olive green of the back and rump, whereas in *alticola* the entire upper parts are nearly uniform blackish-plumbeous, with only a faint tinge of greenish on the back, which is essentially concolor with the crown. In these respects the bird resembles *V. plumbeus*, but its coloring above is darker and dingier, its sides strongly yellowish as in *solitarius*. * * *

Throughout the elevated plateau occupying the southeastern corner of Macon County, this new Vireo was one of the most abundant forest birds. It was found exclusively in open oak and chestnut woods, where its ringing voice, mingling with the rich music of the equally numerous Grosbeaks (*Habia ludoviciana*) and Scarlet Tanagers (*Piranga erythromelas*), was rarely still even at noontide.

Professor Brooks says in his notes: "Mountain vireos are characteristic and abundant birds of the southern highlands, found from the zone of spruce and balsam down to elevations of 1,200 or 1,500 feet in the mountain valleys. I have not found them at corresponding elevations away from the mountains, however; the common name seems abundantly justified."

Bruce P. Tyler (MS.) tells me where he finds this vireo in eastern Tennessee: "With us the ideal home of the mountain vireo is Shady Valley, in Johnson County, Tenn. This lovely valley is located between Holston and Iron Mountains. The floor of the valley is 3,000 to 2,500 feet elevation, decreasing as it departs from the upper reaches of Beaver Dam Creek and extends to 'Back Bone Rock' near Mock's Mill, about 10 miles as the crow flies. The valley is flanked by mountains with ultimate elevations approaching 4,000 feet; and, beyond Iron Mountain, we have White Top and Mount Rodgers, with elevations of 5,678 and 5,719 feet, respectively. These higher peaks reach well into the Canadian Zone. These summits seem, by their proximity, to lend something of the Canadian Zone flavor to Shady Valley. The flora of the valley smacks of the Canadian Zone. Originally the bed of the valley was a cranberry bog. Overmuch 'civilization,' W. P. A., etc., have drained and cleared it until, only by closest search can any cranberry vines be found. The mountain vireo breeds in the upper reaches of the Transition Zone and in the Canadian Zone."

Mount Mitchell, in western North Carolina, is said to be the highest mountain in the eastern half of the United States, rising 6,684 feet above sea level; it was once covered with a dense forest of tall red spruce; but logging and forest fires have destroyed all but a narrow fringe of spruces at the summit. Thomas D. Burleigh (1941) found the mountain vireo to be "a fairly plentiful breeding bird in the fir and spruce woods at the top of the mountain. In the valleys the first spring migrants appear during the latter part of March, but April 12 (1930) is the earliest that this species has been noted in the open spruce woods (5,000 feet), and not until May 4 (1933) has the first venturesome individual been seen at the top of the mountain (6,600 feet). The latest date for occurrence in the fall is September 30, (1930)."

Nesting.—Professor Brooks writes to me from West Virginia: "Woodland openings, trailsides, picnic grounds, and such natural or artificial disturbances of the forest are most frequently chosen as nesting areas by these birds. Yellow birch is a favorite nesting tree, the yellow-brown bark furnishing nesting material and, very often, an effective concealing background for the nest. Nearly every nest I have examined has contained fibers of birch bark. Nests are placed from 6 to 15 feet from the ground, usually just out of reach."

Bruce P. Tyler tells me that, in his Shady Valley region, the nest of the mountain vireo "is placed in the fork of the lower branches of a tree or a fork of a low branch of undergrowth in the woodland. It is more globular than the nests of the red-eyed or white-eyed vireo and somewhat larger." He has sent me a fine photograph (pl. 38) of a nest, taken in this valley on June 12, 1938. "This nest was placed in a red oak tree, 20 feet up and 7 feet out from the trunk of the tree. It was made of grass, shredded bark and plant fiber and covered with lichens, bound together with spider webs. The bird remained on the nest until the limb which supported it was cut off." The nest contained four eggs which had been incubated for three or four days.

Pearson and the Brimleys (1942) say that, in the mountains of North Carolina, "it breeds chiefly in deciduous trees." They record nests in a chestnut, a small sourwood, another chestnut, and an oak.

Mr. Burleigh (1925) seems to be satisfied that, in northeastern Georgia, "two broods are raised each year, the first during the latter

part of April and early May, and the second in June." He says
further:

Nests from which the young had already flown were found early in June,
and my experience would certainly prove the later nestings. The first nest
with eggs was found June 14, holding on that date four well incubated eggs. It
was twenty-five feet from the ground suspended from a fork at the outer end
of a limb of a large hemlock close to a stream in a ravine, at the foot of Brasstown Bald. A second nest, found June 19, also held four well incubated eggs
and was eighteen feet from the ground suspended from a fork at the outer
end of a limb of a beech sapling well up the mountain side. The female was
incubating and was remarkably tame, remaining on the nest until the limb was
cut off and the nest brought within reach, flying only when stroked on the back.
A third nest found June 25 held one fresh egg and was later deserted. It was
twelve feet from the ground at the outer end of a limb of an uprooted ash
sapling in a ravine probably half way up the mountain. These nests were all
alike in construction, being compactly built of grasses, fragments of weed stems
and shreds of bark, lined with fine grasses, vine tendrils and fine hemlock twigs,
and well covered on the outside with, in two cases, fragments of an old hornet's
nest, and invariably numerous green lichens. * * * As confirming my opinion
that two broods are raised each year, I might add here the fact that a fourth
nest was found July 15, in Fannin County, that held newly hatched young.

Mr. Brewster (1888) received what was probably the first nest of
this subspecies ever reported. It was taken by J. S. Carns on May 27,
1887, on Craggy Mountain, Buncombe County, N. C. "It measures
externally 3.25 in diameter by 2.10 in depth. In places the rim is
nearly an inch in thickness. The exterior is beautifully diversified
with white and purplish-brown sheep's wool, grayish lichens, small
strips and fragments of decayed wood, and a few spider's cocoons,
bound firmly to, or hanging loosely from, the framework proper,
which is composed of coarse grass stalks and strips of bark, the latter
partly a reddish-colored inner bark, probably from the hemlock, but
largely the pale gold, sheeny outer bark of the yellow birch (*B. lutea*).
The interior cavity is lined with fine bleached grasses and the reddish
stems of some species of club moss."

R. B. McLaughlin (1888), of Statesville, N. C., found two nests of
the mountain vireo in some high, dry woods, consisting wholly of
pines, such as those in which the pine warbler nests. One nest was in
a small, slim pine, and the other was "attached to the limb of a tall,
slender pine, about forty feet from the ground and ten feet from the
body of the tree." On June 2, while the birds were building the
first nest, they were followed by three young of a previous brood,
which is further evidence that this vireo raises two broods in a season.

Eggs.—The mountain vireo lays ordinarily three or four eggs, most
often four in a full set, and perhaps rarely five, though I find no
record of five. These are similar to those of the northern bluehead,
but averaging slightly larger. The ground color is sometimes creamy
or pinkish white, and the spots are apt to be in lighter shades of

brown, sometimes almost reddish brown, with washed-out edges; some eggs are more heavily marked than those of the northern bird. The measurements of 40 eggs average 19.7 by 14.5 millimeters; the eggs showing the four extremes measure 21.6 by 14.3, 20.2 by 15.0, 18.4 by 14.0, and 21.3 by 12.4 millimeters.

The food of this vireo is included under the report on the type race, and the plumage changes, behavior, and voice are not materially different from those of the blue-headed vireo. Many observers have praised the beautiful song of the mountain vireo, but most of them have compared it with the songs of the redeye or white-eye, which are, of course, inferior or at least less pleasing. But Mr. Brewster (1886) says: "Its song was somewhat like that of *solitarius*, but to my ear much finer, many of the notes being louder and sweeter, and the whole performance more continuous and flowing." And Mr. Wayne (1910) states: "The song of this form is much richer in tone and volume than that of its near relative, the Blue-headed Vireo."

A. L. Pickens thinks this vireo should have specific rating on the merits of its voice, and says in a letter to me: "The mountain vireo takes the standard vireo syllables, with all their distinctness, and adds two syllables like an accompaniment blown on some woodland flute, and the most matter-of-fact oratory of the vireos becomes something worth climbing mountains and pushing through thickets to hear."

VIREO SOLITARIUS PLUMBEUS Coues

PLUMBEOUS VIREO

HABITS

According to the 1931 Check-list, this dull-colored vireo "breeds from northern Nevada, northern Utah, southern Montana, northeastern Wyoming, and southwestern South Dakota south through Arizona and central western Texas to Chihuahua and the mountains of Vera Cruz." It is thus the easternmost of the western races, and there seems to be no breeding race of the species in the center of the United States, that is, the Mississippi Valley region. The species, as a whole, seems to prefer cool, northern forests, mountain regions, or the cooler climate of the Pacific, to the hot dry interior of the country.

Ridgway (1904) describes the plumbeous vireo as "similar to *L. s. alticola*, but back and scapulars entirely gray; rump and upper tail-coverts gray, tinged with olive-green, and sides and flanks much more faintly washed with yellow." The color pattern is the same as in the mountain vireo, the head being practically concolor with the back, but all the colors are much paler and grayer.

The plumbeous vireo is essentially a bird of the mountains and the mountain canyons, during the breeding season. In the Huachuca and the Chiricahua Mountains in Arizona, we found it fairly common in all the wooded canyons up to 7,000 feet, and less common among the pines at 8,000 or 9,000 feet near the summits. We saw the first one in the Chiricahuas on April 26, 1922. Mr. Swarth (1904) says that, in the Huachucas, it is quite abundant in all parts of the mountains during the spring migration, but not so numerous during the summer. In his paper on Arizona mountain birds, Dr. Edgar A. Mearns (1890) writes:

By its loud song this species is known to be a common denizen of the pine forests of this region; but it keeps so near the pine-tops as to be seldom seen, save by tracing to their source the sweet notes one almost constantly hears when riding through these grand forests it being one of the most persistent singers that I have met with. It often visits the spruce woods of the higher zone, a few perhaps breeding there.

In New Mexico, Mrs. Bailey (1928) records it as breeding as low as 6,000 feet in the Guadalupe Mountains, and as high as 8,000 feet "in the coldest part of the Zuni Mountains."

Russell K. Grater writes to me from Zion National Park, Utah: "This is one of the commonest birds in the park during the summer months. Its habitat in the canyons is mainly confined to the boxelder and other broadleaf trees; here among these trees nesting birds are closely distributed for miles along the canyon floor."

Nesting.—On May 26, 1922, in a branch of Ramsay Canyon, in the Huachucas, we found a nest of the plumbeous vireo with the bird sitting on it; it was about 6 feet from the ground at the tip of a lower branch of a small oak growing on the steep mountainside that rose sharply from the bed of the canyon. I tried to photograph it, but the bird would not let me get near enough for a good picture. I was surprised to find the nest empty. The bird would not return to the nest in front of the camera; but after the camera was removed, she promptly returned and settled on the nest as if incubating. My companion, Frank C. Willard, collected this nest, with a set of four nearly fresh eggs, on June 4 and sent it to me. This nest, now before me in its faded condition, must have been a very pretty nest when fresh. The framework, presumably of the usual materials used by vireos, is entirely concealed externally by a great variety of mosses, lichens, and bits of plant down of varied colors, firmly interwoven with and secured in place by narrow strands of fine inner bark, probably cedar, other very fine fibers, numerous bits of fine string and apparently only a little spider silk; these materials completely envelope and conceal the two supporting twigs. It is neatly lined with very fine, yellowish grass tops, from which the seeds had been removed. Its external dimensions are 4 by 3½ in diameter and over 2 inches in depth (it was probably flattened some in packing); the inner cavity measures about 2½ in diameter at the top and 1½ inches in depth; the walls are nearly an inch thick in some places.

There is another set of four eggs in my collection, taken by O. W. Howard in these same mountains on May 31, 1901; the nest was in a maple tree, hung from the fork of a small branch near the extremity of a limb, about 40 feet above ground.

Mr. Willard (1908) says of nests that he has seen in the Huachuca Mountains:

The nests are usually close to the ground, frequently within reaching distance. Oaks, ash, maples and sycamores are selected as nesting sites. Each pair has its claim staked out and ejects all intruders of the same species, altho the other two species are unmolested by Plumbeus even when nesting in close proximity.

In nest building they go as far as a quarter of a mile for material. They feed closer to the nest, however, probably at not over half this distance. The female does all the nest-building but is assisted somewhat by the male in the duties of incubation. He also feeds his mate on the nest, but this is done rather infrequently. My present observations give the time at intervals of from twenty minutes to half an hour. When doing so he sings close by the nest after feeding her and this has helped me locate several. The male also sings when the nest is approached, and once this year I saw one sitting on the nest and singing. Toward evening the male frequently flies down close to the nest and sits within a few inches of it for long periods, being perfectly quiet and motionless all the time.

The nest is a very pretty cup-shaped affair as is usual with this family. It is composed of grass-tops woven into a framework and filled in with oak down and greenish colored oak blossoms and bits of spiders web. The lining is of fine grass tops from which all the seeds have been removed. The general appearance of a normal nest is greenish in color. One nest built in a sycamore was made entirely of white goat hair and fine grass. The hair hung down some inches in a fringe all over and made a handsome ornament.

In Zion National Park, Utah, according to Russell K. Grater (MS.), "nesting begins late in April and continues into June. The nests are uniformly close to the ground, usually being only about 4 to 6 feet up. Made up of fine grasses, bits of small shredded leaves, and the cotton from the poplar trees, it is one of the most perfectly constructed nests found in the region. The nest is invariably on the tip of a long branch, suspended from a fork, and is usually well shaded by other parts of the tree's foliage. The parent birds call incessantly, even while bringing food to the young, becoming silent only when within a few feet of the nest."

Eggs.—The plumbeous vireo lays ordinarily three or four eggs, most commonly four, and rarely five. These are similar to the eggs of the species elsewhere. The measurements of 30 eggs in the United States National Museum average 20.2 by 14.9 millimeters; the eggs showing the four extremes measures 21.7 by 15.0, 21.4 by 15.5, and 18.3 by 14.2 millimeters.

In other respects all the habits of the plumbeous vireo seem to be very similar to those of the eastern blue-headed vireo and need not be reported here.

VIREO SOLITARIUS CASSINI Xantus

CASSIN'S VIREO

HABITS

Cassin's vireo is the westernmost race of the species, breeding from the Rocky Mountains westward and mainly in the Transition Zone, from central British Columbia to northern Lower California. It differs from the eastern blue-headed vireo in being slightly smaller and much duller in color.

In the northern portion of its range, Cassin's vireo seems to prefer the forests of pines and firs, where there is a mixture of oaks or other deciduous trees among the conifers. S. F. Rathbun tells me that it is a regular and not uncommon summer resident about Seattle, Wash., where it prefers the rather open sections of the forest where there is a somewhat scattered growth of trees; he also finds it where there is a mixture of deciduous trees among small firs, but considers it rather partial to oaks.

Gabrielson and Jewett (1940) say that, in Oregon, "it is found in the smaller second growth and in brushy areas either on the hillsides or along the stream bottoms. * * * It breeds commonly and builds its dainty nest low in bushes or trees." Dr. J. C. Merrill (1888) writes: "Unlike most Vireos this one, as observed at Fort Klamath, shows a marked predilection for pines and firs, and is found almost everywhere among these trees. It is also found, but much less frequently, in aspen groves with the Warbling Vireo. The nests are built in low manzanita or buck-rush bushes that grow throughout the pine woods." Grinnell and Storer (1924) write:

The Cassin Vireo is a summer visitant at middle altitudes along the west flank of the Sierra Nevada. Its distribution at nesting time closely parallels the ranges of the golden oak and incense cedar, though the bird does not restrict itself exclusively to these two trees. In and around Yosemite Valley this species and the Western Warbling Vireo are often to be found together, although the Cassin shows preference for the drier portions of the Valley, for example, near and upon the talus slopes along the north and south walls. During the spring migration the Cassin Vireo is a common transient in the western foothill country where, during its passage, it is to be seen in blue oaks and chaparral on dry hillsides. In early fall after the young are grown a few of these vireos wander up into the Hudsonian Zone before taking final leave of the country for the winter.

Howard L. Cogswell writes to me: "In the San Gabriel Mountains, the area where I have seen most of my Cassin's vireos, they are definitely associated in the breeding season with the oaks along the *walls* of the lower mountain canyons and throughout the big-cone spruces and golden-cup oaks and into the lower edges of the pines of the Transition Zone. They are not often found in the alders and sycamores along the bottom of the larger canyons, and in the valley areas occur only in migration."

Nesting.—Thomas D. Burleigh (1930) reports five nests found near Tacoma, Wash. The first "was twelve feet from the ground at the outer end of a limb of a small scrub oak in a stretch of open fir woods, and was built of grasses and usnea moss, lined with fine grasses and bright red moss rootlets, and well ornamented on the outside with white spiders' egg cases and bits of dead leaves. * * * Within the next month four other nests were found, and two of them were in small oaks and two in alder saplings, varying in height from five to ten feet from the ground."

Mr. Rathbun has sent me the following description of two nests of the Cassin's vireo, found in that same region: "The nest is a cup-shaped affair and is attached by its upper edges to the horizontal fork of a limb, generally at no great height. It is neatly made, reflecting skill in its construction. The material used for the outer part of one consisted of pieces of dead leaves of various dull colors, some bits of heavy gray paper, dry gray grasses and a small quantity of greenish-gray moss, these materials being interwoven and bound firmly by tough plant fibers. The lining was entirely of fine, dry grasses. The general color effect of this nest was a composite one, formed of many neutral tints, harmonizing with the lichen-covered limbs of a small oak, in which it was built. The outside of the nest was decorated with pieces of white cocoon."

Of the other, he says: "This nest was attached, pendantly, to a V-shaped fork near the extremity of a lower limb of a young fir, at a height of about 15 feet, the top of the nest being screened from view by a small twig overarching it. The material used consisted of many small pieces of thin, soft, dead leaves, long dry grasses, with a few horsehairs interwoven to help bind them and give strength; the nest was firmly bound to its support by strips of dry moss and vegetable fibers. The lining was of fine fibers, small stems of leaves, and a few horsehairs; the outside of the nest was decorated with a few pieces of white cocoons. On the twigs to which it was attached grew a few lichens, and a few of these were scattered about the upper part of the nest. Diameter outside, $3\frac{1}{4}$ inches; height, $2\frac{1}{4}$ inches; diameter inside, $2\frac{1}{4}$ inches; depth, $1\frac{3}{4}$ inches."

Dawson and Bowles (1909) say that some nests are placed as much as 30 feet above the ground, and Mr. Bowles adds: "They are the quickest as well as the slowest birds in completing their nests that have come under my notice. One pair built a handsome nest and laid four eggs in precisely ten days; while another pair were more than three weeks from the time the nest was started until the eggs were laid. They are the only Vireos that I have ever known to nest in communities.

Single pairs are the rule, but I have found as many as six occupied nests inside of a very small area, the nests being only a few yards apart."

J. Stuart Rowley writes to me: "There is an apple orchard in Tulare County, Calif., at an elevation of about 4,600 feet, where I have had an ideal chance to observe the nesting habits of this vireo. Here it seems that apple trees are favorite nesting trees, and many pairs breed here every year. The first week in June is the height of the egg-laying time, and many nests containing eggs can be found. Often a nest of *cassini* will be found in one tree, while in the very next tree not 20 feet away will be a nest of the western warbling vireo."

In the Yosemite Valley, Grinnell and Storer (1924) found a nest on May 22, 1919. "It was placed in an incense cedar at the edge of Merced River. The nest was on a branch which extended out over the rushing stream and was about 18 feet above the surface of the water." Dr. Grinnell (1908) found another nest "twelve feet from the ground in the lower outer foliage of an incense cedar growing among fire," in the San Bernardino Mountains.

Eggs.—Cassin's vireo lays three to five eggs; four is the usual number, but sets of five are not very rare. They are like the eggs of the eastern races, white or creamy white, and sparingly spotted with different shades of light or dark or reddish brown, the spots apparently averaging lighter and brighter browns than with the eastern blueheaded vireo. The measurements of 40 eggs in the United States National Museum average 19.4 by 14.3 millimeters; the eggs showing the four extremes measure 22.4 by 14.7, 21.3 by 15.2, 17.3 by 14.2, and 18.0 by 13.2 millimeters.

Food.—A separate study of the food of Cassin's vireo was made by Prof. F. E. L. Beal (1907), who examined the contents of 46 stomachs, taken in every month from April to November. He says:

The vegetable food, which was only a little more than 2 percent of the total, was made up of leaf galls, seeds of poison oak, and a few bits of rubbish. Not a trace of fruit was found.

The animal matter amounts to nearly 98 percent of the whole. Hemiptera are the largest item and amount to nearly 51 percent. The various families represented are those of the squash-bugs, leaf-bugs, stink-bugs, shield-bugs, leaf-hoppers, tree-hoppers, the jumping plant-lice, and scales. The latter are represented as usual by the black olive scale, which was contained in four stomachs. Caterpillars, with a few moths, are next in importance and form more than 23 percent of the whole food. They were eaten in every month and are evidently a favorite diet.

[Hymenoptera] amount to over 7 percent, and are mostly wasps, with a few ants. * * * Ladybird beetles were eaten to the extent of a little less than 6 percent, which is quite reasonable as compared with the record of the warbling vireo. * * * Other beetles amount to a little more than 3 percent of the food, and are mostly weevils and small-leaf-beetles (Chrysomelidae). A few flies, grasshoppers, and other insects amount to somewhat more than 2 percent, and these, with 4 percent of spiders, make up the remainder of the animal food.

Fall.—Although most individuals of the species breed in the Pacific States, mainly west of the Rocky Mountains, Cassin's vireos migrate southeastward in the fall, through Utah, Colorado, Arizona, and New Mexico, to their winter resorts in Mexico.

VIREO SOLITARIUS LUCASANUS Brewster

SAN LUCAS VIREO

HABITS

William Brewster (1891), in describing and naming this vireo, says:

This Vireo although averaging considerably smaller than *V. s. cassinii* has a bill as large and stout as in *V. s. alticola.* In the coloring of the upper parts all my spring and summer specimens agree closely with *cassinii* but there is a decided and very constant difference in the color of the flanks and sides, these having quite as much yellow as, but *much* less greenish than, *V. solitarius.* In autumnal plumage the Lower California bird approaches autumnal specimens of *solitarius* very closely, having the upper parts quite as bright olive green, the wing-bands as yellow, and the head nearly as clear ashy. There is also fully as much yellow on the sides, but much less greenish. These characteristics, with the almost total lack of brownish beneath, distinguish it readily from young *cassinii.*

Mr. Brewster (1902) says of its range: "So far as known, this Vireo is strictly confined to the Cape Region, where it is found at all seasons of the year, although most numerously, perhaps, in summer. Its breeding range extends from the coast at San José del Cabo, where it occurs almost exclusively in cultivated grounds about houses, to Miraflores and San José del Rancho, at both of which places it is common. Only a few were seen by Mr. Frazar at Triunfo, and none on the Sierra de la Laguna, while but one was taken (on April 4) at La Paz, which appears to be beyond the northern limits of its usual range."

It is of interest to note that this race seems to be entirely isolated, as no form of the blue-headed vireo species is known to breed in the wide gap between La Paz on the south and the Sierra San Pedro Mártir on the north.

Nesting.—Mr. Brewster (1902) writes: "A nest of *V. s. lucasanus* containing four fresh eggs, found by Mr. Frazar at San José del Rancho on July 15, was suspended in a fork at the extremity of a long, *leafless* branch of an oak at a height of about fifteen feet. It is composed chiefly of a gray, hemp-like fiber mixed with grass stems and thin strips of bark. There are also a few spiders' cocoons loosely attached to the bottom and sides, and apparently intended as ornaments. The interior is very neatly lined with fine, wiry, reddish-brown grass circularly arranged. The nest measures externally 3.00 in diameter by 2.50 in depth; internally, 2.00 in diameter by 1.50 in depth. The walls are half an inch thick in places."

J. Stuart Rowley writes to me: "While walking through the woods on San Bernardo Mountain, on the Gulf slope of the Sierra de la Laguna, I heard the unmistakable song of a solitary vireo, and, by carefully tracing the song to its source, I finally discovered the bird sitting on the nest." Charles E. Doe, who now has this nest in the University of Florida, tells me that it is a beautiful nest, made of fibers and moss, and placed 12 feet from the ground in a small oak; it was taken on May 6, 1933.

Eggs.—Both of the sets mentioned above, the only sets of which I have any record, contained four eggs each. Mr. Brewster's eggs are white, "with a slight creamy tint, and are spotted, chiefly about the larger ends, with reddish brown and black." The measurements of the eight eggs average 20.5 by 14.3 millimeters; the eggs showing the four extremes measure 21.1 by 13.8, 20.5 by 15.3, 19.9 by 14.3, and 20.2 by 13.8 millimeters.

VIREO CALIDRIS BARBATULUS (Cabanis)

BLACK-WHISKERED VIREO

HABITS

Our black-whiskered vireo is an offshoot from a West Indian species, *Vireo calidris*, of which there are at least three other subspecies found in the Lesser Antilles and on islands in the Caribbean Sea. Our bird differs from the type race, *Vireo calidris calidris*, "in much paler and less buffy superciliary stripe and auricular region, grayer pileum, duller olive-green of back, etc., and purer white throat and chest," according to Ridgway (1904).

It is apparently only a summer resident west of Dominica, where it breeds in Haiti, Cuba, Little Cayman, Isle of Pines, Key West, the Dry Tortugas, the Bahama Islands, and on the west coast of Florida, as far north as Anclote Keys.

Arthur H. Howell (1932) records it, also, on Plantation Key, Key Largo, and other Florida keys, as well as at Miami and at Coral Gables. Although I have visited most of these Florida localities several times, I never saw this bird, as I generally left for the north before its arrival. Oscar Baynard told me that it is a common summer resident in Pinellas County, nesting in the red mangroves around the shores of the bays and bayous late in May and in June, and such seem to be its favorite haunts all along the west coast of Florida, though Howell (1932) collected one "from the top of a large oak in a creek bottom at Seven Oaks, a mile or more from Old Tampa Bay."

On the Isle of Pines, according to W. E. Clyde Todd (1916), "it is a common inhabitant of the low thickets and jungles. * * * It was particularly numerous on the slopes and at the foot of the Casas and Caballos Mountains."

Referring to the Bahamas, C. J. Maynard (1896) writes: "It was not, however, until our return to New Providence on May 18th, 1884, that we saw our first specimen of the Black-whiskered Vireo. Their loud, peculiar songs could be heard in all directions, not only in the scrub, but also in the gardens and in the trees along the streets of the city of Nassau. Indeed, the first specimen that I saw was perched on a high limb of one of the fine almond trees which grew among many others on a small public park, known as the Parade, situated to the eastward of the city."

Dr. Glover M. Allen's (1905) experience with it in the Bahamas was somewhat similar; he says: "This vireo is a bird of the more open tree growth, particularly in the neighborhood of cultivated lands. We met with it not infrequently on New Providence and Abaco, but saw none on Great Bahama, from which island it has not yet been reported. Its absence there is doubtless due to a lack of suitable tree growth, at least in the portions hitherto visited. The extensive pine forests seem to be wholly avoided by it. * * * We also found this species on several of the larger cays where there were tall bushes, as at Stranger Cay."

Nesting.—Mr. Baynard (1914) shows a photograph (pl. 42) of a nest and three eggs of the black-whiskered vireo which he found while paddling along the mangroves on the coast of Pinellas County, Fla., of which he says: "It was not over two feet from my face, yet she stayed on her nest until I put forth my hand to touch her. The nest was empty, but evidently completed. * * * I visited this nest every day, but the bird laid an egg only every other day until she had three, then waited two whole days before beginning incubation. The nest was pensile, like all Vireos' nests, but not nearly so deep as most, and made entirely of seaweed, with a few pieces of palmetto fiber and one small feather woven in the side; it was lined nicely with fine, dry grass, and one or two pine-needles."

The construction of the nest described above must have been rather unusual, quite different at least from that of nests of the species elsewhere. For example, Cassin (1854) quotes P. H. Gosse's description of Jamaica nests, as follows:

The nest is rather a neat structure, though made of coarse materials. It is a deep cup, about as large as an ordinary tea-cup, narrowed at the mouth, composed of dried grass, intermixed with silk-cotton, and sparingly with lichen and spiders' nests, and lined with thatch-threads. It is usually suspended between two twigs, or in the fork of one, the margin being over-woven so as to embrace the twigs. This is very neatly performed. Specimens vary much in beauty,—one before me is particularly neat and compact, being almost globular in form, except that about one-fourth of the globe is wanting, as it is a cup. Though the walls are not thick, they are very firm and close, the materials being well woven. These are fibres of grass-like plants, moss, a few dry leaves, flat papery spiders' nests, with a little cotton or down for the over-binding of the edges. It is lined smoothly with fibres, I know not of what plant, as slender as human hair. Another nest, similarly formed, has the cavity almost filled with a mass of white cotton, which looks as if thrust in by man, but that those filaments of the mass are in contact with the sides, are interwoven with the other materials. As it is picked cotton, it must be a bit stolen from some house or yard, not plucked by the bird from the capsule.

A nest, reported by Mr. Todd (1916), was found during the second week in June, on the Isle of Pines, was "placed about fifteen feet from the ground, on a horizontal branch of a hardwood tree." Another nest was found there on April 24, 1909. A set of three eggs in my collection was taken by C. J. Maynard at Nassau, in the Bahamas, on June 24, 1897; the nest was placed in a low tree, about 10 feet up, and was composed of grass, leaves, and fragments of palm fronds, lined with rootlets.

Dean Amadon has sent me the following data on a set of eggs taken by Joseph C. Howell, at Boca Ciega Bay, Pinellas County, Fla., on June 19, 1932: "Eggs two days from hatching. Nest 9 feet up in a red mangrove, suspended from a horizontal limb. The nest tree stood on the edge of a dense clump of red mangroves, which bordered the bayou for miles in both directions; the nest hung out over the water. The bird did not flush until I nearly touched it. Then it returned to within a foot of me, giving a sort of squeal resembling a catbird's 'meow.' The other bird also approached to within 6 feet, but did not scold. Later, both became silent and I lost complete track of them. Outside of nest built almost entirely of materials that were grayish white in color, grass blades, plant down, and dead leaves. There were one or two blackish gray grass blades and a spot of yellow plant down. Not very smoothly lined with fine grass stems. Nest not too firmly affixed to limb by plant down and grass stems."

Eggs.—The black-whiskered vireo usually lays a set of three eggs, but sometimes only two. These are usually somewhat elongated to elliptical-ovate to elliptical-oval. The color is a delicate, pure white, with a pinkish appearance when fresh. They are rather sparingly marked with a few small spots, or minute dots, widely scattered over the egg, of various shades of brown, purplish brown or reddish brown; sometimes the spots are in shades of faint purple or violet-gray, or in very dark brown or blackish. Not all these colors appear in every egg. The measurements of 43 eggs average 21.0 by 15.1 millimeters; the eggs showing the four extremes measure 23.5 by 16.3, 22.8 by 16.5, 18.8 by 14.2, and 19.7 by 13.5 millimeters.

Plumages.—I have seen no small young of this species, but Ridgway (1904) describes the juvenal plumage [of Jamaican vireo], as follows: "Pileum, hindneck, back, scapulars, rump, upper tail-coverts, and lesser wing-coverts plain broccoli brown, inclining to fawn color;

wings (except lesser coverts) and tail as in adults, but greater wing-coverts indistinctly tipped, as well as edged, with pale yellow; superciliary stripe and sides of head buffy whitish, partly separated by a dusky loral and postocular mark; malar region, chin, and throat paler buffy white or vinaceous white; rest of under parts white, the sides, flanks, and under tail-coverts tinged with sulphur yellow."

The small amount of pertinent material available indicates that subsequent molts and plumages parallel those of the closely related red-eyed vireo, with a partial postjuvenal molt, involving the contour plumage and the lesser wing coverts in young birds, and a complete postnuptial molt in adults.

Food.—Dr. Edward A. Chapin's (1925) report on the food of the black-whiskered vireo was based on the examination of only four stomachs, collected in Florida in May and June. He writes:

Of the entire food, 87.5 percent was of animal origin. By far the largest single item was spiders, 39.25 percent of the whole; in one stomach were the remains of 10 individuals of one kind (*Tetragnatha*). Caterpillars and eggs of some moth or butterfly made up 14.25 percent of the food. In one stomach were 10 small earwigs (Forficulidae), which represented about 10 percent of the animal food. Miscellaneous beetles, including weevils from one stomach, made up 18.25 percent, and the remaining 5.75 percent was composed of wasps or bees and assassin bugs (Reduviidae).

The vegetable food, 12.5 percent of the total, was composed of fruit of barberry (*Berberis*) and of ragweed (*Ambrosia*), found in three of the four stomachs.

The number of stomachs examined was far too small to give an adequate picture of the food of this bird, especially as they were collected between May 21 and June 7. The examination of 84 stomachs of the typical race, taken in Puerto Rico, "show that the bird is decidedly frugivorous, inasmuch as wild fruits or berries were detected in 80 of the 84 stomachs examined and amounted to 57.82 percent." Probably birds collected in Florida or Cuba later in the season would show a larger percentage of vegetable food.

Harold H. Bailey (1925) says that in Florida "they feed in the hammocks from the lower bushes to the highest branches, on small spiders, caterpillars, flies, mosquitoes, and most of the small varieties of insects."

Behavior.—Mr. Maynard (1896) writes:

In habit this species is quite peculiar in some ways. They keep well in the tops of the trees, seldom, if ever, feeding in the low scrub. They are exceedingly agile in movement, having a peculiar briskness of action which is quite unvireo-like. They are, almost without exception, shy, and when they perceive an intruder, which they are apt to do very quickly, as they are ever on the alert, they erect the feathers of the head, droop the wings, spread the tail and utter a series of scolding notes quite unlike those of any other Vireo I ever heard. Then after flying restlessly from bough to bough for a moment or two, they utter a shrill scream of anger and off they go, generally flying several hundred yards in a straight line before alighting again. Even while feeding by themselves, they are exceedingly restless birds and a pair will not remain long in one tree. Quickly searching it over, they will leave it, almost invariably taking a long flight before selecting another feeding ground.

This extreme shyness and restlessness described by Mr. Maynard, as observed in the Bahamas, does not seem to be characteristic of the species elsewhere. Dr. Alexander Wetmore (1916) thus refers to the species in Puerto Rico: "Slow and leisurely in habit, they work through the leaves and twigs, sometimes singing for several minutes from one perch and exhibiting no fear." They are said to allow a close approach while incubating, as mentioned by Mr. Baynard above. Dr. Chapman (1892) says of the bird in Cuba: "It is a very tame and unsuspecting bird, and resembles our Red-eyed Vireo both in song and habits. The song, however, is more emphatic and hesitating than that of *V.[ireo] olivaceus.*"

Voice.—Opinions seem to differ, also, on the song of the black-whiskered vireo. Dr. Wetmore (1916) says that the song of the Puerto Rican bird "is a series of couplets, closely resembling that of the red-eyed species, and they have the usual scolding note of the vireos." And Dr. G. M. Allen (1905) says of the Bahaman bird: "The song is somewhat similar to that of the Red-eyed Vireo, but less varied, almost a monotone, delivered in a quiet apathetic way from some hidden perch."

How different is the following account given by Mr. Maynard (1896) for the bird he heard at Nassau!

The song of the Black-whiskered Vireo is loud and clear, noticeable in this character among all other of the smaller species of Bahaman Birds. "Whip Tom Kelly," is the nearest rendering of the lay that I can give, with an occasional fourth syllable added, sounding like "phue." These notes are repeated quite rapidly, with a decided accent on the "kelly." The fourth syllable when given is rather less energetically rendered, being a little plaintive. But the whole song is uttered with such carelessness, not only as to intonation, but also in detail, that it is seldom that the rendering which I have given can be distinctly heard. Either the syllables are run together, as is often the case, or the first one or two are given so low, or omitted altogether, that it is not uncommon to hear the bird uttering the "kelly" only, at rather wide intervals in a preoccupied and careless tone as if too busy about other matters to stop and sing. When heard in the distance on a still morning the notes remind one of the far away song of the Whippoorwill. When heard close at hand the song somewhat recalls the lay of some of the Orioles and the resemblance is partly carried out by the movements of the bird, but unlike the Orioles these Vireos never sing as they fly. Although they sing all day long, unlike the Thick-billed Vireo, they do not begin until sunrise and end at sunset.

It is interesting to note, in Cassin's (1854) account of this species, that the *whip-tom-kelly* note is so characteristic of the bird in Jamaica that it has become a popular name for this vireo. And he quotes Gosse's rendering of its strongly accented notes as *"Sweet-John!— John-to-whit!— Sweet-John-to-whit!— John-t'-whit!— Sweet-John-*

to-whit!" Apparently the song of this species varies considerably in different localities or in different individual birds.

Field marks.—The only field mark that will distinguish the black-whiskered vireo from the red-eyed vireo is the rather inconspicuous black malar stripe, which can be seen only at short range. Its song, however, is usually recognizable.

DISTRIBUTION

Range.—Southwestern Florida and the Bahamas to northern South America.

Breeding range.—The black-whiskered vireo breeds in the Bahamas, being found on all the islands that furnish suitable habitat, in Cuba including the Isle of Pines, on the Florida keys as far west as Key West, and on the islands and mainland of the west coast north to Anclote Key. It has also been found breeding at the south end of Lake Okeechobee.

Winter range.—The winter home is not fully known, but at that time the species is probably found only in South America, where its occurrence has been recorded in the Santa Marta region of Colombia, in British Guiana (possibly migrating), and in the lower Amazon Valley near the mouth of the Rio Tapajóz.

Migration.—A few migration dates are available.

Late date of spring departure from Colombia—Mamatoco, April 15.

Early dates of spring arrival: Cuba—Habana, March 9. Bahamas—New Providence, March 15. Florida—Fort Myers, April 17.

Late dates of fall departure: Florida—Palma Sola, September 9. Bahamas—Nassau, December 8. Cuba—Camagüey, October 1.

Dates of fall arrival are: Panama—Obaldia, Seytember 12. Colombia—Bonda, September 16. British Guiana—Bartica Grove, October 8.

Egg dates.—Bahama Islands: 4 records, June 17 to July 3.

Florida: 5 records, May 25 to June 28.

Isle of Pines: 1 record, April 24.

VIREO FLAVOVIRIDIS FLAVOVIRIDIS (Cassin)

YELLOW-GREEN VIREO

HABITS

CONTRIBUTED BY ALEXANDER FRANK SKUTCH

The long list of migrant birds occurring in Central America is composed almost wholly of winter residents—species that breed farther north and pass the cold months there. With very few exceptions, the birds that nest in this great isthmus are permanent residents. Few kinds indeed can be confidently classified as summer residents, breeding in Central America and passing the nonbreeding season farther south. But in the five republics north of Panama (Central America in the political rather than the geographical sense), four species appear to belong in this category. Of these, the yellow-green vireo's claim to this status rests upon the largest mass of evidence. The other three are flycatchers: the sulphur-bellied flycatcher (*Myiodynastes luteiventris*), the noble flycatcher (*Myiodynastes maculatus nobilis*), and the striped flycatcher (*Legatus albicollis*). It is noteworthy that two of these four birds extend their migrations far north of Central America. Possibly, were bird watchers not so exceedingly few in this area of marvelously varied bird life, other breeding species would be discovered to have similar migratory habits; possibly, too, more widespread observations would show that some of the four listed do not withdraw as completely as we now believe. Where there are so few students to lend confirmatory evidence, one must make general statements with extreme caution.

In Central America the yellow-green vireo is a bird of the Pacific lowlands and lower elevations of the interior. In both Costa Rica and Guatemala it is, during the nesting season, widespread and familiar on the Pacific slope and in the central highlands, up to about 5,000 feet above sea level. Thence it extends down the Caribbean slope through the cleared agricultural lands, but on this side of the isthmus is very rare below the 1,500-foot contour. During my first three years in Central America, spent largely in the Caribbean lowlands of Panama, Honduras, and Guatemala, I did not form the acquaintance of this vireo; but when I began to study the birds of the central highlands and the Pacific slope, I soon became familiar with it. This distribution suggests that, in Costa Rica at least, it was originally a species of the lighter, more open forests of the northern Pacific lowlands, and began to cross the lower passes in the central Cordillera, and invade the Atlantic slope, as heavy primeval forests were replaced by pastures and cultivated fields with scattered trees.

In its mode of life, as in appearance and voice, the yellow-green vireo is the Central American counterpart of its close relation, the red-eyed vireo of North America. It has the same bright red eye, the same deliberate, untiring song, the same habit of hunting restlessly amid the foliage where it is difficult to see, builds its nest according to the same pattern. It avoids the heavy rain forests, rarely if ever venturing into their sunless depths, and is at home in light second-growth woodland, in orchards, hedgerows, and roadside trees. Shady pastures are a favorite haunt of the bird; and the coffee plantations, with their glossy-leafed bushes standing in orderly ranks beneath the evenly spaced shade trees, offer conditions greatly to its liking. But despite the abundance of the yellow-green vireo in the dooryards and plantations of men, and the untiring persistency with which it proclaims its presence during nearly half the year, I have never been able to discover a native name for it, either in Costa Rica or Guatemala. But this lack of a name is hardly surprising in a land where the people as a whole are so indifferent to bird life that kinds so large, abundant, and strikingly beautiful as the trogons are (with the exception of the quetzal) nameless to them.

Spring.—As one would expect with a bird that comes up from the south, the yellow-green vireo appears latest in the more northern parts of its breeding range. In southwestern Tamaulipas, Mexico, Sutton and Pettingill (1942) did not encounter it before April 9. During mid-April it became steadily commoner, until, by the 20th, it was abundant. It began to sing as soon as it arrived. In Guatemala, according to Griscom (1932), it arrives "the first week in April, earliest record late March (Dearborn), but is not generally common or singing until April 15." In central Costa Rica (San José) it arrives, according to Cherrie (1890), in the middle of April. But here in the Térraba Valley of southern Costa Rica, nearer its winter home in South America, it commonly appears early in February. In 1936 I first recorded it at Rivas (3,000 feet) on February 6; the following year, on the 4th; in 1939, on the 8th. In 1942 I first saw the bird at General Viejo on February 15 but heard its voice several days earlier. No sooner have the males arrived than they begin to advertise their return by their song. Since they remain well concealed in the crowns of the full-foliage trees, one is usually first apprised of their homecoming by their voices. Rapidly increasing both in numbers and tunefulness, they are soon singing everywhere along the shady roads through the cultivated districts, the pastures with scattered trees, and the rivers overhung by the epiphyte-laden boughs of the spreading sotacaballo. Their song so greatly resembles that of the red-eyed vireo that, to one newly arrived from the north, their voices lend a homelike touch to an otherwise strange environment.

Nesting.—Just how the yellow-green vireo wins his mate has so far escaped me. At this season, when a score of birds in the surrounding forests are preparing nests never seen by ornithologists, so familiar a bird is apt to receive far less attention than it deserves. Before one is aware of it, he has paired and his mate is beginning to build. My earliest date for the beginning of nest construction is March 18, 1937, a year when rains were frequent the first three months, which here are normally dry. The first egg was laid in this nest on March 27; but my next early record for eggs is April 24 of the same year. Here in the basin of El General (the head of the Térraba Valley), between 2,000 and 3,000 feet above sea level, nests with eggs are not easily found before May, which is the height of the breeding season for this bird, as for the great majority of small passerine birds of the region. Since in normal years the rains begin at the end of March or early in April, the vegetation is by now in its fullest verdure and insect life abundant.

Like other members of her family, the yellow-green vireo chooses for her nest site a V-shaped fork between slender, nearly horizontal branchlets. The 17 nests whose approximate height I have recorded ranged from 5½ to 40 feet above ground. Of the two nests 40 feet up, one was in a shade tree of a coffee plantation near Colomba, Guatemala, and the other in a roadside tree near Alajuela, Costa Rica. Our local birds prefer low positions for their nests; 9 of my 14 records for El General are of nests less than 10 feet above ground; and the highest was 25 feet up. When nesting in bushy pastures, a favorite site is a crotch of the tuete (*Vernonia patens*), a white-flowered composite bush of no great height. But even when they choose a tall tree, the vireos frequently attach their nest to the drooping extremity of one of the lowest branches.

It was in such a position, in a fork at the end of a low bough of an aguacatillo tree (*Persea caerulea*) standing in an open pasture, that I watched a yellow-green vireo build her nest on two bright mornings of March 1937. Since the bird was shy, I sat well concealed in a blind. The nest had already been given its final shape, that of a cup attached by its rim to the supporting branchlets; but the fabric was still exceedingly thin and delicate. The female alone worked. Although she was exactly like her mate in plumage, her silence and his untiring song served well to distinguish the twain. She brought strips of partially decayed grass blades, fibers of various sorts, and cobweb. Standing upon the supporting twig at one side of the nest, she would deposit the material in its bottom. Then, frequently, she would enter the deep cup, and press herself down into it, with bill pointed upward and wings raised above her back, while she shaped it with her entire body. As she flew away again, she usually uttered her sharp little churred call. She did not work very hard; and her visits on the nest were widely spaced. On the first morning, from 7:30 to 8:30, she brought material only 10 times; yet in this hour she labored more actively than during any other of the five that I kept watch. In the next hour she came only eight times; and on the second morning she worked even more slowly.

Her mate remained much of the time among the foliage of the aguacatillo tree in which the nest was being built, singing *viree* in his usual unhurried fashion. Early in the morning, before the female had begun to build, he twice went to the nest, perched a few moments upon one of the supporting twigs at its side, and quivered his wings while he continued to drop his bright notes at measured intervals. Often he followed the female when she flew off to seek more material, and accompanied her too, on her return to the nest. At other times, when he lingered in the tree during her absence, he hurried down and alighted close beside her and soon as she returned to the nest. He also undertook to guard it from intrusion, and drove a Lawrence's elaenia (*E. chiriquensis*) from its neighborhood, then later chased away a silver-throated tanager (*Calospiza icterocephala*) that had ventured too near. But afterward, while the vireos were absent, a Mexican honeycreeper (*Coereba mexicana*), which was doubtless building a dormitory nest somewhere not far off, stole a blade of grass from their nest and flew off unmolested with his small booty.

The completed nest closely resembles that of the red-eyed vireo in form and materials. It is a thick-walled, compact structure, the outer layer composed of dry grass blades, strips of papery bark and of plant epidermis, or similar ribbonlike material, while the inner lining is of fine fibers. It is bound together and attached to the arms of the fork between which it hangs by cobweb used in liberal quantity, and frequently ornamented on the exterior with skeins of white spider web and empty silken egg cases.

Eggs.—Four days may elapse between the completion of the nest and the appearance of the first egg. The others follow on consecutive days. Three is the usual set; but about one-fifth of the nests I have found contained only two. In one case the nest was visited daily during the period of egg-laying, and only two eggs appeared, indicating that at times two constitute the set. The eggs are white, finely speckled with some shade of brown (ranging from light brown to umber and chocolate), the spots usually aggregated in a wreath or cap upon the large end, with perhaps a thin scattering over the remaining surface. The average measurements of eight eggs temporarily removed from their nests in El General are 20.5 x 14.6 mm.; those showing the four extremes measure 22.2 by 15.1, 20.2 by 15.5, 19.4 by 15.1, 19.8 by 13.9 millimeters.

Incubation.—Incubation is performed by the female alone. Commonly she sits facing the crotch in which her nest is hung—I cannot recall having seen a bird face outward from the tree as she incubated. As a rule, she sits steadfastly, allowing a close approach before she quits her eggs. Then she may rise to a higher branch and peer down at the intruder, frequently scolding with her nasal *chaaa*, while she spreads her tail and raises her crown-feathers in a questioning attitude. I have watched two nests for a number of hours continuously during the course of incubation, and since the behavior of the vireos differed materially, it may be well to discuss them separately.

One of these nests was situated about 25 feet up in a sotacaballo tree (*Pithecolobium*) growing along the Río San Antonio, at the edge of a pasture. On the morning of May 12, 1940, I watched for 3 hours, and found the sequence of the female vireo's sessions and recesses to be as follows (the recesses in italics): 39, *19*, 40, *11*, 9, *13*, 16, and *21* minutes. Sometimes while sitting she uttered a sharp, rattling call; and each time she winged away at the end of a session she delivered the same rattle. More rarely she voiced this call as she returned to resume incubation.

Her mate was most attentive. While the female sat, he sang his simple notes incessantly among the surrounding branches. From time to time he went to look into the nest. As his mate returned from a recess to resume incubation, he would hurry up to the nest and stand beside it for a moment. This action, repeated three times in as many hours, seemed an act of courtesy or formality, comparable to the custom of certain male flycatchers and tanagers of accompanying their mates to the doorways of their closed nests as they return to their eggs. Once the male vireo went to the nest while his mate was nearby but not ready to resume sitting. She hurried up to stand beside the nest, too, for a moment; then both flew off again. These visits of the male to the nest kept him informed as to the state of affairs there. As we shall see, he was not tardy in bringing food after the eggs hatched.

The other nest was placed 11 feet above ground in a small *Nectandra* tree in a weedy pasture beside the Buena Vista River. From concealment I made notes on it continuously from dawn to nearly midday (5:15 to 11:33) on the drizzly morning of June 1, 1936. This female vireo was neglected by her mate, who did not once come near the nest during the entire morning. Her sessions on the eggs were of irregular length, and varied from 15 to 61 minutes in no orderly fashion. Her recesses were generally brief and ranged from 6 to 18 minutes; but only twice were they in excess of 9 minutes. She spent a total of 256 minutes on the nest and only 85 away from it. On returning to the nest, she never flew directly to it but always alighted on the other side of the small tree and made her way to it from branch to branch. As she neared her nest she almost invariably announced her coming by the utterance of a rather sharp, nasal *chaa*. Usually she sat in silence; but once, when a male (her mate?) began to sing in a neighboring tree, she answered with a sharp, churred call. Upon leaving the nest she flew directly from its rim, almost always uttering this peculiar churred note early in her flight. Usually she flew to the sotacaballo trees along the bank of the river a hundred feet away; but when the male sang in the trees on the opposite side of the nest, she went there to join him.

During her recesses the female vireo ate many berries, principally of some parasitic loranthaceous bush; and the indigestible seeds of these she regurgitated at frequent intervals while sitting upon the nest. These came up surrounded by a colorless, extremely viscous substance, which caused them to adhere to her bill so that she could not drop them to the ground. Accordingly, to get rid of them, she was obliged to wipe them onto the branch beside the nest. She always sat in the same position, facing the crotch, and invariably attached the seeds to the branch on her left, with the result that a conspicuous mass of them had accumulated here. As she placed another seed on the mass and withdrew her head, a string of slime would frequently pull out between her bill and the seed, so viscous was the substance surrounding it. The newly attached seeds would sometimes slip down over the older ones, to remain adhering to the lower side of the lowest, thus forming short, beadlike chains. While the vireo regurgitates these mistletoe seeds, they pass entirely through the alimentary tract of euphonias, and retaining their adhesive properties as well as their viability, stick to the branches and germinate, to the great detriment of the trees.

The ever-growing mass of seeds seemed to annoy the vireo, and she devoted considerable effort to keeping it small. Frequently, while sitting, she plucked off the seeds in her bill, whence she was able to drop many of the older ones upon which the gum had dried; but others clung so stubbornly that she was constrained to attach them to the mass again in order to free herself of the incumbrance. At times she ate seeds that she had previously attached to the mass; at other times she swallowed again those which had just slipped up into her mouth. Upon leaving the nest for a recess, she almost always carried away a seed, either one newly regurgitated, or one plucked from the mass at her side. Not infrequently she made trips to the nest during her recess for the purpose of carrying away these seeds. On these visits she usually plucked a single seed from the cluster and flew off with it, but on one occasion she swallowed one seed and carried a second in her bill. During the course of a single recess, she made four visits to the nest, and carried away five seeds.

The viscous substance surrounding the mistletoe seeds appeared to be somewhat attractive to insects; and I saw the vireo while incubating eat two flylike creatures which had stuck to the cluster. Thus there was a certain advantage to the bird in this mass of gummy seeds, for it brought food directly to her mouth as she warmed her eggs.

Young.—The incubation period, as determined at two nests, is 14 days. The pink-skinned nestlings have their eyes tightly closed. At first glimpse they appear to be quite naked; but careful scrutiny in a favorable light reveals a few scattered tufts of very short, fine down on the top of the head, back, and wings. The interior of the mouth is yellow, as in the majority of insectivorous passerine birds.

As a rule the nestlings are fed by both parents. If he has been attentive during the course of incubation, the male may begin to bring food quite promptly after the eggs have hatched. This was so of the nest beside the Río San Antonio I had watched during the period of incubation on May 12. The record I made on the spot tells the story quite succinctly:

May 17, 1940, 7:25 A. M. I arrive at the vireos' nest and find the female sitting.

7:32   She leaves the nest, carrying off the cap of a shell from which the nestling has emerged. (Whether the first, second, or third, I cannot tell in this inaccessible nest.)

7:49   The male goes to look into the nest.

7:55   The female sits a few seconds, then leaves. Soon returns to brood.

8:07   She leaves as the male comes with food.

8:10   She feeds a nestling. The male comes with food which he gives to her as she stands above the nest. She passes this on to a nestling, then flies off with the large half of a shell.

8:15   She returns, feeds a nestling, broods.

8:24   The male brings an insect to his mate. She rises up to feed a nestling, then continues to brood.

8:28   She leaves as the male comes with food.

8:29   He brings food again.

8:31   The female delivers food, then departs.

8:34   The male comes singing with food in his bill.

8:36   The female brings food, then broods.

8:39   The male brings food to the female on the nest.

It was easy to distinguish the male by his tireless singing. The female uttered only the sharp rattle already described. The visits the male had been in the habit of making to the nest during the course of incubation kept him well informed of conditions there and ensured his prompt attendance upon the nestlings when they hatched. In the same sotacaballo tree where the vireos nested hung a black, retort-shaped nest of a gray-headed flycatcher (*Rhynchocyclus cinereiceps*). The male apparently never went to look into it while it contained eggs; and as a result of this negligence the nestlings were several days old before he discovered their presence and began to bring food to them.

The nestling vireos are nourished with both animal and vegetable food. Among the former is a variety of winged insects, including big, green tree crickets—which are delivered to the youngsters wings and all—and smooth caterpillars of various kinds. The vegetable food consists of various kinds of berries, and the bright red, arillate seeds of *Clusia*, a genus of thick-leafed epiphytic shrubs and trees with fragrant white or pink blossoms. These red seeds are also an important element in the diet of nestling blue honeycreepers (*Cyanerpes cyanea*). During their first days, the mother vireo keeps the naked nestlings covered most of the time.

Though as a rule the male vireo helps feed his offspring, at the nest where he was so inattentive during the course of incubation (on

June 1, 1936) he also failed to bring food. Yet the mother bird was quite capable of attending her nestlings unaided, even on the cool, darkly overcast morning of June 12, when light drizzles alternated with harder showers during most of my 3-hour watch. The two nestlings, respectively 2 and 3 days old, were kept brooded about two-thirds of the time, from 4 to 17 minutes at a stretch, and left exposed for periods ranging from 2 to 8 minutes, while the mother sought food. She was a skillful hunter and frequently returned with something substantial within 2 or 3 minutes after leaving the nest. Many of the winged insects and caterpillars she brought were so big that the tiny nestlings experienced considerable difficulty in swallowing them, and she was obliged to place them several times in the yellow mouths upstretched before her, until at length they disappeared. She kept her babies well filled; and when, at the end of my watch, they did not readily accept a large insect she brought for them, she swallowed it herself.

Four days later, when the eldest nestling was a week old, I watched this nest again, and again failed to see the male visit it, although I heard a vireo which was probably the parent singing in the trees along the river. The female still brooded most of the time—70 minutes out of 124—in periods ranging from 3 to 11 minutes.

While these nestlings attended by a single parent came safely through the most critical period in their lives, those in the sotacaballo tree beside the Río San Antonio, whose father was so attentive, met some premature end. Apparently they were attacked and killed by ants, for on the morning of May 19, looking closely through the binoculars, I could discern small ants filing in numbers along the branch to which their nest was attached. Several times the female vireo came and stood beside the nest to pluck from it, in quick succession, a great many small objects invisible to me, doubtless ants. Then she would fly off again, uttering her sharp little rattle. Once the father vireo came with an insect in his bill, singing as was his custom, and stood for a few moments above the nest, continuing to sing. At length he carried the insect off and swallowed it and went on singing as before. But during the course of an hour the nestlings were neither fed nor brooded, whence I inferred that they were dead. So much attention given to a nest with dead nestlings implies lack of insight on the part of the parents; but "what should they know of death?"

Despite the apparent security of the cobweb bindings that attach the rim of the nest to the arms of the crotch in which it hangs, it not infrequently becomes detached, on one or both sides, before the young are feathered, or even before the eggs have hatched. On several occasions, I have saved the occupants from disaster by sewing or tying up the nest. Though hummingbirds reinforce the bindings of their nests by continuing to bring fresh cobweb throughout the course of incubation, vireos apparently never take this precaution.

The nestlings are clothed with feathers by their tenth day. At the age of from 12 to 14 days, when they can still scarcely fly, they forsake their swinging cradle. They then rather closely resemble their parents in plumage, the chief difference being the absence, in the fledglings, of the darker margins of the gray crown. Their eyes are brown instead of red.

Food.—In the absence of careful analyses, such as have been made for North American birds, it is only possible to state in general terms the food of the yellow-green vireo. Probably the bulk is made up of insects, spiders, and larvae, which they hunt among the foliage and on the more slender branches, where they are constantly flitting about, pausing now and again to peer to this side and that. But they eat also many berries, such as those of the Loranthaceae, and various arillate seeds.

Behavior.—While I watched the nest attended by the female alone, a second vireo once arrived following close behind her. After delivering the food she had brought, she flew off; and then the stranger alighted upon the rim of the nest, looked in, uttered a few low notes, then hurried away in pursuit of her. Soon she returned, gave an insect to one of the nestlings, and settled in the nest to keep them warm. Then the other vireo, who had followed her to the nest, alighted on the supporting branch close beside it and turned to face her. From the color of his eyes, brighter red than those of the female, I took this bird to be a male. Although full grown, the conspicuous yellow corners of his mouth, and his imperfect plumage, revealed his immaturity. On his perch almost within reach of the nest, he swayed from side to side, voicing the while low, weak notes, and opening wide his mouth, as if begging for food. Then he began to deliver typical vireo song notes, clear but disjointed. The mother seemed to disapprove and opened her mouth threateningly toward him; but he continued his queer performance for several minutes, until she plucked a seed from the cluster beside the nest and flew away with it, with the young male in close pursuit.

Voice.—Like the red-eyed vireo, the yellow-green vireo is among the most tireless and persistent of songsters. His song so closely resembles that of his relative that without hearing the two within a shorter interval of time than is usually possible it is difficult to say how they differ. Sturgis (1928) states that the yellow-green vireo's song "differs more in tone than character from that of *V. olivacea* of the United States * * * The brief phrases of which it consists, are slighter, sharper pitched and less musical than those of its northern relative." She evidently refers, not to the Central American

V. flavoviridis flavoviridis, but to *V. flavoviridis insularis*, the breeding race of the Canal Zone.

In Costa Rica, the yellow-green vireo sings, in a clear, soft, warbling voice, *viree* . . . . . . *viree* . . . . . . *viree* . . . . . . *vireo*. The disyllable is the most common phrase, and an indefinite number may be repeated before the trisyllable is uttered. A brief but distinct interval separates the phrases. The vireo sings like a true master of the art of happy living—he has taken to heart the doctrine of *nil nimis* of the ancients. He is not, like Gray's thrush, a spendthrift of his music, and is too wise to indulge his delight in song with long-continued, passionate outbursts that drain the cup of melody to the very bottom, and oblige the exhausted songster to pass a period of silence while it slowly fills again, and he has recovered the energy and the mood to sing once more. Rather, he takes his pleasure in sweet sounds with moderation, and lets them escape two or three at a time, with pauses between, that he may continue to utter them through the bright, warm days, and need never be silent because he has indulged to excess his love of singing.

I have never, to my knowledge, heard the female sing, and believe her incapable of song. Her characteristic utterance is a sharp, drawn-out call, which I have sometimes in my notes referred to as a rattle, sometimes as a *churr*. She also voices a sharp, nasal *chaaa*. Under the stress of great excitement, both sexes utter harsh, rasping, nasal scolds.

It is perhaps worthy of note in passing that among the local birds, certain individuals of Cherrie's tanager (*Ramphocelus costaricensis*)—the most songful of our tanagers—deliver a song so similar to that of the yellow-green vireo in tone, phrasing, and long duration that I have sometimes been deceived by it. But as a rule the tanager, a bigger bird, sings in a fuller, more forceful voice than the vireo.

Field marks.—The yellow-green vireo is easily distinguished, by voice as well as appearance, from other members of the family resident in its Central American breeding range. The red eye, coupled with the light superciliary stripe, is a very good diagnostic character. But for a brief period in spring, as well as in fall, migrating red-eyed vireos mingle with the yellow-green vireos, and then greater acumen is required for correct identification. The best distinguishing marks are the heavier blackish lines bordering the slate-gray crown of the redeye, and the absence on this bird of the yellow which suffuses the sides and under tail coverts of the yellow-green vireo.

Enemies.—I know of no particular enemies of the adult yellow-green vireo. Doubtless some fall prey to hawks; but I have never witnessed this—indeed, here in El General, I scarcely see two birds captured by hawks in the course of a year. The smaller sets of eggs—

two or three instead of the three to five of the red-eyed vireo, and a
breeding season scarcely longer—indicate that the shorter migrations of this species are accomplished with fewer losses than the long
flights of its northern relative.

The nests are sometimes—probably very frequently—pillaged by
snakes. On May 22, 1940, while passing near a nest situated about 6
feet above ground on a drooping branch of a sotacaballo tree beside the Río Pacuar, I found the parents very much excited, uttering
their nasal rasping scolds with great vehemence. Examination revealed the nest empty; but with a little searching I found, in the grass
below, a small green snake with a partly feathered nestling in its
mouth, already dead. After killing the serpent, I discovered the
second nestling in the grass close by, and returned it to its nest. Had
the nestlings jumped from the nest at the snake's approach, and the
reptile then dropped upon them? As I was about to depart, I espied
a second snake, brown and much larger, in the bushes below the
same tree, on the bank of the river. It had doubtless been attracted
by the commotion and would probably have devoured the second
nestling if this had escaped the green snake—and possibly the smaller
green serpent too.

A very different sort of destroyer of the vireo's eggs and nestlings
is Swainson's toucan (*Rhamphastos swainsonii*). During the months
when most of the smaller birds are nesting, parties of these huge-billed
birds fly from the forest into the scattered trees of the pastures and
plantations, filling the breeding birds with rage and dismay. Their
arrival is heralded by the calls of alarm and distress of anxious parents;
their progress marked by the darting forms of indignant flycatchers;
and wherever they pass they leave a trail of rifled bird nests. It is
probable that the swallow-tailed kite also devours the nestlings of the
yellow-green vireo, for I have seen it pillage nests of other birds that
breed in the same trees.

Once, on a coffee plantation on the Pacific slope of Guatemala, an
Indian, misunderstanding my request that he take me to see any nests
he might find, brought me one of the yellow-green vireo, containing
three half-grown vireo nestlings, and one of the red-eyed cowbird.
All were in a flourishing condition, and but for their unfortunate
removal, the vireo nestlings might have been raised beside their foster-
brother as sometimes happens with the red-eyed vireo. Although I
returned the nest to the tree where the man said it had been found,
next morning all four nestlings were dead.

Fall.—Southern Costa Rica is probably the wettest district on the
generally dry Pacific side of the American Continent between Washington and Colombia. Here, where June is usually a period of heavy
rainfall, the yellow-green vireos cease nesting in this month. My

latest date for the departure of the nestlings is June 23. Thereafter the males rapidly become silent. Farther north, where the climate is drier, they continue to nest through July. Thus I found a nest near Alajuela, Costa Rica (at 3,500 feet elevation), with nestlings on July 7; near Colomba, on the Pacific slope of Guatemala at 3,000 feet, one with eggs on July 18, and another with nestlings on the 26th. Here the males sang much during July. I have no evidence as to a second brood, and I doubt very much that in El General the birds raise more than one in a season.

In September the yellow-green vireos depart for the south. They are now silent; and their withdrawal is an inconspicuous event, in sharp contrast to their song-proclaimed arrival in February. Were it not for the fact that the bird watcher is at this season scanning the treetops for the advent of warblers and other migrants from the north, he would hardly become aware of their departure. My latest dates for this vireo are September 27, 1935 (San Miguel de Desamparados, Costa Rica, 4,500 feet), and September 14, 1936 (El General, 3,000 feet). When my thoughts were again directed to the bird by the request to prepare this account, at the end of September 1942, I began to search for those that earlier in the year had nested in the trees in front of the house, but in vain, for all had silently departed. Griscom states that in Guatemala they have not been found after October 1.

[AUTHOR'S NOTE: Mr. Skutch has asked me to look up the references that I have to certain publications that were not available to him when he wrote the foregoing account. Some of these are rather interesting but, with one exception, there is nothing in them that will add much of sufficient importance to what he has written to warrant quoting from them here. James Lee Peters (1931) has published a comprehensive paper on the status, distribution, and habits of this species and its subspecies, to which the reader is referred for details. But the following items should be included here:

Plumages.—"Juvenile.—No specimens in fresh juvenile plumage seen, but judging from partly moulted juvenals the bird has a plumage like that of *V. olivaceus*, but the lateral underparts with a much more extensive and deeper yellowish wash.

"Immature.—Acquired by a complete post-juvenile moult involving all tracts except the primaries, secondaries, greater wing coverts and tail. In Guatemala this plumage is complete by the beginning of the third week in August.

"Adult winter.—Not distinguishable from immature plumage; acquired by a complete post-nuptial moult beginning about the middle of July and complete before the first of September.

"Nuptial.—The number of wintering specimens available is not sufficient to determine with any exactness how extensive the prenuptial moult is. I have examined specimens in the American Museum taken in western Amazonia between 2 February and 3 April which were undergoing a moult of the primaries. A prenuptial moult of the primaries is an exception among oscine birds."

Winter.—He says on this point: "That the winter home of the species is in Amazonian Colombia, Ecuador, Peru and Bolivia, is, I think well established." He gives a number of records on which this statement is based.

I might add here that I have collected from various sources the measurements of 17 eggs, in addition to those given by Mr. Skutch. These average 20.6 by 14.7 millimeters; the eggs showing the four extremes measure 21.5 by 15.0, 19.9 by 15.3, 19.0 by 14.5, and 21.3 by 14.0 millimeters.

Since the above was written, Richard F. Miller has sent me data on two nests of the yellow-green vireo observed by him in San Luis Potosí on June 20 and 21, 1942. Both nests were quite inaccessible, but the birds were seen to alight upon them. The first was in a large tree with beechlike bark and rhododendronlike leaves, on the bank of a river in a wood; it was about 45 feet up over the stream and suspended from a horizontal fork at the end of a branch about 25 feet long. The second was in an enormous deciduous tree, 5 feet thick, in a meadow containing a few widely scattered trees and near a wood; it was over 15 feet above ground on the lowest limb and suspended from a horizontal fork at its end.]

DISTRIBUTION

Breeding range.—The breeding range of the yellow-green vireo is from northern Mexico (southern Sonora, Nuevo León, and central Tamaulipas) south to eastern Guatemala and western Costa Rica. There is a single breeding record from extreme southern Texas, near Harlingen, in June 1943.

Winter range.—The winter home of this species is in the Amazonian region of Colombia, Ecuador, Peru, and Bolivia.

Casual records.—Besides having nested there once, this vireo has been found three times in Cameron County, Tex.: Fort Brown, August 23, 1877; Brownsville, June 7, 1892; and Mission, September 19, 1937. Also a specimen was collected at Godbout, Quebec, on May 13, 1883; and another near Riverside, Calif., on September 29, 1887.

Egg dates.—Costa Rica: 23 records, March 27 to June 30; 13 records, May 6 to June 3, indicating the height of the season.

Mexico: 2 records, June 20 and 21.

VIREO OLIVACEUS (Linnaeus)

RED-EYED VIREO

HABITS

CONTRIBUTED BY WINSOR MARRETT TYLER

Spring.—The trees are leafing out fast when the red-eyed vireo arrives in New England from its tropical winter home. Many of the spring migrants are already here before him, and his song may pass unnoticed at first, except by an experienced ear, among the chorus of their voices. Only a practiced eye, too, will catch sight of him where, high over our heads, he is singing—a little green bird surrounded by the green leaves of the elms and maples. When we do find him, we see that he is well out on the smaller, drooping branches, constantly moving about among the leaves, hopping along the twigs, or taking short, quick flights to other branches. He is feeding, picking up insects from the leaves all about him, singing as he goes, in short, hurried phrases that do not interrupt his continual search for food. Hour after hour, day after day, he sings from our woodlands, from the trees on the shore of our streams, and from the tall elms along the streets of our towns and villages—like a happy laborer, whistling at his work.

Courtship.—Aretas A. Saunders (1938) writes: "The males sing vigorously between nestings, and on one occasion I observed courtship and a courtship song at this time. The date was July 28, 1933, and the male sang its song in a soft whisper, audible only a short distance. During the singing his wings trembled, and he moved about in front of his intended mate, who sat silently watching and finally flew away, with him in pursuit."

Years ago, late in May 1909, I saw a bit of courtship behavior between a pair of red-eyed vireos. The birds were near at hand, in plain view, not far above my head. My attention was drawn to them by hearing some unfamiliar notes, high-pitched and rather squeaky in tone, but uttered very quietly, made up of fine little trills and some long-drawn-out, faint whistles, not suggesting a vireo at all. At the time I described their actions thus (Tyler, 1912):

The two birds were very near each other; so near that their bills might have touched, although they did not. The male, or at least the bird who played the active role, faced the side of the other bird, so that their bodies were at right angles. * * * He rocked his body, especially his head, from side to side, his bill sweeping over the upper parts of the other bird, never touching her, nor, indeed, coming very near it, for his head was above and a little to one side of her back. In swinging from side to side, he moved slowly, but with a tenseness suggesting strong emotion. In contrast to the fluffy female, the feathers of the male were drawn closely about him, so that he looked slim and sleek. The neck seemed constricted, giving him a strangled appearance.

Three years later, again in May, I caught another glimpse of vireo courtship. A male, with feathers puffed out, perched in a low shrub, was singing in characteristic phrases, but without tone quality, the notes given softly in a whispered voice. He flew toward the other bird, and they darted away together.

Nesting.—The red-eyed vireo builds a dainty little pensile nest suspended usually from a forking, horizontal branch of a shrub, or low branch of a tree, rather below the level of our eyes as we walk through second-growth. The nest is a beautifully finished piece of workmanship, constructed of fine grasses and rootlets, bits of birch bark, and paper from wasps' nests, bound together and to the supporting branches with spider's or caterpillar's webbing, and, perhaps the most constant material, long, narrow, flexible strands of grapevine bark, which help to hold up the cup of the nest. It may be ornamented on the outside with bits of lichen. Dr. Arthur A. Allen (1932) says that it has thinner walls usually than other vireo's nests.

F. N. Whitman (1924) found a nest only 2 feet from the ground, and Charles R. Stockard (1905) speaks of one "situated sixty feet from the ground in the topmost boughs of a gum tree." Five to ten feet elevation is the usual height.

Minna Anthony Common (1934) gives this interesting account of the building of a nest:

July 6, 1933; Found: two pieces of tangled ravellings hanging from fork on a beech branch four feet from the ground. It appears like the starting of a nest. * * *

July 8: We have decided it is a nest, for there are a few more ravellings hanging down a foot or so.

July 9, 1933: Late afternoon: We saw both Red-eyed Vireos (*Vireo olivaceus*) working at the nest. The bunches of untidy ravelling hang lower, but there is no bottom to the nest. Birds are absolutely silent.

July 10: Some loose network may be seen forming a bottom to the nest. Several bits of birch bark have been skillfully intertwined on the outside. Both birds work. The ravellings are mostly caught up.

July 11, 6 a. m.: Saw one bird pull a small, short strand of bark from a dead oak twig. He carried it to the nest and was back for another in four minutes. * * * At the end of the day the nest appeared finished. All loose ravellings had been caught up and fastened. A piece of paper ¾ by 1½ inches in size is spread across the floor of the nest inside.

Francis Hobart Herrick (1935) describes in detail the construction of a red-eyed vireo's nest which he watched from a distance of 10 feet. The following is a condensed account of his report:

With a vireo or an oriole and all such as build similarly suspended nests, the work of construction must needs begin with securing the first fibers to two or more twigs destined to support the future nest. Upon these primary strands is built up a loose, free-hanging fibrous mass, the *primary nest mass*, and this is gradually extended downward while, *pari passu*, the attachment is carried outward along each of the divergent twigs. A rim and bottom are gradually produced in a way to be presently described, and the gap or open side, opposite the first-formed hanging mass, long remains open; with the vireo, as with the oriole, it is filled in last. * * *

The most striking actions of this vireo that I noticed on the first day were as follows: (1) winding silk and fine threads of bast over the forks of the twig at about an inch from their junction; (2) building downward from this support a loose mass of fibers—corresponding to the primary nest mass of the oriole's work—perfectly secured but giving no hint of the beautiful cup-shaped structure that was to appear; (3) carrying the suspension forward and downward until one could recognize part of the concave wall of the future nest, or hardly more than the half of a vertically divided cup; (4) finally, attempting to rest in the imperfect nest and use the breast for molding long before it was physically possible to make such movements effective. * * *

At four o'clock on the second day the frame of this nest was evidently completed. It was composed almost wholly of fine bast, bark strippings, and spider's silk, the latter having been derived from the egg-cocoons of such species as nest on the under side of leaves or against the clapboards of houses. * * *

In reality the work of construction lasted nearly five days, but from the close of the third day until the end of the fifth, active labor gradually slowed down; the hen would sit in her nest-cup for longer and longer intervals, until June 4, or the sixth day from the start, when she remained to lay her first egg, which was deposited after 7:30 o'clock in the morning.

W. J. Erichsen (1919) says of nest building: "A peculiarity of this species which I have noted both in Liberty county [Georgia] and elsewhere is a habit the birds have of destroying partially completed nests built by them. I once watched a pair remove piece by piece the material from a nearly completed nest, and weave it into another which they had begun a few yards distant."

Ora Willis Knight (1908) gives the measurements of a nest as "two and a half inches deep outside by one and a half inside, the external diameter was three and the diameter inside two inches."

Eggs.—[AUTHOR'S NOTE: Four eggs generally make up the set for the red-eyed vireo, but sometimes only three are laid and very rarely five may be found. These are mostly ovate, rarely slightly elongated. They are pure lusterless white, and are usually sparingly marked, chiefly toward the larger end, with fine dots of small spots of reddish brown, or darker browns, or blackish; rarely an egg is nearly or quite immaculate; an occasional set may contain eggs that show large spots or small blotches of light browns, but such cases are rare. The measurements of 50 eggs in the United States National Museum average 20.3 by 14.5 millimeters; the eggs showing the four extremes measure 22.9 by 15.8, 21.8 by 16.3, and 18.3 by 13.2 millimeters.]

Young.—Ora W. Knight (1908) gives the incubation period as 12 to 14 days. M. G. Vaiden, of Rosedale, Miss., writing to Mr. Bent of nests he had studied carefully, found that the eggs hatched in 11 days. He began his count the day after the last egg was laid: in one case it took an extra day.

Samuel A. Harper (MS.) noticed so much irregularity in the incubation of the female in three nests under his observation that none of the eggs hatched.

Aretas A. Saunders (1938) states that "both sexes share in incubation and feeding young" and Forbush (1929) says: "Occasionally a pair may raise two broods in a season."

Francis H. Herrick (1904) remarks: "When the young Vireos were a week old I began to watch their nesting habits at night more closely, and found that, while the male apparently roosted near by, the female invariably slept on the nest. At from fifteen to twenty minutes after sundown she was regularly at her post, and even at this hour usually fast asleep. So profound, indeed, were her slumbers, that I could often enclose her in my hand and stroke her feathers without awaking her. She slept with her head twisted back and buried deep in the feathers between the shoulders. An apparently headless trunk or a little ball of feathers was all that could be seen, and the only motion discernible came from the regular pulsations of breathing." William Brewster (1936) recounts a somewhat similar experience.

T. C. Stephens (1917), from a close study of a nest, found that "75% of the work of feeding was done by the female, while the male did about 25%."

Francis H. Herrick (1904) reports that "the eyes began to open on the fourth day, when the first faint cheeps of the young were audible at a distance of a few feet," and, according to Burns (1921), the young birds leave the next 12 days after hatching.

Young redeyes are very importunate; even when they have reached full size they fly to their parents, begging for food, using a rather long, sustained note that sounds like *theet* and is strangely like the food call of the black-capped chickadee.

My notes, taken in the White Mountains, N. H., some years ago, state: "I was surprised to find parents still feeding their young. On September 8th, one or two young birds (fully grown, of course) followed an adult about, insisting on being fed. The old bird had a green worm in its bill, and one of the young birds, darting toward it, snatched it away from the parent, who tried to escape it seemed. Apparently the family ties were holding by a thread, and the old bird was doing its best to sever them."

Forbush (1929) reports a case of a bird feeding young, on September 15, barely able to fly.

Plumages.—[AUTHOR'S NOTE: Dr. Dwight (1900) calls the natal down of the red-eyed vireo "pale drab-gray" and describes the juvenal plumage as "above, including lesser wing coverts, drab. Wings and tail olive-brown, edged with bright olive-green, brightest on the secondaries and tertiaries. Below, silky white, faintly tinged on the sides and crissum with primrose-yellow. Superciliary stripe dull white; lores and postocular streak dusky. Iris walnut-brown."

The first winter plumage is acquired by a partial postjuvenal molt in August and September "which involves the body plumage, the wing coverts (often the tertiaries) but not the rest of the wings nor the tail. * * * In plumage young and old are practically indistinguishable in the autumn, but the iris of young birds is brown while they remain with us. * * * The iris becomes dull red before the birds return in the spring."

The nuptial plumage is apparently acquired by wear, with very little fading apparent. A complete postnuptial molt for birds of all ages occurs in August and September.]

Food.—Waldo L. McAtee (1926) speaks well of the redeye as a destroyer of harmful insects, saying:

About six-sevenths of the total food of the Red-eye is composed of animal matter, almost exclusively insects, and one-seventh is vegetable. The latter is made up almost entirely of wild fruits which are eaten chiefly in the months from August to October. The favorite kinds are blackberries, elderberries, and fruits of spicebush, dogwood, Virginia creeper, and sassafras.

A third of the total food of this vireo is composed of caterpillars and moths, mainly the former. Tent caterpillars, a beech caterpillar (*Fentonia marthesia*), the hackberry caterpillar (*Chorippe celtis*), and various oak caterpillars (*Acronycta afflicta, Apatela, Notodonta,* and *Anisota*) are among the injurious forms devoured. Mr. Forbush reports the Red-eye to be one of the most effective enemies of the gipsy and browntail moths ('07, p. 205), and Dr. Tothill credits the species with destroying in various years, from 11.4 to 89.5 per cent of the broods of fall webworms in Nova Scotia ('22, pp. 5–26).

Beetles, hymenoptera, bugs, and flies rank next to lepidoptera in importance as food items of the Red-eye. The beetles include a considerable number of forms injurious to trees.

Then follows a list of 43 species. He continues:

Other insects, more or less prejudicial to the welfare of the forest which the Red-eyed Vireo includes in its bill-of-fare are the walking-sticks, cicadas, spittle insects, tree hoppers, leaf hoppers, scale insects, sawflies, and carpenter and other ants.

While we are reciting the good record of this bird we may as well add the names of a few agricultural pests: the striped and spotted cucumber beetles (*Diabrotica vittata,* and *D. 12-punctata*), the click beetles (adults of wireworms), the clover-root weevil (*Sitona hispidula*), the clover leaf weevil (*Hypera punctata*), and the plum curculio (*Conotrachelus nenuphar*).

The only harm done by the Red-eye is the destruction of certain useful parasitic and predatory insects, but in view of the splendid record of the bird in feeding on injurious forms, this may well be overlooked. We may be sure that in its industrious scanning of our woodland trees, the Red-eyed Vireo is ever on the alert to snap up the insects infesting them, by far the most of which are not there for the good of the trees.

To this long list T. C. Stephens (1917) adds other items. He says:

One of the most interesting facts obtained in the study of these Vireos was that land snails formed a considerable portion of the nestling diet. In the food table (Table II) it is shown that the snails stand fifth in numerical abundance. * * *

Some of the snails were specifically identified. Thus twelve snails were recognized as *Succinea avara*, and all of them delivered by the female. At visit No. 210 the male carried one specimen of *Bifidaria armifera*. * * *

At visit No. 264 the female bird brought a spider to the nest which was of a species that I had noticed frequently in the beaks of the parent birds, as well as often in the woods. I was able to take this specimen from the beak of the parent bird and preserve it for later identification. In due time this specimen was identified by Mr. J. H. Emerton as *Epeira trivittata* Keyserling. This is a very common round web spider, whose web is stretched between the branches of the trees at all heights up to fifteen or twenty feet, and would thus be readily found by the foliage gleaning Vireos.

Arthur T. Wayne (1906) makes an interesting observation on the food of the redeye in the Southern States in autumn. He writes:

The controlling influence upon the migration of this bird in the autumn is the presence or absence of the seeds (fruit) of the magnolia (*Magnolia grandiflora*). The fruit of this beautiful tree begins to ripen during the first week of September, but the greater part ripens through October, and many seeds remain in the cones until November. The color is coral-red, and some specimens are about three-fourths of an inch in length, but the great majority average about half an inch. These seeds contain a large amount of oil, and when this vireo has been feeding upon them for any length of time it becomes very obese. There are many beautiful trees on this plantation, and I have often sat on the steps of the old Colonial house and watched these birds while feeding upon the fruit. The tree that has the most fruit attracts nearly all the vireos in a radius of perhaps a quarter of a mile, and I have often counted as many as fifty vireos in one tree. As long as the fruit is to be had, the vireos remain, but as soon as the supply becomes scarce or exhausted, the vireos depart.

Paul Wanamaker, Dean Forest, and Charles L. Bull (1931) report on the food which they fed to an injured young vireo. They say: "In five minutes he was taking blue-bottle flies from our finger-tips, having refused our earlier attempts to feed him bits of earth-worms. A daddy-long-legs was snapped up with great gusto, as were moths, a dragon-fly, a small inch-worm, etc. * * * His entire menu for the first day consisted of: 40 blue-bottle flies; 30 elderberries; 25 grasshoppers; a tentful of tent caterpillars, of which he ate at least 15; 5 moths; 2 daddy-long-legs; 1 dragon-fly; 1 young locust; 1 inch-worm; 1 spider; 1 bee; 1 butterfly—a total of 123 distinct items."

Behavior.—Dayton Stoner (1932) writes thus of the favorite habitat of the red-eyed vireo: "Woodland with an undergrowth of slender saplings from six to ten feet high seems to appeal to this bird most."

Such a situation affords the vireo with a nesting site not far above ground in the low shrubs and a source of food in the high canopy of the overhanging branches. These requirements, however, are often closely approximated in settled communities, so that the redeye, although a forest-loving bird, nevertheless finds congenial surroundings for summer residence in the orchards, gardens, and tree-bordered streets of the built-up sections of the country. It sometimes spends the summer months even in the parks of our large cities with blocks of houses on all sides, such as, rarely, the Public Gardens in Boston, Mass.; but in the main the red-eyed vireo is a woodland bird.

Perley M. Silloway (1923) describes thus the vireo's habitat in the western Adirondack forest: "The Red-eyed Vireo abounds in almost all aspects of the forest except dense bog woods. It lives in clearings where small trees have obtained a standing, in the borders of the Burn, and in open woodlands of every kind. It is one of the birds whose preferences for timber lead them into the virgin forest, but there they require a 'margin' of some sort, usually a brook or a bog, which breaks the forest canopy in some degree. Though it nests most commonly in sapling growth it hunts and sings in the trees, preferably such as form spreading tops at medium height, but it has little to do with evergreens."

A. A. Saunders (1942), writing of the bird in the woodlands of New York State, reports that it is "common in Oak-Hickory, Maple-Beech, Cherry-Aspen, and river valley forests. In the higher Maple-Beech, where hemlock is missing and few birds occur, it is still a common bird. It is also common in mature forests." Saunders also states (1938):

Red-eyed vireos live so much of the time in the trees, hidden among thick foliage, that they are not frequently observed. If it were not for the song, their presence, in spite of their numbers, would be difficult to detect. * * * I have distinguished individuals mainly by the location of their singing trees. This is fairly definite, a particular bird being found in the same tree day after day. Occasionally it leaves the tree and sings elsewhere, but it does not wander from place to place as the blue-head does.

This would seem to be evidence that the red-eyed vireo has definite territory, but I have never observed fighting or jealousy over such territory.

Francis Zirrer, of Hayward, Wis., writes to Mr. Bent of a case of belligerency in the redeye. He says: "During the nesting season some are quite pugnacious. They will attack almost any bird that ventures too close to a nesting tree. The little bird will drop like a stone almost at the head of the culprit. During the nesting season of the pileated woodpecker, when the big birds flew low and silently, like phantoms between the tree trunks and decaying stumps, I have seen this vireo strike the big bird with such force that it nearly lost its balance, looked and acted surprised—and flew away."

The red-eyed vireo is not commonly so tame while on the nest as the solitary, but Ernest Harold Baynes (1922) tells the following astonishing story of his "friendship" with a female redeye:

I knew that vireos have a reputation of being willing to meet one half way in the matter of making friends, so I decided to make an advance. First I went to a dry and sandy spot where I turned over large stones until I found some ants' eggs. Then I selected a dead weed stalk about five feet long and impaled an ant's egg on the sharp end of it. With this I very quietly approached the nest and held out my offering at arm's length, until the white morsel was within reach of the vireo. At first she looked alarmed, then astonished, and a moment later rather bored, for she turned her head away and refused to look at the proffered food. But I waited patiently, holding the tip of the weed stalk within easy reach. At last she turned her head as if the temptation to do so could no longer be resisted. She now showed keen interest in the proceedings, took a sharp look at the white delicacy at the end of the stalk and then as much as to say, "Hello; that *is* an ant's egg, isn't it?" stretched out her neck and took it. * * *

A moment later she confirmed her own opinion by taking another ant's egg in the same way, after which I quietly withdrew, leaving her to digest both her food and her strange experience.

Next day I returned and after she had promptly accepted a few more ants' eggs from the end of the week-stalk, I stepped up a little closer and offered one between my thumb and forefinger. After a little hesitation she took it, and from that moment we were on friendship's footing. She seemed much interested, if not actually pleased, whenever I approached; she would sometimes stretch far out over the rim of the nest in order to make quick connections with the food I brought her, and did not mind in the least if I stroked her on the head or back with my finger. At first she was a little nervous when I stroked her throat, and when I persisted she slipped off the nest. But as she got used to me she minded less and less and would even allow me to lift her off her eggs and put her gently back. * * *

Many people were introduced * * * and children especially experienced ecstatic joy at the privilege of feeding and stroking a wild bird in her own home.

Several times in the course of the past 30 years or so, I have seen a red-eyed vireo acting in a very odd manner. It has occurred when an adult is feeding a full-grown young. The old bird suddenly departs, for a moment, from its normal behavior; it draws its feathers tight to its body and sways slowly from side to side through a wide arc, certainly as great as 90°. If the two birds are facing each other, as they usually are, the bill of the adult points successively far to each side of the young bird, over and over. The old bird gives the impression of being in a sort of trance, or as if it were trying to influence the other bird in some strange way, although the action probably has a more prosaic explanation. Behavior of a similar nature is described under "Courtship." I have never seen any other species of vireo act in this manner.

Arthur B. Williams (1940) describes a very unusual observation:

On July 16, 1934, the writer, while engaged in making a survey of the bird population of a tract of beech and sugar-maple forest near Cleveland, Ohio, noticed a Red-eyed Vireo (*Vireo olivaceus*) plunging into a shallow pool of water at the edge of a woodland brook. This unusual behavior was repeated several times. The bird would work down a small branch overhanging the pool until it was about eight inches above the water. Here attention was fixed at a certain spot in the water below, and shortly the bird would dive in head first as a kingfisher does. It would then fly to a perch in a tree about twenty-five feet away and eat something apparently captured from the water. Once the bird was nearly submerged and had to stop to shake the water off its plumage before eating the morsel.

Voice.—The red-eyed vireo is preeminently famous as a singer. No other of our birds sings so persistently all day long, and because his long-continued series of utterances, given in short, emphatic phrases, going on for hours, calls to mind a lengthy sermon, he has won the title "Preacher." Of this epithet Bradford Torrey (1889), with sly humor, expresses this opinion: "The red-eye's eloquence was never very persuasive to my ear. Its short sentences, its tiresome upward inflections, its everlasting repetitiousness, and its sharp, querulous tone long since became to me an old story; and I have always thought that whoever dubbed this vireo the 'preacher' could have had no very exalted opinion of the clergy."

Nevertheless the preacher sings a cheerful song, and when we study it we find it has its good points as well as its shortcomings. It is tiresome chiefly because most of the phrases end with a rising inflection, giving the impression of a long series of interrogations, the voice seldom coming to rest as before a period. Wilson Flagg (1890) brings out this point very well when he says: "We might suppose him to be repeating moderately, with a pause between each sentence, 'You see it,—you know it,—do you hear me?—do you believe it?' All these strains are delivered with a rising inflection at the close, and with a pause, as if waiting for an answer."

Some characteristic phrases, which I have jotted down while listening to a singing bird, may be written, *cherry-o-wit*, *cheree*, *sissy-a-wit*, *tee-oo*, and many others. At times during the day, and invariably at early dawn, when the bird is not feeding, it sings with almost perfect regularity, the phrases following each other at a rate of from 60 to 80 per minute, and rarely a bird will sing for a considerable period with little variation in his phrases.

There is commonly much variety in the song. A. A. Saunders (MS.) says that the number of different phrases used by an individual bird may be as many as 40, although about 25 is a more usual repertoire. "The pitch of the song," he says, "varies from D ′ ′ ′ ′ to E flat ′ ′ ′, half a tone less than an octave. The quality is clear, but rather colorless, as compared to the other species of vireos. The phrases are composed of two to five notes each, five-note phrases being rather rare. The notes of the phrases are generally joined abruptly and only rarely slurred together. This gives the song a choppy effect, and with the colorless quality gives the effect of talking rather than singing— talking in short, quick, exclamatory or interrogatory sentences."

Several observers have noticed that the bird occasionally introduces a phrase resembling a note of the crested flycatcher, and Francis H. Allen (MS.) says: "I have heard it imitate the olive-sided flycatcher and the bluebird."

William Brewster (1938), writing of birds at Lake Umbagog, Maine, says: "The males sing regularly until late August, and on September 26, 1899, one sang feebly and brokenly," and A. C. Bent says in his notes that he heard a bird singing daily from August 31 to September 14, 1900, in Massachusetts.

Albert R. Brand (1938) gives the approximate mean vibration frequency of the song as 3,600, rather higher than that of the white-eyed and yellow-throated vireos.

The common complaint note may be written *queee*, a discontented, petulant call, inflected downward, about as long as the catbird's snarl.

Field marks.—If an observer is near enough to a redeye to see the vireo bill, the gray crown, bordered by black lines, the black line through the eye, the white underparts, and the unmarked wing, it is an easy bird to identify. The red iris, seen only at very short range, is not a reliable field mark.

The red-eyed vireo in plumage is remarkably like a Tennessee warbler, but the needlelike bill of the warbler and its paler side of the head distinguish the two birds.

Enemies.—In addition to the the danger of capture by small hawks, the red-eyed vireo is subject to attack by the red squirrel, and the chipmunk, as the two following quotations show, respectively. William Brewster (1936) relates this observation made at Concord, Mass., on June 10, 1906:

Again this afternoon Gilbert heard the Vireos crying anxiously. Looking out through the screen door, he saw the Squirrel on the branch within a few inches of the nest, eating something. Presently he dropped a portion of the shell of one of the Vireo's eggs. He then wiped his face with his fore-paws and wiped the latter on the branch. The next minutes he bent forward until his head and fore shoulders disappeared in the nest and almost immediately reappeared on the branch with another egg in his mouth. The Vireos assailed him frantically and one of them struck him with her bill when he was in the nest. Probably because of their attacks, he almost immediately took the second egg off with him, running up the main trunk of the tree until lost to sight in the foliage of its crown.

A. A. Wood (1920) records a similar experience, saying: "Last spring (June 8, 1918) I noticed a Red-eye excited over something, then saw a chipmunk climbing the sapling the bird was in. When he was about eight feet up, the vireo darted down knocking him to the ground. The other bird was on the nest at the end of one of the branches."

In reference to the cowbird's relation to the red-eyed vireo, Herbert Friedmann (1929) says: "This bird is so frequently imposed upon that it is difficult to think of the Cowbird getting along without the pensile, cup-like nests of the Red-eye. No species suffers more and few as much. * * * Occasionally this Vireo covers over, or buries (under a new nest floor), the parasitic eggs as does the Yellow Warbler, but on the other hand it has been known to incubate Cowbirds' eggs even when none of its own were present, and almost always seems not to mind the strange eggs in the least. Three and four of the parasitic eggs are sometimes found in a single nest."

Harold S. Peters (1936) reports the finding of two species of lice and three species of mites in the plumage of this vireo.

Fall.—After its long period of song is over the red-eyed vireo becomes comparatively inconspicuous. In the autumn migration it is not a prominent bird. We meet an individual or two, associated with many of the flocks of warblers as they pass through in September, but perhaps more often we come upon a single bird low down in shrubbery where it is feeding on berries, notably those of the wild and cultivated cornels. Here, in marked contrast to its behavior earlier in the season, it moves about slowly, generally in complete silence, although it may sometimes give a peevish snarl.

It seems strange to see a redeye in this subdued mood, for all through the summer we have associated the bird with constant activity, quickness, and an almost endless stream of loud, exuberant music. Even at this late date, however, the bird is on the watch for insects and continues to examine in its characteristic, careful manner the twigs and what leaves remain on the branches, twisting its neck to peer under the leaves with a sidelong glance.

When it flies it progresses with an easy grace, more rapidly than the warblers and chickadees which are flitting through the treetops at this season, and it surpasses its companions in its precise coordination of movement.

Taverner and Swales (1908), in their study of the fall migration at Point Pelee, report that red-eyed vireos are regular migrants from late in August to late in September, some remaining "well into October," but not many birds are seen on a single day, except on rare occasions.

Alexander F. Skutch writes to Mr. Bent of the migration through Central America thus:

"The red-eye vireo is known in Central America only as a transient, journeying between its winter home in South America and its breeding range in North America. Its migration route, north of the Isthmus of Panama, appears to center in the highlands—where, however, it is seldom recorded as high as 6,000 feet—but extends down the Caribbean slope to sea level and on the Pacific slope to at least 1,500 feet. September is the month when these vireos pass southward in greatest numbers; but stragglers have been recorded in Costa Rica as late as October 28 (Carriker) and November 10 (Skutch). The northward passage begins late in March and is at its height in April, while an occasional straggler may be seen early in May. As they pass through Central America the red-eyed vireos are met singly or in small flocks. I have not heard them sing while migrating."

DISTRIBUTION

Range.—From southern Mackenzie to southern Brazil and Peru.

Breeding range.—The red-eyed vireo breeds **north** to central northern British Columbia (Fort Halkett); southern Mackenzie (mouth of Nahanni River, 8 miles below Fort Wrigley, and probably Blackwater River); central eastern Saskatchewan (south end of Reindeer Lake and Pelican Narrows); north-central Manitoba (Norway House and Oxford House); central Ontario (Lac Seul, Kapuskasing, Lake Abitibi, and probably nearly to the south end of James Bay); southern Quebec (upper St. Maurice River, Quebec, Tadousac, St. Louis and the Forillon Peninsula, Gaspé County, and Anticosti Island); and possibly Newfoundland (St. Anthony and Cape Anguille). **East** to Newfoundland (Cape Anguille); the Maritime Provinces of Canada and the Atlantic Coast States south to central Florida (Kissimmee and Tarpon Springs). **South** to central Florida (Tarpon Springs); and the Gulf States to northeastern Coahuila (Sabinas); southern and central Texas (Houston, Kerrville, Fort Worth, and Decatur); west-central Oklahoma (Cheyenne); central Kansas (Harper and St. John); southern South Dakota (White River and Rapid City); possibly northwestern Wyoming (Newcastle); central and southwestern Montana (Great Falls, Anaconda, and Missoula); northern Idaho (Coeur d'Alene); and northern Oregon (Imnaha, Union, possibly Oakridge, and Portland). Also breeding rarely in Colorado (probaby Clear Creek Valley and possibly Estes Park); and found in summer in northeastern Utah (near Jensen). **West** to western Oregon (Portland); western Washington (Seattle and Bellingham); and western British Columbia (Alberni and Beaver Creek, Vancouver Island, Hagensborg, Hazelton, and Fort Halkett).

That the species is extending its range is evidenced by the fact that previous to 1923 there was only a single record for Oregon, but it has nested in that State since 1924. The first record for Utah was made in 1937 and one was seen in Newfoundland in 1940 where the first specimen was taken in 1946.

Winter range.—The winter home of the red-eyed vireo is in northern South America, **east** at least to Ituribisi River, British Guiana; and the Rio Tapajóz in Brazil. **South** to Matto Grosso, Brazil (Chapada), and possibly Bolivia and southern Peru (Sierra de Carabaya). **West** to central Peru (Sierra de Carabaya and Moyobamba); and the interior valleys of Colombia (Santa Elena and the Santa Marta region).

Migration.—Late dates of spring departure are Ecuador—Río Suno, March 15. Colombia—Don Diego, May 3. Panama—Perme, April 17. Costa Rica—Basin of El General, April 21. Guatemala—Chuntuque, April 26. British Honduras—Mountain Cow, April 17.

Yucatán—Chichen Itzá, April 3. Cuba—Habana, May 17. Bahamas—Cay Lobos, May 2.

Early dates of spring arrival are: El Salvador—San Salvador, April 1. British Honduras—Cayo District, March 23. Cuba—Santiago de las Vegas, April 9. Bahamas—Nassau, March 15. Florida—Pensacola, March 18. Alabama—Greensboro, March 27. Georgia—Savannah, March 17. North Carolina—Statesville, April 5. Virginia—Variety Mills, April 6. West Virginia—French Creek, April 7. District of Columbia—Washington, April 21. Pennsylvania—Pittsburgh, April 26. New York—Buffalo, April 28. Massachusetts—Springfield, April 30. Vermont—St. Johnsbury, May 5. Maine—Waterville, May 7. Quebec—Quebec, May 13. New Brunswick—Scotch Lake, May 2. Nova Scotia—Sidney, May 18. Prince Edward Island—North River, May 18. Louisiana—Thibodaux, March 12. Mississippi—Biloxi, March 24. Arkansas—Monticello, March 24. Tennessee—Nashville, March 30. Kentucky—Bowling Green, April 8. Indiana—Richmond, April 18. Ohio—Oberlin, April 27. Michigan—Kalamazoo, April 25. Ontario—Guelph, May 3. Missouri—St. Louis, April 22. Iowa—Cedar Rapids, April 20. Minnesota—Lanesboro, May 7. Manitoba—Killarney, May 15. Texas—Kerrville, March 30. Kansas—Manhattan, April 20. South Dakota—Rapid City, May 7. North Dakota—Fargo, April 20. Saskatchewan—Regina, May 15. Wyoming—Laramie, May 23. Montana—Bozeman, May 19. Alberta—Camrose, May 14. Mackenzie—Fort Providence, May 15. Idaho—Rupert, May 17. Washington—College Place, May 8. British Columbia—Edgewood, May 12.

Late dates of fall departure are: British Columbia—Okanagan Landing, September 7. Washington—Everson, September 11. Idaho—Bayview, September 16. Mackenzie—Simpson, August 19. Alberta—Glenevis, September 19. Montana—Fortine, September 13. Wyoming—Laramie, September 15. Saskatchewan—Yorkton, September 18. North Dakota—Argusville, September 22. South Dakota—Sioux Falls, September 24. Manitoba—Aweme, September 25. Minnesota—St. Paul, October 1. Iowa—Keokuk, October 1. Missouri—St. Louis, October 10. Arkansas—Helena, October 5. Texas—Cove, October 19. Wisconsin—Superior, October 1. Illinois—Lake Forest, October 6. Michigan—Detroit, October 12. Ontario—Ottawa, October 18. Ohio—Columbus, October 13. Tennessee—Athens, October 5. Mississippi—Bay St. Louis, October 15; Saucier, November 17. Louisiana—New Orleans, October 16. Prince Edward Island—North River, September 17. New Brunswick—St. John, September 24. Nova Scotia—Wolfville, September 21. Quebec—Montreal, September 19. Maine—Bath, September 30. New Hampshire—Dublin, September 29. Massachusetts—Boston, October 19. New York—Rhinebeck, October 20. Pennsylvania—Berwyn, October 26.

District of Columbia—Washington, November 11. West Virginia—
Bluefield, October 8. Virginia—Sweet Briar, October 11. South
Carolina—Clemson College, October 11. Georgia—Athens, October
26. Florida—Fort Myers, November 13. Bahamas—Watling Island, October 5. Cuba—Habana, October 30.

Early dates of fall arrival are: Bahamas—Inagua, September 17.
Cuba—Habana, August 28. Tamaulipas—Matamoros, August 21.
Honduras—Laucetilla, September 1. Guatemala—Pahajachel, Au-
gust 26. Nicaragua—Escondido River, September 10. Costa Rica—
Carrillo, August 31. Panama—Tapia, August 29. Colombia—Bu-
ritaca, September 18.

Only two recovery records for banded red-eyed vireos are available.
One banded at Lansing, Mich., on July 26, 1931, was found dead on
July 30, 1931, about 125 miles away at Harbor Beach, Mich. Another banded at Norristown, Pa., on August 26, 1932, was found dead
on June 7, 1938, about 1½ miles from the place of banding.

Casual records.—A specimen from Greenland was received in Copenhagen in 1844. There are two specimen records from California:
San Diego, October 6, 1914, and Los Angeles, October 10, 1931; and
two from Arizona: Huachuca Mountains, May 20, 1895, and Coyote
Range, September 3, 1934.

Egg dates.—Massachusetts: 54 records, May 25 to July 20; 39 records, June 1 to 15, indicating the height of the season.

Minnesota: 12 records, June 3 to July 2; 9 records, June 3 to 11.

New York: 65 records, May 10 to June 30; 40 records, June 1 to
June 11.

Nova Scotia: 6 records, June 18 to August 16; 3 records, June 26 to
July 5.

Virginia: 6 records, May 17 to June 24; 3 records, May 28 to June 5.

VIREO PHILADELPHICUS (Cassin)

PHILADELPHIA VIREO

HABITS

This vireo was described and named by John Cassin (1851) from
a specimen collected in September 1842 in some woods near Philadelphia. For a number of years thereafter very little was known about
it, though Thure Kumlien wrote to Dr. Brewer (Baird, Brewer, and
Ridgway, 1874) that he had been familiar with the bird in Dane
County, Wis., since 1849, and had "collected it every year since that
period, finding it both in the spring and fall."

William Brewster (1880) was the first to give us any considerable
account of the distribution and habits of the Philadelphia vireo, with
special reference to its occurrence in New England, as observed by him

and others, between 1863 and 1876, including his own introduction to the species at Lake Umbagog in 1872. He says of its haunts there:

Although in the breeding season the species * * * seems to be generally distributed throughout the wooded region about Umbagog, it occurs less commonly in the heavily timbered portions. As upon its first arrival, it chiefly affects the younger growths which have sprung up in the clearings and over old burnt lands. Its favorite haunts are the coppices of wild-cherry and gray birches by roadsides; rocky knolls tufted with black and yellow birches; the various small trees and tall shrubs that fringe the wood-edges; and deserted farms, where cool groves of vigorous young paper-birches and glaucous-foliaged poplars are grouped over the neglected acres, with intervals of sunny openings between. But wherever found, like most of the members of the *Vireosylvia* group, it makes its home in the tops and upper branches of the trees, rather than in the thickets beneath.

Then, 17 years later, came Dr. Jonathan Dwight's (1897) full and interesting account of the Philadelphia vireo, as he had observed it near Tadousac, Quebec, on the Saguenay River. He was struck with the close resemblance between the red-eyed vireo and the Philadelphia, saying: "Both frequent the same localities in the wilderness, but the Philadelphias rather shun civilization and rarely appear, like the Red-eyes, in the village trees. Both prefer to sing in the upper branches, but I have seldom found the Philadelphias in the rambling groves of birches which are the especial delight of the Red-eyes, and they are more partial to the low, bushy, second growth or copses of alders sprinkled with stray trees."

The Philadelphia vireo is now known to breed in the Canadian Zone in southern Canada, from Alberta to New Brunswick, and in the Northern States, from North Dakota to Maine, in all suitable wilderness localities. L. M. Terrill writes to me: "The Philadelphia vireo is common and well distributed in suitable localities wherever I have been in Gaspé, especially in the extensive alder growths in bottomlands and along streams. I also found it among dense patches of mountain maple (*Acer spicatum*) and alders well up on mountain slopes, but it was not as common here as along streams."

Spring.—From its winter home in Central America this vireo migrates northward in spring over most of the United States, at least from the Mississippi Valley eastward. It does not seem to be abundant anywhere, and generally not even common. It is, however, easily overlooked, as it sings very little on migration and often frequents the tree tops, where it moves about in a very leisurely manner and where its colors blend well with the fresh foliage; for these reasons, it may be commoner than is generally supposed. It passes through the States in May, coming along with waves of the later migrating warblers. It is generally seen at this season in the small trees, thickets, and shrubbery bordering streams or marshes, but sometimes in the tree tops of the more open woodlands or in scattered trees.

Among the many attractive bits of nature writing from the pen of that gifted writer, Mr. Brewster's (1880) account of this vireo at Umbagog Lake, Maine, is one of his best:

The Philadelphia Vireos usually arrive at Umbagog during the last week of May, or, if the season be a late one, in early June. They come with the last flight of Warblers, when the forest trees are putting on a drapery of tender green, and the moose-wood is white with snowy blossoms. They are most apt to be found singly at this season, though they not infrequently associate with the various species of Warblers. For some time after their first appearance they are severely silent, and, although by no means shy or suspicious, their habits are so retiring and unobtrusive, that their presence may be easily overlooked. Their motions are essentially like those of all the rest of the genus. A branch shakes, and you catch a glimpse of a pale lemon breast that matches well with the tint of the thin foliage. Then the whole bird appears, hopping slowly out along the limb, and deliberately peering on every side in that nearsighted way peculiar to the tribe. Occasionally its search among the unfolding leaves in rewarded by the discovery of some luckless measuring-worm, which is swallowed with the same indifference that marks all the bird's movements. You begin to feel that nothing can disturb the equanimity of the little philosopher, when it suddenly launches out into the sunshine, and, with an adroit turn, captures a flying insect invisible to human eyes. The next moment there is a dim impression of glancing wings among the trees, and it has vanished. There is little chance of finding it again, for its voice has as yet no place in the chorus that rises from the budding thickets around.

Nesting.—Evidently Ernest T. Seton (1891) was the first to report the discovery of the nest of the Philadelphia vireo, which he found on the west slope of Duck Mountain in Manitoba; his report follows: "On June 9, 1884, near Fort Pelly, on the upper Assiniboine I found a Vireo nesting in a small bluff of poplar and willow. The chosen site was in the twigs of a willow some 10 feet from the ground; the nest was the usual suspended cup formed of fine grass and strips of birch bark. * * * On June 13, the Vireo began to sit on her four eggs. I shot her and found her to correspond exactly with Coues' description of *philadelphicus*, except that the yellow on the breast was quite bright. The eggs closely resembled those of the Red-eyed Vireo, but were destroyed by an unfortunate accident before they were accurately measured."

Although Mr. Brewster (1903) had been more or less familiar with this vireo in the Lake Umbagog region since 1872, it was not until June 14, 1903, that he succeeded in finding its nest. He describes the incident in his inimitable way and gives one of the best descriptions of the nest and its location that I have seen. He had been listening to the song of a vireo, which he suspected might be a Philadelphia; it was concealed in the top of an aspen (*Populus tremuloides*), and he was gathering stones to throw into the tree to make it move, when it occurred to him that some vireos sing on their nests. He writes:

This reflection caused me to drop the stones and begin looking for a nest instead of a bird. A few moments later I saw, through an opening in the foliage, in the very middle of the tree, scarce ten feet below its topmost twigs and fully thirty feet from the ground, a globular object of a light grayish brown color. Holding my glass on it with some difficulty—for I was now actually trembling with excitement—I made it out clearly to be a small, neatly-finished and perfectly new-looking Vireo's nest attached to a short lateral twig of one of the long, upright terminal shoots that formed the crown of the aspen. Looking still more closely I could see the head of the sitting bird and even trace the swelling of his throat and the slight opening of his bill as he uttered his disconnected notes. Soon after this he left the nest and flying to a neighboring tree alighted on a dead twig where I had a clear view of him and quickly satisfied myself that without question he was a Philadelphia Vireo.

The next morning the nest was taken, with the three fresh eggs that it contained; dissection of the female showed that no more eggs would have been laid. Brewster continues:

The nest was hung, after the usual Vireo fashion, in a fork between two diverging, horizontal twigs. One of these, a lateral branch from the upright shoot already mentioned, is rather more than a quarter of an inch in diameter and evidently formed the chief support, as the other twig is scarce thicker than the flower stem of a buttercup. The nest is firmly bound to both for some distance along its rim. It is much longer than broad, measuring externally 3.20 inches in length, 2.75 in width, and 2.65 in depth; internally 2.00 in length, 1.50 in width, and 1.35 in depth. Its walls are more than half an inch thick in places, its bottom almost a full inch. It appears to be chiefly composed of interwoven or closely compacted shreds of grayish or light brown bark, apparently from various species of deciduous trees and shrubs as well as, perhaps, from dried weed stalks. The exterior is beautifully decorated with strips of the thin outer bark of the paper birch, intermingled with a few cottony seed tufts of some native willow still bearing the dehiscent capsules. Most of these materials are firmly held in place by a gossamer-like overwrapping of gray-green shreds of *Usnea*, but here and there a tuft of willow down or a piece of curled or twisted snow-white bark was left free to flutter in every passing breeze. It would be difficult to imagine anything in the way of external covering for a bird's nest more artistically appropriate and effective. The interior, too, is admirably neat and pretty, for it is lined with the dry, tan-colored needles of the white pine (among which are a very few slender blades of grass), arranged circularly in deep layers around the sides and bottom of the cup in which the eggs were laid.

Philipp and Bowdish (1917) found three nests of the Philadelphia vireo in northern New Brunswick in 1916. "The situations where nests were found, as well as where additional birds were observed, were, in every instance, on islands or along the shores of river bottoms, with a growth of willow and alder.

"The nests found were in slender forks of alder, at a height varying from ten to seventeen and one half feet (the latter actual measurement). On June 17, two of these nests held four eggs each, the third five." Their description of the nests is not very different from Mr. Brewster's.

Dr. Harrison F. Lewis (1921) was fortunate enough to have a pair of Philadelphia vireos build their nest in a young rock maple, within 30 feet of the front door of his residence, in the suburbs of the city of

Quebec. He made the best of this unusual opportunity by watching the birds and their nesting activities from June 12 to July 14, 1919, climbing to the nest daily and often more than once a day. As a result of his observations, has has given us a full, accurate, and detailed account of the home life of these birds, to which the reader is referred for details. Although the locality was near the city, it was not strictly urban, for a woodland area of mixed deciduous and coniferous trees, which was two or three square miles in extent, aproached to within about 30 feet of the nesting-tree. He describes the nest as follows:

About four feet from the top of a young Rock Maple which was one of a row of such trees a small twig sprang at a considerable upward incline from the south side of the main stem of the tree, which was here one and one-fourth inches thick. The twig itself is one-fourth of an inch in thickness, and at a distance of one and one-eighth inches from the main trunk it divides at an angle of fifty degrees into two nearly equal parts, each of which is about five inches long and ends in a cluster of leaves. The pensile nest, which was well hidden and shaded by foliage, was hung from the fork between these two small twigs, at a height of twenty-four feet, eight inches, from the ground. Although the lower part of it is roughly circular, the rim is "gathered" to the twigs, so that the opening is shaped like a sector of a circle, with the two twigs as radii, and the outer rim as the arc of the sector. The acute angle between the twigs is filled in for about three-quarters of an inch with nesting material. The "gathering" of the rim of the nest, causing the walls to be incurved at the top, must have been efficacious in retaining eggs and young within it when it tossed and swayed in the breeze, as it did very much in the slender top of the tree. * * *

The outside of the nest is composed of fine strips of the outer bark of White Birches, dead grass blades, coarse white hen feathers, bits of frayed white twine, one spider's white "cocoon," and much spiders' web. The birch bark is much the most conspicuous material. Ends of strips of it have been left loose, so that they flutter in the breeze, breaking up the outline of the nest and helping to conceal it. At points where strips of birch bark cross one another they sometimes seem to possess mutual adherence without visible binding material, as though they had been gummed together, perhaps by the bird's saliva. The nest is fastened to the twigs by spiders' web, strips of birch bark, string, and grass blades. The interior is lined chiefly with fine dead grass stems and flower spikelets, but the lining includes also one or two needles of the White Pine and several white hen feathers, finer than those on the outside of the structure.

The building of the nest was apparently well under way when Dr. Lewis first noticed the birds on June 11, and on June 15 the nest held the first egg. Both birds seemed interested in the construction of the nest, but, as he usually could not distinguish between the sexes, he was not sure that the male did any work on the nest.

Charles E. Doe has sent me his notes on a Philadelphia vireo's nest that he found on a small island at the north end of Moosehead Lake, Maine, in July 1907. On July 7 he saw both birds working on the nest, 35 feet from the ground, attached to a lower limb of a big yellow birch on the edge of some dense spruce timber; there was no other birch in the vicinity. When he found the birds building, on July 7, they had woven only a few strands close up in the crotch of the twig; two days later it was nearly finished, and on the 10th it was all done. On July 15, he wrote in his notes: "The first egg must have been deposited on the 12th, for I climbed to the nest for the first time on the 13th, when it contained two eggs and the bird was on the nest; today, when I climbed to it, she sat very close and allowed me to part the leaves that partly hid the nest; I watched her fully five minutes and then she flew only when I put my hand within six inches of her. Up to then, she had simply raised her head and watched me closely; and how pretty she was with her yellowish white throat! When she flew, she kept out of sight for about ten minutes, and then returned and moved about in a nearby tree, but did not scold as vireos do."

He found another nest in the same locality on June 29, 1909. This was 40 feet from the ground in a thick maple, a lone tree among spruces, on the edge of heavy spruce timber at the top of a ravine. Both nests contained full sets of four eggs each.

Mr. Terrill has sent me a photograph (pl. 45) of a nest that he found 8 feet from the ground in an alder along a small stream; this nest had some birch bark in its composition, as well as a quantity of usnea, which can be seen hanging below the nest; he says that the use of usnea in the nest is diagnostic.

Eggs.—From three to five eggs may constitute a full set for the Philadelphia vireo, four being the commonest number and five very rare. These are very much like the eggs of the red-eyed vireo, though slightly smaller. Mr. Brewster (1903) describes his eggs as "elongate ovate in shape and pure white, sparsely spotted with burnt umber, chocolate and dull black." Philipp and Bowdish (1917) say that their eggs "were white with dark brown spots and specks, the larger spots tending to have a rusty border". Mr. Doe's eggs are marked on the large end with dark reddish brown. The scanty markings are sometimes scattered over the whole surface, but more often nearer the larger end of the egg. The measurements of 50 eggs average 19.2 by 14.0 millimeters; the eggs showing the four extremes measure 21.7 by 14.9, 21.6 by 15.3, 17.8 by 14.0, and 18.5 by 13.0 millimeters.

Young.—Dr. Lewis (1921) found the incubation period for the Philadelphia vireo to be about 14 days. He saw the male relieve the female and sing while incubating on the nest. Mr. Brewster (1903) also saw the male singing on the nest. In the nest that Dr. Lewis studied the first egg hatched on June 29; during that afternoon the pair changed places on the nest at very frequent intervals. "During the hour and twenty-five minutes between 12.40 p. m. and 2.05 p. m. the pair had exchanged places on the nest eight times, the intervals between reliefs being sometimes as short as three, four, or six minutes."

The remaining three eggs hatched during the following two days. "It will be noted that the first, second, and third young birds were hatched in fourteen days after the laying of the first, second, and third eggs, respectively. The time required for the incubation of the fourth egg lies somewhere between thirteen days, three hours, twenty-eight minutes and thirteen days, eleven hours, sixteen minutes [between times of examination]. If all the eggs were warmed alike when a bird was incubating, and if the several eggs required equal amounts of incubation to cause hatching, it would appear that incubation began as soon as the first egg was laid, but that it was more broken and ineffective between the laying of the third and the fourth eggs than at other times."

He gives the following brief outline of the chief events at the nest:

June 15. First egg laid.
June 18. Fourth (last) egg laid.
June 29. First egg hatched.
July 1. Third and fourth eggs hatched.
July 3. First cries of young heard.
July 12. Three oldest nestlings left nest.
July 13. Fourth nestling left nest.
July 14. Last observation of nestlings (two only).

On July 6: "Between 12.51 p. m. and 2.35 p. m. the young were fed at 12.52, 1.17, 1.20, 1.28, 1.39, 1.46, 1.52 (twice), 1.54 (twice), 2.20, 2.27 and 2.29, a total of thirteen feedings in one hour and forty-four minutes. I have recorded two feedings at 1.52 p. m. because at that time I saw the two parent Vireos stand on opposite sides of the nest and both feed the young at once. At 1.54 both birds were in sight near the nest at once and they fed the young in quick succession. At 1.20 and again at 1.52 one of the old birds, after feeding the young, removed excrement from the nest and flew away with it. The young birds were brooded from 12.52 to 1.16, from 1.28 to 1.36, from 1.39 to 1.46, and from 2.29 to 2.35, when I departed for a few minutes."

For an early morning feeding period, he made the following record: "Between 4.00 a. m. and 7.00 a. m. the young were fed at the following times: 4.06, 4.17, 4.29, 4.31, 4.38, 4.39, 4.40, 4.42, 4.45, 4.48, 4.49, 4.50, 4.52, 4.55, 4.56 (twice), 5.30, 5.54, 5.55, 6.00, 6.02, 6.03, 6.04, 6.05, 6.09, 6.12, 6.15, 6.18 (twice), 6.21, 6.28, 6.30 (twice), 6.32, 6.35, and 6.51, a total of thirty-six feedings, or nine for each young bird, in the first three hours of morning activity. * * * Between 4.05 and 4.57 there were sixteen feedings, between 4.57 and 5.53 there was one feeding only, and between 5.53, and 6.53 there were nineteen feedings. It will be observed that the feedings exhibit a marked periodicity, as though the young were given regular meals, with intervals of comparative rest." He noted other evidences of periodicity at other times, and saw some evidence that the parents were not satisfying their own hunger during the periods of rest. "Food which I saw the adult Philadelphia Vireos take to their young consisted largely of naked cater-pillars, brown, green, and whitish, and of flying insects of various kinds."

For two or three days before the last nestling finally left the nest the young birds were more or less restless and frequently hopped about in the tree or fluttered down to the ground, or even made short flights. They were often rescued from the ground and placed in the tree or returned to the nest. At such times the parents were quite excited and aggressive; Dr. Lewis says: "I climbed the tree again and, as I drew near the youngster, one of the parents dashed at me, crest erect, scolding loudly and rapidly. This was continued until I left the tree and was the first scolding I had received from an old bird when I was in the tree."

Dr. Dwight (1897) writes:

It is evident that but one brood is raised in a season. I have seen young birds as early as July 7, comical little chaps largely bare skin and the promise of a tail. At this tender age they are unwilling to essay flight except when urged by anxious parents to make a clumsy, flying leap from one twig to another, but they are knowing enough to keep quiet when they hear a crashing in the bushes, and as they become older they lose no time in moving quickly away. I have found them in alder thickets or along some of the bushy cattle paths which end abruptly at steep walls of rock or lose themselves in small clearings. In fact I never could tell when or where I might run across the birds, young or old, but dur-ing the latter part of July, when the moult is in progress, it is almost impossible to find them anywhere.

Plumages.—Dr. Dwight (1900) describes the natal down as "pale drab-gray." And he says that the juvenal plumage is "similar to *V. olivaceus* and *V. gilvus*, but darker above and distinctly yellow below. Above, wood-brown, darker and olive tinged on the back and wing coverts. Wings and tail clove-brown with olive-green edgings. Below primrose-yellow, auriculars, orbital ring, and superciliary stripe buff-yellow. Lores and postocular streak dusky."

An incomplete postjuvenal molt, involving the contour plumage and the wing coverts, but not the rest of the wings or the tail, begins at the end of July This produces a first-winter plumage, which is prac-tically indistinguishable from the winter plumage of the adult. Dr. Dwight describes this as "similar to the previous plumage but greener with a grayer crown, and brighter yellow below. Above, dull olive-green, slate-gray on the pileum. Below pale canary-yellow, whiter on middle of abdomen. Sides of head pale greenish or grayish buff, superciliary stripe paler; transocular streak dusky." He says that the adult, at this season, is usually paler yellow below with a larger area of white on the abdomen.

There is apparently no prenuptial molt, but specimens taken at the proper season to show it are not available. The sexes are practically alike in all plumages.

Food.—Of the 84 stomachs of the Philadelphia vireo in the collection of the Biological Survey, Dr. Edward A. Chapin (1925) found that only 75, taken in May, June, and September, contained enough food to show the percentages.

All but 4.34 percent of the animal food consisted of insects, the remainder being spiders. Lepidoptera formed the largest item, 24.13 percent of which were caterpillars and 2.17 percent adult moths and butterflies; in September the percentage of these lepidopterous items rose to 45.53, or nearly half of the entire food for the month.

Coleoptera ranked next, 24.82 percent for the year. "The beneficial beetles eaten are almost all of the family Coccinellidae, or ladybirds, well-known as enemies of plant lice and scale insects. Thirteen species of ladybirds have been identified from stomachs of the Philadelphia vireo, and these make up a little more than a fifth of all the beetles consumed, or about 5 percent of the total food." This is a bad showing for this vireo, but it is more than offset by all the injurious beetles destroyed, such as leaf-eating beetles (Chrysomelidae), 7.99 percent; weevils (Rhynchophora), 3.43 percent; wood-boring beetles (Buprestidae and Cerambycidae) and the plant-feeding Elateridae, together, less than 1 percent. The mildly beneficial dung beetles and the leaf-chafers (Scarabaeidae) taken together amount to 6.94 percent.

Of the Hymenoptera, "approximately 14 percent of the annual subsistence of the Philadelphia vireo is composed of wasps, bees, and related insects. Here are to be found some of the most beneficial of all insects, the parasitic ichneumon flies and the minute chalcids. On the other hand, the kinds of ants eaten are usually injurious, especially the large, black, carpenter ants (*Camponotus herculeanus*), and even if some of them do no direct damage they are indirectly injurious in fostering plant lice."

Flies (Diptera) form 11.76 percent of the food, including midges and both injurious and beneficial forms. True bugs (Hemiptera) make up 10.46 percent of the annual food, including the injurious stink bugs but not the useful stink bugs or the beneficial assassin bugs, so that the score is good in this group. Other insects amount to only 1.14 percent.

The seasonal average of vegetable food was but 7.22 percent of the whole, although in September it amounted to 18.71 percent. The fruits identified were bayberries, wild rose hips, and wild grapes, but no cultivated fruits or seeds were found.

Dr. Lewis (1921) says of the feeding habits of this vireo:

The birds fed usually in the border of the woods, among the lower limbs of the Red Oaks and Red Maples, less often among the White Birches or the Rock Maples. The pair which resided among the White Birches a hundred yards behind my house probably fed among them.

I found the Philadelphia Vireos to be rather more active in their feeding habits than are the Red-eyed Vireos. The trick mentioned by Dwight of hanging back-downward, like a Chickadee, from a cluster of leaves while picking insects from it was observed frequently, but the majority of the food of this species seemed to be taken while the birds were on the wing. They would leap repeatedly into the air to snap up passing insects with distinct "click's" of the bill. At other times they were seen hovering like Kinglets before branch-tips while they gathered food therefrom. The work done by this pair of Philadelphia Vireos must have aided greatly in keeping the trees in their vicinity free from insect pests this summer.

Behavior.—Much of the normal behavior of this vireo is described in Mr. Brewster's remarks under "Spring" and in Dr. Lewis's account of its feeding habits above. But Dr. Lewis (1921) wrote on July 3, describing a rather unusual performance:

Observation began at 6.16 a. m., when one bird was on the nest, while no song of the species was to be heard. No change was noticed until 6.24 a. m., when the male began singing among the oaks. A moment later, still singing, he flew to a perch near the nest. The next instant there was a series of excited squeakings, and both birds were away in a mad chase, fighting at frequent intervals with one another, apparently without mercy. They would circle around and around, passing repeatedly through the nesting-tree, then turn face to face in the air and struggle furiously, with much fluttering of wings and sharp clicking of bills, until often they fell nearly to the ground. After the first few seconds the squeakings stopped and shortly afterward the male began to sing as he fought. As the birds passed through the tree they would sometimes alight for a moment, two or three feet apart. After the briefest of pauses the female would attempt to fly back to the nest, when the male would dash after her again and the fight would be resumed.

Voice.—Every observer seems to agree that the song of the Philadelphia vireo closely resembles that of the red-eyed vireo, yet there *is* a subtle difference that a practiced ear can detect, especially if the two are heard at the same time. Mr. Brewster's (1880) first impression follows:

Contrary to what might be expected from the apparently close relationship of the two birds, the song of this species does not in the least resemble that of *Vireo gilvus.* It is, on the other hand, so nearly identical with that of *V. olivaceus* that the most critical ear will, in many cases, find great difficulty in distinguishing between the two. The notes of *philadelphicus* are generally pitched a little higher in the scale, while many of the utterances are feebler, and the whole strain is a trifle more disconnected. But these differences are of a very subtle character, and, like most comparative ones, they are not to be depended upon unless the two species can be heard together. The Philadelphia Vireo has, however, one note which seems to be peculiarly its own, a very abrupt, double-syllabled utterance, with a rising inflection, which comes in with the general song at irregular but not infrequent intervals. I have also, on one or two occasions, heard the male, when in pursuit of his mate, utter a soft *pseuo,* similar to that sometimes used by *Vireo olivaceus* and both sexes when excited or angry have a harsh, petulant note exactly like that of *V. gilvus.*

Referring to the "double-syllabled utterance" mentioned by Mr. Brewster, Dr. Dwight (1897) says:

I would merely emphasize the fact that it is the essence of the song and enters into it at as regular intervals as any of the other notes. It is a liquid note, beginning the song and occupying about three fifths of a second for the two syllables of which it is composed, on both of which considerable emphasis is laid. There seems to be a slight trill or ripple between the syllables when heard close at hand and the inflection rises slightly on the latter. A pause follows, approximating one and two fifths seconds, and the first note is again repeated, less forcibly and slightly varied. Again the pause ensues, and now it is followed by a triple note, not interrogatory and indistinguishable from one of *V. olivaceus*. Again the pause, this time followed by a repetition of the triple note, slightly varied so as to lose some of its sibilance, and after the customary pause of one and two fifths seconds, the song is repeated from the beginning, nearly eight seconds having elapsed in completing one cycle. The four notes may be suggested by the syllables *chŭr-r'wē, chŭr-wē, pst'-ĭ-rĕ, psr'-r-rē.* * * *

The speed at which the song flows is an interesting factor and is remarkably uniform for each individual songster,—in fact, I could almost identify certain Philadelphias and Red-eyes by timing their songs. *V. philadelphicus* sings at the rate of from twenty-two to thirty-six notes a minute, averaging a trifle over twenty-six, while *V. olivaceus* rattles on at the rate of from fifty to seventy, their song rate averaging a trifle over fifty-nine. * * *

The male Vireos are in full voice during June, but toward the end of the month the song period rapidly wanes, and after the first days of July their notes are not very often heard save as a subdued warble at rare intervals.

Also referring to Mr. Brewster's "double-syllabled utterance," Philipp and Bowdish (1917) write: "In our experience with the birds, this distinctive song absolutely predominated with the general impression of a song quite distinctive from that of the Red-eye, or, in fact, of any other Vireo we had heard.

"These birds have the common scolding note characteristic of Vireos, but, in addition, they gave voice to several rather musical, but apparently protesting notes. In one instance, the female sang a subdued but musical reply to the song of her mate who was at a little distance from the nest on which she sat."

Dr. Lewis (1921) also says that it is certain that the female can sing, and that her song is sometimes, at least, made up of notes differing from any heard from the male. "The only songs which I know with certainty were uttered by the female are two loud 'Doodle-ee?'s,' a few very low notes, and the song which she sang just after laying her last egg on June 18. This latter song was very sweet, clear, and simple, and was sung slowly for eight minutes in a low voice. It consisted of a variety of notes, such as 'Hùllit; ee-dò-it; wày-wer; ee-chèw-ee; doo-we?; hùllit-whew!', uttered over and over in a different order each time. The effect was charming."

He seems to differ from Dr. Dwight in the rapidity of the song, for he says: "On June 21 I counted for five minutes the song utterances of a bird which was singing this song [the one mentioned below] among the oaks, and found the number of utterances per minute to be seven, seven, nine, eleven, and six, respectively. A similar count for one minute on June 22 of the utterances of a bird singing this song from the nest showed seventeen utterances to the minute, which I consider to be quite the highest rate at which I heard this song delivered." The discrepancy is perhaps due to the fact that he was counting complete *songs*, while Dr. Dwight was counting individual *notes*.

He says, of the song he counted:

The song heard from the male from June 13 to June 22, inclusive, was simple, but delightful; a low, sweet, gentle "Doo-we? wheé-hooey; doo-we? wheé-hooey," uttered slowly and with long intervals between one utterance and the next. Sometimes the first utterance was elaborated into "Doodle-ee?". * * *

On June 23, and often thereafter, the male Philadelphia Vireo sang a song altogether different from that which I have described. This new song was loud and vigorous, and was readily recognizable as a Vireo's song, although the tone in which it was given was not quite so full as is the tone of the song of the Red-eyed Vireo. It consisted of notes like "S-s-s-cápe! ee-òh-yuh! ee-yòit! chèeb-ly!', and perhaps one or two others, repeated over and over in different orders. * * *

On June 25, when the female had left incubation to feed, the male, while following her through the lower branches of the trees, sang, in a loud voice, "Chee-òw-y! hee-ùh!," over and over again. This song was heard at such times only. Other loud songs which were heard often from this male after June 23 were "Whèe-hoit! s-s-s-jèrry!" and "S-s-s-chèw-ee! whèe-hooey!" After July 4 singing rapidly declined, the last song heard from this species being a few loud notes on July 17, three days after I ceased to find the juvenals. * * *

Other Philadelphia Vireos heard during the nesting-season sang similar loud songs, but the songs of no two of them were exactly alike. * * * I might point out that many common song-phrases of the Red-eyed Vireo, such as its plain little "Huh-huh," do not appear in any recognizable form in the songs of the Philadelphia Vireos heard by me, and that this seems to provide one ready means of distinguishing between the songs of the two species.

He mentions, also, "a mouse-like squeaking, a scolding note, a fine 'It, it, it, it, it,' and (from the female only) a 'Mew, mew'. * * * The 'Mew, mew' of the female apparently indicated readiness for coition."

Field marks.—A glance at the excellent colored plate published with Dr. Dwight's (1897) paper will show that the Philadelphia vireo looks very much like a warbling vireo with a pale yellow breast but slightly greener above and with the stripe over the eye less distinct. It also looks like a red-eyed vireo, minus the gray cap, distinctly bordered with dusky, and with more yellow beneath. The yellow throat and breast of the yellow-throated vireo are a much deeper yellow, and there are two white wing bars on each wing. From the warblers, some of which have a similar color pattern, it can be distinguished by its heavier bill and stockier shape.

Enemies.—We do not know much about the enemies of this vireo. Dr. Friedmann (1934 and 1943) could find only two cases where it was parasitized by cowbirds, one in Alberta and one in Ontario, by the Nevada cowbird and by the eastern cowbird, respectively. Probably cowbirds are not too common in the regions where it breeds. Predators doubtless destroy some eggs, young and adult birds, but this apparently has not been observed. Accidents may account for some mortality.

Fall.—Mr. Brewster (1880) draws this attractive picture of the fall migration in Maine:

At the close of the breeding season, when the brakes are turning brown, and occasional maples along the lake shore begin to glow with the burning tints of autumn, the Philadelphia Vireos join those great congregations of mingled Warblers, Sparrows, Woodpeckers, Titmice, etc., which at this season go trooping through the Maine woods. The specimens taken at Upton, in 1874, were in flocks of this kind, and several of them were shot in low bushes, an apparent exception to the rule previously given. But mixed society among birds, as well as men, is a great leveller of individual traits, and it is by no means uncommon on these occasions to find such tree-loving species as the Bay-breasted, Cape May, Black-burnian, and Blue Yellow-backed Warblers, the Red-bellied Nuthatch, the Golden-crested Kinglet, and many others, consorting with Winter Wrens, Water Thrushes, and Canada Flycatchers in the thickets by wood-paths, or along the banks of ponds or rivers; and I know of no more interesting sight, especially if it be a bright September morning, before the sun has risen above the trees. The dark foliage of the alders and viburnums is frosted with innumerable dewdrops, which fall in sparkling showers where a Warbler hops or a Woodpecker taps on the slender stems. Yellow and gold and scarlet liveries flash among the glossy leaves, as the active little forms appear and disappear, while the constant rustling and low-toned conversational chirping from the depths of the thicket suggest all sorts of pleasing mysteries. It is a pretty picture, this gathering of the birds in the quiet depths of the forest.

Winter.—The Philadelphia vireo spends the winter in Central America. Dickey and van Rossem (1938) call it a "common winter visitant at the upper limits of the Arid Lower Tropical Zone both along the interior and coastal mountains" in El Salvador. Where usually seen, "the altitude was 3,500 feet, and, curiously enough, the species was never seen at any other altitude, even though apparently identical conditions prevailed for at least 500 feet lower. In relative numbers, *philadelphicus* was slightly more common than *gilvus* and invariably outnumbered the latter when especially favorable trees brought the two species together. Sometimes as many as a dozen *philadelphicus* could be found in a single food tree, but otherwise the species was, like most vireos, solitary."

DISTRIBUTION

Range.—Central Canada to Panama.

Breeding range.—The Philadelphia vireo breeds **north** to northeastern Alberta (Chippewyan); central Saskatchewan (Prince Albert); southern Manitoba (Duck Mountain and Winnipeg, and has been recorded in summer at Churchill); central Ontario (Lac Seul, Moose Factory, Lowbush, and Lake Timiskaming); southern Quebec

(Blue Sea Lake, probably Quebec, Tadousac, and the Forillon Peninsula, Gaspé County) ; and southwestern Newfoundland (Tompkins). **East** to Newfoundland. **South** to Newfoundland (Tompkins); northern New Brunswick (Tabusintac, Chatham, and Edmundston) ; northern Maine (probably Sourdnahunk Lake, and Moosehead Lake); northern New Hampshire (Lake Umbagog and Dixville Notch and possibly Franconia) ; probably northern New York (Adirondack region); northern Michigan (Sault Ste. Marie); northern North Dakota (Turtle Mountains) ; eastern Montana (Johnson Lake, probably migrating) ; southern Saskatchewan (Crescent Lake) ; and southern Alberta (Red Deer). **West** to central and eastern Alberta (Red Deer, Camrose, Lac la Biche, and Chippewyan).

Winter range.—The winter home of the Philadelphia vireo is in Central America from northern Guatemala (Volcán de Agua and Secanquim) through El Salvador (Mount Cacaquatique) ; and probably western Nicaragua; the higher portions of western Costa Rica (Liberia, San José, Guayabo, and the valley of El General); to western Panama (Volcán de Chiriquí, Cocoplum, and Altoc Cacao on the Azuero Peninsula). A specimen from Cozumel Island, Mexico, was recorded by O. Salvin in the *Ibis* for 1888 as taken in January "during the last two years." It was probably accidental at that date.

Migration.—Late dates of spring departure are: Costa Rica—San José, April 23. Veracruz—Presidio, May 10. District of Columbia—Washington, May 30. West Virginia—Wheeling, May 24. New York—Geneva, June 5. Mississippi—Deer Island, May 7 (possibly accidental). Texas—Kemah, May 19. Kentucky—Lexington, May 16. Ohio—Youngstown, June 7. Missouri—Grandin, May 24. Illinois—Lake Forest, May 28. Wisconsin—Madison, May 29. Minnesota—Duluth, June 2. South Dakota—Sioux Falls, May 31.

Early dates of spring arrival are: Florida—Pensacola, April 18. District of Columbia—Washington, May 4. Pennsylvania—Doylestown, May 2. New York—Buffalo, May 3. Massachusetts—Lincoln, May 16. Maine—Dover-Foxcroft, May 12. Quebec—Hatley, May 12. New Brunswick—Oromocto, May 18. Arkansas—Winslow, April 24. Missouri—St. Charles, April 26. Tennessee—Memphis, May 2. Kentucky—Versailles, April 30. Ohio—Oberlin, April 26. Ontario—Ottawa, May 13. Michigan—Ann Arbor, May 10. Iowa—Des Moines, May 10. Wisconsin—Madison, May 10. Minnesota—Minneapolis, May 12. Texas—Galveston, April 9. Nebraska—Lincoln, May 16. North Dakota—Fargo, May 24. Manitoba—Margaret, May 15. Saskatchewan—Regina, May 19. Alberta—Chippewyan, May 23.

Late dates of fall departure are: Alberta—Camrose, September 8. Manitoba—Aweme, September 19. Wisconsin—Appleton, September 30. Iowa—Giard, October 1. Louisiana—New Orleans, October 29. Texas—Dallas, October 20. Ontario—Ottawa, September 23. Michigan—Detroit, September 24. Ohio—Columbus, October 12. Illinois—DeKalb, October 10. Tennessee—Nashville, October 10. Mississippi—Bay St. Louis, October 15. Maine—Phillips, October 2. New Hampshire—Dublin, September 29. Massachusetts—Springfield, September 24. New York—Schenectady, October 1. Pennsylvania—McKeesport, October 5. District of Columbia—Washington, October 5. West Virginia—Bluefield, October 2. North Carolina—Swannanoa, October 2. Georgia—Atlanta, October 9. Florida—Pensacola, October 8. In the Atlantic Coast States this species is apparently more common in fall than in spring.

Early dates of fall arrival are: Minnesota—Lanesboro, August 18. Wisconsin—Madison, August 22. Iowa—Forest City, August 31. Michigan—Detroit, August 28. Ohio—Toledo, August 29. Illinois—Glen Ellyn, August 21. Kentucky—Versailles, August 28. Mississippi—Gulfport, September 19. Louisiana—Thibodaux, August 15. New Hampshire—Jaffrey, August 25. Massachusetts—Harvard, September 5. New York—Rochester, August 28. Pennsylvania—Jeffersonville, September 9. District of Columbia—Washington, September 2. Florida—Pensacola, September 28. Guatemala—La Montanita, October 18. Nicaragua—Escondido River, October 21. Costa Rica—San José, October 21. Panama—Cocoplum, Bocas del Toro, October 29.

Casual records.—There is only a single record each for Kansas and Montana, though it is quite possible that this vireo is a fairly regular migrant through both States. In Kansas specimens were collected September 2 and 24, 1922, in Doniphan County; and in Montana one was collected on June 3, 1910, near Johnson Lake, Sheridan County.

Egg dates.—Maine: 4 records, June 15 to July 15.

Manitoba: 3 records, June 9 to 14.

New Brunswick: 8 records, June 15 to 24.

Quebec: 2 records, June 18 and 26.

VIREO GILVUS GILVUS (Vieillot)

EASTERN WARBLING VIREO

HABITS

CONTRIBUTED BY WINSOR MARRETT TYLER

The warbling vireo, if it were not for its song, would not be a notable species, for it is a little bird in leaf-green plumage, inconspicuous as it moves about among the foliage on the highest branches of its favorite elms and poplars where it spends the summer days, surrounded by green leaves and almost hidden by them.

High up in the trees, one of its nearest neighbors is the wood pewee, another leafy-green little bird. But unlike the pewee that sits motionless on its perch, flying out from it now and then into the air to catch its prey, the vireo rambles about among the leafy branchlets, finding its food there.

Spring.—When the warbling vireos arrive in New England early in May, we of their human friends hope that a pair will settle in the roadside trees near our homes, for if they do, although we may rarely see them, we know that the male will entertain us with his delightful song, filling the days with charming, simple melody all through the summer, even on the hottest days of July and August.

The song, as it goes on hour after hour, suggests a spirit of quiet happiness, a contrast to the flaunting, martial bugling of the Baltimore oriole, another of the vireos' neighbors, and to the slow, sweet notes of the wood pewee with their hint of pathos. In the vireo's song there is an air of unhurried calm, a leisureliness we seldom hear in the voice of a bird. Spring brings us greater artists, more proficient technicians, birds of more exuberant joyousness, but no such comfortable and welcome "guest of summer" as the warbling vireo.

Courtship.—We know little in detail of the nesting activities of the warbling vireo, for the bird stays so high above the ground at this season that we rarely see him at short range. Audubon (1842), however, by a fortunate chance, was able to watch the building of a nest under favorable circumstances, and noted a bit of courtship behavior of which he remarks: "During the love days of the pair mentioned above [see below under nesting], the male would spread its little wings and tail, and strut in short circles round the female, pouring out a low warble so sweet and mellow that I can compare it only to the sounds of a good musical box. The female received these attentions without coyness, and I have often thought that these birds had been attached to each other before that season." Audubon also mentions the odd, swaying motion which is characteristic of the red-eyed vireo (q. v.) both in the season of courtship and after the young are fledged. He says: "I observed that they now and then stood in a stiffened attitude, balancing their body from side to side on the joint of the tarsus and toes, as on a hinge, but could not discover the import of this singular action."

Nesting.—Dr. Thomas M. Brewer (Baird, Brewer, and Ridgway, 1874), speaking of the nests, says:

The Warbling Vireo builds its nest usually in more elevated positions than any others of this family. For the most part in the vicinity of dwellings, often over frequented streets, they suspend their elaborately woven and beautiful little basket-like nest, secure from intrusion from their human neighbors, and protected by the near presence of man from all their more dreaded enemies. * * *

The nests of the Warbling Vireo, while they resemble closely those of the other species in all the characteristics of this well-marked family, are yet, as a rule, more carefully, neatly, and closely built. They are usually suspended at the height of from thirty to fifty feet, in the fork of twigs, under and near the extremity of the tree-top, often an elm, protected from the sun and storm by a canopy of leaves, and just out of reach of most enemies. They vary little in size, being about two inches in height and three and a half in their greatest diameter, narrowing, toward their junction with the twigs, to two inches. They are all secured in a very firm manner to the twigs from which they are suspended by a felting of various materials, chiefly soft, flexible, flax-like strips of vegetable fibres, leaves, stems of plants, and strips of bark. With these are interwoven, and carried out around the outer portions of the nest, long strips of soft flexible bark of deciduous trees. They are softly and compactly filled in and lined with fine stems of plants.

William Brewster (1906) writes: "The nest of the Warbling Vireo is ordinarily built at least thirty or forty feet above the ground, at the end of a long, slender branch. Silver-leaved poplars are preferred to all other trees, but where these are not available the birds content themselves with large, spreading white ash trees, or with elms, lindens or maples, while they occasionally choose apple or even pear trees."

A. C. Bent (MS.) writes of a nest which he collected "25 feet from the ground in the top of a pear tree, attached to some small, leafy twigs close to an outer, topmost branch. The nest was deeply hollowed and well made of strips of inner bark of shrubs, various soft fibers, leaves, feathers, spiders' nests and cobwebs; it was lined with fine grasses and horse hair." And Coues (1878) points out that "the nest is quite deeply cupped, with a somewhat contracted brim, for the still greater safety of its precious freight."

M. G. Vaiden (MS.), of Rosedale, Miss., sends to Mr. Bent the following data on nests of the warbling vireo: "A nest 60 feet from the ground, out on a limb, in a crotch of a small limb branching from a larger one. However, the nest was only 14 feet from the trunk of the tree. The nest was very similar to that of the red-eye vireo, but a little heavier material had been used, and there was less workmanship on the outer side, not so much inner bark strips or moss, although there was a dab here and there." Another nest: "At the very top outer branches of a pecan, 90 feet high." A third nest: "In young sycamore tree, out on limb and semipensile, not over 15 feet from the ground on a branch over a little-used dirt road. This was the tallest tree (20 feet) in the vicinity." And A. Dawes Du Bois (MS.) sends the following: "About 40 feet from the ground in top of willow tree on bank of river; about 40 feet up in red oak tree 30 yards from our house; 10½ feet from the ground in apple tree in orchard." Of the second nest he says: "While I was watching the singing bird on the nest, his mate came and replaced him. The change was made as quick as a flash; as he slipped off the nest, his mate slipped instantly into it. A rather stiff wind was blowing, so that the eggs would not have been safe for half a second if left uncovered. However, I found later that, even when there was no wind, the birds changed places rather quickly."

Audubon (1842) gives an account of the building of a nest in a Lombardy poplar which almost touched his window. He says:

Never before had I seen it placed so low, and never before had I an opportunity of examining it, or of observing the particular habits of the species with so much advantage. The nest, although formed nearly in the same manner as several others, which I have since obtained by cutting them down with rifle balls, from the top twigs of the tall trees to which they were attached, instead of being fastened in the fork of a twig, was fixed to the body of the tree, and that of a branch coming off at a very acute angle. The birds were engaged in constructing it during eight days, working chiefly in the morning and evening. * * * One morning I observed both of them at work; they had already attached some slender blades of grass to the knots on the branch and the bark of the trunk, and had given them a circular disposition. They continued working downwards and outwards, until the structure exhibited the form of their delicate tenement. Before the end of the second day, bits of hornets' nests and particles of cornhusks had been attached to it by pushing them between the rows of grass, and fixing them with silky substances. On the third day, the birds were absent, nor could I hear them anywhere in the neighborhood, and thinking that a cat might have caught them from the edge of the roof, I despaired of seeing them again. On the fourth morning, however, their notes attracted my attention before I rose, and I had the pleasure of finding them at their labours. The materials which they now used consisted chiefly of extremely slender grasses, which the birds worked in a circular form within the frame which they had previously made. The little creatures were absent nearly an hour at a time, and returned together bringing the grass, which I concluded they found at a considerable distance. Going into the street to see in what direction they went, I watched them for some time, and followed them as they flew from tree to tree toward the river. There they stopped, and looked as if carefully watching me, on which I retired to a small distance, when they resumed their journey, and led me quite out of the village, to a large meadow, where stood an old hay-stack. They alighted on it, and in a few minutes each had selected a blade of grass. Returning by the same route, they moved so slowly from one tree to another, that my patience was severely tried. Two other days were consumed in travelling for the same kind of grass. On the seventh I saw only the female at work, using wool and horse-hair. The eighth was almost entirely spent by both in smoothing the inside. They would enter the nest, sit in it, turn round, and press the lining, I should suppose a hundred times or more in the course of an hour. * * * In the course of five days, an equal number of eggs was laid.

Eggs.—[AUTHOR'S NOTE: The warbling vireo lays three to five eggs to a set, usually four. These are practically ovate and without any appreciable gloss. They are pure white, with only a few scattered spots of various shades of reddish or darker browns, or blackish, the darker spots being commonest. The measurements of 50 eggs average 19.1 by 14.2 millimeters; the eggs showing the four extremes measure 20.3 by 14.7, 18.7 by 15.1, 17.8 by 13.6, 18.8 by 13.2 millimeters.]

Young.—We meet the young warbling vireos at close range when they come down from their lofty nest and follow their parents about in the shrubbery.   They are odd, pale little birds when we first see them in July, not long from the nest—light brown on the back, with a wash of yellow on the breast and flanks, and hoary about the head, almost white, although they soon lose this latter mark.   A. Dawes Du Bois (MS.) remarks: "The plumage of the fledglings is so pale that they look like little white birds."   The old birds feed them with larvae (often a long, green worm), large moths (after pulling off the wings), and later, when the shrubs have fruited, with cornelberries.

The young birds at this time, as well as the adults, give a curious note which attracts our attention to these family gatherings.   It strongly suggests the distant clipping of garden shears—a sort of sneeze.

Audubon (1842) gives the incubation period as 12 days, and says of the young birds: "On the sixteenth day after their exclusion from the egg, they took to wing, and ascended the branches of the tree, with surprising ease and firmness."

Plumages.—[AUTHOR'S NOTE: Dr. Dwight (1900) calls the natal down "pale wood-brown" and describes the juvenal plumage as "above wood-brown, very pale on pileum and nape, darker and faintly tinged with olive on the back.   *   *   *   Below, white, the crissum tinged with pale primrose-yellow.   Auriculars, orbital ring and superciliary line white."

There is a partial postjuvenal molt, beginning early in August, which involves the contour plumage, and the wing coverts, but not the rest of the wings nor the tail.   This produces a first winter plumage which is practically indistinguishable from the winter plumage of the adult, greener above and more buffy white below than the previous plumage.

Dr. Dwight says that the nuptial plumage is acquired by wear, but Ned Dearborn (1907) found March and April specimens of the western race undergoing a scattered molt on the head and breast.   This may also be true of other vireos, though we have not the proper specimens to show it.]

Food.—In his study of food habits of the vireos, Dr. Edward A. Chapin (1925), summarizing his findings, says:

The economic status of the warbling vireo is in some ways more distinctly unfavorable than that of the other species of this family of birds, especially in its consumption of ladybirds.   In more than a third of the stomachs examined the remains of these beneficial beetles were found.   *   *   *

On the other hand, the injurious insects taken by the warbling vireo make up the greater part of the food.   Lepidopterous remains, including adult moths and butterflies, caterpillars, pupae, and eggs, were taken from about 77 per cent of those examined.   This alone should atone for the bird's injurious proclivities along other lines.   *   *   *   Little if any of the vegetable food taken was obviously cultivated, in most cases being from plants not used for their fruits.   It seems reasonable, then, to class the bird as neither beneficial nor injurious.

Elliott Coues (1878) adds an interesting food item. He says in a footnote: "Prof. Samuel Aughey gives the Warbling Vireo among the birds of Nebraska which destroy the scourge of that country—the grasshopper," quoting him as follows: " 'I frequently saw it light down within a rod of me where locusts abounded and feed on them. This species seemed to eat them in all stages of their growth, and brought them constantly to their nests for their young.' "

Tilford Moore writes to Mr. Bent that he has several times seen one hang upside down from a twig to get food out of an apple blossom.

Behavior.—William Brewster (1906), writing of the bird in eastern Massachusetts, says: "The warbling vireo is a bird of somewhat peculiar and restricted distribution. It shuns extensive tracts of woodland and, indeed, most wild and primitive places, although it nests sparingly in orchard or shade trees near secluded farmhouses, and rather frequently along country roads bordered by rows of large elms or maples. We find it most commonly and regularly, however, in or near village centers such as those of Lexington, Arlington, Belmont and Watertown."

Mr. Brewster is referring here to the early years of this century. I remember that in those days I used to hear warbling vireos about half a mile apart along the main street through Lexington, but before many years, about 1912, we noted a diminution in their numbers; every year fewer and fewer breeding pairs returned, until, early in the 20's, the species became practically unknown in the town, and was rare throughout eastern Massachusetts. However, since about 1938, there has been a decided increase in its numbers.

The warbling vireo is so partial to the lines of trees along our village streets and to isolated trees in open country that, thinking back to the time when this land was covered chiefly by unbroken forest, we wonder where the bird could have found in those days a habitat to its liking. It is thought that the well-watered trees on the border of the broad lanes opened by rivers through the forest were the former habitat of the bird, for these would afford a situation not unlike the vireos' present breeding ground. Aretas A. Saunders (1942) expresses this conjecture: "I believe that the warbling vireo originally inhabited trees along stream borders. With the coming of civilization, shade trees along city streets formed a rather similar habitat, and it adopted such places. This will explain its preference for elms and silver maples, trees that originally were found along stream borders."

In former times, apparently, the warbling vireo was a resident in large cities. Dr. Brewer (Baird, Brewer, and Ridgway, 1874) says: "It is especially abundant among the elms on Boston Common, where at almost any hour of the day, from early in the month of May until long after summer has gone, may be heard the prolonged notes of this, one of the sweetest and most constant of our singers." Henry D. Minot

(1895), speaking of the 1870's, also mentions the birds' occurrence "among the elms of Boston Common."

Many observers have noted the warbling vireo's habit of singing while he is incubating. William Brewster (1937) speaks of it thus: "Soon after leaving the Yellow-throat's nest, I heard our Warbling Vireo singing in the orchard. Thinking that he might be on the nest, I followed up the sound and directly saw the nest in the very top of a rather tall tree attached to the horizontal twigs of a long, *upright* leafy branch. I could see the bird's head distinctly. He raised it high when he sang and his white throat swelled and flashed in the sunlight."

Francis H. Allen (MS.) describes an unusual observation: "I once saw a pair perched in bushes and low trees on a river bank and flying frequently down to the surface of the stream, striking it forcibly, and then returning to their perches, where they preened their feathers. Both birds participated, but not simultaneously. Whether the purpose was for bathing or to take insects from the surface of the water I could not make out, but, intentionally or not, they got their baths. In all cases it was a straight dash to the water at an angle of perhaps 25 or 30 degrees."

Voice.—Wherever we turn in the literature of the warbling vireo we find that the author, after commenting on the bird's inconspicuousness, speaks enthusiastically of its song, pointing out the difference from the songs of the other vireos, the length of the song period, and the charm of the smoothly flowing warble.

The song of the warbling vireo is not broken up into short, exclamatory phrases like those of the other common New England vireos, the red-eyed, the solitary, and the yellow-throated, but continues on in a long series of slow, quietly delivered musical notes increasing in force to the end. The pitch undulates gently to the final note, which is generally the highest and the most strongly accented. Some writers find a resemblance in the song to that of the purple finch, but the finch's notes are very rapid and energetic and have none of the calm deliberateness of the vireo's melody. The most suggestive rendering of the vireo's song, perhaps, is Wilson Flagg's (1890): "Brig-a-dier, Brig-a-dier, Brigate," which, pronounced slowly, brings out the rhythm admirably.

Aretas A. Saunders (MS.) sends to Mr. Bent this summary of the song: "The song of the warbling vireo consists of a series of connected notes, with no two consecutive notes on the same pitch, and is therefore a true warble. Individuals often sing several different songs, and in a number of cases I have recorded from three to seven different songs from one individual. The pitch varies from D $'''''$ to C $\#$ $'''$, half a tone more than an octave. The average song ranges about 3½ tones in pitch. Songs consist of 7 to 25 notes each and vary in length from 1 to 3 seconds. The notes are not all the same length. A common form is made up of one long note followed by two short ones, and when this is repeated several times it is like dactylic feet in poetry. It is common for the song to end on a high note."

In the summer of 1912 a bird that was breeding on Lexington Common, within hearing from my windows, showed a marked departure from the normal song. My notes say: "He often utters a part of his song in a squeaky voice with no whistled quality whatever, the tone becoming so high that it contains a sibilant sound. Sometimes he changes to the squeak in the middle of the song, returning to the whistle before the end; sometimes he ends with the squeak." Strange to say, later in the same year I heard a similar song from another warbling vireo breeding 5 miles from Lexington. This variation, however, must be rare, for I have not heard it since, although I have heard the red-eyed vireo sing in this manner.

The bird often sings until well into September: Mr. Bent has heard it singing daily from August 31 to September 13, inclusive, and my records for 10 years average August 27, the latest being September 18, 1910.

The warbling vireo has two common minor notes; one the sound that resembles the sharp clipping of garden shears, mentioned under "Young," and a complaint note, corresponding, apparently, to the *quee* of the redeye, but with no downward inflection. It is a hard, tense snarl, with sometimes a slight upward inflection, easily recognized as a diagnostic note of the species.

Dr. Jonathan Dwight, Jr. (1897), makes an interesting comment on this latter note. Speaking of a similar note of the Philadelphia vireo, he says: "It does not resemble the corresponding complaint note of *olivaceus*, but is almost exactly like the aggressive *mÿă* of *gilvus*, which has a suggestion of the katydid about it."

Tilford Moore says in his notes: "Today I saw one singing in flight; he finished his song just after alighting but sang three-quarters of it in flight."

Field marks.—The warbling vireo has no mark in its plumage that enables us to identify it at a glance as a species. It has no wing bars, no eye ring, no distinctive lines on the head, like some of the other vireos: it is merely a gray-green little bird, but, from the shape of its bill and its manner in moving about, clearly a vireo. So we have to come to an identification by elimination, by the process of *reductio ad absurdum.*

Yet, before long, when we have seen the bird time and time again, it begins to take on an individuality of its own, as all birds do when we learn to know them well, and we recognize it, not, as we recognize many birds, by some peculiarity of plumage, not even because it lacks any distinctive marks, but because it suggests the definite personality we have attributed to the warbling vireo. The side of the head, marked only by a slight paleness above the eye, has an expression of bland innocence; the delicate coloring of the plumage, with no spot of ornament to set it off, gives an air of quiet refinement, like the bird's song; and the diminutive bill gives the bird a youthful appearance.

Enemies.—Herbert Friedmann (1929) says of the relation of the cowbird to the warbling vireo: "A very common victim. * * * Eaton lists the Warbling Vireo as one of the commonest molothrine victims in New York State, and I have numerous records from other parts of the country. * * * All together over forty records have come to my notice. In common with the other species of its family, this Vireo normally makes no attempt to rid herself of the parasitic eggs." In recent year the warbling vireo has probably suffered more from the spraying of the shade trees with poison than from the natural enemies that commonly beset small arboreal birds. Their nests have been imperiled by the high-pressure spraying that rocks the elm branches at the vital points of the birds' summer distribution, the roadside trees of our country towns.

Winter.—Donald R. Dickey and A. J. van Rossem (1938) speak of the bird on its winter quarters:

The winter home of the eastern warbling vireo can now be stated to be in the foothills of El Salvador and adjacent parts of Central America. * * * On Mt. Cacaguatique in late November and in December, 1925, warbling vireos were abundant at 2,500 feet elevation, all through the berry-bearing trees which provided shade for the coffee groves. From there up to the oak- and pine-covered summit of the mountain (about 4,000 feet) they were also very numerous. In February and March, 1926, both on Volcán de Conchagua and Volcán de San Miguel numbers were observed in similar environments at from 2,500 to 3,500 feet, but much less commonly than in the interior. At Chilata in April, 1927, warbling vireos were migrating and were usually in pairs.

Ludlow Griscom (1932) writes: "It is apparently quite common and generally distributed in Guatemala in winter, arriving principally in October, the earliest date being September 28, 1926."

DISTRIBUTION

Range.—Canada to El Salvador.

Breeding range.—The warbling vireo breeds **north** to northern British Columbia (Atlin, Fort Halkett, and Fort Nelson); southwestern Mackenzie (Wrigley, Simpson, Providence, and Resolution); northeastern Alberta (Chippewyan and McMurray); central Saskatchewan (Wingard and Prince Albert); southern Manitoba (Duck Mountain, Lake St. Martin, and Selkirk; probably to Norway House); southern Ontario (Port Arthur, Lake Nipissing, and Ottawa); southern Quebec (Montreal and Quebec); southern New Brunswick

(Fredericton); Prince Edward Island (Brackley Point); and Nova Scotia (Pictou). **East** to central Nova Scotia (Pictou, Truro, and Halifax); the Atlantic coast of the United States to southern Virginia (Dismal Swamp); through the mountains to northern Alabama (Anniston and Florence). **South** to northern Alabama (Anniston); western Mississippi (Shell Mound and Rodney); southern Louisiana (New Orleans, Houma, and Calcasieu); sparingly in southern Texas Huntsville, Rockport, Marathon, and the Guadalupe Mountains); southern New Mexico (Cloudcroft, Silver City, and the Animas Mountains); southwestern Chihuahua (Bravo and Mina Abundancia); central Sonora (Rancho Santa Bárbara and Magdalena); and southern California (Santa Ysabel and Escondido); also resident in the Cape region of Lower California. **West** to the Pacific coast of California (Escondido, Santa Barbara, San Francisco, and Eureka); Oregon (Grants Pass, Eugene, Tillamook, and Astoria); Washington (La Push, Cape Flattery, and Bellingham); and British Columbia (Victoria, Cape Scott, Kimsquit, Great Glacier, Telegraph Creek, and Atlin).

Winter range.—In winter the warbling vireo is found from southern Veracruz (Orizaba) through southern Oaxaca (Tehuantepec); south-central Chiapas (Comitán); western Guatemala (Finca Carolina, Sacapula, Patulul, and Progreso); to El Salvador (Colimas and Mount Cacaguatique).

The above range includes all the subspecies of the warbling vireo breeding within the Check-list range of which four are recognized. The typical race, the eastern warbling vireo (*V. g. gilvus*), breeds west to eastern Saskatchewan and the eastern edge of the Great Plains and northern Texas. The Oregon warbling vireo (*V. g. leucopolius*) breeds from northern British Columbia (except the coastal area) and southwestern Mackenzie south to northern Nevada and Montana. The western warbling vireo (*V. g. swainsoni*) breeds in the coastal region of British Columbia, Washington, and Oregon, through southern Nevada, to southern Wyoming and Colorado, and south to southern California and western Texas. The Cape warbling vireo (*V. g. victoriae*) breeds in the Cape district of Lower California. Additional races occur in Mexico.[2]

Migration.—Late dates of spring departure from the winter home are: El Salvador—Chilata, April 27. Guatemala—Patulul, April 2. Veracruz—Presidio, May 4.

Early dates of spring arrival are: Alabama—Syllacauga, April 16. Georgia—Macon, April 16. North Carolina—Asheville, April 13. District of Columbia—Washington, April 21. Pennsylvania—

---

[2] The subspecies *leucopolius* and *victoriae* were officially recognized by the A. O. U. Commitee after the manuscript of this bulletin was submitted; hence no separate accounts of them are here included.—EDITOR.

Pittsburgh, April 24. New York—New York, April 28. Massachusetts—Marlboro, April 27. New Hampshire—East Jaffrey, April 27. Maine—Augusta, May 1. Quebec—Montreal, May 16. Louisiana—Chenier au Tigre, March 4. Arkansas—Rogers, April 1. Missouri—St. Louis, April 6. Kentucky—Guthrie, April 5. Indiana—Bloomington, April 21. Michigan—Ann Arbor, April 21. Ohio—Columbus, April 19. Ontario—London, April 29. Iowa—Keokuk, April 24. Wisconsin—New London, April 28. Minnesota—Red Wing, May 2. Manitoba—Aweme, May 15. Texas—Palmetto Park, March 31. Oklahoma—Oklahoma City, April 16. Kansas—Manhattan, April 18. South Dakota—Yankton, April 25. North Dakota—Fargo, May 11. Saskatchewan—Indian Head, May 12. Colorado—Colorado Springs, May 1. Wyoming—Careyhurst, May 10. Montana—Corvallis, May 6. Alberta—Glenevis, May 1. Mackenzie—Simpson, May 22. Arizona—Yuma, March 12. Utah—Provo, May 11. Idaho—Coeur d'Alene, May 3. California—Los Angeles, March 11. Oregon—Eugene, April 12. Washington—Prescott, April 26. British Columbia—Hastings, April 26; Atlin, May 18.

Late dates of fall departure are: British Columbia—Atlin, August 17; Courtenay, September 17. Washington—Yakima, September 19. Oregon—Coos Bay, September 20. California—Berkeley, October 3. Alberta—Glenevis, August 20. Montana—Fortine, September 9. Wyoming—Yellowstone Park, September 29. Colorado—Fort Morgan, September 18. Saskatchewan—Indian Head, September 23. North Dakota—Argusville, September 21. South Dakota—Yankton, September 30. Nebraska—Red Cloud, October 1. Oklahoma—Kenton, September 22. Texas—Brownsville, October 2. Manitoba—Aweme, September 19. Minnesota—St. Paul, September 26. Wisconsin—Racine, October 7. Missouri—St. Louis, September 27. Illinois—Chicago, September 27. Ontario—Ottawa, September 22. Ohio—Toledo, October 11. Tennessee—Knoxville, October 10. Arkansas—Helena, October 5. Maine—Dover-Foxcroft, October 5. Vermont—St. Johnsbury, September 29. Massachusetts—Taunton, October 1. New York—Schenectady, October 1. Pennsylvania—McKeesport, October 7. District of Columbia—Washington, September 12. Georgia—Augusta, October 15.

At a banding station at Northville, S. Dak., 41 warbling vireos were banded over a period of 4 years and four individuals were retrapped in subsequent years:

Banded	Returned
June 11, 1932	August 4, 1933
May 30, 1932	June 12, 1934
May 17, 1933	May 20, 1934
August 20, 1933	May 21, 1934

Egg dates.—California: 82 records, April 26 to July 25; 41 records, May 24 to June 14, indicating the height of the season.

Massachusetts: 11 records, May 20 to June 25; 7 records, May 26 to June 8.

New York: 33 records, May 20 to June 25; 23 records, May 25 to June 6.

Washington: 15 records, May 22 to June 29, 10 records, June 15 to 22.

VIREO GILVUS SWAINSONI Baird

WESTERN WARBLING VIREO

HABITS

The western warbling vireo differs from the eastern race by being smaller, with a relatively smaller bill; "coloration darker, especially the pileum, which is perceptibly (often distinctly) darker than the back; the latter, together with the sides and flanks, usually more strongly olivaceous," according to Ridgway (1904).

It is a widely distributed and very common bird in all suitable localities in the Western States and southern Canada, from the Great Plains to the Pacific slope. It seems to be equally common in the valleys, in the wooded canyons, or in the mountains, up to 6,500 feet in northern Montana and up to 10,000 feet farther south. It lives wherever it can find deciduous trees and shrubbery, showing a decided preference for cottonwoods and aspens. In most places its haunts are in the wilder, uninhabited regions, along the banks of streams and on the edges of woodlands and clearings. But S. F. Rathbun tells me that near Seattle, Wash., it is also found "about the cities and towns, building its nest in some shade tree along the street." He says that at Lake Crescent, Wash., it is "restricted to, or in the vicinity of, the deciduous growth near the lake, or along its shore. Wherever there was a clearing in which might grow the western maple, here would probably be found a pair of the vireos. In some of the wilder parts of the region, particularly the river valleys that are bordered with a deciduous growth of alders and cottonwood, it will be found very common; and in such localities the flow of its song, mingled with the murmur of the running stream, is most pleasing to hear."

Russell K. Grater tells me that, in Zion National Park, Utah, it "is a very common summer resident in the broadleaf trees along the canyon floor and up to elevations around 7,000 feet." Howard L. Cogswell writes to me, from Los Angeles County: "In the breeding season here, the warbling vireo is chiefly a bird of the mountain canyons, or more definitely of the riparian growth (alders, cottonwoods, sycamores, and maples) along the streams from the tree filled gulches in the foothill mesas barely into the lower edge of the pine belt." Dr. Jean M. Linsdale (1938) says that, in the Toyabe Mountains, in Nevada—

the warbling vireo was one of the common species, widespread wherever there
were deciduous trees.   It was of regular occurrence in the groves of aspens and
cottonwoods.   The favorite habitat was in trees 25 to 30 feet high where
there was some undergrowth and leaf litter.   But the birds kept closely within
the crown foliage.   This was the most numerous species in the birches and willows
which lined the streams.   It occurred also, but less commonly, over the ridges
in mountain mahoganies.   Chokecherry thickets provided suitable homes, especially when in fruit in the fall.   Individuals were seen a few times in piñons.
* * *   One was singing in bushes of *Symphoricarpos* on an east-facing ridge
at 8600 feet near Kingston Creek.   The nearest trees were mountain mahogany,
200 to 300 yards distant.

Spring.—The western warbling vireo evidently occurs mainly as a
migrant, in Guatemala, for Ned Dearborn (1907) says: "One was taken
and another seen at El Rancho January 6th.   No more were seen until
March 24th, when they were found at Patulul in abundance, and so
continued, at least, until April 2d.   Seven were collected at Patulul.
At this time, they were passing through the trees in loose flocks and
were evidently migrating.   The March and April specimens were
undergoing a scattered moult, not a general renewal, on head and
breast."

Mr. Cogswell says in his notes: "During the spring migration in
April and early in May, warbling vireos are quite common throughout
Pasadena, Calif., especially sections with oaks and sycamores.   Many
migrants sing constantly during their stay of a few hours or a day or
so in one vicinity."

Mr. Rathbun (MS.) says of the spring migration in western Washington: "At first a few in company will be seen, these little birds seeming to pass on.   Often a day or two elapses before any more are seen;
then once more a few pass by.   This is followed by the appearance of
numbers of the vireos, after which the species is common and will be
found in its accustomed places.   This movement seems to be covered
by a period of about 15 days."

Nesting.—Mr. Rathbun tells me that he finds the nests of the western warbling vireo in maples, alders, and other deciduous trees from
4 to 40 feet above ground, "but, as a rule, one can expect to find them at
some considerable height."   He gives me this good description of a
nest: "This nest was attached in the usual way to a fork of one of the
branches of a young alder tree, which grew at the edge of a clump of the
same kind of growth, the nest being suspended only six feet above the
ground.   Its construction represented the ordinary cup-shaped nest
made by most vireos, and the materials used were similar except in one
marked respect; the outside of this nest was almost entirely of the
dingy-gray, cottony substance from the black cottonwood tree, this
material held in place by means of long blades of green grass; and
there was also tied on the outer side a green alder leaf.   Some of the
blades of grass completely encircled the nest, aiding its attachment

to the fork from which it hung, and, together with spider webs, were used to hold the cottony substance in place. The nest was a beautiful object and harmonized so well with its natural surroundings that it would easily escape notice among the glimmering alder leaves. And so much cottony substance had been used on the outside of the nest that in spots it was fully one-half inch in thickness. This nest was neatly lined with very fine shreds of the outer bark from dry weed stalks; and filaments of spider webs were also utilized to bind the edge of the nest to the fork from which it hung."

Dr. Linsdale (1938) reports four Nevada nests; one was 8 feet up in a chokecherry near the base of a rocky cliff at 8,000 feet altitude in a canyon; and another, found the same day, was 15 feet above ground in an aspen in the same vicinity. Two others were 15 feet above ground in a birch clump and 9 feet up in an aspen, respectively. Frank C. Willard (1908) found a nest in Arizona that was 30 feet from the ground in a sycamore in a canyon.

Grinnell and Storer (1924) report two nests in the Yosemite Valley; one was "4½ feet above the ground at the forking of two almost leafless branches of a coffee berry bush." The other was about 12 feet up and 3 feet out from the trunk of a young black oak. Dr. Grinnell (1908) found a nest 6 feet feet from the ground in an apple tree in the San Bernardino Mountains, and several others in cottonwoods, from 6 to 20 feet above ground.

The best account I can find of the nesting and home of the western warbling vireo is that published by Henry J. Rust (1920), of Coeur d'Alene, Idaho.

His first nest "was suspended from the fork of a small spiraea bush, five feet from the ground, back about ten feet in dense shrubbery along an old roadway"; this nest was torn down and destroyed when the young were about 8 days old. But he found another nest the following year along the same roadway, and watched the birds building it and rearing their young successfully. He took a number of good photographs of it (pls. 46, 47). It was 4½ feet from the ground in a fork of a small willow, and, when first found, "consisted of several blades of dry grass woven over and under, back and forth across the crotch, the loose ends drooping, with several bits of willow down adhering." He continues:

In the afternoon of the next day the rim was finished and rounded out in shape to support the completed nest; some of the loose ends were woven in and out, with a few additional dry grass stems, bits of string and willow down, this forming a part of the body of the nest. Two days later, the 27th, the nest was completed on the outside. When visited on the 30th the lining was in place, consisting of dry grass stems interwoven with ten or twelve strands of horse hair. The nest as completed measured as follows: Diameter outside, 2½ by 3 inches; length 3 inches; diameter inside, 1½ by 2 inches; depth 1¾ inches.

On dissecting the nest after the young had flown, the following materials were noted, besides the dry grass blades and stems already mentioned: Three pieces of white string, 14, 15, and 24½ inches in length, respectively; also a number of small white threads of various lengths up to 6½ inches; 35 detachable bits of down from willow seeds, with many woven in securely; several bits of lichen (*Alectoria fremontii*) ; small strips of ninebark (*Opulaster pauciflorus*) ; three small pieces of old discolored cotton; and, in the rim, bits of matted cow hair. There being four houses less than one hundred yards from the nesting site, the string, horsehair and cotton were no doubt obtained on or near those premises. The balance of the material could have been secured a few feet from the nest. In weaving the long piece of string, one end must have dropped down, and in picking up the loose end it had been passed under a small twig below the nest, forming a long hanging loop that remained in place during the occupancy of the nest, as shown in the photos.

The bulk of the nest, if not the entire structure, was built by the female. The male remained in nearby trees, singing at regular intervals, but he was not noted helping at any time. As in the case of the former nest, several days passed after it was finished before any eggs were laid. The first egg in the second nest was noted on June 4. Visited late in the afternoon of the 7th, the nest contained four eggs, the complete set.

The young willow in which the nest was placed was growing in a small opening about thirty feet from the edge of the old road, and was surrounded by a profusion of green shrubbery that was much to the liking of the vireos. On only two occasions did I note either of the parent birds more than forty yards away from the willow after the nest was completed, until the young had flown. I could not help but note the pretty setting for such an interesting bit of home life. The ground was carpeted with a thick growth of wild sweet pea (*Lathyrus pauciflorus*) which was in full bloom and scenting the air with a sweet odor. One side of the opening was enclosed with buckbrush (*Ceanothus sanguineus*) and ninebark in bloom; beyond there were several large yellow pines and Douglas fir trees; on the other side were service berry bushes, willows, and ocean spray (*Schizonotus discolor*) which extended to a large grove of pine and fir trees in the near distance. In and out through the surroundings were bushes of the large flowering wild rose in full bloom, adding a touch of color to the masses of green and white.

It will be observed from the above records that the western warbling vireo differs decidedly, in its choice of a nesting site, from its eastern relative. The eastern bird builds its nest almost invariably in trees and at a very considerable height, whereas the western bird often builds in bushes or low trees and much nearer the ground. Most of the recorded nests of the western warbling vireo have been placed at not over 12 feet from the ground; and its highest nests, which seem to be exceptional, have been below the average for the eastern bird.

Eggs.—The western warbling vireo lays from three to five eggs, usually four. These are quite indistinguishable from those of the eastern race. The measurements of 40 eggs in the United States National Museum average 18.4 by 13.2 millimeters; the eggs showing the four extremes measure 20.3 by 14.7, 20.1 by 15.0, and 16.8 by 12.2 millimeters.

Young.—Mr. Rust (1920) found that the period of incubation was 12 days, performed by both sexes. "If my visit happened in the morning, and the male was incubating, I could almost touch the nest before he would leave. Then, alighting on a small dead fir tree nine feet from the nest, he would burst into song." He sang at intervals on the nest. "If the female was incubating she quickly became aware of my presence, and at a distance of about five feet, would flit from the nest to a nearby bush, to begin the usual vireo scold." Both parents assisted in feeding the young and in cleaning the nest, which was kept scrupulously clean. The male was very bold in feeding the young, so that Mr. Rust was able to take some photographs of him in the act. "I was able to observe only the male parent feeding at close range, and I was surprised to note the care he took to feed the helpless young before they were strong enough to raise their heads for food." After the young "were several days old the male would sing from the tree as before, then fly direct to the nest and perching on the brim, would sing as if he would burst his throat." "On one occasion," he says, "a male Cassin Purple Finch seemed to share his joy, and, alighting on the singing tree, joined in and sang his best. The same incident occurred again when the young were a week old, but this time the male vireo seemed to resent the intrusion and drove the finch away in a hurry, chasing him some distance. * * * In securing food for the young the female gathered much larger insects than the male, often coming in with a good size caterpillar dangling from her bill. When I was near she would fly back and forth six or eight feet from the nest and scold until the food was either lost or she ate it, I never could tell which. She never fed the young while I was near."

When first hatched the "four naked, dark, yellow-colored young" were all "huddled up in a pile in a corner of the nest." The young gained rapidly in size and strength, but one was found dead in the nest, when five days old. In removing the dead bird, Mr. Rust found that its claws were closed tightly over several strands of horsehair in the lining; this clutching habit seems to be characteristic of young vireos, and might prove very useful in a gale of wind.

At the age of nine days the two stronger young had their eyes open, but one weakling was several days longer in acquiring its eyesight. "At the age of twelve days the young were well feathered and able to perch on the edge of the nest with a little assistance on my part. The parents became very much excited when they saw two of the nestlings out on the edge of the nest and uttered similar chirping notes trying to coax them away. On the fifth day of July they had their pictures taken for the last time; on the sixth the nest was deserted. Two days later I found the parent birds in some dense brush about seventy-five yards from the nest, but could not locate any of the young. After a severe scolding from the parents I retired and left them to their ways in peace."

Plumages.—The plumages and their sequence are similar to those of the eastern warbling vireo, with the probability of a partial prenuptial molt about the head and breast, as noted by Ned Dearborn (1907).

Food.—Prof. F. E. L. Beal (1907) made a study of the western warbling vireo in California, based on the examination of 110 stomachs, collected during the seven months from April to October, inclusive. He writes:

Insects, with a few spiders, amount to over 97 percent of the diet, leaving less than 3 percent of vegetable matter, practically all of which was taken in August and September; it consisted of wild fruit (elderberries), a few seeds of poison oak, a few other seeds, and some rubbish.

Of the animal food the largest item is Lepidoptera; that is, caterpillars, moths, and the like. These amount to something more than 43 percent of the whole. Caterpillars make up the great bulk of this portion of the food and are a very constant and regular article of diet. * * * In April they amount to over 82 percent of the food of the month. Pupae of coddling moths were identified in four stomachs. * * *

Hemiptera are the next most important item of diet, and amount to 21 percent. They consist of stink-bugs, leaf-bugs, leaf-hoppers, spittle-insects, tree-hoppers, and scales. The last were the black olive species (*Saissetia oleae*). Coccinellid beetles, or ladybirds, were eaten to the extent of over 19 percent of the whole. * * * Other beetles, mostly harmful species, amount to more than 7 percent.

Hymenoptera, consisting of a few ants and an occasional wasp made up a little more than 1 percent. "A small number of flies, grasshoppers, and dragon-flies make up a little more than 3 percent of the miscellaneous insects. Spiders were eaten to somewhat less than 2 percent."

Mrs. Wheelock (1904) says: "In the fall this bird becomes very friendly, coming into the orchards and gardens to hunt busily among the leaves for small caterpillars. At this time he is fond of the cornel berries that grow along the mountain brooks, and occasionally condescends to eat mistletoe."

Mr. Rathbun watched a western warbling for a long time while it was busily feeding in some trees, and he says in his notes: "While hunting among the branches and foliage of a tree the vireo sang frequently, and at times the song was given when the bird turned its head from side to side. Often the vireo would poise in the air for an instant to take some insect from beneath a leaf, then begin again its inspection of the twigs and leaves. The bird made this distinction in anything it captured; if the prey was small, it was eaten as soon as taken; but if of large size, it was well minced before being swallowed."

Voice.—All the habits, except as mentioned above, and the song of the western warbling vireo do not seem to differ from those of its eastern relative. It is an equally persistent singer. Mr. Rathbun says in his notes: "Its warbling song is heard incessantly from the time of its arrival until nearly the middle of June, then much less frequently. I have noticed that in the early part of the season the character of the weather has no effect whatever on its tendency to sing, but it does appear to influence the bird later, for then during the cool and lowery days its song is shorter and longer intervals elapse between the renditions. And should a day come that is stormy, then the bird may not be heard at all. During the flood period of its song the singer is seemingly carried away by his efforts, often singing continuously for many seconds, renditions of his song flowing along like the current of a stream. Its song practically ceases by July, and in this month is heard more often in the morning hours. It seems to cease singing sometime in early August, but we have heard it warble a little in September during the time it is moving south."

COEREBA BAHAMENSIS (Reichenbach)

BAHAMA HONEYCREEPER

HABITS

The Bahama honeycreeper is the only one of some 18 species of honeycreepers, or bananaquits, quite generally distributed in the West Indies, the islands in the Caribbean Sea, and in Neotropical regions in South America, that has occurred within the limits of our Check-list and then only as a straggler on the east coast of Florida and in the Florida keys. This species seems to breed only in the Bahama Islands. Apparently there are only two published records of its occurrence in Florida; Baird (Baird, Cassin, and Lawrence, 1858), reported one taken on Indian Key on January 31, 1858; and John T. Nichols (1921) reported one seen at Miami Beach on February 7, 1921.

All visitors to the Bahamas have reported this honeycreeper as abundant on practically all the islands where there are trees or shrubbery. C. J. Maynard (1896), to whom we are mostly indebted for our knowledge of the habits of this species, says: "The Honey Creeper is an abundant and widely distributed species throughout the Bahamas, being found on all of the larger islands which I have visited and they also occur on some of the smaller keys. * * * They inhabit the scrub, and in the neighborhood of settlements live on the borders of the plantations being attracted there by the fruit."

Nesting.—Mr. Maynard found a number of nests during March, April, and May, which seems to cover the nesting season. He says that the nests are—

very large for the size of the birds, supported by forking twigs in a bush, or small tree, with the entrance on one side above the level of the bottom. Composed of the stems of a small vine, hemp-like fiber woven closely, forming either a spherical or balloon-shaped structure. The lining is composed of finer material. Dimensions of nest, externally, 4.40 by 5.00; internal, 3.00 by 3.50; entrance, 1.25 in diameter. * * *

As a rule, neither male nor female pays much attention to the intruder when the nest is visited. In most cases, I find that I have recorded that the female slipped quietly out of the nest and instantly disappeared. This was especially

noticeable when the eggs were fresh.   The nest on the U Key was placed in a low
bush not over three feet from the ground; both parents were present and neither
exhibited the slightest solicitude for the safety of their offspring.   Both were
very tame, coming within a foot of our heads as we sat on the ground near the
nest.   This last mentioned was placed the lowest of any I ever saw and the one
I mentioned as finding in the scrub ten feet up was by far the highest.   The usual
distance from the ground is between four and five feet.   The nests are seldom
fastened securely to the bushes, but are usually laid in the forks formed by
the twigs.

There is one of Mr. Maynard's nests, containing three eggs, in the
Thayer collection in Cambridge.   This had been placed in the slanting forks of a bush and built up fully 4 inches from the fork; it was
made of rootlets, vine tendrils, strips of inner bark, and fine grasses,
mixed with plenty of wool and pappus clusters; it was lined with
finer grass and pappus.

There are three other nests of the Bahama honeycreeper in the same
collection, taken by A. H. Verrill during the first week in May 1904
and 1905.   One of these was in a bamboo thicket 3 feet from the
ground, one 4 feet up in a small bush, and one 6 feet above the earth
in a tree.   They are all bulky nests, containing four, five, and six eggs,
respectively, and made of smilar materials to those mentioned above,
but one contains many dried and skeletonized leaves and dried lichens,
the fine, brown flowing stalks of mosses had been used in one, and the
third contains the dried fronds of some fern.   The largest nest measures 7 by 5 inches in outer diameter.

Eggs.—The Bahama honeycreeper lays three to six eggs in a set.
These are ovate to elongate-ovate and are slightly glossy.   The ground
color is white, or grayish white, speckled and spotted with shades of
"vinaceous-fawn," "Vandyke brown," and "snuff brown."   Frequently
the eggs are so speckled and clouded with "fawn," "brownish drab,"
"auburn," or "bay" that the ground color is practically obscured and
appears to be "vinaceous-fawn."   The markings on all types are more
concentrated at the large end; and on some of the heavily spotted and
clouded varieties, a solid cap of "sorghum brown," with a few very
tiny scrawls of "warm sepia," may be found.   The measurements of
40 eggs average 17.1 by 12.8 millimeters; the eggs showing the four extremes measure **19.0** by 13.1, 17.8 by **14.0, 15.5** by 12.4, and 17.1 by
11.4 millimeters.   (Harris.)

Plumages.—Ridgway (1902) describes the juvenal plumage of the
Bahama honeycreeper as follows: "Above brownish gray or deep drab-
gray, the primaries and rectrices marked with white and (together
with secondaries) edged with paler gray as in adults; lower rump
olive-yellow, much less distinct and more restricted than the pure
yellow patch of adults; sides of head brownish gray, without any white
superciliary stripe or else with this merely indicated; malar region

paler grayish or dull grayish white, faintly tinged with yellow; chin, throat, and upper chest dull yellowish white; rest of under parts similar, the lower chest, breast, and upper abdomen more distinctly yellowish, the sides and flanks strongly tinged with brownish gray; bill and feet as in adults, but the former rather more brownish."

Food.—These honeycreepers are called bananaquits or bananabirds by the natives of the islands, but Mr. Maynard (1896) says: "I do not remember having seen one eat any bananas. They are, however, very fond of sapodillas and will eat them greedily. They also abstract honey from the flowers of various plants and trees. When obtaining honey from flowers, they alight on a convenient twig and insert their bills into the calix, or when this is too deep, as in the case of the long flower of the life leaf, they make an incision near the base, much as is done by bees under similar circumstances and thus remove the honey."

They may also obtain some insects in the blossoms. J. H. Riley (1905) saw them apparently hunting for insects in another way: "They seemed to be very industrious in searching the trees, presumably for insects, crawling up and down like *Mniotilta varia;* indeed, their actions are very warbler-like."

Behavior.—Mr. Maynard (1896) writes:

The flight of this species is swift and strong, quite unlike that of our warblers. They dash quickly through the foliage, alight suddenly, and remain perfectly motionless for a time; then when ready to move again they will fly, even for a short distance, rather than to hop from bough to bough. I have never seen any movement which would suggest creeping, thus it is difficult to say why the name of creeper is applied to the species. They are not at all quarrelsome, and I have seen half a dozen cling together on one sapodilla feeding from an orifice in one side. They are not shy and I have had them alight within a foot or two of my head as I have been standing in the scrub, but they appear to vary individually in this respect. Three, which were brought to me by some children, exhibited different degrees of tameness. One male, which sang the full song, was not at all shy, tasting sweetened water out of a spoon which I held in my hand. Another male was moderately tame, while a female was so shy that she would not allow me to approach her, but flew about the room in which they were all kept, whenever I attempted to offer her food.

Dr. Glover M. Allen (1905) says: "Everywhere on the islands, among bushes and thickets, were little groups of these birds, old and young. They were exceedingly tame and eyed us curiously, often but arm's length away."

John T. Nichols (1921) observed one of these birds at Nassau "taking a morning bath, fluttering in the dew on the broad leaves of a low plant."

Voice.—Mr. Maynard (1896) writes: "The song of the Bahama Honey Creeper consists of a series of low crackling notes, quite unlike the sounds emitted by any other bird, excepting very closely allied species.   They also produce a chattering with the bill when disturbed and utter a sharp chirp of alarm."

Dr. Allen (1905) says: "At New Providence in early July, we occasionally heard the peculiar wirey song of the Honey Creeper which has somewhat the quality of Ruby-Crowned Kinglet's intricate melody with a peculiar faraway and ethereal softness."

DISTRIBUTION

Range.—The Bahama Islands.

Breeding range.—The Bahama honeycreeper, or bananaquit, is resident in the Bahama Islands, occurring on all islands where there is any growth of bushes.   It has occurred a few times in Florida, probably blown west by storms.   Two specimens have been collected: at Indian Key on January 31, 1858, and at Fort Capron on February 11, 1874.   In addition there are three sight records: at Miami on February 7, 1921, and March 23, 1949; and near Cape Sable in May 1922.

LITERATURE CITED

ALEXANDER, HORACE GUNDRY.

1927. A list of the birds observed in Latium, Italy, between June 1911 and February 1916. Compiled from the notes and letters of the late C. J. Alexander. Ibis, 1927, pp. 659–691.

ALLEN, ARTHUR AUGUSTUS.

1930. Cherry bird—the cedar waxwing. Bird-Lore, vol. 32, pp. 298–307.

1932. The red-eyed vireo's family story. Bird-Lore, vol. 34, pp. 353–361.

ALLEN, FRANCIS HENRY.

1922. Some little-known songs of common birds. Natural History, vol. 22, pp. 235–242.

ALLEN, GLOVER MORRILL.

1905. Summer birds in the Bahamas. Auk, vol. 22, pp. 113–133, pl. 1.

ALLEN, JOEL ASAPH.

1874. Notes on the natural history of portions of Dakota and Montana Territories, being the substance of a report to the Secretary of War on the collections made by the North Pacific Railroad Expedition of 1873, Gen. D. S. Stanley, Commander. Proc. Boston Soc. Nat. Hist., vol. 17, pp. 33–85.

1905. Report on the birds collected in north-eastern Siberia by the Jesup North Pacific Expedition, with field notes by the collectors. Bull. Amer. Mus. Nat. Hist., vol. 21, pp. 219–257.

AMERICAN ORNITHOLOGISTS' UNION.

1931. Check-list of North American birds. Ed. 4.

AUDUBON, JOHN JAMES.

1841. The birds of America, vol. 3.

1842. The birds of America, vol. 4.

1844. The birds of America, vol. 7.

AYMAR, GORDON,

1935. Bird flight.

BAGG, AARON CLARK, and ELIOT, SAMUEL ATKINS, JR.

1937. Birds of the Connecticut Valley in Massachusetts.

BAILEY, ALFRED MARSHALL.

1926. Report on the birds of northwestern Alaska and the regions adjacent to Bering Strait, pt. 10. Condor, vol. 28, pp. 165–170.

BAILEY, FLORENCE MERRIAM.

1896. Nesting habits of *Phainopepla nitens* in California. Auk, vol. 13, pp. 38–43.

1904. Scott oriole, gray vireo, and phoebe in northeastern New Mexico. Auk, vol. 21, pp. 392–393.

1928. Birds of New Mexico.

BAILEY, HAROLD HARRIS.

1925. The birds of Florida.

BAIRD, SPENCER FULLERTON.

1865. Review of American birds, in the museum of the Smithsonian Institution. Part 1, North and Middle America. Smithsonian Misc. Coll., No. 181.

BAIRD, S. F.; BREWER, THOMAS MAYO; and RIDGWAY, ROBERT.

1874. A history of North American birds, vol. 1. Land birds.

BAIRD, S. F.; CASSIN, JOHN; and LAWRENCE, GEORGE NEWBOLD.
    1858. Reports of explorations and surveys . . . for a railroad from the
        Mississippi River to the Pacific Ocean. . . , vol. 9, Birds.
BANCROFT, GRIFFING.
    1930. The breeding birds of central Lower California. Condor, vol. 32,
        pp. 20-49.
BANGS, OUTRAM, and BRADLEE, THOMAS STEVENSON.
    1901. The resident land birds of Bermuda. Auk, vol. 18, pp. 249-257.
BAYNARD, OSCAR EDWARD.
    1914. Photographing birds' nests. Bird-Lore, vol. 16, pp. 471-477.
BAYNES, ERNEST HAROLD.
    1922. A vireo as hostess. Bird-Lore, vol. 24, pp. 256-259.
BEAL, FOSTER ELLENBOROUGH LASCELLES.
    1907. Birds of California in relation to the fruit industry. Biol. Surv.
        Bul. 30.
BEAL, F. E. L., and MCATEE, WALDO LEE.
    1912. Food of some well-known birds of forest, farm, and garden. U. S.
        Dept. Agr. Farmers' Bull. 506.
BELDING, LYMAN.
    1883. Catalogue of a collection of birds made near the southern extremity
        of Lower California. Proc. U. S. Nat. Mus., vol. 5, pp. 532-550.
BENSON, MARY B.
    1920. The waxwings' rag bag. Bird-Lore, vol. 22, pp. 286-287.
BERGMAN, STEN.
    1935. Zur Kenntnis nordostasiastischer Vögel.
BERTRAM, G. C. L.; LACK, DAVID; and ROBERTS, BNARI BIRLEY.
    1934. Notes on east Greenland birds, with a discussion of the periodic
        non-breeding among Arctic birds. Ibis, 1934, pp. 816-831.
BICKNELL, EUGENE PINTARD.
    1884. A study of the singing of our birds. Auk, vol. 1, pp. 322-332.
BISHOP, LOUIS BENNETT.
    1900. Birds of the Yukon region, with notes on other species. North Amer.
        Fauna No. 19.
BLAIR, HUGH MOVAY SUTHERLAND.
    1936. On the birds of east Finmark. Ibis, 1936, pp. 280-308, 429-459, 651-
        674.
BLAIR, RICHARD HENRY, and TUCKER, BERNARD WILLIAM.
    1941. Nest-sanitation, by R. H. Blair, with additions from published sources,
        by B. W. Tucker. British Birds, vol. 34, pp. 206-215, 226-235, 250-
        255.
BLAISDELL, FRANK ELLSWORTH.
    1893. Biological notes on *Phainopepla nitens.* Zoe, vol. 3, pp. 312-314.
BLAKISTON, THOMAS WRIGHT.
    1863. On the birds of the interior or British America. Ibis, vol. 5, pp.
        39-155.
BLINCOE, BENEDICT JOSEPH.
    1923. Random notes on the feeding habits of some Kentucky birds. Wilson
        Bull., vol. 35, pp. 63-71.
BOASE, HENRY.
    1926. The display of the pied wagtail. British Birds, vol. 20, pp. 20-22.
BOWLES, CHARLES WILSON, and BOWLES, JOHN HOOPER.
    1892. Nesting of the blue-headed vireo in Massachusetts. Ornithologist
        and Oologist, vol. 17, p. 102.

BRAND, ALBERT RICH.
  1938. Vibration frequencies of passerine bird song. Auk, vol. 55, pp. 263–
    268.
BRANDT, HERBERT WILLIAM.
  1940. Texas bird adventures.
  1943. Alaska bird trails.
BREWSTER, WILLIAM.
  1879. Notes upon the distribution, habits, and nesting of the black-capped
    vireo (*Vireo atricapillus*). Bull. Nuttall Orn. Club, vol. 4, pp. 99–103.
  1880. Notes on the habits and distribution of the Philadelphia vireo (*Vireo
    philadelphicus*). Bull. Nuttall Orn. Club, vol. 5, pp. 1–7.
  1882. On a collection of birds lately made by Mr. F. Stephens in Arizona.
    Bull. Nuttall Orn. Club, vol. 7, pp. 135–147.
  1886. An ornithological reconnaissance in western North Carolina. Auk,
    vol. 3, pp. 94–112.
  1887. Three new forms of North American birds. Auk, vol. 4, pp. 145–149.
  1888. Nest and eggs of the mountain solitary vireo. Ornithologist and
    Oologist, vol. 13, p. 113.
  1891. Descriptions of seven supposed new North American birds. Auk,
    vol. 8, pp. 139–149.
  1902. Birds of the Cape region of Lower California. Bull. Mus. Comp. Zool.,
    vol. 41, No. 1.
  1903. Further notes on the Philadelphia vireo, with description of the nest
    and eggs. Auk, vol. 20, pp. 369–376.
  1906. The birds of the Cambridge region of Massachusetts. Mem. Nuttall
    Orn. Club, No. 4.
  1936. October Farm.
  1937. Concord River.
  1938. The birds of the Lake Umbagog region of Maine, Part 4. Compiled
    by Ludlow Griscom. Bull. Mus. Comp. Zool., vol. 66, pp. 525–620.
BROWN, NATHAN CLIFFORD.
  1906. A great flight of robins and cedar-birds. Auk, vol. 23, pp. 342–343.
BRYANT, HAROLD CHILD.
  1912. Birds in relation to a grasshopper outbreak in California. Univ.
    California Publ. Zool., vol. 11, pp. 1–20.
BRYENS, OSCAR MCKINLEY.
  1925. Some notes on the nesting material of the cedar waxwing. Wilson
    Bull., vol. 37, p. 94.
BUNKER, CHARLES DEAN.
  1910. Habits of the black-capt vireo (*Vireo atricapillus*). Condor, vol. 12,
    pp. 70–73.
BURLEIGH, THOMAS DEARBORN.
  1923. Notes on the breeding birds of Clark's Fork, Bonner County, Idaho.
    Auk, vol. 40, pp. 653–665.
  1925. Notes on the breeding birds of northeastern Georgia. Auk, vol. 42,
    pp. 70–74.
  1930. Notes on the bird life of northwestern Washington. Auk, vol. 47,
    pp. 48–63.
  1941. Bird life on Mt. Mitchell. Auk, vol. 58, pp. 334–345.
BURNS, FRANKLIN LORENZO.
  1915. Comparative periods of deposition and incubation of some North Ameri-
    can birds. Wilson Bull., vol. 27, pp. 275–286.
  1921. Comparative periods of nestling life of some North American Nidicolae.
    Wilson Bull., vol. 33, pp. 177–182.

BUTLIN, SYBIL M.
1940. Display of meadow-pipit. British Birds, vol. 34, pp. 108, 109.

CAMERON, EWEN SOMERLED.
1908. The birds of Custer and Dawson Counties, Montana. Auk, vol. 25, pp. 39–56.

CARRIKER, MELBOURNE ARMSTRONG, Jr.
1910. An annotated list of the birds of Costa Rica, including Cocos Island. Ann. Carnegie Mus., vol. 6, pp. 314–915.

CARTWRIGHT, WILLIAM JAMES.
1924. The increase of the starling. Bird-Lore, vol. 26, pp. 323–326.

CASSIN, JOHN.
1851. Sketch of the birds composing the genera *Vireo*, Vieillot, and *Vireosylvia*, Bonaparte, with a list of the previously known [sic] and descriptions of three new species. Proc. Acad. Nat. Sci. Philadelphia, 1851, pp. 149–154.
1854. Illustrations of the birds of California, Texas, Oregon, British and Russian America.

CHADBOURNE, ARTHUR PATTERSON.
1890. Song of the female butcher bird. Auk, vol. 7, p. 290.

CHAPIN, EDWARD ALBERT.
1925. Food habits of the vireos: A family of insectivorous birds. U. S. Dept. Agr. Dept. Bull. 1355.

CHAPMAN, FRANK MICHLER.
1892. Notes on birds and mammals observed near Trinidad, Cuba, with remarks on the origin of West Indian bird-life. Bull. Amer. Mus. Nat. Hist., vol. 4, pp. 279–330.
1912. Handbook of birds of eastern North America.
1925. The European starling as an American citizen. Natural History, vol. 25, pp. 480–485.

CHAPMAN, F. SPENCER.
1932. Some field-notes on the birds of east Greenland. Geogr. Journ., vol. 79, pp. 493–496.

CHERRIE, GEORGE KRUCK.
1890. North American birds at San José, Costa Rica. Auk, vol. 7, pp. 331–337.

CLARK, AUSTIN HOBART.
1910. The birds collected and observed during the cruise of the United States Fisheries steamer "Albatross" in the North Pacific Ocean, and in the Bering, Okhotsk, Japan and eastern seas, from April to December, 1906. Proc. U. S. Nat. Mus., vol. 38, pp. 25–74.

COMMON, MINNA ANTHONY.
1934. Notes on a red-eyed vireo's nest. Auk, vol. 51, pp. 241–242.

CONGREVE, WILLIAM MAITLAND.
1936. The red-throated pipit. Oologist's Record, vol. 16, pp. 73–78.

CONGREVE, W. M., and FREME, SYDNEY WILLIAM PATRICK.
1930. Seven weeks in eastern and northern Iceland. Ibis, 1930, pp. 193–228.

COOKE, MAY THACHER.
1928. The spread of the European starling in North America (to 1928). U. S. Dept. Agr. Circ. 40.

COTTAM, CLARENCE.
1943. Is the starling population decreasing in northeastern United States? Auk, vol. 60, pp. 439–440.
1944. Starlings feeding on the backs of cattle. Migrant, vol. 15, pp. 24–25.

COUES, ELLIOTT.
    1866. List of the birds of Fort Whipple, Arizona: With which are incorporated all other species ascertained to inhabit the Territory; with brief critical and field notes, descriptions of new species, etc. Proc. Acad. Nat. Sci. Philadelphia, vol. 18, pp. 39–100.
    1874. Birds of the Northwest. U. S. Geol. Surv. Terr. Misc. Publ. No. 3.
    1878. Birds of the Colorado Valley. U. S. Geol. Surv. Terr. Misc. Publ. No. 11.
CRAM, ELOISE BLAINE.
    1930. Birds as a factor in the control of a stomach worm in swine. Auk, vol. 47, pp. 380–384.
CROUCH, JAMES ENSIGN.
    1936. Nesting habits of the cedar waxwing (*Bombycilla cedrorum*). Auk, vol. 53, pp. 1–8.
DAVID, ARMAND, and OUSTALET, ÉMILE.
    1877. Les oiseaux de la Chine.
DAVIS, DAVID EDWARD.
    1937. A cycle in northern shrike emigrations. Auk, vol. 54, pp. 43–49.
DAWSON, WILLIAM LEON.
    1923. The birds of California, vol. 1.
DAWSON, W. L., and BOWLES, JOHN HOOPER.
    1909. The birds of Washington.
DEARBORN, NED.
    1907. Catalogue of a collection of birds from Guatemala. Field Mus. Nat. Hist. Publ. 125, orn. ser., vol. 1, pp. 69–138.
DICKERSON, LAURENCE MAJOR.
    1938. The western frontier of the European starling in the United States as of February, 1937. Condor, vol. 40, pp. 118–123.
DICKEY, DONALD RYDER, and VAN ROSSEM, ADRIAAN JOSEPH.
    1938. The birds of El Salvador. Publ. Field Mus. Nat. Hist., zool. ser., vol. 23.
DICKEY, SAMUEL S.
    1938. The white-eyed vireo in Greene County, Pennsylvania. Cardinal, vol. 4, pp. 158–163.
DIXON, JOSEPH SCATTERGOOD.
    1938. Birds and mammals of Mount McKinley National Park. Nat. Park Service, Fauna Series No. 3.
DU BOIS, ALEXANDER DAWES.
    1940. Nesting habits and behavior of Bell's vireo. Audubon Bull. No. 35, Illinois Audubon Soc.
DWIGHT, JONATHAN, JR.
    1897. A study of the Philadelphia vireo (*Vireo philadelphicus*). Auk, vol. 14, pp. 259–272.
    1900. The sequence of plumage and moults of the passerine birds of New York. Ann. New York Acad. Sci., vol. 13, pp. 73–360, pls. 1–7.
ERICHSEN, WALTER JEFFERSON.
    1919. Some summer birds of Liberty County, Georgia. Auk, vol. 36, pp. 380–393.
ESTERLY, CALVIN OLIN.
    1917. How does the shrike carry its prey? Condor, vol. 19, p. 25.
EVERMANN, BARTON WARREN.
    1882. Black-crested flycatcher. Ornithologist and Oologist, vol. 7, pp. 77–78.
    1886. A list of birds obtained in Ventura County, California. Auk, vol. 3, pp. 179–186.

FELTES, CHARLES HERMAN.
    1935. Notes on banding cedar waxwings in California. Bird-Banding, vol.
        6, p. 104.
    1936. Trapping cedar waxwings in the San Joaquin Valley, California. Con-
        dor, vol. 38, pp. 18–23.
FLAGG, WILSON.
    1890. A year with the birds.
FLOYD, CHARLES BENTON.
    1928. Notes on the invasion of New England and other Atlantic States by
        the northern shrike during the winter of 1926–27. Bull. North-
        eastern Bird-Banding Assoc., vol. 4, pp. 43–49.
FORBUSH, EDWARD HOWE.
    1911. The cedar waxwing. Bird-Lore, vol. 13, pp. 55–58.
    1927. Birds of Massachusetts and other New England States, pt. 2. Land
        birds from bob-whites to grackles.
    1929. Birds of Massachusetts and other New England States. pt. 3. Land
        birds from sparrows to thrushes.
FORD, EDWARD RUSSELL.
    1936. Unusual nest site of the loggerhead shrike (*Lanius ludovicianus
        ludovicianus*). Auk, vol. 53, p. 219.
FRIEDMANN, HERBERT.
    1925. Notes on the birds observed in the lower Rio Grande Valley of Texas
        during May, 1924. Auk, vol. 42, pp. 537–554, pls. 25–29.
    1929. The cowbirds.
    1934. Further additions to the list of birds victimized by the cowbird.
        Wilson Bull., vol. 46, pp. 25–36.
    1937. Further additions to the known avifauna of St. Lawrence Island,
        Alaska. Condor, vol. 39, p. 91.
    1943. Further additions to the list of birds known to be parasitized by cow-
        birds. Auk, vol. 60, pp. 350–356.
GABRIELSON, IRA NOEL.
    1924. Food habits of some winter bird visitants.   U. S. Dept. Agr. Dept.
        Bull. 1249.
GABRIELSON, I. N., and JEWETT, STANLEY GORDON.
    1940. Birds of Oregon.
GÄTKE, HEINRICH.
    1895. Heligoland as an ornithological observatory.
GANDER, FRANK FORREST.
    1927. Phainopepla notes. Bird-Lore, vol. 29, pp. 420–421.
GILMAN, MARSHALL FRENCH.
    1903. The phainopepla. Condor, vol. 6, pp. 42–43.
GOSS, NATHANIEL STICKNEY.
    1891. History of the birds of Kansas.
GREAVES, RICHARD HATHORN.
    1941. Behaviour of white wagtails wintering in Cairo district. Ibis, 1941,
        pp. 459–462.
GREEN, CHARLOTTE HILTON.
    1933. Birds of the South.
GRIMES, SAMUEL ANDREW.
    1928. The loggerhead shrike. Florida Naturalist, new ser., vol. 1, pp. 48–50.

GRINNELL, JOSEPH.
1897. Report on the birds recorded during a visit to the islands of Santa
Barbara, San Nicolas and San Clemente, in the spring of 1897.
Pasadena Acad. Sci., Publ. No. 1.
1900. Birds of the Kotzebue Sound region, Alaska. Pacific Coast Avif.,
No. 1.
1908. The biota of the San Bernardino Mountains. Univ. California Publ.
Zool., vol. 5, pp. 1–170.
1911. Field notes from the San Joaquin Valley. Condor, vol. 13, pp. 109–111.
1914. An account of the mammals and birds of the lower Colorado Valley.
Univ. California Publ. Zool., vol. 12, pp. 51–294.
1922. Northward range of the gray vireo in California. Condor, vol. 24,
pp. 211–212.
GRINNELL, JOSEPH; DIXON, JOSEPH; and LINSDALE, JEAN MYRON.
1930. Vertebrate natural history of a section of northern California through
the Lassen Peak region. Univ. California Publ. Zool., vol. 35,
pp. 1–594.
GRINNELL, JOSEPH, and LINSDALE, JEAN MYRON.
1936. Vertebrate animals of Point Lobos Reserve, 1934–35. Carnegie Inst.
Washington, Publ. No. 481.
GRINNELL, JOSEPH, and STORER, TRACY IRWIN.
1924. Animal life in the Yosemite. Contr. Mus. Vert. Zool., Univ. California.
GRINNELL, JOSEPH, and SWARTH, HARRY SCHELWALDT.
1913. An account of the birds and mammals of the San Jacinto area of
southern California. Univ. California Publ. Zool., vol. 10, pp.
197–406.
GRISCOM, LUDLOW.
1923. Birds of the New York City region. Amer. Mus. Nat. Hist. Handb.
ser. No. 9.
1932. The distribution of bird-life in Guatemala. Bull. Amer. Mus. Nat.
Hist., vol. 64.
HAMILTON, WILLIAM JOHN, JR.
1933. A late nesting waxwing in central New York. Auk, vol. 50, pp.
114–115.
HANNA, G. DALLAS.
1920. Additions to the avifauna of the Pribilof Islands, Alaska, including
four species new to North America. Auk, vol. 37, pp. 248–254.
HANNA, WILSON CREAL.
1924. Weights of about three thousand eggs. Condor, vol. 26, pp. 146–153.
HANTZSCH, BERNHARD.
1905. Beiträg zur Kenntnis der Vogelwelt Islands.
HARRIS, R. D.
1933. Observations on a nest of Sprague's pipit (Anthus spraguei). Can.
Field-Nat., vol. 47, pp. 91–95.
HARTERT, ERNST.
1910. Die Vögel der paläarktischen Fauna, vol. 1.
HARTERT, ERNST, and STEINBACHER, FRIEDRICH.
1938. Die Vögel der paläarktischen Fauna. Ergänzungsband.
HAVILAND, MAUD DORIA.
1915. A summer on the Yenesei.
HELMS, OTTO.
1926. The birds of Angmagsalik. Meddelelser om Grønland, vol. 58, pp. 205–
274.

HENSHAW, HENRY WETHERBEE.
1875. Report upon the ornithological collections made in portions of Nevada, Utah, California, Colorado, New Mexico, and Arizona during the years 1871, 1872, 1873, and 1874. Wheeler's Rep. Expl. Surv. West 100th Merid.
HERRICK, FRANCIS HOBART.
1904. Red-eyed vireos, awake and asleep. Bird-Lore, vol. 6, pp. 113–116.
1935. Wild birds at home.
HERSEY, FRANK SEYMOUR.
1916. A list of the birds observed in Alaska and northeastern Siberia during the summer of 1914. Smithsonian Misc. Coll., vol. 66, No. 2.
HICKS, LAWRENCE EMERSON.
1934. Individual and sexual variations in the European starling. Bird-Banding, vol. 5, pp. 103–118.
HICKS, L. E., and DAMBACH, CHARLES ARTHUR.
1935. A study of the European starling. Cardinal, vol. 4, pp. 25–30.
HØRNING, R.
1939. Birds. In 6. og 7. Thule Expedition til Sydøstgrønland 1931–33. Medd. om Grønland, vol. 108, pp. 1–44.
HOFFMAN, EDWARD CARTER.
1930. Spread of the European starling in America. Wilson Bull., vol. 42, facing p. 80.
HOFFMAN, LOUIS EDWARD.
1933. Phainopepla observed on Barley Flats, San Gabriel Mountains, California. Condor, vol. 35, p. 166.
HOFFMANN, RALPH.
1904. A guide to the birds of New England and eastern New York.
1927. Birds of the Pacific States.
HOLT, ERNEST GOLSAN.
1913. Notes on the loggerhead shrike at Barachias, Montgomery Co., Ala. Auk, vol. 30, pp. 276–277.
HOLT, E. G. and SUTTON, GEORGE MIKSCH.
1926. Notes on birds observed in southern Florida. Ann. Carnegie Mus., vol. 16, pp. 409–439, pls. 39–44.
HONYWILL, ALBERT WILLIAM, JR.
1911. Notes on some summer and fall birds of the Crooked Lake region, Cass and Crow Wing Counties, Minn. Auk, vol. 28, pp. 229–237.
HOWELL, ARTHUR HOLMES.
1932. Florida bird life.
HUTCHINS, JOHN.
1902. The nesting of the yellow-throated vireo. Bird-Lore, vol. 4, pp. 120–123.
JAMESON, EVERETT WILLIAMS, JR.
1942. Speed of the starling. Auk, vol. 59, p. 442.
JEWETT, STANLEY GORDON.
1942. The European starling in California. Condor, vol. 44, p. 79.
JOHNSON, ARCHIBALD.
1938. Nest building behavior in the loggerhead shrike group. Wilson Bull., vol. 50, pp. 246–248.
JOHNSON, HAZEL S.
1933. Notes on the family life of a pair of American pipits. Wilson Bull., vol. 45, pp. 114–117.
JOHNSON, ROBERT ANTHONY.
1935. Notes on the breeding success of starlings. Auk, vol. 52, p. 312.

JONES, CLINTON MILLER.
    1887. Nesting of the blue-headed vireo. Ornithologist and Oologist, vol. 12,
        p. 26.
JOURDAIN, FRANCIS CHARLES ROBERT.
    1938–1939. (See under Witherby, Jourdain, Ticehurst, and Tucker.)
JUDD, SYLVESTER DWIGHT.
    1898. The food of shrikes. Biol. Surv. Bull. 9, pp. 15–26.
KALMBACH, EDWIN RICHARD.
    1922. A comparison of the food habits of British and American starlings.
        Auk, vol. 39, pp. 189–195.
    1932. Winter starling roosts of Washington. Wilson Bull., vol. 44, pp. 65–75.
    1937. Suggestions for combating starling roosts. Wildlife Research and
        Management Leaflet, U. S. Dept. Agr., Biol. Surv. Pamphlet No. 81.
KALMBACH, E. R., and GABRIELSON, IRA NOEL.
    1921. Economic value of the starling in the United States. U. S. Dept. Agr.
        Dept. Bull. 868.
KELLY, WILLIAM N.
    1927. The Japanese starling in Vancouver, B. C. Murrelet, vol. 8, p. 14.
KING, FRANKLIN HIRAM.
    1883. Economic relations of Wisconsin birds. Geology of Wisconsin, vol.
        1, pp. 441–610.
KNIGHT, ORA WILLIS.
    1908. The birds of Maine.
KNOWLTON, GEORGE FRANKLIN, and HARMSTON, FRED CARL.
    1944. Food of white-rumped shrike. Auk, vol. 61, pp. 642–643.
KOPMAN, HENRY HAZLITT.
    1915. List of the birds of Louisiana. Part 7. Auk, vol. 32, pp. 183–194.
LA TOUCHE, JOHN DAVID DIGUES DE.
    1920. Notes on the birds of North-East Chihli, in North China. Ibis, 1920,
        pp. 629–671.
    1925. A handbook of the birds of eastern China, vol 1, pt. 2.
    1926. A handbook of the birds of eastern China, vol. 1, pt. 3.
    1930. A handbook of the birds of eastern China, vol. 1, pt. 5.
LEWIS, HARRISON FLINT.
    1921. A nesting of the Philadelphia vireo. Auk, vol. 38, pp. 26–44, 185–202.
LINCOLN, FREDERICK CHARLES.
    1935. The migration of North American birds. U. S. Dept. Agr. Circ. 363.
    1939. The migration of American birds.
LINSDALE, JEAN MYRON.
    1938. Environmental responses of vertebrates in the Great Basin. Amer.
        Midl. Nat., vol. 19, pp. 1–206.
LLOYD, WILLIAM.
    1887. Birds of Tom Green and Concho Counties, Texas. Auk, vol. 4, pp.
        289–299.
LOEFER, JOHN B., and PATTEN, J. A.
    1941. Starlings at a blackbird roost. Auk, vol. 58, pp. 584–586.
LOTT, WILLIAM.
    1939. A flicker with a family of starlings. Bird-Banding, vol. 10, p. 90.
LUTTRINGER, LEO A., JR.
    1927. Mother robin killed by European starling. Oologist, vol. 44, p. 95.
MACFARLANE, RODERICK ROSS.
    1908. Notes on the mammals and birds of northern Canada. *In* "Through
        the Mackenzie Basin," by Charles Mair.

MACOUN, JOHN, and MACOUN, JAMES MELVILLE.
    1909. Catalogue of Canadian birds.
MAILLIARD, JOSEPH.
    1899. Spring notes on the birds of Santa Cruz Island, Cal., April, 1898.
        Condor, vol. 1, pp. 41–45.
MATHEWS, FERDINAND SCHUYLER.
    1921. Field book of wild birds and their music.
MATTESON, Mrs. E. A.
    1924. Dandy. Bird-Lore, vol. 26, pp. 169–170.
MAYNARD, CHARLES JOHNSON.
    1896. The birds of eastern North America, ed. 2.
McATEE, WALDO LEE.
    1926. The relation of birds to woodlots in New York State.   Roosevelt Wild
        Life Bull., vol. 4, pp. 7–152.
McCOY, HARRIET.
    1927. A waxwing ceremony.   Bird-Lore, vol. 29, pp. 188–189.
McILHENNY, EDWARD AVERY.
    1936. Are starlings a menace to the food supply of our native birds?   Auk,
        vol. 53, pp. 338–339.
McLAUGHLIN, RICHARD BURTON.
    1888. Nesting of the mountain solitary vireo.   Ornithologist and Oologist,
        vol. 13, pp. 113–114.
MEARNS, EDGAR ALEXANDER.
    1890. Observations on the avifauna of portions of Arizona.   Auk, vol. 7,
        pp. 251–264.
    1898. Descriptions of two new birds from the Santa Barbara Islands, south-
        ern California.   Auk, vol. 15, pp. 258–264.
MEINERTZHAGEN, RICHARD.
    1922. Notes on some birds from the Near East and from tropical East
        Africa.   Ibis, 1922, pp. 1–74.
    1930. Nicoll's Birds of Egypt.
MERRILL, JAMES CUSHING.
    1888. Notes on the birds of Fort Klamath, Oregon.   Auk, vol. 5, pp. 357–366.
MILLER, ALDEN HOLMES.
    1928. The molts of the loggerhead shrike, *Lanius ludovicianus* Linnaeus.
        Univ. California Publ. Zool., vol. 30, pp. 393–417.
    1930. Two new races of the loggerhead shrike from western North America.
        Condor, vol. 32, pp. 155–156.
    1931. Systematic revision and natural history of the American shrikes
        (*Lanius*).   Univ. California Publ. Zool., vol. 38, pp. 11–242.
    1933. Postjuvenal molt and the appearance of sexual characteristics of
        plumage in *Phainopepla nitens*.   Univ. California Publ. Zool., vol.
        38, pp. 427–444.
MINOT, HENRY DAVIS.
    1877. The land-birds and game-birds of New England.
    1895. The land-birds and game-birds of New England.   Revised and edited
        by William Brewster.
MOORE, GEORGE A.
    1928. A possible relationship between Bell's vireo and the cowbird.   Wil-
        son Bull., vol. 40, p. 197.
MORLEY, AVERIL.
    1940. Courtship action of male meadow-pipit.   British Birds, vol. 34, p. 65.
MORSE, GEORGE W.
    1927. Bell's vireo.   Double nest.   Oologist, vol. 44, pp. 23–24.

MOUSLEY, HENRY.
  1918. The breeding of the migrant shrike at Hatley, Stanstead County, Quebec, 1916. Auk, vol. 35, pp. 33–36.
MUNRO, JAMES ALEXANDER.
  1922. The "Japanese starling" in Vancouver, British Columbia. Can. Field-Nat., vol. 36, pp. 32–33.
MURIE, OLAUS JOHAN.
  1938. Four birds new to St. Lawrence Island, Alaska. Condor, vol. 40, p. 227.
MYERS, HARRIET WILLIAMS.
  1908. Observations on the nesting habits of the phainopepla. Condor, vol. 10, pp. 72–75.
  1909. Notes on the habits of *Phainopepla nitens*. Condor, vol. 11, pp. 22–23.
NELSON, EDWARD WILLIAM.
  1883. Birds of Bering Sea and the Arctic Ocean. Cruise of the Revenue-Steamer *Corwin* in Alaska and the N. W. Arctic Ocean in 1881, pp. 56–118.
  1887. Report upon natural history collections made in Alaska. U. S. Signal Serv., Arctic ser., No. 3.
NETHERSOLE-THOMPSON, CAROLINE and DESMOND.
  1940. Display of the meadow-pipit. British Birds, vol. 34, p. 109.
  1942. Egg-shell disposal by birds. British Birds, vol. 35, pp. 162–169, 190–200, 214–223, 241–250.
  1943. Nest-site selection by birds. British Birds, vol. 37, pp. 70–74, 88–94, 108–113.
NEWTON, ALFRED.
  1875. Notes on birds which have been found in Greenland. Manual of the natural history, geology, and physics of Greenland and the neighbouring regions ("Arctic Manual"). Edited by T. Rupert Jones, pp. 94–115.
NICE, MARGARET MORSE.
  1929. The fortunes of a pair of Bell vireos. Condor, vol. 31, pp. 13–18.
  1931. The birds of Oklahoma. Revised ed. Publ. Univ. Oklahoma, vol. 3.
  1941. Observations on the behavior of a young cedar waxwing. Condor, vol. 43, pp. 58–64.
NICHOLS, JOHN TREADWELL.
  1921. *Coereba bahamensis* at Miami, Fla. Auk, vol. 38, pp. 461–462.
NICHOLSON, EDWARD MARX, and KOCH, LUDWIG.
  1936. Songs of wild birds.
NIETHAMMER, GÜNTHER.
  1937. Handbuch der deutchen Vogelkunde, vol. 1.
NOBLE, FRANK T.
  1902. A desperate encounter between a loggerhead shrike and a snake. Journ. Maine Orn. Soc., vol. 4, pp. 12–14.
NUTTALL, THOMAS.
  1832. A manual of the ornithology of the United States and Canada. Land birds.
OBERHOLSER, HARRY CHURCH.
  1896. A preliminary list of the birds of Wayne County, Ohio.
  1917. A synopsis of the races of *Bombycilla garrula* (Linnaeus). Auk, vol. 34, pp. 330–333.
  1918. Description of a new *Lanius* from Lower California. Condor, vol. 20, pp. 209–210.
  1938. The bird life of Louisiana. Louisiana Dept. Conservation, Bull. 28.

ODUM, EUGENE PLEASANTS, and PITELKA, FRANK ALOIS.
   1939. Storm mortality in a winter starling roost. Auk, vol. 56, pp. 451–455.
ORCUTT, FRANCIS.
   1928. An incident from the home-life of a yellow-throated vireo. Bird-
        Lore, vol. 30, p. 395.
ORNITHOLOGICAL SOCIETY OF JAPAN.
   1932. A hand-list of the Japanese birds. Third and revised edition.
PALMER, ROBERT HASTINGS.
   1922. The cedar waxwing in Mexico. Condor, vol. 24, pp. 183–184.
PALMER, WILLIAM.
   1898. Our small eastern shrikes. Auk, vol. 15, pp. 244–258.
PALUDAN, KNUD.
   1932. Verbreitung und Winterquartiere des Rassenkreises *Motacilla alba*.
        Journ. für Orn., Jahrg. 80, pp. 392–416.
PANGBURN, CLIFFORD HAYES.
   1919. A three months' list of the birds of Pinellas County, Florida. Auk, vol.
        36, pp. 393–405.
PAULSEN, J. H.
   1846. *In* Ornithologischer Beitrag zur Fauna Groenlands. (Translation
        of Holbøll's "Ornithologiske Beitrag til den grønlandske Fauna.")
PEAKE, E.
   1926. Some notes on bird-song. British Birds, vol. 20, pp. 62–70.
PEARSON, THOMAS GILBERT; BRIMLEY, CLEMENT SAMUEL; and BRIMLEY, HERBERT
   HUTCHINSON.
   1942. Birds of North Carolina. Revised edition.
PEDERSEN, ALVIN.
   1926. Beiträge zur Kenntnis der Säugetier—und Vogelfauna der Ostküste
        Grönlands. Meddelelser om Grønland, vol. 68, pp. 207–249.
   1930. Fortgesetzte Beiträge zur Kenntnis der Säugetier—und Vogelfauna
        der Ostküste Grönlands. Meddelelser om Grønland, vol. 77, pp. 341–
        507.
PETERS, HAROLD SEYMORE.
   1936. A list of external parasites from birds of the eastern part of the
        United States. Bird-Banding, vol. 7, pp. 9–27.
PETERS, JAMES LEE.
   1928. Moults and plumages of the starling *Sturnus vulgaris* Linn. Bull.
        Essex County Orn. Club, 1928, pp. 21–25.
   1931. An account of the yellow-green vireo (*Vireosylva flavovirides* Cassin).
        Auk, vol. 48, pp. 575–587.
PETERSON, ROGER TORY.
   1939. A field guide to the birds.
   1941. A field guide to western birds.
PHILIPP, PHILIP BERNARD, and BOWDISH, BEECHER SCOVILLE.
   1917. Some summer birds of northern New Brunswick. Auk, vol. 34, pp.
        265–275, pls. 7–9.
PHILLIPS, GEORGE G.
   1913. Five little waxwings and how they grew. Bird-Lore, vol. 15, pp. 218–
        220.
PICKWELL, GAYLE.
   1947. The American pipit in its Arctic-alpine home. Auk, vol. 64, pp. 1–14.
PITELKA, FRANK ALOIS, and KOESTNER, ELMER JOSEPH.
   1942. Breeding behavior of Bell's vireo in Illinois. Wilson Bull., vol. 54,
        pp. 97–106.

PLESKE, THEODORE.
   1928. Birds of the Eurasian tundra.   Mem. Boston Soc. Nat. Hist., vol. 6,
      pp. 111–485, pls. 16–37.
POPHAM, HUGH LEYBORNE.
   1897. Notes on birds observed on the Yenisei River, Siberia, in 1895.   Ibis,
      1897, pp. 89–108.
PREBLE, EDWARD ALEXANDER.
   1908. A biological investigation of the Athabaska-Mackenzie region.   North
      Amer. Fauna, No. 27.
   1921. Philadelphia vireo in Montana.   Condor, vol. 23, p. 138.
PREBLE, EDWARD ALEXANDER, and McATEE, WALDO LEE.
   1923. A biological survey of the Pribilof Islands, Alaska.   North Amer.
      Fauna, No. 46.
RATHBUN, SAMUEL FREDERICK.
   1934. Notes on the speed of birds in flight.   Murrelet, vol. 15, pp. 23–24.
REID, PHILIP SAVILE GREY.
   1884. Contributions to the natural history of the Bermudas.   Part 4: The
      birds of Bermuda.   U. S. Nat. Mus. Bull. 25, pp. 163–279.
REIMANN, EDWARD JOSEPH.
   1938. Loggerhead shrikes and snakes.   Auk, vol. 55, p. 540.
RICHMOND, CHARLES WALLACE.
   1888. An annotated list of birds breeding in the District of Columbia.   Auk,
      vol. 5, pp. 18–25.
RIDGWAY, ROBERT.
   1883. *Anthus cervinus* (Pallas) in Lower California.   Proc. U. S. Nat Mus.,
      vol. 6, pp. 156–157.
   1889. The ornithology of Illinois.
   1902 The birds of North and Middle America.   U. S. Nat. Mus. Bull. 50, pt. 2.
   1904. The birds of North and Middle America.   U. S. Nat. Mus. Bull. 50, pt. 3.
RILEY, JOSEPH HARVEY.
   1905. List of birds collected or observed during the Bahama Expedition of
      the Geographic Society of Baltimore.   Auk, vol. 22, pp. 349–360.
RILEY, J. H., and WETMORE, ALEXANDER.
   1928. An erroneous record for the Japanese pipit in Alaska.   Condor, vol. 30,
      p. 193.
ROBERTS, THOMAS SADLER.
   1932. The birds of Minnesota, vol. 2.
ROBERTSON, JOHN McBRAIR.
   1930. Roads and birds.   Condor, vol. 32, pp. 142–146.
ROGERS, CHARLES HENRY.
   1907. Cedar waxwings and sapsuckers.   Wilson Bull., vol. 19, pp. 31–32.
RUST, HENRY JUDSON.
   1920. The home life of the western warbling vireo.   Condor, vol. 22, pp. 85–94.
SAUNDERS, ARETAS ANDREWS.
   1911. A study of the nesting of the cedar waxwing.   Auk, vol. 28, pp. 323–329.
   1915. The fearless white-eyed vireo.   Wilson Bull., vol. 27, pp. 316–321.
   1935. A guide to bird songs.
   1938. Studies of breeding birds in the Allegany State Park.   New York State
      Mus. Bull. 318.
   1942. Summer birds of the Allegany State Park.   New York State Mus.
      Handbook 18.
SAUNDERS, WILLIAM EDWIN, and DALE, EDGAR MELVILLE SEARLE.
   1933. A history and list of the birds of Middlesex County, Ontario, Canada.
      Trans. Roy. Can. Inst., vol. 19, pp. 161–248.

SCHEFFER, THEO[PHILUS] H., and COTTAM, CLARENCE.
    1935. The crested myna, or Chinese starling, in the Pacific Northwest.
        U. S. Dept. Agr. Techn. Bull. 467.
SCOTT, WILLIAM EARL DODGE.
    1885. On the breeding habits of some Arizona birds. Auk, vol. 2, pp. 242–246,
        321–326.
    1888. On the avifauna of Pinal County, with remarks on some birds of Pima
        and Gila Counties, Arizona. Auk, vol. 5, pp. 29–36, 159–168.
SEEBOHM, HENRY.
    1879. Contributions to the ornithology of Siberia. Ibis, 1879, pp. 1–18.
    1901. The birds of Siberia.
SEEBOHM, HENRY, and HARVIE-BROWN, JOHN ALEXANDER.
    1876. Notes on the birds of the lower Petchora. Ibis, 1876, pp. 108–126,
        215–230, 289–311, 434–456.
SETON, ERNEST THOMPSON.
    1891. The birds of Manitoba. Proc. U. S. Nat. Mus., vol. 13, pp. 457–643.
    1911. The Arctic prairies.
SHAW, TSEN-HWANG.
    1936. The birds of Hopei Province. Zoologica Sinica, ser. b. The vertebrates
        of China, vol. 15, fasc. 2, pp. 529–974, figs. 304–506, pls. 14–25.
SHELLEY, LEWIS ORMAN.
    1935. Flickers attacked by starlings. Auk, vol. 52, p. 93.
SHERMAN, ALTHEA ROSINA.
    1921. The Bohemian waxwing in Iowa in vast numbers. Auk, vol. 38,
        pp. 278–279.
SILLOWAY, PERLEY MILTON.
    1903. The birds of Fergus County, Montana. Fergus County Free High
        School Bull. 1.
    1904. Afield at Flathead. Condor, vol. 6, pp. 12–14.
    1923. Relation of summer birds to the western Adirondack forest. Roose-
        velt Wild Life Bull., vol. 1, pp. 397–486.
SIMMONS, GEORGE FINLAY.
    1915. On the nesting of certain birds in Texas. Auk, vol. 32, pp. 317–331.
    1925. Birds of the Austin region.
SKINNER, MILTON PHILO.
    1928. A guide to the winter birds of the North Carolina sandhills.
SOMMER, JOSEPH B.
    1937. Parasites of the European starling in Illinois. Auk, vol. 54, pp. 50–54.
STAEBLER, ARTHUR EUGENE, and CASE, LESLIE D.
    1940. Community bathing of the cedar waxwing. Wilson Bull., vol. 52,
        p. 281.
STEGMANN, BORIS.
    1936. Die Vögel des nördlichen Baikal. Journ. für. Orn., Jahrg. 84, pp.
        58–139.
STEPHENS, FRANK.
    1878. *Vireo vicinior* in California. Bull. Nuttall Orn. Club, vol. 3, p. 42.
    1890. A new vireo from California. Auk, vol. 7, pp. 159–160.
STEPHENS, THOMAS CALDERWOOD.
    1917. A study of the red-eyed vireo's nest which contained a cowbird's egg.
        Bull. Lab. Nat. Hist. State Univ. Iowa, vol. 7, pp. 25–38.
STEVENS, CAROLINE M.
    1911. An observation on the development of the social instinct in cedar wax-
        wings. Journ. Maine Orn. Soc., vol. 13, pp. 9–11.

STEVENSON, JAMES.
  1933. Bird notes from Mount Pinos, California. Condor, vol. 35, p. 79.
STOCKARD, CHARLES RUPERT.
  1905. Nesting habits of birds in Mississippi. Auk, vol. 22, pp. 146–158,
    273–285.
STONE, WITMER.
  1937. Bird studies at Old Cape May, vol. 2.
STONER, DAYTON.
  1932. Ornithology of the Oneida Lake region: With reference to the late
    spring summer seasons. Roosevelt Wild Life Annals, vol. 2, Nos.
    3 and 4.
STRABALA, LONY B.
  1926. The starling vs. the flicker. Oologist, vol. 43, pp. 93–95.
STRODE, WILLIAM SMITH.
  1889. The food habits of the shrikes. Ornithologist and Oologist, vol. 14,
    p. 26.
STURGIS, BERTHA BEMENT.
  1928. Field book of birds of the Panama Canal Zone.
SUTTON, GEORGE MIKSCH, and PETTINGILL, OLIN SEWALL, JR.
  1942. Birds of the Gómez Farias region, southwestern Tamaulipas. Auk,
    vol. 59, pp. 1–34.
SWAINSON, WILLIAM, and RICHARDSON, JOHN.
  1831. Fauna Boreali-Americana, vol. 2. The birds.
SWARTH, HARRY SCHELWALDT.
  1904. Birds of the Huachuca Mountains, Arizona. Pacific Coast Avif., No. 4.
  1922. Birds and mammals of the Stikine River region of northern British
    Columbia and southeastern Alaska. Univ. California Publ. Zool.,
    vol. 24, pp. 125–314.
  1926. Report on a collection of birds and mammals from the Atlin region,
    northern British Columbia. Univ. California Publ. Zool., vol. 30,
    pp. 51–162.
  1928. Occurrence of some Asiatic birds in Alaska. Proc. California Acad.
    Sci., ser. 4, vol. 17, pp. 247–251.
  1934. Birds of Nunivak Island, Alaska. Pacific Coast Avif., No. 22.
TACZANOWSKI, LADISLAS.
  1872–1873. Bericht über die ornithologischen Untersuchungen der Dr.
    Dybowski in Ost-Siberien. Journ. für Orn., Jahrg. 20, pp. 340–366,
    433–454; Jahrg. 21, pp. 81–119.
TAVERNER, PERCY ALGERNON.
  1934. Birds of Canada. Department of Mines, Nat. Mus. Canada, Bull. 72,
    biol. ser. No. 19.
TAVERNER, P. A., and SWALES, BRADSHAW HALL.
  1908. The birds of Point Pelee. Wilson Bull., vol. 20, pp. 107–129.
TAYLOR, WALTER PENN.
  1918. Bohemian waxwing (*Bombycilla garrula*) breeding within the United
    States. Auk, vol. 35, pp. 226–227.
TESCHEMAKER, W. E.
  1913. Nesting of the white wagtail. Avicultural Mag., ser. 3, vol. 4, pp.
    323–327, 1 pl.
THAYER, JOHN ELIOT, and BANGS, OUTRAM.
  1914. Notes on the birds and mammals of the Arctic coast of East Siberia.
    Birds. Proc. New England Zool. Club, vol. 5, pp. 1–48.
  1921. The black-backed Kamchatkan wagtail, *Motacilla lugens* Kittlitz, in
    Alaska. Auk, vol. 38, p. 460.

398 BULLETIN 197, UNITED STATES NATIONAL MUSEUM

THOMAS, EDWARD SINCLAIR.
  1934. A study of starlings banded at Columbus, Ohio. Bird-Banding, vol.
    5, pp. 118–128.
TICEHURST, NORMAN FREDERIC.
  1938. (See under Witherby, Jourdain, Ticehurst, and Tucker.)
TODD, WALTER EDMOND CLYDE.
  1916. The birds of the Isle of Pines. Ann. Carnegie Mus., vol. 10, Nos.
    1, 2, art. 11, pp. 146–296, pls. 22–27.
TORREY, BRADFORD.
  1885. Birds in the bush.
  1889. A rambler's lease.
  1904. Nature's invitation.
TOTHILL, JOHN DOUGLAS.
  1922. The natural control of the fall webworm (*Hyphantria cunea* Drury) in
    Canada. Dominion Dept. Agr., new ser., Bull. 3.
TOWNSEND, CHARLES WENDELL.
  1920. Supplement to the birds of Essex County, Massachusetts. Mem.
    Nuttall Orn. Club, No. 5.
  1933. Some winter activities of the northern shrike. Bull. Essex County
    Orn. Club, No. 15, pp. 22–27.
TOWNSEND, C. W., and ALLEN, GLOVER MORRILL.
  1907. Birds of Labrador. Proc. Boston Soc. Nat. Hist., vol. 33, pp. 277–428,
    pl. 29.
TRAUTMAN, MILTON BERNARD.
  1940. The birds of Buckeye Lake, Ohio. Misc. Publ. Mus. Zool. Univ.
    Michigan, No. 44.
TRAUTMAN, M. B., and VAN TYNE, JOSSELYN.
  1935. The occurrence of Sprague's pipit in Michigan. Auk, vol. 52, pp.
    457–458.
TURNER, LUCIEN MCSHAN.
  1885. List of the birds of Labrador, including Ungava, East Main, Moose,
    and Gulf Districts of the Hudson Bay Company, together with the
    Island of Anticosti. Proc. U. S. Nat. Mus., vol. 8, pp. 233–254.
  1886. Contributions to the natural history of Alaska. U. S. Signal Service,
    Arctic series, Publ. No. 2.
TYLER, WINSOR MARRETT.
  1912. A vireo courtship. Bird-Lore, vol. 14, pp. 229–230.
  1933. The starling as a mimic. Auk, vol. 50, p. 363.
URNER, CHARLES ANDERSON.
  1936. Bird mental capacity. Proc. Linnean Soc. New York, No. 47, pp.
    98–99.
VAN FLEET, CLARK CROCKER.
  1919. A short paper on the Hutton vireo. Condor, vol. 21, pp. 162–165.
VAN ROSSEM, ADRIAAN JOSEPH.
  1932. The avifauna of Tiburon Island, Sonora, Mexico, with descriptions
    of four new races. Trans. San Diego Soc. Nat. Hist., vol. 7,
    pp. 119–150.
VAN SOMEREN, VICTOR GURNET LOGAN.
  1931. Catalogue of the European and Asiatic migrants to Kenya and
    Uganda. Journ. East Africa and Uganda Nat. Hist. Soc., Special
    Supplement No. 4.
VAN TYNE, JOSSELYN, and SUTTON, GEORGE MIKSCH.
  1937. The birds of Brewster County, Texas. Misc. Publ. Mus. Zool. Univ.
    Michigan, No. 37.

VAUGHAN, ROBERT E., and JONES, KENNETH, HURLSTONE.
  1913. The birds of Hong Kong, Macao, and the West River or Si Kiang in
      South-East China, with special reference to their nidification and
      seasonal movements. Ibis, 1913, pp. 17-76, 163-201.
WALKINSHAW, LAWRENCE H.
  1948. Nestings of some passerine birds in western Alaska. Condor, vol. 50,
      pp. 64-70.
WANAMAKER, PAUL; FOREST, DEAN; and BULL, CHARLES LIVINGSTON.
  1931. "Puree." Bird Lore, vol. 33, pp. 400-402.
WAYNE, ARTHUR TREZEVANT.
  1906. A contribution to the ornithology of South Carolina, chiefly the coast
      region. Auk, vol. 23, pp. 56-68.
  1910. Birds of South Carolina. Contr. Charleston Mus., No. 1.
  1919. Early nesting of the loggerhead shrike (Lanius ludovicianus ludovi-
      cianus) at Savannah, Ga. Auk, vol. 36, p. 288.
WEIGOLD, HUGO.
  1926. Masse, Gewichte und Zub nach Alter und Geschlecht bei Helgoländer
      Zugvögeln.
WETMORE, ALEXANDER.
  1916. Birds of Porto Rico. U. S. Dept. Agr. Dept. Bull. 326.
  1926. The migrations of birds.
  1939. Notes on the birds of Tennessee. Proc. U. S. Nat. Mus., vol. 86,
      pp. 175-243.
WEYGANDT, CORNELIUS.
  1907. A study of the solitary vireo. Cassinia, No. 10, pp. 10-15.
WHEELOCK, IRENE GROSVENOR.
  1904. Birds of California.
WHITMAN, F. N.
  1924. The nest of the red-eyed vireo. Bird-Lore, vol. 26, pp. 256-257.
WHITTLE, HELEN GRANGER.
  1928. The biography of a cedar waxwing. Bull. Northeastern Bird Band-
      ing Assoc., vol. 4, pp. 77-83.
WILLARD, FRANCIS COTTLE.
  1908. Three vireos: Nesting notes from the Huachuca Mountains. Condor,
      vol. 10, pp. 230-234.
WILLIAMS, ARTHUR BALDWIN.
  1940. Red-eyed vireo captures food under water. Auk, vol. 57, p. 114.
WILLIAMS, JOHN GEORGE.
  1941. The birds of the Varanger Peninsula, East Finmark. Ibis, 1941,
      pp. 245-264.
WILSON, ALEXANDER, and BONAPARTE, CHARLES LUCIEN.
  1832. American ornithology.
WING, LEONARD.
  1939. Birds of the upper peninsula of Michigan. State Coll. Washington
      Res. Studies, vol. 7, pp, 163-198.
  1943. Spread of the starling and English sparrow. Auk, vol. 60, pp. 74-87.
WINGE, HERLUF.
  1898. Grønlands Fugle. Medd. om Grønland, vol. 21, pp. 3-316.
WITHERBY, HARRY FORBES.
  1919. A practical handbook of British birds, vol. 1.
WITHERBY, H. F.; JOURDAIN, FRANCIS CHARLES ROBERT; TICEHURST, NORMAN
    FREDERIC; and TUCKER, BERNARD WILLIAM.
  1938. The handbook of British birds, vol. 1.
  1939. The handbook of British birds, vol. 3.

WOOD, ALBERT ANDREW.
    1920. An annotated list of the birds of Coldstream, Ontario, vicinity. Can.
        Field-Nat., vol. 34, pp. 47–53.
WOOD, CASEY ALBERT.
    1924. The starling family at home and abroad. Condor, vol. 26, pp. 123–136,
        fig. 41.
WRIGHT, ALBERT HAZEN, and HARPER, FRANCIS.
    1913. A biological reconnaissance of Okefinokee Swamp: The birds. Auk,
        vol. 30, pp. 477–505, pls. 14–20.
WRIGHT, HORACE WINSLOW.
    1921. Bohemian waxwing (*Bombycilla garrula*) in New Zealand. Auk, vol.
        38, pp. 59–78.
YAMASHINA, MARQUIS YOSHIMARO.
    1931. Die Vögel der Kurilen. Journ. für Orn., Jahrg. 79, pp. 491–541.
YARRELL, WILLIAM.
    1874. A history of British birds, ed. 4, vol. 1. Edited by Alfred Newton.
ZANDER, H.
    1854. Kurze Uebersicht der europäischen Pieper, *Anthus* Bechst. Journ.
        für Orn., 1853, Suppl., pp. 60–65.

INDEX

Accentor, mountain, 1.
Accentors, 1.
aeneus, Quiscalus quiscula, 201.
Aethiopsar cristatellus cristatellus, 215.
alascensis, Motacilla flava, 19.
Alaska yellow wagtail, 19.
alba, Motacilla, 5, 6, 10, 13, 18.
    Motacilla alba, 3, 18.
albicollis, Legatus, 322.
Alexander, H. G., on meadow pipit, 47,
    48.
Allen, A. A., on cedar waxwing, 85, 92.
    on red-eyed vireo, 336.
Allen, F. H., on American pipit, 31, 33.
    on blue-headed vireo, 299.
    on eastern warbling vireo, 368.
    on northern shrike, 123.
    on red-eyed vireo, 343.
    on starling, 206, 207, 209.
    on white-eyed vireo, 234.
    on yellow-throated vireo, 285.
Allen, G. M., on Bahama honeycreeper,
    381, 382.
    on black-whiskered vireo, 317, 320.
Allen, J. A., on Sprague's pipit, 54, 55,
    60.
    on Swinhoe's wagtail, 14.
alticola, Anthus spinoletta, 37.
    Vireo solitarius, 304, 305, 309, 315.
Amadon, Dean, on black-whiskered
    vireo, 318.
American pipit, 25, 41, 45, 51.
anthonyi, Lanius ludovicianus, 147,
    180, 181.
Anthony's vireo, 246.
Anthus cervinus, 48.
    ludovicianus, 55.
    pratensis, 40.
    spinoletta, 51.
    spinoletta alticola, 37.
    spinoletta japonicus, 38, 39.
    spinoletta pacificus, 36.
    spinoletta rubescens, 25, 37, 39.
    spraguei, 52.
    trivialis, 45, 51.
Arizona vireo, 262, 263.
arizonae, Spizella socialis, 157.
    vireo belli, 262, 263, 265.
Armstrong, F. B., 241.
    on Stephens's vireo, 251.
ater, Molothrus ater, 201.
Atkins, J. W., 239.
atricapillus, Vireo, 222.

Audubon, J. J., on American pipit, 31.
    on Bell's vireo, 253.
    on Bohemian waxwing, 72.
    on cedar waxwing, 89, 95.
    on eastern warbling vireo, 365, 366.
    on loggerhead shrike, 132, 138, 141,
    142, 144.
    on migrant shrike, 149.
    on Sprague's pipit, 52, 54.
Aymar, Gordon, on loggerhead shrike, 140.

Bachman, John, on loggerhead shrike,
    132, 135, 138, 141, 144.
Bagg, A. C., on blue-headed vireo, 297.
Bagg, A. C., and Eliot, S. A., Jr., on
    yellow-throated vireo, 286, 287.
Bahama honeycreeper, 379.
bahamensis, Coereba, 379.
Bailey, A. M., on Swinhoe's wagtail, 13,
    14.
Bailey, Florence M., on gray vireo, 270,
    272.
    on phainopepla, 105, 110, 112.
    on plumbeous vireo, 310.
Bailey, H. H., on black-whiskered vireo,
    319.
Baird, S. F., on Bahama honeycreeper,
    379.
    on Bohemian waxwing, 65.
Baird, S. F., Brewer, T. M., and Ridg-
    way, Robert, on Bell's vireo, 256.
Bancroft, Griffing, on Nelson's shrike,
    180.
Bangs, Outram. (See under Thayer,
    T. E.)
Bangs, Outram, and Bradlee, T. S., on
    Bermuda vireo, 239.
barbatulus, Vireo calidris, 316.
Baynard, O. E., 316.
    on black-whiskered vireo, 317.
Baynes, E. H., on red-eyed vireo, 341.
Beal, F. E. L., 117.
    on Cassin's vireo, 314.
    on Hutton's vireo, 245.
    on western warbling vireo, 378.
Beal, F. E. L., and McAtee, W. L., on
    California shrike, 172, 173.
    on loggerhead shrike, 137.
Belding, Lyman, 252.
    on Swinhoe's wagtail, 13.
Bell, J. G., 253.
belli, Vireo, 157, 223, 254.
    Vireo belli, 253, 262, 263.

401

PLATES

PLATE 1

Alaska.

Herbert Brandt.

NEST OF ALASKA YELLOW WAGTAIL

PLATE 2

Howard Cleaves.

Adult.

Hopedale, Labrador, July 21, 1912.

A. C. Bent.

Nest.

AMERICAN PIPIT.

PLATE 3

Howard Cleaves.

YOUNG AMERICAN PIPIT IN NEST.

PLATE 4

Gayle Pickwell.

AMERICAN PIPIT FEEDING YOUNG.

Mount Rainier, Wash.

PLATE 5

Kittson County, Minn., June 16, 1929.   W. J. Breckenridge.

NESTING SITE AND NEST OF SPRAGUE'S PIPIT.

PLATE 6

Belvedere, Alberta, June 5, 1927.   R. H. Rauch.

NEST OF BOHEMIAN WAXWING.

PLATE 7

W. C. Hanna.

Atlin Lake, British Columbia.

Colorado Museum of Natural History.

ADULTS IN WINTER AND NEST OF BOHEMIAN WAXWING.

PLATE 8

S. A. Grimes.

NEST OF CEDAR WAXWING.

Erie County, N. Y., July 24, 1926.

PLATE 9

H. M. Halliday.

CEDAR WAXWING ON NEST

Near Toronto, Ontario.

PLATE 10

A. D. Cruickshank.

ADULT AND YOUNG CEDAR WAXWINGS.

PLATE 11

Near Toronto, Ontario.   H. M. Halliday.

FLEDGLING CEDAR WAXWINGS

PLATE 12

Maine, July 27, 1940.   Eliot Porter.

CEDAR WAXWING AND YOUNG.

PLATE 13

Azusa, Calif., May 24, 1933.   R. S. Woods.

Azusa, Calif. June 1943.   R. S. Woods.

ADULT MALE PHAINOPEPLA AND NEST.

PLATE 14

Female at nest.

Imperial County, Calif.   E. N. Harrison.

Male at nest.

PHAINOPEPLAS.

PLATE 15

Churchill, Manitoba.   A. A. Allen.

Pair at nest.

H. M. Halliday.

Shrike and its prey.

NORTHERN SHRIKES.

PLATE 16

Duval County, Fla., April 1932.

NEST OF LOGGERHEAD SHRIKE.

PLATE 17

A. D. Cruickshank.

Duval County, Fla., May 1, 1930.   S. A. Grimes.

ADULT AND JUVENAL LOGGERHEAD SHRIKES.

PLATE 18

Owen Durfee.

Coos County, N. H., May 18, 1903.

Whitney, Vt., May 7, 1915.

NESTING TREES OF MIGRANT SHRIKE.

PLATE 19

MIGRANT SHRIKE.

PLATE 20

MIGRANT SHRIKES.

Near Toronto, Ontario.

PLATE 21

Walter Colvin.

NEST OF WHITE-RUMPED SHRIKE.

Kay County, Okla., April 22, 1924.

PLATE 22

Los Angeles County, Calif., April 8, 1930.   J. S. Rowley.

Moss Landing, Calif.   Gayle Pickwell..

CALIFORNIA SHRIKE.

PLATE 23

A. D. Cruickshank.

ADULT STARLINGS.

PLATE 24

J. H. Gerard.

ROOSTING STARLINGS.

PLATE 25

H. K. Job.

A. C. Bent.

Swansea, Mass., June 6, 1908.

NESTING SITE AND NEST OF WHITE-EYED VIREO.

PLATE 26

S. A. Grimes.

WHITE-EYED VIREO AT NEST.

Duval County, Fla., May 1933.

PLATE 27

Near Johnson City, Tenn., June 6, 1945.   B. P. Tyler.

NEST OF WHITE-EYED VIREO.

PLATE 28

Arizona.   F. C. Willard.

HABITAT AND NEST OF STEPHENS'S VIREO.

PLATE 29

Walter Colvin.

NEST OF BELL'S VIREO.

Ojai, Calif.

LEAST VIREO.

A. J. van Rossem.

PLATE 30

Arizona.   Eliot Porter.

ARIZONA VIREO AND NEST.

PLATE 31

San Bernardino County, Calif., June 23, 1935.   A. J. van Rossem.

W. C. Hanna.

HABITAT AND NEST OF GRAY VIREO.

PLATE 32

A. J. van Rossem.

July 1, 1935.

San Bernardino County, Calif., May 26, 1935.

NESTS OF GRAY VIREO.

PLATE 33

Duval County, Fla., April 17, 1933.   S. A. Grimes.

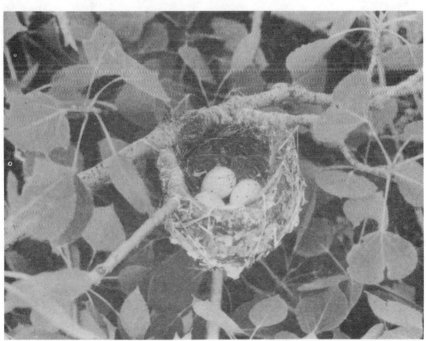

Pennington County, Minn., June 17, 1933.   S. A. Grimes.

NESTS OF YELLOW-THROATED VIREO.

PLATE 34

Duval County, Fla.   S. A. Grimes.

YELLOW-THROATED VIREO.

PLATE 35

Young.

Duval County, Fla.   S. A. Grimes.

YELLOW-THROATED VIREO.

PLATE 36

Enfield, Conn., May 19, 1913.   H. K. Job.

Allen Frost.

BLUE-HEADED VIREOS.

PLATE 37

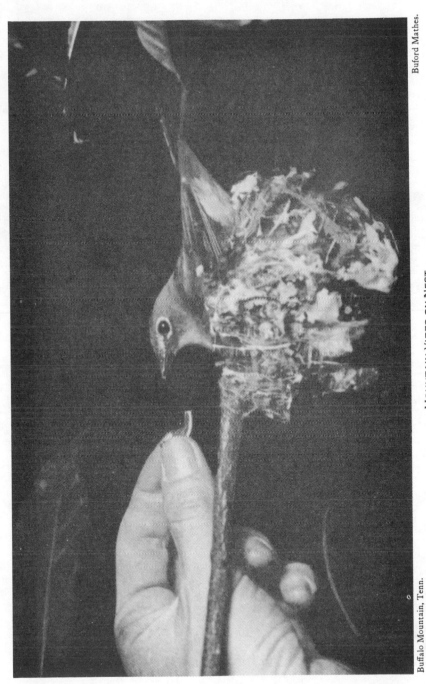

Buford Mathes.

Buffalo Mountain, Tenn.

MOUNTAIN VIREO ON NEST.

PLATE 38

R. P. Tyler.

NEST OF MOUNTAIN VIREO.

Tennessee, June 12, 1938.

PLATE 39

H. J. Rust.

Coeur d'Alene, Idaho.

NESTING SITE AND NEST OF CASSIN'S VIREO.

PLATE 40

Oregon. W. L. Finley.

CASSIN'S VIREO.

J. E. Patterson.

PLATE 41

Idaho. H. J. Rust.

Oregon. W. L. Finley.

CASSIN'S VIREOS.

PLATE 42

O. E. Baynard.

NEST OF BLACK-WHISKERED VIREO.

Clearwater, Fla.

PLATE 43

Taunton, Mass., June 12, 1940.   Grice & Grice.

NEST OF RED-EYED VIREO.

PLATE 44

Eliot Porter.

RED-EYED VIREO.

Maine, July 17, 1939

PLATE 45

Perce, Quebec, June 26, 1930.   L. M. Terrill.

PHILADELPHIA VIREO ON NEST.

PLATE 46

MALE WESTERN WARBLING VIREO.

PLATE 47

Idaho.

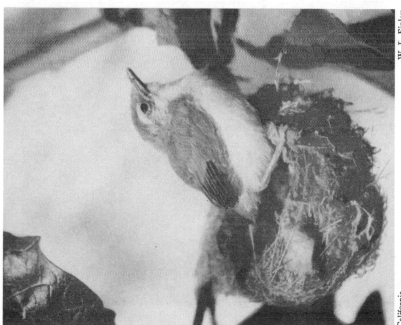

California.

W. L. Finley.

YOUNG AND NEST OF WESTERN WARBLING VIREO.

PLATE 48

Gayle Pickwell.

Santa Clara County, Calif.

WESTERN WARBLING VIREO.

A CATALOGUE OF SELECTED DOVER BOOKS
IN ALL FIELDS OF INTEREST

A CATALOGUE OF SELECTED DOVER BOOKS
IN ALL FIELDS OF INTEREST

AMERICA'S OLD MASTERS, James T. Flexner. Four men emerged unexpectedly from provincial 18th century America to leadership in European art: Benjamin West, J. S. Copley, C. R. Peale, Gilbert Stuart. Brilliant coverage of lives and contributions. Revised, 1967 edition. 69 plates. 365pp. of text.

21806-6 Paperbound $3.00

FIRST FLOWERS OF OUR WILDERNESS: AMERICAN PAINTING, THE COLONIAL PERIOD, James T. Flexner. Painters, and regional painting traditions from earliest Colonial times up to the emergence of Copley, West and Peale Sr., Foster, Gustavus Hesselius, Feke, John Smibert and many anonymous painters in the primitive manner. Engaging presentation, with 162 illustrations. xxii + 368pp.

22180-6 Paperbound $3.50

THE LIGHT OF DISTANT SKIES: AMERICAN PAINTING, 1760-1835, James T. Flexner. The great generation of early American painters goes to Europe to learn and to teach: West, Copley, Gilbert Stuart and others. Allston, Trumbull, Morse; also contemporary American painters—primitives, derivatives, academics—who remained in America. 102 illustrations. xiii + 306pp. 22179-2 Paperbound $3.50

A HISTORY OF THE RISE AND PROGRESS OF THE ARTS OF DESIGN IN THE UNITED STATES, William Dunlap. Much the richest mine of information on early American painters, sculptors, architects, engravers, miniaturists, etc. The only source of information for scores of artists, the major primary source for many others. Unabridged reprint of rare original 1834 edition, with new introduction by James T. Flexner, and 394 new illustrations. Edited by Rita Weiss. 6⅝ x 9⅝.

21695-0, 21696-9, 21697-7 Three volumes, Paperbound $13.50

EPOCHS OF CHINESE AND JAPANESE ART, Ernest F. Fenollosa. From primitive Chinese art to the 20th century, thorough history, explanation of every important art period and form, including Japanese woodcuts; main stress on China and Japan, but Tibet, Korea also included. Still unexcelled for its detailed, rich coverage of cultural background, aesthetic elements, diffusion studies, particularly of the historical period. 2nd, 1913 edition. 242 illustrations. lii + 439pp. of text.

20364-6, 20365-4 Two volumes, Paperbound $6.00

THE GENTLE ART OF MAKING ENEMIES, James A. M. Whistler. Greatest wit of his day deflates Oscar Wilde, Ruskin, Swinburne; strikes back at inane critics, exhibitions, art journalism; aesthetics of impressionist revolution in most striking form. Highly readable classic by great painter. Reproduction of edition designed by Whistler. Introduction by Alfred Werner. xxxvi + 334pp.

21875-9 Paperbound $2.50

VISUAL ILLUSIONS: THEIR CAUSES, CHARACTERISTICS, AND APPLICATIONS, Matthew Luckiesh. Thorough description and discussion of optical illusion, geometric and perspective, particularly; size and shape distortions, illusions of color, of motion; natural illusions; use of illusion in art and magic, industry, etc. Most useful today with op art, also for classical art. Scores of effects illustrated. Introduction by William H. Ittleson. 100 illustrations. xxi + 252pp.

21530-X Paperbound $2.00

A HANDBOOK OF ANATOMY FOR ART STUDENTS, Arthur Thomson. Thorough, virtually exhaustive coverage of skeletal structure, musculature, etc. Full text, supplemented by anatomical diagrams and drawings and by photographs of undraped figures. Unique in its comparison of male and female forms, pointing out differences of contour, texture, form. 211 figures, 40 drawings, 86 photographs. xx + 459pp. 5⅜ x 8⅜.

21163-0 Paperbound $3.50

150 MASTERPIECES OF DRAWING, Selected by Anthony Toney. Full page reproductions of drawings from the early 16th to the end of the 18th century, all beautifully reproduced: Rembrandt, Michelangelo, Dürer, Fragonard, Urs, Graf, Wouwerman, many others. First-rate browsing book, model book for artists. xviii + 150pp. 8⅜ x 11¼.

21032-4 Paperbound $2.50

THE LATER WORK OF AUBREY BEARDSLEY, Aubrey Beardsley. Exotic, erotic, ironic masterpieces in full maturity: Comedy Ballet, Venus and Tannhauser, Pierrot, Lysistrata, Rape of the Lock, Savoy material, Ali Baba, Volpone, etc. This material revolutionized the art world, and is still powerful, fresh, brilliant. With *The Early Work,* all Beardsley's finest work. 174 plates, 2 in color. xiv + 176pp. 8⅛ x 11.

21817-1 Paperbound $3.00

DRAWINGS OF REMBRANDT, Rembrandt van Rijn. Complete reproduction of fabulously rare edition by Lippmann and Hofstede de Groot, completely reedited, updated, improved by Prof. Seymour Slive, Fogg Museum. Portraits, Biblical sketches, landscapes, Oriental types, nudes, episodes from classical mythology—All Rembrandt's fertile genius. Also selection of drawings by his pupils and followers. "Stunning volumes," *Saturday Review.* 550 illustrations. lxxviii + 552pp. 9⅛ x 12¼.

21485-0, 21486-9 Two volumes, Paperbound $10.00

THE DISASTERS OF WAR, Francisco Goya. One of the masterpieces of Western civilization—83 etchings that record Goya's shattering, bitter reaction to the Napoleonic war that swept through Spain after the insurrection of 1808 and to war in general. Reprint of the first edition, with three additional plates from Boston's Museum of Fine Arts. All plates facsimile size. Introduction by Philip Hofer, Fogg Museum. v + 97pp. 9⅜ x 8¼.

21872-4 Paperbound $2.00

GRAPHIC WORKS OF ODILON REDON. Largest collection of Redon's graphic works ever assembled: 172 lithographs, 28 etchings and engravings, 9 drawings. These include some of his most famous works. All the plates from *Odilon Redon: oeuvre graphique complet,* plus additional plates. New introduction and caption translations by Alfred Werner. 209 illustrations. xxvii + 209pp. 9⅛ x 12¼.

21966-8 Paperbound $4.00

DESIGN BY ACCIDENT; A BOOK OF "ACCIDENTAL EFFECTS" FOR ARTISTS AND DESIGNERS, James F. O'Brien. Create your own unique, striking, imaginative effects by "controlled accident" interaction of materials: paints and lacquers, oil and water based paints, splatter, crackling materials, shatter, similar items. Everything you do will be different; first book on this limitless art, so useful to both fine artist and commercial artist. Full instructions. 192 plates showing "accidents," 8 in color. viii + 215pp. 8⅜ x 11¼. 21942-9 Paperbound $3.50

THE BOOK OF SIGNS, Rudolf Koch. Famed German type designer draws 493 beautiful symbols: religious, mystical, alchemical, imperial, property marks, runes, etc. Remarkable fusion of traditional and modern. Good for suggestions of timelessness, smartness, modernity. Text. vi + 104pp. 6⅛ x 9¼. 20162-7 Paperbound $1.25

HISTORY OF INDIAN AND INDONESIAN ART, Ananda K. Coomaraswamy. An unabridged republication of one of the finest books by a great scholar in Eastern art. Rich in descriptive material, history, social backgrounds; Sunga reliefs, Rajput paintings, Gupta temples, Burmese frescoes, textiles, jewelry, sculpture, etc. 400 photos. viii + 423pp. 6⅜ x 9¾. 21436-2 Paperbound $5.00

PRIMITIVE ART, Franz Boas. America's foremost anthropologist surveys textiles, ceramics, woodcarving, basketry, metalwork, etc.; patterns, technology, creation of symbols, style origins. All areas of world, but very full on Northwest Coast Indians. More than 350 illustrations of baskets, boxes, totem poles, weapons, etc. 378 pp. 20025-6 Paperbound $3.00

THE GENTLEMAN AND CABINET MAKER'S DIRECTOR, Thomas Chippendale. Full reprint (third edition, 1762) of most influential furniture book of all time, by master cabinetmaker. 200 plates, illustrating chairs, sofas, mirrors, tables, cabinets, plus 24 photographs of surviving pieces. Biographical introduction by N. Bienenstock. vi + 249pp. 9⅞ x 12¾. 21601-2 Paperbound $4.00

AMERICAN ANTIQUE FURNITURE, Edgar G. Miller, Jr. The basic coverage of all American furniture before 1840. Individual chapters cover type of furniture— clocks, tables, sideboards, etc.—chronologically, with inexhaustible wealth of data. More than 2100 photographs, all identified, commented on. Essential to all early American collectors. Introduction by H. E. Keyes. vi + 1106pp. 7⅞ x 10¾. 21599-7, 21600-4 Two volumes, Paperbound $11.00

PENNSYLVANIA DUTCH AMERICAN FOLK ART, Henry J. Kauffman. 279 photos, 28 drawings of tulipware, Fraktur script, painted tinware, toys, flowered furniture, quilts, samplers, hex signs, house interiors, etc. Full descriptive text. Excellent for tourist, rewarding for designer, collector. Map. 146pp. 7⅞ x 10¾. 21205-X Paperbound $2.50

EARLY NEW ENGLAND GRAVESTONE RUBBINGS, Edmund V. Gillon, Jr. 43 photographs, 226 carefully reproduced rubbings show heavily symbolic, sometimes macabre early gravestones, up to early 19th century. Remarkable early American primitive art, occasionally strikingly beautiful; always powerful. Text. xxvi + 207pp. 8⅜ x 11¼. 21380-3 Paperbound $3.50

ALPHABETS AND ORNAMENTS, Ernst Lehner. Well-known pictorial source for decorative alphabets, script examples, cartouches, frames, decorative title pages, calligraphic initials, borders, similar material. 14th to 19th century, mostly European. Useful in almost any graphic arts designing, varied styles. 750 illustrations. 256pp. 7 x 10.   21905-4 Paperbound $4.00

PAINTING: A CREATIVE APPROACH, Norman Colquhoun. For the beginner simple guide provides an instructive approach to painting: major stumbling blocks for beginner; overcoming them, technical points; paints and pigments; oil painting; watercolor and other media and color. New section on "plastic" paints. Glossary. Formerly *Paint Your Own Pictures.* 221pp.   22000-1 Paperbound $1.75

THE ENJOYMENT AND USE OF COLOR, Walter Sargent. Explanation of the relations between colors themselves and between colors in nature and art, including hundreds of little-known facts about color values, intensities, effects of high and low illumination, complementary colors. Many practical hints for painters, references to great masters. 7 color plates, 29 illustrations. x + 274pp.
20944-X Paperbound $2.75

THE NOTEBOOKS OF LEONARDO DA VINCI, compiled and edited by Jean Paul Richter. 1566 extracts from original manuscripts reveal the full range of Leonardo's versatile genius: all his writings on painting, sculpture, architecture, anatomy, astronomy, geography, topography, physiology, mining, music, etc., in both Italian and English, with 186 plates of manuscript pages and more than 500 additional drawings. Includes studies for the Last Supper, the lost Sforza monument, and other works. Total of xlvii + 866pp. 7⅞ x 10¾.
22572-0, 22573-9 Two volumes, Paperbound $10.00

MONTGOMERY WARD CATALOGUE OF 1895. Tea gowns, yards of flannel and pillow-case lace, stereoscopes, books of gospel hymns, the New Improved Singer Sewing Machine, side saddles, milk skimmers, straight-edged razors, high-button shoes, spittoons, and on and on . . . listing some 25,000 items, practically all illustrated. Essential to the shoppers of the 1890's, it is our truest record of the spirit of the period. Unaltered reprint of Issue No. 57, Spring and Summer 1895. Introduction by Boris Emmet. Innumerable illustrations. xiii + 624pp. 8½ x 11⅝.
22377-9 Paperbound $6.95

THE CRYSTAL PALACE EXHIBITION ILLUSTRATED CATALOGUE (LONDON, 1851). One of the wonders of the modern world—the Crystal Palace Exhibition in which all the nations of the civilized world exhibited their achievements in the arts and sciences—presented in an equally important illustrated catalogue. More than 1700 items pictured with accompanying text—ceramics, textiles, cast-iron work, carpets, pianos, sleds, razors, wall-papers, billiard tables, beehives, silverware and hundreds of other artifacts—represent the focal point of Victorian culture in the Western World. Probably the largest collection of Victorian decorative art ever assembled— indispensable for antiquarians and designers. Unabridged republication of the Art-Journal Catalogue of the Great Exhibition of 1851, with all terminal essays. New introduction by John Gloag, F.S.A. xxxiv + 426pp. 9 x 12.
22503-8 Paperbound $4.50

A HISTORY OF COSTUME, Carl Köhler. Definitive history, based on surviving pieces of clothing primarily, and paintings, statues, etc. secondarily. Highly readable text, supplemented by 594 illustrations of costumes of the ancient Mediterranean peoples, Greece and Rome, the Teutonic prehistoric period; costumes of the Middle Ages, Renaissance, Baroque, 18th and 19th centuries. Clear, measured patterns are provided for many clothing articles. Approach is practical throughout. Enlarged by Emma von Sichart. 464pp.   21030-8 Paperbound $3.50

ORIENTAL RUGS, ANTIQUE AND MODERN, Walter A. Hawley. A complete and authoritative treatise on the Oriental rug—where they are made, by whom and how, designs and symbols, characteristics in detail of the six major groups, how to distinguish them and how to buy them. Detailed technical data is provided on periods, weaves, warps, wefts, textures, sides, ends and knots, although no technical background is required for an understanding. 11 color plates, 80 halftones, 4 maps. vi + 320pp. 6⅛ x 9⅛.   22366-3 Paperbound $5.00

TEN BOOKS ON ARCHITECTURE, Vitruvius. By any standards the most important book on architecture ever written. Early Roman discussion of aesthetics of building, construction methods, orders, sites, and every other aspect of architecture has inspired, instructed architecture for about 2,000 years. Stands behind Palladio, Michelangelo, Bramante, Wren, countless others. Definitive Morris H. Morgan translation. 68 illustrations. xii + 331pp.   20645-9 Paperbound $3.00

THE FOUR BOOKS OF ARCHITECTURE, Andrea Palladio. Translated into every major Western European language in the two centuries following its publication in 1570, this has been one of the most influential books in the history of architecture. Complete reprint of the 1738 Isaac Ware edition. New introduction by Adolf Placzek, Columbia Univ. 216 plates. xxii + 110pp. of text. 9½ x 12¾.
21308-0 Clothbound $10.00

STICKS AND STONES: A STUDY OF AMERICAN ARCHITECTURE AND CIVILIZATION, Lewis Mumford.One of the great classics of American cultural history. American architecture from the medieval-inspired earliest forms to the early 20th century; evolution of structure and style, and reciprocal influences on environment. 21 photographic illustrations. 238pp.   20202-X Paperbound $2.00

THE AMERICAN BUILDER'S COMPANION, Asher Benjamin. The most widely used early 19th century architectural style and source book, for colonial up into Greek Revival periods. Extensive development of geometry of carpentering, construction of sashes, frames, doors, stairs; plans and elevations of domestic and other buildings. Hundreds of thousands of houses were built according to this book, now invaluable to historians, architects, restorers, etc. 1827 edition. 59 plates. 114pp. 7⅞ x 10¾.
22236-5 Paperbound $3.50

DUTCH HOUSES IN THE HUDSON VALLEY BEFORE 1776, Helen Wilkinson Reynolds. The standard survey of the Dutch colonial house and outbuildings, with constructional features, decoration, and local history associated with individual homesteads. Introduction by Franklin D. Roosevelt. Map. 150 illustrations. 469pp. 6⅝ x 9¼.   21469-9 Paperbound $4.00

THE ARCHITECTURE OF COUNTRY HOUSES, Andrew J. Downing. Together with Vaux's *Villas and Cottages* this is the basic book for Hudson River Gothic architecture of the middle Victorian period. Full, sound discussions of general aspects of housing, architecture, style, decoration, furnishing, together with scores of detailed house plans, illustrations of specific buildings, accompanied by full text. Perhaps the most influential single American architectural book. 1850 edition. Introduction by J. Stewart Johnson. 321 figures, 34 architectural designs. xvi + 560pp.

22003-6 Paperbound $4.00

LOST EXAMPLES OF COLONIAL ARCHITECTURE, John Mead Howells. Full-page photographs of buildings that have disappeared or been so altered as to be denatured, including many designed by major early American architects. 245 plates. xvii + 248pp. 7⅞ x 10¾. 21143-6 Paperbound $3.50

DOMESTIC ARCHITECTURE OF THE AMERICAN COLONIES AND OF THE EARLY REPUBLIC, Fiske Kimball. Foremost architect and restorer of Williamsburg and Monticello covers nearly 200 homes between 1620-1825. Architectural details, construction, style features, special fixtures, floor plans, etc. Generally considered finest work in its area. 219 illustrations of houses, doorways, windows, capital mantels. xx + 314pp. 7⅞ x 10¾. 21743-4 Paperbound $4.00

EARLY AMERICAN ROOMS: 1650-1858, edited by Russell Hawes Kettell. Tour of 12 rooms, each representative of a different era in American history and each furnished, decorated, designed and occupied in the style of the era. 72 plans and elevations, 8-page color section, etc., show fabrics, wall papers, arrangements, etc. Full descriptive text. xvii + 200pp. of text. 8⅜ x 11¼. 21633-0 Paperbound $5.00

THE FITZWILLIAM VIRGINAL BOOK, edited by J. Fuller Maitland and W. B. Squire. Full modern printing of famous early 17th-century ms. volume of 300 works by Morley, Byrd, Bull, Gibbons, etc. For piano or other modern keyboard instrument; easy to read format. xxxvi + 938pp. 8⅜ x 11. 21068-5, 21069-3 Two volumes, Paperbound $10.00

KEYBOARD MUSIC, Johann Sebastian Bach. Bach Gesellschaft edition. A rich selection of Bach's masterpieces for the harpsichord: the six English Suites, six French Suites, the six Partitas (Clavierübung part I), the Goldberg Variations (Clavierübung part IV), the fifteen Two-Part Inventions and the fifteen Three-Part Sinfonias. Clearly reproduced on large sheets with ample margins; eminently playable. vi + 312pp. 8⅛ x 11. 22360-4 Paperbound $5.00

THE MUSIC OF BACH: AN INTRODUCTION, Charles Sanford Terry. A fine, nontechnical introduction to Bach's music, both instrumental and vocal. Covers organ music, chamber music, passion music, other types. Analyzes themes, developments, innovations. x + 114pp. 21075-8 Paperbound $1.25

BEETHOVEN AND HIS NINE SYMPHONIES, Sir George Grove. Noted British musicologist provides best history, analysis, commentary on symphonies. Very thorough, rigorously accurate; necessary to both advanced student and amateur music lover. 436 musical passages. vii + 407 pp. 20334-4 Paperbound $2.75

JOHANN SEBASTIAN BACH, Philipp Spitta. One of the great classics of musicology, this definitive analysis of Bach's music (and life) has never been surpassed. Lucid, nontechnical analyses of hundreds of pieces (30 pages devoted to St. Matthew Passion, 26 to B Minor Mass). Also includes major analysis of 18th-century music. 450 musical examples. 40-page musical supplement. Total of xx + 1799pp.
(EUK) 22278-0, 22279-9 Two volumes, Clothbound $17.50

MOZART AND HIS PIANO CONCERTOS, Cuthbert Girdlestone. The only full-length study of an important area of Mozart's creativity. Provides detailed analyses of all 23 concertos, traces inspirational sources. 417 musical examples. Second edition. 509pp.
21271-8 Paperbound $3.50

THE PERFECT WAGNERITE: A COMMENTARY ON THE NIBLUNG'S RING, George Bernard Shaw. Brilliant and still relevant criticism in remarkable essays on Wagner's Ring cycle, Shaw's ideas on political and social ideology behind the plots, role of Leitmotifs, vocal requisites, etc. Prefaces. xxi + 136pp.
(USO) 21707-8 Paperbound $1.50

DON GIOVANNI, W. A. Mozart. Complete libretto, modern English translation; biographies of composer and librettist; accounts of early performances and critical reaction. Lavishly illustrated. All the material you need to understand and appreciate this great work. Dover Opera Guide and Libretto Series; translated and introduced by Ellen Bleiler. 92 illustrations. 209pp.
21134-7 Paperbound $2.00

HIGH FIDELITY SYSTEMS: A LAYMAN'S GUIDE, Roy F. Allison. All the basic information you need for setting up your own audio system: high fidelity and stereo record players, tape records, F.M. Connections, adjusting tone arm, cartridge, checking needle alignment, positioning speakers, phasing speakers, adjusting hums, trouble-shooting, maintenance, and similar topics. Enlarged 1965 edition. More than 50 charts, diagrams, photos. iv + 91pp.
21514-8 Paperbound $1.25

REPRODUCTION OF SOUND, Edgar Villchur. Thorough coverage for laymen of high fidelity systems, reproducing systems in general, needles, amplifiers, preamps, loudspeakers, feedback, explaining physical background. "A rare talent for making technicalities vividly comprehensible," R. Darrell, *High Fidelity.* 69 figures. iv + 92pp.
21515-6 Paperbound $1.25

HEAR ME TALKIN' TO YA: THE STORY OF JAZZ AS TOLD BY THE MEN WHO MADE IT, Nat Shapiro and Nat Hentoff. Louis Armstrong, Fats Waller, Jo Jones, Clarence Williams, Billy Holiday, Duke Ellington, Jelly Roll Morton and dozens of other jazz greats tell how it was in Chicago's South Side, New Orleans, depression Harlem and the modern West Coast as jazz was born and grew. xvi + 429pp.
21726-4 Paperbound $2.50

FABLES OF AESOP, translated by Sir Roger L'Estrange. A reproduction of the very rare 1931 Paris edition; a selection of the most interesting fables, together with 50 imaginative drawings by Alexander Calder. v + 128pp. 6½x9¼.
21780-9 Paperbound $1.50

AGAINST THE GRAIN (A REBOURS), Joris K. Huysmans. Filled with weird images, evidences of a bizarre imagination, exotic experiments with hallucinatory drugs, rich tastes and smells and the diversions of its sybarite hero Duc Jean des Esseintes, this classic novel pushed 19th-century literary decadence to its limits. Full unabridged edition. Do not confuse this with abridged editions generally sold. Introduction by Havelock Ellis. xlix + 206pp. 22190-3 Paperbound $2.00

VARIORUM SHAKESPEARE: HAMLET. Edited by Horace H. Furness; a landmark of American scholarship. Exhaustive footnotes and appendices treat all doubtful words and phrases, as well as suggested critical emendations throughout the play's history. First volume contains editor's own text, collated with all Quartos and Folios. Second volume contains full first Quarto, translations of Shakespeare's sources (Belleforest, and Saxo Grammaticus), Der Bestrafte Brudermord, and many essays on critical and historical points of interest by major authorities of past and present. Includes details of staging and costuming over the years. By far the best edition available for serious students of Shakespeare. Total of xx + 905pp. 21004-9, 21005-7, 2 volumes, Paperbound $7.00

A LIFE OF WILLIAM SHAKESPEARE, Sir Sidney Lee. This is the standard life of Shakespeare, summarizing everything known about Shakespeare and his plays. Incredibly rich in material, broad in coverage, clear and judicious, it has served thousands as the best introduction to Shakespeare. 1931 edition. 9 plates. xxix |- 792pp. (USO) 21967-4 Paperbound $3.75

MASTERS OF THE DRAMA, John Gassner. Most comprehensive history of the drama in print, covering every tradition from Greeks to modern Europe and America, including India, Far East, etc. Covers more than 800 dramatists, 2000 plays, with biographical material, plot summaries, theatre history, criticism, etc. "Best of its kind in English," *New Republic*. 77 illustrations. xxii + 890pp. 20100-7 Clothbound $8.50

THE EVOLUTION OF THE ENGLISH LANGUAGE, George McKnight. The growth of English, from the 14th century to the present. Unusual, non-technical account presents basic information in very interesting form: sound shifts, change in grammar and syntax, vocabulary growth, similar topics. Abundantly illustrated with quotations. Formerly *Modern English in the Making*. xii + 590pp. 21932-1 Paperbound $3.50

AN ETYMOLOGICAL DICTIONARY OF MODERN ENGLISH, Ernest Weekley. Fullest, richest work of its sort, by foremost British lexicographer. Detailed word histories, including many colloquial and archaic words; extensive quotations. Do not confuse this with the Concise Etymological Dictionary, which is much abridged. Total of xxvii + 830pp. 6½ x 9¼. 21873-2, 21874-0 Two volumes, Paperbound $6.00

FLATLAND: A ROMANCE OF MANY DIMENSIONS, E. A. Abbott. Classic of science-fiction explores ramifications of life in a two-dimensional world, and what happens when a three-dimensional being intrudes. Amusing reading, but also useful as introduction to thought about hyperspace. Introduction by Banesh Hoffmann. 16 illustrations. xx + 103pp. 20001-9 Paperbound $1.00

POEMS OF ANNE BRADSTREET, edited with an introduction by Robert Hutchinson. A new selection of poems by America's first poet and perhaps the first significant woman poet in the English language. 48 poems display her development in works of considerable variety—love poems, domestic poems, religious meditations, formal elegies, "quaternions," etc. Notes, bibliography. viii + 222pp.

22160-1 Paperbound $2.50

THREE GOTHIC NOVELS: THE CASTLE OF OTRANTO BY HORACE WALPOLE; VATHEK BY WILLIAM BECKFORD; THE VAMPYRE BY JOHN POLIDORI, WITH FRAGMENT OF A NOVEL BY LORD BYRON, edited by E. F. Bleiler. The first Gothic novel, by Walpole; the finest Oriental tale in English, by Beckford; powerful Romantic supernatural story in versions by Polidori and Byron. All extremely important in history of literature; all still exciting, packed with supernatural thrills, ghosts, haunted castles, magic, etc. xl + 291pp.

21232-7 Paperbound $2.50

THE BEST TALES OF HOFFMANN, E. T. A. Hoffmann. 10 of Hoffmann's most important stories, in modern re-editings of standard translations: Nutcracker and the King of Mice, Signor Formica, Automata, The Sandman, Rath Krespel, The Golden Flowerpot, Master Martin the Cooper, The Mines of Falun, The King's Betrothed, A New Year's Eve Adventure. 7 illustrations by Hoffmann. Edited by E. F. Bleiler. xxxix + 419pp. 21793-0 Paperbound $3.00

GHOST AND HORROR STORIES OF AMBROSE BIERCE, Ambrose Bierce. 23 strikingly modern stories of the horrors latent in the human mind: The Eyes of the Panther, The Damned Thing, An Occurrence at Owl Creek Bridge, An Inhabitant of Carcosa, etc., plus the dream-essay, Visions of the Night. Edited by E. F. Bleiler. xxii + 199pp. 20767-6 Paperbound $1.50

BEST GHOST STORIES OF J. S. LEFANU, J. Sheridan LeFanu. Finest stories by Victorian master often considered greatest supernatural writer of all. Carmilla, Green Tea, The Haunted Baronet, The Familiar, and 12 others. Most never before available in the U. S. A. Edited by E. F. Bleiler. 8 illustrations from Victorian publications. xvii + 467pp. 20415-4 Paperbound $3.00

MATHEMATICAL FOUNDATIONS OF INFORMATION THEORY, A. I. Khinchin. Comprehensive introduction to work of Shannon, McMillan, Feinstein and Khinchin, placing these investigations on a rigorous mathematical basis. Covers entropy concept in probability theory, uniqueness theorem, Shannon's inequality, ergodic sources, the E property, martingale concept, noise, Feinstein's fundamental lemma, Shanon's first and second theorems. Translated by R. A. Silverman and M. D. Friedman. iii + 120pp. 60434-9 Paperbound $1.75

SEVEN SCIENCE FICTION NOVELS, H. G. Wells. The standard collection of the great novels. Complete, unabridged. *First Men in the Moon, Island of Dr. Moreau, War of the Worlds, Food of the Gods, Invisible Man, Time Machine, In the Days of the Comet.* Not only science fiction fans, but every educated person owes it to himself to read these novels. 1015pp. (USO) 20264-X Clothbound $5.00

LAST AND FIRST MEN AND STAR MAKER, TWO SCIENCE FICTION NOVELS, Olaf Stapledon. Greatest future histories in science fiction. In the first, human intelligence is the "hero," through strange paths of evolution, interplanetary invasions, incredible technologies, near extinctions and reemergences. Star Maker describes the quest of a band of star rovers for intelligence itself, through time and space: weird inhuman civilizations, crustacean minds, symbiotic worlds, etc. Complete, unabridged. v + 438pp.   (USO) 21962-3 Paperbound $2.50

THREE PROPHETIC NOVELS, H. G. WELLS. Stages of a consistently planned future for mankind. *When the Sleeper Wakes,* and *A Story of the Days to Come,* anticipate *Brave New World* and *1984,* in the 21st Century; *The Time Machine,* only complete version in print, shows farther future and the end of mankind. All show Wells's greatest gifts as storyteller and novelist. Edited by E. F. Bleiler. x + 335pp.   (USO) 20605-X Paperbound $2.50

THE ,DEVIL'S DICTIONARY, Ambrose Bierce. America's own Oscar Wilde— Ambrose Bierce—offers his barbed iconoclastic wisdom in over 1,000 definitions hailed by H. L. Mencken as "some of the most gorgeous witticisms in the English language." 145pp.   20487-1 Paperbound $1.25

MAX AND MORITZ, Wilhelm Busch. Great children's classic, father of comic strip, of two bad boys, Max and Moritz. Also Ker and Plunk (Plisch und Plumm), Cat and Mouse, Deceitful Henry, Ice-Peter, The Boy and the Pipe, and five other pieces. Original German, with English translation. Edited by H. Arthur Klein; translations by various hands and H. Arthur Klein. vi + 216pp.
20181-3 Paperbound $2.00

PIGS IS PIGS AND OTHER FAVORITES, Ellis Parker Butler. The title story is one of the best humor short stories, as Mike Flannery obfuscates biology and English. Also included, That Pup of Murchison's, The Great American Pie Company, and Perkins of Portland. 14 illustrations. v + 109pp.   21532-6 Paperbound $1.25

THE PETERKIN PAPERS, Lucretia P. Hale. It takes genius to be as stupidly mad as the Peterkins, as they decide to become wise, celebrate the "Fourth," keep a cow, and otherwise strain the resources of the Lady from Philadelphia. Basic book of American humor. 153 illustrations. 219pp.   20794-3 Paperbound $1.50

PERRAULT'S FAIRY TALES, translated by A. E. Johnson and S. R. Littlewood, with 34 full-page illustrations by Gustave Doré. All the original Perrault stories— Cinderella, Sleeping Beauty, Bluebeard, Little Red Riding Hood, Puss in Boots, Tom Thumb, etc.—with their witty verse morals and the magnificent illustrations of Doré. One of the five or six great books of European fairy tales. viii + 117pp. 8⅛ x 11.   22311-6 Paperbound $2.00

OLD HUNGARIAN FAIRY TALES, Baroness Orczy. Favorites translated and adapted by author of the *Scarlet Pimpernel.* Eight fairy tales include "The Suitors of Princess Fire-Fly," "The Twin Hunchbacks," "Mr. Cuttlefish's Love Story," and "The Enchanted Cat." This little volume of magic and adventure will captivate children as it has for generations. 90 drawings by Montagu Barstow. 96pp.
22293-4 Paperbound $1.95

THE RED FAIRY BOOK, Andrew Lang. Lang's color fairy books have long been children's favorites. This volume includes Rapunzel, Jack and the Bean-stalk and 35 other stories, familiar and unfamiliar. 4 plates, 93 illustrations x + 367pp.
21673-X Paperbound $2.50

THE BLUE FAIRY BOOK, Andrew Lang. Lang's tales come from all countries and all times. Here are 37 tales from Grimm, the Arabian Nights, Greek Mythology, and other fascinating sources. 8 plates, 130 illustrations. xi + 390pp.
21437-0 Paperbound $2.50

HOUSEHOLD STORIES BY THE BROTHERS GRIMM. Classic English-language edition of the well-known tales — Rumpelstiltskin, Snow White, Hansel and Gretel, The Twelve Brothers, Faithful John, Rapunzel, Tom Thumb (52 stories in all). Translated into simple, straightforward English by Lucy Crane. Ornamented with headpieces, vignettes, elaborate decorative initials and a dozen full-page illustrations by Walter Crane. x + 269pp.
21080-4 Paperbound $2.00

THE MERRY ADVENTURES OF ROBIN HOOD, Howard Pyle. The finest modern versions of the traditional ballads and tales about the great English outlaw. Howard Pyle's complete prose version, with every word, every illustration of the first edition. Do not confuse this facsimile of the original (1883) with modern editions that change text or illustrations. 23 plates plus many page decorations. xxii + 296pp.
22043-5 Paperbound $2.50

THE STORY OF KING ARTHUR AND HIS KNIGHTS, Howard Pyle. The finest children's version of the life of King Arthur; brilliantly retold by Pyle, with 48 of his most imaginative illustrations. xviii + 313pp. 6⅛ x 9¼.
21445-1 Paperbound $2.50

THE WONDERFUL WIZARD OF OZ, L. Frank Baum. America's finest children's book in facsimile of first edition with all Denslow illustrations in full color. The edition a child should have. Introduction by Martin Gardner. 23 color plates, scores of drawings. iv + 267pp.
20691-2 Paperbound $2.50

THE MARVELOUS LAND OF OZ, L. Frank Baum. The second Oz book, every bit as imaginative as the Wizard. The hero is a boy named Tip, but the Scarecrow and the Tin Woodman are back, as is the Oz magic. 16 color plates, 120 drawings by John R. Neill. 287pp.
20692-0 Paperbound $2.50

THE MAGICAL MONARCH OF MO, L. Frank Baum. Remarkable adventures in a land even stranger than Oz. The best of Baum's books not in the Oz series. 15 color plates and dozens of drawings by Frank Verbeck. xviii + 237pp.
21892-9 Paperbound $2.25

THE BAD CHILD'S BOOK OF BEASTS, MORE BEASTS FOR WORSE CHILDREN, A MORAL ALPHABET, Hilaire Belloc. Three complete humor classics in one volume. Be kind to the frog, and do not call him names . . . and 28 other whimsical animals. Familiar favorites and some not so well known. Illustrated by Basil Blackwell. 156pp.
(USO) 20749-8 Paperbound $1.50

EAST O' THE SUN AND WEST O' THE MOON, George W. Dasent. Considered the best of all translations of these Norwegian folk tales, this collection has been enjoyed by generations of children (and folklorists too). Includes True and Untrue, Why the Sea is Salt, East O' the Sun and West O' the Moon, Why the Bear is Stumpy-Tailed, Boots and the Troll, The Cock and the Hen, Rich Peter the Pedlar, and 52 more. The only edition with all 59 tales. 77 illustrations by Erik Werenskiold and Theodor Kittelsen. xv + 418pp. 22521-6 Paperbound $3.50

GOOPS AND HOW TO BE THEM, Gelett Burgess. Classic of tongue-in-cheek humor, masquerading as etiquette book. 87 verses, twice as many cartoons, show mischievous Goops as they demonstrate to children virtues of table manners, neatness, courtesy, etc. Favorite for generations. viii + 88pp. 6½ x 9¼.
22233-0 Paperbound $1.25

ALICE'S ADVENTURES UNDER GROUND, Lewis Carroll. The first version, quite different from the final Alice in Wonderland, printed out by Carroll himself with his own illustrations. Complete facsimile of the "million dollar" manuscript Carroll gave to Alice Liddell in 1864. Introduction by Martin Gardner. viii + 96pp. Title and dedication pages in color. 21482-6 Paperbound $1.25

THE BROWNIES, THEIR BOOK, Palmer Cox. Small as mice, cunning as foxes, exuberant and full of mischief, the Brownies go to the zoo, toy shop, seashore, circus, etc., in 24 verse adventures and 266 illustrations. Long a favorite, since their first appearance in St. Nicholas Magazine. xi + 144pp. 6⅝ x 9¼.
21265-3 Paperbound $1.75

SONGS OF CHILDHOOD, Walter De La Mare. Published (under the pseudonym Walter Ramal) when De La Mare was only 29, this charming collection has long been a favorite children's book. A facsimile of the first edition in paper, the 47 poems capture the simplicity of the nursery rhyme and the ballad, including such lyrics as I Met Eve, Tartary, The Silver Penny. vii + 106pp. (USO) 21972-0 Paperbound
$1.25

THE COMPLETE NONSENSE OF EDWARD LEAR, Edward Lear. The finest 19th-century humorist-cartoonist in full: all nonsense limericks, zany alphabets, Owl and Pussycat, songs, nonsense botany, and more than 500 illustrations by Lear himself. Edited by Holbrook Jackson. xxix + 287pp. (USO) 20167-8 Paperbound $2.00

BILLY WHISKERS: THE AUTOBIOGRAPHY OF A GOAT, Frances Trego Montgomery. A favorite of children since the early 20th century, here are the escapades of that rambunctious, irresistible and mischievous goat—Billy Whiskers. Much in the spirit of Peck's Bad Boy, this is a book that children never tire of reading or hearing. All the original familiar illustrations by W. H. Fry are included: 6 color plates, 18 black and white drawings. 159pp. 22345-0 Paperbound $2.00

MOTHER GOOSE MELODIES. Faithful republication of the fabulously rare Munroe and Francis "copyright 1833" Boston edition—the most important Mother Goose collection, usually referred to as the "original." Familiar rhymes plus many rare ones, with wonderful old woodcut illustrations. Edited by E. F. Bleiler. 128pp. 4½ x 6⅜. 22577-1 Paperbound $1.00

Two Little Savages; Being the Adventures of Two Boys Who Lived as Indians and What They Learned, Ernest Thompson Seton. Great classic of nature and boyhood provides a vast range of woodlore in most palatable form, a genuinely entertaining story. Two farm boys build a teepee in woods and live in it for a month, working out Indian solutions to living problems, star lore, birds and animals, plants, etc. 293 illustrations. vii + 286pp.

20985-7 Paperbound $2.50

Peter Piper's Practical Principles of Plain & Perfect Pronunciation. Alliterative jingles and tongue-twisters of surprising charm, that made their first appearance in America about 1830. Republished in full with the spirited woodcut illustrations from this earliest American edition. 32pp. 4½ x 6⅜.

22560-7 Paperbound $1.00

Science Experiments and Amusements for Children, Charles Vivian. 73 easy experiments, requiring only materials found at home or easily available, such as candles, coins, steel wool, etc.; illustrate basic phenomena like vacuum, simple chemical reaction, etc. All safe. Modern, well-planned. Formerly *Science Games for Children.* 102 photos, numerous drawings. 96pp. 6⅛ x 9¼.

21856-2 Paperbound $1.25

An Introduction to Chess Moves and Tactics Simply Explained, Leonard Barden. Informal intermediate introduction, quite strong in explaining reasons for moves. Covers basic material, tactics, important openings, traps, positional play in middle game, end game. Attempts to isolate patterns and recurrent configurations. Formerly *Chess.* 58 figures. 102pp. (USO) 21210-6 Paperbound $1.25

Lasker's Manual of Chess, Dr. Emanuel Lasker. Lasker was not only one of the five great World Champions, he was also one of the ablest expositors, theorists, and analysts. In many ways, his Manual, permeated with his philosophy of battle, filled with keen insights, is one of the greatest works ever written on chess. Filled with analyzed games by the great players. A single-volume library that will profit almost any chess player, beginner or master. 308 diagrams. xli x 349pp.

20640-8 Paperbound $2.75

The Master Book of Mathematical Recreations, Fred Schuh. In opinion of many the finest work ever prepared on mathematical puzzles, stunts, recreations; exhaustively thorough explanations of mathematics involved, analysis of effects, citation of puzzles and games. Mathematics involved is elementary. Translated by F. Göbel. 194 figures. xxiv + 430pp. 22134-2 Paperbound $3.00

Mathematics, Magic and Mystery, Martin Gardner. Puzzle editor for Scientific American explains mathematics behind various mystifying tricks: card tricks, stage "mind reading," coin and match tricks, counting out games, geometric dissections, etc. Probability sets, theory of numbers clearly explained. Also provides more than 400 tricks, guaranteed to work, that you can do. 135 illustrations. xii + 176pp.

20335-2 Paperbound $1.50

MATHEMATICAL PUZZLES FOR BEGINNERS AND ENTHUSIASTS, Geoffrey Mott-Smith. 189 puzzles from easy to difficult—involving arithmetic, logic, algebra, properties of digits, probability, etc.—for enjoyment and mental stimulus. Explanation of mathematical principles behind the puzzles. 135 illustrations. viii + 248pp.
20198-8 Paperbound $1.75

PAPER FOLDING FOR BEGINNERS, William D. Murray and Francis J. Rigney. Easiest book on the market, clearest instructions on making interesting, beautiful origami. Sail boats, cups, roosters, frogs that move legs, bonbon boxes, standing birds, etc. 40 projects; more than 275 diagrams and photographs. 94pp.
20713-7 Paperbound $1.00

TRICKS AND GAMES ON THE POOL TABLE, Fred Herrmann. 79 tricks and games—some solitaires, some for two or more players, some competitive games—to entertain you between formal games. Mystifying shots and throws, unusual caroms, tricks involving such props as cork, coins, a hat, etc. Formerly *Fun on the Pool Table*. 77 figures. 95pp.
21814-7 Paperbound $1.00

HAND SHADOWS TO BE THROWN UPON THE WALL: A SERIES OF NOVEL AND AMUSING FIGURES FORMED BY THE HAND, Henry Bursill. Delightful picturebook from great-grandfather's day shows how to make 18 different hand shadows: a bird that flies, duck that quacks, dog that wags his tail, camel, goose, deer, boy, turtle, etc. Only book of its sort. vi + 33pp. 6½ x 9¼.   21779-5 Paperbound $1.00

WHITTLING AND WOODCARVING, E. J. Tangerman. 18th printing of best book on market. "If you can cut a potato you can carve" toys and puzzles, chains, chessmen, caricatures, masks, frames, woodcut blocks, surface patterns, much more. Information on tools, woods, techniques. Also goes into serious wood sculpture from Middle Ages to present, East and West. 464 photos, figures. x + 293pp.
20965-2 Paperbound $2.00

HISTORY OF PHILOSOPHY, Julián Marias. Possibly the clearest, most easily followed, best planned, most useful one-volume history of philosophy on the market; neither skimpy nor overfull. Full details on system of every major philosopher and dozens of less important thinkers from pre-Socratics up to Existentialism and later. Strong on many European figures usually omitted. Has gone through dozens of editions in Europe. 1966 edition, translated by Stanley Appelbaum and Clarence Strowbridge. xviii + 505pp.   21739-6 Paperbound $3.50

YOGA: A SCIENTIFIC EVALUATION, Kovoor T. Behanan. Scientific but non-technical study of physiological results of yoga exercises; done under auspices of Yale U. Relations to Indian thought, to psychoanalysis, etc. 16 photos. xxiii + 270pp.
20505-3 Paperbound $2.50

Prices subject to change without notice.
Available at your book dealer or write for free catalogue to Dept. GI, Dover Publications, Inc., 180 Varick St., N. Y., N. Y. 10014. Dover publishes more than 150 books each year on science, elementary and advanced mathematics, biology, music, art, literary history, social sciences and other areas.

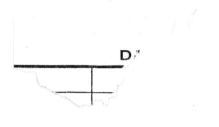